THE UNIVERSITY OF
WINCHESTER

Martial Rose Library
Tel: 01962 827306

To be returned on or before the day marked above, subject to recall.

LAND OF NECESSITY

CONSUMER CULTURE IN THE
United States–Mexico Borderlands

Edited by Alexis McCrossen

Duke University Press   Durham and London   2009

Designed by Heather Hensley

Typeset in Minion Pro by Keystone Typesetting,
Inc.

Library of Congress Cataloging-in-Publication
Data appear on the last printed page of this book.

Published in cooperation with the William P.
Clements Center for Southwest Studies, Southern
Methodist University

TO MY FATHER

Preston G. McCrossen (1933–2005)

"As American as the Southwest"

Contents

Maps

Cover of order form, McCrossen Handwoven Textiles, Santa Fe, New Mexico, ca. 1942–47. George McCrossen Papers, Center for Southwest Research, University Libraries, University of New Mexico.

Acknowledgments

The genesis of this volume illustrates how scholars benefit from reaching beyond their expertise, from thinking together, and from teaching. The summer before I started my first faculty appointment at Southern Methodist University, my dissertation advisor, David D. Hall, gave me a collection of essays about consumption in eighteenth-century British North America (*Of Consuming Interests: The Style of Life in the Eighteenth Century*), which, along with his good guidance about the early modern European world, led me to locate the origins of consumer culture in the seventeenth and eighteenth centuries, long before assembly lines, department stores, and slick-paper magazines. Thus the undergraduate course on the history of consumer culture that I teach at SMU begins several centuries earlier than comparable courses at other institutions. Doing so has habituated me to seeing consumer culture in places that have been overlooked (one-room dwellings) or characterized only as "material culture" (native American communities).

At the same time as I developed my approach to the history of consumer culture, my association with the Clements Center at SMU as a member of its Executive Board, particularly my good fortune in getting to know many of its fellows, including the inestimable Raul Ramos, Flannery Burke, and Sam Truett, piqued my scholarly interest in the borderlands. So, when David Weber and Sherry Smith agreed to fund a Clements Center Symposium under my aegis, investigating consumer culture in the U.S.-Mexico borderlands seemed particularly appealing. That so many scholars responded to the open call for papers confirmed my sense that there was indeed something to this subject other than my own effort to bring various interests together under one rubric.

It is thus natural that I would be as grateful as I am for the assistance of several different academic units at SMU and to colleagues at SMU and elsewhere. I deeply appreciate the Clements Center's logistical and financial support: it paid for and took care of the many logistics associated with meetings in Taos and Dallas during the 2005–6 academic year. The Center also subvened the publication of this volume; while SMU's Clements Department of History contributed to the expenses associated with illustrating the volume; and SMU's Dedman College provided me with a semester's leave during which I edited the volume's marvelous essays and finished writing my own contributions. The department's secretary, Sharron Pierson, was so helpful during critical moments of the book's production, and the Clements Center's dynamic duo—Andrea Boardman and Ruth Ann Elmore—did much of the hard work associated with bringing me and the contributors together for two very productive meetings. Russell Martin, director of SMU's DeGoyler Library, mounted a show about business in the U.S.-Mexico borderlands that coincided with a conference at which the volume's contributors presented their work. My gratitude extends to Howard Campbell, Josiah McC. Heyman, Mauricio Tenorio, Melissa Wright, and the two anonymous readers for Duke University Press: they read all the volume's essays with sharp eyes and then took the time to fashion useful suggestions for the contributors and me. Above all else, I am deeply grateful to the twelve contributors to this volume: they are wonderful scholars, generous interlocutors, and creative thinkers.

This volume showcases scholarly essays, but images are nearly as important as text in the volume as a whole. The contributors and I thank the many librarians who assisted us in our image hunts, the photographers who have allowed us to reproduce their depictions of the borderlands and consumer culture, and SMU's History Department, the Clements Center, and Duke University Press for making it financially possible to add a visual component to the volume. We are deeply grateful for the opportunity to so heavily illustrate an edited collection of essays. I want to thank my editor Valerie Millholland and her assistant Miriam Angress for accommodating the inclusion of so many illustrations. That they believed in the book made it possible for it to take what I hope is compelling form.

I have dedicated Land of Necessity to my recently deceased father, Preston G. McCrossen, who would have loved every contribution and every contributor had he had the chance. He devoted his life to the notion that the economy matters, not because it could lead to wealth for the few, but because if and when its fruits were equitably shared, it could foster cultural and social vitality. In this lifelong endeavor my father sat at the feet of his father, George McCrossen, a radical, an aesthete, as well as a businessman. With his wife Helen and brother Preston (my father's namesake), George was part of a migratory stream of Americans disaffected with machine civilization. They fled to the U.S. Southwest, a region that to them embodied the exotic, the foreign, and the forbidden. Cheap land made it possible for them to lead lives that seemed to them more authentic and more ethical than the lives of their counterparts in America's cities. They perhaps recognized that consumerism exercised as significant a power over the borderlands and its sojourners as it did on the residents of the cities they left behind, Detroit and New York City. After all, after a go at designing, producing and marketing handmade textiles, my grandfather ran a small advertising company with offices on Santa Fe's "Radio Plaza."

I thank my friend Amy Greenberg, my mother Macon McCrossen, and my husband Adam Herring for sharing a dream of a just and beautiful society with me and for inspiring much that constitutes my share of this volume. I am especially grateful to Adam for the innumerable ways that he has helped to bring this volume to fruition, including taking photographs of our favorite taco stand and an Omnilife storefront. Finally, my young daughter Annie Herring deserves more than a nod for enduring the indignity of being upstaged by "Mommy's book," for giving me a few pep talks as I worked on its many components, and for reminding me more than once that, in her words, "different people say different things."

Alexis McCrossen
Dallas, Texas
October 2008

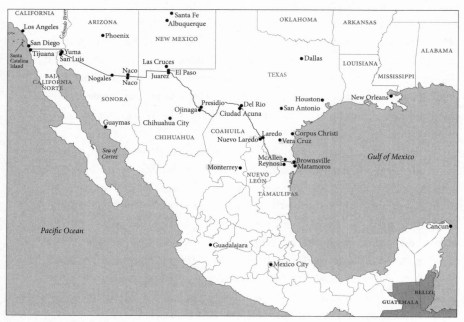

U.S.-Mexico Borderlands, ca. 2005.

Alexis McCrossen

Introduction
Land of Necessity

Since the early 1850s when the nearly 2,000-mile-long boundary line between the United States and Mexico was drawn and the "American System of Manufacture" using interchangeable, standardized parts was perfected, the convergence of broad demographic, economic, political, and international developments in the U.S.-Mexico borderlands unleashed necessity, a force as strong as desire in forging a culture and society rooted in the imperatives of market-oriented consumption. Though its importance is uncontestable, scholars have hitherto rarely explored the role of necessity in consumer culture. Indeed, it is widely assumed that where necessity reigns, consumer culture is anemic. This volume seeks to demonstrate otherwise, not simply because privation defines the experience of many borderlanders past and present, but because even amidst excess (of time, money, things) necessity plays a defining role in shaping social life and cultural patterns. In doing so, the contributors to *Land of Necessity* shed new light on the history of the U.S.-Mexico borderlands, while also opening up new terrain for scholarly inquiry into consumer culture.

The volume first took shape in the 2005–2006 Symposium of the William P. Clements, Jr., Center for Southwest Studies, which is associated with Southern Methodist University and directed by its founder, the historian David Weber. In the fall of 2005, the contributors to this volume (with the exception of Robert Perez), Valerie Millholland, the editor of all things Latin American for Duke University Press, and I met at SMU's satellite campus, Fort Burgwin, near Taos, New Mexico. We met for several days on end, discussing early drafts of our papers, finding common threads that ran through our seemingly disparate research agendas, scholarly inclinations, and ideological commitments. The following spring we presented our findings to a full house on SMU's campus in Dallas, Texas, this time with Robert Perez among us, as well as the borderlands ethnographer Melissa Wright. Over the summer the contributors revised their essays. Several months later, yeoman-like, they revised their essays yet again in response to critique rendered by reviewers for Duke University Press' editorial department. The compelling and rich essays that resulted from this process are testament to the seriousness with which each scholar approached the subject and the benefits of well-funded collaborative endeavors.

Despite the many opportunities to work face-to-face with the volume's contributors, for some time I remained stumped about how to bring the volume together and about how to provide useful framing for the essays. As a historian, my instinct led me to attempt to weave together the histories of the U.S.-Mexico borderlands and consumer culture. The result is two essays. One, titled "Drawing Boundaries," provides an overview of the origins of consumer culture and of the U.S.-Mexico borderlands. While few boundaries were in place in the early modern period when this story begins, through the nineteenth century and into the twentieth, strenuous efforts were made on behalf of separating nations, peoples, and markets. Of course countervailing forces against separation (in the case, for instance, of peoples living in the borderlands) and toward integration (in the case, for instance, of international markets for commodities) complicated nationalistic and imperialistic designs. My other essay, "Disrupting Boundaries," casts the borderlands as an exemplary site with which to study and think about globalization. What is more, it shows that the exigencies of necessity have not dissipated even with the tremendous improvements (worldwide and in the borderlands itself) in the capacity to efficiently produce and transport both foodstuffs and consumer goods. Much like the sweep of Parts II and III, which open with Amy Greenberg's essay about the official U.S. inspection of the borderlands' seemingly barren land in the 1850s and close with Sarah Hill's textual and visual evocation of present-day overflowing landfills, junkyards, and secondhand markets, my essays in Part I dwell on scarcity and necessity in the borderlands: initially of goods, eventually of purchasing power. This emphasis is not meant to obscure the borderlands' abundance of resources and surfeit of luxuries, but to bring into focus the mutually constitutive nature of scarcity and abundance, needs and wants.

Thus, the key words *national, transnational, scarcity, abundance, desire, luxury,* and *necessity* are the volume's pivot points. Its essays explore the relationships between these key words over time, finding moments of imbalance and periods of reconfiguration. They point toward significant aspects of the development of consumer culture in general, not just in the borderlands. They explore social and cultural formations that develop as a result of the coexistence of national and transnational forces, scarce and abundant resources, structures of feeling rooted in both desire and necessity. The essays visit houses, tourist districts, cinemas, retail venues, factories, fields, junkyards, Indian reservations, resorts, and beaches to recover some of the ways that national, binational, and transnational forces fashioned public and private sites of consumption. Amy Greenberg, Rachel St. John, and Lawrence Culver, all historians, lay out the framework for understanding the skepticism of U.S. citizens about the "American-ness" of the border region, while Laura Serna, also a historian, and Sarah Hill, a cultural anthropologist, do the same for Mexican incredulity about the border region's *mexicanidad.* How native peoples, migrants, and residents of the borderlands make do with scarce purchasing power amidst the region's material abundance is the focus of the essays contributed by the historians Josef Barton and Robert Perez and the cultural anthropologists Peter Cahn and Sarah Hill.

As is likely obvious, initially it was the contrast between scarcity and abundance that attracted me to the borderlands as a site of study, but gradually other vectors came into view, not the least of which was that extending between necessity and desire. While few would deny the central role *necessity* plays in human behavior, most scholars of consumer culture are far more attentive to the machinations of *desire.* In part this is because consumer culture has been narrated as the consequence of an enormous leap from subsistence to abundance. In accounting for vast economic change, scholars until very recently lost sight of the persistence of necessity, even among the groups with means to fulfill some of their never-ending desires. By no means does this volume wish to suggest that necessity alone is the key to understanding consumer culture in the U.S.-Mexico borderlands, or other regions deemed "marginal" due to their uneven economic development. Instead, its goal is to incorporate into the study of consumer culture the insights of scholars, anthropologists in particular, who have studied the processes and attendant consequences of rising market dependency for the very stuff of life—water, fuel, food, and shelter.

Mexican consul Salvador Duhart, Marilyn Monroe, and Captain Roberto Pini at a publicity event for Pan American Airways, ca. 1950. *Los Angeles Daily News* photograph, courtesy *Los Angeles Times* Photographic Archive, Department of Special Collections, Charles E. Young Research Library, University of California, Los Angeles.

The map drawn on the belly of a Compañia Mexicana jet, to which movie star Marilyn Monroe is pointing in this photograph, depicts more than one geographical fact about the history of consumer capitalism in the U.S.-Mexico borderlands. The borderlands are framed to the south by Mexico City, the second-largest city in the world, and to the north by Los Angeles, the eighth-largest city in the world. Until 1800, Mexico City was the New World's capital of trade and merchandising. During the next fifty years the borderlands began to squirm out of Mexico City's grip, but for several decades even after much of the region became U.S. territory, Mexico City remained its fulcrum and reference point. By the 1880s, though, multiple railroad connections to U.S. cities and ports finished the work of the Santa Fe Trail in reorienting the region toward the United States. Over the course of the twentieth century, movie and television production, automobile orientation, and the jet airplane as manufactured product and transportation—all significant contributors to the emergence of consumer culture in the United States—fostered circuits of exchange that strengthened the magnetism of Los Angeles, for Mexicans and Americans alike.

As much as consumer culture is a transnational phenomenon, it seems that the various forms it takes contribute more to the perpetuation of perceptions of national differences than to their diminution. Likewise, as much as consumer culture is the consequence of mind-boggling productivity, the forms it has taken thus far have not abolished either necessity or scarcity. The study of consumer culture as a set of dynamic policies and practices, as well as consumer goods, can highlight the similarities, mutual dependencies, and shared histories that bind together the United States and Mexico, and its rich and poor peoples living on both sides of the line. Reflections on the contributors' essays, one by cultural anthropologists Howard Campbell and Josiah McC. Heyman and the other by a cultural historian of modern Mexico, Mauricio Tenorio-Trillo, bring the volume to a close. Professors Campbell and Heyman argue persuasively that the line between necessity and desire does not run parallel with the boundary line separating the United States and Mexico. They point to *socioeconomic class* as perhaps the most salient category in which to organize analysis of consumption in the borderlands. Professor Tenorio-Trillo also underscores the salience of class, questioning the tendency to accept as fact that the border divides the two nations. He points to how scholars, including contributors to this very volume, tend to reify senses and convictions of national differences.

In the course of gathering illustrations for this volume I came to appreciate all the more the importance of investigating consumer capitalism, culture, and society in the U.S.-Mexico borderlands. Themes run through the book's illustrations that the essays only touch upon, if that. For instance, consider the forms carts, railroads, and automobiles take in some of the volume's photos. Or gaze at the signage, which encompasses hand painted and neon, which beckons and repels ("No Spanish"). Or look at the various architectural spaces, such as homes, hotels, stores, streets, factories, that shape lived spaces of consumption. Not only are there abundant historic images of the borderlands in archives, some of which are digitized and stored on the Website of the Library of Congress, the El Paso Public Library, the University of New Mexico, the University of Texas's Center for American History, and Yale University's Beinecke Library, but thousands of photographs of the U.S.-Mexico border are posted on photo-sharing Web sites, such as *Flickr* and *Wikimedia*. In addition to rich archival and print sources, as well as the essays in this volume, these repositories of visual sources should help to open up further understandings of the region and of consumption.

I

HISTORIES OF NATIONS,
CONSUMERS, AND BORDERLANDS

On the border, 1914. Photographic postcard, courtesy Research Library, The Getty Research Institute, Los Angeles, California, piece ID: 89.r.46-b16.21. Across the image is scrawled "Well—good by love the old-man is comming [*sic*] now. I will see you later on the border." On the verso it reads: "Dear John—Well Ole kid here I am just finished dinner across the border. See you Sunday. Your pal Dean."

Alexis McCrossen

Drawing Boundaries between Markets, Nations, and Peoples, 1650–1940

> When the political boundary has evolved by a system of contraction out of the wide waste zone to the nicely determined line, that line, nevertheless, is always encased, as it were, in a zone of contact wherein are mingled the elements of either side.
>
> ELLEN CHURCHILL SEMPLE (1911)

At the same time that Europeans began to settle North America in the sixteenth and seventeenth centuries, international markets for commodities, finished goods, labor, and capital began to form, while Western Europeans were taking the first steps toward the largest increase in per capita productivity in history. Each development begot formal and informal efforts to draw and maintain boundaries around territories, peoples, and markets, such that the "wide waste zone" to which the geographer Ellen Semple refers shrank to the width of a "nicely determined line." Out of this process whereby political lines were drawn developed the very circumstances—"the zone of contact"—that would lead to the attenuation of the defensive purpose of the border.[1] Nations require boundaries to delimit and separate territories and peoples, but markets are attracted to territorial and political boundaries, clustering around them, pushing against them, maximizing opportunities rising out of the accumulation of asymmetries in such close proximity.

The borderline separating the United States and Mexico after an 1828 "treaty of limits" became ever more visible with each decade—moving from a set of impressions keyed to landmarks, to agreed-upon geographic coordinates (which would

Panorama of Nogales, Arizona, 1909. Photograph distributed by West Coast Art Co., held by Library of Congress, Prints and Photographs Division, PAN US GEOG—Arizona no. 70.

Nogales, Arizona left, and Nogales, Sonora, separated by a high concrete and steel fence, January 30, 2007. Photograph by Gordon Hyde, licensed by Creative Commons Attribution ShareAlike 2.5.

Photographs of the borderline running through Nogales illustrate the tensions between the national and transnational. When the boundary line was drawn in 1853–54, it ran through the almost nonexistent settlement of "Nogales." The railroad tracks reveal how a north-south axis of exchange made Nogales a single city in practice, despite the dusty boundary line that visually separated it into two towns, one in Arizona, the other in Sonora. The 1909 photograph asks whether the no man's land of the borderline or the bustling market of the railroad would prevail. Nearly one hundred years later, a fortified fence makes the boundary line visible: roads, buildings, and cars encroach on the borderline. It should be noted that an on-duty U.S. soldier took the 2007 photo.

be revised on occasion as the accuracy of surveying tools improved), to lines on official maps, to boundary monuments. By the 1880s, it was possible to stroll along wide, dusty streets that marked the line in border cities, stepping across the north-south railroad tracks that bisected the boundary. But soon wooden and barbed wire fences, and then chain link fences, and now electric fences, walls, and a multitude of barriers, went up, with the intention of rendering the line visible, but what is more, immutable and unpassable, as natural and imposing as an ocean or set of cliffs. And yet, people, enterprises, and wealth have clustered along the borderline, attracted, rather than repelled, by it, despite the ever-heavier policing of the line itself, increasing restrictions placed on border crossing, and the accumulating dangers, such as murder, lurking in the border's shadows.[2] In this context, then, it is clear that drawing boundaries contributed to the particular development of consumer culture in the U.S.-Mexico borderlands that this volume investigates.

With broad strokes this essay explores the emergence of markets and nations between the sixteenth and twentieth centuries. In doing so, it focuses on the lands stretching from the Gulf Coast along the scrubby banks of the Rio Grande River, through the mineral-rich deserts of the present-day states of Arizona and Sonora, and across the California peninsula. This region initially seemed of little consequence in the intertwined struggles to define, promote, and protect the American and Mexican nation-states, economies, and peoples. But, as the essay shows, as nationalism and market-oriented capitalism each intensified after the middle decades of the nineteenth century, the U.S.-Mexico borderlands assumed astonishing significance. In this transnational region strenuous governmental and individual efforts were made to control, at times to prevent altogether, and quite often to facilitate, the passage of people, capital, commodities, and goods across the international border.

In the 1930s these tendencies toward national fortification increased. They resulted in the expulsion of unknown numbers of people of Mexican descent from the United States. Asserting its own national sovereignty, Mexico nationalized its oil industry, as well as hundreds of thousands of acres of Mexican land, some of it along the border. At the same time, each nation invested in public works projects meant to build up enterprise in their borderlands and encouraged a moderate amount of trade with each other by reducing tariffs after 1934. Ultimately, enhanced transportation, agricultural, and industrial infrastructures trumped nationalist and ethnocentric tendencies toward shoring up firm boundaries. Since the 1940s, the dissolution of boundaries between the two nations' peoples and markets has been the rule, despite the heavy patrolling of the border since the 1960s. That a transnational consumer culture and society had been developing in the borderlands for at least half a century prior to the 1930s only contributed further to undermining the geopolitical boundaries that were drawn and redrawn with such exactitude over the course of the nineteenth century.

Scarcity by and large defined human life across space and time before the seventeenth century. At that time, a multitude of factors—not least of which was what economic historian Jan de Vries has identified as "*the industrious revolution*"—set the stage for its retreat. It is likely that during the 1500s, investment and interest in trade networks, expansion of towns and cities, increased agricultural productivity, and population growth together combined to motivate certain groups to abandon what economists call "target income behavior" (working just to meet needs). As more members of households worked more intensely than before, productivity in western Europe and parts of the Mediterranean basin increased. Households devoted smaller proportions of their labor to securing food and shelter than before, while planning production for the market and engaging in discretionary spending. It was increased work effort, rather than application of new technologies, that first begot rising surplus: thus the nomenclature "industrious revolution."[3] Which came first, surplus goods or surplus income, is endlessly debatable, so gradual and intertwined were their earliest appearance. What is known is that together they created a favorable climate for innovation and experimentation in agriculture and manufacturing, the construction of numerous public buildings and private homes, the extension of trade networks, and migration to cities and faraway lands.[4]

Two such distant places, the present-day eastern seaboard of the United States and the greater valley of Mexico, highlight the pivotal role trade played in the expansion of the world of goods *and* in the formation of nation-states. Mercantile trade with Asia, European colonization of the Americas and Caribbean, and the brutal harnessing of a tractable labor force on New World plantations, along with greater household productivity in northern Europe and the British North American colonies resulted in the trade of what might be considered the first mass-consumed non-subsistence goods: tobacco, tea, and sugar. In the eighteenth century, British officials implemented protectionist policies in the effort to favor not only merchants but also industrialists, particularly those running textile and ceramics factories. The British regulated trade in these goods, in part to raise revenue, and in part to maintain sovereignty over distant colonial holdings.[5]

Between 1720 and 1770, British North American per capita consumption of "the baubles of Britain," as historian T. H. Breen memorably called tea, shoe buckles, candle wax, and other British imports, increased 50 percent. Although, as Breen explains, "the rich and well-born had been buying imported goods from distant lands for as long as societies have kept records," it was the first time that the marketplace offered "an opportunity to become a consumer" to nearly everyone. The extensive choice and variety of items at increasingly lower prices resulted in "a shared language of goods." As resentments over taxes and imperial regulations rose after 1760, diverse colonists stretching from Massachusetts to Georgia participated in a range of ritualistic actions centered on consumer goods—boycotts, destruction of tea, pledges against imports—that in Breen's view contributed to the emergence of a common sensibility as "American." This new nationalist consciousness, in turn, contributed to the Declaration of Independence, the subsequent armed struggle against Britain, and the formation of a new nation altogether.[6]

In contrast, the role of consumer consciousness and needs has a far smaller place in historical interpretations of the Mexican quest for independence from Spain. At stake was far greater wealth than that extracted from British New World colonies, in the form of the minerals silver and gold, the dyes cochineal and indigo, and the stimulants sugar and tobacco, so the Spanish too instituted strict trading regulations and practices. Until the late sixteenth century, when the Pacific port of Acapulco opened up trade with Manila, and thus all of Asia, Veracruz was the sole destination of the Spanish galleons, large cargo ships that traveled in fleets, whose shipments were then loaded onto carts that traveled the well-worn road to Mexico City. In 1629, when handfuls of British colonists were barely eking out a subsistence in New England and Virginia and Native Americans still had effective control over present-day California, New Mexico, and Texas, the mayor of one of New Spain's smaller cities, Oaxaca, wrote, "It seems to me that one of the good and most important businesses in this land is merchandise. . . . The profit is so sure and so large that a well-stocked shop here is the richest thing in the world." Spanish clothing, paper, and wine, European velvet, damask, and linen, Asian spices, silks, and ceramics, he maintained, could be turned into gold: he called it "alchemy," so taken with the possibilities of trade in consumer goods was this merchant in a provincial Mexican town.[7] And it was so throughout New Spain, with Mexico City and its hinterlands becoming the center of Spanish colonial trade, merchandising, agriculture, and manufacturing.

Over the course of the seventeenth and eighteenth centuries, as the creole communities in New Spain's interior became self-sufficient in terms of the production of textiles, foodstuffs, agricultural implements, and housewares, all similar to like goods imported from Spain, they tended to seek only imports of what one historian has called "the luxurious, the novel, the status-conferring."[8] On New Spain's northern edge, even after the 1690s when Spain established permanent outposts in the present-day border states, trade goods arrived once or at best twice a year via ox cart or mule train. Here the Spanish tried to regulate local trade, especially in symbolically potent goods like medicine and liquor.[9] Hispanic material culture contributed to settlers' ongoing sense of themselves as Spanish, particularly as they intermarried with the native populations of the New World. The *casta* system depended not just on bloodlines, but on the skilled deployment of the clothing, foodstuffs, household items, and religious paraphernalia that underpinned Hispanic identity. Thus *creoles* were able to lay claim to Spain, and to develop as did colonial Britons an "imagined community" of Spaniards in the New World.[10] We are only just beginning to understand how unassimilated native populations incorporated Spanish material culture into their daily lives and ritual practices, but there is little doubt about whether they did so.

While the dynamics differed from the "market revolution" tearing Britain's North American colonies away from the home country, after the 1750s the demand for and availability of foreign goods undermined the Spanish Empire's control over its northernmost regions. Due to the enfeeblement of the Spanish crown, foreign ships crowded Veracruz's port, while imported goods spilled out of Mexico City's stores. In response, Spain's Bourbon reforms of the 1760s and 1770s sought to foster a similar pattern of development as in the British Empire: Spain would manufacture and export consumer goods, and its colonies would supply the raw materials. But New Spain would follow its own path, despite the mother country's policies. In part this was because, unlike British North America, it was self-sufficient in terms of necessities due to vigorous intercolonial trade, the work of skilled artisans, and *obrajes* (workshops) that employed as many as fifty hands well before any such enterprise on the Atlantic seaboard hired half as many. Furthermore, New Spain's large indigenous populations consumed but a few Spanish goods, whereas native people in the British colonies, especially the Iroquois and Cherokees, ably and eagerly traded for European consumer goods. Finally, New Spain's creole elite desired French and English—not Spanish—manufactured goods. Thus, while there may be as of yet undiscovered connections between emergent Mexican nationalism and common consumption habits developed under Spanish rule, they likely did not animate the Mexican quest for independence.

Demand for and availability of foreign goods also contributed to the unraveling of the northern edges of Mexico. When the newly independent Mexico opened up trade with foreigners (1821), the flood of what one historian characterizes as "colorful, exotic, and cheap *efectos de comercio*" (trade goods) via the Santa Fé Mexican Trail and Texas settlements elicited nationalist fears about the strength of the borderlands as a barrier against North Americans.[11]

As the traffic increased in volume and value, particularly after the inauguration of wagons on the trail, low grade conflict between traders and native Americans ensued, increasing in intensity until caravans of traders traveled together, seeking safety in numbers. The talented chronicler of the Santa Fé trade, merchant and traveler Josiah Gregg, described how the "arrival of a caravan at Santa Fé changes the aspect of the place at once." He favorably contrasted "the bustle, noise and activity of a lively market town" with what he perceived as its usual "idleness and stagnation."[12] Even two decades after the opening of trade, direct trade did not replace the trickle from Santa Fé to Chihuahua, due to a combination of high import tariffs, the "derecho de consumo" (consumption duty), the "tedious ordeal of custom-houses on the frontier," and the scrutiny the cargo underwent when passing through every town.[13] Nevertheless, between 1824 and 1831 traders did take small amounts of U.S. goods to Sonora and California, and eventually the Chihuahua trade, through New Mexico, was large enough that some contemporaries estimated it being worth two to three million dollars annually.[14] Nowhere was Mexico more vulnerable to encroachment than on its northern frontier, porous as it was to foreign consumer goods, stolen horses and cattle, traders traveling solo or in groups, itinerant bands of Indian warriors, and foreign armies.[15]

By the time of Mexico's independence, Western European nations and the United States were in the midst of a second industrial revolution, whose enormity made abundance appear to be "a great historical force," as the historian David Potter put it.[16] Whereas an increase in total household work time and effort haphazardly led to the seventeenth century's industrious revolution, and the use of machines in new spaces devoted only to production, called factories, resulted in the first industrial revolution, the second industrial revolution was due to technological and organizational innovations leading to astounding increases in productivity beginning in the 1780s. Previously, mills used the energy of moving water, animals, and wind to process agricultural commodities like grain, cotton, wool, and wood. But when steam engines harnessed the power of coal to operate boats, railroads, printing presses, and farming and factory machinery, the volume and speed of transportation, communication, and production together reached unimaginable levels. Engineers, machinists, journalists, accountants, and, above all else, managers innovated and applied organizational techniques in order to keep up with the demands of the new technologies.[17] The consequent heaps of output in turn generated what became the central problem of industrial capitalism: distribution.

Capitalist solutions to the distribution problem initially set store in the search for new markets, which in the nineteenth-century United States took many shapes, including deepening trade networks with Europe, pursuing the imperialist ideology of Manifest Destiny, and expanding the nation's territorial size. European demand for U.S. agricultural commodities, especially cotton, increased after the American Revolution, and by the 1820s international markets for American-made consumer goods, like clocks, began to grow as well. As the United States looked to Asia and Latin America for raw materials and consumer markets, it came to see Mexico, particularly its northernmost territory, as a geographic impediment. U.S. trade interests and its desire to open up new markets provided a strong impetus for the formation of the Republic of Texas (1836–45), the U.S. annexation of Texas (1845), and the U.S.-Mexico War (1846–48). At the war's conclusion, the United States gained half of Mexico's territory through the Treaty of Guadalupe Hidalgo and the Gadsden Purchase (1853–54). What is known today as the Southwest and California increased the size of the United States by one quarter. Access to Pacific ports spurred dreams of entering into, and even capturing, the Asian market. The Mexican market did not seem to beckon, though in time it would. (Today the United States and Mexico are among each other's principal trading partners; the United States as a whole only does more business with Canada and China. Statistics can hardly capture the enormity of this trade; during the last two decades of the twentieth century, residents of northern Mexico spent more than five million dollars *a day* in four Texas border towns.[18])

When surveyors first demarcated the border between the United States and Mexico, there was no premonition that the region would yield abundance in the form of raw or processed goods or have sufficient population density to warrant the name "market." The aridity of much of the borderlands reinforced the notion that the region could not sustain economic growth. Since the border was meant to generate an "empty zone" so that each nation would have a buffer against the other, its seeming emptiness was a boon.[19] For some time the boundary line itself warded off trade and economic development, largely because both Mexico and the United States enacted tariffs that diminished the extent of border cities' hinterlands. Indian raids, but one practice along the spectrum of underground economic activity of the borderlands' native peoples, further exacerbated the fragile commercial situation on both sides of the border.

Until the 1880s, inhabitants faced shortages and scarcity because centers of agriculture and manufacturing were accessible only by carts, stagecoaches, and horses. Shortages and scarcity were the norm. Residents on the Mexican side of the border could barely provision themselves, so they relied on "their neighbors in the United States," according to one Ciudad Juárez newspaperman's lament, from whom they bought "not only clothes, but bread, lard, sugar, and other consumer goods."[20] Further straining their resources, they also had to pay high import duties of up to 40 percent. The few general stores on the U.S. side were not especially well stocked: shipping to border outposts was unreliable at best.

Things changed within a few decades in such dramatic ways that the borderlands were swept up into the new economy. By the 1880s, the daunting amount of agricultural commodities and processed goods in the United States demanded either political or economic adjustments: the excess, some of which rotted or was sunk or burned, gave rise in the United States to political movements such as populism and socialism, as well as to images of greedy entrepreneurs being buried alive by the commodities they hoarded, as in the climatic moment of the Frank Norris novel *The Octopus* (1901), when a silo of wheat erupts. Succeeding in labeling this excess as "surplus," capitalists discovered the economic and cultural necessity of "marketing." Marketing practices, too varied and complex for incorporation into existing business and cultural institutions, gave rise to "institutions of abundance," such as the advertising agency.[21] Initially, marketing encompassed a variety of wholesale, retail, and advertising strategies meant to dispose of surplus. By 1900 or so it also determined what and how much would be manufactured. With the emergence of what historian Susan Strasser has identified as "marketing-driven production," advertising assumed responsibility for spreading awareness of "new problems" that could be solved only by adopting "new habits," which in turn generated "new needs" that marketing-driven production promised to meet.[22] Ultimately, it was marketing, more than the actual production of surplus goods, that fomented the set of social, ideological, economic, and political conditions summed up in the appellation "consumer culture."

But the vast dissonance between the newly arrived economy of abundance and the still hardscrabble nature of everyday life was startling enough to foment sustained critiques of capitalism, political revolutions, as well as sustained defenses of the system which had produced so much stuff. In the United States and around the world, the standard of living—as an anthropometric measure of well-being and as an aspiration—remained low: through 1900, nearly three-quarters of all Americans lived in the kind of wrenching poverty that results in short life expectancy and high infant mortality. Clearly things were worse elsewhere, as evidenced alone by the high levels of immigration to the United States between 1870 and 1920.[23] The standard of living in Mexico before the twentieth century is hard to determine, however some measures, such as availability of food, suggest that it was no worse than in the U.S.[24]

A few political philosophies rejecting free-market capitalism as the solution to the distribution problem emerged during the middle decades of the nineteenth century, most notably socialism and Marxism. Anti-capitalist political revolutions, particularly in Russia (1917–21) and China (1933–49), dramatically introduced (and sustained, until recently) state-centered solutions to the problem of distribution. In contrast, U.S., Western European, and Japanese commercial and political leaders developed capitalist-friendly solutions to the problem of distribution, largely based on the equation of the surplus of commodities with abundance, rather than with excess or maldistribution.[25]

Most scholarly studies of consumption make the same move as did politicians and businessmen when they proclaimed abundance, so swept away are their authors by the visions of the new economy's tremendous productivity: from a factory where a hand would roll one hundred cigarettes a day to one where a machine rolled 120,000 an hour boggles the imagination. So in terms of the historical narrative, scarcity gets left aside as ever more details pile up about the institutional, social, and cultural adaptations to abundance. Scholars have plumbed the depths of retail, advertising, and commodities, but few address the informal economy, purchasing power, or consumers themselves. With some exceptions, the paradigm of abundance frames the study of consumer capitalism almost unquestioningly, despite scarcity's persistence. To be sure, "abundance rising" is an apt description of the increase in productivity throughout the world, as is one historian's assessment of this process as "astounding and transformative" and another's description of it as "the most significant event in modern history."[26] Nevertheless, transcending the parameters that abundance has set for research on consumer capitalism opens up new rich veins of inquiry.

Because late-nineteenth-century Mexicans faced a radically different socioeconomic situation than did many residents of the United States, they were unable to develop vital institutions of abundance. Since perhaps as many as nine in ten Mexicans had little to no expendable income in 1900, Mexican manufacturers, in the analysis of one economic historian, "faced a very insecure and limited consumer goods market." The prognosis was much the same for the market for intermediate and producer goods. With a home market "in transition to modernity," it was nearly impossible for Mexican industry to get a foothold, let alone prosper. As a consequence, Mexican manufacturers faced a severe version of "the problem of excess capacity."[27] Forming oligopolies and monopolies would limit production, avoid market saturation, and thus keep prices stable, if not high. However, because only a handful of Mexicans had any disposable income, implementation of economies of scale in which unlimited production would result in lower profit margins per unit sold, but higher overall profits due to volume sales, was an unrealistic strategy. The United States was home to a large market of consumers who could be reached through marketing campaigns, but the Mexican consumer market was small. So, Mexican manufacturers did not invest heavily in improving manufacturing capacity or in the sorts of vast marketing schemes that in the end remade the economy, culture, and society of the United States.

In the midst of each nation's crises of distribution, the borderlands attracted settlement and investment. After the subjugation of Native American raiders, entrepreneurs in the U.S. Southwest strengthened the region's connections to the American commercial centers through investment in railroads. So anemic was Mexico's transportation system that it was only in 1873 that the first tracks extended between Mexico City and Veracruz, the nation's primary port. In contrast, thousands of miles of railroad tracks zigzagged throughout the United States: a transcontinental railroad was completed in 1869, railroads arrived in El Paso and other regional border towns in the first years of the 1880s, and by 1900 railroad lines connected U.S. border cities to Chicago, cities on both coasts, and Gulf ports. In the 1880s, U.S. businessmen invested in connecting the border region to Mexico's interior: they funded the extension of two railroad lines between the border and Mexico City, and financed two more before 1910. Additionally, tangled railroad routes connected border towns and mines to the gulf ports of Matamoras and Tampico.[28]

During this period, foreign investors acquired concessions from the administration of Mexican president Porfirio Díaz (1876–1910) to invest in railroads, cash-crop operations, smelters, and mines throughout northern Mexico. Soon 70 percent of investment in northern Mexico was foreign, much of it from the United States. The region's mines, particularly its copper ones, yielded great wealth, due to rising demand as communications cables reached around the globe and power lines electrified cities, businesses, and homes. Much to the consternation of the Díaz administration, the United States dominated the transnational region, due to heavy investment in production and transportation between 1870 and 1900. Most of the commodities extracted

Photographic view of
Albuquerque looking Northwest,
ca. 1880–85. Photograph courtesy Cobb Memorial Collection,
Center for Southwest Research,
University Libraries, University
of New Mexico.

Santa Fe R.R. streamliner, the
"Super Chief," being serviced at
the depot, Albuquerque, N.M.,
1943. Photograph by Jack Delano,
Library of Congress, Prints and
Photographs Division, FSA/OWI
Collection, LC-USW36–689.

When the railroad arrived in New Mexico territory in 1880, it was located two miles from the town of Albuquerque. Mule-drawn trolleys connected the emerging commercial hub to "Old Town," where new arrivals of European, Chinese, Mexican, and African descent found room and board among locals de-scended from the Spanish, Pueblo, Navajo, and Apache. Lines through El Paso, Dodge City, and Barstow connected Albuquerque to the greater United States and Mexico: to the south to New Orleans and Mexico, to the north and east to Kansas City, Chicago, and New York, and to the west to San Diego, Los Angeles, and Oakland. What became known as "new town" sprang to life, here seen in the row of newly erected buildings, the L-shaped adobe warehouse in the foreground, and the boxcar that served as the first train depot until the permanent one was built in 1901. For the next half-century, the Santa Fe Railway's south-north tracks multiplied, securing Albuquerque's status as the region's shipping center. Its large passenger depot welcomed visitors to the Southwest, while its extensive yards made the railroad Albuquerque's largest employer through the 1950s.

from Mexico's northern states entered the global market via rail connections between U.S. border cities and U.S. ports, rather than via the scattered Mexican rail lines and underdeveloped Mexican Gulf ports.[29]

As the region's growing trade entrepôts thus situated on the U.S. side of the border attracted Americans and Mexicans, as well as Chinese and other nationals, everyday consumer goods—particularly food, housing, and clothing—elicited strong ethnic, national, and class associations. The migrants with the most capital, U.S. citizens, Americanized the demography, economy, built environment, culture, society, and politics of border and Southwestern cities. For instance, historian Oscar Martinez describes how brick and frame buildings, paved streets, fraternal clubs, churches, and a high school transformed El Paso from a "sleepy adobe village" into an American city. The town's population increased from 736 the year the first railroad and bank arrived (1881) to 100,000 in 1920, while the proportion of people of Mexican descent living in the city dipped from nearly all to just over half the population, in part because of housing and employment discrimination. Self-proclaimed "Americans" assumed that "Mexicans" would reside on the other side of the border or at the very least remain separate, if not invisible, in their own neighborhoods. Their expectations were not fully met, but the gradual emergence of "American" and "Mexican" districts in U.S. border towns worked to reinforce national, as well as ethnic, senses of difference.[30]

In 1885, the Díaz administration lifted all import duties in the region in order to encourage commerce on the Mexican side of the border, which it hoped would counteract the encroaching Americanization of the region. A few years earlier, in 1883, a handful of U.S. and Mexican officials had proposed a customs union that would have regarded "Mexico and the United States as integral parts of one commercial system."[31] Much too far ahead of its time, this proposal for a borderless, transnational economic zone defied the nationalist principles at the heart of what historians call "the age of tariffs." One Mexican observer of Mexico's economic policies and fortunes explained that the nation "surrounds her people with an almost impassable tariff wall." However, in the Porfirian *zona libre* (1885–1905) along the border with the United States, consumers were exempt from import duties. But, a provision in the U.S. tariff code allowed European and Asian goods to enter the United States duty-free if they were reexported, so U.S. import-export businesses profited by selling Asian and European consumer goods to Mexican retail enterprises operating in the "free zone." Retailers operating on the U.S. side of the border, however, struggled: they complained that "nearly all articles of necessity and luxury"

Discrimination, Dimmitt, Texas, 1949. Photograph by Russell Lee, courtesy Russell Lee Photograph Collection, box 3y183, negative no. 4. e_r1_14646_0038, Center for American History, University of Texas, Austin.

In the purportedly neutral marketplace in the United States, racial and ethnic groups were confined to particular days and times during which they could shop, go to fairs and amusement parks, or otherwise participate in the market for goods, services, and experiences. What is more, many of the most alluring institutions of consumption, such as department stores, hotels, self-service grocery stores, cafés, and lunch counters, were typically off-limits to peoples of African, Mexican, Indian, and Asian descent. In the Southwest, such marketplace discrimination reverberated beyond limiting choice and access, for in barring "Spanish or Mexicans" and promising to "serve White's *only*," this Dimmitt, Texas, diner and many other segregated commercial sites contributed to the social construction of Mexican national origins as nonwhite. A little more than a decade after this photograph was taken, lunch counter sit-ins and other consumer protests underscored the fundamental importance of sites of consumption for the articulation of group and national rights, especially the right to freely participate in the market.

could be "purchased on the other side much cheaper" than in their stores.[32] Despite the apparent advantages the *zona libre* gave to Mexican retailers and consumers patronizing Mexican stores, they were only temporary.

Since the economic prosperity of the northern border states was largely to the profit of foreigners, it seemed to threaten *mexicanidad*, that is, Mexican national integrity. The increased volume and value of cross-border trade destabilized the centuries-old trade circuit between Europe, the port of Veracruz, and Mexico City. As northern Mexico entered the orbit of the United States, new trade circuits developed that threatened to overshadow Veracruz as a trade hub. In response to northern Mexico's commercial development, Mexican lawmakers implemented Article 696 (1891), which placed an astounding internal tariff of 90 percent on goods made or even assembled in the *zona libre*. Typically, protective duties are imposed on articles of foreign provenance; clearly, Mexican lawmakers viewed northern states' positive industrial and commercial prospects with suspicion.[33] Little could be done to stymie the development of the region's extractive industries, however, particularly since foreign concerns owned and operated them. But a variety of Mexican political interests were determined to erect barriers to the development of manufacturing in northern Mexico. Well into the twentieth century, it was assumed that industrial production fortified national integrity and independence. Furthermore, making things—processing raw materials into finished goods—was the most exalted, and potentially profitable, form of economic activity. So the Mexican state, with its sense of national destiny rooted in its interior, tried to keep its periphery in a subordinate economic position. Nevertheless, manufacturing did develop in some Mexican border states: Nuevo Léon's largest city, Monterrey, for instance, was well on its way to becoming Mexico's center of steel, beer, glass, and textile production well before 1910.[34]

In the United States, high productivity in agriculture and manufacturing created such an immense surplus of goods that producers could barely eke out a profit: supply outstripped demand so intensely that wholesale prices often slipped below the costs of production. Simply increasing access to goods—through wholesalers, mail-order firms, department stores, and troops of salesmen—did not generate sufficient demand to raise prices.

The unprecedented task of generating demand *and* raising prices pushed producers to attempt to differentiate like products for a mass market. This innovation, however, was beyond the expertise of most manufacturers, wholesalers, and retailers. Stepping into the breach were advertising agencies, the preeminent "institutions of abundance." They innovated a welter of techniques meant to differentiate like products: packaging, branding, and trademarking together transformed barrels of crackers into different types of varying quality sold at set prices. National advertising campaigns taught consumers to differentiate between seemingly like choices. The multiplication of branded goods diminished the appearance of surplus, thus allowing prices to stabilize, and even rise. Advertising for packaged and branded goods, which initially pitched "use value" and reliability, built clusters of connections identifying the brand with "the good life," while also making subjective appeals that tapped into the anxieties and dreams of particular target markets.[35] Branded goods, the single most important contribution advertising agencies made to the forma-tion of consumer culture, have tended toward reinforcing nationalist identities, preoccupations, and fears. Regardless of where it is bottled, Coke, for instance, is American, as are Levi's, and the National Basketball Association. To be sure, some brands trade on regional and local preferences; consider Pacific Coffee sold in 1917 from twenty-two branches extending from San Diego to Oakland, or Old El Paso Foods which began catering to a local market in the 1920s.[36]

While branded goods have played an immense role in the development of consumer preferences, their manufacturers have not homogenized tastes, nor have they achieved mastery over demand. Instead, "fashion intermediaries," who often stand outside the manufacturing and promotional sectors, have at once divined and shaped many of the things ordinary consumers want. They included shopkeepers who listened attentively to their customers so as to develop a sense of what goods to stock, artisans and then art directors and industrial designers who drew on the preoccupations of the era for decorative motifs, inventors who sought to master new techniques that brought color, elaborate design, and other qualities to durable (and nondurable) consumer goods, home economists who assessed how women cleaned house, cooked meals, and tended to children so as to make suggestions for practical products, or U.S. State Department officials who filed reports with the U.S. Bureau of Foreign Commerce about the tastes and preferences of the communities where they were posted. These independent agents, and many others, played vital roles as the economy shifted, in the apt formulation of historian Susan Strasser, from production-oriented marketing to marketing-oriented produc-tion.[37] Note the admonition of a U.S. consular official posted to Nogales that "American manufacturers are gradually learning that in order to sell their goods they must accommodate themselves to the wants and peculiarities of their customers, and not attempt to impose their own ideas upon them."[38] This is but one voice from consular officials posted throughout Mexico about the necessity of attending to who Mexicans are and assessing their needs and wants, rather than sending overstocks and seconds, or imagining what they might desire, or worse yet, what might be good for them.[39] As an 1887 article in the Mexican scholarly press observed, "the establishment of ways of com-munication between the zones of production and the markets of consump-tion" is "a great element for the development of public riches."[40]

In extending their reach to the borderlands, emergent institutions of abun-dance, particularly mail-order firms and department stores, introduced new consumer products as well as branded goods to the region. The Mesilla Valley's

Amador family, for instance, stocked its thriving general store in Las Cruces, New Mexico, with necessities and luxuries—bicycles, furs, lingerie, sewing machines, saddles, whips, tobacco, and processed foods including the American Biscuit Company's "Uneeda Biscuit"—that a host of regional and national suppliers, including Chicago's mail-order giants, Montgomery Ward and Sears and Roebuck, shipped via railroad. Well into the twentieth century, mail order reached millions of households throughout the United States living at a remove from commercial centers.[41]

Thanks to the *zona libre*, the borderlands' first department stores emulating the grand emporiums of London and Paris opened in Mexican, not U.S., border towns. Within two decades, however, they and most other commercial businesses had moved to the U.S. side of the border: the efficiencies of the U.S. transportation and communications networks trumped the *zona libre*'s absence of tariffs. By 1910, 130 wholesale companies that traded in sixty different lines of staples, many of which initially opened in Ciudad Juárez, were operating in El Paso. The owners of the department store La Ciudad de Londres (1884–99), for instance, closed its doors in Ciudad Juárez one year before opening El Paso's White House Department Store (1900–84), which became part of a long-lived regional chain extending to San Francisco. Its competitor, the Popular Dry Goods Company, "the Popular," also initially opened for business in Ciudad Juárez under the name Las Tres B.B.B. (*buena, bonita*, and *barata*, or "good, pretty, and cheap") before moving its display and inventories to El Paso.[42]

More important than expanding retail choices, mail-order catalogues and department stores cultivated consumerist knowledge and desires, while at the same time incorporating and developing local and regional tastes and styles. Their *departments* literally categorized and organized the ever-multiplying array of manufactured goods. Catalogue illustrations and text fostered private daydreams in which the transformative power of objects promised self-realization. Department stores fed and stimulated sensual appetites in their insistence on display, initially under and behind glass, then in lifestyle arrangements dependent on staging and mannequins, and ultimately in bins, open shelves, and on racks beckoning browsers to touch, feel, smell, try.[43] One historian of the borderlands suggests that department stores, the most dazzling of the institutions of abundance, were modern "borderlands institutions," similar to Spanish missions and presidios. He shows how Tucson's Jácome's Department Store (1896–1980) fostered a common borderlands identity among the residents of northern Sonora and southern Arizona through ritualistic

La Feria. The Fair Store at Overland Street, El Paso, ca. 1900–1902. Photograph by Otis A. Aultman, courtesy Aultman Collection, A355, El Paso Public Library.

In 1897 the merchants who had operated the Juárez department store Las Tres B. B. B. (*buena*, *bonita*, and *barata*) opened La Feria, here pictured, in El Paso. The substantial brick building sported plate-glass windows essential for display; display windows, glass cases, and large shop floors were all vital to transforming the world of goods from inventory into the stuff of dreams. In 1902, its owners renamed La Feria, which occupied only the ground floor, The Popular Dry Goods Company. Fifteen years later, flush with revenue and assured of a large customer base, they moved "The Popular," as it was known, into a six-story building, where it grew into the largest department store in the region. In the 1960s several branches opened in the shopping malls that became part of El Paso's commercial landscape. Due in part to the negative impact of Mexico's *peso* devaluations on cross-border shopping, and in part to the competition of big-box retail, The Popular closed all its branches in 1995.

grand opening ceremonies for a new store building, the deployment of local decorative motifs and historical figures, and policies that welcomed a multi-ethnic, multinational, and cross-class clientele.[44] Other regional department stores followed different trajectories, though they too might be considered borderlands institutions. Take Goldwater's, the outlet started as a small dry goods concern in 1860 in the Arizona border town of Gila City, in Yuma County, by the grandfather of U.S. Senator and 1964 Republican presidential candidate, Barry Goldwater. A century later, its display and sale of luxury goods reinforced the class and ethnic status of Phoenix and Albuquerque's Anglo elite, much as Neiman Marcus had been doing in Dallas since 1907.[45] Borderlands' department stores, as well as local grocery and variety stores, melded the aesthetics of the borderlands and of abundance such that they reflected and reinforced class and ethnic identities far more trenchantly than national ones.

In contrast, national chain stores, restaurants, hotels, and gas stations, which by and large sold branded goods and standardized services, mostly emphasized the primacy of the nation and corporation in their operations, products, and aesthetics. However, because the borderlands had low population density, seemed foreign, and were distant from centers of manufacturing, national chains expressed little interest in the region. F. W. Woolworth's and Co., for instance, which introduced the five and dime retail concept in the 1870s, had more than 1,000 branches in the 1920s, but none in the borderlands until the 1930s. Between 1912 and 1930, the Great Atlantic and Pacific Tea Company, known as the "A & P," opened more than 16,000 grocery stores, of which only a handful were in Texas and California. Other national chains made few inroads into the region as well, although by the First World War, cigar, shoe, and clothing chains could be found in the U.S. borderlands larger cities.[46]

While anti–chain store sentiment resulted in as many as forty states imposing special regulations and taxes on the largest chain stores in the 1920s, it is likely that nowhere was the political animus as deep as in Texas, home to Wright Patman, who as Congressman in the 1930s authored and attempted to push through Federal regulations hampering the operations of national chains.[47] In contrast, locally owned businesses that had multiple branches, some of which extended through the region, although technically "chains," did not attract scrutiny. So the Helply-Selfly Grocery, Fort Worth's knockoff of the national chain, Piggly Wiggly, expanded to thirteen stores by 1927. It, like other local and regional chains, sold heavily-advertised national brands as well as in-house brands and local foodstuffs, while introducing parking spaces for automobiles, expanding retail floor space, providing carts for shoppers, and making other adjustments to incorporate the automobile.[48]

California's and Texas's larger cities were sites too of innovations in commerce seeking to address the needs of consumers living in automobile-oriented communities. In the 1910s and 1920s, Los Angeles was "the staging ground," in the words of an urban historian, for commercial forms that catered to consumers who drove cars.[49] During the middle decades of the twentieth century, gas stations, supermarkets, auto-convenient strips of retail businesses, and drive-through restaurants spread throughout the U.S. and Mexican borderlands. While many of these new commercial venues were independently owned, some were franchises, and still more were branches of regional or national chain operations. Perhaps the single most auto-oriented retail form is the shopping mall. It too has borderlands origins. In 1931, a suburb of Dallas became home to one of the first outdoor shopping malls in the United States,

Highland Park Village, whose Spanish-revival architecture emphasized Texas's northernmost city's ties to the border. A few years later, in 1934, the California grocery chain Safeway opened a store in this prototypical outdoor shopping mall.[50] Nevertheless, despite the penetration of chain stores, shopping malls, and other avatars of the new retail into cities in the U.S. borderlands, through the 1950s most borderlands' residents likely first encountered branded goods, potent signs and symbols of abundance, in small shops with uncertain inventories and even less reliable accounting.

Although nearly all businesses always sorely needed customers, well into the 1960s race, ethnicity, and nationality restricted access to the marketplace, as well as to its many services, throughout the United States, Mexico, and the borderlands. The availability of some branded goods, like Coca-Cola and Ivory soap, made it possible to aspire to be a modern American, but their advertising campaigns, built on exclusionary visual and textual rhetorics, reflected a reality of exclusionary politics and segregated marketplaces. Before the dollar was desegregated, to paraphrase a pioneering historical study about African-American consumers, advertising pitches conflated the modern, the American, and the white, while many commercial venues reinforced these associations by barring or limiting access.[51] Nevertheless, the consumption of canned foods, ready-made clothing and shoes, or cinematic dramas conveyed the awareness of participating in "modern life" regardless of racial status or origins. With the legal dismantling of racial and ethnic barriers to entering the market, only purchasing power remains as a factor limiting access. Rather than a mass market of white Americans, multiple segmented markets coexist, in which appeals are pitched to the cultural preferences and purchasing power of racial, ethnic, and national groups.[52] Contemporary marketing specialists, more so perhaps than scholars, recognize that rather than one type of borderlands consumer, there are many, with identities rooted in particular configurations of ethnicity, nationality, class, religion, gender, and sexual orientation.[53]

As powerful as advertising and its attendant cultural practices are, the central governments of the United States and Mexico may well be the most influential and far-reaching institutions of abundance. In the United States, government policies and services gradually and imperfectly balanced businesses' insistence on ever-increasing profit, consumers' demands for marketplace protection, and American expectations for unfettered and equal access to "the good life." The slavish intent of the Díaz administration to modernize Mexico at any cost arose in part out of the desire to facilitate the emergence

Small store owner, Corpus Christi, Texas, 1949. Photograph by Russell Lee, courtesy Russell Lee Photograph Collection, box 3y183, negative no. 2_r1_13943iiac_0001, Center for American History, University of Texas at Austin.

While this midcentury borderlands *tienda*, or corner store, might seem anachronistic (after all its façade suggests that it was not a chain store or even one with self-service or other characteristics of "modern" retail), it reveals how older retail forms incorporated elements of the new consumer culture. Evident is the outcome of the revolution in packaging—tin cans, bottles, and paper boxes—that eliminated most retail in bulk commodities. In the 1890s, the high output of processed goods necessitated branding—Dr. Pepper, Barq's, Camels, Cools, KC Baking Powder—as a marketing strategy which would differentiate like products and thus offset the downward pressure on prices that oversupply creates. Small and large store owners alike found themselves at the mercy of brands, since customers requested them by name and often would not accept substitutes. In the 1920s slogans tied multimedia campaigns together—store posters proclaiming "good for life," "made in the South," or "So Mild!" echoed jingles heard on the radio, which themselves repeated ad copy in magazines and newspapers. Well through midcentury, the small shop was a vital conduit for branded goods, especially to geographically and economically marginalized consumers.

Downtown El Paso, ca. 1910–20. Photograph by Otis A. Aultman, courtesy Aultman Collection, A412, El Paso Public Library.

During the 1910s, the many signs and symbols of consumer capitalism saturated downtown El Paso, as well as other U.S. cities in and beyond the borderlands. Electric signs, painted signs, telephone poles and wires, sidewalks, and theater marques together frame the White House Department Store, the city bank, the local newspaper headquarters, and the town hall.

of a consumption-oriented economy, but its concessions instead contributed to the unraveling of the nation. Gilded Age politicians in the United States handed out railroad subsidies, passed and repealed tariffs, and dangerously fooled around with the currency, while remaining mostly impervious to the travails of farmers, workers, and propertyless people. Despite measures in the United States that served consumers as well as businesses, such as the extension of the post office's services to rural areas (1896), the initiation of parcel post (1912), the creation of the Department of Commerce (1902), and the establishment of the Food and Drug Administration (1906), the U.S. government has tended to favor business needs over those of consumers. (Consider the battles to impose consumer safety standards on automobiles and cigarettes, not coincidentally the twentieth century's most profitable, dangerous, and symbolically charged mass-produced items.[54])

In addition to government agencies and policies, established cultural institutions such as commercial publishing houses, museums, and schools also contributed to the new consumer-oriented economic order in the United States and Mexico.[55] In the 1880s and 1890s, "slick paper" magazines, as they were known at the time, with full-page color advertisements punctuating tales about "consuming subjects" were distributed nationally. In the 1930s and 1940s, comics (*historietas*) performed a similar role in Mexico. Furthermore, newspapers in the United States and Mexico introduced the fashion, automotive, and lifestyle pages, while also joining a global network of media enterprises connected by transoceanic cables, wireless communications, and news services.[56] Soon entirely new forms of communication—moving pictures, radio, and eventually television—heralded the "information age." The forms that each medium took hewed to a consumer-oriented order, in which discernment, discontent, and desire were as necessary as disposable income.[57] Vocational and business schools trained secretaries, accountants, marketing specialists, managers, and a host of other professionals and semi-professionals necessary to the new economy. Museums and other venues for exhibitions, such as world's fairs, purposefully fostered attention to design, hosted fashion shows, and in many cases—through taxonomic displays of peoples and objects —reinforced notions of racial, cultural, and national superiority that in turn supported imperialist and capitalist relations at home and abroad.[58]

A new structure of values that cast the cultivation of image, desire, and pleasure as positive economic and personal attributes undergirded innovations in institutional practices and forms. New quantitative measures, such as "the masses" and "the standard of living," recalibrated vices into virtues: materialism was recast as "pious consumption" and "keeping up with the Joneses" ousted envy. Perhaps most far-reaching was the "therapeutic ethos," which emerged from mainstream Protestant promises in the 1880s and 1890s that salvation—indeed, self-realization—could begin here on earth through the consumption of uplifting goods, experiences, and places. Leisure, mass culture, vacations, and tourism augmented the middle-class value system, remaking theater into a site of uplift rather than corruption, Sunday into a day of recreation rather than of rest, night into a time for adult fun, rural areas into pleasure resorts, and the Southwest into a scenic place where one could marvel at "untouched nature" found in the landscapes and peoples. Advertisers in the 1920s adopted a ministerial stance, preaching the gospel of consumption in as many venues as possible, above all advertisements themselves.[59] The therapeutic ethos is as integral to consumer capitalism today in the United States and Mexico as it was a hundred years ago. Peter Cahn, for instance, highlights the profound complexity of the relationships between religious outlooks and capitalist practices through his ethnographic research into contemporary Mexican religious practices and beliefs.[60]

"Desire" and "pleasure" were another set of conditions that gained positive associations after the turn of the twentieth century. As economists like Simon Patten, journalists like Charles Lummis, fabulists like the author of *The Wizard of Oz*, L. Frank Baum, and Hollywood movie studios refashioned desire and pleasure as uplifting, popular culture oriented its diversions around them. Despite ongoing ambivalence about how passions erode moral sensibilities, the efforts to arouse desire and provide pleasure became fundamental aspects of economic and personal practices in the U.S. and eventually elsewhere. Throughout the second half of the twentieth century, popular culture let loose the currents—most easily encompassed in the idea of "image"—that would erode indifference or outright hostility to accumulation, luxury, and consumption itself. Surplus cast as *abundance*, rather than as *over-supply*, eased the task of recalibrating attitudes toward materialists and sensualists, such that each could join the ranks of virtuous citizens. Part of this far-reaching adjustment in attitudes hinged upon the expansion of notions of *usefulness* so that *necessity* could become a subjective and dynamic consideration. Marketers played an important role in this process, identifying, as the historian Susan Strasser has shown, "new needs," which mandated "new habits," and, thus, "new products." The elasticity of the meanings of *necessity* and *luxury* provided ample room within which new structures of feeling based on desire, pleasure, and appearance took shape.[61]

In contrast to the multifaceted U.S. response to abundance, in the Mexican borderlands after the turn of the century, no such ideological sleight of hand was necessary. The problem of distribution presented itself in the age-old shape of scarcity: scarcity of imported goods due to the end of the *zona libre* (1905), scarcity of water due to drought (1906–08), scarcity of food and fuel due to a subsistence crisis across Mexico (1907–08). Many residents left, while those who stayed began to cater to their U.S. neighbors' demands for entertainment and services, selling caricatures of Mexico in the forms of souvenirs, tourist attractions like Ciudad Juárez's bullring (1903) and racetrack (1905), and services available in *zonas de tolerencia*, not to mention vast tracts of Mexican land.[62] Spending time and money across the border took on an aura of abandon, of leaving behind the ethics of work and thrift, which reinforced notions of U.S. superiority, a theme that historians, anthropologists, and social critics develop in their research about the economic development of the borderlands in the twentieth century. What could be called the "in-and-out" variant of borderlands tourism, both in terms of time spent across the border and the nature of the services sought, contributed to the spread of exploita-

Detained at the refugee camp, El Paso, 1914. Photographic postcard, Yale Collection of Western Americana, Beinecke Rare Book and Manuscript Library, Yale University, Image ID 1066553. Manuscript caption on verso reads: "Electronically charged fence."

A high, electrified barbed-wire fence here encloses five of the hundreds of thousands of refugees from the Mexican Revolution who found their way across the border, seeking not only a safe haven but also, in many cases, respite from scarcity. The empty bottle, parched earth, and dirty clothing suggest a collective need for water; the girls' boots and smocked, collared, buttoned, and pleated dresses indicate that other consumer needs had been met. This refugee camp, a site of scarcity and "making do" and emblem of Mexico's impoverishment, was but a few miles from El Paso's downtown, seen in the contemporaneous photograph found on page 30.

tive attitudes and conditions that continue, a century later, to characterize the region. Scarcity amidst an abundance of wealth generated from the region's natural resources transformed Mexican border towns during the first decade of the twentieth century. Lacking access to the various safety valves that in the United States diffused rising discontent about inequality, such as an open frontier (until 1890), an expanding economy, racial scapegoating, and the quest for empire (after 1898), Mexico's solution to the distribution problem was the one of last resort: civil war.

Put bluntly, the Mexican Revolution (1910–20) ruined the immediate prospects for Mexico's border states to benefit from rising transnational flows of capital, labor, and commodities. Not only did it drive out residents and disrupt industrial and agricultural activities; its leaders also undercut the viability of what commerce remained on the Mexican side of the border through redistributive policies, while ceding to U.S. border merchants opportunities to get rich. For instance, Pancho Villa confiscated clothing, shoes, and other apparel, as well as candy, from Chihuahua City merchants, which he then handed out to the city's impoverished. In a further effort to solve the distribution problem his

Rebel troops passing through street in Chihuahua, 1914. Photograph, Library of Congress, Prints and Photographs Division, LC-USZ62–71101.

Pictured here are the cavalry troops of the provisional governor of the northern Mexican state of Chihuahua, Pancho Villa, riding in single file down the main street of the state capital, Chihuahua City. The electric and telephone wires, street lights, sidewalks, and multistoried buildings are representative of the economic and technological modernization of northern Mexico before the revolution. The factions fighting in northern Mexico, above all Villa's, depended on the region's well-developed railroad networks to transport supplies and troops, just as much as they did on the region's modern cities.

way, Villa set price ceilings for meat, wheat, and corn, while giving away milk, meat, and bread. In the meantime, merchants, builders, and smugglers operating in U.S. border cities and states met Mexican wartime demand for goods ranging from five rail carloads of canned sardines to 40,000 pairs of shoes and khaki shirts for Villa's troops, to guns and cannon for all of the armed factions, including the federal army. The militarization of the region, seen not only in Mexico, but also in fortified U.S. military outposts, particularly El Paso's Fort Bliss (1877) and San Diego's naval base (1898), further increased demand for staples, supplies, and services, nearly all of which was met by U.S.-owned businesses.[63]

The shift of business to the U.S. side of the border during the revolution alone did not contribute to northern Mexico's economic decay. Instead, blame ought to include missed opportunities for long-term development, summed up in the words *modernization, expansion,* and *maintenance*. Some of the world's first branded goods, such as Quaker Oats, Uneeda Biscuit, Campbell's Soup, and Crisco, expanded the market for agricultural commodities such as oats, wheat, barley, vegetables, and even cottonseed oil, in which some large-scale borderlands farmers participated. The use of refrigerated railroad cars after the 1880s further stimulated the mass market for perishable foods, especially fresh fruits and vegetables, in large U.S. cities. To meet this demand, large-scale cash crop cultivation transformed much of Texas's Rio Grande Valley and California's Imperial Valley. When the First World War laid siege to Europe's agricultural acreage, large-scale farming operations in California and Texas further profited from surging demand for staples. Furthermore, rising wartime demand for copper and petroleum led to the expansion of mining, drilling, and processing operations on the U.S. side of the border. Once the fighting was over in Mexico and Europe, the United States had leapt far ahead of Mexico. In the aftermath of the 1910s, the Mexican state oriented itself toward land reform and nationalization of industries and mines: rather than concede economic opportunities to foreigners, it hoped to provide Mexicans with the means of self-subsistence. Not until the 1970s did much of northern Mexico's agricultural infrastructure modernize with hydrology projects, highway building, and refrigerated trucks.[64]

There are other ways, too, that the Mexican Revolution and the First World War tilted the balance toward U.S. dominance in the region. U.S. cities in the region grew rapidly, while Mexican ones stagnated. The populations of San Diego and Los Angeles, for instance, nearly quadrupled during the two decades after 1910. Filmmakers, who in 1910 began relocating their industry to the Southwest, particularly Los Angeles, captured the international market for movies during the war, which provided them with lasting advantages in one of the consumer culture's most important venues. Along with oil, aviation, shipping, and shipbuilding, the film business contributed to Los Angeles's growth, such that by 1930 it was the fifth largest city in the Unites States. Five times as many people made Los Angeles their home as lived in the ten largest cities in the Mexican borderlands; 132,577 residents made Monterrey the largest Mexican borderlands city, followed by Ciudad Juaréz, which was home to 39,666 people, while Tijuana's minuscule population of 8,384 put it in seventh place.[65] Mexican border cities' relatively small size and slow growth prior to the Great Depression further exacerbated northern Mexico's disadvantages in the region's transnational economy.

Through the first half of the twentieth century, nationalist preoccupations with building a strong central state in Mexico and with protecting the economic gains that the U.S. had achieved affected the borderlands nearly as much as had the Mexican Revolution and the First World War. The U.S.

U.S. Troops in El Paso, 1915. Photographic postcard, Yale Collection of Western Americana, Beinecke Rare Book and Manuscript Library, Yale University, Image ID 2017309.

The militarization of the border, as signified by U.S. troops marching down one of El Paso's main corridors, at first gave rise to saloons and other places of amusement in U.S. border towns, while also boosting local construction, transportation, and wholesale businesses. Over the course of the 1910s, the formidable strength of U.S. armed forces—particularly after the American Expeditionary Forces' contribution to the Allied victory in Europe—in contrast with the disarray of the Mexican Federalists and revolutionary factions only exacerbated the sense of imbalance between the two nations. Since the 1920s, Mexican border towns catered to the recreational needs of U.S. sailors and soldiers. Beginning in the 1970s another wave of militarization along the border began, this time in response at first to narcotics smuggling, and later to concerns about national security related to unauthorized entry of people into the United States.

President Calvin Coolidge declared in the 1920s that "the business of America is business," but he did not nationalize industry or redistribute land as did his Mexico City counterparts. Clearly each nation diverged from the other considerably in terms of its political approach to fostering economic growth, but nationalism deeply informed each set of efforts. In the shape of commercial regulation and initiative, it paradoxically contributed to the region's binationalism and eventually its transnationalism. Specific consumer needs and desires propelled large numbers of people across the border in both directions, providing further impetus to the development of an asymmetrical regional economy. Inequalities among peoples rising from class, ethnic, and national position flourished, as did illegal and criminal enterprises whose very existence depended on the border.

U.S. preoccupation with Protestant versions of morality further exacerbated the region's uneven economic development. Through the 1910s, local and state U.S. morals laws prohibited the sale of alcohol and sex, the sponsorship of animal racing and blood sports, and the facilitation of gambling. These measures were part of a broad set of responses to the cumulative effects of modernity, particularly high levels of immigration to the Atlantic coast during the previous four decades, new concentrations of wealth and populations in large cities, and emergent cultural obsessions with novelty, youth, and sex. In the wake of Prohibition, saloons, breweries, distilleries, brothels, racetracks, and casinos moved just south of the border, remaining in the orbit of millions of people in the United States, living in cities such as Los Angeles and El Paso. In this way the border became modern, for it offered a safety valve for people unwilling to adhere to vice regulations promising tradition and stability. Despite the significant revenue Mexican border towns generated catering to the vice and tourist trade, on balance, U.S. border cities prospered far more than did Mexican ones during the 1920s. They hosted numerous national and regional conventions, boarded and conveyed hundreds of thousands, if not more, U.S. residents heading across the border, continued to refine, process, and ship the region's agricultural and mineral commodities, and also met most U.S. and Mexican retail demands.

The preoccupation of Mexican nationalism with the need for a strong central state cast the border region as in need of fortification against foreign capitalists, who were exploiting Mexico's valuable natural resources, and against U.S. tourists, who were responsible for the "cities of whores" strung along the Mexican side of the border.[66] During the 1920s and 1930s the Mexican federal government claimed significant amounts of previously private land and resources for the nation. The intent of Article 27 of Mexico's 1917 Constitution was to reclaim Mexico for Mexicans: not only does it mandate that all natural resources in Mexico are national property whose private exploitation is only permissible through concessions, but it also forbids foreigners from owning land within sixty-two miles of Mexico's territorial borders and thirty-one miles of its coasts. These provisions entailed nationalization: by the end of the 1930s, the Mexican state had nationalized its petroleum industry, seized millions of acres of U.S.-owned land along Mexico's coasts and northern border, and redistributed one hundred million acres of land.[67] Taxes and licensing fees on some of the millions of dollars of revenue saloons, bars, lounges, brothels, and casinos generated in the 1920s hastened the region's partial modernization, through public works projects that included the construction of modern irrigation systems, public utilities, roads, railroads, and schools, but in 1934 Mexico banned vice industries from border towns.[68]

Fortification against U.S. mass-produced goods, however, proved impos-

Mexican police officers with confiscated opium and cocaine drugs, Tijuana, Baja California, 1930. Photograph courtesy Photograph Collection, San Diego Historical Society.

The Harrison Act (1914) gave the U.S. Treasury the power to tax and regulate the distribution and sale of opium and cocaine, but the use of narcotics in the United States would not be prohibited until after the Second World War. Despite a 1926 Mexican law banning poppy cultivation, opium grown in the Mexican state of Sinaloa was exported to the United States, mostly through Mexicali and Tijuana. Though the origins of these "*drogas heroicas*" (narcotics), here neatly displayed as though for sale in a grocery store, are unknown, it may be that Manuel Proto and Guillermo McAlpin, Tijuana policemen, seized them from traffickers doing business in the border town, rather than from smugglers seeking to move them into the United States. In the 1960s, what had become an insatiable U.S. market for marijuana and narcotics transformed northern Mexico into the home of more than three hundred clandestine airfields. The magnitude of the trade was so great that the U.S. government launched "Operation Intercept" against cross-border drug smuggling in 1969. It is estimated that as of 2007, at least 70 percent of controlled substances enter the United States via the border with Mexico.

sible. Northern Mexico's anemic commercial infrastructure, Mexico's late and poorly capitalized entry into mass production, and the allure, as well as availability, of U.S. consumer goods together worked to the advantage of U.S. retailers in the borderlands during the 1920s. Most people living on the Mexican side of the border shopped in U.S. border towns for provisions, including medicines, milk, and tinned foods, as well as for durable consumer goods like automobiles. A 1926 study reveals the enormity of this trade. That year, *juarenses* spent ten times as much in El Paso ($15 million) as in their own city: in U.S. stores they bought "fruits, vegetables, staple items, canned meats, clothing, shoes, cars, furniture, office supplies, medicines, perfumes, soaps,

Two men sitting in Maxwell Auto, San Diego, 1922. Photograph courtesy Photograph Collection, San Diego Historical Society.

U.S. car dealers in the borderlands, like San Diego's local dealer for Maxwell-Chrysler, the Merritt Company, served customers living on both sides of the border. In 1920, San Diego had no more than three auto dealerships, but by 1930, the city of 150,000 hosted twenty-six businesses catering to demands for automobiles, parts, and repairs, a number that increased to nearly fifty by 1940, despite the decline in U.S. and Mexican consumer spending throughout the 1930s.

glass, construction materials, hardware goods, and many other products," while in Mexico they bought, according to one study, "national goods," identified as coffee, tropical fruits, beans, straw hats, and alcoholic beverages.[69] The residents of Nogales and Mexicali spent four hundred times as much across the border as in their own towns. Since Mexican national identity, *mexicanidad*, was in part instilled through the consumption of Mexican-made products, and in part projected through the patronage of Mexican businesses, borderlanders' dependence on U.S. retail contributed to the suspicion with which central Mexicans approached the northern border and its residents. Nevertheless, throughout the twentieth century, except during times of severe economic crisis, residents of the Mexican borderlands have avidly done their shopping across the border.[70]

For the most part, few observers, until quite recently, have included border-crossing Mexican shoppers among "modern consumers." The modern consumer, rendered iconic in popular visual and print culture, connotes the affluent and the comfortable classes. Consider, in contrast, what the anthropologist Josiah Heyman identifies as the "consumer proletariat": people alienated from the means of production *and* consumption. Heyman concludes that after 1900, borderlanders ceased to directly provision their households, as they once had by growing crops, raising animals, gathering firewood, drawing water, weaving textiles, and sewing clothes. As "producers" without land, tools, or capital, they had no choice but to sell their labor to farming, mine, railroad, and other operations. As "consumers" without access to springs, fields, or commons, they had to turn to the market for tinned foods, factory-made tortillas, water, fuel, and ready-made clothing. This state of affairs, known as "market dependency," irked and threatened the central Mexican government when it considered its northernmost citizens. Around the world, in fits and starts since the seventeenth century, large numbers of people have experienced similar shifts from self-sufficiency to market dependency. In the borderlands, descendants of indigenous peoples, Spanish colonists, and Anglo settlers began to make the transition in the 1880s; by the 1940s market-dependency was the rule.[71]

As borderlanders, like residents of industrial and global cities, became market-oriented producers and consumers, they had to hone what the historian Susan Porter Benson has identified as consumption practices rooted in "self-denial, rather than self-fulfillment."[72] She shows how U.S. working classes in the 1920s and 1930s acted as "inconspicuous consumers," unlike the "conspicuous consumers" social critic Thorstein Veblen first taunted in his 1899 classic, *Theory of the Leisure Class*. In short, Benson's work contravenes the widely held notion that "a rising and inclusive tide" of consumption swept across the United States during the twentieth century.[73] Other historians too are working to shift focus from the peoples who have "adapted to abundance" toward the many who have made do with scarcity. Consumer practices in the U.S.–Mexico borderlands present further opportunities to assess self-denial and inconspicuous consumption within the context of rising levels of material abundance, particularly in the 1920s and 1930s, pivotal decades in this matrix.[74]

After the international economic collapse of 1929, it appeared conclusive that scarcity would persist despite the maturation of economies and cultures of abundance. But the worldwide collapse of capitalist economies due to overproduction and underconsumption seemed to discredit consumer capitalism as *the* answer to the problem of distribution. In places where fascism took hold or where communism tightened its grip, state-centered solutions to the problem of distribution gained traction. In the United States, displaced

"The house that Jack built," Los Angeles, 1928. Courtesy *Herald-Examiner* Collection, Los Angeles Public Library.

The Los Angeles *Herald-Examiner* captioned this photograph: "Here are Jack Donovan, film actor, and the 'house that Jack built' and sold to Mae Murray, famous star, for $50,000." Houses like this, and the movie stars like Jack who built them, became symbols of a new culture oriented toward purchase, display, and pleasure—a consumer culture—that served to underscore the contrast between abundance and scarcity, but also to push the specter of scarcity to the margins of the nation, that is, to rural areas, urban ghettoes, and the border region.

sharecroppers, tenant farmers, unskilled young men, and industrial workers were among the most likely to consider the viability of forms of distribution other than market-oriented ones, but various ideological, political, and social conditions foreclosed those possibilities. Certainly, there were Americans of all economic positions who took the opportunity, created by capitalism's crisis, to reject greed and materialism; in some cases they even elected representatives to political office.

But "plenty," which had defined the United States since its inception, would continue to underpin political and economic commitments to democracy and capitalism. Grassroots consumer activism did flourish in response to hoarding and stockpiling (especially of food), discriminatory hiring practices (the slogan "don't shop where you can't work" adorned picket signs in Chicago and New York City), and dried-up sources of consumer credit. Sales of durable goods like automobiles and home appliances plummeted, but debtors were loath to miss monthly installment payments for what they already possessed, particularly their automobiles. Millions of Americans reverted to the homegrown and homemade; in doing so they purchased seeds, bulk textiles, glass jars, and other producer goods, but they did not lose their taste for consumer goods. Instead, they dreamt about what they might buy when times got better.[75]

New Deal programs stepped up efforts of the U.S. federal government to foster a well-run, well-regulated, and subsidized consumer economy. An alphabet soup of programs aimed to relieve privation, to reform financial institutions and instruments, and to regulate market relationships. The resultant programs and policies deepened consumerism's roots through the electrification of rural areas, the construction of roads, bridges, harbors, and airports, the formation of federal agencies to underwrite consumer loans for purchases ranging from houses to electric appliances, and the stabilization of purchasing power through Social Security insurance and the minimum wage laws. These programs, as well as FDR's failed effort during the Second World War to amend the Bill of Rights with the guarantee to all U.S. citizens of an "American standard of living" (which Congress trimmed down to the G. I. Bill of Rights), transformed the U.S. government from an enthusiastic bystander into an active participant in consumer society. The Great Depression was "the defining moment" in the nation's history for a number of reasons, not the least of which was that the political response to it enshrined abundance as the nation's primary concern.[76]

The attenuation of border crossing for labor, leisure, or commerce during the 1930s contributed to the sense that, in the words of two historians, the border was "finally starting to harden into the clearly marked boundar[y] that appeared on most national maps."[77] That Mexico so fiercely sought economic independence from the United States through the 1930s added to the hardening of the border. After U.S. president Franklin Delano Roosevelt lifted Prohibition in 1933 and Mexican president Lázaro Cárdenas banned the vice industries in 1934, revenues from vice tourism in Mexico declined precipitously, and so with them went the economic fortunes of Mexican border towns and residents. In the attempt to provision border residents, the Mexican government reestablished duty-free zones in communities along the border with California and Arizona.[78] At the same time a large but unknown number of people of Mexican descent, half of whom might have been U.S. citizens, were forcibly expulsed from the United States. They swelled the populations of Mexico's border towns to unmanageable proportions. Attempting to prevent their return to the U.S., as well as the entry of other immigrants, the

Aztec Brewery, San Diego, ca. 1937. Photograph courtesy Photograph Collection, San Diego Historical Society.

Southwestern regional architecture during the 1930s embraced a visual aesthetic that incorporated a host of symbols from each side of the border. At San Diego's Aztec Brewery, built after the repeal of Prohibition (1933), the mural above the fermenting vats shows an "Indian" in Plains Indian headdress paying homage to hops and barley bursting forth from the Aztec calendar. The tiled floor and wainscoting, stuccoed walls, and fancy ironwork characterized period libraries, town halls, post offices, and hotel lobbies. Many of the rooms in the brewery were decorated as elaborately as this one, combining the Aztec motif with that of beer.

U.S. firmed up its border patrol and entry requirements.[79] Openings remained. A regional aesthetics flourished in commercial spaces such as department stores, trading posts, grocery stores, bars and restaurants, hotels, gas stations, stage and movie theaters, concert halls, and breweries. It did so too in public spaces like post offices, customs houses, railroad stations, fairgrounds, and schools, where the U.S. Works Progress Administration funded new construction and the addition of decorative elements, particularly murals, that showcased distinctive regional types and motifs. Transnational transportation and communications systems operated, with railroads and automobiles, as well as radio waves, transversing the borderline. Tourism maintained a foothold, though it was far less lucrative than it had been during the previous two decades. Cross-border kinship ties persisted. Trade barriers actually loosened after the implementation of the Reciprocal Trade Agreement Act, which gave the U.S. president the power to reduce tariffs by half in exchange for similar concessions from foreign governments. So U.S.-Mexico trade, which had hit a low in 1933 after more than a decade of gains, doubled by 1939.[80] It was these continuities, rather than the drawing and redrawing of the borderline between the U.S. and Mexico during the ninety years since the conclusion of the U.S.-

Mexico War, that accounted for the particular shape and vitality of the region's consumer culture, as well as its dramatic contrasts.

Notes

I acknowledge with gratitude the help of the following friends and colleagues. Penn State University's Amy Greenberg read the very first, very short draft of this essay, added some insight about the U.S.-Mexico War, and watched it grow and grow. SMU's Ben Johnson and David Weber commented on an early version of the essay; thanks especially to Ben for identifying an incorrectly captioned photograph. Northwestern University's Gerry Cadava and University of Texas, El Paso's Julia Camacho each read versions of the essay, and graciously and enthusiastically shared their own unpublished research about the U.S.-Mexico borderlands. University of California, Berkeley's Brian DeLay insightfully critiqued the penultimate version of this essay; his comments about the nineteenth-century borderlands were particularly helpful. My own Adam Herring answered so many questions, from ones about Latin American material culture to others about theoretical issues. Special thanks to Adam, Amy Greenberg, and Neal McTighe for helping me in various ways write this essay, take it apart, and put it back together.

Notes fully cite primary sources and specialized secondary sources. Full bibliographic details for all other citations are in the volume's selected bibliography.

1. Ellen Churchill Semple, *Influences of Geographic Environment on the Basis of Ratzel's System of Anthropo-Geography* (New York: Henry Holt and Company, 1911), 221.

2. The first agreement between the United States and Mexico about their shared border was signed in 1828; subsequently six more agreements about the boundary line itself were negotiated prior to the 1910 Chamizal Agreement (Herzog, *Where North Meets South*, Table 2, 36). The geographer Lawrence Herzog points out that after an agreement made in 1925 to exchange information about smuggling, the emphasis in binational treaties and agreements shifted from maintenance of the border line to management of the border region (38). On militarization of the border, see Dunn, *Militarization of the U.S.-Mexico Border, 1978–1992*. On the murder rate in Ciudad Juárez—more than 100 murders a month in the city of 1.5 million—during the first ten months of 2008, see Alicia A. Caldwell, " 'There's No Law Over There': Juárez Living Up to Its Violent Reputation," *Albuquerque Journal*, October 19, 2008. On the relation between neoliberal forms of capitalist development, the international border, and Juárez's femicides, see Wright, *Disposable Women*.

3. On the world economy after 1500, see Wallerstein, *Modern World System*; Findlay and O'Rourke, "Commodity Market Integration, 1500–2000." On the "industrious revolution," the industrial revolution, and the "reallocation of household resources," see the following publications by Jan de Vries: *Industrious Revolution*; "Purchasing Power"; "Industrial Revolution." On the rising volume of global trade and its consequences for consumption patterns in Europe, Asia, and Latin America, see Brewer and Porter, eds., *Consumption*; Clunas, "Modernity, Global and Local"; Adshead, *Material Culture*;

Bauer, *Goods, Power, History*; Brewer and Trentmann, eds., *Consuming Cultures*; Trentmann, "Modern Evolution of the Consumer"; Stearns, "Stages of Consumerism"; Stearns, *Consumerism in World History*. On U.S. consumer culture, see Strasser, "Making Consumption"; Steigerwald, "All Hail the Republic of Choice"; Blanke, "Consumer Culture"; Cross, *All-Consuming Century*; Zukin, *Point of Purchase*.

4. Historians' competing views about the relationship between demand and supply reflect divergent understandings of human nature. Nevertheless, scholars have attended far more closely to supply than to demand as a causative factor in the industrial and consumer revolutions. Economic historian Jan de Vries's investigation of Western European household productivity, income and wages, and spending patterns provides evidence of the early importance of demand during the rise of capitalism. That demand came before surplus is the contention of historian Jeremy Presthold's article "Global Repercussions" about trade between Massachusetts, East Africa, and India in the eighteenth century. See also Presthold, *Domesticating the World*. Two painstaking studies, Roche's *History of Everyday Things*, about early modern France, and Bruegel's *Farm, Shop, Landing*, about the U.S. Hudson Valley from 1800 to 1850, make strong cases that surplus preceded demand.

5. On the origins of mass consumption in the Atlantic world, see de Vries, *Industrious Revolution*; Shammas, "Changes in English and Anglo-American Consumption"; Walsh, "Peopling, Producing, and Consuming"; Carr and Walsh, "Changing Lifestyles"; McCusker and Menard, eds., *Economy of British America*; Agnew, "Coming Up for Air"; Bushman, *Refinement of America*; Nater, "Colonial Tobacco."

6. Breen, *Marketplace of Revolution*, 61, 65; Breen, " 'Baubles of Britain,' " 87, 80.

7. Juan Peláez de Berrío, quoted in Bakewell, *History of Latin America*, 202.

8. Bakewell, *History of Latin America*, 229. On colonial Mexican trade with Spain, see 198–201.

9. On trade regulation on the Spanish frontier, see Reséndez, "Getting Cured." On Latin American producers and global consumers, see Topik, Marichal, and Frank, eds., *Silver to Cocaine*; Bértola and Williamson, "Globalization in Latin America before 1940."

10. Ilona Katzew, *Casta Painting: Images of Race in Eighteenth-Century Mexico* (New Haven: Yale University Press, 2004); Magali M. Carrera, *Imagining Identity in New Spain: Race, Lineage, and the Colonial Body in Portraiture and Casta Paintings* (Austin: University of Texas Press, 2003); Colin M. MacLachlan and Jaime E. Rodríguez, *The Forging of the Cosmic Race: A Reinterpretation of Colonial Mexico*, expanded edition (Berkeley: University of California Press, 1990).

11. Reséndez, "Getting Cured," 78.

12. Josiah Gregg, *Commerce of the Prairies*, edited by Max L. Moorhead (1844; Norman: University of Oklahoma Press, 1954), 16–21, quotes on p. 80.

13. Ibid., n. 1, 226, chapter 9, quote on p. 265.

14. Ibid., 333.

15. On eighteenth-century trade between Mexico and Spain, see Bakewell, *History of Latin America*, 182, 266. On trade in the Spanish borderlands, see Weber, *Mexican Fron-*

tier; Lorey, *U.S.-Mexican Border*, 24–25; Reséndez, "Getting Cured"; Martha Works, "Creating Trading Places on the New Mexican Frontier," *Geographical Review* 82 (1992): 268–81; Linda Devereaux, "Philip Nolan and His 'Wild Horse,'" *Texana* 12 (1974): 88–100. On trade relations between the United States and Mexico prior to 1846, see Gregg, *Commerce of the Prairies, op. cit.*; Salvucci, "Origins and Progress," 700–16. On Native American consumption habits in British North America, see Colin Calloway, *New Worlds for All: Indians, Europeans, and the Remaking of Early America* (Baltimore: Johns Hopkins University Press, 1998), esp. chap. 3; Nancy Shoemaker, *A Strange Likeness: Becoming Red and White in Eighteenth-Century North America* (New York: Oxford University Press, 2004), 53–54, 77–78.

16. Potter, *People of Plenty*, 166.

17. On the industrial revolution in the United States, see Sellers, *Market Revolution*; Bruegel, *Farm, Shop, Landing*; Clark, *Roots of Rural Capitalism*; Chandler, *Visible Hand*; Scranton, *Endless Novelty*.

18. On Americans' search for markets, see Albert Weinberg, *Manifest Destiny: A Study of Nationalist Expansionism in American History* (Baltimore: Johns Hopkins University Press, 1935); Jacobson, *Barbarian Virtues*; Hoganson, *Consumers' Imperium*. On the 1820s and 1830s international market for U.S.-made clocks, see Donald Hoke, *Ingenious Yankees: The Rise of the American System of Manufactures in the Private Sector* (New York: Columbia University Press, 1990), 186. On the search for markets as cause for the U.S.-Mexico War, see Graebner, *Empire on the Pacific*; Weeks, *Building the Continental Empire*; Hietala, *Manifest Design*, chap. 3; Salvucci, "Origins and Progress," 714–16, 728, 734–35. On Mexican shopping in Texas border towns between 1978 and 2001, see Keith and Coronado, "Texas Border Benefits from Retail Sale to Mexican Nationals," in *The Face of Texas: Jobs, People, Business, Change* (Dallas: Federal Reserve of Dallas, 2005), 24–26.

19. On "empty zones," see Herzog, *North Meets South*, xi. On buffers, see Herzog, ed., *Shared Space*, 2.

20. Editorial in *El Eco de la Frontera* (April 22, 1856), quoted in Martinez, *Border Boom Town*, 12.

21. Potter, "The Institution of Abundance: Advertising," *People of Plenty*, chap. 8.

22. Strasser, *Satisfaction Guaranteed*; Strasser, "Woolworth to Wal-Mart." On anxieties about surplus, see Mark Seltzer, *Bodies and Machines* (New York: Routledge, 1992), esp. part 1, " Naturalist Machine"; Horowitz, *Anxieties of Affluence*.

23. On standards of living in the United States and the world since 1700, see Komlos, *Biological Standard of Living*; Easterlin, "Worldwide Standard of Living"; Voth, "Living Standards"; Kanbur, "Standard of Living"; Storper, "Lived Effects of the Contemporary Economy"; Hart, "Commoditisation and the Standard of Living"; David Igler, "Diseased Goods: Global Exchanges in the Eastern Pacific Basin, 1770–1850," *American Historical Review* 109 (2004): 693–719. On contemporary standards of living in the United States, see Slesnick, *Living Standards in the United States*; Slesnick, *Consumption and Social Welfare*. The vast literature on U.S. social history addresses in great depth and detail the standard of living for various people living in various regions and various

times. Two works that give an especially helpful snapshot of the second half of the nineteenth century are Edgar Martin, *American Consumption Levels on the Eve of the Civil War* (Chicago: University of Chicago Press, 1942); Henry Bedford, ed., *Their Lives & Numbers: The Condition of Working People in Massachusetts, 1870–1900* (Ithaca: Cornell University Press, 1995).

24. Based on analysis of a cross-class, cross-region sample of Mexicans' height and weight, historian Moramay López-Alonso concludes, in an article titled "Growth and Inequality," that the biological standard of living in Mexico saw a decline between 1870 and 1930. About wages and prices in Mexico prior to 1910, see Gómez-Galvarriato, "The Impact of Revolution"; Gómez-Galvarriato, *Evolution of Prices and Real Wages*; and Gómez-Galvarriato, *Political Economy of Protectionism*. On twentieth-century Latin American standards of living, see Astorga, Berges, and Fitzgerald, "Standard of Living."

25. On political responses to maldistribution and inequality, see Thompson, "Social Opulence"; Sen, *Inequality Re-examined*. The idea of "standard of living" itself was a political response to the maldistribution of rising levels of abundance. About the emergence and development of the idea of the standard of living, see Glickman, "Inventing the American Standard of Living," in *A Living Wage*, chap. 4; Sen, "Standard of Living."

26. The phrase "abundance rising" is from Joel Mokyr, *The Gifts of Athena: Historical Origins of the Knowledge Economy* (Princeton: Princeton University Press, 2002), 110, quoted in Rosalind Williams, "Opening the Big Box," *Technology and Culture* 48 (2007): 104–16, quote on p. 111.

27. Haber, *Industry and Underdevelopment*, 27–29, 44. According to Haber, most Mexican manufacturing enterprises prior to the Mexican Revolution were barely profitable (103). See also Coatsworth, *Growth against Development*; Coatsworth, "Obstacles to Economic Growth"; Weiner, *Race, Nation and Markets*.

28. On borderlands railroads, see Haber, *Industry and Underdevelopment*, 14–15, 64; Hart, *Empire and Revolution*, 106–30; Salas, *In the Shadow of Eagles*, chaps. 6 and 9; Martinez, *Border Boom Town*, 32–33; Ficker and Connolly, "Los ferrocarriles."

29. On borderlands mining, 1850–1940, see Hart, *Empire and Revolution*, 131–66; Truett, *Fugitive Landscapes*; Calderón, *Mexican Coal Mining Labor*; Salas, *In the Shadow of the Eagles*, chaps. 2 and 8; Kortheuer, "Compagnie du Boléo"; Perales, "Smeltertown"; Monica Perales, "Fighting to Stay in Smeltertown: Lead Contamination and Environmental Justice in a Mexican American Community," *Western Historical Quarterly* 39 (2008): 41–64. On U.S. financial investment in Mexico, 1870–1910, see Hart, *Empire and Revolution*, 73–105; Haber, *Industry and Underdevelopment*, 12; Gómez-Galvarriato and Recio, "Indispensable Service of Banks"; Gómez-Galvarriato, *Foreign and Mexican Companies*.

30. On nationalism and consumer goods, see Breen, *Marketplace*; Frank, *Buy American*; Tiersten, *Marianne in the Market*; Gerth, *China Made*; Burke, *Lifebuoy Men, Lux Women*. On the Americanization of border and Southwestern cities, see Martinez, *Border Boom Town*, 20–22, 33–34; Lorey, *U.S.-Mexican Border*, 36–37; García, *Desert Immigrants*, 30; Wood, "Anticipating the Colonias"; Wilson, *Myth of Santa Fe*. On El

Paso's population, see Mario García, *Desert Immigrants*, 13, 31, 235; Martinez, *Border Boom Town*, appendix, table 3, p. 160.

31. Congressman Abram S. Hewitt in 1885, quoted in Salvucci, "Origins and Progress," 723; Romero, *Mexico and the United States*, 431.

32. *Lone Star*, April 11, 1885, quoted in Martinez, *Border Boom Town*, 25. On the *zona libre*, see Pérez Herrera, *La zona libre*; Bell and Smallwood, *"Zona Libre"*; Lorey, *U.S.-Mexican Border*, 32, 50; Martinez, *Border Boom Town*, 15–17; Salas, *In the Shadow of the Eagles*, chap. 7. A useful period source on the *zona libre* is Romero, *Mexico and the United States* (1898), 439–94. On California merchants' trade with the borderlands in the 1880s and 1890s, see Romero, "Transnational Commercial Orbits."

33. On Article 696 of Mexico's 1891 Tariff Law, see Romero, *Mexico and the United States*, 441; Sánchez, *Becoming Mexican American*, 47; Martinez, *Border Boom Town*, 20, 25, 27–29. On Mexican tariff policies, import trade, and export trade, 1821–1910, see Beatty, *Institutions and Investment*, chap. 3; Beatty, "Commercial Policy in Porfirian Mexico"; Ficker, "Institutional Change and Foreign Trade"; Ficker, "Import Trade Policy"; Gómez-Galvarriato, *Foreign and Mexican Companies*; Haber, "Political Economy of Industrialization"; Márquez, "Tariff Protection"; Márquez, "Commercial Monopolies and External Trade"; Reséndez, "Masonic Connections"; Reséndez, "Getting Cured and Getting Drunk"; Riguzzi, *¿La reciprocidad imposible?*; Salvucci, "Origins and Progress"; Salvucci, "Export-Led Industrialization."

34. On economic development in northern Mexico before 1910, see Haber, *Industry and Underdevelopment*, 163–4, 178–80; Hibino, "Cervecería Cuauhtemoc"; Mora-Torres, *Making of the Mexican Border*; Saragoza, *Monterrey Elite*; Wasserman, *Capitalists, Caciques, and Revolution*; Wasserman, *Persistent Oligarchs*; Gómez-Galvarriato, *Foreign and Mexican Companies*. On "centralism" in the development of Mexico's political economy prior to 1846, see Reséndez, "Masonic Connections."

35. On the history of advertising and marketing in the United States, see Strasser, *Satisfaction Guaranteed*; Marchand, *Advertising*; Fox, *Mirror Makers*; Lears, *Fables of Abundance*; Laird, *Advertising*; Garvey, *Adman in the Parlor*. On advertising in northern Mexico, see Bunker, "'Consumers of Good Taste.'" On the history of advertising in Mexico, see Moreno, *Yankee Don't Go Home!*; Moreno, "J. Walter Thompson"; Fejes, "Growth of Multinational Advertising Agencies."

36. On Pacific Coffee, see "Who is this Sellers?" *Simmons Spice Mill* (Los Angeles) 40 (April, 1917), 393. On Old El Paso Foods, see Kenneth Kiple, *A Moveable Feast: Ten Millennia of Food Globalization* (New York: Cambridge University Press, 2007), 234.

37. On production-driven marketing versus marketing-driven production, see Strasser, *Satisfaction Guaranteed*, 53. About "fashion intermediaries" in the durable household goods economic sector, see Blaszczyk, *Imagining Consumers*. Most studies of consumer culture discuss fashion intermediaries, even if they do not use the term, or subscribe to the view that producers simply seek to meet consumer demand.

38. Report from Nogales J. F. Darnall, dated October 25, 1901, in *Commercial Relations*

of the United States with Foreign Countries during the Year 1901 (Washington, D.C.: GPO, 1902): 1:482–83, quote on p. 482.

39. See Andrew D. Barlow, Report from Mexico City, dated December—, 1901, in *Commercial Relations, op. cit.*, 1:436–62, esp. p. 454; Louis Kaiser, Report from Mazatlan, dated October 17, 1901, in *Commercial Relations, op. cit.*, 1:471–79, esp. 472–73, 475–76; Charles W. Kindrick, Report from Ciudad Juárez, dated November 4, 1901, in *Commercial Relations, op. cit.*, 1:463–67; W. W. Mills, Report from Chihuahua, dated October 17, 1901, in *Commercial Relations, op. cit.*, 1:467–68; P. Merrill Griffith, Report from Matamoras, dated October 4, 1901, in *Commercial Relations, op. cit.*, 1:469–71; Philip C. Hanna, Report from Monterey, dated July 30, 1901, in *Commercial Relations, op. cit.*, 1:479–82; Darnall, Report from Nogales, *op. cit.*; Samuel Bennett, Report from Saltillo, dated October 3, 1901, in *Commercial Relations, op. cit.*, 1:483–84.

40. M. Zapta Real, "The Depression of Trade and Agriculture in Mexico," translated from the *Mexican Economist*, in *Reports from the Consuls of the United States* 22 (April-June, 1887), 471–77.

41. Amador Family Papers, 1836–1949, Collection Ms. 4, Rio Grande Historical Collections, New Mexico State University Library. On mail-order retail, see Strasser, *Satisfaction Guaranteed*; Tedlow, *New and Improved*; Blanke, *Sowing the American Dream*. On department stores, see Rosalind Williams, *Dream Worlds*; Leach, *Land of Desire*; Strasser, *Satisfaction Guaranteed*, 206–11; Koehn, *Brand New*, 91–130.

42. On borderlands department stores, see Martinez, *Border Boom Town*, 32; Hernandez and Marquez, "White House Department Store"; Popular Dry Goods Company Collection, C. L. Sonnichsen Special Collections Department, University of Texas, El Paso; Cadava, "Ethnic Histories of Tucson," chap. 3; Klasson, "T. C. Power & Brother."

43. On commerce's appeal to imagination, see Leach, *Land of Desire*; Campbell, *Romantic Ethic*; Lears, *Fables of Abundance*.

44. Cadava, "Ethnic Histories of Tucson," chap. 3.

45. Goldwater's eventually moved to Phoenix, and by 1961, when it opened a branch in Scottsdale, it was the region's luxury department store. The family sold the business in 1963 to the Associated Dry Goods Corporation, which retained the store's name and style. In the 1970s, branches of Goldwater's opened in the Arizona towns Phoenix, Mesa, and Tucson, and in Albuquerque, New Mexico.

46. On chain stores in the United States, see Tedlow, *New and Improved*, chap. 4; Strasser, "Woolworth to Wal-Mart"; Lebhar, *Chain Stores in America*; Liebs, *Main Street to Miracle Mile*, 121–29; Pitrone, *F.W. Woolworth*; Raucher, "Dime Store Chains." On national and local chains in Texas before the 1930s, see Buenger and Buenger, *Texas Merchant*, 37–38, 54–55. On national chains in Los Angeles before 1930, see Longstreth, *The Drive-In, the Supermarket*, 8–9, 105, 115.

47. Mitchell, *Big-Box Swindle*, 205–10.

48. Buenger and Buenger, *Texas Merchant*, 37.

49. Longstreth, *The Drive-In, the Supermarket*, 9.

50. On Highland Park Village, see Longstreth, "The Diffusion of the Community Shopping Center Concept," 276–79. On the development of automobile-oriented commerce, see Liebs, *Main Street to Miracle Mile*; Jakle and Sculle, *Gas Station in America*; Longstreth, *The Drive-In, the Supermarket*; Longstreth, *City Center to Regional Mall*. On franchises, see Marx, "Development of the Franchise"; Clarke, *Trust and Power*, chap. 6. On the development of automobile-oriented commerce in the borderlands, see Arreola and Curtis, *Mexican Border Cities*; Herzog, *Where North Meets South*; Herzog, *From Aztec to High Tech*.

51. Weems, Jr., *Desegregating the Dollar*. On marketplace discrimination, see Cohen, *Consumers' Republic*, 41–53, 83–100, 167–91, 200–227, 370–83. On marketplace discrimination in the borderlands, see Serna, "'As a Mexican I Feel It's My Duty'"; Serna, "'We're Going Yankee.'"

52. Venkatesh, "Ethnoconsumerism." On marketing to ethnic minorities, see Dávila, *Latinos, Inc.*; Peñaloza, "Multiculturalism"; Weems Jr., "'Bling-Bling'"; Chin, *Purchasing Power*; Dorsey, *Pachangas*, esp. chap. titled "Budgirls."

53. On the diversity of borderlands consumers, see Vila, *Crossing Borders*; Vila, *Border Identifications*; Vila, ed., *Ethnography*; Campbell, "Tale of Two Families."

54. Cohen, *Consumers' Republic*, 28–31, 100–9, 345–97; Jacobs, "'How About Some Meat?'"; Brandt, *Cigarette Century*; Nader, *Unsafe at Any Speed*; Glickman, *Buying Power*. Several recent exposés reveal the collusion between government, business, and experts to hide the possible effects of mass-produced products; see Paul Blanc, *How Everyday Products Make People Sick: Toxins at Home and in the Workplace* (Berkeley: Univerity of California Press, 2007); Michael Pollan, *The Omnivore's Dilemma: A Natural History of Four Meals* (New York: Penguin Press, 2006); Mark Schapiro, *Exposed: The Toxic Chemistry of Everyday Products and What's At Stake for American Power* (White River Junction: Chelsea Green Publishing, 2007); Eric Schlosser, *Fast Food Nation: The Dark Side of the All-American Meal* (New York: Houghton Mifflin, 2001).

55. Carson, Hoffman, and Albert, eds., *Of Consuming Interests*, and Leach, *Land of Desire*, address most of these institutional developments between the eighteenth and early twentieth centuries.

56. On U.S. commercial publishing, see Scanlon, *Inarticulate Longings*; Ohmann, *Selling Culture*; Garvey, *Adman in the Parlor*. On Mexican commercial publishing, see Gruesz, *Ambassadors*; Mraz, "Today, Tomorrow, and Always"; Bartra, "The Seduction of Innocents," esp. pp. 302–19.

57. On electronic media in the United States, Mexico, and the borderlands over the course of the twentieth century, see Winseck and Pike, *Communications*; Beatty, "Approaches to Technology Transfer"; Smulyan, *Selling Radio*; Hilmes, *Only Connect*, chaps. 3–7; Baughman, *Republic of Mass Culture*, 30–90; Alisky, "Early Mexican Broadcasting"; Paxman and Saragoza, "Globalization and Latin Media Powers"; Sánchez-Ruiz, "Globalization, Cultural Industries, and Free Trade"; Hernández and McAnany, "Cultural Industries in the Free Trade Age"; McAnany and Wilkinson, eds., *Mass Media and Free Trade*; Moran, "The Development of Spanish-Language Television in San

Diego"; Maria Arbelaez, "Low-Budget Films for *Fronterizos* and Mexican Migrants in the United States," *Journal of the Southwest* 43 (2001): 637–57; Mari Castañeda Paredes, "Reorganization of Spanish-Language Media Marketing"; Claire Fox, "Fan Letters."

58. On world's fairs, schools, and museums, see Rydell, *All the World's a Fair*; Tenorio Trillo, *Mexico at the World's Fairs*; Joel Spring, *Educating the Consumer Citizen: A History of the Marriage of Schools, Advertising, and Media* (Mahwah: Lawrence Erlbaum Associates, 2003); Steven Conn, *Museums and American Intellectual Life, 1876–1926* (Chicago: University of Chicago Press, 1998).

59. On structure of values, see Leach, *Land of Desire*, 235. On the masses, see Zakim, *Ready-Made Democracy*. On the U.S. standard of living, see Glickman, *Living Wage*. On pious consumption, see Merish, *Sentimental Materialism*. On envy, see Matt, *Keeping Up*. On the therapeutic ethos, see Lears, "From Salvation to Self-Realization"; Marchand, *Advertising*. On mass culture, Sundays, nights, leisure, vacations, and tourism, see McCrossen, *Holy Day*; Schivelbusch, *Disenchanted Night*; Schmidt, *Consumer Rites*; Aron, *Working at Play*; Dye, *All Aboard for Santa Fe*.

60. On the therapeutic ethos in contemporary Mexico, see the following studies by Peter Cahn: *All Religions Are Good in Tzintzuntzan: Evangelicals in Catholic Mexico* (Austin: University of Texas Press, 2003); "Building Down and Dreaming Up: Finding Faith in a Mexican Multilevel Marketer," *American Ethnologist* 33 (2006): 126–42; "Saints with Glasses: Mexican Catholics in Alcoholics Anonymous," *Journal of Contemporary Religion* 20 (2005): 217–29.

61. Leach, *Land of Desire*, 233–44; Horowitz, *Morality of Spending*, chap. 3; McCrossen, *Holy Day*, 104–10, 180–81 n. 32; Strasser, *Satisfaction Guaranteed*, chap. 4.

62. On the market for caricatures of "Mexico" and vice in Mexican border towns between 1890 and 1930, see Martinez, *Border Boom Town*, 30–33; Lorey, *U.S.-Mexican Border*, 62; Arreola and Curtis, *Mexican Border Cities*, 77; Gabbert, "Prostitution"; Curtis and Arreola, "*Zonas de Tolerencia*." On U.S. real estate speculation and development in the Mexican borderlands, see Hart, *Empire and Revolution*, chaps. 6–8; Kerig, "Yankee Enclave"; St. John, "Line in the Sand."

63. On the Mexican Revolution's economic effect on borderlands, see Hart, *Empire and Revolution*, chaps. 9–10; Beezley, *Judas at the Jockey Club*; Mora-Torres, *Making of the Mexican Border*. On Pancho Villa's redistribution of wealth, see Lorey, *U.S.-Mexican Border*, 65. On suppliers for revolutionary factions, see Romo, *Ringside Seat*, 216; Lorey, *U.S.-Mexican Border*, 41, 43–44, 67; Sandos, "Northern Separatism"; Hernández Sáenz, "Smuggling for the Revolution"; "Millions Smuggled Over Mexican Line," *New York Times*, September 7, 1919. On the U.S. military presence in the Southwest prior to the 1920s, see Herzog, *North Meets South*, 95, 104; Metz, *Desert Army*; Andreas, *Border Games*, 33.

64. On Mexico's missed opportunities as a consequence of the Mexican Revolution, see Lorey, *U.S.-Mexican Border*, 43; Martinez, *Border Boom Town*, 52; Hart, *Empire and Revolution*, 271–342. On refrigeration and agricultural markets, see Strasser, *Satisfaction Guaranteed*; Pilcher, "Fajitas"; Pilcher, *Sausage Rebellion*. On 1990s cross-border trade in cash crops, see Alvarez, *Mangos*.

65. On U.S. film exports, 1910–1930, see Thompson, *Exporting Entertainment*, chap. 3. On southern California labor relations, 1900–1940, see Camarillo, *Changing Society*; Guerin-Gonzales, *Mexican Workers*; Sánchez, *Becoming Mexican American*; Garcia, *World of Its Own*. On borderlands urban population size in 1930, see Ricardo Romo, *East Los Angeles: History of a Barrio* (Austin: University of Texas Press, 2005), table 1, 58.

66. Castillo, Rangel Gomez, and Delgado, "Border Lives," 401.

67. On Mexican nationalization of land, industry, coasts, and borders, 1920–1940, see Hart, *Empire and Revolution*, 364–72, 380–90, 403–31; Santiago, *Ecology of Oil*; Brown, "Structure of the Foreign-Owned Petroleum Industry"; Knight, "Politics of the Expropriation"; Adams, *Bordering the Future*, chap. 3; Haber, Razo, and Maurer, *Politics of Property Rights*.

68. On Mexican vice industries, see Lorey, *U.S.-Mexican Border*, 45–46, 78–80; Martinez, *Border Boom Town*, 57–77; Herzog, "Political Economy"; Bowman, "U.S.-Mexico Border."

69. Martinez, *Border Boom Town*, 64.

70. On the 1926 survey of border consumption, see Gamio, *Mexican Immigration*; Casey Walsh, "Eugenic Acculturation: Manuel Gamio, Migration Studies, and the Anthropology of Development in Mexico, 1910–1940," *Latin American Perspectives* 31 (2004): 118–45. On Mexican cross-border shopping, see Adkisson and Zimmerman, "Retail Trade on the U.S.-Mexico Border"; Guo, Vasquez-Parraga, and Wang, "An Exploration Study of Motives for Mexican Nationals to Shop in the U.S."; Phillips and Coronado, "Texas Border Benefits from Retail Sales to Mexican Nationals." On Canadian cross-border shopping, see Lord, Putrevu, and Parsa, "Cross-Border Consumer"; Timothy and Butler, "Cross-Border Shopping"; Simmons and Kamikihara, "Field Observations."

71. On the proletarianization of Mexicans in the borderlands, see Heyman, "Working for Beans"; Heyman, *Life and Labor*; Foley, *White Scourge*; Vargas, *Proletarians of the North*; Vargas, *Labor Rights*; Peck, *Reinventing Free Labor*. On the case against the "proletarianization" paradigm for borderlands, see Wilson, *Subsidizing Capitalism*. Nearly all the published works of Sarah Hill, Melissa Wright, and Josiah McC. Heyman address the situation of consumers in the borderlands. See also Mitchell, *Coyote Nation*; Alvarez, Jr., *Familia*; Rodríguez and Hagan, "Transborder Community"; Ojeda de la Peña, "Transborder Families"; Velasco Ortiz, "Women, Migration, and Household Survival Strategies"; Hansen, "Difference a Line Makes"; Campbell, "Tale of Two Families"; Campbell, "Chicano Lite"; Cook, *Understanding Commodity Cultures*, chap. 9.

72. Benson, "Gender, Generation, and Consumption," 240.

73. Roy Rosenzweig and Jean-Christophe Agnew, "In Memoriam: Susan Porter Benson," *AHA Perspectives* (October 2005), 55. See Benson's posthumously published monograph, *Household Accounts*, as well as "Living on the Margin" and "Gender, Generation, and Consumption."

74. On U.S. working-class (urban and rural) consumption, see Ownby, *American Dreams in Mississippi*; Heinze, *Adapting to Abundance*; Hurley, *Diners, Bowling Alleys*; Nickles, " 'More Is Better': Mass Consumption, Gender, and Class Identity"; Blanke,

"Consumer Choice, Consumer Agency"; Blanke, *Sowing the American Dream*. The historian Frank Trentmann's published essays provide further admonitions to move the field toward inclusion of consumers with little disposable income; see especially "Bread, Milk and Democracy"; "Beyond Consumerism"; "The Modern Evolution of the Consumer"; "Knowing Consumers." See also Brewer and Trentmann, eds., *Consuming Cultures, Global Perspectives*.

75. On the survival of consumer-oriented values and practices during the 1930s, see Renouard, "Predicaments of Plenty"; Hill, Hirschman, and Bauman, "Consumer Survival"; Elvins, "Shopping for Recovery"; Marchand, *Advertising*, chaps. 6, 9, and 10. On grassroots consumer activism in the 1930s, see Cohen, *Consumers' Republic*, chap. 1; Jacobs, *Pocketbook Politics*, chaps. 3 and 4; Stole, *Advertising on Trial*; Glickman, *Buying Power*, chaps. 6 and 7. On the "Don't buy where you can't work" campaign, see Cheryl Greenberg, *"Or Does It Explode?" Black Harlem in the Great Depression* (New York: Oxford University Press, 1991), chaps. 4 and 5. On installment payments and consumer debt servicing in the U.S. during the 1930s, see Calder, *Financing the American Dream*; Olney, "Avoiding Default."

76. Michael Bordo, Claudia Goldin, and Eugene White, eds., *The Defining Moment: The Great Depression and the American Economy in the Twentieth Century* (Chicago: University of Chicago Press, 1998). On the New Deal, see Cohen, *Consumers' Republic*, chaps. 1 and 2; Jacobs, *Pocketbook Politics*, chaps. 5 and 6; McElvaine, *Great Depression*. On the American standard of living and FDR, see Sunstein, *Second Bill of Rights*; Cohen, *Consumers' Republic*, 18–61, 137–46. On the U.S. political shift from a "producerist" to "consumerist" orientation, 1800–1960, see McGovern, *Sold American*; Donohue, *Freedom from Want*; Jacobs, *Pocketbook Politics*, 95–175; Glickman, *Living Wage*, 133–62; Cross, "Corralling Consumer Culture."

77. Truett and Young, "Making Transnational History," 19.

78. About Mexican duty-free zones in the 1930s, see Ganster and Lorey, *U.S.-Mexican Border*, 77–78.

79. On the U.S. expulsion of people of Mexican origins, see Balderrama and Rodríguez, *Decade of Betrayal*; Hoffman, *Unwanted Mexican Americans*; Carreras de Velasco, *Los mexicanos*; Guerin-Gonzalez, *Mexican Workers*; Vargas, *Labor Rights*, chap. 1. On the implementation of U.S. border controls, see Stern, "Buildings"; Stern, *Eugenic Nation*, chap. 2; Garcia, *Operation Wetback*; Nevins, *Operation Gatekeeper*; Spener, "Logic and Contradictions of Intensified Border Enforcement"; Maril, *Patrolling Chaos*; Payan, *U.S.-Mexico Border Wars*.

80. On regional aesthetics in the 1930s, see Berglund, "Western Living"; Herzog, *From Aztec to High Tech*, chaps. 3 and 4; Wilson, *Myth of Santa Fe*. On regional transportation and communications during the 1930s, see Lorey, *U.S.-Mexican Border*, chap. 4. On Mexican tourism, 1930–1950, see Saragoza, "Selling of Mexico"; Ganster and Lorey, *U.S.-Mexican Border*, 84–5. Ganster and Lorey estimate that in 1940 15 percent of border crossers into Mexico were tourists, whereas by 1960, 27 percent were tourists.

Alexis McCrossen

Disrupting Boundaries
Consumer Capitalism and Culture in the
U.S.-Mexico Borderlands, 1940–2008

> The turnover and sheer quantity and variety of consump-
> tion practices continuously disrupt conventional bound-
> aries of all kinds.
> VICTORIA DE GRAZIA (1996)

The dynamics of capitalism and nationalism along the
1,952-mile-long boundary line between the United States
and Mexico—drawn in the early 1850s after the Treaty of
Guadalupe Hidalgo (1848) concluded the U.S.-Mexico War—
provide endless examples of how "consumption practices con-
tinuously disrupt conventional boundaries." Take the ceaseless
cross-border traffic in necessities ranging from pinto beans to
blue jeans, in luxuries such as fine liqueurs and knockoff designer handbags, in contraband extending from marijuana to
exotic animals, and in industrial by-products like chemical
wastes and cardboard. Or consider Mexican "border blasters,"
radio stations that operated just south of the border for half a
century after 1931 to avoid U.S. communications regulations.
Or review the player stats from Los Tecolotes de los Dos Laredos, a professional baseball team that represented both Laredos
in each nation's minor leagues near the end of the twentieth
century.[1] Or instead, surf through the thousands of border
photographs and videos posted on content-sharing Web sites
like Flickr and YouTube, artifacts of the production and circulation of images, an elemental and essential aspect of consumer capitalism. Although the boundary line was meant to
demarcate and separate the two nations, it has instead fostered

the growth of a transnational region and economy that exemplifies the central features of contemporary global capitalism: inequality and hybridity.[2]

Since the 1970s, when powerful and powerless transnational actors—particularly corporations and stateless populations—seemed to elude the control of nation-states, scholars have begun to chafe against the nation-centered organization of the academy and of inquiry itself. Although there is an extensive and important corpus of scholarship on subjects such as capitalism, diasporas, and religion, the taken-for-granted way of viewing history, politics, and peoples through the prism of the nation has shaped the academy since the Enlightenment. Curriculum, graduate training, positions, and publishing are mostly organized along national lines. Various academic initiatives have sought to transcend the boundaries between disciplines and subfields, but even in cases where a field seemed universal—women's studies, for instance—practitioners tended to cluster into nation-oriented subfields. In the 1990s, scholars whose work was out of place within nation-centered studies moved toward questioning theoretical and real geopolitical boundaries and borders.[3] The nation-state paradigm remains strong due to institutional and political structures that facilitate the study of nations, as well as the continued geopolitical salience of nations. Nevertheless, scholars are turning to the micro, the local, the transnational, the international, the nongovernmental, and above all else, the global, to investigate and explain what they consider the pressing problems of their fields.

Within this dramatic and far-reaching academic revisionism, borderlands in general have gained recognition as a site where the simultaneous persistence and disintegration of the nation-state stand out in sharp relief. In heeding social theorist Arjun Appadurai's 1993 call to "think ourselves beyond the nation," historians, anthropologists, and other scholars are directly questioning what historian David Thelen identifies as the "faith that the border can keep people and nations apart."[4] Borderlands have been recognized as sites where scholars can untangle national from transnational histories, trajectories, and conditions. In the U.S.-Mexico borderlands, the visibility of the "tug of war between the transnational and the national" attracts scholarly and media attention.[5] As scholars, publishers, and academic institutions invest resources in understanding the region, they join the push to partially divest the academy of a nation-centric approach to organizing research and teaching.

Academic interest in borderlands no doubt also springs from the rising economic importance of borderland regions to the global economy. Since the 1970s, border areas and cities have been closely linked to and dependent on

"Station XER," Villa Acuña, Coahuila, Mexico, 1931. Library of Congress, Prints and Photographs Division, LC-USZ62–97961, copyright Lippe Studio, Del Rio, Texas, permission granted by Rosantina Calvetti, Warren Studio and Photography, Del Rio, Texas.

Station XER, home to the notorious self-proclaimed Dr. John ("Goat Gland") Brinkley, was one of several "border blasters" set up just south of the border after the passage of the U.S. Radio Act of 1927. Built across the Rio Grande from Del Rio, Texas, in Ciudad Acuña, Coahuila, in 1931 with $350,000 worth of equipment and broadcasting at 100,000 kW, until 1939 it aired Brinkley's sales pitches for a variety of treatments meant to enhance male sexual performance. Similar stations abounded along the border in the 1930s, licensed by the Mexican government, but oriented toward serving markets in the United States. After the Second World War, evangelical preachers who could not get on U.S. radio due to their solicitation of "donations" in exchange for prayers promising to rescue listeners from disease and poverty, leased air time from the station, which was renamed XERA. In 1959 a marketing company, incorporated in Texas as Inter-American Radio Advertising, acquired the facilities, boosted its capacity to 250,000 kW, and then recruited a disc jockey whose madcap style and on-air sales offers became famous: Wolfman Jack.

international trade, not only because of lowered trade barriers, but also because efficiencies in transportation due to container shipping lowered shipping costs in most instances to less than 1 percent of the total cost of production and distribution.[6] Not only did the implementation of the North American Free Trade Agreement (NAFTA) in 1993 increase the volume and profitability of trade between Canada, the United States, and Mexico, it also contributed to rising levels of exchange with Pacific Rim countries, particularly China. The force of globalization hits borderlands quite hard: the transitions making borders into economic bridges rather than barriers are hardly nice or easy. Extant transnational communities in border regions thus are among the first to grapple with the positive and negative effects of trade liberalization.[7]

After the United States entered into the Second World War, permeability characterized the border once again, as it had prior to the economic contraction of the 1930s. U.S. capital moved south, in particular reopening mines and smelters, while Mexican laborers headed north to fields, factories, and construction sites. The U.S. and Mexican governments initiated a guest-worker system, the Bracero Program (1942–64), through which millions of Mexican men crossed the border on temporary work permits. Defense-related manufacturing and processing industries contributed to the economic and population growth of U.S. border states—even that most remote and underdeveloped one, New Mexico, where the Manhattan Project ushered in the establishment of Sandia and Los Alamos National Laboratories, as well as the White Sands Missile Range and several Air Force bases. Mexican border cities and towns flush with displaced peoples of Mexican descent continued to grow, especially after becoming jumping-off points for millions of Mexican migrants heading to the United States. Once in the United States, Mexican migrants worked for low wages while consuming mass-produced goods. On their return to Mexico, they brought back new ideas about consumption, along with suitcases, sacks, and boxes of consumer goods associated with the United States.[8]

By the end of 1945, not only had the United States won the war, dominated its allies, and mostly avoided depredations and damages to its own territory, but it now stood ready to export consumer democracy, in the shape of the Marshall Plan, the International Monetary Fund, the World Bank, tariff and trade agreements, and corporate investments, not to mention U.S.-made consumer goods. Immediately after the war, European and Japanese demand for agricultural commodities and manufactured goods, in combination with that of African, Asian, and Latin American countries, resulted in what one of the first students of globalization, the economist Raymond Vernon, called an "export bonanza" for the United States.[9] Massive amounts of U.S. funding for the reconstruction of "the free world's" economies were channeled into industries that produced consumer goods and defense matériel, often through the offices of U.S. corporations, who profited from the opportunity to expand overseas product lines and manufacturing. Furthermore, U.S. television and radio programs, Hollywood movies, and popular branded goods like Ford, Coca-Cola, and Wrigley's chewing gum saturated the United States, Mexico, and many other parts of the world.[10] In all, it was promised that development aimed toward establishing a consumer economy would lay the best groundwork for the worldwide rise of democracy.

Dramatic innovations in U.S. manufacturing and marketing during the 1950s fortified this ideological linkage of capitalism with democracy. Flexible production, in which small batches were efficiently manufactured and then sold to targeted consumer markets, which had been identified through sophisticated demographic and psychological analysis, nurtured individualistic self-fashioning and expression, each considered essential to democracy and capitalism. Simultaneously, explosive social movements insisting that group-based identities replace the monolithic (though raced, gendered, and classed) "American" identity further pushed the shift away from the mass market toward a segmented one. Significantly, just when U.S. electoral politics had achieved a commendable measure of inclusivity with the 1965 Voting Rights Act, political campaigns shifted from pitching appeals to the mass electorate toward interest group politics. Politicians relied on the new marketing to cobble together segmented markets (interest groups) into winning coalitions.[11]

At the same time as segmented marketing remade U.S. commerce, society, and politics, the United States was engaged in a global competition against the Soviet Union, whose solution to the problem of scarcity was state-run production and distribution. During what was known as the Cold War (1947–89), the United States championed the freedom to choose where to work, what to buy, and for whom to vote; it asserted that capitalism, free markets, and democracy together created abundance, pointing to fully stocked grocery stores, parking lots with row upon row of brand-new cars, and single-family houses with backyards, picture windows, and electric kitchens. Soviet bloc residents, on the other hand, faced shortages and made do with shoddy goods, largely because their manufacturing sector's concentration on military and capital goods resulted in the production of undifferentiated batches of consumer goods. Competition between capitalism and communism in the arena of consumption simmered and sometimes boiled over, perhaps best exemplified by the 1959 "Kitchen Debates" between the U.S. vice president Richard Nixon and the Russian premier Nikita Khrushchev. In them, "the American standard of living," as embodied in the all-electric kitchen, Pepsi, and television, wreaked psychic havoc on the boisterous Khrushchev.[12]

U.S. foreign policy makers reporting to Truman, Eisenhower, and Kennedy insisted that prioritizing material needs and desires would result in the common good, which included improved living standards. The international economic development programs the United States funded sought to promote the development of consumer-oriented economies. But they did not promote consumer choice or protection. U.S. governmental and nongovernmental agencies claimed, according to one historian, that greater access to consumer goods could work "wholly to transform the universe of the marginalized and disempowered."[13] In retrospect the cultural anthropologists Jean and John Comaroff coined the term "millennial capitalism" to describe this misguided developmental ideology.[14] The convictions that in the United States resided a "people of plenty" and that millennial capitalism would bring well-being to the world each contributed to the postwar sense that the border with Mexico separated two worlds, one superior to the other based on its access to and deployment of abundance. Mexican efforts to produce a material culture that was modern, yet imbued with *mexicanidad* and *indigenismo*, only reinforced this tendency to view the border as a stark dividing line.[15]

In the 1950s and 1960s, as part of the battle over modes and ideologies of distribution, nationalism swept through the parts of the world that were economically underdeveloped, a group to which Mexico belonged. Despite its underemployed and undereducated population, its underdeveloped industrial infrastructure, its inefficient agricultural sector, its high foreign debt, and its late entry into mass production, the Mexican government gambled that a nationalized consumer economy built on *mexicanidad* would protect it from foreign dependency, particularly on the United States. Likewise, it encouraged the use of indigenous design for consumer goods, hoping to cash in on *indigenismo*, a Latin American nation-building strategy reaching back to the nineteenth and early twentieth centuries.[16] Tradition and authenticity characterized these cultural styles. Mexican peasants made "timeless" handicrafts. Others showcased pre-Columbian and colonial ruins and relics to extend the nation's patrimony to the ancients of civilizations past, including the Aztec, Mayan, Roman, and Greek. Places and goods imbued with characteristics and symbols of the folk, the primitive, and the ancient attracted Western intellectuals and dreamers, who, uneasy with capitalism and disdainful of the mass-produced, were prone to antimodernist positions and places.[17] But this aesthetic—handmade, authentic, one-of-a-kind, indigenous, traditional—did little to add luster to shoddy Mexican-made mass-produced items, such as can openers, ready-made clothing, radio and television sets, refrigerators, or automobiles, which were just as much the stuff of everyday life in Mexico as in the United States.

Still, in an attempt to foster national economic growth, Mexico sponsored what are known as import-substitution policies—high import tariffs, subsidies for internal improvements, and loans for new factories—in order to encourage, if not force, Mexicans to "buy Mexican."[18] These policies stimulated the expansion of Mexican manufacturing. Nevertheless, Mexicans living in the northern states continued to cross the border to "buy American," attracted by low prices, large inventories, the latest styles, and the ease of automobile-oriented retail. In the 1950s, the drive-through originated in southern California, joining the shopping strips and centers that proliferated after a revision to the 1954 tax code made it advantageous to build such structures. U.S. downtown retail sectors near the international boundary line remained vibrant due to the persistence and increase in foot traffic from Mexico, while at the same time suburban growth stimulated the construction of automobile-oriented retail districts on the edges of borderland cities.[19] As they had earlier, border-crossing consumers defied expectations that the boundary line should separate the two nations. It did contribute to divisions, but the lines separating the rich from the poor, capital from labor, the new from the used, the American from the Mexican, "the best" from the substandard, the authentic from the fake, the machine-made from the handmade, the up-to-date from the behind-the-times were not entirely congruent with the boundary line. Transnational social, cultural, and economic conditions, more so than the border, account for the region's stark contrasts.

In the 1960s, two Mexican initiatives, one focused on tourism and the other on assembly of consumer goods, aimed to extract benefits from the density of contradictory possibilities gathered along the permeable northern border. In 1961, the Mexican state introduced a state-funded development agency known as PRONAF (Program Nacional Fronterizo), which aimed to improve living conditions along the border, as well as to generate revenue. In keeping with economic policies of the 1950s, Mexico also persisted with import-substitution policies. PRONAF encouraged the sale of Mexican goods—and of the experience of Mexico itself—to foreigners. It tried to entice U.S. consumers to cross the border to buy Mexican, whether hotel rooms and restaurant meals, duty-free imports, or indigenous arts and crafts. Antonio Bermúdez, the director of Mexico's nationalized oil company PEMEX before he was named head of PRONAF, tried to make the border into "a great show window," and thus Mexico into an emporium of goods and services for the world's richest consumers, Americans.[20] State-run curio shops stocked folk arts representing Mexico's many traditions, jewelry and souvenirs, indigenous foods, spices, and liquors.[21] PRONAF funded the building of American-style hotels with Mexican decorative motifs, beautifying public spaces, and opening a few shopping centers. Despite these efforts, during the 1960s the U.S. side of the border became, in the words of the Mexican diplomat and scholar Carlos Ferrat, "a big mall for the Mexicans."[22] In keeping with the metaphor, Mexico remained an adult amusement park for Americans, who found packaged leisure on its beaches and in its resorts, as well as elsewhere in the Caribbean and Central America.[23]

Sticking with a consumer-oriented vision of economic development, PRONAF introduced a new version of the *zona libre* in 1971: the *artículos ganchos* ("hook goods") program, which was meant to keep pesos (and dollars) in Mexico. Duty-free imports were placed on display alongside articles of Mexican manufacture in shops Mexicans frequented. Thus drawn into stores by displays of desirable imports, but exposed to Mexican goods, Mexicans would, so the theory went, buy Mexican out of national pride. In practice, the *artículos ganchos* program simply helped to meet, and feed, the demands for imported goods among Mexicans. Recognizing that well-stocked modern retail venues attracted customers, the Mexican government also handed out subsidies to developers of shopping malls in Mexican border cities.[24] Taken together, Mexico's consumer-oriented programs did not move its borderlands into the forefront of international tourism, fill up the treasury with consumer dollars, or wean northern Mexicans from their preference for American goods. In retrospect it may be that U.S. marketing models overly influenced PRONAF's policymakers, whose strategizing was hampered by naïve consumer psychology and wishful economic policy. Nevertheless, the Mexican government recognized the centrality of the consumer—as tourist, as shopper, as citizen—to national economic health, just as the United States government had a few decades earlier.

Instead of trying to sell the experience of Mexico and Mexican-made goods, as PRONAF had attempted, another set of development policies fostered the sale of Mexico's cheapest and most abundant commodity, labor. Initiated in 1965 in response to the social crisis brought on by the end of the Bracero Program the previous year, the Border Industrialization Program (BIP) facilitated the establishment of *maquiladoras*, assembly plants operating along the border in a zone exempted from import and export duties. Mexican labor assembled Asian-made components into computer keyboards, refrigerators, radios, and televisions, which were then moved across the nearby border, destined for U.S. warehouses and stores. The BIP would not have succeeded were it not for low transportation costs, due in large part to the development of a smooth system for the transfer of standardized forty-foot-long containers from cargo ships, to railroad cars, to truck beds. The container was to global production of consumer goods what the moving assembly line was to Ford's organization of factory production.[25] At each point in the commodity chain, waived import and export duties, along with low transportation costs, reconfigured production in order to take advantage of low labor costs and lax workplace regulations. Through the 1970s and 1980s, the *maquiladora* sector grew, as did duty-free zones (frequently known as "Special Economic Zones" or "Export Processing Zones") in other parts of Mexico, Central America, Latin America, as well as throughout the developing world, including China's Pearl River Delta, eight enclaves in India, and ports in Germany, Portugal, and France.[26]

In the 1990s, when large numbers of Chinese factories entered into the production of consumer goods for export, competitive pressures further pressed upon the border's assembly plants. Downward pressure on already low wages and rapidly changing and widely divergent demands contributed to inhumane living conditions and unsafe workplaces in the border's industrialized cities. The costs of the goods assembled in the Mexican export zone, and other export zones, ought to include rendering the region into one of the world's environmental disaster areas, its cities into overcrowded, underserviced landscapes, and many of its residents, particularly women, into a vulnerable population.[27] Instead, prices are low, export zones sites of devastation, and natural agencies inundated with requests of help.

Stagnating and in some cases decreasing real wages (purchasing power) for U.S. and Mexican working and middle classes followed the emergence of the *maquiladora* system. In the United States, the oil shocks and inflationary spirals of the early 1970s, the closing of many factories in what became known as the "rust belt," and the shift to a service-based economy contributed to flattening wages, rising prices for automobiles and houses, and increasing income inequality.[28] As in the United States, Mexico's rate of inflation began to skyrocket in the early 1970s. But it was far worse in Mexico, hitting 100 percent in 1976, precipitating an official devaluation of the peso. Since the 1970s, more and more women and children in Mexico have entered the workforce as household purchasing power has plummeted. While not as dramatic in terms of sheer numbers in the United States, it is also the case that more members of households are working in order to compensate for the decline in the sole breadwinner's purchasing power. In all, over the course of the twentieth century, Mexican householders "reallocated their productive resources," namely their own labor, such that large numbers of women and children entered into wage work on both sides of the border. In part as a consequence of this, Mexico's standard of living has risen as well.[29]

Promotoras, 2006. Promotional photograph by David Maung for the documentary *Maquilápolis*, directed by Vicki Funari and Sergio de la Torre, courtesy of Vicki Funari.

Multinational corporations own thousands of assembly plants, known as *maquiladoras*, which began to appear in the cities of the U.S.-Mexico borderlands during the late 1960s. *Maquiladora* workers, like these women, earn subsistence wages or less for finishing electronics, clothing, and other consumer goods that are shipped north across the border. As the costs of transportation decreased due to the standardization of container shipping in the 1970s, similar manufacturing arrangements developed in innumerable duty-free export zones around the world. Because today transportation costs account for perhaps 1 percent of the final costs of most consumer goods, proximity to the United States no longer provides a geographical advantage over distant labor markets. Thus, in this context, there is little hope that manufacturing along the border will improve the standard of living for Mexicans, who now compete in a global, rather than a local or regional, labor market.

In 1982, Mexico's peso devaluation set off a series of crises, the worst of which, from a humanitarian perspective, was plummeting purchasing power, which fell between 40 and 50 percent over the next four years. Mexican spending in U.S. border cities declined so dramatically that many retailers faced bankruptcy, until a "Border Aid Program" signed by the U.S. president, Californian Ronald Reagan, helped to bail them out. The peso devaluation of 1995 made matters worse for most Mexicans, one in three of whom until the end of the century lived on less than two dollars a day.[30] One pungent reflection on this state of affairs concluded that Mexicans' "hopes went underground and then emerged in unreflective and destructive ways."[31] Swelling numbers saw no other choice but to migrate to the United States, if for no other reaons than the dollars that they could send back to secure a competency for their families, which amounted to 16.6 billion dollars in 2005.[32]

The outsourcing and offshoring of U.S. manufacturing and the significant economic setbacks cutting into United States and Mexican wages since the 1970s have coincided with the boom in "discounting," and the concomitant "logistics revolution" in product distribution. These developments characterize the years between the opening of the first Wal-Mart in the United States in 1962 and then of Mexico's first one in 1991. Today this retail corporation is the largest private employer in Canada, the United States, and Mexico. As the historian Nelson Lichtenstein posits, Wal-Mart is "the template for world capitalism" in which the retailer is "king and the manufacturer his vassal."[33] Although Edward Filene opened his Boston bargain basement in 1909, discounting only developed as a widespread retail practice in the 1950s and 1960s: the same year that Wal-Mart opened its first store, 1962, so did the discounters K-mart, Woolco, and Target. An era of manufacturers' control over prices ended in 1975 when the U.S. Congress passed the Consumer Goods Pricing Act, which abolished the practice of "retail price maintenance" through which manufacturers could insist that retailers sell their products above certain price levels. The logistics revolution that gave Wal-Mart and other discounters so much power over manufacturing and sales depended on the use of new technologies developed in the 1960s and 1970s: computer systems, the Universal Product Code, scanning technologies, and the standard shipping container, which can be moved from ship's hull to rail car to truck bed before its contents are unloaded into the back of any one of thousands of big-box stores. These developments in the scale and efficiency of retail and manufacturing are built on a foundation of labor exploitation. Wal-Mart and other discount corporations discriminate against female and foreign workers in terms of pay, promotions, and benefits, and externalize other labor costs such as health insurance and workers' compensation. While prices have never been lower than in 2007 and store inventories never more closely attuned to market demands, the Wal-Mart template of "always low prices" depends on correspondingly always low wages.[34]

Thus, partially due to labor relations mandated by the Wal-Marts of the present age, many residents of the U.S.-Mexico borderlands today live in a relatively new form of poverty in terms of world history, born primarily out of limited household purchasing power rather than the result of a scarcity of goods. Although "the visual landscape, divided at the border," as one geographer observes, "serves to underscore the vast economic gap separating the two nations," poverty is everywhere evident in the U.S. Southwest, even despite its relatively high per capita income in relation to the Mexican north. Nowhere is this poverty more evident than in areas historically occupied by peoples of

Mexican and Native American descent.[35] All four U.S. border states have higher poverty rates than the national average, five of the seven poorest metropolitan areas in the United States are on the border, and of the many very poor counties strung along the U.S. side of the border, several have rates of poverty comparable to their Mexican neighbors, including Starr County, Texas, where more than half the residents live in poverty. The disparity between the compensation of low-wage workers and corporate bosses in the borderlands and across the United States is astounding: managers of assembly plants in Juárez make more than $2,000 a week, while employees earn between $25 and $100 a week, and while CEO annual compensation is 364 times more than that of the lowest-paid employees.[36]

Since the 1980s, easy access to consumer credit has compensated, at least in the short run, for decreasing real wages and income inequality. Young adults, the working classes, and even the unemployed have been able to bolster their purchasing power with credit cards, mortgages, and other consumer loans that were previously off-limits to people without assets or demonstrated earning power. To be sure, borderlanders, like poor people in many places, have long resorted to pawn shops, small loan operators, and neighbors and kin for loans. Payday loan companies have made inroads into Mexico, as have foreign-owned banks offering credit cards and auto loans. By the same token, some banks in Mexico, such as Citigroup, which owns Banamex, are investing in cross-border consumer banking services, particularly the consumer banking sector. Branches of Mexican banks are now operating along the U.S. side of the border.[37]

In Mexican border towns today, the near absence of public utilities, transportation, and welfare services exacerbates the negative impact of many households' low wages and lack of consumer credit. Through the end of the twentieth century, half of all residents living on the Mexican side of the border faced day-to-day crises of provisioning, which became almost insurmountable challenges during the peso devaluations of the 1980s and 1990s. Northern Mexicans spent as much as two-thirds of their household income on food.[38] What we could call the *sovereignty of the tortilla*, but for the fact of eight-for-a-dollar packages of Top Ramen instant noodles, continues to cast the borderlands onto the same terrain as early modern French cities, eighteenth-century English villages and cities, or nineteenth-century cities in the United States, where everyone but a lucky few spent all their income on food and shelter.[39] According to the official Mexican measure of poverty, which sets a threshold below which an individual cannot adequately feed herself, 18 percent of the

Llanito, New Mexico, 1970. Albuquerque, photograph by Danny Lyon, courtesy Danny Lyon, Edwynn Houk Gallery, and the George Eastman House.

Not just because of their perch on the edge of the nation, but also because of their relative poverty, the residents of the U.S. borderlands also belong to what social critic Michael Harrington identified as the "other America," when his 1962 exposé of that name drew attention to the 22 percent of Americans who lived below the official poverty line and the other quarter of the population who hovered near it. Despite the rapid and initial success of U.S. President Lyndon Baines Johnson's "War on Poverty," which cut the number of Americans living in poverty to a bit less than 13 percent over the six years following 1964, nearly a quarter of New Mexicans lived in poverty in 1970 when this photo was taken. Then and now, a higher proportion of residents of the four states abutting the border live in poverty than in nearly all other U.S. states. Borderlands poverty has many different faces. In New Mexico, many descendants of Spanish and Mexican settlers own land and their homes, but are poor nevertheless due to few jobs and low wages. Old trucks, like the one pictured here, are not just junk; they are the materials for some New Mexicans' engagement with the region's car culture, in which tinkering and customizing result in automobiles whose very form—low riding—proscribes mobility, speed, and convenience and thus stands in opposition to the dominant culture's preoccupations.

population is poor. Using the U.S. federal government's definitions of poverty, which take into account a range of "decencies" in addition to necessities like food, about 86 percent of all Mexicans live in poverty, in contrast with 12 percent of U.S. residents. "Decencies," as Josiah Heyman judiciously formulates them, "are neither strict necessities nor luxuries; people can reasonably be expected to own them at some point during a lifetime, and they convey to the household a standing above abject poverty but below ostentation." To be sure, *norteños* with perhaps a handful of decencies are better off than many Mexicans living to their south, which is but one of the many reasons that dozens of buses packed with migrants arrive from the interior daily.[40]

Understanding the dynamics of scarcity within consumer culture requires more than close investigation into "the culture of poverty," despite the nomen-

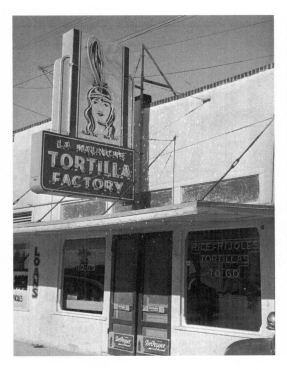

Tortilla factory, Corpus Christi, Texas, 1949. Photograph by Russell Lee, courtesy Russell Lee Photograph Collection, box 37183, negative no. e_r1_13943iidf_0005, Center for American History, University of Texas at Austin.

If the tortilla was sovereign in many borderlands' homes in 1949, it was likely that it was made in a factory such as Corpus Christi's La Malinche, where customers could also get rice, *frijoles*, and other Mexican food "to go." The adjacent storefront offering loans and "*Dineros Abonos Faciles*" (easy installment money) likely served locals and migrants whose purchasing power was minimal due to unemployment, low wages, or a combination thereof. For many members of the poor and working classes across the United States and Mexico, borrowing was one of a host of practices that constituted making do amidst abundance.

clature "consumer culture of poverty" that two marketing specialists have introduced recently.[41] Rather, it shifts attention to practices of making do—the creative use, conservation, and reuse of resources. Mike Davis, a historian and social critic, calls Tijuana's residents "consummate *bricoleurs*," in praise of their exercise of choice and agency in building expressive homes, yards, and streetscapes out of the debris of the border's nationalist versions of capitalism.[42] Lowriders in the borderlands further exemplify creative reuse of mass-produced commodities, while tinkering with and driving secondhand cars and "junkers" demonstrate another side of making do, as does "souping up" and then drag racing hot-rods.[43] In open air marketplaces, as well as large warehouses, cash-poor borderlanders dig through mountains of used clothing, sort through old machine tools, and carefully examine discarded household appliances and decorative items. The United States exports nearly one billion dollars' worth of used clothing a year, much of which is smuggled into Mexico. Clearly, making do—based on enormous formal and informal circuits of exchange—does not preclude participation in the consumer economy.[44]

Today, as in the past, people working in the overlapping low-wage and informal economies are consumerism's constituent parts, yet they live in its shadows, crevices, and in-between spaces, where consumption happens differently than in the living rooms, bars, and bedrooms represented on television.[45] Here they cobble together practices, languages, and consumer goods from what is at hand. The built environment of squatters' shacks and mirror-plated high-rises makes visible the tensions between abundance and scarcity, between modernity and hybridity.[46] In this sense, modernity, understood as the increased scale of movement of goods, capital, and people, must also be understood as what cultural historian Mauricio Tenorio recognizes as not just Mexican, but all the poor's "continual, tiresome, expensive, hopeless, and yet unavoidable attempt" to provide for themselves in a market economy.[47]

Extending commodity-chain analysis into the realm of "making do" opens up the study of what the cultural theorist Arjun Appadurai terms "the social life of things." Ultimately such analysis, which brings together economic, cultural, social, and theoretical considerations, emphasizes the positive consequences of hybridity.[48] Some borderlanders speak a new language (Spanglish), which among other things facilitates consumption of mass-produced culture, durable consumer goods, and food, including foods such as fajitas, puffy tacos, *queso*, and Frito pies.[49] Hybrid music permeates the borderlands: *banda*, "border *corridos*," *narcocorridos*, the *conjunto* of slain Tejana pop star Selena.[50] Cross-border circuits extend between clinics, pharmacies, dentists' chairs, hospitals, *botánicas*, and nutrition centers.[51] The various uses to which consumers put everyday products, such as spray-painted murals and bottle-topped walls, dramatically underscore the hybridity of low-income borderlanders' consumption practices.

Over the last few decades, U.S. and Mexican household adjustments to always limited and at times declining purchasing power seem unable to keep pace with transnational flows of culture and capital, which themselves create, exacerbate, and then advertise the stark contrasts between scarcity and abundance. The ever-increasing availability of ever-cheaper mass-produced goods confounds economists and households alike. How can people starve when food is so cheap? How can there be deprivation with the low prices of big-box retailers like Wal-Mart? How could anybody within the vicinity of a dollar store want for anything?[52]

Simultaneous with the tremendous increase in the volume of global trade since 1980 has been a remarkable decrease in extreme poverty throughout the world: today a billion people live on a dollar a day, twenty years ago two billion did. There are many plausible explanations for this, one of which is the liberalization of trade. Mexico's elimination of barriers to trade—at first unilaterally in 1985 and then with NAFTA in 1994—appears to have increased purchasing power across the board. In the early twenty-first century, the richest Mexican households had 6 percent more disposable income than they had in the 1980s, and even the poorer households had 2 percent more.[53] Paradoxically, capitalism fosters senses of deprivation amidst abundance. Studies of affluent societies, like William Leach's landmark study of the United States, titled *Land of Desire*, explore the amplification of relative, rather than real, measures of deprivation. Heedlessly and shamelessly, marketing campaigns peddle diet foods, light beers, and automobiles in a world of hungry, thirsty, and shoeless people. It is no wonder that in the borderlands, as in other impoverished and not so impoverished places, real senses of need and necessity compete with relative wants and desires, giving rise to both tremendous hope and profound despair. Words and images fail to fully capture the lived experience of the vast majority around the world who live in and make possible the global consumer economy.

Poverty, necessity, and the culture of desire along the lengthy border heighten the opportunity for and allure of informal economic activity, which in its totality accounts for the yearly exchange of billions of dollars' worth of goods and services on the black market. Today borders between nations create "opportune space[s]," as one economist puts it, instead of "empty zones." Many commodity circuits depend on the border's alchemical magic to create value. Consider the quotidian hiring of undocumented workers or the spectacular movement of millions of dollars' worth of contraband.[54] Since the colonial era border crossings have rendered some trade goods into contraband. Regulation of the drug trade faces enforcement obstacles inherent in the very long borderline running through mostly uninhabited territory. The asymmetry of markets, laws, and enforcement on and between each side of the border creates the opportunity to profit through underground exchange, both criminal and informal. Abolishing tariffs and deregulating industry have not diminished the incentives for underground economic activity; instead, huge quantities of criminal and informal goods and services have joined the global flow of commodities, information, and services. Since the 1990s, "global illicit trade," according to the editor of *Foreign Policy*, Moisés Naím, has "moved away from fixed hierarchies and toward decentralized networks; away from controlling leaders and toward multiple, closely linked, dispersed agents and cells; away from rigid lines of control and exchange and toward constantly shifting transactions as opportunities dictate."[55] In doing so, it has saturated the world's borderlands.

Criminal and informal underground exchange, each so vital to the border-lands' consumer culture, are also integral to consumer culture throughout the United States, Mexico, and the world. It is estimated that the underground economy accounts for 10 percent of the United States Gross Domestic Product (GDP), about 50 percent of Mexico's, and as much as three-quarters of Nigeria's and Thailand's, each home to global cities (Lagos and Bangkok) that match the U.S.-Mexico borderlands as environmental and human wastelands.[56] The combination of the social conditions of global cities and the opportunistic features of the border itself render the borderlands into a particularly rich site for criminal and informal economic activity.

It is the border's simultaneous status as a trade barrier and bridge that enhances the profitability of the criminal procurement and trade in controlled substances, including narcotics, in stolen and regulated goods such as guns, horses, and automobiles, and in human beings for the purpose of illegal forms of labor, such as sex work or slavery.[57] Moving drugs, guns, stolen goods, sex workers, and slaves across the border enhances, rather than creates, their market value. The region has always provided opportunities for criminal economic activity, but smuggling and other illegal acts have considerably increased in volume and profitability since the 1960s. NAFTA, which removed most trade barriers, ironically brought more criminal enterprise to the region. In the 1990s, 80 percent of the marijuana, 70 percent of the cocaine, and 30 percent of the heroin in the United States came via Mexico, most of it across the border. Each year, perhaps as many as ten thousand sex workers cross the border into the United States. Thousands of other unlucky migrants who entrusted themselves to *coyotes*—guides for illegal border crossing—have found themselves enslaved; their freedom of contract denied, they are confined to fields and sweatshops and the back rooms of restaurants throughout the United States, where they work without receiving wages under physical threats of violence. Money laundering became so extensive in the 1990s, after many restrictions on the movement of currency were lifted, that a *Journal of Money Laundering Control* began regular publication in 1997.[58] The borderline itself, border cities with few public services but large, deracinated populations, neoliberal economic reforms, and tightening border security—each contributes to the florescence of criminal activity, much of which is related to trade.

Informal economic activity also flourishes in the borderlands. At least one-third of its residents sustain themselves through the unregulated production and consumption of legal goods and services. Unlike the criminal penalties for smuggling narcotics, arms, stolen goods, and humans, misdemeanor citations, fines, and deportation are the punishments meted out for informal economic activity. It too relies on the border to enhance the value of services and goods. Movement across the border adds to the exchange value of goods or services circulating in the informal economy. Avoiding payment of duties on manufactured goods, whether iron nails and factory-made textiles in the 1830s or consumer electronics in the 1970s, or slipping through customs or around a blockade, as did cotton brokers during the Civil War, generates profit for the smuggler and savings for the customer.[59] After the U.S. Chinese Exclusion Act (1882), customs officials took bribes from Chinese migrants wishing to cross the border into the United States. Tequileros, rum runners, and other smugglers during the Prohibition era (1920–33) profited from the transformation of distilled spirits from legal into illicit goods through the simple measure of a border crossing.[60] Today, millions of dollars are made through transporting discarded and used goods, such as clothing, auto parts, tools, and appliances, from the United States into Mexico without paying import duties. Further millions are made in the smuggling of Chinese-made consumer goods into Mexico.[61] Above all else, the way that border crossing transforms the unemployed or underemployed into the employed exemplifies the border's propensity to enhance market value through unregulated flows. Crossing the border in all these cases enriches the market value of commodities ranging from used shoes to male labor in slaughterhouses, from transistor radios to female household labor. Such forms of shadow production perforce beget what we could call *shadow consumption*, which often, though not always, takes place in the interstices of the economy, society, and culture: in streets, alleys, squatters' shacks, *colonias*, automobiles, junkyards, and elsewhere.

The warrantless cross-border movement of so many tons of commodities and so many millions of people is so overwhelming in its extent that many of the fears and hopes associated with new forms of transnational capital and society are localized in the body of the "illegal alien," whose flesh and bones symbolize the irrepressibility of criminal, informal, and formal economic flows. More than a hundred years ago, when mature forms of consumer capitalism and culture debuted in Western cosmopolitan centers, it was the body of the female consumer, especially the insatiable kleptomaniac, who absorbed the anxieties about market capitalism's restructuring of social relations from household patriarchy to workplace paternalism.[62] At the dawn of the twenty-first century it is the bodies of paragons of the underground economy—illegal aliens, street peddlers, drug dealers, hawkers—who absorb similar blows. In a deft ethnographic essay about Mumbai's hawkers—known as

Zapatos, near international bridge, El Paso Street, El Paso, Texas, November 25, 2006. Photograph by Carlos Vigueras, courtesy of photographer.

The informal economic sector, which sustains perhaps as many as a third of borderlands residents, can be found nearly everywhere, including on a street near the international bridge between Mexico and the United States.

pheriwalas—the social theorist Arvind Rajagopal examines how these exemplars of India's informal economy have been cast as "symbols of metropolitan space gone out of control." His account of the affluent minority's vision of Mumbai's streets "as but the circuitry of the formal economy in which they themselves work" could well describe nationalist dreams for the border as a line separating the two nations and as a conduit channelling the orderly exchange of goods, capital, and labor (only when officially demanded).[63] Illegal aliens and smugglers, who defy the formal purposes of the border, bear a similar weight to that of *pheriwalas*: they are symbols of out-of-control transnational space and economies. Nationalism demands regulated borders, but capitalism might not. Consider the fact that when trade restrictions are lifted along borders between less developed and more developed countries, illegal immigration and organized smuggling increase as does legal trade.[64]

Smugglers, illegal aliens, and street vendors all challenge the legal and vernacular distinctions between informal and formal markets. What is more, they disrupt the logic of categorical divisions altogether. What does nation mean when people, money, and goods come and go? What differentiates private from public spaces? One nation from another? The illegal alien, the

Undocumented Mexican immigrants apprehended by U.S. Border Patrol, May 3, 1950. *Los Angeles Times* news photograph, courtesy *Los Angeles Times* Photographic Archive, Department of Special Collections, Charles E. Young Research Library, University of California, Los Angeles.

The alchemical power of the border between the United States and Mexico makes a person "illegal" when he or she crosses it without papers, transforms an hour of his or her labor on one side into the same wage he or she would earn on the other after working for a week, and renders what on one side would be considered substandard pay into high wages on the other. When published in the *Los Angeles Times*, the caption to this photograph read: "Closing in—While Pilot Ed Parker circles overhead, *la migra*, in the person of two border patrolmen, order four line-jumping Mexican nationals over to a jeep. They were questioned briefly, taken back to Mexicali and left on the other side of the border—only to try again in desperate battle to get into the United States for high farm wages." A few years after this photograph was published, in 1954, the U.S. Border Patrol initiated "Operation Wetback." The agency deported eighty thousand Mexican nationals, some of whom it intercepted during border crossings, others whom it picked up on work sites and in residential areas.

smuggler, and the *pheriwala* at once signify outmoded, illegal, and "ancient means of circulating," but they also represent the widespread availability of low-wage labor, contraband, cheap goods, and even, as Rajagopal insists, "human servitude." Few dispute the dependency of India's, Mexico's, and the United States' "haves" on the "have nots." And yet, in Mumbai, bulldozers raze haphazard newspaper stands and food carts, Indian television scapegoats the *pheriwala*, and in the United States Minutemen, the Immigration and Naturalization Service, and City Councils try to run undocumented immigrants out of the country.[65] Ports of entry tighten, proposals for border fences abound, soldiers roam the borderline with guns, and hundreds of migrants die of thirst and exposure as they seek to cross the border in lightly patrolled, but rough and dangerous areas.

Nationalist resistance against globalization first took the form of tariffs, barriers to trade meant to foster national industries and protect citizens from corrupting imports. During the era of free trade, its form is immigration restriction, which takes preeminence to the detriment of markets.[66] The U.S. Border Patrol's implementation of new rules requiring that it inspect U.S. citizens' papers creates long waits at ports of entry, in part stymieing trade by holding up the hundreds of thousands of trailer trucks responsible for moving 80 percent of the $332 billion in trade between the two countries. The news media and Hollywood too foster a sense of panic and alarm about an open border.[67] An impenetrable border would severely harm the economies of each country, as well as affect the lifestyles of the many Americans and Mexicans who depend on some combination of cheap labor, controlled substances, black-market merchandise, and low-cost licit goods. Calls for border security are not simply nationalist; they are also expressions of denial and discomfort with the contemporary solution to the distribution problem.

Over the past quarter of a century, national interests have led to U.S. and Mexican insistence on dismantling trade barriers and implementing other neoliberal policies, such that today the border is porous enough that billions of dollars' worth of goods and capital flow freely and legally.[68] Simultaneously, however, the geographic fact of the border's permeability contributes to the heavy flow of undocumented migrants and illegal goods across it. Dispatching members of each nation's military, enforcement agencies, and police departments to secure the border contributes to, but is not entirely responsible for, the exploitative and criminal forms transnationalism has taken in the twenty-first century borderlands. The ubiquity of depictions of the borderlands as "a no man's land or a war zone" in many contemporary popular genres deflects attention from the fact that since 1950 the U.S.-Mexico borderlands has been one of the fastest-growing regions in the world.[69] It belongs with several other cross-border regions and most global cities as a place where people, capital, and goods amass in a large and unprecedented manner: the region is a "staging ground" for globalization.[70] The free movement of goods and capital across the border, at the same time that governments attempt to box in people, is but one of the effects of globalization on the working classes. The historian Néstor Rodríguez characterizes "the battle for the border" as being between nation-states and what he identifies as "working-class communities in peripheral countries" who cross borders out of the necessity "to spatially reorganize their base of social reproduction," which depends on participation in the economy for consumer goods and services.[71]

The confrontation of national sovereign states and "transnational actors with varying prospects of power, orientations, identities and networks," as one geographer explains, is the crux of globalization.[72] Nowhere is this more evident than along the U.S.-Mexican border. The "placelessness of community, labour and capital," characteristic of the fragmentation of nation-states, also describes a global consumer culture where brand loyalties foster distended communities, where the labor producing and packaging the unending supply of consumer goods could be located anywhere or nowhere, so negligible are the rewards it receives, and the capital behind the whole scheme, multinational in its origins, is hard to pinpoint.[73] Particularly instructive is the Latin American intellectual Néstor García Canclini's warning that the aesthetics of "fragmentation," "recomposition," and "hybridity" obscure how globalization "reorders differences and inequalities without eliminating them."[74]

Consumer goods themselves, however, as particular kinds of objects with certain forms of branding, have firm identities that situate them within particular national groupings: "made in the U.S.A.," "*à la francaise,*" "China-made," "*muy Mexicano.*" It is thus evident that globalization is not erasing the meaning of borders or wiping out national and regional differences. It is still one world very divided, where local and regional tastes, class distinctions, and political problems persist, exacerbated by the arrival of multinational firms and neoliberal political policies.[75] Despite the many ways that the border as a place and as a condition disrupts the boundaries between scarcity, abundance, the national, and the transnational, very real boundaries nevertheless remain fixed, dividing the borderlands such that despite all else, it is a land of necessity for most who make it their home.

Notes

Thanks to Tel Aviv University's Michael Zakim for his careful critique of my arguments concerning capitalism in this essay; to the co-editor of *Business History Review*, Walter Friedman, for his helpful suggestions about how to approach business history in the borderlands; and to Adam Herring for everything else.

Notes fully cite primary sources and specialized secondary sources. Full bibliographic details for all other citations are in the volume's selected bibliography.

1. The source for the epigraph is de Grazia, "Empowering Women," 279. On border trade in necessities, see Martinez, *Border Boom Town*, 12, 14, 22–23, 64, 85, 119, 123, 129; and Arreola and Curtis, *Mexican Border Cities*, 56. On border trade in luxuries, see Reséndez, "Getting Cured"; Sandoval, "American Invasion"; and Martinez, *Border Boom Town*, 22, 24. On border waste disposal, see Tiefenbacher, "*Frontera Química.*" On border blasters, see Fowler and Crawford, *Border Radio*, 1, 8–13, 103–6, 135–46, 155. On the "Two Laredos' " baseball team, see Klein, *Baseball on the Border*.

2. On inequality in the U.S.-Mexico borderlands, see Anderson and Gerber, *Fifty Years of Change*; Ruíz, *Rim of Mexico*; Ceballos Ramírez, ed., *Encuentro*; Dohan, *Price of Poverty*; Martinez, ed., *Border People*; and Richardson and Resendiz, *Edge of the Law*. On global inequality, see Sen, *Inequality Re-examined*; Sen, "Globalization"; Lindert and Williamson, "Does Globalization Make the World More Unequal?"; Storper, "Lived Effects of the Contemporary Economy"; Ravallion, "Debate on Globalization"; Dorman, "Globalization, the Transformation of Capital, and the Erosion of Black and Latino Living Standards"; and Ann Harrison, ed., *Globalization and Poverty* (Chicago: University of Chicago Press, 2007). On borderlands hybrid forms and practices, see Arreola and Curtis, *Mexican Border Cities*; Campbell, "Chicano Lite"; Canclini, *Hybrid Cultures*, 234–41; Fox, *Fence and the River*; Herzog, *Aztec to High Tech*; Dear and Leclerc, eds., *Postborder City*; Richardson, *Batos, Bolillos, Pochos, & Pelados*; Vanderwood, *Juan Soldado*; and Wasserman, "Borderlands Mall." On global hybrid forms and practices, see Bhabha, *Location of Culture*; Appadurai, *Modernity at Large*; Canclini, *Hybrid Cultures*; Yúdice, *Expediency of Culture*; Kraidy, *Hybridity, or the Cultural Logic of Globalization*; Jameson and Miyoshi, eds., *Cultures of Globalization*, part 4; and Kanishka Chowdhury, "It's All within Your Reach: Globalization and the Ideologies of Postnationalism and Hybridity," *Cultural Logic: An Electronic Journal of Marxist Theory and Practice* 5 (2002).

3. On the nation-state paradigm, see Anderson, *Imagined Communities*; Eric Hobsbawm, *Nations and Nationalism since 1780: Programme, Myth, Reality* (New York: Cambridge University Press, 1992); and Arjun Appadurai, "Patriotism and Its Futures," *Public Culture* 5 (1993): 411–29. On nationalism and academic disciplines, see Michèle Lamont and Virág Molnár, "The Study of Boundaries in the Social Sciences," *Annual Review of Sociology* 28 (2002): 167–95; Ernest Gellner, *Nations and Nationalism* (Ithaca: Cornell University Press, 1983); Prasenjit Duara, *Rescuing History from the Nation: Questioning Narratives of Modern China* (Chicago: University of Chicago Press, 1995);

and Patrick Geary, *The Myth of Nations: The Medieval Origins of Europe* (Princeton: Princeton University Press, 2002).

4. Appadurai, "Patriotism and Its Futures," *op. cit.*, 411; David Thelen, "Rethinking History and the Nation-State: Mexico and the United States," *Journal of American History* 86 (1999): 439–52, quote p. 439.

5. Truett and Young, "Making Transnational History," 20.

6. On the container revolution, which began in the 1950s, but was systematized internationally by the 1970s, see Levinson, *The Box.*

7. On the borderlands, globalization, and NAFTA, see Chen, *As Borders Bend*, especially pp. 231–61; Papademetriou and Meyers, eds., *Caught in the Middle*; Gutmann, "For Whom the Taco Bells Toll"; Cook, *Understanding Commodity Cultures*, chap. 10; Adkisson and Zimmerman, "Retail Trade on the U.S.-Mexico Border"; and Barrera, "U.S.-Mexican Border." On the globalization of transnational communities, see Wilson and Dissanayake, eds., *Global/Local*; Mosco and Schiller, "Integrating a Continent"; Vaughan, "Transnational Processes"; and Staudt, *Free Trade?*, 31–57.

8. On U.S. capital in Mexico after 1940, see Hart, *Empire and Revolution*, chap. 13. On the Bracero Program, see Calavita, *Inside the State*; Driscoll, *Tracks North*; Cohen, "Masculine Sweat." On Mexican migrant laborers' exposure to the U.S. consumer economy, see Massey and Liang, "Long-Term Consequences"; Sánchez, *Becoming Mexican American*, chaps. 4, 8, and 9.

9. Vernon, *Storm over the Multinationals*, 60.

10. On the U.S. role in building "consumer democracies" in western Europe and Japan, see de Grazia, "Changing Consumption Regimes"; Kroen, "Renegotiating the Social Contract in Post-War Europe"; Paolo Scrivano, "Signs of Americanization in Italian Domestic Life: Italy's Postwar Conversion to Consumerism," *Journal of Contemporary History* 40 (2005): 317–40; Greg Castillo, "Domesticating the Cold War: Household Consumption as Propaganda in Marshall Plan Germany," *Journal of Contemporary History* 40 (2005): 261–88; Pence, "'Shopping for an 'Economic Miracle'"; Wildt, "Changes in Consumption as Social Practice in West Germany during the 1950s." On U.S. consumer culture in Europe after the Second World War, see Richard Kuisel, "Coca-Cola and the Cold War: The French Face Americanization, 1948–1953," *French Historical Studies* 17 (1991): 96–116; Pells, *Not Like Us*, chaps. 2, 3, and 7; de Grazia, *Irresistible Empire*. On U.S. consumer goods and corporations in Mexico after the Second World War, see Moreno, "J. Walter Thompson"; Moreno, *Yankee Don't Go Home!*

11. On how the segmented market eclipsed the mass market, see Cohen, *Consumers' Republic*, 292–397. On segmented retailing since the 1970s, see Lichtenstein, ed., *Wal-Mart*; Brown, *Revolution at the Checkout*; Chris Anderson, *The Long Tail: Why the Future of Business Is Selling Less of More* (New York: Hyperion, 2006). On flexible production, see Joseph B. Pine II, *Mass Customization: The New Frontier in Business Competition* (Boston: Harvard Business School Press, 1993); Frederick Abernathy, John Dunlop, Janice Hammond, and David Weil, *A Stitch in Time: Lean Retailing and the*

Transformation of Manufacturing (New York: Oxford University Press, 1999). In *Ready-Made Democracy*, historian Michael Zakim explores the ideology of individualism within the political economy of democratic capitalism.

12. On the Soviet bloc consumer economy, see Julie Hessler, *A Social History of Soviet Trade: Trade Policy, Retail Practices, and Consumption, 1917–1953* (Princeton: Princeton University Press, 2004); Mark Landsman, *Dictatorship and Demand: The Politics of Consumerism in East Germany* (Cambridge: Harvard University Press, 2005); Heldmann, "Negotiating Consumption in a Dictatorship"; Steiner, "Dissolution of the 'Dictatorship over Needs'?" On the "standard of living" as a cold war weapon, see Robert Haddow, *Pavilions of Plenty: Exhibiting American Culture Abroad in the 1950s* (Washington, D.C.: Smithsonian Institution Press, 1997); Castillo, "Domesticating the Cold War"; Laura Belmont, "Exporting America: The U.S. Propaganda Offensive, 1945–1959," in Casey Blake, ed., *The Arts of Democracy: Art, Public Culture, and the State* (Philadelphia: University of Pennsylvania Press, 2007), 123–50; Elizabeth Borgwardt, *A New Deal for the World: America's Vision for Human Rights* (Cambridge: Belknap Press of Harvard University Press, 2005). On the 1959 "kitchen debates," see Susan Reid, "Cold War in the Kitchen: Gender and the De-Stalinization of Consumer Taste in the Soviet Union under Khrushchev," *Slavic Review* 61 (2002): 211–52; Susan Reid, "The Khrushchev Kitchen: Domesticating the Scientific-Technological Revolution," *Journal of Contemporary History* 40 (2005): 289–316; Cynthia Lee Henthorn, *From Submarines to Suburbs: Selling a Better America, 1939–1959* (Athens: Ohio University Press, 2006), 1–18.

13. Matthew Hilton, "Consumers and the State since the Second World War," *Annals of the American Academy of Political and Social Science* 611 (2007): 66–81, quote p. 79.

14. Comaroff and Comaroff, "Millennial Capitalism," 4, 2.

15. On aesthetics, politics, and attitudes toward plenty in the U.S. after the Second World War, see Nickles, " 'More Is Better': Mass Consumption, Gender, and Class Identity in Postwar America"; Jacobs, "Politics of Plenty"; Karal Ann Marling, *As Seen on TV: The Visual Culture of Everyday Life in the 1950s* (Cambridge: Harvard University Press, 1996); Lears, "Reconsidering Abundance." On Mexican responses to U.S. consumer culture after the Second World War, see Morris, *Gringolandia*, 215–42; Zolov, *Refried Elvis*.

16. On *mexicanidad* and economic policy, see Moreno, *Yankee Don't Go Home!*; Miller, *Red, White, and Green*; Hill, "Wasted Resources." On *indigenismo*, economic policy, and material culture, see Alan Knight, "Racism, Revolution, and *Indigenismo*: Mexico 1910–1940," in Richard Graham, ed., *The Idea of Race in Latin America* (Austin: University of Texas Press, 1990), 71–114; David Brading, "Manuel Gamio and Official *Indigenismo* in Mexico," *Bulletin of Latin American Research* 7 (1988): 75–89; Héctor Díaz-Polanco et al., *Indigenismo, modernización y marginalidad: Una revisión crítica* (Mexico City: Juan Pablos, 1987); Analisa Taylor, "The Ends of *Indigenismo* in Mexico," *Journal of Latin American Cultural Studies* 14 (2005): 75–86; Lise Nelson, "Artesania, Mobility and the Crafting of Indigenous Identities among Purhépechan Women in Mexico," *Journal of Latin American Geography* 5 (2006): 51–77; Judith Friedlander, "The National Indigenist Institute of Mexico Reinvents the Indian: The Pame Example," *American Ethnologist* 13

(1986): 363–67; Ana María Alonso, "Conforming Disconformity: *Mestizaje*, Hybridity, and the Aesthetics of Mexican Nationalism," *Cultural Anthropology* 19 (2004): 459–90; Vaughan and Lewis, eds., Batra, "The Seduction of Innocents"; *Eagle and the Virgin*.

17. On U.S. and European responses to Mexican material culture after the Second World War, see Tenorio Trillo, "Cosmopolitan Mexican Summer"; Harner, "*Muebles Rústicos*"; González, *Culture of Empire*, chap. 2; Delpar, *Enormous Vogue*; Pilcher, " 'Montezuma's Revenge' "; Boardman, *Destination México*; Schreiber, "The Cold War Culture of Political Exile"; Rebecca Schreiber, "Exile, Transnationalism, and the Politics of Form in Cold War Mexico," in Sandhya Shukla and Heidi Tinsman, eds., *Imagining Our Americas: Nation, Empire, and Region* (Durham: Duke University Press, 2007), 282–312. The economist and consumer activist Stuart Chase's *Mexico: A Study of Two Cultures* (1931) remains a key source to understanding the force of Mexico's material culture in shaping foreign response to the nation as a whole.

18. On Mexican economic development after the Second World War, see Anderson and Gerber, *Fifty Years of Change*; Hart, *Empire and Revolution*, 432–58; Moreno, *Yankee Don't Go Home!*; Babb, *Managing Mexico*, 75–136; Franko, *Puzzle*, chaps. 3 and 4; Durand, Massey, and Parrado, "The New Era of Mexican Migration."

19. On Mexican consumption practices in the borderlands during the 1940s and 1950s, see Lorey, *U.S.-Mexican Border*, 85, 88–89; Heyman, "Imports," 170–73; Niblo, *Mexico in the 1940s*. On car-oriented commerce in the U.S., see Longstreth, *Drive-In*; Longstreth, *City Center*; Jakle and Sculle, *Gas Station in America*; Hanchett, "U.S. Tax Policy"; Cohen, "Town Center."

20. Bermúdez quoted in Fernández-Kelly, *For We Are Sold*, 24.

21. On PRONAF, see Lorey, *U.S.-Mexican Border*, 103–16; Arreola and Curtis, *Mexican Border Cities*, 88–89, 104.

22. Ferrat, "Mexico, the Latin American Nation," 478.

23. Ward, *Packaged Vacations*.

24. On the *artículos ganchos* program, see Herzog, *North Meets South*, 147; Lorey, *U.S.-Mexican Border*, 113. On 1970s Mexican shopping center development, see Herzog, *North Meets South*, 147; Wasserman, "Borderlands Mall."

25. On the Border Industrialization Program and *maquiladoras*, see Anderson and Gerber, *Fifty Years of Change*; Herzog, *North Meets South*, 48–52, 146–47; Fernández-Kelly, *For We Are Sold*, 26; Lorey, *U.S.-Mexican Border*, 107–8; Kopinak, *Desert Capitalism*; Sklair, *Assembling for Development*; Adams, *Bordering the Future*, chap. 5; Cowie, *Capital Moves*, chaps. 6 and 7. On container shipping, see Levinson, *The Box*, chaps. 9–14.

26. On global sweatshops, see Cowie, "Century of Sweat."

27. On Chinese competition with Mexican manufacturing, see Adams, *Bordering the Future*, chap. 4. On the borderlands environment, see Greenberg, "The Tragedy of Commoditization"; Fernández and Carson, eds., *Both Sides of the Border*; Young, ed., *The Social Ecology and Economic Development of Ciudad Juárez*; Sarah Hill, "The Chamizal 'Tipping' Point? El Paso's Garbage in 1910," *Password* 50 (2005): 142–49; Kazimi et al., "Emissions from Heavy-Duty Trucks"; Sánchez, "Binational Cooperation." On the

environmental impact of a consumer society, see Princen, Maniates, and Conca, eds., *Confronting Consumption*; Klingle, "Spaces of Consumption." On female *maquiladora* workers, see Salzinger, "Manufacturing Sexual Subjects"; Salzinger, *Genders in Production*; Iglesias Prieto, *Beautiful Flowers*; Collins, *Threads*, chap. 5; Wright, *Disposable Women*; Wright, "Crossing the Factory Frontier"; Wright, "Maquiladora Mestizas"; Wright, "Dialectics of Still Life."

28. On declining wages, inflation, and increasing inequality in the United States, see Ryscavage, *Income Inequality*, chaps. 3 and 6; Piketty and Saez, "Income Inequality"; Jacobs, "Inflation."

29. On Mexican wages, inflation, and peso devaluations, see Bortz, "Prices and Wages in Tijuana and San Diego"; Lustig, *Mexico*, 2, 14–27, 61–95, 154–71, 201–12. See also Lustig's tables, especially table 3.2, "Evolution of Real Wages and Per Capita Private Consumption, 1981–1990"; table 3.4, "Wage and Nonwage Income, 1981–1990"; table 3.12, "Income Distribution in Mexico, Selected Years, 1963–1989"; and table 7.13, "Real Wages and Unemployment, 1989–1996." On the effects of the peso devaluations on Mexicans, see Lomnitz, "Times of Crisis"; Heyman, "Working for Beans"; Heyman, "Political Ecology," 113–14. On reallocation of household resources, see de Vries, "Purchasing Power," 113–21; Maynes, "Gender, Labor, and Globalization in Historical Perspective"; Casey and Martens, eds., *Gender and Consumption*. On women and children in the workforce in the Mexican North, see Salzinger, *Genders in Production*; Wright, "Crossing the Factory Frontier"; Sklair, *Assembling for Development*; Peña, *Terror of the Machine*; Salzinger, "Manufacturing Sexual Subjects"; Bacon, *Children of* NAFTA, 30–39, 215. For an overview of world currency crises, 1980–2000, see Bordo and Flandreau, "Core, Periphery, Exchange Rate Regimes, and Globalization."

30. On the effects of peso devaluations on retail sales in U.S. border cities, see Lorey, *U.S.-Mexican Border*, 102–3; Patrick and Renforth, "Effects of Peso Devaluation"; Yoskowitz and Pisani, "Penetration of the Mexican Peso into U.S. Retail Operations"; Prock, "The Peso Devaluations"; Diehl, "Effects of Peso Devaluation"; Phillips and Coronado, "Texas Border Benefits from Retail Sales to Mexican Nationals."

31. Lomnitz, "Times of Crisis," 147.

32. On remittances, see "Mexico: It's Hot South of the Border," *Business Week*, March 7, 2005; Jason DeParle, "Western Union Empire Moves Migrant Cash Home," *New York Times*, November 22, 2007; López-Córdova, "Globalization, Migration, and Development"; Mishra, "Emigration and Wages"; McKenzie, "Beyond Remittances"; Massey and Parrado, "Migradollars"; Garza and Lowell, eds., *Sending Money Home*.

33. Lichtenstein, "Wal-Mart," 4–5.

34. On the development of Wal-Mart, see Strasser, "Woolworth to Wal-Mart"; Tilly, "Wal-Mart in Mexico"; Bonacich and Hardie, "Wal-Mart and the Logistics Revolution." On Wal-Mart labor practices, see Adams, "Making the New Shop Floor"; Seligman, "Patriarchy at the Checkout Counter."

35. Herzog, *North Meets South*, 250. Per capita annual income is nearly three times higher on the U.S. side of the border than on the Mexican.

36. On borderlands income data, see Bane and Zenteno, table 9, "Poverty and Place in North America," 22; Anderson and Gerber, *Fifty Years of Change on the U.S.-Mexico Border; At the Cross Roads: US/Mexico Border Counties in Transition*, http://www.borderlands.org, accessed June 15, 2006; "Who Makes What in Ciudad Juárez?" *Frontera NorteSur*, July–September, 2007, http://www.nmsu.edu/frontera/comm.html, accessed July 23, 2007; "2006 Trends in CEO Pay," http://www.aflcio.org/corporatewatch/pay watch/pay/index.cfm, accessed January 9, 2008.

37. On pawnbroking, see Tebbutt, *Making Ends Meet*; Woloson, "In Hock"; McCants, "Goods at Pawn." On consumer credit, see Calder, *Financing the American Dream*; Olegario, *Culture of Credit*; Olney, *Buy Now*; Olney, "Avoiding Default." On lending in Mexico, see Francois, *Culture of Everyday Credit*; "Mexico: It's Hot South of the Border," *op. cit.* On Mexican banks in the borderlands, see Elisabeth Malkin, "Spanish Bank Courts Hispanic Customers in United States," *New York Times*, September 22, 2004.

38. On poverty in Mexico and the Mexican borderlands, see Bane and Zenteno, "Poverty and Place," 6, 13–14; Heyman, "Working for Beans"; Pardinas, "Fighting Poverty"; Hufbauer and Schott, NAFTA *Revisited*, 50–51; Betts and Slottje, *Crisis on the Rio Grande*, 33; Stoddard and Hedderson, *Trends and Patterns*; Anderson and Gerber, *Fifty Years of Change*.

39. On the "sovereignty of bread," see Roche, *History of Everyday Things*, 60. On Ramen noodles, see Marla Dickerson, "Steeped in a New Tradition: Instant Ramen Noodles are Supplanting Beans and Rice for Many in Mexico," *Los Angeles Times*, October 21, 2005.

40. On decencies, see Heyman, "Imports," 164. On Mexican measures of poverty, see Executive Summary, *Mexico: Income Generation and Social Protection for the Poor*, World Bank Report (2004), http://siteresources.worldbank.org/INTMEXICO/Resources/Executive_Summary.pdf, accessed 8 January 2008, table 1, "Share of Population in Poverty," and table 5, "Extreme Poverty Trends, by Region."

41. Hill and Gaines, "Consumer Culture of Poverty."

42. Davis, *Magical Urbanism*, 26. For a fascinating historical account of "making do," see Rockman, *Scraping By*.

43. On lowriders, see Plascencia, "Low Riding in the Southwest"; Bright, "Heart Like a Car"; Bright, "Nightmares in the New Metropolis"; Chappell, "Lowrider Cruising Spaces"; Best, *Fast Cars*, chap. 1; Stone, "*Bajito y Suavecito*." On car culture, see Franz, *Tinkering*.

44. On secondhand trade in borderlands, see Helen Thorpe, "Great Hand-Me-Down Heap," *New York Times*, October 15, 2000; Ojeda-Benitez, Armijo de Vega, and Ramírez-Barreto, "Potential for Recycling"; O'Day and López, "Organizing the Underground NAFTA."

45. In terms of shadows, consider ethnographer Pierrette Hondagneu-Sotelo's *Doméstica: Immigrant Workers Cleaning and Caring in the Shadows of Affluence* (Berkeley: University of California Press, 2007), a powerful account about the "shadow of affluence" in which migrants work in U.S. homes.

46. On the borderlands built environment, see Arreola and Curtis, *Mexican Border*

Cities; Herzog, *North Meets South*; Peñaloza, "*Atravesando Fronteras*/Border Crossings"; Oberle, "*Se Venden Aquí*: Latino Commercial Landscapes"; Saldívar, *Border Matters*; Canclini, *Hybrid Cultures*, 234–49.

47. Tenorio-Trillo, *Mexico at the World's Fairs*, 12.

48. Appadurai, *Social Life of Things*. For another view on "the social life of things," see van Binsbergen and Geschiere, eds., *Commodification*. On commodity chain analysis, see Hopkins and Wallerstein, "Commodity Chains"; Gereffi and Korzeniewicz, eds., *Commodity Chains*; Raikes, Jensen, and Ponte, "Global Commodity Chain"; Topik, Marichal, and Frank, eds., *From Silver to Cocaine*.

49. On Spanglish, see Hill, "*Hasta La Vista*, Baby"; Morales, *Living in Spanglish*; Stavans, *Spanglish*. On borderlands food, see Campbell, "Chicano Lite"; Pilcher, "Tex-Mex, Cal-Mex, New Mex, or Whose Mex?"; Pilcher, "Industrial Tortillas and Folkloric Pepsi"; Pilcher, "Taco Bell, Maseca, and Slow Food."

50. On borderlands music, see Dorsey, *Pachangas*; Habell-Pallán, *Loca Motion*, chap. 6; Edberg, *El Narcotraficante*; Wald, "Polka *Contrabandista*"; Wald, *Narcocorrido*; Simonett, *Banda*; Kun, "Aural Border"; Kun, *Audiotopia*, 152–54, 185, 193–200; Coronado, "Selena's Good Buy"; Paredes, *Texas-Mexican Cancionero*.

51. On the borderlands health-care consumer market, see Gabriele Judkins, "Persistence of the U.S.-Mexico Border: Expansion of Medical Tourism amid Trade Liberalization," *Journal of Latin American Geography* 6 (2007): 11–32; Oberle and Arreola, "Mexican Medical Border Towns"; Tomes, "Merchants of Health."

52. On big-box retail, see Spector, *Category Killers*; Lichtenstein, ed., *Wal-Mart*. On borderlands food scarcity, 1980–2000, see McDonald, "NAFTA and Basic Food Production." On Wal-Mart in Mexico, see Tilly, "Wal-Mart in Mexico."

53. On globalization and poverty in Mexico, see Ann Harrison, "Globalization and Poverty: An Introduction," and Gordon Hanson, "Globalization, Labor Income, and Poverty in Mexico," both in Harrison, ed., *Globalization and Poverty*, op. cit.

54. Staudt, "Informality Knows No Borders," 128; Herzog, *North Meets South*, xi.

55. On "global illicit trade," see Naím, *Illicit*, 7.

56. On the informal economy, see Venkatesh, *Off the Books*; Schneider and Enste, *Shadow Economy*; Schneider and Enste, "Shadow Economies"; Castells and Portes, "World Underneath"; Portes, Castells, and Benton, eds., *Informal Economy*; Fernández-Kelly and Shefner, eds., *Out of the Shadows*; Saskia Sassen, *Cities in a World Economy* (Thousand Oaks: Pine Forge Press, 1995). On the underground economy's share of national GDPs, see Schlosser, *Reefer Madness*, 5; Schneider and Enste, *Shadow Economy*, table 4.1.

57. On the border as a trade bridge and barrier, see Chen, *As Borders Bend*.

58. Peter Andreas's brilliant discussion of contemporary criminal activity in the borderlands, *Border Games*, shows how heightened forms of regulation and enforcement enhance the profitability of criminal economic activity. For example, social scientist Ken Dermota shows that after the implementation of NAFTA, the drug traffic from Colombia increasingly was routed through Mexico and across the border into the U.S.

("Snow Business: Drugs and the Spirit of Capitalism," *World Policy Journal* 16 (1999–2000): 15–24.) See also Bowman, "The U.S.-Mexico Border as Locator of Innovation and Vice." For 1990s drug-smuggling data, see Recio, "Drugs and Alcohol," 21–22. On narcotics smuggling and control, see Taylor, *American Diplomacy*; Astorga, *El siglo de las drogas*; Astorga, "Drug Trafficking"; González and Tienda, eds., *Drug Connection*; Andreas, *Border Games*, chaps. 3 and 4; van Schendel and Abraham, eds., *Illicit Flows*; Perramond, "Desert Traffic"; Campbell, "Drug Trafficking Stories"; Schlosser, *Reefer Madness*; Fernandez, *United States-Mexico Border*, 126–27; Griffith, "Border Crossings: Race, Class, and Smuggling in Pacific Coast Chinese Immigrant Society," *Western Historical Quarterly* 35 (2004): 473–92; Brouwer, "Trends in Production." On cross-border traffic in human beings for sex and for indentured and enslaved work, see Peter Landesman, " Girls Next Door," *New York Times*, January 25, 2004; Bowe, *Nobodies*; Zhang, *Smuggling and Trafficking*. On money laundering, see Jim Thomas, "What is the Informal Economy, Anyway?" SAIA *Review* 21 (winter–spring 2001): 1–11; *Cuellar v. United States* 553 U.S. (2008) Slip Opinion No. 06-1546.

59. On criminal vs. informal economic activity, see Staudt, *Free Trade?* 1–9, 58–90. On informal economic activity in the borderlands, see Richardson and Resendiz, *Edge of Law*; Staudt, *Free Trade?*; Ward, *Colonias*. On smuggling to avoid tariffs and blockades, see Barger, "Furs, Hides, and a Little Larceny"; Reséndez, "Getting Cured"; Mayo, "Consuls and Silver Contraband"; Jorge Hernández, "Merchants and Mercenaries: Anglo-Americans in Mexico's Northeast," *New Mexico Historical Review* 75 (2000): 43–75; Jorge Hernández, "Trading across the Border: National Customs Guards in Nuevo Leon," *Southwestern Historical Quarterly* 100 (1997): 433–50; Homer Hickham, "The Contrabandistas," *Air & Space/Smithsonian* 11 (1996): 62–67; Lebergott, "Through the Blockade."

60. On human smuggling during the U.S. era of Chinese exclusion (1882–1934), see Griffith, "Border Crossings" *op. cit.*; Patrick Ettinger, " 'We Sometimes Wonder What They Will Spring on Us Next': Immigrants and Border Enforcement in the American West, 1882–1930," *Western Historical Quarterly* 37 (2006): 159–81; George Paulson, "The Yellow Peril and Nogales: The Ordeal of Collector William M. Hoey," *Arizona and the West* 13 (1971): 113–28. On smuggling Chinese across the border during 1990s, see Ko-lin Chin, *Smuggled Chinese: Clandestine Immigration to the United States* (Pittsburgh: Temple University Press, 1999), chap. 6. On smuggling during Prohibition, see Recio, "Drugs and Alcohol"; Shawn Lay, "Imperial Outpost on the Border: El Paso's Frontier Klan No. 100," in Shawn Lay, ed., *The Invisible Empire in the West: Toward a New Historical Appraisal of the Ku Klux Klan of the 1920s* (Urbana: University of Illinois Press, 1992), 67–96; George Diaz, "Tracking Tequileros: The Bloody Origins of a Border Ballad," *Journal of South Texas* 17 (2004): 61–77; Haldeen Braddy, "Running Contraband on the Rio Grande," *Southern Folklore Quarterly* 25 (1961): 101–12; Pete Flores, "Cordova Island," *Password* 40 (1995): 35–41.

61. On smuggled *used* U.S. goods, see O'Day and López, "Organizing the Underground NAFTA"; Medina, "Informal Transborder Recycling"; Medina, "Scavenging on the Bor-

der"; Thorpe, "Great Hand-Me-Down Heap," *op. cit.* On smuggled *stolen* U.S. goods, see Sean Holstege and Samuel Murillo, "U.S., Mexico Unite to Fight Car Thieves," *Arizona Republic*, December 10, 2007. On smuggled *Chinese-made* consumer goods, see Mary Jordan, "Mexico Now Feels Pinch of Cheap Labor," *Washington Post*, December 3, 2003.

62. On kleptomania, see Elaine Abelson, *When Ladies Go A-Thieving: Middle-Class Shoplifters in the Victorian Department Store* (New York: Oxford University Press, 1989); Kerry Seagrave, *Shoplifting: A Social History* (Jefferson: McFarland, 2001), chap. 1; Tammy Whitlock, *Crime, Gender, and Consumer Culture in Nineteenth-Century England* (Aldershot, UK: Ashgate, 2005), chaps. 6 and 7.

63. Rajagopal, "The Violence of Commodity Aesthetics," 94, 92. On Los Angeles street peddlers, see Margaret Crawford, "Blurring the Boundaries: Public Space and Private Life," in John Chase, Margaret Crawford, and John Kaliski, eds., *Everyday Urbanism* (New York: Monacelli, 1999), 22–35. On "illegal aliens," see Ngai, *Impossible Subjects*; Nevins, *Operation Gatekeeper*; Chacón and Davis, *No One Is Illegal.*

64. On the effect of lifting trade restrictions, see Andreas, "Escalation of U.S. Immigration Control"; Andreas, *Border Games*; Payan, *Three U.S.-Mexico Border Wars.* On borderless capitalism, see Mosco and Schiller, eds., *Continental Order?*

65. Rajagopal, "The Violence of Commodity Aesthetics," 96, 99, 103.

66. On immigration between 2000 and 2007, see Julia Preston, "Immigration at Record Level, Analysis Finds," *New York Times*, November 29, 2007. On Mexican migrants as beyond control of nation-states, see Durand, Massey, and Parrado, "The New Era of Mexican Migration to the United States." On consumption and globalization, see Storper, "Lived Effects of the Contemporary Economy," 376; Comaroff and Comaroff, eds., *Millennial Capitalism.* On globalization and borders, see Ganster and Lorey, eds., *Borders and Border Politics in a Globalizing World*; Hu-Dehart, "Globalization and Its Discontents."

67. On border fences and walls, see Ralph Blumenthal, "Some Texans Fear Border Fence Will Sever Routine of Daily Life," *New York Times*, June 20, 2007; Randal Archibold, "28-Mile Virtual Fence Is Rising Along the Border," *New York Times*, June 26, 2007; Julia Preston, "Environmental Laws Waived to Press Work on Border Fence," *New York Times*, October 23, 2007. On the militarization of the borderlands, see Dunn, *Militarization*; Andreas, *Border Games*; Spener, "The Logic and Contradictions of Intensified Border Enforcement in Texas"; Maril, *Patrolling Chaos*; Payan, *Three U.S.-Mexico Border Wars*; Toro, "The Internationalization of Police"; Toro, *Mexico's "War" on Drugs.* On long waits at border ports of entry, see Julia Preston, "Tighter Border Delays Re-entry by U.S. Citizens," *New York Times*, October 21, 2007. On media representations of border, see Monica Soderlund, "The Role of News Media in Shaping and Transforming the Public Perception of Mexican Immigration and the Laws Involved," *Law & Psychology Review* 31 (2007): 167–77; Sarah Hill, "Purity and Danger on the U.S.-Mexico Border, 1991–1994," *South Atlantic Quarterly* 105 (fall 2006): 777–99.

68. On the concept of a porous border, see Saldaña-Portillo, "Shadow of NAFTA," 757, 753.

69. Claire Fox, "The Portable Border: Site-Specificity, Art, and the U.S.-Mexico Frontier," *Social Text* 41 (1994): 61–82, quote p. 71. On fast rate of growth of U.S.-Mexico borderlands, see Herzog, *North Meets South*, 30, 35.

70. On similarities between border regions and global cities, see Saskia Sassen, ed., *Global Networks, Linked Cities* (New York: Routledge, 2002), part 2; Perkmann and Sum, eds., *Globalization*, 3–5; Anderson and Wever, "Borders." A definitive work on global cities is Saskia Sassen, *The Global City: New York, London, Tokyo* (1991; Princeton: Princeton University Press, 2001). On the border as globalization's "staging ground," see Sadowski-Smith, ed., *Globalization*, 6; Herzog, *North Meets South*, 138–42; Hu-Dehart, "Globalization and Its Discontents"; Perkman and Sum, eds., *Globalization, Regionalization, and Cross-Border Regions*; Ganster and Lorey, eds., *Borders and Border Politics in a Globalizing World*.

71. Néstor Rodríguez, "The Battle for the Border: Notes on Autonomous Migration, Transnational Communities, and the State," in Susanne Jonas and Suzanne Dod Thomas, eds., *Immigration: A Civil Rights Issue for the Americas* (Lanham: Rowman & Littlefield, 1999): 27–44.

72. Ulrich Beck, *What Is Globalization?*, translated by Patrick Camiller (Cambridge: Polity Press, 2000), 10–11.

73. Ibid., 12.

74. Canclini, *Consumers and Citizens*, 3. On globalized U.S.-Mexico borderlands, see Canclini, *Hybrid Cultures*; Ortiz-Gonzales, *El Paso*; Herzog, "Globalization of the Barrio."

75. On globalization and Americanization, see Saskia Sassen, *Globalization and Its Discontents: Essays on the New Mobility of People and Money* (New York: The New Press, 2007); William Marling, *How "American" Is Globalization?* (Baltimore: Johns Hopkins University Press, 2006); Hoganson, "Stuff It"; Bordo, Taylor, and Williamson, eds., *Globalization in Historical Perspective*; Tarrow, *New Transnational Activism*; Wilson and Dissanayake, eds., *Global/Local*. For global economic indicators, see Peter Dicken, *Global Shift, Fifth Edition: Mapping the Changing Contours of the World Economy* (New York: Guilford Press, 2007).

II

NATIONAL AND TRANSNATIONAL
CIRCUITS OF CONSUMPTION

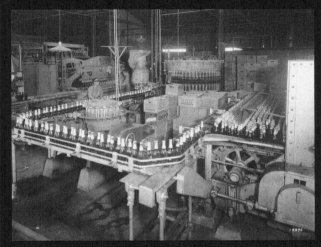

Aztec Brewery, San Diego, ca. 1937. Photograph courtesy Photograph Collection,
San Diego Historical Society.

South El Paso children with a donkey, ca. 1900–1909. Photograph by Otis Aultman, courtesy Aultman Collection, A525, El Paso Public Library.

Amy S. Greenberg

Domesticating the Border

Manifest Destiny and the "Comforts of Life" in the
U.S.-Mexico Boundary Commission and Gadsden
Purchase, 1848–1854

> One's desire for a frontier life will not be increased by
> a perusal of the chapters of this section . . . the scarcity
> of most of the necessaries and all of the comforts of
> life, impress us that a sojourn at El Paso must be
> more exciting than agreeable, and we prefer taking our
> author's account of it to making the experiment.
> *PROVIDENCE JOURNAL*, JUNE 6, 1854

In the course of a short but devastating war in the late 1840s,
Mexico lost almost half of her territory to the United States.
The present-day border between the two countries was not
finalized, however, until December of 1853, when the Gadsden
Purchase added an extra 45,535 square miles to the American
Southwest. The Gadsden Purchase, like the war that preceded
it, was particularly contentious in the northeastern United
States. Critics asserted that the land in question, in Chihuahua
and Sonora's Mesilla Valley, was both "worthless" and "barren," and totally unsuited for what Americans understood as
civilized life. Among the most glaring weaknesses of the larger
borderlands region was the lack of "most of the necessaries and
all of the comforts of life," as the Providence, Rhode Island,
Journal put it.[1]

In the view of northern critics, the Gadsden Purchase was a
prime example of a southern slave power attempting to corrupt
the political process to its own ends: in this case acquiring more
land for slavery and hopefully a southern transcontinental rail-

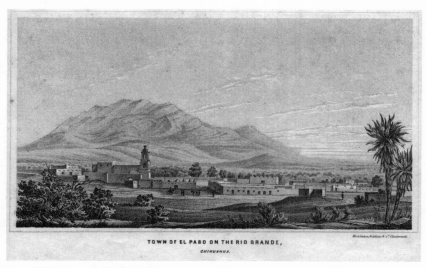

TOWN OF EL PASO ON THE RIO GRANDE,
CHIHUAHUA.

Town of El Paso on the Rio Grande, 1854. Lithograph by Carl Schuchard, courtesy Archives and Special Collections, New Mexico State University Library, ID NMLCU/RGHC 03390014.

road route. Like the U.S.-Mexico War, the purchase exacerbated sectional tensions that would result in another, far bloodier war, only a few years later. That the Gadsden territory was defined in northern public discourse by its stunted trade, lack of consumer goods, and primitive family homes was to a large degree attributable to one Rhode Island Whig, John Russell Bartlett. Bartlett's political position should have placed him at the forefront of proponents of Manifest Destiny in the early 1850s, but he became, instead, the leading voice condemning acquisition of territory in the U.S.-Mexico borderlands. As this essay will explore, his prolific writings from and about the region both shaped and reflected a conflict between divergent views of the place of consumption and domesticity in American society and the potential value of the borderlands within American civilization.

Bartlett was appointed the American commissioner of the U.S.-Mexico Boundary Commission, directed by the 1848 Treaty of Guadalupe Hidalgo to chart the new postwar boundary from San Diego to the mouth of the Rio Grande. The treaty granted the international commission the power to resolve any differences of opinion on the location of the boundary line. Its agreements were to have the force of treaty, but Congress—believing that the results of the survey, known as the Bartlett-Conde agreement, were too favorable to Mexico—disbanded the Boundary Commission after three and a half years of work. Bartlett was publicly humiliated in Congress, while Mexico was brazenly

John Russell Bartlett. Engraving, from Bartlett's *Personal Narrative of Explorations and Incidents in Texas, New Mexico, California, Sonora, and Chihuahua*, v. 1, 1854.

John R. Bartlett, a member of the Whig Party, as the first American commissioner of the U.S.-Mexico Boundary Commission, led a three-year cooperative effort to map the border between the U.S. and Mexico. Bringing a view of domesticity that was informed by the intertwined cultures of uplift and consumption, Bartlett was confounded by the region's apparent absence of domestic comforts. Nevertheless, as a student of Native Americans, he did not disparage the region, despite seeing little opportunity for American-style settlement and development. After the U.S. Congress refused to ratify the Bartlett-Conde agreement, which Bartlett had prepared with his Mexican counterpart, Pedro García Conde, who died in December 1851, negotiations resulting in the Gadsden Purchase ensued.

intimidated into agreeing to the Gadsden Purchase soon after. A new joint commission under the direction of Major William Emory completed the marking of the two-thousand-mile post-Gadsden borderline from December of 1854 to October 1855. The failure of the Bartlett-led U.S.-Mexico Boundary Commission, one of America's first politically sanctioned cross-cultural efforts, caused an enormous scandal in the early 1850s. Yet it is barely remembered today.[2]

Bartlett, a notable scholar of Native American ethnology, gained his position thanks to his political connections to the Whig Party, then in power.[3] He joined the Boundary Survey for the money, for the adventure, and for the chance to examine the *terra incognita* of the Southwest. He spent millions of the government's dollars on meandering travels through the region, studying the flora, fauna, people, and land on both sides of the new boundary line. The result was one of the finest travelogues ever written of the region, his *Personal Narrative of Explorations and Incidents in Texas, New Mexico, California, Sonora, and Chihuahua*, published in 1854. Bartlett anonymously authored a number of articles in American newspapers while he was commissioner, and journalists traveling with the commission further disseminated his views in the popular press.[4]

Bartlett's replacement, William Emory, was in many ways his predecessor's

William H. Emory. Photograph, from George F. Price, *Across the Continent with the Fifth Cavalry*, 1883.

William H. Emory was the chief astronomer and surveyor of the Bartlett-led U.S.-Mexico Boundary Commission prior to 1854. After the treaty of Guadalupe Hidalgo was signed, resulting in the Gadsden Purchase, Democrats in the U.S. Congress, with the approval of U.S. President James Polk, appointed him the U.S. Boundary Commissioner. Emory brought a considerably different attitude toward consumption, set of political commitments, and perspective of the borderlands to his task than did Bartlett.

opposite. Emory was a skilled topographical engineer and a career Army officer from a southern slaveholding family who had worked on the survey of the northeastern boundary between the United States and Canada, an 1844 map of Texas, and an 1846 military reconnaissance of the Gila River. Emory had chafed under Bartlett's command as chief astronomer and surveyor for the Bartlett-led commission. He refused to sign on to the Bartlett-Conde agreement when Bartlett first drafted it. Emory's actions while directing the boundary survey suggest that he was committed to a southern expansionist position and was willing to adjust his professional opinion in order to support the desires of congressional expansionists.[5] Bartlett's account was "a publication that would irritate Emory for years while he worked on his own narrative," eventually published in 1859 at government expense as *Report on the United States and Mexican Boundary Survey, made under the Direction of the Secretary of the Interior*.[6]

Bartlett's Mexican counterpart on the commission was the nationalist general Pedro García Conde, a former military commander of Chihuahua. Conde, who died of illness in December of 1851 while conducting the survey, left few personal papers or publications, so his opinions about the boundary commission are somewhat obscure. As boundary commissioner, Conde was a superb advocate for Mexican interests, but they were Mexico's interests broadly understood. Although Conde was himself from northern Mexico, his allegiance lay with Mexico City; at one point he attempted to trade land along the Gila River to the United States in return for land on the Pacific Coast, suggesting the relative value he placed on the two regions. Many *fronterizos*, residents of Mexico's northern frontier region, opposed the treaty of Guadalupe Hidalgo and wanted to continue fighting the United States. They were understandably wary of the entire boundary commission.[7]

Unlike the politically savvy Conde, Bartlett entered the job with neither surveying nor diplomatic experience. His nepotistic appointments produced a remarkably unqualified body of officers. Many of the problems that plagued the boundary commission during his tenure were outside his control, like the political squabbling in Washington that held up commission funds and the difficulty of travel though the deserts and mountains of the region. But other problems were of his own making. The dearth of supplies and their expense was partially due to the simultaneous beginnings of gold fever, but the ineptitude (some said outright corruption) of Bartlett's brother, appointed to handle those supplies, exacerbated the situation. Difficulties with the Apaches, who had terrorized Mexican residents of the region for decades, were probably inevitable, but in refusing to share alcohol with the Native Americans he encountered, the teetotaler Bartlett helped alienate potential allies. Violence and drunkenness among soldiers is traditionally common, but he had no clear plan as to how to control and discipline troublemakers, and certainly the number of murders perpetrated against and by his soldiers was unusually high. A more experienced traveler would have known to pack enough water to make it through the desert without losing the majority of his livestock. Perhaps a better diplomat would have understood the implications of the fact that the Treaty of Guadalupe Hidalgo was based on Disturnell's inaccurate 1847 map of Mexico, which located the boundary 35 miles north and 175 miles east of its actual location. When Bartlett and Conde agreed to split the difference between two radically different views of where the southern boundary of Arizona should be placed, opposition in Congress was immediate and violent. On the eve of an administration and party change, the fact that an antislavery Whig appointee, from Rhode Island no less, might compromise with Mexico over the question of southern territory was too much for congressional Democrats, especially southern ones, to bear.[8]

Some lawmakers suggested that Bartlett, the political neophyte, had been duped by the "shrewd" Conde, an insult made all the more painful given the low regard in which many Americans held Mexican men.[9] Mexicans,

Disturnell's 1847 treaty map of Mexico. Library of Congress, Geography and Map Division.

John Disturnell's 1847 map plagiarized portions of two previous maps, which were themselves inaccurate. He placed the Rio Grande two degrees too far west, and incorrectly located the town of Paso (now Ciudad Juárez).

especially *fronterizos*, were also outraged by the compromise, believing it too generous to the United States. Most historians, however, have agreed that Bartlett and Conde's compromise position was exactly what the treaty makers of both countries intended. It was a good compromise in keeping with the spirit and law of the treaty.[10]

Historians have posited a variety of explanations for the failure of the Bartlett-Conde agreement, ranging from the ineptitude of commission members, to the start of the California Gold Rush, to the shift of political power in Washington in 1853 following the election of Democrat Franklin Pierce to the presidency.[11] Both Whigs and northerners generally were highly skeptical of both Bartlett's dismissal and the Gadsden Purchase. In 1854, when the Gadsden Treaty was being debated in Congress, the New York *Herald* asked its readers "why it is that we shall have to pay so much money for such a God-forsaken country as this proposed new cession from the deserts of Mexico." Its editor suggested that it was "a master stroke of 'South Carolina diplomacy'" that would provide an "ample margin for the addition of three or four slave states to [the] glorious Union." Southerners, on the other hand, believed that Bartlett had deliberately given away a key portion of the only topographically viable transcontinental railroad route in the far Southwest—running along the southwestern wagon trail—when he agreed on the location of the border with his Mexican counterpart.[12]

This essay suggests that competing views of the market, of consumption, and of the place of domesticity in the U.S.-Mexico borderlands were also contributing factors to the failure of the Bartlett-led commission and to the ultimate resolution of the international boundary with the Gadsden Purchase. Southern Democratic expansionists and their northern Whig opponents held dramatically different views of the worthiness of the region for annexation, views that clearly shaped their willingness to compromise, or to continue fighting, over the placement of the border. While Bartlett and Emory both openly questioned the suitability of much of the territory in question for trade, farming, and the placement of middle-class homes, complete with the material trappings that would enable "civilized" domestic life, for the Democrats these were far less significant concerns than they were for the Whigs. By placing the debates over the border in their cultural context, it becomes apparent that more than a railroad was at stake in the question of a compromise agreement: the role of consumption within American culture in the 1850s was also under consideration.

It is fair to say that Whigs were firm supporters of the expansion of American industry at home and American commerce abroad in the 1840s and early 1850s, while the Democratic Party, during that period, claimed the continuing expansion of American territorial boundaries as their particular political issue.[13] Furthermore, each party professed commitment to the central role of the home, the family, and women in American life. Whigs, on the whole, were more willing than Democrats to transfer control of household matters to women, were more supportive of women's rights movements, and were more willing to share the political spotlight with women. Divisions between the parties on expansionism and gender were far from clean ones, however, because the ideologies of domesticity and expansionism were not necessarily opposed.[14]

Historians of European imperialism have long asserted that empire, in Britain especially, "was intimately wedded to the Western reinvention of domesticity."[15] The same can be said of the United States. Catharine Beecher, probably the antebellum era's leading exponent of domestic ideology, declared in her 1841 *Treatise on Domestic Economy* that "the Disposer of events"

Anglo-American home interior. Engraved frontispiece, from Catharine Beecher and Harriet Beecher Stowe, *The American Woman's Home*, 1869.

designed that America should "go forth as the cynosure of nations, to guide them to the light." In the years before the U.S.-Mexico War, women's domesticating force legitimated territorial expansionism, justifying violence against Native Americans in the name of protecting white womanhood, and allowing Americans to cast the settlement of the West as a civilizing venture. Middle-class women from the northeast, in particular, who settled the West envisioned their actions as patriotic and understood themselves as agents of American civilization, while politicians utilized images of female settlement to promote Manifest Destiny. Domesticity and national expansion were thus mutually reinforcing.[16]

One of the central tenets of domestic ideology was the consumption of consumer goods. Catharine Beecher directed women to purchase "superfluities" in order to promote the national economy, pointing out that consumption of such goods "is as indispensable to promote industry, virtue, and religion, as any direct giving of money and time." The primary place where a woman could devote her energy as a consumer was in the home. The popular women's magazine *Godey's Lady's Book* regularly offered tips on decorating a household in a tasteful manner, and Beecher and other authors of domestic guides lavished attention on creating a comfortable oasis for one's family through interior decorating.[17]

Interior decoration not only enabled the expression of domestic virtue in the antebellum era, it also became an important class marker. In the 1840s and 1850s, a period of increasing class stratification, the family home became a key site for the expression of the "cultured" or "refined" practices that the emerging middle class presented to distinguish itself from the lower orders. The prominent architectural pattern-book author Andrew Jackson Downing asserted in 1847 that a refined domestic environment presented an "unfailing barrier against vice, immorality, and bad habits." Famed landscape architect and designer Calvert Vaux claimed that an "all-encircling civilization," expressed through a tastefully decorated home, was "within reach of every class," implying that the failure of a home to adhere to the standards these authors set forth was clear evidence of the unworthiness of its occupants.[18]

In order to express the refinement of its owners, the proper family home of the 1840s and 1850s required an increasing number of improvements over houses that were viewed as perfectly acceptable in the first decades of the century, including the presence of a parlor, carpets, an attractive yard, plastered walls, a fireplace mantle, and possibly a library. The invention and dissemination of the corn broom in the first half of the century meant that new standards of floor cleanliness were demanded by refined homeowners, and the dramatic increase in carpet sales during the same period indicates how deeply this idea of refinement impacted purchasing habits. The ostensible purpose of all this refinement was to create a comfortable retreat from the harsh outside world, conducive to moral family life. Increasingly, according to historian Richard Bushman, "coarse living in rude dwellings repelled people who were trying to bring refinement into their homes and their lives."[19]

Both antebellum domestic manuals and novels promised that the appropriate deployment of tasteful domestic objects could be spiritualizing, civilizing, and humanizing, while linking these domestic environments with the civilizing process of domesticated expansionism. Whigs, in particular, upheld the view that consumption could be an almost religious activity, which would promote the moral uplift of both a woman's home and the larger environment in which she lived. Democrats, on the other hand, were perpetually wary that luxuries could lead to corruption and emasculation. Ideological opposition between Whiggism and Jacksonianism was roughly translated, in the writings of some women writers, into the distinction between the refined and un-cultured classes. As the literary scholar Lori Merish has written, " 'pious con-sumption' was written into a Whig historical narrative of moral and economic 'progress,' " which became a key instrument of acculturation within America's civilizing mission. Consumption was directly linked with expansionism in the writing of many antebellum women writers. Eliza Farnham's 1846 novel *Life in Prairie Land*, for instance, explicitly defined an ideal of white, civilized domes-ticity, against the deficiently developed homes and womanhood present on the western frontier.[20]

When the boundary commission began its work, then, it did so in a politi-cal environment in which Democrats were largely unquestioning of the posi-tive value that the continued territorial growth of the country represented, regardless of the character of any new land that might be annexed (so long as it was not densely populated by racial inferiors). Whigs, on the other hand, were more ambivalent about the issue, since territorial growth could lead to the weakening of America's centralized political structure. At the same time, the refined family home was heavily loaded with both class and gender signifi-cance, particularly to domesticated women and their political supporters in the Whig party. And there was a clear precedent, on the western frontier, for Whigs to affirm territorial expansionism as a means for the spread of middle-class American values, in large part through the vehicle of the refined middle-class household. A Whig appointee to the U.S.-Mexico Boundary Commission would put these beliefs into action in the borderlands.

Although Pedro García Conde left little record of his views of the U.S.-Mexico border region before his untimely death, his willingness to trade away land on the border suggests that his views of the frontier were similar to those of other Mexican officials. Mexicans have never celebrated their arid and mountainous northern frontier, or *el norte*, in the same romantic manner that U.S. residents have embraced their frontier. Indeed, from Mexican indepen-dence up until the U.S.-Mexico War, the relationship between the periphery, which sought political independence and free trade, and the central state, which demanded political and economic authority over *el norte*, was far from comfortable. "Contraband was a fact of life in independent Mexico," even in the bustling ports of the Gulf and Pacific Coasts, but even contraband trade was limited in the border region by the mountains, lack of roads, and few navigable rivers that physically isolated *el norte* from central Mexico.[21]

Fronterizos, from Nuevo León to Sonora, grew increasingly hostile to the central state, which proved unable to protect the region from Indian raids and unwilling to aid trade in the region. For Mexico City, especially after 1848 according to historian Juan Mora-Torres, "the border represented nothing but a series of new problems it was incapable of solving: secessionist movements, Indian and Texan raiders, uncontrolled contraband, and all kinds of threatening diplomatic disputes with Washington." Physically, economically, and culturally isolated from the seat of power, *el norte* was easy for authorities in central Mexico to dismiss. Debates in Mexico over the *Tratado de la Mesilla* (Gadsden Treaty) suggest that Mexican officials outside of *el norte* saw little intrinsic value to the region. In his negotiations with Bartlett, Conde expressed more concern for the residents of the contested area, many of whom had moved south to the Mesilla Valley after the war, than he did about the value of the land itself to Mexico.[22]

In contrast, both Bartlett and Emory recognized the potential value of the disputed territory to a country gripped by a belief in its Manifest Destiny to spread across the continent. Bartlett wrote, "Mexican indolence can not stand by the side of the energy and industry of the Americans and Europeans; and the newcomers are rapidly elbowing the old settlers to one side." Emory was yet more enthusiastic, so steeped in America's destiny that in his report on the Gila River reconnaissance, he described witnessing a mirage "on the north side of the Gila (mountains), a perfect representation of the capitol, with dome, wings, and portico, all complete." Emory's boundary commission narrative travels from east to west, from Texas to the Pacific, although that is not the direction his survey took. He claimed that to trace in the account the actual direction of the commission's journey would "not be convenient." The narrative as Emory shaped it cohered with Manifest Destiny's course: the forward march of progress toward the sunset. Emory, like many Democrats, expected Manifest Destiny to continue its march inexorably forward.[23]

The illustrations in both Emory's and Bartlett's volumes also supported the idea of Manifest Destiny, presenting a vision of the Southwest often closer to Albany than Albuquerque. Offering few portraits of the hostile Apache and Comanche who decimated agriculture, commerce, and industry from Tamaulipas to Sonora, Emory's volume, in particular, focused on romanticized images of peaceful and domesticated Native Americans from tribes friendly to the commission, including the Maricopa and Pima. Bartlett, who entered his job hoping to study Native American cultures, also offered images in his writing of "peaceful natives who were agriculturalists already converted to European ways."[24] The result of these artistic choices was to present a visual portrait of territory open to Manifest Destiny, where the landscape was familiar

Interior of Indian huts, California. Engraving by Jocelyn-Annin Whitney, in John Russell Bartlett, *Personal Narrative of Explorations and Incidents in Texas, New Mexico, California, Sonora, and Chihuahua*, v. 2, 1854.

enough to settle comfortably and where Native Americans were themselves domesticated and presented no threat to emigrants.[25]

But Bartlett's faith in Manifest Destiny wavered during his excursions. He never grew comfortable in the terrain of the Southwest. Bartlett first expressed his misgivings as an anonymous "correspondent" of the boundary commission to the Providence *Journal*. Writing in May of 1851 from Fronteras, Sonora, he described "toiling across these sterile plains, where no tree affords a friendly shade, the sun glowing fiercely, the wind hot from the parched earth cracking the lips and burning the eyes, the thought will suggest itself is this the land for which we paid so dearly and which is to be surveyed and kept at such a cost? As far as the eye can see stretches one unbroken waste, barren, wild and worthless." A year before Bartlett and Conde reached their agreement, which was then rejected by Congress, Bartlett had already reached a conclusion about the value of Sonora to the United States: it was worthless.[26] While Emory agreed that much of the Southwest was unsuitable for, as he put it, "the notion entertained of farming in the Eastern States," he expressed a faith in the agricultural potential of many areas under proper irrigation. Bartlett was less sanguine. He wrote in his 1854 narrative that "much has been said about the great value of the Mesilla valley [the Gadsden Purchase area], but of this fertile land not one tenth part can ever be regularly and successfully cultivated, owing to the uncertainty in the supply of water." Furthermore, "a mistaken idea prevails in regard to the great advantage of artificial irrigation over that of natural rains," since "when water is most needed, the supply is the scantiest."[27]

Bartlett's reservations were hardly limited to the agricultural advantages of the region. Like any good Whig, he was concerned with the suitability of the region to American trade, and what he found, especially in Chihuahua and Sonora, made him wary. American traders had long had an influence on the economic, social, and political development of Mexico's northeast. Anglo-American colonies in Mexico emerged as commercial outposts of Louisiana in the early decades of the nineteenth century, and trade was crucial to the definition of space in northeastern Mexico. In many cases, trade routes helped align *fronterizos* with the United States, from which goods flowed more or less freely, and away from Mexico City, which strongly inhibited trade in the north through the *alcabala*, a substantial tax on all transported goods. Furthermore, merchants in Mexico City and Veracruz controlled much of Mexico's trade, even after the gulf port of Matamoros opened up to (highly taxed) international trade in 1826. As historian Andrés Reséndez has documented, Mexicans on the northern frontier were affected by the American market revolution in the decades before the war. A spirit of mercantile enterprise spread among residents of the region such that *fronterizos* became enthusiastic consumers of both American medicines and alcohol. Commercial relations with the United States tested national loyalties among *fronterizos* as Mexico struggled to prevent dependency on valuable U.S. trade and desirable consumer goods.[28]

The Santa Fe trade was, of course, world renowned and profitable in the 1840s. Emory himself noted in his 1846 reconnaissance of the Gila River that the Santa Fe trade alone merited the annexation of New Mexico to the United States. American consumer goods had made deep inroads into northeastern Mexico by the late 1840s. Advertisements in a Matamoros newspaper during the U.S.-Mexico War offered a wide array of dry goods, including clothing, shoes, and hats, as well as groceries, patent medicines, and hardware, for sale in both Spanish and English, and the ability to purchase such goods was central to the self-perception of the emerging Mexican middle class in the region.[29]

Most trade in the region was contraband, however, especially after the start of the U.S.-Mexico War effectively made the Rio Grande the boundary between the two countries. Before the war, two-thirds of all imported goods in northern Mexico passed through Matamoros, but that port quickly declined as a commercial center when smugglers realized they could easily move goods across the river away from the tax collectors of the city. New towns sprang up along the Rio Grande to handle the illicit trade, and newspapers from the period featured ads from traders willing to "receive and forward freight at almost any point on the Rio Grande," letters in support of smuggling, and articles bemoaning the commercial decline of Matamoros. A typically enthusiastic newspaper account of the founding of one new town, Rio Grande City, on the American side of the border, focused almost entirely on its "highly advantageous" commercial position opposite a populous Mexican valley. "The river is navigable to the place during the whole year, and we understand large quantities of goods are now being sent there for sale. They are not subject to duties under the Mexican tariff, when shipped to this point from an American port." In fact, those goods *would* be subject to duties once they crossed the river into Mexico, unless, of course, they were smuggled.[30]

The spread of American consumer goods in some portions of the border region in the late 1840s is suggested by a telling anecdote. The Boston *Herald* reported that the commissioners, finding no suitable vessel, used "a thick, square sided, greenish looking bottle, labeled and stamped, 'Dr. Townsend's Sarsaparilla, Albany, New York,'" to mark the initial boundary point on the Pacific Coast. They placed documentation of the fact in the soda container, "said bottle being fitted with an iron stopper for the occasion. Little did S. P. Townsend dream of the undying honor that was about to be conferred on his name and that of his drug."[31]

Nonetheless, Bartlett was repeatedly thwarted by the difficulties of obtaining goods in northern Mexico, and he was shocked by the stunted nature of commerce in the region. Early on, newspaper correspondents from the commission openly bemoaned the lack of trade in El Paso del Norte (Ciudad Juárez) and their complaints continued throughout the journey. The further west they traveled, the worse things became. The explosion of illicit trade was largely limited to Mexico's northeast, where the Rio Grande marked the southern edges of Texas. The lack of rivers and roads further west limited the licit and illicit spread of commercial goods. To make matters worse, a blockade of Sonora's primary port on the Gulf of California, Guaymas, during the U.S.-Mexico War effectively paralyzed trade in the region for a year and a half, and the Gold Rush, starting in 1849, drained both population and resources from the area in exchange for a serious cholera epidemic that further devastated Guaymas. There was little sarsaparilla, or any other goods, available to residents of this area.

Bartlett (writing as "G.T.") expressed amazement at the primitive state of trade in Fronteras, Sonora, in a letter to the Providence *Journal*. "It is difficult to make" the people of the region "believe that we are not a party of traders, and every hour in the day we have calls to sell needles, thread, and a hundred little articles." Arispe, the former capital of Sonora, was no better. "We find the same scarcity of provisions here as at the other towns we have stopped at. . . . The few stores in the place are miserably furnished. . . . We were fairly beset by persons who came to buy, and who could not be persuaded that we did not come to trade." Bartlett concluded while in Guaymas that "a regular supply of any article cannot be depended upon in this country—a constant occupation is not consistent with the nature of the people."[32] Scarcity and idleness, in Bartlett's view, characterized the region.

Some might see these conditions as ripe for exploitation by the canny American trader, a view taken by one letter writer from the commission. "T." wrote to the Providence *Journal* that after watching the painstaking work of corn shelling in the region, he imagined how Mexican men "would stare to see a 'Patent Yankee Corn Sheller' which would send the corn and cobs out in separate directions as fast as they could supply them." Indeed, if the Chihuahua and Sonora borderlands were closer to Matamoros or other gulf ports where Americans and Europeans traded, the Yankee corn sheller might already have been for sale. But Mexico's primitive transportation networks, identified by one historian as second only to its protectionist economic policies as the key factor in its nineteenth-century underdevelopment, limited foreign trade in the Chihuahua-Sonora borderlands even under the best of circumstances.[33]

Bartlett was not sure that the commercial Americanization of the border was desirable or even possible, both because Americans seemed to have a negative influence on the morals and habits of the Mexicans with whom they came in contact, and also because of the apparent lawlessness of society in northern Mexico. *Fronterizos*, who viewed Mexico City with suspicion, were accustomed to their independence from governance. In a region far from the control of either the United States or Mexico, borderlands residents "rather than states," as historian Juan Mora-Torres explains, "shaped social relations." Faced with what was essentially a "feudal frontier," in Howard Lamar's memorable characterization, Bartlett's confidence wavered, a situation that was not improved by the fact that several former employees of the boundary commission were tried and convicted for murder in New Mexico during the course of the survey.[34]

Adobe home with beehive oven, El Paso, ca. 1910. Photograph by Otis A. Aultman, courtesy Aultman Photo Collection, AQ411, El Paso Public Library.

Murderous employees would have concerned any commissioner, but Bartlett, like other Whigs, linked social disorder with the absence of strong social institutions, and he turned to those institutions for a solution.[35] Based on the amount of attention that Bartlett's narrative and letters devote to houses, their construction, and their furnishing, the foremost civilizing institution missing from the border, in his opinion, was the well-ordered family home. From independence forward, the Mexican middle class (the self-proclaimed *gente decente*), like Bartlett, upheld the family home as the antidote to political turmoil and social instability. But the *gente decente* embraced neither refinement nor consumption at mid-century in the same manner that middle-class northeastern U.S. residents did: indeed, the rejection of luxury was a hallmark of idealized womanhood among this class in Mexico. Even if refined household furnishings had been available in the borderlands, there might not have been a market for them among the *gente decente*. Bartlett, time and again, found the homes of even the wealthy border residents lacking. These were not the "comfortable" homes he and other refined Americans venerated back in the United States. These were not the sorts of homes that could civilize the region.[36]

The average family home in the United States changed dramatically over the first half of the nineteenth century, not only in its furnishings, but also in exterior style, internal division of space, and construction technique. The adobe homes of the borderlands, by contrast, were essentially the same in 1860 as they had been one or even two hundred years earlier: boxes composed of sun-dried bricks of mud and straw, coated in two layers of adobe plaster, and topped with a dirt roof supported by stripped tree trunks and split cedar, sticks, or saplings. From their earliest forays into the region, and particularly after the opening of the Santa Fe Trail in 1821, travelers from the United States commented unfavorably on these structures. In 1806 the explorer Zebulon Pike compared the adobe homes of Santa Fe, New Mexico, to "flat-bottomed boats."[37]

In Bartlett's perception, however, the overriding problem with the adobe homes on the border was not that they were made out of mud, but that they lacked proper furnishings and domestic goods. Bartlett remarked in his narrative upon the absence of wood floors and glass windows in the region, as well as further problems.[38] A "member of the Mexican Boundary Commission" (possibly Bartlett himself), writing to the Providence *Journal* about El Paso, openly dismissed the town, in large part because of the interior furnishings of its houses. The correspondent expressed wonder that there was not "in the place a single wood floor," while in the best homes they cover the dirt floors with "old canvass, or a very common kind of domestic carpeting, always the same color, that is a dirty white, with black stripes." Even the wealthiest man in El Paso, whose carpet was "inferior to the poorest homespun carpeting" in the northeastern United States, furnished his rooms with only "pine benches" and "rude wooden chairs," and decorated them with "a small looking glass a foot square, and a few gaudy prints." In another house, "there was no furniture but three chairs," so the family sat on "buffalo skins around the fire; the half clad children nesting themselves in the warm folds of the skin." Overall, the correspondent concluded, "the people of El Paso are the most primitive I ever saw." Compared to the increasingly elaborate furnishings and decorations that Anglo-American pattern books upheld as ideal in the 1850s, these homes appeared woefully inadequate.[39] What chance did domesticity have to flourish in such a setting? The reviewer of Bartlett's *Personal Narrative* for the Providence *Journal* didn't see much of a chance at all. Bartlett's description of El Paso, and "the scarcity of most of the necessaries and all of the comforts of life" convinced the reviewer to stay home.[40]

Domestic space remained on Bartlett's mind. When writing to his wife, who remained in Rhode Island, Bartlett focused on the domestic sphere, both back home and on the border. Drawing on the language of domestic

Interior in a simple Gothic style. Engraving in Andrew Jackson Downing, *The Architecture of Country Houses*, 1850.

refinement common to pattern books, women's novels, and domestic guides, he wrote early on in his travels how he wished "to be in good comfortable houses, with good fires, instead of canvas tents." After a lengthy discussion of the construction technique of adobe houses, he expressed anxiety to his wife about getting his "room fitted up" in Secorro, Texas, and pleasure at the prospect of spending a week in "the most beautiful" house in the region, which was also "very handsomely fitted up." H.C.C., a correspondent to the Providence *Journal*, was happy to report not long after that Commissioner Bartlett had moved his quarters into a house with "large glass windows" and mortared walls, but "no plank floors, because that would cost nearly as much as a whole building."[41]

Bartlett was not entirely critical of the domestic arrangements on the frontier. Writing as G.T. to the Providence *Journal*, he noted that "some of the private dwellings" in Hermosillo "are well built, and of pleasant exterior; the court yards filled with flowering shrubs, and the interior well, often handsomely furnished." For the most part, however, Bartlett reserved his admiration for the German settlers of Texas, who closely conformed to the standards of middle-class American domesticity. They won his praise for "articles of taste" that adorned their "rude" houses, including "a choice library of scientific books" and a "fine harpsichord." Here, at last, were some settlers who "impart to the pioneer population by which they are surrounded that love for refined enjoyments in which it is deficient." The New York *Herald* printed a letter "from our Texas Correspondent" that also praised the Germans of Texas, "by far the best in Texas as regards industry, wealth, and morality." Their homes, wrote the correspondent, were "abodes of men of the highest intelligence and refinement." Mr. Berne, on the Guadalupe River, owned a "large and very choice library" in five languages, while Mr. Rapp was "a regular Professor of Geology." A correspondent to the Providence *Journal* from the commission generally bemoaned the lack of "civilization" in Texas but praised the Germans, who alone among residents of the region seemed to appreciate comfort and culture. One man, living in a log cabin whose external appearance would not lead one to "expect to find the ordinary comforts of life," had inside it "an extensive library" of standard works of literature and scientific books, as well as "several fine copies of Murillo and other masters." This correspondent also complimented the owner of the harpsichord.[42]

In each of these accounts, it is commercial goods—from furniture, to books, to musical instruments, to artworks—that are highlighted as key to a cultured and admirable domestic sphere. The Germans were praiseworthy precisely because they conformed to the emerging norms of domestic ideology, not only by consuming goods in the service of domestic bliss, but also through their restrained and refined masculine practices. Frederick Law Olmsted, another northeastern Whig traveler through the borderlands in the 1850s, was similarly impressed by the domestic arrangements of the German settlers of Texas, while caustically critical of the homes of American slave owners. Like Bartlett, whose work he repeatedly referenced, Olmsted equated the interior furnishings of homes in the region with the morality of their occupants.[43]

Bartlett's views of manhood and consumption extended as well to Native Americans. While noting the "savage beauty" and "fine manly forms" of several individuals, Bartlett saved his greatest praise for "a remarkably fine-looking young man, of athletic form, which he took pride in displaying. He wore no garment but a breech-cloth and a necklace of bone. . . . At first he strutted around the camp, with the evident design of making a sensation, and to convince us that he felt it a condescension to associate with us," but ultimately he revealed his discernment, and his sentimental nature, by attempting to buy a cameo portrait of a beautiful woman from one of the soldiers. Both the Indian's attempted act of consumption, and the implied veneration for beauty, validated him in Bartlett's eyes. Emory, on the other hand, not only found Bartlett's views of Native Americans overly romantic, but testified that "the wild Indians must be exterminated."[44]

While Emory devoted a great deal of attention to military matters and the placement of military fortifications in his three-volume report on the boundary commission, he paid virtually no attention to domestic settings. The sole mention of a family home included in the report is a general reference to the living arrangements of the Maricopa tribe, which Emory himself did not author. His single reference to the interior of a house is in the context of religious commentary. "In almost every house" in the town of Presidio del Norte "is found, in addition to the cross, a figure of our Saviour, which is sometimes so very grotesque that piety itself cannot divest it of its ridiculous appearance." If Emory had an opinion about the furnishings of homes in the region, he did not choose to share it with his readers. Most likely, his disinterest in domestic settings reflected his dismissal of the significance of domesticity on the frontier and to politics.[45]

Emory shared none of Bartlett's misgivings about the unfolding of Manifest Destiny on the frontier. While Bartlett was less than sanguine about the possibility of the Americanization of the border region, especially given the lack of orderly family homes and limited trade that made the settlement of such homes difficult, Emory viewed the current disorder of the borderlands as something to be overcome through the proper use of the American military, followed by the introduction of the transcontinental railroad that he lobbied hard to obtain territory for, and finally the gradual settlement of preferably slave-owning frontier families. Emory willingly admitted that "miserably built mud town(s)" marred the border, but this hardly dampened his enthusiasm. Whatever the current limitations of the region, Emory insisted that it was "undeniable" that the Gadsden Treaty had "secured to us what before did not exist . . . the most feasible if not the only practicable route for a railway to the Pacific." Emory was so enthusiastic about further expansion in the region, in fact, that although he claimed to hate "filibusterism," the unsanctioned attacks by American adventurers looking to gain new territory for the United States that were common in the 1850s, while working on the survey in 1855 he secretly conspired with residents of Chihuahua who hoped to see their state annexed to the United States.[46]

Bartlett openly questioned the value of the Chihuahua-Sonora borderlands to the United States, since they seemed unsuitable for farming and peripheral

Interior of de la Peña house, Santa Fe, New Mexico, 1912. Photograph by Jesse Nussbaum, courtesy Palace of the Governors, Santa Fe, New Mexico, ID: MNM/DCA, negative no. 015335.

to the flow of goods that would enable the settlement of well-furnished family homes. As a subscriber to domestic ideology that linked refined homes with civilization, he was more than willing to compromise with Mexico on the location of the boundary; other Whigs, sharing his views of the link between consumer goods and civilization, supported his position. Believing that compromise was a virtue rather than a sign of weakness, Bartlett emphasized his diplomacy and cooperation with the Mexican commissioner and officers both in his report to Congress, and in his narrative of the boundary commission. The Democratic expansionists who controlled Congress were more concerned with land for a railroad than the use of that land to families, and they were uncomfortable with both the ideology of domesticity and the spread of a consumer-oriented market. It is not surprising that Emory, along with congressional Democrats, should so loudly protest Bartlett's compromise.[47]

Although Bartlett was dismissed from the boundary commission, and the Democratic Congress refused to publish his *Personal Narrative* at government expense, his opinions, spread and reinforced by journalists, politicians, and his own publications, in the short term influenced debates over further expansion into Mexico. In the long term, Bartlett's views contributed to American perceptions of the borderlands and Mexico itself as uninhabitable and undomesticated. His two-volume *Personal Narrative* met with generally positive reviews upon publication in 1854 and sold well, becoming "for many years the standard guide for travelers coming to or passing through the area."[48] Gadsden Purchase opponents drew on images of the Mesilla Valley remarkably similar to those found in Bartlett's letters to the Providence *Journal*. A letter writer to the Washington, D.C. *National Intelligencer* opposed the plan because "nearly all of it [the region] is a barren waste, uncultivable and uninhabitable." The New York *Herald* similarly dismissed the region, concluding with the question whether "any body can tell us what we are to make of this new territory except a common place of refuge for the final extinction of our Indian tribes by starvation"?[49]

Bartlett's views of the value of the Chihuahua-Sonora borderlands also appear to have impacted congressional debate over the bill. Democratic representative Thomas Hart Benton, of Missouri, who opposed a southern railroad line in favor of one through his own state, cited Bartlett in his speech against the Gadsden Purchase, arguing that "as land," the Mesilla Valley was "worth nothing" and was "uninhabitable by man." Other Democratic representatives agreed with their Whig opponents that the land in question was "not of much importance on account of its intrinsic value"; its potential as a secure southern railroad route was its attraction for them.[50]

Many literary reviews of Bartlett's *Narrative*, like the one in the Providence *Journal* that read Bartlett's publication as a cautionary tale against frontier life, affirmed Bartlett's antiexpansionist stance. Venturing past general praise to note Bartlett's particular views of gender, domesticity, and consumption, these reviews questioned the rationale for expansion into the region. In 1855 the Cincinnati publication *Ladies' Repository* offered readers a two-page review of Bartlett's *Personal Narrative*, which focused almost exclusively on the domestic aspects of Bartlett's narrative. Specifically, it explored the marriage rites and homes of the Maricopa Indians, the issue of female abduction in the area, and the appearance of both men and women in the Native American tribes the boundary commission encountered.[51] The review echoed Bartlett's overall assessment that much of the region was made up of "rocky wilds and barren plains, in which man can not live"—meaning, of course, white men, and more importantly, white women. At the same time, however, the review asserted that "brave" men were already living there. This was not virgin land, but a landscape in which proper families of Indian extraction lived in "solid" homes in an already domesticated landscape.[52] Another reviewer who was impressed with the cultured existence of Texas Germans, despite the primitive nature of their homes and furnishing, concluded nevertheless that much of the border region was "a barren, desolate waste" that could "never be rendered useful for man or beast, except as a public highway."[53] These reviews, and others like them, furthered the impression that there was little potential or room for American settlement in the region.[54]

Bartlett's narrative, so bound up with consumption, was itself offered up in the Episcopalian church's official organ, *The Churchman*, as something to be consumed by anti-expansionist northeasterners at leisure. It recommended his volumes "as an excellent summer companion to the tourists who, while enjoying the easy luxuries of Saratoga, West Point, or Newport, would enhance their satisfaction by the survey of distant portions of their widely-extended country, traveled over under less agreeable circumstances." Another journal, the New York *Albion*, suggested that the volumes, which deserved "a place in every well-appointed American library," were objects that could themselves contribute to the refinement of a family home.[55]

The U.S.-Mexico War had a dramatic impact on the rise of consumer culture in the borderlands. Merchants on both sides of the new borderline grew wealthy from smuggling, and new towns sprang up along the Rio Grande in order to facilitate the burgeoning illegal trade, while the once-thriving port cities of Matamoros and Guaymas stagnated. As both Bartlett and Emory's accounts reveal, *fronterizos*, particularly to the west of Texas, were desperate for consumer goods of all sorts. With a clear eye to the significance of this issue, U.S. Secretary of State William Marcy instructed James Gadsden to include the statement that the United States was anxious to establish "intimate commercial relations on liberal terms" in his boundary negotiations with Mexico in 1853. That same year Mexico established a duty-free border zone in Tamaulipas in order to counter smuggling from Texas to Mexico, eventually extending that zone to Coahuila, Chihuahua, and Nuevo León, despite protests of American officials.[56] The state of borderlands consumer culture was still uncomfortably, indeed unacceptably primitive in the eyes of some Americans, who placed a moral value on ownership of objects, particularly in the context of the family home.

Competing visions of the relationship between consumption and settlement, as well as partisanship and the desire among southern Democrats for a workable southern railroad route, shaped congressional debates over the Bartlett-

Conde agreement. The Democrat Emory rationalized expansion into Chihuahua and Sonora in part because he saw no need for market penetration of the region prior to its settlement. For John Bartlett, as for many sympathetic Whigs, the U.S.-Mexico borderlands were less than fully desirable because they could not easily be integrated into the market. The region did not lend itself to the distribution of consumer goods: the comfortably furnished households that he associated with a well-ordered society were few and far between, and the likelihood that families would be able to replicate the conditions of American domesticity was remote. These issues did not concern Emory, who argued that military outposts could maintain and Americanize the region. Democratic expansionists saw the region as existing beyond the mandates of production or consumption, a place through which a railroad could run connecting Southern markets with the Pacific coast. In response to expansionist plans that did not take into account the region's inhabitants, other Whig voices besides Bartlett's, like those of the *Ladies' Repository*, asserted that the current inhabitants of the region were deserving of their land because they already conformed to standards of consumption that marked them as civilized, while their consumption of American goods and adoption of a consumption-based ideology of domesticity would gradually Americanize them. Although a sarsaparilla bottle marked the initial point in the U.S.-Mexico boundary, these debates about the relationship between expansion, settlement, and consumption would continue to inform U.S. policies and attitudes toward the border region and Mexico long after Bartlett's and Emory's work was done.

Abbreviations

AF	*American Flag* (Matamoras)
Bancroft-Brown	Henry Box Brown Papers, Bancroft Library, University of California at Berkeley
Bartlett *Narrative*	John Russell Bartlett, *Personal Narrative of Explorations and Incidents in Texas, New Mexico, California, Sonora, and Chihuahua*, 2 volumes (New York: D. Appleton and Co., 1854)
BP 11	Bartlett Papers, Brown University Library, microfilm reel 11
Emory *Report*	William H. Emory, *Report on the United States and Mexican Boundary Survey, made under the Direction of the Secretary of the Interior*, 31st cong., 1st session, ex. doc. no. 135 (Washington, D.C.: Cornelius Wendel, printer, 1859).
G.T.	Pseudonym under which John Russell Bartlett published dispatches from the boundary commission's travels

Huntington-Bartlett   John R. Bartlett Papers, Huntington Library, San Marino, Calif.

NY-H   New York *Herald*

PJ   Providence *Journal*, Bartlett Papers, Brown University Library, microfilm reel 11

Notes

For their invaluable assistance on this essay I am indebted to the participants of the Clements Center symposium on borderlands consumer culture (particularly the indomitable Alexis McCrossen), the lively audience at "Ten Views: Consumer Cultures Meet the U.S.-Mexico Borderlands," and the readers for Duke University Press.

Notes fully cite primary sources and specialized secondary sources. Full bibliographic details for all other citations are in the volume's selected bibliography.

1. Book review, "Personal Narrative of Explorations and Incidents," PJ, June 6, 1854; Letter from G.T., "Mexican Boundary Commission. Fronteras, State of Sonora, Mexico, May 25th, 1851," PJ, n.d.

2. Treaty of Peace, Friendship, Limits, and Settlement, signed at Guadalupe Hidalgo February 2, 1848, reprinted in Bevans, ed., *United States Treaties*, 9:791–806; Rebert, *Gran Línea*, 23–26.

3. Bartlett was actually the fourth man appointed to the job. James Polk appointed A. H. Sevier, who died before the Senate could confirm him. John B. Weller was appointed less than a month before Polk's term ended, and the Whigs replaced him after about five months on politically motivated grounds. John C. Frémont accepted the job only until something better—the chance for a seat in the Senate—came along.

4. On Bartlett's interest in the tribes of the Southwest, see Bartlett to Henry Box Brown, May 8, 1852; Bartlett to Brown, May 20, 1852; Brown to Bartlett, May 2, 1852, all in Bancroft-Brown. Bartlett referred to the region as "terra incognita" in an 1851 letter to Issac G. Strain, February 3, 1851, Huntington-Bartlett.

5. Emory *Report*, 1:xxvi. Although Robert Blair Campbell was the official commissioner as of May 1853, because, according to William Goetzmann, Emory "for all practical purposes directed the entire survey," I will refer to Emory in this essay as Bartlett's replacement (*Army Exploration*, 194, 129). See also, Emory, "Running the Line," 235–36. On Emory and the Mexican commission, see Sepúlveda, *La frontera norte*, 74–75; Martinez, "Surveying and Marking," 18.

6. David Norris, James Milligan, and Odie Faulk, *William H. Emory: Soldier-Scientist* (Tucson: University of Arizona Press, 1998), 134.

7. Werne, "Pedro García Conde," 113–29; Martinez, *U.S.-Mexico Borderlands*, 18; José Salazar Ylarregui, *Datos de los trabajos astronómicos y topográficos despuestos en forma de diarío* (Mexico: Impr. de J. R. Navarro, 1850), 8–12; Goetzmann, *Army Exploration*, 162–63.

8. As William Goetzmann has put it, "The Whigs were thus easily labeled the party of

the great land give-away and an obstacle in the path of Manifest Destiny" (*Army Exploration*, 188–93). See also Werne, "Partisan Politics," 329–46; Haskell, "John Russell Bartlett," 138–40; Faulk, *Too Far North*, 39, 58, 74; Emory, "Running the Line," 221–65.

9. See, for instance, speech of V. E. Howard, July 6, 1852, *Congressional Globe*, 32nd Cong., 1st sess,. Appendix, 25, 776; speech of John Weller, ibid., 801.

10. Goetzmann, *Army Exploration*, 188–93; Escoto Ochoa, *Integración y desintegración*, 126; Faulk, *Too Far North*, 63. A few historians still maintain that Bartlett was duped. See, for instance, Norris, Milligan, and Faulk, *William H. Emory*, *op. cit.*, 111, 127.

11. For differing interpretations of the reasons for the failure of the Bartlett-Conde agreement, see Werne, "Partisan Politics," 329–46; Ochoa, *Integración y desintegración*, 120–49; Zorrilla, *Historia de las relaciones*, 1:336–42; Sepúlveda, *La frontera norte*, 71–77; Goetzmann, "United States–Mexican Boundary Survey," 164–90.

12. "Gen. Gadsden's Treaty—Curious and Interesting Disclosures," NY-H, January 28, 1854; John G. Parke, *Report of Explorations for that Portion of a Railway Route, Near the 32d Parallel of Latitude, Lying Between Dona Ana, on the Rio Grande, and Pimas Villages, on the Gila* (Washington, D.C.: Corps of Topographical Engineers, 1855); Edward Wallace, *The Great Reconnaissance: Soldiers, Artists, and Scientists on the Frontier, 1848–1861* (Boston: Little, Brown, 1955), 90; Goetzmann, *Army Exploration*, 177; *Treaty of Boundaries*, signed on December 30, 1853, in Bevans, *United States Treaties*, 9:812–16; Emory, "Running the Line," 250. The search for a workable route was a major concern of the survey. In 1851, in fact, "the American parties spent so much time looking for routes for a railroad and a wagon road that the Mexican Government protested to the Government of the United States against the delays and consequent expense caused thereby" (Robert Russel, *Improvement of Communication with the Pacific Coast as an Issue in American Politics, 1783–1864* [Cedar Rapids, Iowa: Torch Press, 1948], 134). Even today Amtrak dips into Mexico for topographical reasons on its southern route.

13. Lawrence Kohl, *The Politics of Individualism: Parties and the American Character in the Jacksonian Era* (New York: Oxford University Press, 1989); Michael Holt, *The Rise and Fall of the American Whig Party: Jacksonian Politics and the Onset of the Civil War* (New York: Oxford University Press, 1999), 951–52.

14. On women and the Whig party, see Elizabeth Varon, *We Mean to be Counted: White Women and Politics in Antebellum Virginia* (Chapel Hill: University of North Carolina Press, 1998), 3, 5; Ronald Zboray and Mary Saracino Zboray, "Gender Slurs in Boston's Partisan Press during the 1840s," *Journal of American Studies* 34 (2000): 413–46; Daniel Walker Howe, "The Evangelical Movement and Political Culture in the North during the Second Party System," *Journal of American History* 77 (1991): 1216–39. On domesticity, see Katherine Kish Sklar, *Catharine Beecher: A Study in American Domesticity* (New Haven: Yale University Press, 1973); Mary Ryan, *Cradle of the Middle Class: The Family in Oneida County, New York, 1790–1865* (New York: Cambridge University Press, 1981); Nancy Cott, *Bonds of Womanhood: "Woman's Sphere" in New England, 1780–1835* (New Haven: Yale University Press, 1997).

15. Anne McClintock, *Imperial Leather: Race, Gender, and Sexuality in the Colonial Context* (New York: Routledge, 1995), 17; Hansen, ed., *African Encounters*; George, "Homes in the Empire," 95–127.

16. Catharine Beecher, *A Treatise on Domestic Economy for the Use of Young Ladies at Home and at School* (Boston: T. H. Webb and Co., 1841), 12. See also Catharine Beecher and Harriet Beecher Stowe, *The American Woman's Home* (1869; Watkins Glen, N.Y.: American Life Foundation, 1979), 458–59; Lynnea Magnuson, "In the Service of Columbia: Gendered Politics and Manifest Destiny Expansion" (Ph.D. diss., University of Illinois at Urbana-Champaign, 2000), 129; Kaplan, *Anarchy of Empire*, 23–50. On Beecher's role in formulating and promoting domesticity, see Sklar, *Catharine Beecher, op. cit.*

17. Beecher, *Treatise on Domestic Economy, op. cit.*, 172; Sklar, *Catharine Beecher, op. cit.*, 306–7. Not surprisingly, support for domesticity was strongest where market penetration was most pronounced and goods were being produced that needed to be purchased. This was one reason why domesticity was stronger in the somewhat more economically-developed Northeast than in the largely rural South.

18. Andrew Jackson Downing, *Cottage Residences: Rural Architecture and Landscape Gardening* (New York: Wiley and Putnam, 1842); Calvert Vaux, *Villas and Cottages: A Series of Designs Prepared for Execution in the United States,* 2nd ed. (New York: Harper and Brothers, 1864), 37–38.

19. Bushman, *Refinement of America*, 238–79, quote on p. 275.

20. Merish, *Sentimental Materialism*, 21, 88–134, quotes on pp. 15, 91; Richards, *Commodity Culture*, 104.

21. Weber, "Turner, the Boltonians, and the Borderlands," 66–81; Francaviglia, "Geographic and Cartographic Legacy," 1–18; Mayo, "Consuls and Silver Contraband," 389–411, quote on p. 390. The emerging Mexican middle class attempted to ameliorate the disorderly aspects of social life in *el norte* through legislation and social pressure, with limited success. French, *Peaceful and Working People*, 87–97; Staples, *"Policía y Buen Gobierno,"* 115–26.

22. Mora-Torres, *Making of the Mexican Border*, quote on p. 23; Basante, "Los especuladores y el debate parlamentario norteamericano," 293–378; Vázquez and Meyer, *United States and Mexico*, 48; *El Universal* (Mexico City), May 15, 1853.

23. Bartlett *Narrative*, 1:40; Ross Calvin, ed., *Lieutenant Emory Reports: A Reprint of W. H. Emory's Notes of a Military Reconnaissance* (1848; Albuquerque: University of New Mexico Press, 1951), 139. See also Emory *Report*, 1:39, 53.

24. Sweeny, "Drawing Borders," 33; Emory, "Running the Line," 242–46. On hostile Indian tribes, see DeLay, *War of a Thousand Deserts*.

25. J. Fred Rippy, *The United States and Mexico* (New York: F. S. Crofts and Co., 1931), 80–81.

26. G.T., "Mexican Boundary Commission, Fronteras, State of Sonora, Mexico, May 25th, 1851," PJ, n.d. This passage appears with almost exactly the same wording in Bartlett *Narrative*, 1:247.

27. Emory *Report*, 1:49; Bartlett *Narrative*, 1:187–88. Bartlett was not the only American appointed in the region at the time who questioned its desirability. Colonel Edwin V. Sumner, the military commander of New Mexico, was also unenthusiastic about the region. In 1852 he wrote to the U.S. secretary of war that the entire Southwest was a "heavy burden" for the United States to carry. Sumner to secretary of war, Santa Fe, May 27, 1852, *Senate Executive Document* 1, 32nd Cong., 2nd Sess., 1852, 23.

28. Reséndez, *Changing National Identities*, 38–40, 105, 117; Mora-Torres, *Making of the Mexican Border*, 21, 29.

29. Emory, "Notes on a military reconnaissance from Fort Leavenworth in Missouri to San Diego in California, Including Parts of the Arkansas, Del Norte, and Gila Rivers," *Senate Executive Document* 7, 30th Congress, 1st sess., 1848, 11, 386; Norris, Milligan, and Faulk, *William H. Emory, op. cit.*, 34–36; Mora-Torres, *Making of the Mexican Border*, 31; AF, April 23, 1847–November 20, 1847.

30. On freight anywhere on river, see AF, October 16, October 2, May 5, 1847. In support of smuggling, see AF, October 2, 1847. On the decline of Matamoros, see AF, October 23, 1847. On the establishment of "Rio Grande City," see AF, August 11, 1847. The Veracruz *Free American* reported on January 11, 1848, that both Mexicans and Americans were flocking to the U.S. side of the Rio Grande in expectation of the boundary settlement.

31. "From our New Mexican Correspondent—The U.S. Boundary Commission, &c, &c," correspondence of the *Boston Herald*, Dona Ana (New Mexico), April 28, 1851, in BP 11.

32. Voss, *Periphery of Nineteenth-Century Mexico*, 110–12; "Mexican Boundary Commission. Camp M'Duffie, October 27, 1850," PJ, n.d.; Letter from T, "Mexican Boundary Commission. El Paso, Texas, March 14, 1851," PJ, n.d.; G.T., "Mexican Boundary Commission. Fronteras, State of Sonora, Mexico, May 26, 1851," PJ, n.d.; G.T., "Mexican Boundary Commission. Arispe, Sonora, Mexico, June 1, 1851," PJ, n.d.; G.T., "Mexican Boundary Commission. Guaymas, Sonora, Mexico, November, 1851," PJ, n.d.

33. Letter from T, "Mexican Boundary Commission. El Paso, Texas, March 14, 1851," PJ, n.d.; Coatsworth, "Obstacles to Economic Growth."

34. Mora-Torres, *Making of the Mexican Border*, 11; Lamar, *Far Southwest*, 92. *Fronterizos*, already accustomed to fending for themselves in a contested territory far from Mexico City, developed their own culture, enforced their own laws, and increasingly viewed the central government as a force of unwanted domination. "After three decades of Mexican rule," the historian Juan Mora-Torres concludes, "the *vecinos* had concluded that the Mexican state was predatory, taxing and otherwise preying on their meager resources" (*Making of the Mexican Border*, 29). On what David Weber has called Mexico's "disaffected periphery" during the years between Mexican independence and the U.S.-Mexico War, see Weber, *Mexican Frontier*, quotation on p. 276; DeLay, *War of a Thousand Deserts*; Bartlett *Narrative*, 1:161.

35. Kohl, *Politics of Individualism, op. cit.*, 145–85.

36. On class and consumption in Chihuahua in a later period, see French, *Peaceful and Working People*, 87–97; Jean Franco, *Plotting Women: Gender and Representation in Mexico* (New York: Columbia University Press, 1999), 81. About California's adobe homes in

the Spanish period, see Mason, "Adobe Interiors." The architectural historian Agnesa Lufkin Reeve describes several adobe homes of northern New Mexico's very richest inhabitants in the 1840s as luxuriously furnished, but these homes were outside the range of the boundary survey (Reeve, *From Hacienda to Bungalow*, 8–18, 33–35). The fiction of mid-twentieth-century *tejana* author Jovita González suggests that Spanish-Mexican communities understood the importance of domesticity to Anglo-Americans and deliberately displayed "Spanish" houses as a way to claim "whiteness" in the years following the war. See Marci McMahon, "Politicizing Spanish-Mexican Domesticity, Redefining Fronteras: Jovita González's *Caballero* and Cleofas Jaramillo's *Romance of a Little Village Girl*," *Frontiers: A Journal of Women Studies* 28 (2007): 232–59.

37. Reeve, *From Hacienda to Bungalow*, 3–8; Pike quoted in Reeve, 5.

38. Bartlett *Narrative*, 1:190.

39. "Mexican Boundary Commission. El Paso, New Mexico, Nov. 19, 1850," PJ, n.d.

40. Book review, "Personal Narrative of Explorations and Incidents," *op. cit.*

41. Bartlett letter to "my dear wife," December 18, 1850, Secorro, Texas, BP 11; Letter from H.C.C., "Mexican Boundary Commission. El Paso, Dec. 29, 1850," PJ, n.d.

42. Letter from G.T., "Mexican Boundary Commission. Hermosillo, Sonora, Mexico, October 26, 1851," PJ, n.d.; Bartlett *Narrative*, 1:54–56; "From Our Texas Correspondent," November 19, 1850, NY-H, n.d., BP 11; "Mexican Boundary Commission. Camp M'Duffie, October 27, 1850," PJ, n.d.

43. Beecher and Stowe, *American Woman's Home, op. cit.*, 19, 23, 42; Clark Jr., *American Family Home*, 32–33; Frederick Law Olmsted, *Journey through Texas, or a Saddle-Trip on the Southwestern Frontier* (1857; Lincoln: University of Nebraska Press, 2004), 47–55, 143–45, 189, 311, 201. On restrained masculine practices and expansionism, see Greenberg, *Manifest Manhood*.

44. Bartlett *Narrative*, 1:79–80, 328, 445, and 2:264; "From Our Texas Correspondent," *op. cit.*; Emory *Report*, 1:64. The *New York Herald*'s correspondence "From Our Texas Correspondent" reported that the man was "a young" Lipan "warrior named Tealchjah" who was enchanted by the miniature portrait of a female friend of the author's.

45. Emory *Report*, 1:110–11, quote on p. 85. Emory does not once mention furniture, furnishings, or interior decoration of homes in his report.

46. Emory *Report*, 1:51, 85; Robert May, *Manifest Destiny's Underworld: Filibustering in Antebellum America* (Chapel Hill: University of North Carolina Press, 2002), 20.

47. One historian has concluded that Bartlett and Conde "set an example of understanding, teamwork and good humor that might well have been emulated in Washington and Mexico City." Robert Utley, *The International Boundary, United States and Mexico: A History of Frontier Dispute and Cooperation, 1848–1963* (Santa Fe: Department of the Interior, 1964), 6.

48. Odie B. Faulk, "A Letter from John R. Bartlett at Camp Yuma, 1852," *Journal of Arizona History* 6 (Winter 1965): 212–13.

49. Letter from C, *National Intelligencer*, n.d. in BP 11; "Gen. Gadsden's Treaty—Very Like a Plundering Operation upon the Treasury," February 7, 1854, NY-H.

50. *Congressional Globe*, 33rd Cong., 1st sess., 1536–49, Benton speech quotes, Appendix, 1034, 1035. See also speech of Rufus W. Peckham, ibid., 1030.

51. "An Excursion to the Copa-Maricopa Indians upon the River Gila," *Ladies' Repository* 15 (January 1855): 15–16. The Pee Posh, or Maricopa, were known as the Cocomaricopa by the Spanish. Although by 1800 they had formed a confederacy with the Pima, Bartlett seems to differentiate between the two in his narrative. I refer to them as the Maricopa for the sake of clarity. "Pee Posh," in Bary Pritzker, ed., *Native Americans: An Encyclopedia of History, Culture, and People* (Santa Barbara: ABC-CLIO, 1998), 76–78.

52. "An Excursion to the Copa-Maricopa Indians upon the River Gila," *op. cit.*, 15.

53. "Travels," *New York Quarterly Review* II (July 1854): 303–6, quotation on p. 306. For further examples of praise for the Germans' lifestyle as recounted by Bartlett, see also the review in *The Churchman*, n.d., in BP 11.

54. "C.C.S.," *The Christian Examiner and Religious Miscellany* 57 (September 1854): 244–67. This made the point that in the Sonoran village of Bacuachi, "a house surrounded by foliage with a grassy lawn, which makes a country house so attractive, even though it is but a humble cottage, is unknown here" (250).

55. *The Churchman*, n.d. in BP 11; *The Albion*, June 17, 1854, 13.

56. Rippy, *United States and Mexico, op. cit.* 130; Vázquez and Meyer, *United States and Mexico*, 76.

Rachel St. John

Selling the Border
Trading Land, Attracting Tourists, and Marketing
American Consumption on the Baja California Border,
1900–1934

In 1920, the Sunset Inn, a Tijuana casino, launched an advertising campaign in San Diego newspapers. "The Border's Open!" it announced, "everyday to everybody." An illustration of people and cars streaming across the line underscored the point.[1] Thanks to advertisements like this one and the opportunities they offered an eager U.S. market, in the 1920s these promotional visions became reality. Crowds of people and lines of cars regularly amassed on the boundary line as millions of American consumers headed south to partake in the border experience.

This marked a striking transformation of the Baja California border from an isolated and undeveloped region to a site of intense American consumption. For its first fifty years, this boundary line had seen little traffic. In 1900, fewer than four hundred people lived in Tijuana; Mexicali did not yet exist.[2] After the turn of the century, however, the border became a site of American consumption. By the 1920s, throngs of transborder travelers en route to Mexicali and Tijuana jammed the Calexico and San Ysidro ports of entry. Most of these crossers were Americans. Working-class thrill seekers, middle-class families, upper-class investors, and Hollywood stars all came to the border, willing to pay for goods, services, and experiences that they believed the border offered. Not only could they buy postcards, cheap land, and illicit liquor, but they could also consume the novelty of crossing the international boundary

Get Passports at Federal Building (Postoffice). No Passports Issued at Border!

TIJUANA

The drought's over.
"*EVERYTHING*"
as usual

Dining, Dancing
Refreshing, Fascinating
Diversions
And a bit of
quaint Old Mexico

BORDER'S OPEN *EVERY DAY to EVERYBODY*

Advertisement, *San Diego Union*, **September 14, 1920.**

Following the cessation of First World War passport restrictions, the proprietors of the Sunset Inn, a nightclub and gambling establishment in Tijuana, launched a major advertising campaign in San Diego newspapers. This advertisement, depicting a stream of people rushing toward the Inn, emphasized the ease with which American customers could secure passports and cross the border.

line, the excitement of experiencing an exotic foreign culture, and the freedom of drinking and gambling outside Prohibition-era America.

The characteristics that drew Americans to the border were the result of the synergetic, if unsynchronized, efforts by tourism promoters, vice purveyors, and real estate developers to market the advantages of the Baja California border. Linking shopping for curios, buying real estate, and partaking of prohibited vices, both American and Mexican boosters constructed a consumers' border that offered investment opportunities, exotic experiences, and illicit activities unavailable in the United States. As it had in the 1850s boundary commissions described by Amy Greenberg in the previous essay, consumption came to define American ideas and interest in the border in the first third of the twentieth century.

Promoters, however, offered only a narrow view of the border. The border, of course, was not just a place of American consumption, but also a political frontier, a site of binational economic exchange, and the home of a growing number of Mexican citizens. Yet the promoters' images came to dominate

Automobiles at the border of the United States and Mexico, San Ysidro, 1920. Photograph courtesy Photograph Collection, San Diego Historical Society.

This photograph taken of one of the border crossings between the United States and Mexico illustrates the extent of cross-border automobile traffic as early as 1920.

representations of the border, and Mexicans, on both the local and national level, had to struggle to assert their national identity and autonomy along the border. Historians have written extensively about the political, economic, social, and cultural ramifications of American investment, tourism, and vice, but they have only rarely explored how and why Americans were attracted to the border.[3] Through an analysis of border promotion, this essay begins to improve our understanding of American ideas about and interest in the border during the first four decades of the twentieth century.

While promotions mask the history of the urban spaces, economic connections, and political conflicts to which American consumption contributed, they open an illuminating window into how promoters' perceptions of Americans' needs and desires gave meaning to the boundary line. In advertisements, articles, and promotional correspondence, the international boundary line emerged as a place distinct from the larger U.S.-Mexico borderlands in which it was situated. While border promoters tapped into the borderlands aesthetic, which, as Lawrence Culver shows in his essay in this volume, was so prevalent in Southern California at this time, the selling of the border itself depended on the legal, political, economic, and symbolic significance of the boundary line. In marketing the Baja California border, promoters emphasized not the shared history of the United States and Mexico in the borderlands, but rather the stark divide between those two nations along the boundary line. From novelty landmark to exotic foreign country to inexpensive ranchland to playground of illicit pleasures, the border seemed to offer a full menu for Americans seeking adventure, opportunity, and vice.

Waiting in lines to cross the boundary line, Americans demonstrated how successfully promoters had transformed the border into a magnet of American consumption. The money they carried financed the construction of ranches, railroads, and public works that not only connected Baja California to American markets but also began to elevate the importance of the territory and improve its connections with the Mexican republic. At the same time, thanks to the successful selling of the border, Americans' perceptions that the border should serve their interests became pervasive. By the time American consumption of border services and goods reached its peak in the 1920s, the border had become a flashpoint of local and international conflict where disputes arose concerning which nation controlled the boundary line.

Acquiring and Consuming Land along the Baja California Border

The origins of American consumption along the Baja California border lay in land. Both Mexican government officials and private landowners were eager to attract American businessmen who had the capital to buy and develop border ranchlands. Once Americans had purchased land on the border, they in turn marketed their property to other American investors and renters. In their correspondence and contracts, land promoters created an image of the border as a space that offered the best of both nations. As they bought, sold, and developed border ranchlands over the following decades, these men reinforced the conception of the Baja California border as both of, and apart from, the United States and thus an ideal site for American investment.

The American market in land along the border developed around the turn of the century, as a Southern California real estate boom, the development of irrigation and transportation infrastructure, and the Mexican government's pursuit of foreign investment coincided. Under the rule of Porfirio Díaz (1876–1910), the Mexican government embraced foreign investment as the key to national development. In order to encourage investment, Mexican officials cultivated relationships with American capitalists and facilitated the acquisition and development of land, natural resources, and railroads.[4] Along the Baja California border, Díaz appointees granted American investors permits for landownership, concessions for railroads and irrigation works, and exemptions from customs duties.[5] Among the investors they helped to attract were a group of Southern California land speculators who saw the potential to extend their regional real estate empire south of the border. Organizing as Mexican land companies, these men bought vast tracts of land along the boundary line. The San Ysidro Ranch Company (SYRC) purchased approximately 35,000 acres near Tijuana, while *Los Angeles Times* chief Harrison Gray Otis's Colorado River Land Company (CRLC) secured control of more than 860,000 acres extending south from the boundary line through the Colorado River delta.[6]

For these Southern California investors, the land immediately adjacent to the boundary line was of particular interest because it combined the advantages of a foreign investment, including the Mexican government's incentives, with the convenience and security of a familiar regional market. The promotional correspondence exchanged between the new landowners and other prospective American investors emphasized the access and oversight made possible by their properties' proximity to Los Angeles and San Diego. The SYRC prospectus stressed that it was "a pleasant and easy motor ride . . . from Los Angeles to the property" and that a new rail line would soon increase the investors' access, as well as the value of their investment.[7] By the 1910s, two transborder rail lines—the Ferrocarril Tijuana y Tecate and the Inter-California Railroad—linked Baja California to rail networks and markets north of the line.[8]

Promoters stressed that land along the Baja California border was not only nearby, but virtually identical to land under development in San Diego and California's Imperial Valley. "This country," noted a CRLC report, "lies just south of the Imperial Valley of the United States, and is in fact a continuation of the same."[9] The informal sales literature exchanged between American businessmen interested in buying and leasing Baja California borderlands was replete with similar comparisons. "The land is as good as the best upland of Southern California," the original owner of the San Ysidro Ranch promised new investors.[10] The CRLC made such comparisons so often that its president worried that the people of the Imperial Valley would accuse them of "stealing their thunder."[11]

In addition to touting its similarity with U.S. properties in the region, promoters also highlighted the particular benefits of Mexican land—low prices and unspoiled terrain. Real estate south of the border sold for a fraction of the price of comparable property north of the line; along the Tijuana River, Mexican land went for one hundred and fifty dollars an acre, while similar lands on the American side cost four or five hundred dollars an acre.[12] The cost of these properties, a potential investor was told, were "what would be considered bargain prices when compared to prices demanded on this side of the line."[13] Real estate developers also stressed that Mexican lands were unspoiled, putting a positive spin on the lack of irrigation works or other improvements. Investors in the SYRC raved about the abundance of small game on their undeveloped land and formed a hunting club to take advantage of its resources.[14]

In addition to the economic advantages of investing in borderlands, real estate investors also emphasized the romantic allure of owning ranchland on the Mexican border. "[My wife and I] have some sentiment left about the property," wrote an early owner of the San Ysidro Ranch, recalling that it was there that his wife had "learned to shoot, hunt, camp, ride in a Mexican saddle."[15] Harrison Gray Otis referred to the CRLC's property by the evocative designation of the "Rancho of the Two Flags."[16] Writing in the 1930s, Henry Keller reminisced about one reason he and the other stockholders in the SYRC had been predisposed to buy land in Mexico: "Many of us had grown up with and counted among our intimate friends members of the fine old Spanish families of Southern California, and spoke their tongue."[17] Keller's reference to "the fine old Spanish families of Southern California" reflected the romanticization of California's Hispanic heritage that, as Lawrence Culver discusses in his essay, was so popular in California at this time.[18] By buying borderlands, Americans not only gained a potentially profitable investment but also bought into a romantic vision of Mexico and the border. The ideas about the border that American real estate investors marshaled in the marketing of their properties contributed to the characterization of the border as a space where the United States and Mexico came together, as if for the convenience of American investors. Drawn by these discussions, American investors bought, sold, and developed border ranches, tying the Baja California borderlands ever more tightly to the United States while integrating this real estate into a broader economy of borderlands consumption.

"All Aboard for This Trip to a Foreign Land!":
Cultural Tourism and the Selling of Exotic Mexico on the Border

While only a few wealthy investors engaged in the border real estate market, many more middle-class Americans consumed border goods and experiences as tourists.[19] Like land sales, tourism depended on promoters' abilities to convince American consumers that the border combined the convenience and security of the United States with the particular appeal of Mexico. Tourism promotions emphasized the exotic and romantic qualities of Mexican culture. A visit to the border, they promised, would provide the adventure of foreign travel without the inconvenience or expense of an overseas journey.

Tourism promoters constructed a version of Mexican culture that they hoped to sell to Americans on the blank slates of the small and recently established cities of Tijuana and Mexicali. These promoters, most of whom were recent arrivals on the border themselves, were a varied and cosmopolitan group. While American capitalists controlled most of the transportation and larger vice-related establishments, a small group of Mexicans and recent European immigrants established curio shops and staged cultural exhibitions. This ethnic and national division among entrepreneurs was not unique to the Baja California borderlands, as Laura Isabel Serna shows in her essay in this volume about moving-picture exhibition in the borderlands. Together promoters blanketed the Southern California market with advertisements that stressed the novelty and romance of crossing the boundary line. By the 1910s, thousands of American tourists from all parts of the United States visited Tijuana annually. For many, their trip across the border was their first to Mexico.[20]

Border tourism initially emerged as a component of an extended tour of Southern California. Tijuana, explained one article, "is a place of special interest to tourists visiting Southern California from the fact that it lies in Mexico, just over the line dividing the territory of the two republics."[21] Travel articles in U.S. newspapers cast a Tijuana excursion as an easy day trip. As one advertisement noted, Tijuana was "a foreign land 'within a stone throw.'" A wide offering of private cars, stages, auto services, busses, and railroads assured this accessibility: more than fifteen busses and five trains ran from San Diego to Tijuana each day of the summer of 1915.[22]

Once at the boundary line, border tourism began. Promoters sold the border crossing as a novel symbolic experience that tourists could consume.[23] "The unusual experience of leaving the United States behind and crossing the international boundary line into a foreign country," one article noted, "is one that provides keen pleasure to the visitor."[24] Advertisements in San Diego newspapers urged Americans to visit the border and "mail home a postal from the foreign land; have a photo taken astride the international boundary line!"[25] The boundary monument became a landmark where many tourists posed for photos.[26]

Once across the boundary line, tourists sought Mexican encounters, sights, experiences, and souvenirs to satisfy their expectations of foreign adventure.

However, aside from the boundary monuments and customs houses, the first border tourists would have seen little evidence that they had left U.S. territory. With its dusty roads and wooden buildings, Tijuana looked like any other town in the U.S. West in 1900. It was left to local border entrepreneurs to provide a variety of goods and services that fulfilled one postcard's promise that "the little Mexican village of Tijuana" is "typical of its country, as though it were a hundred miles from the border."[27] In doing so, they not only responded to tourists' expectations but also shaped tourists' perceptions of what was, in fact, Mexican; they sold their version of Mexico.

To satisfy Americans' desires, promoters developed an array of "Mexican" activities. Visitors to Southern California could easily have met Mexican people, tasted Mexican food, and purchased Mexican goods without leaving the United States, but across the boundary line these activities' purported authenticity and exoticism intensified. Antonio Elosúa's "Typical Mexican Fair" promised tourists "everything Mexican," including a bullfight, a local Mexican regimental band, Mexican dancing girls, cockfights, gambling, a cabaret, and a Mexican café.[28] Restaurants offered "Spanish dinners" consisting of "frijoles," "tortillas," "the genuine chili and tamales of the Mexicans," and a "bewilder [sic] array of dishes" which would "surprise and delight the palate of the guest not accustomed to Spanish cooking."[29] When rebel forces invaded Tijuana in 1911, even the Mexican Revolution became a tourist attraction. Southern Californians, like Americans elsewhere on the border, flocked to the boundary line for a better view of the battles (as Laura Isabel Serna discusses in the next essay, screenings of newsreel footage and fictional recreations of battles drew similar crowds.) Photographs taken of the spectators at the battle of Tijuana portray a paradelike quality, with the crowd gathered to watch the bloodshed arranged beside the border as if seated in a grandstand. After the battle, tourists flooded into Tijuana, paying the rebels twenty-five cents to view the battle site.[30]

From the standpoint of many American tourists, the Mexican soldiers, like most of the Mexicans with whom they came into contact along the border, were part of the scenery. Viewing Mexicans became a central part of cultural tourism along the border. "The 'soldados' or soldiers of the fort in picturesque uniforms, natives in the sombreros and serapes of the Mexican race, bright-eyed senoritas and sedate senoras," noted a 1920 article in the San Diego Union, "unite to make a picture of striking color and great charm."[31] Rather than providing Americans with an opportunity to meet and engage with Mexican citizens, a trip to Tijuana more often offered contrived interactions with performers and salespeople who reinforced preexisting conceptions of Mexicans

Crowd watching the Battle of Tijuana from the boundary line, June 22, 1911. Photograph courtesy Photograph Collection, San Diego Historical Society.

While Tijuana saw only limited violence during the Mexican Revolution, its few battles drew the attention of residents and tourists from the United States. Crowds like this one gathered at the border to watch the battle and afterwards flooded into Tijuana to view the destruction firsthand.

as exotic, romantic, and primitive. Promoters did not create these stereotypes, but they adopted and disseminated them in the many images of Mexican people with which they filled advertisements, curio stores, postcards, and entertainment events. Illustrated with sketches of seductive women, costumed dancers, and swarthy horsemen, advertisements for Tijuana promised that "roguish eyed *senoritas*" and "gaily costumed *senors* [*sic*]" would entertain visitors.[32] The Sunset Inn used images of men wearing large sombreros and a dark-haired woman in a low-cut dress dancing with castanets to underscore its description of Tijuana as "refreshing," "fascinating," "quaint," and "exotic."[33] In romanticizing Mexicans, promoters placed particular emphasis on the Spanish aspects of Mexican ethnicity. Publicity for bullfights gave top billing to matadors and bulls imported from Spain and dancing exhibitions featured "Spanish" dancers.[34]

While these performances and images emphasized Mexico's exotic qualities, other tourist attractions and commodities presenting Mexican people as primitive or comic were more pejorative. Postcards featured photographs of Mexicans, some labeled as "peons," barefoot and dressed in simple clothes,

Advertisement, *San Diego Union*, September 12, 1920.

This advertisement for the Sunset Inn used both words and images to reinforce the idea of Tijuana as foreign and alluring.

frequently seated on the ground or engaged in menial labor.[35] With a cartoon of a Mexican man dwarfed by an enormous sombrero, another Sunset Inn advertisement poked fun at Mexican dress.[36] These condescending depictions of Mexicans were highlighted in the ubiquitous photographs of tourists swathed in serapes and sombreros, often astride donkeys.[37] As one article explained, "the staid and dignified visitor usually lays aside his dignity and mounts one of the patient beasts to pose in a photo as a '*caballo*' or mounted cavalier, a picture to be shown and laughed over on the return home."[38] At a time when the Mexican government was promoting modernization and industrial growth, these caricatures reflected and reinforced negative stereotypes of Mexico and Mexicans as primitive.[39]

Curio shops perpetuated these stereotypes, further shaping the way tourists experienced Tijuana. The serapes and sombreros in which tourists posed came from the well-stocked shelves of a number of border specialty stores that both created and catered to tourists' expectations. Souvenirs, ranging from postal cards and Tijuana pennants to a variety of handmade goods, offered tourists a reminder of their foreign adventures and a piece of an imagined Mexico to

Advertisement, *San Diego Union*, September 16, 1920.

This caricature of a grinning man in an oversized sombrero humorously portrayed Mexicans.

show their friends and family at home. Alexander Savín's Bazaar Mexicano advertised "Mexican Souvenirs," which included "Fine Mexican Cigars and Cigarettes," "Mexican Carved Leather Goods," "Indian and Mexican Art Goods," and "Mexican and Indian Blankets (*Serapes*)."[40] The Big Curio Store sold "Mexican drawn work, Mexican Blankets and Handwoven Mexican Straw Hats" and featured "typical clay figures, real Mexican looking." Ranging from matadors to portly peons, the figurines lined store shelves, reinforcing the notion that Mexicans were meant for Americans' amusement and entertainment.[41] By purchasing these curios, American tourists consumed a construction of Mexican culture and contributed to its dispersal throughout the United States.[42]

The border tourist industry commodified Mexican culture in order to amuse, entertain, and ultimately profit. Responding to Americans' desires to consume the sights, sounds, and material goods of an exotic, foreign country, border promoters created their own version of Mexican culture, drawing from a range of cultural practices and stereotypes while emphasizing the national distinctions signified by the boundary line. At the same time that they sought

Tourists in Tijuana, ca. 1920. Photograph courtesy Photograph Collection, San Diego Historical Society.

Photographers set up businesses on the border to cater to tourists by providing serapes, sombreros, and signs indicating a borderline location: the resulting photographs were a ubiquitous part of the Tijuana tourist experience.

to construct an atmosphere of exoticism and national difference, the rise of Progressive-era moral reforms within the United States heightened the legal distinctions between the United States and Mexico. These distinctions would make the emergence of border vice districts possible and redefine American consumer practices along the border.

"Everybody Goes Where Everything Goes": The Rise of Border Vice Districts

Cultural tourism and the novelty of the border provided the foundation for border tourism, but it was the legal significance embedded in the boundary line that enabled the tourist industry to reach its apex on the Baja California border. More than a symbol of cultural differences, the boundary line marked the divide between Baja California's permissive legal climate and increasingly restrictive moral laws in the United States. Gradually pushed out of California cities during the first two decades of the twentieth century, vice purveyors relocated across the border, just out of reach of local, state, and federal laws but well within reach of American consumers. Soon gambling, drinking, horseracing, and other activities prohibited under American law became the central features of border tourism.[43] As such, they became intertwined with American tourists' conceptions of Mexico and Mexican culture. In addition to

Miguel González's Big Curio Store, Tijuana, 1912. Photograph courtesy Photograph Collection, San Diego Historical Society.

A number of border curio stores catered to the tourist trade with sombreros, serapes, postcards, pennants, and a variety of other items advertised as authentically Mexican.

exotic, romantic, and occasionally violent, the border appeared freewheeling, scandalous, and ever more dependent on American consumption.

Vice permeated consumer culture on the border. Throughout the early twentieth century, as "dry" and antisaloon laws spread from the local to the national level, liquor became the driving force of border consumption. According to local rumor, the first Mexicali business had been no more than a plank under a mesquite tree from which an enterprising businessman sold mescal and tequila to the Americans laboring to build the dry town of Calexico on the U.S. side of the line.[44] By 1905, three different Mexicali establishments advertised their stock of domestic and imported liquors in the *Calexico Chronicle*.[45] Along with sales of souvenirs and Mexican cultural artifacts, curio shops and other border businesses did a brisk trade in liquor. With state laws shutting down saloons, First World War restrictions on the manufacture and sale of alcohol, and, finally, the imposition of nationwide Prohibition after the passage of the Eighteenth Amendment and the Volstead Act in 1920, more and more border entrepreneurs recognized the profitability of producing and

Automobiles parked in front of Blue Fox Café and ABC Bar in Tijuana, December 1928. Photograph courtesy Photograph Collection, San Diego Historical Society.

With its many bars, Avenida Revolución became the heart of Tijuana's vice-tourism district.

selling liquor, as did American saloon owners who moved their businesses across the boundary line.[46] Marvin Allen, Frank B. Byer, and Carl Withington were among the most successful of these American transplants. Pushed out of Bakersfield in 1913, the trio first founded The Owl (or El Tecolote) in Mexicali and later the Tivoli Bar in Tijuana. By 1924, they had expanded into brewing, importing European spirits, gambling, and racing and were reported to be making as much as $40,000 to $100,000 a week from just one of their clubs in Mexicali.[47] They were not the only entrepreneurs profiting from liquor sales: Miguel González, owner of the Big Curio Store, opened the Mexicali Brewery; Herman Cohen ran the San Francisco Bar; Miguel Calette Anaya established the Blue Fox Cafe; and M. Escobedo managed the Tijuana Bar and Café. The list goes on and on, including not just American and Mexican proprietors, but European and Asian ones as well. Even the American heavyweight boxer Jack Johnson operated two Tijuana nightclubs, one of which catered exclusively to African Americans. Following the passage of the Volstead Act, the number of saloons in Tijuana doubled, from thirty to sixty, in a mere four years.[48]

Alcohol was not the only guilty pleasure that Americans sought south of the border. Casinos, prizefights, racetracks, and brothels crowded border vice districts. As California passed a series of moral reform laws, including the

Grandstand and Race Track at Tijuana, ca. 1925. Photograph courtesy Union-Tribune Collection, San Diego Historical Society.

With horseracing outlawed in California, Tijuana's Agua Caliente racetrack drew hundreds of thousands of American spectators across the border during the 1910s and 1920s.

Walker-Otis Anti–Race Track Betting Bill in 1909, the Red Light Abatement Act in 1913, and a law outlawing prizefighting in 1916, prostitutes, pimps, and race and fight promoters moved across the border.[49] In one two- to three-year period, 700 American women relocated to brothels in Tijuana and Mexicali. As with other vice businesses, Americans operated many of the brothels, but Asian immigrants, including Patricio Mee Hong and Soo Yasuhara, also controlled a significant share of the market. Home to numerous brothels, saloons, and opium dens, Mexicali's Chinatown in particular became synonymous with vice.[50] Following the legalization of gambling in Baja California by federal decree in 1908, both American and Mexican promoters launched plans to build casinos, dog tracks, and horse tracks. In 1915, Antonio Elosúa, a Mexican citizen, secured a gaming permit that enabled him to include boxing, gambling, and races in his "Typical Mexican Fair." Securing a government concession the same year, an American-owned enterprise soon eclipsed Elosúa's operations. Operated by a Los Angeles racing promoter and a San Francisco boxing promoter, the Lower California Jockey Club racetrack opened to great fanfare on January 1, 1916. Thousands of Americans attended the races, many taking advantage of the new San Diego and South Eastern Railroad branch line to the track.[51]

By the 1920s, the border was home to a substantial and diversified vice economy. Racetracks, bars, dance halls, brothels, and casinos catered to Americans of all classes. The predominantly middle- and working-class residents of the agricultural Imperial Valley, along with visiting salesmen and investors, frequented the many bars and brothels of Mexicali.[52] Tijuana, by contrast, was home to high-end resorts and racetracks that drew on the booming populations in San Diego and Los Angeles. The Tijuana vice industry achieved its pinnacle with the opening of the Agua Caliente resort and casino in 1929. Built with American funds on land owned by Governor Abelardo Rodríguez, Agua Caliente consisted of a 500-room hotel, casino, spa, swimming pool, golf course, gardens, private radio station, airport, and both greyhound- and horse-racing tracks. Opulent resorts like Agua Caliente attracted such celebrities as Buster Keaton, Jack Dempsey, Charlie Chaplin, and Al Capone.[53] While the Hollywood illuminati stole the spotlight, many middle-class Americans also ventured south to gamble, drink, and watch the races. One American, who worked parking cars and selling cigars and cigarettes in Tijuana, remembered that even small businessmen from San Diego frequented the upscale casinos, where they gambled and tipped extravagantly.[54]

There was never any doubt that border vice promoters built these establishments for American consumers, consequently their advertising efforts concentrated on the American market. San Diego newspapers covered all of the horse races and regularly ran advertisements for Tijuana establishments and special events.[55] Each week the A.B.W. Club in Mexicali printed a full-page advertisement in the *Calexico Chronicle* informing its patrons of scheduled performances.[56] Regardless of the nationality of their owners, most saloons and casinos, like the Blue Fox Café and Sunset Inn, had English names. One observer noted that "flaring electric signs" faced the American border, luring customers to the "debauch emporiums." While signs advertising "legitimate Mexican enterprises are usually in Spanish," he continued, "the vice and booze signs are in the English language."[57]

In marketing vice establishments, border promoters depicted the border as exotic, freewheeling, and liberating. Symbols of "Old Mexico" and "Jazz-Age America" commingled in advertisements for Tijuana's and Mexicali's nightclubs and bars. One advertisement for the Sunset Inn coupled the offer of a "bit of quaint Old Mexico" with illustrations of a jazz band, a modern couple

Advertisement, *San Diego Union*, September 15, 1920.

With its depiction of a jazz band, dancing, and a beautiful young flapper enjoying a cocktail and cigarettes, this advertisement for the Sunset Inn blended images of the jazz age with the promise of "a bit of quaint Old Mexico."

on the dance floor, and a young flapper seated at a table adorned with a cocktail and cigarettes. Another ad for the Tivoli Bar showed a mariachi strumming a guitar in the shadow of a Spanish colonial building, but dispensed with the romantic rhetoric in favor of the flagrant announcement: "No Music! No Dancing! No Entertainment! JUST CHOICE OLD "BOOZE!"[58] Despite the crass simplicity of the Tivoli Inn's advertisement, border vice districts offered more than liquor to Prohibition-era Americans; they offered freedom. Asking, as did one advertisement, "Would you escape the rigid conventionalities which limit one's enjoyment in this country?" promoters lured Americans across the line with promises not just of drinks and diversions, but of temporary reprieves from the restrictions of American society.[59] Border vice districts made it possible, in the words of the U.S. consul in Mexicali, "for the nearby residents of the United States to step across the border and there to enjoy certain privileges and perform certain acts which are illegal in the country and state of their actual residence."[60]

Promoters repeatedly stressed that it was in fact just that easy to simply step across the border. Filling San Diego newspapers with information about where tourists could obtain passports and board auto stages and trains, they emphasized the accessibility and convenience of the border vice districts.[61] Just across the border, Americans found a growing number of hotels with modern, "American" amenities.[62] As a U.S. official noted, Agua Caliente had "an ideal location for attracting visitors from the United States"—"two miles from the border crossing at San Ysidro, California, but a paved highway extends to the door of the hotel." American entrepreneurs planned another hotel that would literally straddle the border for their compatriots' convenience: "The beach attractions and some of the cottages will be situated on United States soil, the hotel and bar, and the casino to be in Mexico."[63]

By all accounts, these marketing efforts were incredibly successful. On Labor Day, 1927, sixteen thousand automobiles passed into Tijuana from the United States. In 1931, the first year in which the U.S. government kept official statistics of border crossings, over five million people entered Tijuana through the San Ysidro port of entry.[64] One investigation noted that in 1929 Americans were responsible for 95 percent of all money spent in "pleasure resorts" on the Mexican side of the border.[65] Reformers and officials alike were forced to assume, as one American consul did in 1922, that "without American exploitation and support local vice conditions would undoubtedly be much less deplorable than they have been in the past and still are."[66] According to one critic, the Americanization of Tijuana was complete: "At Tia Juana [sic], these Mexicans find on their side of the line, an American town, run by American capital, harboring American underworld women and American white slavers, the medium of exchange being American money, and all this unbridled debauchery being accomplished through the medium of the American language."[67] Although advertisements for Tijuana in San Diego newspapers continued to urge tourists to "visit this quaint Mexican village and send a post card from a foreign land," another American consul concluded that, excepting the presence of Mexican government officials, "there is little Mexican about the village."[68]

In these reports, the border appeared to have, in fact, become the playground of American consumers. Promoters had so successfully emphasized the aspects of the border that appealed to Americans that Mexican culture and authority had faded from view. Despite the growth of local Mexican populations, expanding infrastructure, and economic development along the border, most Americans did not look beyond the vice districts to which they and their fellow citizens flocked.[69] With the spread of this proprietary view along the U.S. side of the line, internal American political and cultural divisions became displaced onto the border.

Border Closings and the Control of American Consumption

As the border vice districts flourished, moral reformers on both sides of the boundary petitioned Mexican officials to outlaw them. When Baja California officials refused to accede to these demands, Mexican reformers and nationalists complained, to no avail, that their border cities had been abandoned to the worst of American whims. At the same time, American reformers turned to their own government, arguing that the predominance of Americans in the vice districts gave U.S. officials the right to regulate Americans' consumption by preventing them from crossing the border altogether.

The border vice districts posed a double threat to the morality and national integrity of the Mexican communities of Tijuana and Mexicali. As historian Eric Michael Schantz has detailed, many local Mexican residents demanded government suppression of the drinking, gambling, and prostitution that threatened the social and commercial health of local families and businesses.[70] Their attitudes reflected the outlook of a binational reform movement that encompassed both the United States' sweeping prohibitions and the Mexican government's regulatory approach to vice.[71] Beyond the presumed dangers of vice, Mexican reformers also recognized that American dominance was a menace to Mexican sovereignty. The former police officer and labor organizer Julio Dunn Legaspy recalled that in the 1920s Americans "controlled all the activities, even their own authorities who gave them protection." It was "as if Tijuana was an American city," he explained, adding, "the Mexicans did not have the right to work, not even in the vice dens. It felt as if we were in a foreign country."[72] In response to these conditions, Mexican nationalists and labor organizers like Legaspy demanded that territorial officials close American-owned vice establishments, or at least require that they hire Mexicans.[73]

The border vice districts also enraged American reformers, but for different reasons. The well-publicized propensity of Americans to drink, gamble, and visit brothels across the boundary line undermined reformers' hard-fought efforts to protect American society from the perils of vice. Their concern was less for Baja California's border communities than for the vice districts' effects on the Americans who visited them. In 1924, U.S. Secretary of State Charles Evans Hughes opined that conditions at Tijuana and Mexicali represented a "grave menace to the health and welfare of American communities."[74] One San Diego pastor complained that Tijuana was a "moral sink hole, and a constant source of disease and disgrace."[75]

While American demand was the root of the problem, reformers sought a supply-side solution (as they had done in the United States) by petitioning the Mexican government to initiate reforms along the border. These pleas placed the blame on the Americans who, as both purveyors and consumers of vice, drove the growth of the border vice districts. "Inasmuch as [the opening of a racetrack and gambling and prostitution resort at Tijuana] is not a Mexican affair, but a matter capitalized and run by American money and men to avoid and defeat the laws of our nation and state," wrote one reformer, "we hope, Sir, that the American Government at Washington will find a way to request Mexican Authorities to forbear granting the necessary permission."[76] Many Americans asked that the Mexican government establish a fifty-mile-wide "dry-zone" (a vice-free zone) adjacent to the boundary line. As one San Diego resident suggested, "[Mexican president] Obregón should move the hell holes fifty miles from the border."[77]

Mexican officials did not establish a vice-free zone, but they did prove receptive to a number of other vice-curbing measures demanded by American and Mexican reformers.[78] This was particularly true on the level of the federal government. Mexico, like the United States, initiated many nationwide moral reforms during the early twentieth century.[79] After reasserting federal power over the Baja California peninsula with the removal of independent governor Estéban Cantú in 1920, Mexico's president Álvaro Obregón initiated a number of measures curbing the vice industry. In 1922, the American consul noted that with the support of the Mexican federal government, Baja California had witnessed "gradual improvement in conditions relative to gambling and the drug traffic."[80] The Mexican federal government proved particularly receptive to cooperating with the United States in controlling the flourishing drug trade, with prohibitions on the importation of opium in 1916 and all narcotics in 1923.[81]

Baja California officials were also responsive to demands to regulate, if not eradicate, border vice districts. In 1915, Governor Cantú announced a plan of heavy taxation that he claimed would eliminate all "vicious vices."[82] As in other parts of Mexico, territorial officials regulated prostitution along the border, requiring prostitutes to register with local governments and deporting unwanted foreign prostitutes.[83] In 1926, governor of Baja California Abelardo Rodríguez launched a major wave of reforms after the Peteets, an American family of four, committed suicide following a horrific trip to Tijuana during which the two daughters were said to have been drugged and raped. Within days of the suicides, Rodríguez ordered fifty-two saloons to close, required those remaining to pay a $10,000 bond as security against future violations, prohibited all women from entering bars without male escorts, and expelled "Mexican undesirables," entertainers, and "women of suspicious character" from the city.[84]

Local officials, however, remained reluctant to completely shut down the vice districts, and with good reason—vice was extremely profitable for them personally. Kickbacks and payoffs were pervasive. During their time in office both Cantú and Rodríguez came under attack for their close association with American investors; charges included the claim that Rodríguez accepted bribes from the owners of the Agua Caliente Casino in exchange for ignoring violations of national antivice laws. Reformers on both sides of the border, Americans and Mexicans alike, protested against these abuses of government power and demanded federal intervention to uphold national morality laws.[85]

While these officials' behavior was not beyond reproach, their personal greed was but one reason they encouraged the development of the border vice districts. Despite the social disorder that went along with it, vice tourism provided a much-needed economic stimulus to the isolated and often overlooked territory of Northern Baja California. Although many casinos preferred to hire American workers, public sentiment and the demands of the Mexican labor movement resulted in a 1925 court decision that required companies to employ Mexican nationals as at least 50 percent of their workforce. Thanks to this law and continued pressure by local unions, large numbers of Mexicans eventually found work in the vice service industry.[86] The money American tourists spent also helped fill territorial coffers and fund public works. Taxes and licensing fees diverted some of the profits of saloons, brothels, casinos, and racetracks to the territorial government. During Cantú's administration, the government of Baja California collected between thirteen and fifteen thousand dollars each month from one Mexicali brothel alone. With this increased income, Cantú was able to build a high school in Mexicali and to improve the roads throughout the district. When the capitol of Baja California burned down in 1921, gambling concessions financed its reconstruction.[87] In the twenties, Governor Rodríguez used funds derived from vice taxes and concessions to finance such progressive public works as a theater and library in Mexicali. All along the border, American vice underwrote progressive improvements in Mexican territory.

Faced with Baja California officials who were unwilling to give up personal and public advantages of vice dollars, American reformers denounced them as corrupt and turned instead to the U.S. government. Writing from Mexicali, American consul H. C. von Struve concluded, "the only solution, so far as a solution is possible, lies in the power of the United States government."[88] While the U.S. government could not legislate morality in the vice districts, it could, argued reformers, control American access via the border. Associating vice with the thriving border nightlife, reformers argued that border ports of entry should be closed at night to limit American crossings to daytime business hours. In a letter to the secretary of state, Consul von Struve laid out the rationale for nighttime closures: vice establishments were dependent on "the patronage of transient Americans who visit Tijuana and Mexicali from nearby American territory at night after the close of ordinary business and return to American territory almost invariably the same night." Thus, "if the ports of Calexico and Tijuana were closed to all passage—foot passengers as well as vehicles—from seven or eight o'clock at night until six o'clock in the morning," he explained, "it is believed that the vice centers of Mexicali and Tijuana would be deprived of at least seventy five per cent of their profitable patronage and would therefore no longer be able to pay sufficient legitimate or illegitimate revenues to enable their further existence except on a very small scale."[89]

Despite opposition from some Americans, including officials who were not sure whether the government had the right to prevent U.S. citizens from coming and going as they pleased, U.S. border officials succumbed to public pressure and established early closing hours at border ports of entry. In 1924, the U.S. State Department notified the Mexican government that due to the "flagrant immoralities" at Tijuana and Mexicali, the California–Baja California border would be closed after nine at night. Two years later, after outrage erupted over the Peteet suicides, reformers convinced the U.S. government to close the San Ysidro port of entry at 6 p.m.[90]

While American reformers applauded these developments, many Mexicans, who both understood and explicitly rejected the Americans' characterization of border spaces as threatening to U.S. citizens alone, were indignant. The *Excelsior* newspaper reported that early closing hours were "an insult" to "national honor" that discriminated "against Mexico because of the absence of similar closing regulations on the Canadian border."[91] The Mexicali and Tijuana chambers of commerce, comprised of both Mexican and American nationals who did business in the border towns, also condemned the closing hours as discriminatory. The Mexicali Chamber of Commerce denounced the reformers as "a craven political organization" that was slandering Mexicans and "engendering hatred between the two nations."[92] "[W]e do not consider ourselves an inferior race whose contact means danger at night hours nor as a body afflicted with an infectious plague," wrote representatives of the Tijuana

U.S. Customs closing the line at 9 p.m. at Tijuana, 1924. Photograph courtesy Photograph Collection, San Diego Historical Society.

In response to protests by American reformers, in 1924 the U.S. Customs Service began closing the San Ysidro port of entry at 9 p.m. every night—to the consternation of many crossers, including the unknown man in this photograph. Two years later in 1926, following the Peteet suicides, the Customs Service pushed the closing time back to 6 p.m.

Chamber of Commerce to President Herbert Hoover in 1929, "and consequently request equal consideration and the same treatment accorded other peoples."[93] Angered by the unilateral border closing measures, Governor Rodríguez attempted to retaliate by establishing his own border controls—temporarily initiating registration requirements in 1924 and closing the border to nighttime railroad traffic in 1929. While ultimately unsuccessful, Rodríguez's efforts represented a symbolic reassertion of Mexican sovereignty.[94]

In the end, Rodríguez's resistance was unnecessary. Although Consul von Struve reported that drinking, gambling, and prostitution fell off by 50 to 90 percent in Tijuana and that arrests and drunk driving had decreased in Mexicali and Calexico after the establishment of the nine o'clock closing time in 1924, border businesses, including a number of resort hotels that provided overnight accommodations, continued to thrive.[95] As long as American prohibitions and Mexican acquiescence lasted, the border, as the Sunset Inn had advertised in 1920, was open for business. The border vice districts only began to decline with the onset of the Great Depression, the return of horseracing to

California, and the repeal of Prohibition in 1933. Shortly after his election in 1934, Mexican President Lázaro Cárdenas finally brought the heyday of border vice to an end when he decided to close the border casinos as part of his wide-reaching nationalist project.[96]

The legacy of border promotion, however, remained. True to border promoters' promises, the Baja California border was open to Americans, creating both opportunities and inconveniences for citizens of both nations. Lured south by advertisements that proclaimed the border the perfect place to buy land, experience an exotic foreign culture, and access forbidden vices, American consumers both discovered and contributed to the development of cultural images, urban environments, and international relations that have been remarkably persistent. The emphasis on the American market replaced the ideal of foreign travel—an opportunity for novel experiences and cultural exchange—with contrived encounters and cultural stereotypes. Furthermore, it transformed the American demand for vice into a problem of Mexican supply. These ideas about the border resonate into the present century. For many Americans, border towns remained synonymous with the tourist kitsch and moral depravity of the 1910s and 1920s. It was this image of the border, as Evan Ward describes in his essay about Mexico's promotion of tourism in this volume, that PRONAF would struggle to replace in the 1960s. Similarly, the idea that the border is the source of the U.S. drug problem continues to define the U.S. war on drugs today, as Robert Perez explores in his essay about smuggling in this volume. Between 1900 and 1934, promoters transformed the border into a site of American consumption; it was left to the Mexicans and Americans on both sides of the line to live with the consequences of the reality they created.

Abbreviations

CC	*Calexico Chronicle*
CRLC Papers	Colorado River Land Company Papers, Sherman Library, Corona Del Mar, California
IIH–UABC	Instituto de Investigaciones Históricas, Universidad Autónoma de Baja California, Tijuana, Baja California
Keller Papers	Henry W. Keller Papers, The Huntington Library, San Marino, California
RG 59, NACP	U.S. State Department Decimal Files, 1910–29, Records of the State Department, Record Group 59, National Archives, College Park, Maryland

SDET	*San Diego Evening Tribune*
SDHS	San Diego Historical Society
SDS	*San Diego Sun*
SDU	*San Diego Union*

Notes

The author thanks Southern Methodist University, the Clements Center for Southwest Studies, and all of the participants in this volume for their support and suggestions.

Notes fully cite primary sources and specialized secondary sources. Full bibliographic details for all other citations are in the volume's selected bibliography.

1. Advertisement, SDU, September 14, 1920, 10.

2. Taylor, "Wild Frontier," 204–29.

3. Ibid.; Schantz, "All Night at the Owl"; Cabeza de Baca and Cabeza de Baca, " 'Shame Suicides' "; Schantz, "Mexicali Rose"; C. de Baca, "Moral Renovation of the Californias"; Arreola and Curtis, *Mexican Border Cities*, 77–117; Profitt, *Tijuana*, 185–215; Price, *Tijuana*, 46–69; Piñera Ramírez and Ortiz Figueroa, eds., *Historia de Tijuana*, vol. 1; Vanderwood, *Juan Soldado*, 76–87; Ruiz, *On the Rim of Mexico*. A notable exception to this latter point is chapter 5 of Schantz, "Mexicali Rose," which explores the differences in vice tourism in Mexicali and Tijuana.

4. For a discussion of Díaz and U.S. investment in Mexico, see Hart, *Empire and Revolution*; Katz, *Secret War*; Pletcher, *Diplomacy of Trade*.

5. St. John, "Line in the Sand"; Kerig, "Yankee Enclave"; John A. Kirchner, *Baja California Railroads* (Los Angeles: Dawson's Book Shop, 1988).

6. Boxes 19–33, Keller Papers; CRLC Papers.

7. "Outline of a Proposed Hunting Reserve in Mexico near San Diego," box 21, folder 2; Edwards to Keller, June 27, 1910, box 23, folder 13, both in Keller Papers.

8. Kirchner, *Baja California Railroads*, op. cit., 63–69, 74, 92–119.

9. See the following documents in the Anderson Portfolios, CRLC Papers: "Report of the Soil Expert, Mr. J. Garnett Holmes," folder 29; Otis to Diaz, April 11, 1906, folder 37; and Anderson to Javier Arrangoiz, March 15, 1905, folder 21.

10. Edwards to Keller, June 27, 1910, box 23, folder 13, Keller Papers.

11. Otis to Chandler, August 19, 1909, Anderson Portfolios, folder 35, CRLC Papers.

12. Keller to Tolle, September 16, 1916, box 32, folder 9, Keller Papers.

13. Keller to Wattles, April 26, 1916, box 33, folder 11, Keller Papers.

14. Keller to Powell, March 30, 1911, box 29, folder 17, Keller Papers.

15. Edwards to Keller, October 14, 1925, box 23, folder 13, Keller Papers.

16. Otis to Creel, September 3 and 4, 1907, Anderson Portfolios, folder 37, CRLC Papers.

17. Keller to Pérez Treviño, June 10, 1930, box 29, folder 13, Keller Papers.

18. In addition to Lawrence Culver's essay in this volume, see also Carey McWilliams, *Southern California: An Island on the Land* (New York: Duell, Sloan, and Pearce, 1946); Kevin Starr, *Inventing the Dream: California through the Progressive Era* (New York: Oxford University Press, 1985); Deverell, *Whitewashed Adobe*.

19. For general studies of tourism, see Timothy, ed., *Tourism and Political Boundaries*; Krakover and Gradus, eds., *Tourism in Frontier Areas*; MacCannell, *The Tourist: A New Theory of the Leisure Class*; Sharon Gmelch, ed., *Tourists and Tourism: A Reader* (Long Grove: Waveland Press, 2004); Rothman, *Devil's Bargains*.

20. "Tijuana the Mecca for Thousands of Tourists Annually," SDU, January 1, 1910; "Fair Attractions Pack Tijuana with Tourists," SDU, July 26, 1915.

21. "Tijuana the Mecca for Thousands of Tourists Annually," *op. cit.*

22. SDU, December 29, 1929, 3; After its completion in 1919, the San Diego and Arizona Railway also connected San Diego to the border. "Tijuana Fair Attracts Hosts across Border," SDU, August 25, 1915; Advertisement, SDU, August 27, 1915, no page; "Richly Scenic Region Traversed by S.D. & A. Ry.," SDU, January 1, 1920.

23. Dallen J. Timothy has described how tourists' fascination with political divides has caused boundary lines to become tourist attractions around the world. Timothy, ed., *Tourism and Political Boundaries*, 54–55.

24. "Thousands of Tourists Visit Quaint Mexican Town Yearly," SDU, January 1, 1920.

25. Advertisements in SDU, January 29, 1920, 2; January 30, 1920, 2; Advertisements in SDS, January 3, 1920, 4; January 27, 1920, 10.

26. "Tijuana the Mecca for Thousands of Tourists Annually," *op. cit.*; "Thousands of Tourists Visit Quaint Mexican Town Yearly," *op. cit.* For photographs of boundary markers, see the SDHS Photograph Collection. Boundary markers and monuments have become tourist attractions on international borders throughout the world. Timothy, ed., *Tourism and Political Boundaries*, 43–49.

27. Postcard in author's collection, published by Curt Teich and Co., Chicago.

28. Advertisement, SDU, July 10, 1915, 7.

29. Advertisement, SDU, January 1, 1920, 8; January 1, 1910, section 6, 3.

30. "Quiet Reigns at Tijuana," SDU, May 11, 1911; Profitt, *Tijuana*, 188. For an overview of the revolution in Baja California, see Blaisdell, *Desert Revolution*. For accounts of battles elsewhere on the border, see Samponaro and Vanderwood, *Border Fury*; Martinez, ed., *Fragments of the Mexican Revolution*.

31. "Thousands of Tourists Visit Quaint Mexican Town Yearly," *op. cit.*

32. Advertisements, SDS, January 3, 1920, 12; January 6, 1920, 8; January 13, 1920, 12; January 22, 1920, 12; and January 24, 1920, 4; Advertisements, SDU, January 29, 1920, 2; January 31, 1920, 12.

33. Advertisement, SDU, September 12, 1920, 10.

34. "Mexicali Will Have Bullfight," CC, April 27, 1915; "Thousands of Tourists Visit Quaint Mexican Town Yearly," *op. cit.* Border promoters also incorporated other foreign elements into their entertainments. The A.B.W. Club in Mexicali featured "Papinta, Hula Hula Dancer" and "Elysiah, the Dancer from Egypt." Mexicali's Chinatown was also a popular attraction for border tourists. Advertisement, CC, January 11, 1924, 6; Schantz, "Mexicali Rose," 386–94. The emphasis on blending foreign cultures and performers was evident throughout U.S. entertainment culture at this time. See Kasson, *Amusing the Million*. For a discussion of similar practices of performance and bodily display in cultural tourism in Hawai'i, see Desmond, *Staging Tourism*, 2–141.

35. "The Big Curio Store" postcard, from postcard folder published by the Western Novelty and Publishing Co., Los Angeles, in author's collection.

36. Advertisement, SDU, September 16, 1920, 7.

37. Photographs of Tijuana tourists, SDHS Photograph Collection.

38. "Thousands of Tourists Visit Quaint Mexican Town Yearly," op. cit.

39. Whether taking on the guise of "Mexicans" had a more complex meaning for any of these American tourists, as Philip J. Deloria has argued dressing up as Indians did for generations of Americans (*Playing Indian*), is difficult to know from these images and their descriptions.

40. Advertisement, SDU, January 1, 1910, section 6, 3. Savín, a Mexican-born son of French immigrants, opened the Bazaar Mexicano in 1886. C. de Baca, "Moral Renovation of the Californias," 31.

41. "Big Curio Store" postcard," op. cit.; Advertisement, SDU, January 1, 1910, section 6, 3. Jorge Ibs, a German immigrant, started the Big Curio Store, which his Mexican son-in-law, Miguel González, later operated. See C. de Baca, "Moral Renovation of the Californias," 80. For examples of the figurines for sale, see photographs labeled "Senorita the Clerk" and "Senorita the Teacher" in the SDHS, Photograph Collection.

42. The dispersal of postcards is indicative of the spread of these ideas. In my personal collection alone I have postcards sent from Tijuana to California, Colorado, Washington, New Hampshire, New York, and Toronto.

43. The studies of tourism in Tijuana cited earlier address vice tourism as well. Border vice districts that cater to tourists are a common feature of international boundary lines. Timothy, ed., *Tourism and Political Boundaries*, 69–77; Goodovitch, "Legalization of Casino Gambling"; Felsenstein and Freeman, "Gambling on the Border."

44. Otis B. Tout, *The First Thirty Years, 1901–1931: Being an Account of the Principal Events in the History of Imperial Valley, Southern California, U.S.A.* (San Diego: Otis B. Tout, 1931), 273.

45. Advertisements, CC, July 20, 1905.

46. Woods, "Penchant for Probity."

47. Schantz, "Mexicali Rose," 365–74; H. C. von Struve to Secretary of State, February 12, 1924, 812.40622/42, (M274, roll 148), RG 59, NACP.

48. Advertisement, SDU, January 2, 1922, 8; Oral history of Miguel Calette Anaya, in Piñera Ramírez and Ortiz Figueroa, eds., *Historia de Tijuana*, 1:108; C. de Baca, "Moral Renovation of the Californias," 77–81; Price, *Tijuana*, 51; Taylor, "Wild Frontier," 212–16.

49. Woods, "Penchant for Probity." For a discussion of the suppression of prostitution in San Diego, see McKanna Jr., "Prostitutes, Progressives, and Police." Morality laws had a long history in the United States, but it was not until the first decades of the twentieth century that reformers succeeded in making morality a nationwide priority. For a discussion of earlier state attempts to control morality in the United States, see William Novak, *The People's Welfare: Law and Regulation in Nineteenth-Century America* (Chapel Hill: The University of North Carolina Press, 1996), 149–90.

50. C. de Baca, "Moral Renovation of the Californias," 78; Schantz, "All Night at the Owl," 115–18.

51. *Mexicali*, 268–69; Gobernación to the Administrador of the Aduana, January 3, 1913, folder IIH: 1913.1 [5.5], Fondo Gobernación, IIH-UABC; Taylor, "Wild Frontier," 210–15; Price, *Tijuana*, 49–51.

52. Schantz, "Mexicali Rose," 50.

53. Piñera Ramírez and Ortiz Figueroa, eds., *Historia de Tijuana*, 1:114–28; Taylor, "Wild Frontier," 218–19.

54. Leonard Rottman, oral history interview, June 18, 1972, SDHS; "Agua Caliente Premier Pleasure Resort of America," SDU, January 1, 1930; Lugo Jr., "El Casino de Agua Caliente," in Piñera-Ramirez and Ortiz Figueroa, eds., *Historia de Tijuana* 1:115; Proffitt, *Tijuana*, 196; Price, *Tijuana*, 52; Taylor, "Wild Frontier," 220.

55. Advertisements, SDU, July 16, 1915, 6; January 29, 1920, 2; June 29, 1928, 11; "Thousands Greet Revival of Racing at Tijuana," SDU, November 12, 1916; "Agua Caliente Racing Season Opens Today," SDU, December 28, 1929; "Field of 114 to Tee Off in Caliente Open," SDU, January 20, 1930.

56. Advertisements, CC, January 11, 1924, 6; January 25, 1924, 4; February 1, 1924, 6.

57. Grant to Secretary of State, October 14, 1924, 711.129/13, (M314, roll 28), RG 59, NACP.

58. Advertisement, SDU, January 2, 1922, 8; Schantz, "Mexicali Rose," 405–12. During this period, promoters increasingly incorporated other exotic performances, cuisines, and comparisons into their offerings for border tourists. For instance, the Vernon Club featured hula dancers, the Garden Café offered French and Italian dinners, and the Agua Caliente Resort and Casino called itself "America's Deauville." Advertisement, SDU, January 2, 1922, 8; postcard published by Western Publishing and Novelty Co, Los Angeles, in author's collection.

59. Advertisement, SDU, January 2, 1922, 8.

60. Frank Bohr, Consul, Mexicali, to Secretary of State, September 26, 1928, 812.4054/81, (M274, roll 148), RG 59, NACP.

61. Advertisements, SDU, September 13, 1920, 16; September 14, 1920, 10; September 15, 1920, 7; September 16, 1920, 7; January 2, 1925, 15; February 7, 1926, sports section, 4.

62. "Hotel de Seville Soon to Rise above Tijuana," SDU, June 3, 1928.

63. Report re: Development of Pleasure Resorts in the Ensenada District, September 30, 1929, 812.4061/8, (M274, roll 148), RG 59, NACP.

64. Price, *Tijuana*, 57.

65. "Report re: Development of Pleasure Resorts in the Ensenada District," *op. cit.*; Price, *Tijuana*, 57.

66. Von Struve to Secretary of State, November 28, 1922, 812.40622/25, (M274, roll 148), RG 59, NACP.

67. Grant to Secretary of State, October 14, 1924, *op. cit.*

68. Burdett to Secretary of State, August 8, 1921, 812.40622/16, (M274, roll 148), RG 59, NACP.

69. Arreola and Curtis, *Mexican Border Cities*, 77; Proffitt, *Tijuana*; Price, *Tijuana*; Piñera Ramírez and Ortiz Figueroa, eds., *Historia de Tijuana*, vol. 1; *Mexicali*, vol. 1.

70. Schantz, "Mexicali Rose," 66.

71. For Mexican moral reform movements, see Schantz, "Mexicali Rose"; C. de Baca, "Moral Renovation of the Californias"; French, *A Peaceful and Working People*; Bliss, "Science of Redemption."

72. As quoted in Piñera Ramírez and Ortiz Figueroa, eds., *Historia de Tijuana*, 1:100, author's translation.

73. Piñera Ramírez and Ortiz Figueroa, eds., *Historia de Tijuana*, 1:100–1; Schantz, "Mexicali Rose"; C. de Baca, "Moral Renovation of the Californias"; Vanderwood, *Juan Soldado*, 100; Taylor, "Wild Frontier," 219–21.

74. Secretary of State to Embassy, Mexico City, February 26, 1924, 812.40622/42, (M274, roll 148), RG 59, NACP.

75. Lincoln A. Ferris to Newton Baker, Secretary of War, August 1, 1919, 812.40622/4 (M274, roll 148), RG 59, NACP.

76. Ibid.

77. Webster to Hughes, September 3, 1928, 711.129/4, (M314, roll 28), RG 59, NACP; von Struve to Secretary of State Hughes, February 12, 1924, *op. cit.*; Henry Goddard Leach to Secretary of State Hughes, June 18, 1923, 711.129/2; Ashurst to Secretary of State Hughes, May 2, 1923, 711.129/1; W. Mellon, Secretary of the Treasury, to Secretary of State Hughes, April 19, 1924, 812.40622/74; all in (M274, roll 148), RG 59, NACP. "Rep. Swing Requests Mexican Treaty for 50-Mile Vice Zone," SDS, February 17, 1926.

78. According to one author, Obregón ordered the creation of a fifty-mile-wide "dry zone" along the northern border in 1923. Toro, *Mexico's "War" on Drugs*, 7–10. However, the continued growth of border vice districts and the persistence of American demands for just such a measure indicate that it either quickly lapsed or was simply not enforced.

79. French, *A Peaceful and Working People*; Bliss, "Science of Redemption."

80. Von Struve to Secretary of State, November 28, 1922, *op. cit.*

81. "Treaty Series, No. 732: Convention of the United States and Mexico to Prevent Smuggling and for Certain Other Objects," (Washington, D.C.: GPO, 1926), 711.129, (M314, roll 28), RG 59, NACP.

82. "Cantu Says No Export Duty on Cotton," CC, January 5, 1915. For a further discussion of the class implications of this policy, see Schantz, "Mexicali Rose," 165–66.

83. Schantz, "Mexicali Rose," 126–45; Schantz, "All Night at the Owl," 106; Bliss, "Science of Redemption."

84. "Governor Orders Closing of 52 Tijuana Saloons, Following Peteet Findings," SDU, February 15, 1926; "Close Saloons to Unescorted Women," SDET, February 16, 1926. For more on the events surrounding the Peteet suicides, see St. John, "Line in the Sand," 252–55; Cabeza de Baca and Cabeza de Baca, " 'Shame Suicides.' "

85. Von Struve to Secretary of State, November 28, 1922, *op. cit.*; "Letters Sent to Pres. Diaz—Chamber of Commerce Communication Which Will Explain Conditions across the Line," CC, September 30, 1909; *Mexicali*, 1:268–69; Taylor, "Wild Frontier," 212–18; Toro, *Mexico's "War" on Drugs*, 8–9; Schantz, "Mexicali Rose," 58–75.

86. Abelardo L. Rodríguez, *Memoria administrativa del gobierno del Distrito Norte de*

Baja California, 1924–1927 (Tijuana: Universidad Autónoma de Baja California, 1993), 279–82; Piñera-Ramírez and Ortiz Figueroa, eds., *Historia de Tijuana*, 1:114–29; Taylor, "Wild Frontier," 218–20.

87. William C. Burdett to Secretary of State, August 8, 1921, *op. cit.*; Rodríguez, *Memoria administrativa, op. cit.*, 279–82; Taylor, "Wild Frontier," 218–20; *Mexicali*, 1:268–69.

88. Resolution of the Calexico Rotary Club, May 10, 1923, 812.40622/27; Glasgow, Secretary of Calexico Klan, to Secretary of State Hughes, May 11, 1923, 812.40622/31; both in (M274, roll 148), RG 59, NACP.

89. Von Struve to Secretary of State, n.d., 812.40622/37, (M274, roll 148), RG 59, NACP. See also L. D. McCartney to Calvin Coolidge, September 25, 1923, 812.40622/35; Ashurst to Secretary of State, April 1, 1924, 812.40622/89; A. W. Mellon to Secretary of State, April 19, 1924, 812.40622/74; and other letters in (M274, roll 148), RG 59, NACP.

90. By 1929, ports of entry along the U.S.-Mexico border had a variety of closing hours. All ports in Arizona, New Mexico, and Texas (with the exception of El Paso and San Luis) closed at midnight. The line closed at 9 p.m. in El Paso and Calexico, 7 p.m. in San Luis, and 6 p.m. in Andrade and Tijuana. See Secretary of State to Embassy Mexico City, February 26, 1924, *op. cit.*; "Early Border Closing Is Now In Effect," SDET, February 18, 1926; "Tijuana Hopes Ban Will End," SDS, February 18, 1926; RCT, Division of Mexican Affairs, to Clark, February 23, 1929, 711.12157/77, (M314, roll 20), RG 59, NACP. For the debates among Americans over nighttime closures, see St. John, "Line in the Sand," 278–79, 282–86, 290–94.

91. Clipping from *Excelsior* (Mexico City), June 17, 1929, attached to Dwight W. Morrow to Secretary of State, June 17, 1929, 711.12157/125, (M314, roll 20), RG 59, NACP.

92. Mexicali Chamber of Commerce to U.S. President Herbert Hoover, June 11, 1929, 711.12157/99, (M314, roll 20), RG 59, NACP.

93. Tia Juana Chamber of Commerce to U.S. President Herbert Hoover, June 18, 1929, 711.12157/122, (M314, roll 20), RG 59, NACP.

94. About Rodríguez's resistance, see St. John, "Line in the Sand," 287–90; von Struve to Secretary of State, March 8, 1924, 812.40622/47, (M274, roll 148, RG 59), NACP; von Struve to Secretary of State, March 31, 1924, 812.40622/65, (M274, roll 148), RG 59, NACP; Rodríguez to General Manager of the Tijuana & Tecate Railway Co., June 8, 1929, 711.12157/102, (M314, roll 20), RG 59, NACP; Mercier, SD & AZ RR, to Stimson, June 11, 1929, 711.12157/102, (M314, roll 20), RG 59, NACP; Chas. W. Doherty to Secretary of State, September 18, 1929, 711.12157/152, (M314, roll 20), RG 59, NACP.

95. Von Struve to Secretary of State, March 31, 1924, 812.40622/65, (M274, roll 148), RG 59, NACP; "Agua Caliente Premier Pleasure Resort of America," SDU, January 1, 1930; Advertisement, SDU, January 1, 1931, 5; "Hotel de Seville Soon to Rise Above Tijuana," SDU, June 3, 1928.

96. Despite this decline, tourism remained central to Tijuana's economy. Taylor, "Wild Frontier," 219–23; Arreola and Curtis, *Mexican Border Cities*, 77–117.

Laura Isabel Serna

Cinema on the U.S.-Mexico Border
American Motion Pictures and Mexican Audiences,
1896–1930

On August 11, 1927, the Mexican national weekly *México en Rotograbado* referred to the opening of a movie theater, the Cine Alcázar in Ciudad Juárez, Chihuahua, as a "patriotic act." The magazine lauded the cinema's proprietors (the Calderón brothers, Rafael and Enrique, and their associate Juan Salas Porras) for their activities "in favor of cultural diffusion."[1] Ciudad Juárez, just across the U.S.-Mexico border from El Paso, Texas, was far from the seat of Mexican political, social, and cultural power—Mexico City—and yet, the activities of its citizenry, as the *México en Rotograbado* article suggests, were perceived as contributing to the country's modernization and progress. In northern Mexico, as in the country's capital, motion picture exhibition and consumption formed part of a set of social practices that promoted education, signified modernity, and contributed to the nation-building project, despite the fact that most of the films being distributed and exhibited were products of U.S. film studios.[2]

Along the U.S.-Mexico border, these nation-building activities extended across from Mexico and into the United States. For example, in addition to owning a circuit of movie theaters in northern Mexico, the Calderón brothers and Juan Salas Porras (and other Mexican entrepreneurs) also owned movie theaters and film-related businesses that served the large Mexican population in El Paso, Texas, and the surrounding area.[3] These movie theaters that served the Mexican community in south Texas formed part of Mexican cinematic culture (a cultural formation composed of exhibition, the social space of the movie theater, and the films themselves). Though technically in the United States, these cinemas constituted a transnational social space, parallel to Anglo film culture, that contributed to Mexico's postrevolutionary nation-building project, a project that included Mexicans living on both sides of the border.[4]

This contention runs counter to scholarship that characterizes U.S. mass culture solely as an instrument of cultural imperialism and Americanization. Narratives of Mexican national cinema generally acknowledge the predominance of U.S. film in Mexico while focusing on the few nationally produced silent films as early evidence of an authentic Mexican film culture and precursor to the Golden Age of Mexican cinema (typically dated from the mid-1930s to the 1940s).[5] Even Aurelio de los Reyes's magisterial two-volume social history of cinema in Mexico from 1896–1920, *Cine y sociedad*, which pays the most attention to the presence of U.S. film in Mexico, dwells primarily on the activities of the national industry.[6]

Similarly, most scholars of Chicano history have perceived cinema as a peripheral part of immigrant life that was antithetical to migrants' "traditional" culture or as a pastime engaged in primarily by their second-generation children.[7] For example, in his social history of the Mexican community in El Paso, historian Mario T. García notes the increasing popularity of motion pictures among Mexican audiences in El Paso in the 1920s but leaves unexamined their role in community life and fails to contextualize motion picture exhibition in the transnational commercial culture that characterized the region. American films, he writes, functioned as "an acculturating influence" for Mexican audiences, exposing them to "American material and cultural values and mores."[8] Thus, for García, motion picture exhibition functioned solely as an Americanizing force, rather than, for example, constituting a part of Mexico's experience of modern life.

The consumption of U.S. motion pictures could, though it seems paradoxical, nurture Mexican national identity. Thus, rather than assuming that the mere presence of U.S. cultural formations—in this case silent cinema—indicates cultural hegemony, I focus on the local and national factors that influenced the social meanings that Mexicans living along the border in the twenties created out of the consumption of U.S. mass culture. First, I offer a brief history of early motion picture exhibition in El Paso and Ciudad Juárez. Then I examine how the Mexican entrepreneurs who purposefully created motion picture exhibition venues for Mexican audiences on the U.S. side of the border positioned themselves as agents of modernity and social progress. Finally, I consider the ways in which cinema exhibition in Mexican theaters in

El Paso connected border residents not only to American mass culture but also to processes of modernization at the heart of postrevolutionary Mexican nation building.[9]

While much has been written about the border as a site of spectacle, where scenes of violence and racial difference were packaged for Anglo audiences, we know far less about the experience of moviegoing for local Mexican audiences.[10] While conducting research for this essay, I found myself at the City of El Paso's historic preservation office with a list of addresses that had been the sites of Mexican movie theaters in the 1920s. I was told no one had ever asked about these properties and was directed to a map of the historical district of El Paso. Besides one well-known theater, El Colón, the history of Mexican moviegoing in El Paso fell, literally, outside of the boundaries of the city's official historical memory. Through this preliminary study of Mexican movie exhibition in El Paso, I hope to offer a corrective to this neglect, even if we can only catch opaque glimpses of borderland Mexican audiences' reception of U.S. film and film culture.

Early Motion Picture Exhibition along the U.S.-Mexico Border

Although Anglo entrepreneurs introduced moving pictures in some borderland cities, including El Paso, before 1900, it was itinerant Mexican exhibitors who brought what would constitute Mexican cinema culture to the borderlands. After Lumière representatives introduced the *cinématographe* at Mexico City's Droguería Plateros (a drugstore on Plateros St.) in 1896, sixteen moving-picture theaters quickly sprouted up in the capital, in addition to thirty *jacalones* (temporary structures dedicated to cinema exhibition placed in public spaces). Curious and (most likely) upper-middle-class *juarenses* who were anxious to see the new invention attended a moving-picture exhibition in the fall of 1896 at El Paso's Myar Opera House. Several years passed before Mexican audiences on the border had the chance to view other offerings.[11] As the vogue for moving pictures in Mexico City faded, entrepreneurs began to seek audiences outside of the capital, fanning out across the provinces.[12] Where there were theaters—usually in any city or large town of consequence—they arranged to offer short runs of *vistas* they obtained from dealers in Mexico City or through connections abroad. When they could, exhibitors took the railroads introduced as part of the Porfiriato's modernizing efforts, but it was not uncommon for them to ride horses or mules, or even go on foot to reach out-of-the-way places, including the cities, towns, *rancherías*, haciendas, and pueblos along the northern border.

Northern routes of itinerant Mexican film exhibitors, 1897–1908. Based on maps in Aurelio de Los Reyes's *Cine y sociedad en México, 1896–1930* (1996).

Itinerant exhibitors whose circuits reached the northern border typically crossed into the United States in quest of Mexican audiences. As the film historian Aurelio de los Reyes's careful research shows, one such exhibitor, Carlos Mongrand, a French immigrant to Mexico, went from Chihuahua through Ciudad Juárez to Hachita, New Mexico, and Douglas, Arizona. Moving west, he passed through the Sonoran towns of Agua Prieta, Cananea, and Naco, before entering the United States again to show films in Bisbee and Nogales, Arizona. After traveling along the Pacific coast of Mexico as far south as Mazatlán, he retraced his route along the border, giving mostly Mexican audiences another opportunity to see his stock of films, which may have been augmented by new titles he was sent while on the road. Other exhibitors, including Federico Bovi, regularly covered Piedras Negras, Nuevo Laredo, Ciudad Juárez, and Matamoros, in addition to visiting small towns in the southwestern United States. Likewise, Enrique Moulinié went as far north as the Sonoran border town Nogales. Guillermo Becerril and the Stahl brothers went from Mazatlán, to Hermosillo, and finally Chihuahua, though their exact routes are unclear.[13] In all, it is likely that some settlements hosted several different itinerant exhibitors, who would have screened moving pictures made in European and U.S. studios.

The itinerant exhibitors' activities followed long-standing patterns of the circulation of popular entertainment. Anecdotal evidence indicates that lantern slide shows and panoramas circulated, at least at the annual Feria de Juárez, before itinerant film exhibitors began making Ciudad Juárez and El Paso stopping points on their routes. Theatrical troupes, circuses, and other attractions traveled similar circuits, often (as itinerant movie exhibitors would do later) following the calendar of local religious celebrations.[14] The programs of these itinerant entertainers ensured that Mexican audiences along the border were exposed, at least periodically, to motion pictures, and that this exposure constituted not a radical break with popular culture but rather continuity in terms of the conditions under which they were presented.

Between 1896 and 1910, U.S. cinematic culture in El Paso was similar to that found in Ciudad Juárez: it also emanated from a national commercial center, New York City and its environs, and was a novelty act. Initially theater managers and itinerant exhibitors incorporated moving pictures into existing entertainment spectacles, considering it just another act in their repertoire. However, El Paso, the larger and wealthier of the twin border cities, had many more entertainment venues that drew audiences from both sides of the border. In the 1880s and 1890s, after the railroad arrived (1881) and El Paso gained importance as a commercial hub, saloons, casinos, and dance halls vied with legitimate theater houses such as the National Theater, Schultz Opera House, and the Myar Opera House, which showcased live theater and vaudeville. This thriving entertainment scene garnered the city the tag "the Broadway of the Southwest." After civic reformers successfully campaigned to rid El Paso of gambling and prostitution (which did not eradicate these activities, but only moved them over the border), some El Paso entertainment impresarios began to offer the public movies instead of vice. For example, in 1905, when the city prohibited gambling, a popular gaming establishment called the Wig Wam became a nickelodeon. Soon, theaters such as the Bijou, the Lyric, the Majestic, and the Crawford offered combined programs of vaudeville, stock theater, and motion pictures. The less elaborate second-run theaters like the OK, the Iris, the Grecian, the Unique, and the Princess began showing motion pictures almost exclusively.

It was only after the turn of the century that motion pictures were exhibited on a regular basis in Ciudad Juárez. In 1903, the city council agreed to underwrite the construction of a theater, in part in the hopes of persuading *juarenses* to spend their leisure dollars in Juárez rather than across the border in El Paso.[15] Used for a variety of purposes—theater, *zarzuela* (light opera), concerts, official meetings, civic celebrations, and film exhibition—the Teatro-Juárez became a central part of public and community life. By the end of the decade, however, as movie exhibition had overtaken almost every other use, the building became known simply as Cine Juárez. Two different companies, one managed by local businessman Silvio Lacoma and the other by a company called the Empresa Cinematógrafo y Variedades, rented the theater for stretches at a time to offer motion picture programs. Shortly after the Battle of Juárez (1911), two additional cinemas, neither as luxurious nor well designed as the Cine Juárez, sprung up in Ciudad Juárez—the Cine Azteca (built in 1912) and the Cine Anahuac (built in 1913).[16] Over the course of the first two decades of the twentieth century, investment in tourist venues like saloons, curio shops, and a bullring, along with increasing political and economic instability, served to stymie investment in theaters for locals in Ciudad Juárez.[17]

Within this competitive context, showmen in Ciudad Juárez tried to distinguish their programs from those found across the border. They often emphasized the continental origins of their pictures, in order to differentiate them from the westerns or comedies screened in El Paso. Sometimes exhibitors directly made competitive comparisons: the Empresa promised its motion pictures were "superior" and "the admission much cheaper than in El Paso, Texas." Furthermore, combining motion pictures with the staging of zarzuela appealed to audience members who were already fans of variety and theatrical troupes popular across the Southwest.[18] The activities of itinerant exhibitors, referred to as tragaleguas (literally "league eaters"), and local entrepreneurs like the Empresa Company and Lacoma, ensured that residents of the northern border region were not left out of Mexico's growing cinematic culture. At the border, emergent Mexican and U.S. cinematic cultures met and overlapped.

Although initially El Paso and Juárez residents mingled at movie exhibitions, by the First World War cinematic spaces were differentiated. Reports suggest that an audience drawn from both sides of the Rio Grande watched the first moving picture exhibition in El Paso in 1896.[19] Likewise, historian Mario T. García found no evidence that "the early movie houses such as the Crawford, the Grand, the Little Wigwam, and the Bijou specifically excluded Mexicans during the first years of the twentieth century."[20] During and after the Mexican revolution, however, movie exhibition on the border's binational character shifted. El Paso's Anglo and Mexican populations increasingly went to different theaters, and when Juárez residents crossed the border, they tended to find themselves in "Mexican" theaters. The growth of "Mexican" theaters in El Paso accelerated during the revolutionary years, perhaps due to the large numbers of displaced Mexicans—wealthy expatriates and poorer refugees alike—living in the area. Signal among these theaters were The Mexican (ca. 1908), Teatro Cristal (ca. 1913), Silvio Lacomo's Teatro Estrella (ca. 1913), and Félix Padilla's and Pedro Maseo's Imperial Theater (1915) in East El Paso. Mexican workers living in Smeltertown, the local lead-processing plant's company town, could attend the imaginatively named Smelter Theater, which was in operation off and on from 1914 through 1926, or a theater owned and operated by Ramón Barca in 1916.[21] After the revolution, the two cities' Anglo and Mexican populations occupied clearly marked, separate cinematic spaces.

Mexican Theaters in El Paso: Exhibitors as Agents of Modernity

When the silent screen star Pola Negri stopped in El Paso on her way from Los Angeles to New York City in 1927, both the *El Paso Daily Herald* and *El Continental*, the region's leading Spanish-language newspaper, interviewed her.[22] The bilingual publicity buzz around the celebrity's quick visit suggests that Mexican and Anglo audiences along the border were equally invested in film culture, sharing a great deal in terms of their tastes in films and stars. Nevertheless, the interest in Negri developed in two distinct spheres of cinematic culture, determined by the racial, ethnic, and class distinctions drawn between El Paso and Ciudad Juárez residents. A distinct Mexican audience emerged over the course of the 1920s, in part due to the effect of hardening racial, ethnic, and national lines between communities in the borderlands.

With the end of the Mexican Revolution in sight, U.S. film distributors recognized that "a unique market" of Mexican ticket buyers had taken shape across the Southwest, especially along the border. As *Moving Picture World*, an industry publication, declared in 1918, "the peace which reigns from Matamoros to Juárez"—that is, along the border—was nurturing a "good transborder trade" in film.[23] Mexican exhibitors from northern Mexico went to Texas to obtain film stock and other equipment, American entrepreneurs invested in Mexican theaters, and distributors took into consideration Mexican sensibilities. For example, *The Vitagraph Family*, a weekly publication of the Vitagraph Company, praised the manager of the Vitagraph Exchange in Dallas for his attention to the "number of theatres on the Mexican border which cater strictly to Spanish audiences."[24] The manager of the Aztec Theater in the Texas border town of Eagle Pass warned that "should a border town house run a film which in the least reflects upon the Mexican people, he's immediately in trouble."[25]

Mainstream theaters in El Paso likely practiced de facto segregation—discouraging certain types of patrons based on appearance or class or relegating Mexican patrons to the galleries that were typically reserved for African Americans.[26] Regardless of the severity or prevalence of segregation, a clear market existed for theaters dedicated to serving Mexican audiences. When Mexican theaters opened, movie attendance increased among Mexicans.[27] By 1925, a large enough audience existed to support eleven Mexican movie theaters in El Paso.[28] These theaters, which ran the gamut in terms of size and elegance, served elite Mexican expatriates, the large working class from Mexican communities on both sides of the border, and poorer refugees who belonged to neither class.

The emergence of theaters that exclusively served Mexican audiences reflected the U.S. tendency, particularly marked in Texas and other former states of the Confederacy, toward de jure and de facto racial segregation. In the United States, the cinema, like other spaces of consumer culture, became a "theater of racial difference" where the nation's racial pecking order was imposed and resisted.[29] For example, in a study of Mexican communities across Texas conducted in 1920, a researcher noted that many of the "better" movie theaters discouraged Mexican patronage with signs that read "Mexicans not wanted."[30] Motion picture theaters in cities like Dallas and Austin were reported as having "one side exclusively for Mexicans," and "even educated cultured Mexicans" were "sometimes roughly ordered to stay on their side." Mexican audiences not only resisted this expression of white supremacy but also jockeyed for status, distancing themselves from African Americans through protests and boycotts. In one Gulf Coast community, members of a Mexican mutual benefit society agreed to boycott a local theater as long as its management insisted on seating them with African Americans. In a neighboring town, fliers protesting a similar policy succeeded in convincing the theater manager to allow Mexicans to sit with Anglos.[31] The conciliatory responses of some movie-theater owners point to the fact that in some cases, particularly in smaller towns, they could not afford to lose their Mexican patronage.

As one investigator suggested, the racial and class conflict beneath the surface, which he delicately called "this difficulty," could be "avoided when practicable by separate theaters in the Mexican quarter."[32] In El Paso, theaters opened by Mexican film exhibitors and entertainment entrepreneurs joined other commercial establishments owned by a mix of Mexican and European immigrant merchants who sold goods and services to the Mexican residents of both El Paso and Ciudad Juárez. Most were located in the blocks closest to the

"Mexican man in front of movie theater," San Antonio, Texas, March, 1939. Photograph by Russell Lee, Library of Congress, Prints and Photographs Division, FSA/OWI Collection, LC-DIG-fsa-8a25630.

The two signs near the theater's entrance, in the photograph's background, are in Spanish, which, along with the photograph's caption, suggest that this was one of the hundreds of "Mexican theaters" in the border region. Although the poster advertises a Hollywood film with distinctly American stars, audiences in this theater likely would have maintained a strong sense of Mexican identity while viewing *City Streets* (Columbia, 1938) and other films produced in the United States.

international border crossing, part of the Mexican barrio known as El Chihuahuita, with a few scattered east of downtown El Paso. The two largest Mexican theaters, The Colón and The Alcázar, were, for example, both located on the 300 block of South El Paso Street, whose array of small shops over the course of the 1920s became increasingly Mexican. By 1928, two-thirds of the block's shops were owned by Mexicans, some of whom owned several businesses.[33] Silvio Lacoma, who began operating two theaters in Ciudad Juárez a decade earlier, built The Colón after finding that his El Paso theaters, The Cristal and The Estrella, were lucrative operations.

The businessmen like Lacoma who opened these cinemas were part of a transnational commercial class. Their enterprises spread across the border region into northern Mexico and the southwestern United States, and sometimes linked the borderlands to New York City, Mexico City, and Los Angeles in transnational chains of commerce. The Calderón–Salas Porras consortium and the activities of Juan de la Cruz Alarcón illustrate the commercial possibilities of distribution—whether of consumer goods, musical instruments, musical recordings, printed works or movies, all available in large quantities due to

Teatro Colón, El Paso, Texas, 1980. Photograph by David Kaminsky, Library of Congress, Prints and Photographs Division, HABS TEX, 71-ELPA, 4–32.

The concentration of businesses around the Teatro Colón oriented toward a Mexican market segment increased over the half century since 1930. The advertised movie, *El Chicano justiciero* (1974, 1977), is an example of the Mexican film industry's increased attention, even in run-of-the-mill westerns, to immigration issues during the 1970s and 1980s. The movie was filmed in northern Mexico near the border.

the marvels of mass production—to a Mexican market in the border region and beyond.

Before becoming involved in motion picture exhibition, the Calderón brothers, Rafael and Juan, owned a Ciudad Chihuahua department store, El Nuevo Mundo, that specialized in the distribution of imported dry goods from Europe and the United States. Their future partner in the film business, the young Juan Salas Porras, was the store's manager.[34] In addition to their retail business, the Calderón brothers also held an interest in Calderón Hermanos Sucesores, Inc., the oldest house of Mexican music in the United States, which sold Columbia gramophones, musical instruments, and records in Texas. To capitalize this business, they sold shares to groups of "completely Mexican" investors.[35] In the late teens, the three associates decided to add motion picture exhibition in both Ciudad Chihuahua and Ciudad Juárez to their array of commercial enterprises.

The Calderón–Salas Porras consortium pursued a simultaneously modern and nationalist approach to cinema exhibition. Their entrance into the field involved a study-tour in San Antonio, where they learned how the business operated and bought their first manual film projector. They then proceeded to acquire a set of cinemas in Chihuahua—the Alcázar, Apollo, Ideal, and Estrella—and took over the Teatro Centenario, a former live stage that had, like the Teatro Juárez, been adapted for use as a cinema.[36] In February of 1922, the company held a grand opening for Ciudad Juárez's Teatro-Cine Alcázar, which had previously been the extremely "popular" (in the sense of appealing to the working classes) Cinema Anahuac.[37] Over the next five years they opened more theaters in Ciudad Chihuahua and the northern parts of the states of Zacatecas and Durango. They sent films to each of the theaters in the circuit in turn, thus maximizing their investment in film rental costs. The crowning moment of their cinematic endeavors came a few years later, with the construction of the new Alcázar Theater on the corner of Second and Victoria streets in Ciudad Juárez, the project praised in *México en Rotograbado*. The exhibition of the monumental epic *Ben-Hur*, starring Durango native Ramón Navarro, marked the theater's grand opening in January 1927. Unlike many other theaters, the Alcázar had been constructed specifically as a *movie* theater with padded seats, security lights, emergency exits, sanitary facilities, a candy counter, and automated projectors.[38] At the opening festivities, the respected local poet and literary critic Manuel Roche y Chabre welcomed the public to the new theater with a prepared speech. While the text is lost to us today, we can imagine that he might have celebrated the modern characteristics of the theater and praised yet another example of the region's development and culture.

The conviction that film culture belonged in the company of other modern cultural practices can be seen in the ways that the Calderón–Salas Porras circuit combined movie exhibition with other cultural events and expressions. All of their theaters featured vaudeville, touring stock theater, and performances by renowned Mexican actors, writers, and playwrights. Their new theaters adopted a modern architectural aesthetic that made use (as did many of the most up-to-date movie palaces in the United States, such as the Aztec Theater in San Antonio) of pre-Columbian motifs and design elements, which in Mexico referenced the country's glorious, if mythologized, indigenous past.[39] For example, the 1,600-seat Cine El Azteca, built in Ciudad Chihuahua in 1929 under the direction of Mexican architects Manuel O'Reilly and Carlos Arróniz, combined this aesthetic with a nationalist scene depicting the founding of the city of Tenochtitlán (Mexico City) on the theater's curtain.[40] The

Cine Azteca, Ciudad Chihuahua, Chihuahua, Mexico, 2006. Photograph by Nahum Ordoñez, courtesy of photographer.

The pre-Columbian motifs that graced the theater's façade are still visible on the building, which is now used as a bank.

sounds of the theater's house band, the Aztec Jazz Boys, forged another symbolic link between Mexico's pre-Columbian past and another marker of modernity, jazz music.

The Calderón–Salas Porras outfit faced competition from Juan de la Cruz Alarcón, whose distribution company, International Pictures Company (also known as the International Amusement Company), distributed U.S.-produced silent films throughout Mexico from its offices in New York, El Paso, and Mexico City. By 1919, Alarcón, a former newspaperman, and his associates owned six theaters in El Paso and were the exclusive distributors for Vitagraph productions in Mexico, Guatemala, and El Salvador, making the company the only legitimate source for Vitagraph films in the region.[41] While the Calderón brothers concentrated on a diverse set of commercial enterprises ranging from retail to entertainment, Alarcón situated himself as the leader of film distribution and exhibition not only in the border region, but also in Mexico and Central America.

Alarcón saw the professionalization of the motion picture business—distribution and exhibition—as the key to the successful use of the cinema as an agent of modernity. Like the Calderóns, he made a careful, professional study of the Mexican market for U.S. films, sending an employee on a trip through

Circuito Alcazar logo, 1931.
Engraving redrawn by
Creative Design Resources,
original courtesy of the
Bancroft Library, University
of California, Berkeley.

The Calderón Brothers'
logo, found on their business stationery, shows the
geographic reach of their
cinema interests.

Mexico to get "exact information as to what the people want in picture shows, how much they will pay, and so on." Alarcón declared in an El Paso newspaper that chief among his purposes in entering the movie exhibition and distribution business was the "education and democratization of the Mexican people by means of film." He confidently claimed that in terms of education, which was what he thought "the Mexican people need," cinema was in a position to do "something . . . worth while—more than the government perhaps." Its democratic space, in which the "lower, middle, and higher classes" could mix, would expose the "peon" to members of the "better class," thus inspiring the working-class moviegoer to "take more pride in himself, dress better and more cleanly." Selective programming choices that included the latest features and the most popular stars would only add to the uplifting social space of the cinema.[42] For example, despite the sold-out houses for Vitagraph series such as *Barreras infranqueables* (*Uncrossable Barriers*) and *El torbellino* (*The Whirlwind*), Alarcón decided to "continue to . . . improve the cinema shows in the Mexican theaters," by screening "art films" with the "notable actresses of the Select Pictures Corp."[43]

The Calderón–Salas Porras consortium and the activities of Juan de la Cruz Alarcón illustrate how despite transnational business practices promoting a primarily U.S.-made product, Mexican theaters contributed to the development of a distinct version of *mexicanidad*, rather than an Americanized class of Mexicans. Alarcón and the Calderón brothers capitalized on and contributed to a process of modernization in Mexico that counted commercialized leisure among the hallmarks of civilization and progress (much as did many of their Anglo counterparts). A strong nationalist rhetoric linking the growth of commercial culture with the future of the nation overlaid their vision. In their view, cinema as a leisure activity educated, uplifted, and encouraged patriotism in audience members, while as a business it contributed to Mexico's economic modernization.

Alarcón's International Picture Co. and the Calderón–Salas Porras outfits dominated the movie-exhibition business in the El Paso–Ciudad Juárez area, but several other entrepreneurs tried to enter the market. For example, in 1918 Comacho de León and Company began building a theater "up to date in every particular," with six hundred seats "of the most up to date pattern, similar to those used in several El Paso theaters," which would be the fourth theater in the Plaza de Constitución area of Ciudad Juárez.[44] Likewise, in 1919, Lacoma and Quinn Company, owners of the Estrella and the Cristal, which served El Paso's Mexican community, announced the construction of a new theater on the southwest corner of Second and El Paso Streets, which would combine "the newest ideas in theater construction" with the seating plan "used in the best class theaters in Mexico."[45]

Though these announcements were made in the English-language press, the theaters were clearly marked as distinctly Mexican spaces. In announcing the new theater to be built in Ciudad Juárez, the newspaper's account focused on the process used to create subtitles for the intertitles of the films shown in Juárez. Similarly, Lacoma and Quinn's new theater, with all of its architectural and technological wonders, was destined to offer entertainment "mostly by artists of the Latin races" for Mexican audiences.[46] Inaugurated with combined programming that mixed the "highest quality" motion pictures with live entertainment, the theater was leased in 1921 to a Mr. Goldberg, owner of the Standard Candy Company and a part owner of the Follies Review Company, which performed at the Texas Grand in El Paso.[47] By the mid-1920s, the theater had reverted to Mexican ownership when it became part of the Calderón–Salas Porras exhibition circuit, the Circuito Alcázar.

This theater, the Colón, would become a centerpiece in the lives of El Paso's Mexican community members (despite English-language journalists' jabs at the name, which they read with an American accent). By 1927, Spanish-language journalists were describing the Calderón brothers with laudatory adjectives such as "active" and "wise." Their business was praised for bringing

Teatro Colón, El Paso, Texas, 1930. Photograph courtesy Viviana Garcia Bresne.

Employees of the Calderón Brothers stand outside the Teatro Colón on South El Paso Street with crates containing a new Western Electric sound projector—described as *"modernísimo y costoso"* (very modern and costly). They planned to inaugurate it by showing *The Hollywood Revue* (Metro Goldwyn Mayer, 1929).

"not only good films, but also spectacles worthy of the Mexican Colony [in El Paso]."[48] Providing Mexican audiences with modern entertainment in architectural spaces specifically coded as modern not only filled a market niche neglected by Anglo entrepreneurs, it also positioned cinema owners, along with other Mexican businessmen, as agents of modernity.

Border Audiences and Mexican Modernity

Though the activities of Mexican exhibitors offer us a picture of the social function they hoped cinema would perform, we know far less about the ways in which Mexican audiences responded to the films they saw. Most theaters in El Paso and Ciudad Juárez operated without pause throughout the 1920s due to the frequency with which Mexican spectators went to the cinema. In large urban centers like El Paso and in small towns across Texas, movie theaters became centers of both recreation and community life for their Mexican audiences. The Colón and the Cine Alcázar were considered "favored center[s] of diversions" for El Paso's Mexican community.[49] Moviegoing, the "favorite diversion," went hand in hand with activities promoting national and community values. In El Paso–Juárez, for example, Mexican residents were urged not to miss William Duncan, "the king of courage," appearing in *El torbellino*, "the last word in dramatic series," or the three rolls of film taken during the recent *fiestas patrias* (independence day celebrations), presumably in Ciudad Juárez, which featured "all the Mexicans."[50] The Teatro Julimes, in Canutillo, Texas, slightly northwest of El Paso, not only showed motion pictures but also doubled as a community center that hosted events and celebrations, like the 1924 "Función Teatral a Beneficio de la Alianza Hispano-Americana" (Theatrical Benefit for the Hispanic American Alliance), which featured local talent dancing, singing, reciting poetry and prose, and a "beautiful" seven-part film.[51] These community-building activities—functions offered at "precios populares" (popular prices) or in support of local public works and charity projects—harkened back to the practices of early exhibitors, who, following their predecessors, circus and fair performers, had often ingratiated themselves with sometimes recalcitrant local elites by contributing a portion of their profits to local causes.[52] The social space of Mexican theaters offered the chance to celebrate and build national identity; in the U.S., this form of community building took on an oppositional character due to the prevalence of racist attitudes and actions directed toward Mexicans.

The social space of the cinema also offered Mexican audiences in the El Paso–Juárez region a place to rehearse the modern cultural styles they saw on the screen. For example, films and events that took place in movie theaters promoted the new ideals of womanhood. This was no less true in the El Paso–Juárez region than in Mexico City. In March of 1920, for example, the "elegant" Teatro Rex in El Paso exhibited the photographs of contestants in a beauty contest sponsored by a local Spanish-language newspaper. In this instance, the aspirant beauty queens occupied a similar set of social spaces as movie stars, whose images regularly adorned the entrances and lobbies of movie theaters.[53] Likewise, the cinemas of El Paso's Mexican community formed the backdrop for dramatic scenes from real life, which highlighted changing family and social relations. In 1923, it was reported that a sixteen-year-old candy store employee had poisoned herself after being scolded by her mother for chatting with her boyfriend in El Paso's Cine Alcázar.[54] Other reports made it clear that the new cultural styles that were causing a stir in Mexico City and other cities were showing up on the border as well. For example, a 1924 article published on the front page of the El Paso Spanish-language newspaper *La Patria* sensationalized the scandals caused by women bobbing their hair and the trend among men who cut their hair "wanting to imitate Valentino."[55]

While the encounter with new cultural styles on the screen gave rise to imitation, other cinematic representations—especially the mostly stereotypical

Alameda Theater located at 3301 Alameda St., El Paso, ca. 1918. Photograph by Otis Aultman, courtesy Aultman Collection, A257, El Paso Public Library.

After the Alameda Theater opened, a mixed clientele patronized it. It was located a few blocks down the street from the Imperial Theater, which Félix Padilla and his partner Pedro Maseo ran from 1916 to 1922. According to the *El Paso Herald*, in 1917 the Alameda showed a photoplay about the battle of Carrizal, a failed expedition into Mexico of black U.S. soldiers from segregated units. This film and others like it may have added to the tensions between Mexican and African American residents of El Paso.

depiction of Mexico and Mexicans—clearly rankled Mexicans' patriotic sensibilities.[56] A unique film project begun in the late 1920s by El Paso film exhibitor Félix Padilla and completed by his son Edmundo offers further clues about how Mexicans received such representations.[57] After operating a movie theater for a short time in the teens and early 1920s, Félix Padilla turned his hand to itinerant exhibition. It was during this period that he, with Edmundo's help, began production of his own film, *La venganza de Pancho Villa*. Padilla used the materials he had on hand—American feature films from the teens, Mexican documentary footage of the revolution, still photographs, and some very brief scenes he shot himself—to tell his own version of the revolutionary general's life.

Félix Padilla undertook his only venture as a filmmaker a decade after U.S. film companies had released countless newsreels and dramas about the Revolution, casting the revolutionary leader "Pancho Villa" in starring roles. These films reflected the U.S. government's changing stance toward the war and its protagonists, while at the same time feeding American audiences' hunger for news about the conflict and reinforcing long-held racial and cultural stereotypes. While early portrayals of Villa tended to be positive, though still racialized, later films in which he took on the features of a villain reflected the shift of United States support toward other revolutionary leaders. Padilla's film, an example of what is called a "compilation film," went through a number of iterations, exemplified by the change of title from *Pancho Villa en Columbus* (*Pancho Villa in Columbus*), to *La venganza de guerillero* (*The Revenge of the Warrior*), to *Hazanas de Pancho Villa* (*Feats of Pancho Villa*), before Padilla finally settled on *La venganza de Pancho Villa* (*Pancho Villa's Vengeance*).[58] The narrative of the film—in its essence an action film—roughly recounts the life of Villa such that he appears as a nationalist hero, rather than as an emblematic figure whose rise from humble origins underscores a critical view of Mexican society as it was prior to and during the Revolution.

Padilla's film was never screened in Mexico City, the cosmopolitan center of Mexican political, social, and cultural life. It did, however, make the rounds across a wide swathe of northern Mexico and southeastern Texas. In addition to showing the film in small towns, perhaps borrowing a church wall or setting up a tent, Padilla rented the film to cinema owners in exchange for a percentage of the ticket sales. Members of audiences in places like Cárdenas, San Luís Potosí, Tampico, and Tamaulipas in Mexico, along with Big Spring and the town of Canutillo (just outside El Paso) in Texas, paid from five to forty cents to see the film. No mention of the film has been found in local newspapers, making it difficult to gauge the public's response. One theater owner wrote to Padilla in 1931 declaring that "the exhibition of your films [referring to the multiple reels] . . . during the present month of June has been a complete success." He was so pleased that he informed Padilla that he would have no problem "recommending them to all the theaters with Mexican clientele."[59]

That Padilla's film—in which a Pancho Villa, constructed out of recycled images, many of them stereotypical, was an avenger rather than a bandit—was popular with Mexican audiences on the border is no surprise. Mexicans on both sides of the border had witnessed the events of the Revolution at close range, including the U.S. preparations for possible intervention and the incursion of General Pershing's men into Mexican territory. Although it is incontestable that many Mexican audiences would have been receptive to the portrayal of Villa as avenger, Padilla's project also points to another direction in Mexican cinematic culture. Félix and Edmundo, like their perhaps more professional counterparts in Mexico City, offered border audiences alternative

Shooting movie near El Paso, ca. 1922. Photograph by Otis Aultman, courtesy Aultman Collection, A5056, El Paso Public Library.

There is little information about this photograph apart from the notes on the verso side of the print "Indians of N.A.—Apache (Geronimo's Group)." The oft-repeated representation of cowboys and Indians in U.S. and Hollywood film is but one example of how the discourses of race and nation provided fodder for cinematic narratives.

representations of Mexican history and other national subjects that drew on U.S. cinema's techniques and narrative practices. They created nationalist narratives out of a visual vocabulary with which their audiences were already familiar.

The way other national and racial groups were depicted in U.S. cinematic productions offered a foil against which Mexican filmmakers could create their own representations. As the national industry developed, the screen became another space for the construction of national and racial identities. Padilla's homegrown and regionally circulated film would find its industrialized and national counterparts in the productions of the Mexican film industry, based in the capital, which offered narratives and visions of national identity for domestic and international consumption. Padilla's filmmaking effort joined film distribution, exhibition, and consumption in the U.S.-Mexico borderlands as vital nationalistic instruments. Cinema—a cultural formation composed of exhibition, the social space of the movie theater, and the films themselves—was part of Mexico's own progress and modernization. In the space of the cinema, Mexican audiences affirmed their national identity as Mexican. They also experimented with the new gender ideals, modes of self-presentation, and social practices presented on the screen: each was a hallmark of the "modern" as it seeped into the lives of ordinary people. Nowhere was this process more freighted than in the border region, where a competing nationalism—Americanism—made strong and vigorous claims on all that was modern.

Cinema would continue to hold an important place in the cultural life of the border region, such that contemporary cultural critics celebrate what Claire Fox identifies as a "bi-national film culture unique to the U.S.-Mexico border region." She points in particular to "the region's uneven configuration of mass media" as partly responsible for this film culture.[60] Some of the businessmen involved in cinema exhibition in El Paso–Juárez between 1905 and 1930 used their experience and capital to promote the growth of a Mexican film industry: Juan de la Cruz Alarcón, for example, became a major early investor in the Compania Nacional Productora de Películas.[61] Though many smaller Mexican theaters folded and their buildings were converted to other uses, the Colón played an important role in the social and cultural life of El Paso's Mexican community, as did its competition across the street, the Alcázar. Each theater reliably and proudly showed Mexican films of the 1930s and 1940s, movies from the "golden age" of Mexican national cinema, alongside U.S.-produced fare, which included Hollywood's blockbusters. As the century progressed, cinema persisted as an important social space for the cultivation of modern Mexican identities, whether as entrepreneur, exhibitor, filmmaker, spectator, or consumer.

Abbreviations

CM	*Cine Mundial* (New York City)
CON	*El Continental* (El Paso)
EPH	*Herald* (El Paso, Texas)
EPMT	*Morning Times* (El Paso)
LRI	*La Revista Internacional* (Ciudad Juárez)
MPW	*Moving Picture World* (New York City)
MR	*México en Rotograbado* (Mexico City)
PAT	*La Patria* (El Paso)
REP	*La República* (El Paso)
TB	Silvestre Terrazas Collection, Bancroft Library, University of California, Berkeley
UNI	*El Universal* (Mexico City)
UT-CAH	Center for American History, University of Texas, Austin
VF	*Vitagraph Family* (New York City)

Notes

I am grateful to the David Rockefeller Center for Latin American Studies at Harvard University and the Ford Foundation Doctoral Fellowship Program for supporting the research for this essay. I also thank Alexis McCrossen for guiding this volume through conception to publication. Thank you also to the Arias family, Ernesto Chavez, Viviana García Bresne, and the staff of the Library Special Collections Department at the University of Texas, El Paso, especially Susan Novick.

Notes fully cite primary sources and specialized secondary sources. Full bibliographic details for all other citations are in the volume's selected bibliography.

1. "La empresa Calderón y Salas Porras ensancha a su campo de acción," MR, August 11, 1927.

2. In the 1920s American silent film dominated the Mexican market: 78 percent of the films screened in Mexico during this period came from U.S. film studios. Throughout the decade, an average of five hundred American titles were screened each year. María Luisa Amador and Jorge Ayala Blanco, *Cartelera cinematográfica, 1920–1929* (Mexico City: UNAM, 1999), 465–69.

3. I use the term "Mexican" to refer to both Mexican nationals and Mexican Americans. In *Walls and Mirrors*, historian David Gutiérrez uses the term "ethnic Mexicans" to refer to both these groups. Until the 1930s, most migrants thought of themselves as *mexicanos* rather than as Mexican Americans. While communities in regions with Mexican populations that preceded the Treaty of Guadalupe Hidalgo may have identified themselves as *hispanos* or *tejanos* or *nuevo mexicanos*, one of Mexico's first anthropologists, Manuel Gamio, observed that "Mexicans, though they may be American citizens of the second or third generations, nevertheless remained or were kept apart socially, and were almost always called Mexicans." Gamio, *Mexican Immigration*, 53. Certainly, before the emergence of organizations such as LULAC in the Southwest in the 1940s, consciousness of membership in an American "ethnic" group was quite rare and greatly overshadowed by consciousness of membership in the imagined community of "Mexico." The historian George J. Sánchez discusses the development of an ethnic Mexican American and later Chicano identity in *Becoming Mexican American*. See also Guerin-Gonzales, *Mexican Workers*.

4. "Mexican movie theater" more accurately describes the social composition of the audience served than "Spanish-language theater." Intertitles may have been in English or Spanish, or both languages. What is more, using language as the primary means of identifying these theaters obscures the U.S. origins of the films by suggesting that the films were made in Spanish or produced in Spanish-speaking countries.

5. This tendency can be located in the extensive body of literature that documents scant production and its protagonists, and in the historical narratives that have been produced about Mexican national cinema in general. On the former, see Federico Davalos Orozco and Esperanza Vazquez Bernal, *Filmografía general del cine mexicano (1906–1931)* (Puebla, Mexico: Universidad Autónoma de Puebla, 1985); Aurelio de los Reyes,

Los orígenes del cine en México (1896–1900) (Mexico City: Fondo de Cultura Económica, 1983). On the latter, see Emilio García Riera, *Historia del cine mexicano* (Mexico City: Secretaría de Educación Pública, 1986); Mora, *Mexican Cinema*.

6. Aurelio de los Reyes, *Cine y sociedad*, 2 volumes (Mexico City: UNAM, 1993 and 1996).

7. See, for example, Ruíz, "Flapper and the Chaperone," in *Out of the Shadows*; and Sánchez, *Becoming Mexican American*. George Sánchez writes that the Los Angeles–based film industry helped Mexicans living in Southern California in the 1920s to "retain old values, but also played a role in cultural change" (173).

8. García, *Desert Immigrants*, 208, 211–12.

9. Cynthia Farah Haines's unpublished manuscript (in the author's possession), "The Golden Age of the Silver Screen: Theatres and Film Exhibition in El Paso, Texas, 1896–1960s," is the only work to include what she calls "Spanish-language theaters" in accounts of El Paso's moviegoing history. Scattered sources and incomplete archival material compound the challenges of writing a social history of cinema in the borderlands. As Willivaldo Delgadillo and Maribel Limongi note in *Mirada desenterrada*, the history of cinema in the border region during this period is difficult to write, in part because state and municipal archives often fell victim to the vagaries of the Revolution and the ignorance (or zeal) of bureaucrats who disposed of old papers to make room in municipal archives (24). Getting at spectators' opinions about specific films or their experience of moviegoing is likewise difficult. The profession of film critic was in its infancy in the major metropolitan newspapers published in Mexico City and almost nonexistent in the provinces. Many times accounts of specific films were mere plot summaries or thinly disguised advertisements. See Miquel, *Por las pantallas*.

10. See Britton, *Revolution and Ideology*; Fox, *Fence and the River*; Samponaro and Vanderwood, *Border Fury*; Margarita de Orellana, *La mirada circular: el cine norteamericano de la Revolución Mexicana, 1911-1917* (Mexico City: Joaquin Mortiz, 1991).

11. Delgadillo and Limongi, *Mirada desenterrada*, 20.

12. The most comprehensive study of this period in Mexican cinema can be found in de los Reyes, *Cine y sociedad*, vol. 1, *op. cit.*

13. Ibid., 42–45.

14. Delgadillo and Limongi, in *Mirada desenterrada*, cite a local resident who remembered seeing such shows as a child at the annual *fería* (39). On the activities of Spanish-language theater troupes in Texas, see Ramírez, *Footlights across the Border*; Kanellos, *History of Hispanic Theatre*.

15. Archivo Historico de Ciudad Juárez, Actos de Cabildo, September 11, 1904.

16. Siegifrid F. Pallin, in business with a projectionist named Leonardo Lujan, owned the Cine Azteca. The wood structure burned to the ground about six months after it was built in November of 1912. Delgadillo and Limongi, *Mirada desenterrada*, 84.

17. Delgadillo and Limongi, *Mirada desenterrada*, 140.

18. LRI, May 6, 1910, cited in Delgadillo and Limongi, *Mirada desenterrada*, 85. On the *zarzuela* tradition in the United States, see Sturman, *Zarzuela*. On Spanish-language performance traditions in Texas, see Ramírez, *Footlights across the Border*.

19. Delgadillo and Limongi, *Mirada desenterrada*, 20.

20. García, *Desert Immigrants*, 211. Emphasis in original.

21. Haines, *Golden Age, op. cit.*, 19.

22. José M. Pena, "A ojo de pajaro," CON, July 8, 1927.

23. "Screen 'Coming Back' in Mexico," MPW, July 27, 1918, 527.

24. "Spanish Heralds," VF 12 (April 20, 1918), 32. See also "Down Rio Way," VF 12 (May 18, 1918), 48.

25. "Picture Theater Problems in Border Towns," MPW, January 26, 1918, 559.

26. The historian Wilbert H. Timmons observes that the Anglo commercial elite looked down on the Mexican working classes who made up the majority of El Paso's Mexican community (*El Paso*, 162).

27. García, *Desert Immigrants*, 211.

28. Romo, *Ringside Seat*, 180.

29. In *Making Whiteness*, the historian Grace Hale uses this phrase to describe the segregated South during Reconstruction, which she dates from 1890 to 1940 (284).

30. Social data on Mexican people in Fort Worth, Texas, gathered December 6–8, 1920, typescript, UT-CAH.

31. Taylor, *American-Mexican Frontier*, 252, 265.

32. National Conference Concerning Mexicans and Spanish-Americans in the United States, *Report of Commission on International and Interracial Factors in the Problem of Mexicans in the United States* (1926), 21. This document is in the UT-CAH archives.

33. This analysis is based on my study of the El Paso city directories from 1922 to 1928, which are held in the Special Collections of the University of Texas at El Paso.

34. The extent of the Calderón brothers' commercial holdings in Chihuahua is difficult to ascertain in comprehensive detail. According to their correspondence with newspaper publisher and member of the local elite Silvestre Terrazas, they held a range of businesses in addition to department stores and movie theaters. See Correspondence, TB. Biographical information on Salas Porras is drawn from the Cámara de Comercio, Servicio y Turismo de Chihuahua website, http://www.canacochihuahua.com.mx/A_presi_salasporras.htm, accessed June 2, 2005. Juan Salas Porras, son of a lawyer, Francisco Salas, and Doña Ignacia Porras, received a scant primary education in his hometown of Hidalgo de Para, but according to a local *cronista*, displayed an uncanny knack for numbers and accounting, which is how he became the manager of the Calderón's store.

35. Letter from Ángel Calderón to Silvestre Terrazas, May 20, 1916, TB.

36. On the early history of cinema in Ciudad Chihuahua, see Montemayor, "El cine silente"; Montemayor, *Cien años de cine en Chihuahua*. Before the Revolution, the Teatro Centenario had been, along with the Salon Rosa, the property of Eduardo Albafull, a Spanish national, who also had business interests in railroads and mining. Albafull was forced to leave Chihuahua in 1913, and his theaters were taken over by the Villista forces. He returned to Chihuahua in 1916 but went back to Spain after renting the Centenario to the Calderón brothers. (Montemayor, "El cine silente," 24–26.)

37. "Año nueva! Vida Nueva! Cine Nuevo!," advertisement in REP, January 1, 1922, n.p.

38. It is unlikely that the Alcázar was wired for sound when it first opened, but the Calderón brothers quickly updated it after sound technology was introduced in Mexico City in the spring of 1929. But, it was the first movie theater in the state of Chihuahua to exhibit sound films, beginning with *El cantante de jazz* (*The Jazz Singer*), which was screened in November 1929. About sound film in Mexico, see Federico Dávalos Orozco, "The Birth of the Film Industry and the Emergence of Sound," in Joanne Hershfield and David Maciel, eds., *Mexico's Cinema: A Century of Film and Filmmakers* (Wilmington: Scholarly Resources, 1999), chap. 2.

39. On the use of exotic architectural motifs in the design of movie theaters in the United States, see Koszarski, *Evening's Entertainment*, 226–50. On the use of pre-Columbian motifs in modern Mexican architecture, see Tenorio Trillo, *Artilugio de la nación moderna*, 141–72.

40. The building that housed the Cine El Azteca still stands. One can still see the original decorative elements of the façade, the arch over the stage, and other architectural elements. (Montemayor, "El cine silente," 94.)

41. Advertisement, CM, 3, no. 7 (July 1919), n.p.

42. All the quotations in this paragraph come from the article "El Pasoan Plans to Educate Peon with Movie Show," EPMT, August 17, 1919.

43. "Siguen siendo los favoritos las series en Méjico," CM 5 (January 1920), 154; "Lo que dice el gerente de la Compañía Internacional de Diversiones de El Paso," REP, January 26, 1920.

44. "New Theater to Cost $6000," EPH, February 13, 1918.

45. "New Theater to be Built Here," EPH, April 12, 1919. The Estrella opened in 1913 and operated, according to listings in the El Paso City Directory, until 1925. The Cristal opened in 1919 and operated under that name until 1922.

46. "New Theater to Be Built Here," *op. cit.*

47. "Quinn Leases Colon House to Goldberg," EPH, June 8, 1921.

48. "El publico mexicano espera con ansia loca contemplar *Los cuatros jinetes del Apocalipsis*, la obra maestra de Rodolfo Valentino," CON, February 1, 1927.

49. "Dolores Cassinelli en el Alcázar," REP, March 15, 1920.

50. "El publico Mexicano espera," *op. cit.*

51. "Función teatral a beneficio de la Alianza Hispano-Americana," CON, February 12, 1927.

52. Juan Felipe Leal, Carlos Arturo Flores, and Eduardo Barraza, *Anales del cine en México, 1895–1911. 1899: ¡A los barrios y a la provincia!* (Mexico City: Ediciones Gráficos Eón/Voyeur, 2003), 92.

53. "De nuestro concurso de muchachas bonitas," REP, March 15, 1920.

54. "Muchacha envenenada," REP, May 19, 1923.

55. "Interesante entrevista con varias pelonas de C. Juárez y El Paso sobre su posición," PAT, August 1, 1924.

56. Serna, " 'As a Mexican I Feel It's My Duty.' "

57. *La venganza de Pancho Villa* (ca. 1935) is now, after having been restored, part of the American Film Institute's collection, along with other films, including a reel of the serial *Liberty Daughter of the U.S.A.*, which were found in the family's garage. A close analysis of the film is the topic of a separate work in progress.

58. A compilation film recombines footage from other sources. The footage used in compilation films need not necessarily have any obvious relationship (though in this case they do); the relationship is created in their reconfiguration. See William Wees, *Recycled Images: The Art and Politics of Found Footage Films* (New York: Anthology Film Archives, 1993), 35; Michael Zyrd, "Found Footage Film as Discursive Metahistory: Craig Baldwin's Tribulation 99," *Moving Image* 3 (2003): 40–61.

59. Letter from Fernando Carrasco to Edmundo Padilla, Cantunillo, Texas, June 25, 1931, Padilla Papers, private collection, El Paso, Texas.

60. Fox, "Fan Letters to Cultural Industries."

61. "Inauguración de los estudios donde se producirán películas habladas," UNI, July 30, 1931.

Lawrence Culver

Promoting the Pacific Borderlands
Leisure and Labor in Southern California, 1870–1950

In the late nineteenth century, southern California emerged as a contact point between Mexico and the United States. It also served as the birthplace of a new sort of American West— not an archetypal Anglo-American homesteading frontier, but rather a precursor to the urbanized West of the twentieth century. Americans had previously conceived of the West as a place of labor, where land, minerals, forests, and animals were transformed into wealth through work. What promoters of Los Angeles came to call the "Great Southwest" was perceived as a very different place—one that promised a life of leisure to the middle class. Other locales, such as the resort hotels of the Colorado Rockies, or the tourist spectacles of Yellowstone or Yosemite, also offered an escape from work. The crucial difference, however, was that those places offered leisure as a vacation. Southern California would offer leisure as a permanent way of life.

As Amy Greenberg's essay in this volume demonstrates, Anglo-Americans were at first unsure if the arid Southwest, which they had taken from Mexico, could be made profitable. Tourism proved a key strategy for pursuing economic development in southern California and the Southwest, as well as in Mexican border communities, as Rachel St. John's essay about Tijuana illustrates. Laura Serna's essay shows how investment in local movie theaters in El Paso-Ciudad Juárez flourished at the same time the twin border cities became vibrant tourist attractions. In fact, when Mexican government officials began to pursue tourism as a means of national development and modernization in the 1920s and 1930s, and intensified this effort again in the 1960s and 1970s as Evan Ward's essay demonstrates, they viewed the success of southern California as a key model. Though the region lay on the U.S. side of the border, it benefited from its proximity to the border, particularly due to the inexpensive labor of immigrants and borderlands residents.[1]

The promotion of leisure in southern California had profound and problematic consequences for the region and for the nation. While Anglo tourists and residents could enjoy recreation in the warm climate and scenery of the region, their leisure depended upon the labor of others. For Mexicans, Mexican Americans, and Native Americans, as well as other groups, the Anglo reinvention of the borderlands as a region of leisure meant the continuation of a far older regional labor system—one based on race, as well as citizenship. Native Americans had labored at missions in the Spanish era, and then on Mexican California cattle ranchos. After annexation, Native Americans, Mexican Californios, and more recent Mexican immigrants labored for the Anglo-American inheritors of a preexisting labor system. That labor system made possible the culture of leisure that emerged in southern California, which democratized leisure for Anglo-Americans by exploiting the labor of others.

Examining the promotion of leisure across the borderlands, especially in the region's largest city, Los Angeles, demonstrates that the borderlands were not a periphery removed from the evolution of consumer capitalism. It was, in fact, a region that played an important role in shaping consumer culture in the United States during the twentieth century. The history of modern American leisure—as well as that of American suburbia, which also promised a leisured life—is inextricably connected to the labor relations of the U.S.-Mexico borderlands.

This essay traces the themes of labor and leisure by examining the promotion of southern California and the borderlands to tourists and potential residents during the late nineteenth and early twentieth centuries. Tourist leisure and resident labor at two resorts in the Pacific U.S.-Mexico borderlands, Catalina Island and Palm Springs, provide an example of these mechanisms at work. Over time, tourist leisure became resident leisure, as vacationers built seasonal and permanent residences—houses adapted to the climate and emerging leisure culture of the Pacific borderlands. These houses proved highly influential in the region and across the nation, and demonstrate how the evolution of a leisure-oriented consumer culture and tourist culture in southern California contributed to the appearance and culture of modern American suburbia.

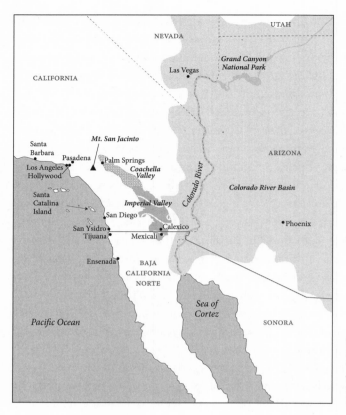

The Pacific Borderlands and "Greater Southwest," 1900–1955. Prepared by Creative Design Resources.

The Early Promotion of Southern California and the "Great Southwest"

One of the first books to focus on southern California extensively was written by Charles Nordhoff, a journalist: *California: For Health, Pleasure, and Residence*, published in 1873. Nordhoff, a Prussian immigrant who spent his later childhood in Ohio, proved a devout believer in American democracy and capitalism, yet he was troubled by the urbanization and monopolistic business practices of the Gilded Age. Most of all, this immigrant was appalled by what he saw as the inundation of eastern cities by a "semi-barbarous foreign population" of southern and eastern European immigrants.[2]

Nordhoff's book posited southern California as a place where middling white farmers could live in a citrus-scented agricultural utopia—a veritable Jeffersonian Polynesia. It was the region's seemingly magical climate that made this new Eden possible. Here, in "the first tropical land our race has thoroughly mastered," Anglo-Americans could enjoy "the delights of the tropics, without their penalties." Enervated by the rush of modern life and threatened by "un-American" immigrants, Americans could here be cured of illness and regain their vitality, without falling prey to the diseases of more humid tropical climes. In an era when disease was common and tuberculosis a constant danger, a climate that encouraged health would prove irresistible.[3]

In addition to climate, moreover, Nordhoff asserted that southern California possessed other resources of significant value. His prose made it clear that this new land would prosper not from the labor of diligent white farmers, but instead through the deployment of workers drawn from the resident non-Anglo population. Nordhoff asserted, for example, that the Chinese made excellent servants. As for Californio rancho families, he pronounced them picturesque and the "moderate" pace of their lives admirable. Nordhoff, however, devoted the most space to discussing another group—Native Americans. One chapter was unambiguously titled "The Indians as Laborers." In southern California, Nordhoff asserted, "it was thought a great advantage for a man to 'have' Indians"—claiming that that they were docile, knew how to handle horses, and would work for little money. For Nordhoff, Californian Indians, already accustomed to mission and rancho labor, were "a useful people," totally unlike the "brutal Apache."[4]

Here was a fundamental difference from other, earlier American "Wests." Elsewhere Anglo-Americans had pushed Indians away, confined them to reservations, or, especially in Gold Rush–era northern California, attempted to exterminate them. In southern California, however, they would provide essential labor, along with Mexican and Asian immigrants. This was especially true at citrus orchards—more like plantations—which Nordhoff predicted would bring wealth to wise investors. Nordhoff, who espoused hope for southern California as a refuge for yeoman farmers, instead used the region's climate and existing population to imagine a future which shared more with the antebellum South or colonized tropics in the possession of France and England than it did with the homesteads of the archetypal Anglo-American West.

Nordhoff's promotional efforts hit a receptive chord across the United States. In its review of the book, *The Nation* pronounced Nordhoff "an excellent *raconteur*," with the tone "of a man who half expects his audience to put their tongues in their cheeks at which he is telling them." The magazine, however, scoffed at his book's attempt to herald an agricultural utopia in an age of industry: "If he had any purpose more than another in writing it, we should say it was to recommend the climate to invalids, and not to preach the superiority of agriculture to mining as a means of comfortable living and even of affluence." The elite eastern press might have dismissed the attributes of distant southern California, but others did not. The book would sell three million copies by the end of the century.[5] Many more books about California by other authors would follow. While guidebooks aimed at tourists and settlers sometimes found a ready market, travel to the region, and settlement within it, remained slow.

This changed in the 1880s, largely due to the railroad. When the Southern Pacific Railroad constructed a route connecting Los Angeles with California's Central Valley in 1879, and built another line to southern California from Arizona, a new regional center, Los Angeles, began to emerge. Fares and shipping rates, however, remained prohibitively high. When the Atchison, Topeka, and Santa Fe Railroad completed a line connecting Los Angeles to the east in 1885, the Southern Pacific Railroad's monopoly ended. The resulting fare and rate war between different railway lines produced the region's first boom.

A primary architect of the Anglo-American reinvention of the borderlands arrived in southern California the same year as the Atchison, Topeka, and Santa Fe Railroad. For the rest of his career, the author and editor Charles Fletcher Lummis would promote himself, the region he came to call the "Great Southwest," and the city he proclaimed to be its capital, Los Angeles. Many others also promoted tourism, settlement, and development in southern California and the borderlands. Unlike earlier boosters, however, Lummis did not present this region as merely an interesting vacation destination or a promising locale for agricultural or real estate developments. His "Great Southwest" offered leisure as a way of life.[6]

Though Lummis was perhaps unequalled in his adulation of all things southwestern, he was not alone in urging Americans to rest. An increasing number of his fellow citizens—particularly in the urban Northeast and Lummis's native New England—called on Americans to embrace a more leisurely life. Others, from philosopher John Ruskin to Henry David Thoreau, also advocated a return to nature, or the pursuit of the "simple life." Their arguments were buttressed by changing realities and perceptions in American society. As the nation grew more prosperous, both the middle and upper classes began to shed the old Puritan abhorrence of leisure. Some individuals also fretted that their society was too mercenary, and that American culture could never be refined until its citizens renounced their unending pursuit of the almighty dollar. At the other end of the socioeconomic spectrum, social reformers and some physicians charged that industrial workers were trapped in mindless, menial labor that threatened their physical and mental health. Like Lummis, these other proponents of leisure argued that rest could be curative, restoring vigor to a nation that had been rendered effete by Victorian manners and enervated by the closing of the frontier.[7]

Lummis strove to popularize the scenery and cultures of the region he called the "Great Southwest." In reality, his books actually described a fairly limited region of northern Arizona and New Mexico: specifically, an area within a forty-mile band north and south of the Santa Fe Railroad.[8] Lummis's glorification of the U.S. Southwest obviously aided the railroad, as well as cities such as Albuquerque and Santa Fe. Yet, his efforts above all else promoted Los Angeles.

By annexing the entire region as a vast recreational hinterland, Los Angeles gained added allure—and a means of combating more cosmopolitan San Francisco, which had long promoted Yosemite and the Sierras as additional attractions for visitors. Tourists riding trains bound for San Francisco also passed through the Colorado Rockies. The route to southern California offered no comparable mountain vistas. Instead, it offered an exotic world to tourists—all of it accessible from the Santa Fe Railway. The Fred Harvey hotels along its route, which numbered fifteen by 1901, sold Indian crafts and exotic regional atmosphere along with meals and accommodations.[9]

Lummis's first book on the Southwest, *The Land of Poco Tiempo*, was published in 1893 while he was living in Isleta Pueblo, south of Albuquerque. It served as the Urtext for the emerging Anglo-American fascination with the region, and in coming decades it helped to popularize everything from regional tourism to "Santa Fe style" architecture and interior decor. In this book, Lummis presented a Pueblo culture that was balanced and contented, unlike supposedly harried Anglo-American culture. His writing recast the borderlands as a landscape of leisure. *The Land of Poco Tiempo* took its title from a Spanish phrase he loosely translated as "pretty soon." In the title chapter of the book, Lummis asked, "Why hurry with the hurrying world? The 'Pretty Soon' of New Spain is better than the 'Now! Now!' of the haggard United States. The opiate sun soothes to rest, the adobe is made to lean against, the hush of the day-long noon would not be broken. Let us not hasten—*mañana* will do. Better still, *pasado mañana*."[10]

Yet even as he promoted the U.S. Southwest as a realm of leisure, Lummis presented Mexico in an entirely different light. Instead of rest and relaxation, Mexico offered Anglo-Americans industriousness and easy money. According to Lummis, Mexico did not warrant description as "quaint" or picturesque.

Four Great
Scenic Routes

Go One Way, Return Another—
and See the Whole Pacific Coast

SOUTHERN PACIFIC offers to the westbound traveler a wide choice of routes going and returning, and a network of rail lines on the Pacific Coast, with convenient connections that afford easy access to all of the points of scenic and romantic interest in America's great playground.

Only the main stems of the principal routes and a few of the outstanding attractions are indicated on the accompanying outline map.

The best way for the traveler to see all of the Pacific Coast is to go west over one Southern Pacific route, return another, and to use the Coast and Valley Lines in California and the Siskiyou

and Cascade Lines of the Shasta Route through Oregon.

In this booklet are separate descriptions of Sunset, Golden State, Overland and Shasta Routes. At the end of the description of each route are several itineraries suggesting optional plans for seeing the points of interest on the Pacific Coast, depending upon the route to be taken in returning East.

On page 15 is a list of Southern Pacific representatives, who are located in nearly all large cities throughout this country and Europe. These men and their capable staffs will gladly help you arrange the details of your trip.

During your trip you will find Southern Pacific employes everywhere eager to assist you in every way that they can.

Map printed in Southern Pacific Railroad brochure, "How to Best See the Pacific Coast," 1931. Courtesy Ephemera Collection, DeGoyler Library, Southern Methodist University, Dallas.

Instead of the Rockies or the Sierras, tourists bound for Los Angeles could see the Grand Canyon. Dismissed a few decades before as a barren wasteland, the borderlands would prove so attractive that even the Southern Pacific Railway began to funnel tourists to California on a longer and more profitable southerly route originating in New Orleans.

Instead, Mexico was "an ambitious marcher in the procession of nations."[11] Moreover, it was the ideal location for Anglo investment: "the kingdom of Something for Nothing." Lummis proved unambiguous on this point. He asserted that Mexican labor was inexpensive, contented, and unlikely to strike. This docility, Lummis claimed, was due to the "fact" that "twelve days' work in the year is enough to supply one peon with the necessities of life."[12] While he depicted the U.S. Southwest as an escape from capitalism, Lummis presented Mexico as another sort of fantasy—a place where Anglos could enrich themselves without guilt or compunction, and even congratulate themselves for playing a part in a neighboring nation's modernization.

In 1895 Lummis became editor of *Land of Sunshine*, a promotional magazine showcasing the opportunities for recreation and leisure throughout Los Angeles, southern California, and the "Great Southwest." The magazine, sold through subscriptions and distributed by the Los Angeles Chamber of Commerce back east as a promotional tool, provided Lummis with a large and regionally diverse audience for his gospel of leisure.[13] In Lummis's estimation, the new residents of Los Angeles were "destined to show an astonished world

Cast and crew of Nestor Film Studio, Sunset Boulevard and Gower Street, Los Angeles, 1911. Photograph courtesy Security Pacific Collection, Los Angeles Public Library.

The assembled cast and crew of the Nestor Film Studio, the first motion picture studio in Hollywood, illustrate the scale and diversity of early film shoots. While the public focused on celebrity actors, film-making also employed writers, directors, technicians, costume designers, cameramen, and day laborers. Films such as the ones produced by the Nestor Film Studio played an important role in creating archetypal myths about the history of the borderlands and the American West.

the spectacle of Americans having a good time."[14] The city boasted beach resorts, as well as the resort of Santa Catalina Island. In the deserts to Los Angeles's east there were still more attractions, including the oasis of Palm Springs.[15] With *Land of Sunshine*, Lummis was but one of a host of editors using new print technologies to bring color, advertising copy, and themed essays about the "good life" to nationally-circulated magazines promoting fashion, home decoration, and travel.

In 1911, when a new industry based on the development of a new medium and method of promotion, film, was well on its way to shifting its center of U.S. production from New York City to Los Angeles, *Land of Sunshine* ceased publication. Southern California's inexpensive land, labor, and electricity, along with its diverse scenery for outdoor filming locations, attracted film studios. The easy access to the U.S.-Mexico border proved a boon, especially whenever patent agents and Pinkerton detectives arrived trying to enforce Thomas Edison's patents on motion picture production equipment. But it was the confluence of the region's leisure culture and the film industries' penchant for depicting people at play that rendered promotional magazines secondary to the movies in the promotion of southern California.

Film, and the community it created—Hollywood—also played a crucial function in the development of the city and region. Lummis, who might have seen film as yet another way to promote his gospel of leisure, instead loathed it as crass entertainment.[16] The irony of this view was that whatever else film

"Pickfair," Beverley Hills, ca. 1925. Photograph courtesy Security Pacific Collection, Los Angeles Public Library.

At Pickfair, a mansion built in the new suburb of Beverly Hills, Hollywood stars Mary Pickford and Douglas Fairbanks popularized a new way of life. Unattainable for most Americans in the 1920s, their residential lifestyle, complete with a private backyard and swimming pool, would become the suburban ideal by the 1950s.

taught the masses, it added to their fascination with California. It showcased the mountains, coasts, and deserts of southern California, as well as the streetscapes of Los Angeles, lined with palm and orange trees and filled with pleasant bungalows. Motion pictures told the world—as no single booster ever could—that southern California might be a wonderful place for recreation, or for residence. Some films went so far as to make relocation to California a central theme, such as *It's a Gift* (1934), in which W. C. Fields plays a cantankerous Midwesterner who uses his inheritance to buy a southern California citrus orchard. Other films simply used Los Angeles as a backdrop—filling movie theaters around the world with images of the bungalows and palm trees which occupied the background of Laurel and Hardy comedies and innumerable other films.

Early film studio productions, often society melodramas, were replete with depictions of the rich and glamorous. They showed filmgoers a way of living, a world of material wealth and, above all, a world of leisure. Celebrities, whether acting in films or appearing in 1930s newsreels frolicking at Catalina, Palm Springs, or other area resorts, served as models of, and ambassadors for,

Actress Jane Wyman sitting in lounge chair on California beach, September 1935. *Los Angeles Times* news photograph, courtesy *Los Angeles Times* Photographic Archive, Collection 1429, Department of Special Collections, Charles E. Young Research Library, University of California, Los Angeles.

Hollywood films and celebrity newsreels popularized California beach culture and sunbathing as well as ever-shrinking swimming attire, and aided the growth of beach and poolside recreation, as well as a more openly sensual popular culture.

leisure. Hollywood, though certainly not the only source for a new culture of consumerism and leisure, popularized this lifestyle. The fact that the nation's growing middle class accepted and emulated this life of consumerism and leisure would have profound implications for southern California and the nation as a whole. From Nordhoff to Lummis to the newsreel, the promotion of southern California and the U.S.-Mexico borderlands as a place of leisure for Anglo-Americans proved an immense success. The consequences of that success, both positive and problematic, were apparent at resorts across the region.[17]

Two such resorts were Catalina Island, located twenty-six miles off the coast of Los Angeles, and Palm Springs, located one hundred miles east of Los Angeles in the arid Coachella Valley. Each resort demonstrated how the leisure industry changed the region, drawing Anglos who perceived a landscape of recreation to a place others knew through subsistence strategies. These resorts also demonstrated the extent to which Anglo leisure depended on Mexican and Native American labor.

Catalina Island and Resort Recreation in the Pacific Borderlands

One of the largest of the Channel Islands, mountainous Catalina Island rises more than two thousand feet above the Pacific, with a total land area of approximately seventy-five square miles. The Banning family, who dominated shipping in southern California, bought it in 1888. At Catalina, their corporation, the Santa Catalina Island Company (scic), created the first corporate resort in the United States, a precursor to later corporate resorts such as Sun Valley and Vail. The scic operated passenger ships and hotels, controlled access to the island, and employed large numbers of workers.

Once a haven for southern California fishermen and sheepherders, the island's new tourist service economy employed many people of color. The most numerous were Mexicans and Mexican Americans, hired to labor on ships, in hotels, and for construction projects. The restaurant staff of the scic's Metropole Hotel was African American, as were the porters on its steamships. The hotel's bellhops were Japanese. Many other people not deemed "Anglos" found employment at the resort's other hotels and restaurants, or as domestic employees in vacation residences. By the 1910s, Catalina also possessed a sizeable population of eastern Europeans, mostly Slovaks, who took jobs in the tourist service industry. Avalon, the only town on Catalina, exhibited the same racial discrimination found in much of the United States in this era. A small section of Avalon, known as "Sonoratown," was where Mexicans and other people of color barred from Anglo neighborhoods lived.[18]

Catalina served as a popular summer destination for Anglo southern Californians fleeing the heat of the mainland for a cooler marine climate. Foremost among them were affluent residents of Pasadena, a suburb of Los Angeles. During the hot Pasadena summers, it sometimes seemed as if the entire town had relocated to the Pacific, with Catalina serving as "Newport, Miami and Narragansett Pier all rolled into one."[19] One such Pasadenan was Charles Frederick Holder. Born in 1851 in Lynn, Massachusetts, Holder attended the U.S. Naval Academy but left before graduating. He served for several years as the assistant curator of zoology at the American Museum of Natural History in New York, and he authored a number of books, including biographies of Charles Darwin and Louis Agassiz. In 1885, Holder came to southern California to recuperate from a lung infection aggravated by overwork. Enamored with the region, Holder decided to stay. In 1891, he became professor and chair of the Department of Zoology at the newly established Throop University, later renamed the California Institute of Technology.[20]

Catalina Island, with its claims to healthfulness and distinctive flora and fauna, was an encapsulation of everything Holder loved about southern California. In books such as *Santa Catalina: An Isle of Summer* (1895), he rhapsodized about his subject, calling it "a bit of southern California anchored offshore" and "nearer the perfect insular resort than any I know of." Catalina again featured prominently in his *Life in the Open: Sport with Rod, Gun, Horse and Hound in Southern California* (1906) and *The Channel Islands of California: A Book for the Angler, Sportsman, and Tourist* (1910). These books contained a substantial amount of natural history and observations of flora and fauna, but also copious southern California boosterism and tourist information, particularly on deep-sea fishing, Holder's favorite of all "true manly sports."[21]

While amazed by the abundance of marine life at Catalina, Holder was appalled by what he saw as the wanton destruction of the island's fish, so in 1898, Holder founded the Catalina Island Tuna Club, which combined conservationist policies with a glorification of the rugged outdoor lifestyle. Initially, active membership, open solely to men, could be attained only by reeling in a tuna of at least one hundred pounds, or a swordfish of two hundred pounds, with rod and reel without assistance. The club's membership rolls, which included honorary members, contained a variety of local and national notables, such as Henry Huntington, George S. Patton, Stanford University president David Starr Jordan, and polar explorer Admiral Robert E. Peary. Membership also came to include many prominent conservationists of the progressive era, including forester Gifford Pinchot and U.S. president Theodore Roosevelt. The Tuna Club's constitution stated that the organization would work to achieve "the protection of the game fishes of the state of California, and to encourage and foster the catching of all fishes, and especially tuna, yellowtail, sea bass, etc., with the lightest rod and reel tackle," and to discourage "unsportsmanlike" commercial fishing. Distinctions such as these bore close parallels to class-based distinctions characterizing attitudes toward hunting: those with the money to hunt for leisure were sportsmen, while those who hunted for subsistence were "poachers." Additionally, club bylaws divided fish into game species, to be treated with care, and non-game species to be hunted at will. Thus, members took great pains to catch trophy tuna in a "manly" manner but enjoyed the sport of shooting at the island's iridescent flying fish with buckshot.[22]

Along with drawing distinctions between the working and elite classes' motivations to fish, emphasis on racial differences among fishermen also

Charles Frederick Holder with fish gaffer Joe Pesciado and trophy tuna, Avalon, Catalina Island, California, 1898. Photograph courtesy Catalina Island Museum Archives, Avalon, California.

Holder, Catalina's most prolific proponent of sport fishing, and Pesciado, its best-known gaffer, pose together with a large tuna. Similar photographs became iconic souvenirs for countless Catalina tourists.

underpinned the Catalina Island Tuna Club's conceptualization of conservation. This economic and ethnocentric nationalism underpinned newspaper stories perhaps meant to taint the fish ethnic fishmongers sold from small stands, baskets, and shops throughout California's coastal towns. In 1909, for example, the *Los Angeles Times* reported that a group of Japanese fishermen illegally harvested abalone near the outlet of Avalon's sewer. As an aside, the article remarked that whites considered abalone inedible.[23] Californian Anglos who complained about "foreign" fishermen typically conflated the ethnicity of most commercial fishermen in California—typically Asian, Mexican, or Italian—with their nationality. One critic of state fishing regulations epitomized this view, describing the "foreign fishing nations" represented by nearly three-quarters "of the people engaged in commercial net fishing." The critic complained that they "are not even citizens of the United States, yet we permit them to directly . . . dictate the laws governing the taking of our fish and our national food supply."[24] Through implication and innuendo, Holder and his allies blamed racialized "foreigners" for the depredations to what had once been one of the richest fisheries along the Pacific coast, the waters off Catalina Island, where by 1912 the annual catch was just a quarter of what it had been in

1885. In addition to their complaints about overfishing by "foreigners," Holder and other members of the Tuna Club lamented the disappearance of "big fish." The island's famous big tuna were nearly gone—thanks in part to the Tuna Club's trophy hunters—as were its once-abundant abalone.[25]

That the views of Holder and other members of the Tuna Club were mired in class and racial prejudices no doubt helped persuade local and state authorities, who held similar prejudices, to implement conservation measures. Ultimately, Catalina's waters, up to a three-mile radius from shore, were classified as a fish preserve where only recreational hook-and-line fishing would be permitted. Commercial net fishing was banned. After 1913, local fishermen—mostly working-class "ethnics"—either had to relocate, find new employment, or make the transition from fisherman to recreational fishing guide.

One fisherman who made this transition was "Mexican Joe" Pesciado, whose last name must have been chosen to fit his profession. Born in Sonora, Pesciado originally came to Catalina as a child in the 1850s and fished and hunted to provide food for sheep-herding operations on the island. When the island developed as a tourist center, Pesciado partnered with another fisherman, George Michaelis, to operate a charter fishing boat in Avalon. "Mexican Joe" became a fixture in Avalon and was the community's best-known "gaffer": one of the many fishing guides who helped anglers haul in their catch. He appeared in countless photos of tourists posing with their numerous —and sometimes gargantuan—prizes.

As on the mainland, Mexicans and other members of racialized groups served Anglos both as laborers and as part of the exotic southern California scenery.[26] To be sure, fishing boats were an inescapable part of Avalon's picturesqueness, but many were no longer seaworthy—just listing hulks dotting the shoreline. In Avalon, old fishing boats had been "adapted to ornamental garden purposes" by being towed ashore, "filled with earth and planted with flowers." These strange, marooned garden planters, as much as anything else, testified to the socioeconomic change underway on the island, which would only accelerate after 1919, when the Bannings sold Catalina to Chicago chewing-gum magnate William Wrigley. Wrigley, an entrepreneur of the new consumer culture, turned Catalina into one of the most popular tourist destinations in the American West during the 1920s.[27]

Making the Desert Resort Residential in Palm Springs

Another tourist attraction that grew in the 1920s and 1930s was Palm Springs. While Palm Springs was just one of many places transformed by the regional promotion of leisure, the history of this resort, perhaps more than any other in the Pacific borderlands, demonstrates how the consumption of leisure at a resort presaged broader transformations in modern consumer culture, particularly the birth of a new consumer-oriented suburban culture. In the early twentieth century, most tourists avoided the Mojave and Colorado deserts that lay to the east and north of coastal southern California. One hundred miles east of Los Angeles lays the Coachella Valley, part of the Colorado Desert that stretches south to Mexico and the Sea of Cortez. On the western edge of the valley stands Mount San Jacinto, one of the tallest peaks in southern California. Along its eastern flank runs a series of canyons, lined with the only native palm trees in the entire continental United States. While a lush island setting amidst fish-rich waters near a growing city seemed a natural choice for a resort, an arid stark location such as this one could hardly have been less likely.

Near the mouth of one of Mount San Jacinto's canyons (Tahquitz Canyon) stood a grove of palms. In their midst, a hot spring issued from the sandy earth, creating a small pool. The spring lay on the reservation lands of the Agua Caliente band of the Cahuilla Indians. This was the oasis that would serve as the nucleus for Palm Springs, which became one of southern California's signature resorts. Initially a failed agricultural venture in the 1890s, and then a tiny settlement of tuberculosis patients in the 1910s, over the next three decades this community emerged as one of the most famous resorts in the United States. The first resort hotel, the Desert Inn, was opened by Nellie Coffman in 1909. Coffman had visited the tiny community previously to recuperate from a persistent cough, and she believed that someday the desert valley would become a "sand box" for playful Angelenos. Coffman's intuition proved prescient. Her small hotel, later expanded into a large resort, served as the nucleus of a sprawling assemblage of resorts, motels, stores, golf courses, and vacation-home tracts. First drawing the wintering rich, the resort gradually began to draw middle-class auto tourists and day-trippers from Los Angeles as well.[28]

As at Catalina, Palm Springs relied upon the laborers and labor relations of the borderlands. That Agua Caliente Indians should take jobs in the growing resort was no surprise, nor that local Mexican Americans and Mexican immigrants would as well. Both groups already served as agricultural laborers in the orchards and farms surrounding Riverside, Redlands, and San Bernardino to the west of the Coachella Valley. By 1920, Cahuilla women were serving as maids and laundresses in the Desert Inn and other hotels, and Cahuilla men worked as gardeners and gathered firewood. Mexican men also found employment as gardeners. The Desert Inn had two cooks—one Chinese, the other African American. Many other Asians also took jobs in Palm Springs, such as Filipino Segundo Rigonan, who worked at the Desert Inn, and with other Filipino employees lived in a bungalow called the "Manila Cottage." Employee housing at the Desert Inn may have been segregated, but at least the hotel provided lodging for its employees. White workers could usually secure adequate rooms nearby, but other workers often could not, as almost all existing housing in the resort was reserved for Anglos only. Many workers lived in ramshackle cabins and lean-tos constructed on Agua Caliente reservation land, which encompassed much of the territory surrounding the resort town.[29]

In the desert Coachella Valley, desert vistas and date palm cultivation provided a new cultural trope ripe for theme-oriented marketing. An early manifestation of southern California's tourist leisure culture was "theming," in which history or fantasy was used to shape a physical environment conducive to recreation, shopping, or residential life. Though the term was not coined until 1955, when Disneyland opened showcasing themed areas, such as Fantasyland, Main Street, U.S.A., or Tomorrowland, since the 1910s Indian and Hispanic cultures had been utilized in the theming of towns like Santa Fe and Santa Barbara, or of tourist districts in border towns like Tijuana and Ciudad Juárez. In Palm Springs, the desert landscape would be used to fashion an Orientalist theme dependent for its effect on dates, palm trees, and camels.

Agricultural entrepreneurs came to the interior desert hoping to replicate the success of the citrus industry in coastal southern California with the cultivation of dates. Health guru and cereal magnate W. K. Kellogg supported the effort, believing that fresh dates were more healthful than those packed and shipped from overseas.[30] Once date cultivation proved successful it provided a useful thematic element for the promotion of tourism in the Coachella Valley.[31] Accordingly, the racial posturing already utilized to posit Anglo-Americans as the heirs of the Spanish padres and Mexican rancho dons was now used to link them and the southern California landscapes they inhabited to a far more ancient past: "From earliest days, humanity has hovered on the desert's edge . . . Egypt, Babylon, Chaldea, all cradles of the race, were desert lands . . . The first civilization knew the desert and loved it. We of the present are also succumbing to its lure." Some developers even hired Cahuillas and Mexicans bedecked in Arabian Nights garb to greet tourists at the train station and then lead them by camel across the desert to their resorts. If any tourists did, in fact, brave a camel ride, few likely submitted to it again. Motion sickness—not to mention camels' propensities for biting and spitting—was a

Tourists riding camels in the Coachella Valley, 1928. Photographic print in *The Walled Oasis of Biskra "In the Coachella Valley": An Interpretation of the American Desert in the Algerian Manner*, courtesy Special Collections, Charles E. Young Research Library, University of California, Los Angeles.

This image, which appeared in a promotional brochure for a resort near Palm Springs that was never built, illustrates the Coachella Valley's Orientalist fantasy at its most florid. The "Arabs" depicted here are most likely local Cahuilla Indians.

regular hazard. Wagons, trains, and then automobiles quickly replaced the camel caravan as the best means of transit from the outlying train depot to Palm Springs itself.[32]

From Recreation to Residence in Southern California

Though southern California was promoted for decades as a place to play, it was also promoted as a place to live. Purchasing a home was—and is—the largest act of consumption most Americans ever commit, and southern California played an important part in this aspect of modern consumer culture. Promoters hoped that some portion of all those people who visited the region would return to stay. This aspect of regional promotion—residential, rather than recreational—had a long history in southern California. In his books and in the magazine *Land of Sunshine*, Charles Lummis touted regional architecture as suited for modern buildings, lauding the cooling properties of thick adobe walls and the social possibilities of a backyard patio.

While in his early writing and editorial work for *Land of Sunshine* Lummis extolled the borderlands as leisure space, he also depicted it as an ideal space for modern living. This interest in architecture and in making a home—

literally and figuratively—in the Southwest dated back to his first book written at Isleta Pueblo, *The Land of Poco Tiempo* (1893). The book included photographs of what he identified as a "typical Pueblo interior"—a whitewashed adobe room, with blankets and pottery artfully arranged in a seemingly indigenous Arts and Crafts aesthetic. Yet this was, in fact, not a "typical" borderlands or even Pueblo residence. Rather than documenting the actual living quarters of Isletas, Lummis had simply decorated and photographed his own room in the pueblo. Showcasing still other southwestern homes and gardens, Lummis's *Land of Sunshine* functioned as one of many shelter magazines that appeared late in the nineteenth century. Periodicals such as *House Beautiful*, *House and Garden*, *The Bungalow*, and Gustav Stickley's *The Craftsman* offered readers a comforting vision of modes of living, building, and decorating that would improve home life in a world that often seemed unpredictable or threatening. *Land of Sunshine*, however, did not simply promote homes. It promoted all of southern California and the Great Southwest as shelter from a rapidly changing world many Americans found troubling.[33]

With income from editing *Land of Sunshine*, Lummis did far more than decorate a room. He built a house in the 1890s to incorporate the region's history and climatic advantages. Aided by Pueblo workers from Isleta, Lummis constructed his Arts and Crafts–influenced Spanish Revival stone house, which he named El Alisal, in the Arroyo Seco neighborhood northeast of downtown Los Angeles. Here he displayed his vast collection of artifacts from the U.S. Southwest, Mexico, and South America. Built of cobblestones excavated from the adjacent arroyo, El Alisal included a mission bell built into its exterior façade, a reminder of Lummis's role in founding the California Landmarks Club to preserve and restore the state's Spanish missions. The home's thick walls moderated interior temperatures, and a courtyard patio, adapted from Hispanic architecture and shaded by a venerable sycamore tree, served as an outdoor social space. A large parlor took up most of the first floor, and Lummis named this the "Museo," filling it with artifacts, craft objects, and photographs from his travels. The room served as the setting for his Southwest "salon"—an eclectic assemblage of writers, artists, intellectuals, boosters, and others who shared his infatuation with the region.

Helen Hunt Jackson's novel *Ramona* (1884), with its nostalgic evocation of the California rancho past, carried a similar implicit message as did *Land of Poco Tiempo*, *Land of Sunshine*, and El Alisal. Vast numbers of eastern and Midwestern tourists travelled to ranchos, missions, and other sites with purported links to the events of the novel. In the process, they saw adobe homes

Exterior view of the Charles Fletcher Lummis home, El Alisal, under construction, Los Angeles, 1890s. Photograph courtesy Lummis Photograph Collection, Southwest Museum, Autry National Center, Los Angeles, photo ID #P35397.

To connect his home to regional culture and landscape, Lummis utilized water-rounded rocks from the Arroyo Seco streambed adjacent to the house and even incorporated a mission bell from one of the California missions.

that were pleasant, rather than stereotypically primitive, with shaded verandas, thick adobe walls that moderated temperatures, and traditional furniture and decorative art objects. The restoration of historic California adobes and Spanish missions reinforced this impression. Restored adobe homes, such as the De le Guerra Adobe in Santa Barbara, and the adobes restored as part of the restoration of Olivera Street and the Los Angeles Plaza, were crammed with antiques and art objects, furnished far more luxuriously than they had been in the Mexican era. Likewise, the rebuilt missions were surrounded by gardens of roses and other flowers, rather than the crops raised by Indian neophytes. Though actual historic sites, these missions and adobes conveyed impressions which owed more to *Better Homes and Gardens* than they did to history. *Ramona* tourism and refurbished historic sites cast "Southwestern" architecture as a viable style Anglos could adopt. It contributed to the craze for Mission and Spanish Revival architecture, furniture, and décor, which remade Santa Fe, New Mexico and Santa Barbara and left an indelible architectural imprint on southern California as well as the U.S. Southwest.[34]

Southern California did, in fact, influence the Arts and Crafts movement's

Interior view of the Charles Fletcher Lummis home, El Alisal. Los Angeles, ca. 1900. Photograph courtesy Lummis Photograph Collection, Southwest Museum, Autry National Center, Los Angeles, ID #P35714.

The large room on the first floor at El Alisal, which Lummis called the "Museo," showcased his vast collection of Native American pottery and textiles, as well as his photographs of the region and books on regional history, literature, and folklore. The Museo served as the setting for his Southwest salon of artists, boosters, and writers, and its contents would later become the nucleus of the Southwest Museum's collections, now under the aegis of the Autry National Center.

most famous proponent. In 1904 Gustav Stickley, editor of *The Craftsman* magazine and purveyor of Arts and Crafts furniture and houses, visited Palm Springs with his wife and daughters. Southern California booster George Wharton James, who accompanied them, would soon become associate editor of *The Craftsman*. Stickley's magazine carried an increasing number of articles about and advertisements for California, reinforcing the notion that southern California offered architectural, geographic, and cultural forms of shelter. In real estate developments across southern California, the bungalow, the archetypal Arts and Crafts residence, served as housing for hundreds of thousands of new arrivals to the region. After his visit, Stickley even considered Palm Springs as the prospective site for a new community constructed entirely around the precepts of the "simple life."[35]

That community never came to fruition, and subsequent residential development in Palm Springs rarely seemed to embody the simple life. Yet residences in Palm Springs, from mission revival to modernist, did reflect some aspects of the philosophies of Stickley and Lummis. They often reflected regional culture in some superficial form, and were constructed to take advantage of the warm climate and spectacular landscapes of the region. They also shared one other characteristic with Stickley's houses and furniture: they may have been intended to perpetuate the simple life, but they were almost never inexpensive. In this consumerist way, discriminating vacationers could do more than simply winter in Palm Springs. Now, the affluent owners of vacation homes could live a genteel life in the desert, purportedly even one in tune with its environment. One developer's florid promotional literature made this explicit: "Those who quest and seek for beauty have built here habitations of their own, some so lovely as to seem real bits of Paradise. These houses dot the landscape like jewels. Built largely of native material, they blend with their surroundings admirably, and their tiled roofs, pools, patios, balconies, gardens of desert growth, [and] splashing fountains, add their own charms to the establishment of Nature herself."[36] Such home-building "seekers of beauty" included razor magnate King Gillette and cereal mogul W. K. Kellogg.

In case some homebuyers were less discriminating—or not effectively discriminated against—the developer also assured buyers that "carefully drawn restrictions protect the home owner and permanently maintain the high standards of the property, and while homes need not be pretentious, they must conform to an attractive style of architecture, and plans must be approved by an Art Jury." If this language were not clear enough, another developer stated that "careful discrimination in the matter of lot buyers is also being made, as to race, desirability, etc., thus ensuring a high order of neighbors." Though isolated from larger urban areas, residential development in Palm Springs reflected the racial segregation and racist zoning practices endemic in Los Angeles and many other urban and suburban regions. The influx of affluent white sojourners—as well as a growing tide of auto tourists—helped the resort town weather the Depression with relative comfort. During the 1930s, a Palm Springs promotional magazine featured Hollywood figures such as Walt Disney, Shirley Temple, Delores Del Rio, Martha Raye, Andy Rooney, Jack Benny, Leslie Howard, and Cary Grant, as well as business tycoons such as Benjamin Fairless, CEO of U.S. Steel, and Walter P. Chrysler.[37]

While celebrities and the affluent had been building and buying vacation homes in Palm Springs for some time, residential development in the resort town accelerated in the 1930s. One of the most exclusive new resort housing developments, Smoke Tree Ranch, appeared late in the decade. Created out of a former dude ranch, it carefully maintained a rustic atmosphere: houses were required to be one story and constructed in "rustic" architectural style. Homes sat wide apart on large lots, which were required to be maintained as desert, with no lawns or nonnative shade trees. Roads were narrow and initially unpaved. In contrast to the "country" atmosphere, the gated community hosted a club with hotel-like amenities, including a restaurant, a swimming pool, tennis courts, and maid service.[38] Walt Disney, King Gillette, and the Weyerhaeuser family, among many others, would build homes here. Disney would keep his Smoke Tree Ranch home until the 1950s, when he sold it to raise funds for his newly proposed theme park, Disneyland.

Yet if Smoke Tree Ranch offered a new model for resort design, its houses also served as models for homes intended for year-round residence. Low-slung and rambling, fusing rustic wood and stone with some modernist elements, the houses in Smoke Tree Ranch looked unlike much of the existing architecture in Palm Springs, particularly those structures of a Spanish or Moorish revival design, and in the rest of the region. From the perspective of a decade or two later, however, these homes were instantly recognizable. They were clear early examples of the "ranch" house—the domestic architectural style that would carpet the floor of the San Fernando Valley after the Second World War before appearing in virtually every community in the United States in the 1950s and 1960s. The houses in Smoke Tree Ranch, though located behind a security gate, were replicated innumerable times in national architectural and general circulation magazines. They and other Palm Springs resort homes would also appear in celebrity magazines, newsreels, and films. Dropped improbably among cacti, ocotillos, and wispy, aptly named smoke trees, these houses offered a simple façade to the street but seclusion and amenities to their inhabitants. They would serve as models of a resort-style architecture, leavened by a rustic simplicity and purported harmony with the landscape, that proved a dominant domestic architectural idiom of the United States in the twentieth century.[39]

The movement of family social life and leisure time into the backyard, and the construction of patios, barbecues, and swimming pools, allowed suburbanites to live a resort lifestyle year-round, at least as long as weather permitted. Ranch-style house pattern books, published by *Sunset* magazine and other periodicals, proved widely popular. One example, the *Sunset Western Ranch House*, published in 1946, remained in print at the end of the twentieth century. It presents the ranch house as a uniquely Southwestern architectural form, derived from the haciendas and rancho homes of the Mexican Californio era. Though connecting the ranch style to a regional past, the book casts it as perfectly suited to the modern age. Though many houses in this and other pattern books avoided the avant-garde appearance of modern-

Dick Richards home, Smoke Tree Ranch, Palm Springs, California, 1930s. Photograph copyright held by Palm Springs Historical Society, Palm Springs, California, courtesy Palm Springs Historical Society, Palm Springs, California.

This structure, with its low, horizontal orientation and outdoor patio, is an early example of a ranch house, the archetypal residence of postwar suburbia. The roof beams extending beyond the exterior walls recall the *vigas* of traditional adobe architecture and were a common feature in older mission and Spanish revival designs. The large corner window on the right, however, where two windows meet at a right angle with no wall separating them, was a hallmark of many modernist architects, such as Richard Neutra, who would later design several iconic homes in the Palm Springs area.

ist homes in Palm Springs, the houses functioned in remarkably similar ways. The mitigation of heat and excess sunlight was a recurring theme, for these could prove problematic not only in Palm Springs, but in many parts of the Sunbelt, particularly if homeowners took the authors' advice to "turn your living towards the sun." The spread of ranch houses throughout the United States, though not solely a consequence of residential developments in Palm Springs, demonstrates the extent of the influence of resort leisure in the Southwest on national urban and suburban development.[40]

Charles Nordhoff and Charles Fletcher Lummis imagined an escape from modernity in the leisure of the "Great Southwest," which was not a region removed from modern life, but a place that emerged in response to consumer culture's emphasis on domestic and recreational consumption. Resorts played no small role in the development of this lifestyle. They capitalized on the

Prospective homebuyers, Maryvale, Arizona, 1955. Photograph courtesy John F. Long Properties, LLP, Phoenix, Arizona.

When completed, Maryvale, a housing development in Phoenix, became home to one hundred thousand residents. It was also the first of many large housing developments in the United States built in ranch style.

new—and sometimes highly problematic—recreational perceptions and uses of nature. In particular, the orientation of resorts like Palm Springs to the recreational family home and private club set a powerful example that in post–Second World War America permeated suburban developers' plans and, more importantly, suburbanites' dreams. In the great southwest of Anglo-Americans like Nordhoff and Lummis, capitalism, urbanism, and materialism took lasting form in themed tourist attractions, ranch houses, and the ranch style.[41] Americans would discover the culture of leisure not in one of New Mexico's Native American Pueblos or one of California's ranchos, but rather in the backyards and swimming pools of middle-class American suburbia. Over time, this suburban landscape spread not only leisure, but also perpetuated exploitative labor and race relations of the borderlands, throughout the postwar Sunbelt and much of the United States.

Abbreviations

BRL	Braun Research Library, Southwest Museum of the American Indian, Autry National Center, Los Angeles
CIM	Catalina Island Museum Archives, Avalon, California
HL	Huntington Library, San Marino, California
LAT	*Los Angeles Times*

PSPL	Palm Springs Public Library
RCL	History and Genealogy Department, Richard J. Riordan Central Library, Los Angeles
SC	Seaver Center for Western History Research, Natural History Museum of Los Angeles County
UCLA	Special Collections, Young Research Library, University of California, Los Angeles
UCR	Special Collections, Rivera Library, University of California, Riverside

Notes

I would like to thank all the participants for their insights and advice, and particularly Alexis McCrossen for her repeated careful readings of this essay.

Notes fully cite primary sources and specialized secondary sources. Full bibliographic details for all other citations are in the volume's selected bibliography.

1. Berger, *Development of Mexico's Tourism Industry*, 15. Studies of tourism in the U.S. Southwest include Rothman, ed., *Culture of Tourism*; Rothman, *Devil's Bargains*; Wrobel and Long, eds., *Seeing and Being Seen*; Wilson, *Myth of Santa Fe*.

2. Charles Nordhoff, *California: For Health, Pleasure, and Residence* (New York: Harper and Brothers, 1873), 18.

3. Nordhoff, *California, op. cit.*, 11. See also John Baur, "Charles Nordhoff, Publicist Par Excellence," *Ventura County Historical Society Quarterly* 19 (1974): 2–11; John Baur, *The Health Seekers of Southern California, 1870–1900* (San Marino: The Huntington Library, 1959); Elias, *Los Angeles*.

4. Nordhoff, *California, op. cit.*, 137–39, 155–56.

5. *The Nation*, December 5, 1872, 369; Baur, "Charles Nordhoff," *op. cit.*, 6.

6. For general information about Lummis, see Thompson, *American Character*; Turbesé Lummis Fiske, *Charles F. Lummis: The Man and His West* (Norman: University of Oklahoma Press, 1975); Edwin Bingham, *Charles F. Lummis: Editor of the Southwest* (San Marino: Huntington Library, 1955).

7. Shi, *Simple Life*; Rodgers, *Work Ethic*, chap. 4, "Play, Repose, and Plenty."

8. Charles F. Lummis, *Land of Poco Tiempo* (New York: Charles Scribner's Sons, 1893), 1; Martin Padget, "Travel, Exoticism, and the Writing of Region: Charles Fletcher Lummis and the 'Creation' of the Southwest," *Journal of the Southwest* 37 (1995): 421–49, quote p. 433; Weigle and Babcock, eds., *Great Southwest*, 2; *Out West*, February 1905.

9. Cultural geographer J. Valerie Fifer discusses the competition between various cities and states in the Western tourist market in *American Progress*. See also Pomeroy, *In Search of the Golden West*; Hyde, *American Vision*; Weigle and Babcock, eds., *Great Southwest*.

10. Lummis, *Land of Poco Tiempo, op. cit.*, 1.

11. Charles Lummis, *Awakening of a Nation: Mexico of Today* (New York: Harper and Brothers, 1898), 3, 74.

12. Ibid., 76.

13. Charles Fletcher Lummis, "As I Remember," 238, Lummis Collection, BRL. See also Franklin Walker, *A Literary History of Southern California* (Berkeley: University of California Press, 1950); Bingham, *Charles F. Lummis, op. cit.* Subscription information is derived from the *Land of Sunshine* and *Out West* materials included in the Lummis Collection, BRL.

14. Charles F. Lummis, *Land of Sunshine* 6 (May 1897): 261.

15. *Land of Sunshine* 15 (July 1901); "Where the Date Palm Grows," *Land of Sunshine* 13 (August 1900).

16. Thompson, *American Character*, 293.

17. May, *Screening Out the Past*.

18. Gary Steven Okun, "Avalon, California: Structure and Function of an Island Town" (M.A. thesis, University of California, Los Angeles, 1976), 18; LAT July 15, 1909; Squirrel 'Duke' D'Arcy interview, interviewed by Chuck Liddell, Joe Guin, and Lloyd Rathburn, February 25, 1976, Oral History Program, CIM.

19. Harry Carr, *Los Angeles: City of Dreams* (New York: D. Appleton—Century Company, 1935), 301. Local histories of Catalina include Adelaide LeMert Doran, *Ranch That Was Robbins': Santa Catalina Island—A Source Book* (Los Angeles: Arthur H. Clark Company, 1963); and William Stanford White and Steven Tice, *Santa Catalina Island: Its Magic, People, and History* (San Dimas: White Limited Edition, 1997). See also Okun, "Avalon, California," *op. cit.*

20. Hancock Banning Jr., "The Banning Family in Southern California," UCLA Oral History Archives, UCLA; McWilliams, *Southern California*, 147; White and Tice, *Santa Catalina Island, op. cit.*, 73–77.

21. Charles Frederick Holder, *Santa Catalina, an Isle of Summer: Its History, Climate, Sports and Antiquities* (San Francisco: Murdock, 1895), 42, 95–96; Charles Frederick Holder, *Channel Islands of California: A Book for the Angler, Sportsman, and Tourist* (Chicago: A. C. McClurg, 1910), v; Charles Frederick Holder, *Life in the Open: Sport with Rod, Gun, Horse, and Hound in Southern California* (New York: G. P. Putnam's Sons, 1906). For analysis of progressive-era conceptualizations of masculinity, see Bederman, *Manliness and Civilization*.

22. "Annual Tournaments, The Tuna Club—Catalina Island, California—1898–1916," Ephemera Collection, SC; Doran, *Ranch That Was Robbins', op. cit.*, 123–24. For an analysis of the intersections of class and conservation, see Louis Warren, *The Hunter's Game: Poachers and Conservationists in Twentieth-Century America* (New Haven: Yale University Press, 1999); Karl Jacoby, *Crimes against Nature: Squatters, Poachers, Thieves, and the Hidden History of American Conservation* (Berkeley: University of California Press, 2001).

23. LAT, April 21, 1909. See also LAT, June 23, 1894.

24. "Captain George Farnsworth to Governor Olson," quoted in Santa Catalina Island

Company Press Release, June 1940, CIM. See also Arthur McEvoy, *The Fisherman's Problem: Ecology and the Law in the California Fisheries, 1850–1980* (New York: Cambridge University Press, 1986).

25. Doran, *Ranch that was Robbins'*, *op. cit.*, 30–37, 95–98.

26. "Locally Famous Woman Dies on Catalina Island," LAT, 1915, clipping in General Personages—Pesciado File, CIM; "Early Days in California: Santa Catalina Island, Chapter IX," LAT, May 1, 1918. See also White and Tice, *Santa Catalina Island, op. cit.*, 184.

27. "Permit to Land at Santa Catalina Island for the Purpose of Fishing," box 5, Banning Company Collection, HL; Edholm, "The Seaward Suburbs of Los Angeles," *Out West* 30 (May 1909): 459.

28. The historiography of Palm Springs is limited. Local histories include two problematic accounts: Katherine Ainsworth, *The McCallum Saga: The Story of the Founding of Palm Springs* (Palm Desert, Calif: Desert-Southwest, Inc., 1965); Ed Ainsworth, *Golden Checkerboard* (Palm Springs: Palm Springs Desert Museum, 1973). See also two dissertations: Thomas Jensen, "Palm Springs, California: Its Evolution and Functions" (Ph.D. diss., University of California, Los Angeles, 1954); and Rachel Shaw, "Evolving Ecoscape: An Environmental and Cultural History of Palm Springs, California, and the Agua Caliente Indian Reservation, 1877–1939" (Ph.D. diss., University of California, San Diego, 1999). Important sources for the history of the Agua Caliente Indians include Harry James, *The Cahuilla Indians* (Banning, Calif.: Malki Museum Press, 1960); John Lowell Bean, *Mukat's People: The Cahuilla Indians of Southern California* (Berkeley: University of California Press, 1972); and George Hayward Phillips, *Chiefs and Challengers: Indian Resistance and Cooperation in Southern California* (Berkeley: University of California Press, 1975).

29. A. Ross Bourne, "Some Major Aspects of the Historical Development of Palm Springs between 1880 and 1938," (M.A. thesis, Occidental College, 1953), 15; Marjorie Belle Bright, *Nellie's Boardinghouse: A Dual Biography of Nellie Coffman and Palm Springs* (Palm Springs: ECT Publications, 1981), 136–37; Jensen, "Palm Springs," *op. cit.*, 86.

30. J. Kellogg, Mecca, Calif., to Lawrence Paul Williams, March 17, 1921; "First Official Bulletin Issued by International Festival of Dates Association, Indio, California, 1921," 50; both in Lawrence Paul Williams Papers, UCR.

31. *Coachella Valley Submarine*, 1919, Ephemera Collection, SC, offers a boosterist view of the local date industry.

32. "Palm Springs: The Oasis of Delight," Hugh Evans and Company, ca. 1930, Ephemera Collection, SC; Elizabeth W. Richards, "A Look into Palm Springs' Past," Santa Fe Federal Savings and Loan Association, ca. 1960, RCL; Charles S. Jones, "Walled Oasis of Biskara: An Interpretation of the American Desert in the Algerian Manner," 1928, UCLA.

33. I am indebted to Denise S. Spooner for her interpretation of *Land of Sunshine* as a shelter magazine in "Something There Is That Loves a Wall: Constructing the Landscape of Community in Southern California," paper presented at the Los Angeles History Research Group, April 2004.

34. DeLyser, *Ramona Memories*.

35. David Cathers, *Gustav Stickley* (New York: Phaidon, 2003), 107–16; George Wharton James, *Wonders of the Colorado Desert* (Boston: Little, Brown, and Company, 1911), 287–88.

36. "Palm Springs: Oasis of Delight," *op. cit.*

37. Ibid.; " 'Our Araby' Palm Springs, Merito Vista," pamphlet, ca.1935, Ephemera Collection, SC; Elizabeth Coffman Kieley and Thomas Kieley, interview by author, Palm Springs, Calif., August 25, 2003; *Palm Springs Life* (Palm Springs: The Chaffey Company, Inc., 1938), PSPL.

38. Ad for Smoke Tree Ranch, *Palm Springs Life* (1938), 37.

39. *Palm Springs Life* (1938), *op. cit.*, PSPL; Alan Hess and Andrew Danish, *Palm Springs Weekend: The Architecture and Design of a Midcentury Oasis* (San Francisco: Chronicle Books, 2001), 60–65.

40. Cliff May et al., *Sunset Western Ranch House* (San Francisco: Lane Publishing Company, 1946), 84.

41. *Palm Springs Life*, *op. cit.*; Hess and Danish, *Palm Springs Weekend*, *op. cit.*, 60–65. The "ranch" style first appeared in house-style magazines and plan books in the mid-1930s, though it did not become widely popular until after the Second World War. See also Berglund, "Western Living *Sunset* Style"; Merry Ovnick, *Los Angeles: The End of the Rainbow* (Los Angeles: Balcony Press, 1994), 285–95.

Evan R. Ward

Finding Mexico's Great Show Window
A Tale of Two Borderlands, 1960–1975

The need for foreign currency, historical concerns for national respectability, and efforts to present a modern face of Mexico to the rest of the world influenced the plans of Adolfo López Mateos (1958–64) to make the border into a "show window" through the National Border Program (PRONAF). Established in 1961, PRONAF subsidized the cost of certain nationally produced goods, encouraged modern marketing strategies, and fostered North American tourism in Mexican border cities. Tourism and shopping in the border region were not new, as the preceding essays show, but Mexico's efforts to improve the image of its border cities as attractive destinations for upscale shopping and family tourism portended significant change, but it would ironically bring large-scale manufacturing, rather than tourism, to the region. What is more, it provided the momentum for the development of a tourist borderlands along Mexico's coastlines.

Both global and national forces influenced the plans for PRONAF. On the global scale, developing economies in countries such as Spain and Greece turned to tourism as a means for balancing foreign exchange in the post–Second World War era.[1] In Latin America, economists, such as Argentine Raul Prebisch, advocated for government-directed national production to replace foreign imports. Tourism was directly involved in the effort to capture funds for modernization on two levels. First, tax revenues would be increased by convincing affluent Latin Americans who spent large sums of money shopping abroad, particularly in Europe, to shop at home. Second, bringing tourists to Latin American countries could also generate needed funds for modernization and debt reduction. As early as 1949, the United Nations Economic Council on Latin America acknowledged tourism as one strategy for national development.[2] PRONAF, however, did not bring family- or resort-oriented tourism.

The consumer orientation of PRONAF made way for the emergence of the Border Industrialization Program (BIP), which gave rise to in-bond factories, *maquiladoras*, where employees assembled parts into finished consumer goods that were then shipped duty-free to U.S. locations.[3] At the same time, the Mexican government also devised effective ways to entice American consumers to Mexico as tourists: it fostered the creation of new "borderlands" cities on Mexico's Caribbean and Pacific coasts, including the resort towns of Cancún, Ixtapa, and Los Cabos, which were planned and built by a collaboration between Banco de México and FONATUR (the tourism arm of the Mexican state). As a result, American tourists—particularly those outside of the Southwest—were drawn to Mexico for somewhat different reasons and in quite different ways than the tourists who went to border towns during the twenties, the heyday of the border as a tourist site that Rachel St. John analyzes in her essay in this volume. In effect, these peripheral, planned cities on the coast became the locus of the new borderlands between the United States and Mexico, for it was here that the two nations now met, and here new boundaries between them were now drawn.

Ultimately, the Mexican state pursued tourism development along its northern border region and its Caribbean and Pacific coasts. While bringing tourists to the territorial border had been the conventional goal for PRONAF, the changing tastes, preferences, and modes of travel of American tourists made them more likely to seek out coastal towns than to head to border cities. PRONAF spent millions of pesos building border crossings to greet American tourists who crossed the international boundary line, but American vacationers' preferences had shifted to exotic resort locations like Baja California and Cozumel, accessible primarily by jet air service. While the visible legacy of Bermúdez's efforts along Mexico's Caribbean and Pacific shores is negligible, he was one of the first to simultaneously conceptualize Quintana Roo and Baja California as borderlands of leisure and consumerism. The avalanche of mass tourism that followed in places such as Los Cabos and Cancún attests to the accuracy of his premonitions, linking, in the process, the territorial border to the coastal borderlands as zones of development of consumer-oriented businesses.

MEXICO HAS AN ENORMOUS SHOW WINDOW 1600 MILES LONG, ADJOINING THE UNITED STATES, THE COUNTRY WITH THE HIGHEST PURCHASING POTENTIAL.

THIS ENORMOUS SHOW WINDOW MUST BE MADE INTO A GREAT COMMERCIAL, RECREATIONAL AND CULTURAL AVENUE.

Cartoon in *National Border Program/Programa Nacional Fronterizo* (Mexico City: PRONAF, 1961).

Casting the U.S.-Mexican border as "an enormous show window 1,600 miles long," idealized Mexico's ability to transform its border space into a giant shopping center.

Antonio Bermúdez and the Evolution of PRONAF

Although the face of the former president of Mexico, Adolfo López Mateos, graces the pages of many of PRONAF's oversized brochures, and his name still adorns the wide boulevards of Mexico's border cities, it was largely the pioneering work of Chihuahua native Antonio Bermúdez that brought the program to the border region. A former president of Mexico's state-owned petroleum company, Petroleos Mexicanos (PEMEX), Bermúdez brought little direct experience in consumer-related fields to his appointment as head of PRONAF, though he did have the requisite political and business pedigrees. Bermúdez's progressive management style, staunch nationalism, and border heritage made him an excellent fit for the position. His familiarity with the northern border gave him clear insight into how Mexico could improve its economic position vis-à-vis the United States. As early as 1927, when he served as president of the Cámara Nacional de Comercia de Ciudad Juárez (Chamber of Commerce of Juárez), Bermúdez passionately preached against foreign economic dependency: "Increase the exportation of Mexican products, lower the importation of foreign articles. This is the base that we understand to be fundamental to uplift and improve the economy of our country."[4] Twenty years later, Bermúdez was simultaneously elected to serve as a senator from the state of Chihuahua and asked to direct PEMEX, where over the course of

Cartoon in *National Border Program/Programa Nacional Fronterizo* (Mexico City: PRONAF, 1961).

This illustration demonstrates with great simplicity and some humor how it was thought that Mexico would benefit from intensified cross-border consumerism.

twelve years he assisted in the conclusion of disputes with foreign oil companies and developed new refineries. He hoped that "dominion over its petroleum" would give Mexico the resources, both fiscal and moral, to pursue "its own economic development."[5]

Tapped to head PRONAF in 1960, Bermúdez focused on the United States in his efforts to generate more revenue out of the region near the border. On the one hand, the proximity of U.S. banks, shops, and even real estate drained Mexican wealth out of the region: "Millions and millions of pesos, converted to dollars," Bermúdez lamented, "were deposited in North American banks, invested in the purchase of houses, and spent on North American products."[6] On the other hand, the fact that Americans consumed 93 percent (his calculations) of what they produced and exported the other 7 percent offered "an example to follow and imitate."[7] Dual-purpose surveys that the U.S.-based Real Estate Research Corporation conducted for PRONAF in Tijuana, Ciudad Juárez, and Matamoros in 1962 underscored Bermúdez's concern regarding the dependence of Mexican consumers on the United States, while at the same time painting a bleak picture of U.S. tourist consumer activities in Mexico. Although there was some regional variation, the studies pinpointed as problems the absence of retail stores and dearth of tourist attractions in Mexico's border towns. One finding alone will serve to illustrate the reports' characterization of Mexican border residents as unduly dependent on the United States: a surprising 40 percent of Mexicans interviewed in Matamoras in 1962 revealed that they made their last purchase of milk in the Texas town of Brownsville.[8] Some Mexican residents of U.S. border towns did cross into Mexico on a regular basis to buy Mexican foodstuffs, particularly at the open-air markets, but in general, the Real Estate Research Corporation's interviews revealed that few American tourists stayed overnight, spent more than twenty dollars, or made return visits.[9]

Nevertheless, the Mexican border cities had great economic potential because of their proximity to large markets of U.S. consumers. As a consequence, PRONAF sought to make the border a "show window" for Mexico, as well as its exotic consumer goods, leisure spaces, and services. Initially, PRONAF programs did not attempt to improve border cities' retail sectors (except in terms of artisan crafts), focusing instead on improving the tourist infrastructure, perhaps because American tourists had greater purchasing power than locals. The program was ambitious, because in order to encourage families (whose large numbers due to the baby boom heralded "family-oriented" consumption patterns) to visit Mexico, it had to "transform the environs of the border towns." While achieving this goal required, in part, the reduction of the availability (or the visibility) of cheap liquor, prostitutes, narcotics, gambling, and other vice products and services, PRONAF initially focused on the beautification of border cities.[10] The Mexican modernist architect Mario Pani—who had designed hotels, the Ciudad Universitaria, and the showcase of middle-class Mexican consumerism, the suburban Ciudad Satélite, in Mexico City—was hired on commission to produce a proposal for modernizing the façade for the border cities.[11] Sleek exteriors exuding Mexico's quest for modernity, with dignified interiors reflecting the nation's history, would showcase Mexico's progress and heritage. Located near the U.S.-Mexican border on new wide thoroughfares, with beautiful gates at the international boundary, Pani's centers would include cultural venues, upscale hotels, and, most importantly, retail sites.[12]

Integrated development plans aimed to serve tourists and locals, a dual function that captivated Bermúdez, who later noted in his memoirs that he pushed PRONAF to prioritize "the construction of modern shopping centers that with their attractive presentation captivate the view of the customer, inviting him to visit them and make purchases." Sounding more like Victor

Gruen, famed Austrian architect and developer of the first enclosed shopping center, than the ex-director of PEMEX, Bermúdez continued, "Shopping centers are a vital necessity and each day evolve and improve the appearance and presentation of those in the principal countries of the world." The border region needed modern forms of retail that would offer "aesthetics and Mexican-flavored style," as well as "economic convenience." In recognizing that well-designed, modern stores alone could not change the dynamics of the border's consumer culture, Bermúdez also called for merchants to aggressively market Mexican products to foreigners and nationals alike. He prodded them to build parking lots, keep their stores clean, train their employees "to take care of their customers," and offer "products that can compete with any other on the basis of quality, price, and presentation."[13]

Bermúdez's optimism about PRONAF seemed boundless. International shopping centers were slated for every major city along the border with the United States, and also minor cities such as San Luis Río Colorado, Sonoita, and Villa Acuña. In addition to planning the construction of warehouses, PRONAF slated a less prosaic and far more enticing array of luxury hotels, motels, trailer courts, shopping centers (international and local), colleges, art museums, exposition centers, convention halls, auditoriums, dance schools, conservatories, bullrings, *charro* stadiums, zoos, elaborate ports of entry, and country clubs for Tijuana, Ciudad Juárez, and Matamoros. A full program of "cultural festivals of symphonic music, ballet, [and] high-quality Mexican and foreign motion pictures" would be presented in "first-rate theaters," while at the same time, boxing and horseracing, euphemistically referred to as "sporting events which have a high drawing power," would continue to find venues in border towns.[14]

While evidence of PRONAF's accomplishments can be found in the built environment of nearly all the border cities, Ciudad Juárez was its primary beneficiary. Shopping centers were constructed in Matamoros, Piedras Negras, Nogales, and Ensenada (where a hotel was also constructed), while grand international gateways went up in several cities, including Nogales. But it was in Juárez that an ultramodern museum dedicated to ancient, colonial, and modern Mexican art, a shopping center, a convention hall designed by Mario Pani, a market featuring Mexican handicrafts, several supermarkets, a *charro* stadium, and the posh Camino Real Hotel would all be built in what came to be known as the Zona Pronaf. The Camino Real Hotel, more than any of the other components of this remarkable mixed-use cultural and commercial center, pleased Bermúdez. "A great quantity of North Americans, principally family tourists,"

Bermúdez noted, "continually occupy this hotel."[15] The synergy between the commercial and cultural components of the Zona Pronaf was exhibited both in displays of Mexico's past in the Museo de Arte e Historia and indigenous Mexican handicrafts in the nearby Centro Artesanal. Perhaps the greatest contribution of PRONAF to Ciudad Juárez was the development of a business zone where hotels and shopping outlets have continued to congregate.

Although PRONAF went into decline after Bermúdez's departure from its directorship in 1965, the programs initiated during the previous four years did alter border cities' commercial landscapes. Local, state, and federal funds flowed into the border region for the first time since the 1920s. This is nowhere more evident than in Tijuana, a city that received very little initial support from PRONAF. Today, Olmec statuary heads stand as cultural reminders of Mexico's past on Avenida Revolución, summer book fairs provide an alternative form of leisure to the ubiquitous bars and clubs, and the transformation of Avenida de los Héroes into an elegant boulevard dotted with trees, arbors, and impressive cultural institutions owes some debt to the vision of Antonio Bermúdez as realized through PRONAF's development programs in the 1960s.[16]

The Demise of PRONAF

PRONAF fell far short of its goals of increasing domestic consumption of Mexican-made goods and foreign consumption of Mexican tourist services. The structural inequities between the two national economies were simply too great for consumer-oriented programs alone to succeed. What is more, the Mexican government did not fully understand the dynamic nature of the consumer economy. For instance, it mistakenly subsidized certain items produced nationally, such as cotton clothing, shoes, soaps, and canned seafood, that neither tourists nor Mexican nationals were inclined to buy. PRONAF fell short, as one Mexican critic contended, because it "tried to go head to head, using basically artificial means, with the most industrialized country in the world."[17] That country, the United States, was witnessing its own commercial revolution during the 1960s, characterized by a boom in shopping center construction, patents for brand-name consumer goods, and flashy advertising campaigns. Just as Mario Pani was drawing his first plans for PRONAF-subsidized communities and shopping centers in 1961, the outdoor shopping center Fashion Valley Mall was completed in suburban San Diego. With easy freeway access, Fashion Valley was just one of San Diego's shopping centers. Two decades later the downtown Horton Plaza was completed. Despite the proliferation of shopping centers in Mexican border cities after 1976, including Plaza Río Tijuana, their lack of architectural sophistication and tenant mix discouraged upwardly mobile Mexicans from abandoning their weekend shopping pilgrimages to malls north of the border.[18]

Furthermore, despite the "Zona Pronaf" and other similar tourist developments, the extent and quality of tourism did not improve largely because of tourists' expectations about the border. Most visitors to Mexico's border cities lived in nearby U.S. border cities and only entered Mexico to patronize nightclubs, bars, and prostitutes.[19] While some of the cultural events PRONAF sponsored were meant to counteract the impression of debauchery on the Mexican border, as well as the reality of poverty in many of its districts, they simply were not appealing to the majority of tourists, who were seeking leisure, rather than uplift. A 1963 book fair held at the Ciudad Juárez Pronaf Center, for example, featured a lecture entitled "Latin American Historical and Sociological Studies in the United States" and a recital of Spanish poems by the Argentine Rafael Acevedo.[20] This is hardly what tourists were seeking.

PRONAF was active during a period in which the very nature of tourism was changing: Bermúdez might have read *The Image*, which cultural critic and historian Daniel Boorstin published in 1961, to learn that American tourists craved "elaborately contrived indirect experience." They wanted to travel to *landscapes of accommodation*—where they could stay in "American-style" hotels and "remain out of contact with foreign peoples"—rather than to *landscapes of negotiation*.[21] Transforming the border, where a tourist might encounter "vast stretches of land marked by misery and hopelessness," from a landscape of negotiation to one of accommodation would prove to be too much for PRONAF.[22] In addition, while Bermúdez and Pani were busy planning elaborate automobile gateways to Mexico, many American tourists interested in crossing international boundaries were boarding increasingly affordable jet airplanes.[23]

Perhaps the most salient reason for PRONAF's demise in the mid-1970s surfaced twenty years *before* Antonio Bermúdez assumed control of the agency: the 1942 creation of the Bracero Program, which drew tens of thousands of Mexicans, if not more, to the border region. When the program was terminated in 1964, private and public officials in Mexico looked for a way to employ the thousands of *braceros* who were returning to Mexico. This wave of return migrants included Antonio Bermúdez's brother, Jaime, who eventually opened the first industrial park for in-bond factories in Ciudad Juárez, under the mandates of the BIP.[24] From the standpoint of tourists, who were in search of picturesque views and romantic settings, the presence of assembly factories, known as *maquiladoras*, merely added to the region's rough image. Visits to border cities, which came to be known more for their factories than their tourist attractions, would continue to be made on the way to somewhere else, or simply as a short diversion.[25] The assembly of consumer goods (for instance, televisions) and subsequent duty-free export of them to the United States would become the basis for the border region's economic development. It was the production of consumer goods, rather than the consumption of consumer services, that would bring Mexico's borderlands to economic maturity.

"Projects farther South": The Transformation of "Border" Tourism

The rise and fall of PRONAF is only a part of the epic transformation of foreign tourism and consumer culture along Mexico's periphery during the 1960s. At the same time that Antonio Bermúdez was wrapping up his five-year tenure as director of PRONAF, Banco de México officials were also considering tourism as a means of boosting Mexico's foreign reserves. It is important to note that Bermúdez and PRONAF sought to develop tourism and consumer-related activities not just on the territorial border, but also along the entire periphery of the country.[26] While PRONAF activities mainly targeted the northern border cities, Bermúdez spent significant amounts of time and money south of the border along Baja California's coasts, where he initiated development plans for beach resorts.

By 1966 PRONAF spent more money on tourism development at Ensenada and Punto Estero in Baja California than in any of the cities that lay directly adjacent to the international boundary line, save Ciudad Juárez and Nogales. In part this was because of the recognition that the overlay of vice tourism was too thick in border cities to attract families seeking resort experiences described by Lawrence Culver in the previous essay in this volume. PRONAF's attempted reconditioning and expansion of the storied Hotel Playa Ensenada manifested its intention to develop Ensenada into a tourist attraction, a goal it eventually fulfilled. Part of Bermúdez's attraction to Ensenada was its distance from the borderline: it was an ideal site for family tourism because, as Bermúdez explained, it was "a clean city," by which he referred "especially to its moral cleanliness." In his view, there was "no room for centers of vice, nor prostitution, nor second- or third-class bars."[27] At Punto Estero, Bermúdez opined that water resorts "including a hotel and yacht club" would attract "rich people who enjoy water sports and are attracted by the Mexican ambience."[28]

In retrospect, Bermúdez realized that PRONAF's efforts to build a series of

International Airports in the U.S.-Mexico border region, 2007.

marinas up and down Punto Estero's coastline, which languished, had opened the doors "for the development of similar projects farther south," where, in his view, "the mild nature of the climate" contributed to the creation of "an enormous and important source of tourism." He was especially optimistic about the development of the frontier state of Quintana Roo, where Cozumel and Islas Mujeres were, in his assessment, "the most beautiful sites of the Caribbean and entire world." Bermúdez mused that "promoters of international and national tourism will ask themselves why they did not promote it better, because in addition to possessing crystalline and transparent waters without equal in other parts," these sites enjoyed "a delicious climate and a great quantity and diversity of fish." In taking into account the short distance between Florida and Quintana Roo, Bermúdez speculated that perhaps Cuban tourist attractions could relocate to the Mexican peninsula.[29]

Despite his prescient comments related to the potential for international tourism in both Baja California and Quintana Roo, Bermúdez's memoirs make no reference to direct coordination with the Banco de México, or other entities, in underwriting tourist development in those coastal regions. Indeed, he was only one of several groups and individuals in Mexico who recognized the development potential of tourism in Baja California and along the Caribbean coast.[30] PRONAF's publicity bulletins from the second half of the 1960s indicate that discussions about how to develop beach tourism were frequent and focused on the southeastern coast of Mexico. But, until 1968, a center for tourism on the southeastern coast was not identified, although Chetumal's archaeological ruins, sandy beaches, and new airport made it a likely site.[31] Throughout the 1960s and into the 1970s, the secretary of the treasury, Antonio Ortiz Meña, consistently insisted on the development of programs that could capture foreign revenue through tourism. It was Ortiz Meña who helped launch PRONAF in 1960, appointed Bermúdez as its director in 1961, and then established FONATUR, which in 1969 began planning the tourist resorts of Cancún and Ixtapa.[32]

Tourism Creates a New U.S.-Mexico Borderlands

The efforts of FONATUR and Banco de México to design resorts largely intended for North American tourists gave rise to a series of new decentralized "border towns" along Mexico's coastlines. The involvement of Mexico's federal authorities in developing Cancún, Los Cabos, Ixtapa, Loreto, Huatulco, Playa del Carmen, and other new tourist towns differentiated these new resorts from earlier ones, like Acapulco, which had been an international destination since the 1940s.[33] Cancún was the first of the resorts that the Banco de México and FONATUR engineered. While others have ably told the story of Cancún's genesis and evolution, comparing its development with the efforts made to similarly transform several border cities provides insight into the transnational consumer culture binding the United States and Mexico.[34]

Two Banco de México executives, Antonio Enríquez Savignac and Rodrigo Gómez, realized in the 1960s that beach tourism could be profitable.[35] In the late 1960s, Savignac explains, "tourism to Mexico had been growing consistently and successfully to various destinations, especially to our Pacific coast, without any of the usual government planning, fiscal incentives, or loans." Savignac and Gómez organized two federal agencies, INFRATUR (Fondo Nacional de Fomento Turismo) (responsible for implementing tourist strategies) and FOGATUR (National Trust Fund for Tourist Infrastructure) (responsible for funding hotel development), which both merged into FONATUR (Tourism Guarantee and Promotion Fund) in 1974. Unlike Bermúdez's work in the border cities, Savignac and his associates found the greatest possibility for profitable tourism in undeveloped areas far from the U.S. market: they carefully selected uninhabited locations along Mexico's coasts. Their search for the perfect beaches began with "intensive studies, both in the field and the office." Savignac describes the fieldwork as "wild, beautiful, and challenging." He continues, "We covered Mexico's 10,000 kilometers [6,250 miles or so] of marvelous, varied, spectacular and still mostly pristine coastline by plane, boat, jeep, horse and on foot, measuring anything measurable (beach length, width, slope, composition, tides, vegetation, fauna, communications, available infrastructure such as roads, water, rivers, and many, many more things) and assessing the equally important unquantifiable variables (the existence and frequency of dangerous or nuisance species such as sharks, moray eels, snakes, aggressive ants, mosquitoes, malaria, or other contagious or endemic diseases; the attitude of the local population, customs, fears, habits and again, many, many more things)." His office then analyzed sea and air temperatures, wind quality, natural disasters, and sun patterns. With the input of travel experts, politicians, and hoteliers, five sites for development were selected: Cancún, Ixtapa, Los Cabos, Huatulco, and Loreto.[36] None, it is worth noting, were along the two-thousand-mile-long border with the United States, the home of the target market for these resorts.

The dependence on air travel to channel tourists to the new coastal resorts further highlights the border region's drawbacks as a tourist site. Even if PRONAF had developed "must see" entertainment, luxury shopping, and five-star hotels in its border towns, the lack of scheduled airplane access to the region was (and continues to be) problematic for all travelers. Both Mexican and American border cities were drastically underserviced, making access from the East Coast, Midwest, and even West Coast difficult, except for by car. While many roads led to the border, the airplane was becoming the carrier of choice for tourists. At first, the idea of isolated resorts dependent on jets seemed madness. Savignac recounted, "Everyone agreed unanimously that we Banco de México technocrats were absolutely mad. Building an instant mega–resort destination in the jungle, 1,800 kilometers [1,118 miles] from Mexico City, away from the tried and true tourist paths to Mexico's coast was absolute, undiluted folly. But . . . what the heck!!! If Banco de México wanted to pour all that money into their organizations and regions, they would tolerate our eccentricities."[37]

Despite the fact that FONATUR was a government venture, Mexico's state-owned airlines resisted offering regular service from Mexico City to the coastal resort and bristled even more at the thought of international carriers flying directly into Cancún. With the completion of Cancún's airport, the number of Cancún's "border crossings" increased markedly. When coupled with the peso devaluations in the early 1980s, Cancún soon came to exemplify "mass tourism." The seeming accessibility of Mexico's border cities—"just a step away"—

Cancún beach, 2003. Photograph by Keith Pomakis, use licensed by Creative Commons Attribution Share-Alike 2.5.

The sandy beach, protected inlet, cabañas, high-rise hotels, and older low-rise pyramidal hotel together create a landscape of accommodation, epitomizing the new coastal borderlands where the United States and Mexico meet.—A.M.

ironically undermined their potential to become tourist resorts, which required the easy access of the jet airplane and seclusion from all but the exotic symbols of the host culture and the unceasing service labor of its people.

Further highlighting the border region's dissonance with the *landscape of accommodation* is the contrast between the architecture of the FONATUR resorts and Mario Pani's modernist designs for PRONAF's border cities. Under the criteria for design set forth by FONATUR, hotels needed to incorporate pyramids, thatched roofs, and extensive interior and exterior landscaping in keeping with a Caribbean aesthetic.[38] For example, architect Ricardo Legoretta's first phase of the Cancún Camino Real, completed in the early 1970s, which resembles an elongated Mayan pyramid, showcases elements of contemporary Mexican architecture, including large geometric objects placed throughout the hotel, brilliant colors, and moving water.[39]

Cancún's shopping zones also incorporated an indigenous aesthetic, while embracing modern conveniences necessary to retail. As one Banco de México planner explained, "Inside the tourist zone, the most important sector of

Las Ventanas al Paraiso, A Rosewood Resort, Los Cabos, Baja California, Mexico, 2005. Permission courtesy Rosewood Hotels and Resorts.

This coastal resort not only reflects the aesthetic tendency of designers to mimic the natural flow of sea and ocean water but also gestures toward *mexicanidad* seen in the use of building materials found in Baja California.

private investment will be that related to the construction of a shopping center, where the various demands for goods and services in Cancún can be satisfied." It was decided to adapt Mayan architectural features from nearby, but only "to such a degree that they blend with the practical design of a modern shopping center." The shopping area, according to the developer, would become "a site of marvelous attractiveness" that incorporated Mayan motifs.[40] Subsequent FONATUR architectural regulations outlined similar plans to meld Mexico's cultural patrimony into commercially viable spaces. A 1993 document enumerating the architectural guidelines for hotels, homes, and shops built in Ixtapa, for example, encourages designers to "seek a national identity."[41] The coastal border towns have now become the aesthetic and architectural face of Mexico, offering a setting that looks like Mexico but feels like the United States. Bermúdez had envisioned a similar fate for Ciudad Juárez, Matamoros, and Tijuana, but the border cities could not be razed, and so only a few modernist façades went up. The show window showcased a *landscape of negotiation*, a site of challenging differences.

Finally, Mexicans, North Americans, Europeans, and multinational groups invested in FONATUR's projects, while PRONAF's depended almost exclusively on private Mexican investment. In the wake of the peso devaluations of the early 1980s, FONATUR appealed to North American and European hoteliers to invest in tourist cities like Cancún. The arrival of European investors, particularly the Spanish, offered FONATUR a luxury that Bermúdez never could have dreamed of on the northern border: international partners that diversified FONATUR's client base away from an exclusive dependence on American investors or consumers. Not only did Marriott, Ritz Carlton, Westin, and Hilton build properties after the peso devaluations of the 1980s, Spanish hotel companies like Sol Meliá also extended their Caribbean presence into Mexico's new borderlands, as did other Spanish chains like Oasis, Occidental, Barcelo, Riu, and Iberostar. A range of factors facilitated the ease with which the Spanish hoteliers adapted to Mexico, including the willingness of Spanish officials to diplomatically intervene on their behalf.[42] The presence of European hotel operators in FONATUR resort cities has resulted in large numbers of Europeans, in addition to Americans, coming to Mexico on vacation, thus decreasing Mexico's reliance on American consumer dollars.

Flying Over the U.S.-Mexico Border on the Way to the "New" Borderlands

PRONAF and the Banco de México's efforts to capture foreign currency through tourism and retail during the 1960s profoundly transformed the trajectory of Mexican tourism, as well as the development of the U.S.-Mexico border region. Beginning with PRONAF in 1961, Mexican officials, including Antonio Bermúdez, looked for ways to combine cultural activities, shopping, and tourism to entice American consumers across the border. An important part of this process involved using American technical expertise and marketing methods. Numerous factors, however, conspired to thwart PRONAF's efforts to boost border tourism and retail sales, not the least of which was the border region's demographic growth. The introduction of the *maquiladora* program, the demise of the Bracero Program, and weakness of the tourism infrastructure, among other things, rendered PRONAF ineffective. Most importantly, however, the absence in border cities of entertainment options for families, the developing taste for resorts, and the growing preference for jet travel diminished the importance of the border to Mexico's tourist economy.

Despite setbacks on the northern border, Bermúdez sensed that the development of beach and water-sport tourism in isolated locales could lure affluent Americans to Mexico for trips that extended beyond several days.

Administrators within Banco de México also initiated efforts to build integrated, decentralized resort cities on Mexico's Caribbean and Pacific peripheries. Not only did Cancún, Los Cabos, Ixtapa, Huatulco, and Loreto become new points of contact between the United States and Mexico, they often were the *only* point of contact. As the nature and geographical location of U.S.-Mexican tourism shifted from the territorial border to Mexico's coastal peripheries, tourists began staying an average of four to five nights per vacation, instead of twenty-four hours or less. Air travel facilitated the arrival of millions of tourists a year, and Mexican architects and contractors built a sophisticated hotel superstructure often reflective of Mexican culture and heritage. Peso devaluations and a simultaneous arrival of European and American hotel chains conspired to make tourism even more affordable, as spacious hotels opened thousands of rooms to tourists in the late 1980s and throughout the 1990s. Antonio Bermúdez had envisioned the Mexican border city as a tourist Mecca, but the combination of geography, demography, and history rendered the beach resort far more amenable for the promotion of the consumption of Mexican goods and services. Ironically, however, were Antonio Bermúdez alive today, he would probably not be surprised to learn that Los Cabos and Cancún are now home to some of Mexico's most exclusive hotels, largest resorts, and fanciest retail venues, though he did himself try to site these consumer institutions adjacent to Mexico's largest show window, the physical border with the United States.

Abbreviations

FONATUR	Fondo Nacional de Fomento al Turismo
PNF	Programa Nacional Fronterizo
PNF-BM	Programa Nacional Fronterizo, PRONAF *Boletín Mensual* (Mexico City: PRONAF, 1961–1968)
PNF-CJ	Programa Nacional Fronterizo, *Proyecto de un nuevo centro commercial en Ciudad Juárez, Chihuahua: Análisis económico* (Mexico City: PRONAF, 1962)
PNF-Guía	Programa Nacional Fronterizo, *Guía oficial: Museo de arte e historia, Ciudad Juárez, Chihuahua* (Mexico City: PRONAF, 1964)
PNF-Matamoros	Programa Nacional Fronterizo, *Proyecto de un nuevo centro commercial en Matamoros, Tamaulipas: Análisis económico* (Mexico City: PRONAF, 1962)
PNF-NBP	Programa Nacional Fronterizo, *National Border Program/ Programa Nacional Fronterizo* (Mexico City: PRONAF, 1961)

| PNF-Nogales | Programa Nacional Fronterizo, *Nogales, Sonora* (Mexico City: PRONAF, n.d.) |
| PNF-Tijuana | Programa Nacional Fronterizo, *Tijuana, Baja California* (Mexico City: PRONAF, n.d.) |

Notes

I would like to thank the College of Arts and Sciences at the University of North Alabama for a research grant that made this article possible. Mrs. Sue Nazworth, at the University of North Alabama Library, also provided indispensable help. FONATUR, Rosewood Hotels and Resorts, Ana Lilian Moya Grijalva, and Alba Rosa López at the Colegio de Sonora (Hermosillo) assisted with documentation and images. The author is responsible for all translations from Spanish.

Notes fully cite primary sources and specialized secondary sources. Full bibliographic details for all other citations are in the volume's selected bibliography.

1. Williams and Shaw, eds., *Tourism and Economic Development.*

2. Michael Clancy, *Exporting Paradise: Tourism and Development in Mexico* (Amsterdam: Pergamon, 2001); Berger, *The Development of Mexico's Tourism Industry.*

3. Sklair, *Assembling for Development*; Hansen, "Origins of the *Maquila* Industry"; Kopinak, *Desert Capitalism*; Iglesias Prieto, *Beautiful Flowers.*

4. Antonio J. Bermúdez, *El rescate del mercado fronterizo: una obra al servicio de México* (Mexico City: Ediciones Eufesa, 1966), 15. See also Hill, "Wasted Resources."

5. Antonio J. Bermúdez, *Doce años al servicio de la industria petrolera mexicana, 1947–1958* (Mexico City: Editoriales Comaval, S.A., 1960), 17, 12.

6. Bermúdez, *El rescate, op. cit.,* 18–19.

7. Ibid., 19–20. Bermúdez's idealization of Mexican nationalism and American business practices reflects the transnational business relationships explored in Moreno, *Yankee Don't Go Home!*

8. PNF-CJ, 11, 13; PNF-Matamoros, 13–16.

9. PNF-CJ, 9–10; PNF-Matamoros, 10–13, 19.

10. Bermúdez, *El rescate, op. cit.,* 24–27.

11. For a general overview of Mario Pani's work, see two essays in Edward Burian, ed., *Modernity and the Architecture of Mexico* (Austin: University of Texas Press, 1997): Celia Ester Arrendondo Zambrano, "Modernity in Mexico: The Case of the Ciudad Universitaria," 91–106; and Louise Merles, "The Architecture and Urbanism of Mario Pani; Creativity and Compromise," 169–90.

12. PNF-NBP.

13. Bermúdez, *El rescate, op. cit.,* 106–7, 46. About the mall architect Gruen, see Hardwick, *Mall Maker.*

14. These bold plans are outlined in PNF-NBP.

15. Bermúdez, *El rescate, op. cit.,* 47.

16. Herzog, *From Aztec to High Tech,* 78–90.

17. Rogelio López Lucio, "El Programa Nacional Fronterizo: sus efectos en la industria y el comercio," (Mexico City: n.p., 1970), 131. See also Interdepartmental Graduate Planning Program, *The Nature of United States—Mexico Border Development: Investigation into the Effects and Potential of* PRONAF (Austin: Interdepartmental Graduate Planning Program, School of Architecture, Division of Extension, The University of Texas, Austin, 1966).

18. Herzog examines Tijuana's contemporary shopping centers within the context of a discussion on public space and transnational architecture in *From Aztec to High Tech*, 165–76. Several journalists have captured the impact of Mexican consumerism in the United States. See Richard Marosi, "Mexicans Head North to Snare Holiday Bargains," *Los Angeles Times*, December 23, 2005; "U.S. Lures Mexican Shoppers," *New York Times*, November 17, 1984; Shannon McMahon, "Border Boost: Mexican Consumers Pour Billions Annually into San Diego's Economy," *San Diego Union-Tribune*, August 7, 2005.

19. López Lucio, "El Programa Nacional Fronterizo," *op. cit.*, 128–37.

20. Ronald Hilton, "Hispanic American Report" (1963): 645–646, reprinted in *Hispania* as "Hispanic World," 47 (1964): 160–61.

21. Boorstin, *The Image*, 99.

22. Hilton, "Hispanic World," *op. cit.*, 161.

23. Boardman, *Destination México*, 95–97.

24. Bermúdez Internacional, "Grupo Bermúdez and the Historical Roots of Bermúdez International," http://www.bermudezinternational.com/Information/history.html, accessed May 10, 2006.

25. Arreola and Curtis, *Mexican Border Cities*, 77–106.

26. PRONAF *Boletín Mensual* (PNF-BM) served as the promotional newsletter for Bermúdez's organization from its inception in the early 1960s until the early 1970s. While the publication's articles were mostly about the northern border, they discussed tourism development in Quintana Roo and the Mexican Caribbean. Articles also illustrate the intense interest of Bermúdez and PRONAF in developing beach tourism along Baja California's Pacific coast. One, for example, discusses ongoing discussions between groups in the United States and Mexico to build a highway from Tijuana to San José del Cabo: "Nuevo incentivos para los turistas," PNF-BM, 6, no 57 (February 1966).

27. Bermúdez, *El rescate, op. cit.*, 35, 67; Bonifaz de Novelo, "Hotel Riviera del Pacífico" and "Ensenada se encuentra de placemes," PNF-BM, 4, no. 35 (April 1964), both publicize PRONAF's resort development plans in the Ensenada area.

28. Bermúdez, *El rescate, op. cit.*, 68.

29. Ibid., 59.

30. Consejo Nacional de Turismo report, "Incorporación del turismo del cáribe al sureste de México: Ensayo económico turístico de Mercado," May 1965, author's personal collection; Departamento de Turismo del Gobierno de México report, *Testimonio de una política en materia de turismo*, 1964, author's personal collection; *Estudio general del desarrollo del turismo en México*, n.d., commissioned by Impulsora de Empresas Turisticas, S.A. de C.V., Banco de México Library.

31. To trace Bermúdez's and PRONAF's interest in developing a coastal tourist borderlands, see "Primera reunión de turismo del sudeste," PNF-BM, 2 (June 1962); "Nuevos servicos aereos en Quintana Roo," PNF-BM, 6 (February 1966); "Quintana Roo y sus grandes atractivos," PNF-BM, 6 (March 1966); "Quintana Roo va ganando la preferencia del turismo," PNF-BM, 6 (June 1966); "Gran centro turistico en Bacalar, Q.R.," PNF-BM, 6 (August 1966); "Reconocimiento fronterizo por la obra del presidente Diaz Ordaz," PNF-BM, 7 (January 1967); "Impulso al turismo en el sudeste de México," PNF-BM, 7 (April 1967); "Aumenta el interés turístico por Cozumel, Q.R.," PNF-BM, 7 (May 1967).

32. FONATUR, *30 años de inversión con buen destino* (Mexico City: FONATUR, 2004), 20. Ortiz Meña gives his own interpretation of tourism development in the 1960s in Mexico in his memoirs, *El desarrollo estabilizador: reflexiones sobre una época* (Mexico City: El Colegio de México, 1998).

33. See Hart, *Empire and Revolution*, 411–14.

34. Fernando Martí's classic journalistic account of the origins and development of Cancún are compiled in *Cancún, fantasía de banqueros: la construcción de una ciudad turistica a partir de cero: una narración periodística* (F. Martí, 1985). See also Daniel Hiernaux-Nicolas, "Cancun Bliss," in Dennis Judd and Susan Fainstein, eds., *The Tourist City* (New Haven: Yale University Press, 1999), 124–39; Clancy, *Exporting Paradise, op. cit.*; Berger, *The Development of Mexico's Tourism Industry*.

35. FONATUR, *30 años de inversión, op. cit.*, 19.

36. The quotations and information in the preceding paragraph are from Antonio Enrique Savignac, "Tourism as a Tool for Development: A Case History," Fifth ICCA Conference, Cancún, Quintana Roo, November 5, 2001.

37. Ibid.

38. Fernando Martí, *Cancún: Paradise Invented* (México: Impresora Formal, 1998), 87.

39. FONATUR, *Cancún* (Mexico City: FONATUR, 1982), 70; Martí, *Cancún: Paradise Invented, op. cit.*, 110.

40. Fondo de Promoción de Infraestructura Turística, "Proyecto de desarrollo turístico en Cancun, Q.R.," Banco de México, n.d., Library, Secretaría de Turismo, Mexico City.

41. FONATUR, "Reglamento de imagen arquitectónica, Ixtapa, Gro.," April 1993. Javier Sordo Madaleno designed Mexico's most photographed hotel, the Westin Regina Los Cabos, to reflect the surrounding landscape in monumental Mexican style. One of the best examples of the monumental Mexican style is Las Ventanas al Paraíso, a Rosewood Resort, in Los Cabos, designed in the style of contemporary Mexican architecture and built entirely with elements found on the peninsula. The landscaping was also completed using only plants found in Baja California. See Kira L. Gould, "Las Ventanas al Paraíso, Cabo San Lucas, Mexico," *Architectural Record* (November 1998), 118.

42. Author's correspondence with Ricardo Alvarado Guerrero, May 2003.

III

CONSUMPTION IN NATIONAL AND TRANSNATIONAL SPACES

"Employment Agency Sign," Corpus Christi, Texas, 1949. Photograph by Russell Lee, courtesy Russell Lee Photograph Collection, box 3y183, negative no. e_r1_13918ef_0014, Center for American History, University of Texas, Austin.

A typical Mexican home on the border, ca. 1910–1914. Photographic postcard print from Yale Collection of Western Americana, Beinecke Rare Book and Manuscript Library, Yale University, Image ID 1066829.

Josef Barton

At the Edge of the Storm
Northern Mexico's Rural Peoples in a New Regime
of Consumption, 1880–1940

No one knows why the local justice took an inventory of José Silva's estate. On a miserably hot day in August 1918, after having walked ten kilometers from his village of Presa de Guadalupe to a vast stand of *agave lechuguilla*, Silva had died while harvesting *ixtle* fiber used in sacking. As the justice Hilario Dávila inspected the scene under the mesquite tree where the harvester had fallen, he gathered Silva's tools, directed two men to carry his body back to the settlement, then returned to the dead man's palm-thatched *jacal*. There, in the 96 square feet of a dirt-floored hut, Dávila pursued his inquest. In one column he listed tools and in another durable household goods, which were limited to an iron pot and tripod, two ceramic jars (filled with a little corn and a few beans), a chair, a table, a blanket, and a cornhusk mattress. At the bottom of the official inquest form, the justice tersely closed the case: "Nothing of value."[1]

Not so. This man's death, in a remote corner of the northern Mexican state of Coahuila, was testimony of the intensification of a new regime of consumption, one that would end with all production and consumption occurring within the confines of the market. Among José Silva's household goods, the local justice found some items that told of the dead man's world: two small sacks of seed corn and beans, receipts for sales of *ixtle* fiber, paid-up accounts from company stores, and punched railway tickets. These were tokens of the migratory harvester's annual harvest of his own corn and beans in late June, his twice-yearly extraction and sale of Coahuilan agave fiber in

Harvester carrying sack of *ixtle* fiber, Hacienda Aguanueva, Coahuila, ca. 1914. Photograph, courtesy Charles M. Freeman Collection of Mexico Photographs, Harry Hunt Ransom Humanities Center, University of Texas, Austin.

January and July, his annual chopping of young Texas cotton in April, and his picking of mature bolls in August and September. The few steps between his *jacal* and his tiny fields of corn and beans defined his local limits of provisioning, his trails between his strips of *ixtle* and the nearest railroad sidings traced the regional boundaries of wage labor, and his journeys on the Ferrocarriles Nacionales de México and the Atchison, Topeka, & Santa Fe Railroad outlined his transnational circuit of migratory work. These glinting rails, in turn, set the perimeters of his world, for at either end lay the defining institutions of his strategies of consumption: the *tienda de raya* of the Hacienda de San Carlos, an enterprise recently assembled from the ruins of older estates in southwestern Coahuila, and the company store of the Caney Cattle & Pasture Company, newly created in the wetlands of coastal Texas.[2] In his travels along railways, then, José Silva strung together habits of provisioning and strategies of consumption whose meager results the local justice noted.

But Silva's was no solitary struggle. For several years, he had joined his fellow harvesters in protests against the Hacienda de San Carlos's avid cutting of ever more distant agave stands, even as the estate forced harvesters from their tiny corn and bean fields and charged higher and higher prices for beans

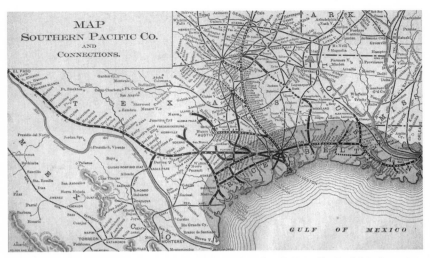

Railroads in Texas and Mexico, 1893. From Southern Pacific Railroad's *Texas Rice Book* (1893), courtesy Ephemera Collection, DeGoyler Library, Southern Methodist University, Dallas, Texas.

and corn at its store. All this, as one of their leaders wrote in a petition, "and yet there are many fields around here that need nothing more than hands to work them, but now we poor have to invade the lands of other poor families to survive."[3] Even as they improvised to make common cause, the people with whom José Silva joined hardly hung together on ties forged out of tradition or long acquaintance as neighbors. They were, in fact, most of them strangers to each other, neighbors for fleeting moments. In the early twentieth century, three of every four residents of Coahuila had recently migrated from nearby settlements in the Sierra El Toro and Sierra Piñones.[4] The very harvesters who were resisting the hacienda's efforts at expropriation, in 1917, themselves evicted recent migrants from the miserably unproductive corn rows that they cultivated along railways and roads.[5]

Yet, in the midst of mounting conflict, displaced rural Mexicans discovered that they possessed weapons of resistance, made potent by their very own entrance into the market as producers and as consumers. In their day-to-day provisioning of households, women expanded their control over gardening plots and fanned out into multiplying local markets and regional trading centers. In breaching previous limits on their provisioning and marketing activities, women built new networks that helped them take the lead in thieving corn and beans, in invading hacienda lands and neighbors' plots, in boycotting company stores, in starting rotating credit associations, and in founding consumer and producer cooperatives.[6] The death of José Silva came, then, at a moment of danger and possibility—*al filo del agua*, as the Mexican idiom has it: at the edge of the storm—when land-poor rural dwellers in northern Mexico joined old strategies of spreading their work across many locations with new instrumentalities of collective action, driven by imperatives of consumption, albeit subsistence consumption.

Recent anthropological and historical scholarship insists that people make themselves into consumers in the contexts of their own projects of surviving and provisioning.[7] The focus of this essay, then, is on women and men who began in local places with whatever assets were at hand, who entered new arenas of production and consumption, and who struggled to join their individual abilities with collective resources in order to make their way.[8] Rather than beginning with the large context of markets and the long era of consumerism, I start with the miniature world of the *ixtle* harvesters, the poorest of the poor in northern Mexico and the U.S. Southwest, who nevertheless spent their days and years becoming modern consumers.

The *ixtle* harvesters' journey traced the swift transformation of peasants into migratory men and provisioning women. Together they produced one of the essential elements of a global consumer economy—all that fiber to make sacking—while consuming some of the food and clothing that were poured out by the Mexican and U.S. economies. This pathway marked a jagged boundary between a strategy of provisioning in which market-oriented consumption played a small part and a "regime of consumption" in which the buying and selling of commodities was embedded in social and cultural relations.[9] On one side of this divide, harvesters still followed a gambit of fitfully purchasing consumer goods, a practice that relied on their own local provisioning and left them only occasionally dependent on the flow of consumer goods through their households. But once across the threshold of the market economy, peasants had to speed the flow of commodities through their households, since they relied more and more on purchased provisions and less and less on ones of their own making.[10] Mexican *ixtle* harvesters sought to sustain themselves in a local world of provisioning even as they crossed into a boundless arena of consumption.

Like José Silva, Mexican peasants and migrant laborers juggled scarce but complex assets into improvisational survival strategies, whose rootedness in grueling, physical labor has attracted the attention of countless historians and sympathies of many others, but whose new involvement in what social anthropologist Arjun Appadurai calls "the work of consumption" has been unremarked upon. Appadurai observes that mastering consumption's "multiple rhythms and how to integrate them is not just work—it is the hardest sort of work, the work of the imagination . . . , [for] the work of consumption is as fully social as it is symbolic, no less work for involving the discipline of the imagination."[11] As rural Mexicans submitted to the disciplines of markets and states, they also turned to collective life and new instruments of dissent. To peer into these local worlds is, in turn, to situate this account of consumption in dynamic spaces that producers and consumers were themselves defining. Here, in these emergent social forms—part networks, part movements, part organizations—we can grasp an early stage of globalization from below.[12] Nowhere was the struggle accompanying the entry into the regime of consumption more dramatic—or more hidden—than in the far reaches of the borderlands between Mexico and the United States.

To grasp the hazards and promise of this passage requires both conceptual work and historical context. Dispossession, displacement, and loss were the common lot of the poor in the nineteenth and twentieth centuries. Among the many dimensions of modernity that have shaped the lives of the poor—the growth of interdependent global markets, the gathering power of the state, the pull of ethnic and national identities—the networks of collaboration and new movements of solidarity easing access to mass-produced goods demand further research.[13] Newly constituted communities at once tried to preserve older forms of community, to accommodate them to the modern world, and to use them to shape global changes to local purposes.[14] In doing so, activists offered new meanings for consumption, for they rewove its thread into their design for reconstructing local worlds. As their repertories of collective assertion widened to include social movements, they claimed not only human rights, but consumer rights as well. Through these efforts the land-hungry rural poor in northern Mexico seized upon and transformed consumption to make their own worlds habitable and meaningful.

As they did so, memories, habits, and strategies shaped in response to scarcity played no small role. In the half century from the late 1840s to the early 1890s, allied mercantile and landed elites achieved dominance over commercial exchange across northern Mexico.[15] As they accumulated land and wealth, they acquired luxury goods. Since these great families of commerce and agriculture controlled access to credit, channels of distribution, means of transportation, and entry into local settlements, they imposed tight limits upon the households of both the small provincial middle class and the local peasantry.[16] Peasants and laborers sought some of their necessary clothing and foodstuffs in tiny rural stores stocked almost wholly with locally produced commodities. Shops, however, were rare. For instance, in rural Coahuila in the early 1880s there was just one store for every five hundred people; even one of the poorest rural counties in the United States a few decades later had one store for every three hundred people.[17] The scarcity of hard currency exceeded only that of stores. Within a rural order dominated by merchants and landowners, then, rural peoples confronted a regime of consumption marked by a scarcity of goods and minimal, if not absent, purchasing power.

Transnational economic change destabilized the social order, which had been based on abundance for the few and scarcity for the many. Following the completion of the great north-south railroads in the late 1880s, commercial elites gained new access to national and international markets for agricultural commodities.[18] Furthermore, an enormous transfer of public lands into private ownership resulted in the remaking of the landlord class. Initially, a great tide of foreign investment swept away the old estate owners and pushed forward new rural capitalists. The new rural elites, in turn, formed alliances with an emerging industrial class, all of whom relentlessly sought status through every means possible, including conspicuous consumption.[19]

By joining their consolidated control over recently opened agricultural lands with dominance over transporting and marketing agricultural commodities, this scrambling class undercut familial control of merchandising, which overturned the old regime of consumption. The new entrepreneurial elite ventured into new forms of advertising, distribution, and retail, their efforts resulting in a flood of new products into the towns and cities of northern Mexico. The increased traffic in goods carried in its train innovations in business organization, commercial associations, and merchandising knowledge, currents that often swept American entrepreneurs and catalog-lugging salespersons far into Mexico's hinterlands. Soon idealized in revisionist handbooks of business organization, these practices penetrated deep into the borderlands. By the first decade of the twentieth century, a new regime of consumption rooted in forms of both industrial and commercial capitalism had broken the hold of northern Mexico's old elites.[20] What is more, these new capitalistic forms pushed the land-poor and landless into new markets for their labor and for their necessities.

Local and transnational industrial and commercial capitalists relentlessly excluded rural peoples from resources.[21] After they consolidated their hold on the northern state governments, they limited customary patterns of landholding and excluded new claimants to land. Growing numbers of migrants and laborers were denied customary access to land, timber, and water.[22] As a consequence, northern rural laborers crowded onto fewer and fewer acres, now more dependent than ever on wages earned working in factories in the desert throughout northern Mexico, like La Laguna in Durango or the Agricultural Company of San Diego in Coahuila.[23] The new regime of consumption swallowed everyone: provided with abundant cheap labor, landowning Mexicans, Americans, and Europeans expanded their operations, while their own appetites for mass-produced goods, ranging from automobiles to department store ready-made fashion, were insatiable. Denied the means to survive apart from the market, landless Mexicans improvised their means of survival, finding themselves in company stores buying the beans their parents' generation had grown for themselves. What emerged was a permanent consumer revolution spurred by capitalist power, a central theme in the history of twentieth-century Mexico and the United States.

Within this revolution, the ordinary people of northern Mexico struggled to claim community—their source for survival, security, and honor.[24] The price of their struggle, as the political theorist Antonio Gramsci captured it when thinking about Europeans in the 1920s and 1930s, was lives passed in a state of "alarmed defense." He points to how this permanent mobilization left "traces of autonomous initiative" in the documentary record.[25] The remnants, when rewoven, reveal how ordinary men and women left to the margins nevertheless made themselves into consumers and made their homes and communities into in-between spaces.

The remnants of José Silva's life reveal what is to be expected: he moved through northern Mexico and the U.S. Southwest, as did and do many other Mexican peasants, in quest of work.[26] Despite fitful early-twentieth-century efforts by Mexico and the United States to formalize the control of peoples' motions across the region, migrants flowed largely unregulated, their movements quickly responsive to burgeoning enclaves of agricultural and extractive growth. They founded hundreds of new settlements that became villages and towns throughout the borderlands.[27] From Tijuana and San Diego to Brownsville and Matamoros wound this great modern frontier, where, in making their own lives, rural Mexicans on the move in turn shaped an in-between space where neither the old nor the new regime of consumption reigned.[28]

This new world opened imperceptibly, initially through the intensification of old ways of provisioning and of socializing. Consider the revealing vantage offered from the sprawling border municipality of Guerrero, a loose gathering of barely one thousand men, women, and children scattered among thirty tiny settlements on 1,235 square miles southeast of Piedras Negras (then Ciudad Porfirio Díaz) in the Mexican state of Coahuila. In small knots of houses and fields along streams and roads, rural laborers seized upon the breakup of old haciendas and the consolidation of new enterprises to find niches in which to pursue their projects of survival. In the early 1890s, new investors, big and small, consolidated their control over several modernizing haciendas and many small operations and promptly attacked the customary rights of laborers to work small plots to grow corn and beans and to graze livestock on common pastures.[29] In response, resident hacienda workers, small cultivators, and laborers struggled to develop new means of supplying their daily rations: they used their carts and oxen to carry cotton and corn to Piedras Negras, went high into the sierra to cut timber, and negotiated for small fields on which to cultivate cotton on shares.[30] Guerrero's people also made use of their durable assets of family and neighborhood: now a collection of kin and neighbors allied with a nearby settlement in reclaiming access to a spring from an aggressive landlord.[31]

In such multiplying contests over land, water, and markets across two decades, rural women and men developed ever more complex responses that ranged from forcing higher yields from their small plots, to seasonal labor on local work gangs, to migration into onion and cotton fields across south Texas. Even as great agricultural enterprises consolidated their control over lengthening stretches of this frontier, rural peoples mounted armed resistance and attacked the claims of the agricultural companies. And within these new communities, women defended their customary claims on subsistence plots against the advances of small agriculturalists bent on appropriating them.[32] Moreover, in the 1920s, men and women both expanded their repertory of collective responses to include union locals and cooperative stores. In a precarious equipoise between defending against an external threat and consolidating gendered practices of cultivating land and provisioning households,

Guerrero's people formed a new terrain along the border. And as always they relied on a complex network of human relationships.[33]

For most, living amidst capitalist transformation meant redoubling effort.[34] *How* northern Mexican rural peoples managed was, in one sense, a question of place. No conventional map captures the space through which they moved. Consider the expansion of the great hacienda of Aguanueva in the border state of Coahuila. Linked to both national and international markets by the Ferrocarriles Nacionales de México in the late nineteenth century, the hacienda produced enormous quantities of maize, wheat, beans, and *ixtle* on its lands and ran large herds of cattle and goats on its pastures. Production soared in the 1890s as new markets opened for its agricultural exports. After the turn of the century, wider recruitment drew three of every five of its seasonal laborers from Coahuila's Huachichil and Hediondita mountains and the distant villages of Gómez Farías, San Antonio, and Noria.[35]

In response to the international demand for industrial fibers, the hacienda consolidated control over fiber production, replacing harvesters like José Silva who exchanged *ixtle* for credit or currency with hired gangs of wage laborers to work the *ixtle*. At first, the ejected harvesters fought back by expanding cultivation of the *ixtle* plants higher in the sierra and building new cart routes to the railway for contact with North American middlemen seeking the fiber.[36] But when the hacienda clear-cut stands of highland timber to supply its construction crews with ties for new railroad spurs, the harvesters faced a complete loss of cooking and heating fuel, as well as the materials for charcoal making. Without fuel, these *serranos* (displaced residents) sought wages and provisions through migratory labor that encompassed Aguanueva and its neighboring haciendas, the newly opened mines in the region, and the expanding agricultural and extractive operations on the northern border. Moving in circles, the laborers maintained ties to both their communities and the estate.[37]

Only in the twentieth century did these displaced *ixtle* harvesters break out of their circle to connect with a wider world. Across Coahuila, peasants energized by the sociability found in homes, taverns, and communities entered into campaigns against expanding haciendas. Continued migration into new communities, as well as rapid expansion of hacienda operations, pushed villagers to diversify their strategies for claiming access to resources and provisions.[38] Now began a prolonged struggle on many fronts: defending rights to land and water in court, claiming access to stands of *ixtle* on land enclosed by expanding operations, searching for wage labor in more distant agricultural and industrial operations, and raiding the haciendas' stores. Still the haciendas' grip tightened, and by 1910, across a swathe of southern Coahuila, less than a quarter of rural households retained rights in land and water, resources even this fortunate remnant soon began to lose.[39] In this moment of mounting crisis, the revolution fell upon rural communities with extraordinary force. Even though villagers' first response was to furnish soldiers and supplies, as uncertainties deepened, communities began in 1913 to invade the haciendas and to reclaim their lands, thus challenging the provisioning regime that had changed their lives.[40]

Making their new resistance possible was the appearance of a new community of laborers on the hacienda of Aguanueva, whose holdings by 1911 were worked by 900 resident workers, 400 seasonal laborers, and hundreds more day laborers; 150 to 200 families lived in the settlement of San Miguel, in contrast to twenty-five men and women a decade earlier.[41] Yet the village was no mere human lump. Even in the years of peak *ixtle* production, the laborers successfully bargained with the hacienda for time to cultivate and harvest their own fields.[42] In San Miguel, this drive for autonomy took an insurrectionary form during the revolution. The villagers provided supplies and munitions to revolutionary troops first in 1911, again two years later.[43]

In 1916, as a powerful unionization drive got underway on the hacienda, San Miguel once more took the lead. When the hacienda's workers struck in January, the owner tried to hire scabs from the surrounding communities of Aguanueva's determined *serranos*, but strikers, most of whom continued to keep up their links to their highland communities of origin, convinced the migrants to stay off the job. Mobilized as they had never been in 1911 or 1913, the hacienda laborers fought for two years to break Aguanueva's hold on their lives.[44] Although the struggle was costly—San Miguel, the core of migrant and worker resistance, lost half its population to emigration between 1917 and 1919—still they acted. Out of their mobilization emerged new patterns of leisure-oriented, community-focused consumption.[45]

In the course of momentous transitions to wage labor and market-oriented provisioning, San Miguel's people asserted their autonomy, both amongst themselves and against the expanding reach of the hacienda's owners and managers. Catch a brief glimpse of the remarkable concatenation of market exchanges in San Miguel. Here was a lively trade in liquor, in peasant-manufactured fiber products, in transportation from field to market, in stolen goods, and in grain. The taverns of San Miguel, secret in the 1890s but increasingly open after 1905, formed the nodes of association for workers on the

Train at Cerro del Mercado station, Durango, 1914. Photograph, courtesy Charles M. Freeman Collection of Mexico Photographs, Harry Hunt Ransom Humanities Center, University of Texas, Austin.

sprawling hacienda and residents of the bordering *serrano* communities.[46] By the early twentieth century these dingy dives were among the few autonomous institutions of northern rural communities, places to gather information about jobs and wages, exchange accounts about working conditions, and pick up news about the oppositional politics of northern Mexico. Joined to the taverns were the great cockfights of the north, where people from several communities and regions gathered to hear ballad singers and colporteurs carrying news of the larger world, where political talk flowed as freely as mezcal, and where workers made contact with labor contractors from Tampico and Baja California and from Texas and California.[47]

In a time of improvisatory reconstructions of community, women's kaleidoscopic innovations endlessly shuffled older strategies of provisioning and new necessities of consumption. After 1915, a cohort of women sowed small plots near their residences in burgeoning new settlements like San Miguel, as well as on land they reclaimed from decimated haciendas, idled mines, and abandoned rural factories. In doing so, they supplied corn, beans, and vegetables to their households and to local markets.[48] These female gardeners confronted conventions rooted in landholding and gender. In a silent struggle that unfolded in a tiny clump of houses called Rancho de Vega between 1915 and 1921, eight women managed to gain control of nearly a quarter of the arable land. With their newly secured resources, they succeeded in consolidating their hold on provisioning, since they now had strong leverage in production and marketing. Soon they entered regional trading centers as well, where they not only occupied marketing stalls but also commanded a new public visibility. Established merchants blocked their further advance, but these eight women nonetheless gained a visible role in the marketplace, an advantage that other women defended by forming rotating credit societies and organizing producers' and consumers' cooperatives. In one new town after another, women like them blended old and new resources in the quest to satisfy household needs and pursue opportunities in the market. In so doing, they succeeded in shifting the balance of power from adult men to adult women in households and communities. Hence, women gained a permanent public presence in the consumer society that was permeating the borderlands, a presence that remains salient, as Peter Cahn's essay in this volume amply demonstrates.[49]

In these flexible mobilizations, the social forms that rural peoples created—a blend of networks, movements, and organizations—worked to take control of spaces of consumption, particularly sites and forms of exchange. To grasp how this effort proceeded, revisit once more Presa de Guadalupe, the village where José Silva had met his death in 1918. In this young settlement, formed just twenty years earlier, women cultivators and male *ixtle* harvesters boycotted the Hacienda de San Carlos's *tienda de raya*.[50] During the decade after the Mexican Revolution had run its course, *ejidos*, collective agrarian communities, established cooperative stores and credit associations across northern Mexico. In consolidating control over their members' resources, they sought to counter the haciendas' economies of scale, which made their marketplace transactions—whether buying or selling commodities—both more profitable and more possible than those of individuals.[51] Coahuila's rural peoples, as did those in other regions, seized an opportunity to organize newly complex provisioning regimes into projects for cooperative consumption. As the agents of land reform scattered across northern Mexico in the 1920s, they took agrarian censuses that revealed snapshots of this new direction. In one settlement after another, communities had organized rural unions, established cooperative stores, and broken the hold of the *tienda de raya*.[52]

But a biting irony lay at the heart of this remarkable transition. In the act of seizing the political and economic initiative, communities had made permanent the very discipline of market-oriented consumption that they had sought to fend off. And so the necessity of straddling the worlds of local provisioning and distant migration, a strategy that had sustained them during the previous half century, became all the more imperative. A final glimpse of the inner workings of the little settlement of San Miguel reveals much: in the 1920s, the village sent laborers into the nearby irrigated cotton fields of La Laguna, the cotton kingdom in the northern states of Coahuila and Durango, the sugar plantations of both the Gulf coast state of Veracruz and the Pacific coast state of Michoacán, and the booming oil fields of Tampico on the Gulf of Mexico.[53] In these migratory movements, the men and women of Guerrero, of Presa de Guadalupe, of San Miguel, and of places like them, entered into situations that demanded their compliance with new work routines, new time constraints, and new provisioning habits. Even as northern Mexico's rural peoples opened their own pathways to survival, they fastened upon themselves the disciplines of modern consumption.

And yet they continued to search for alternatives, most astonishingly in the flaring gyres of their migrations. One of these seekers was Vicente Lira, who had first entered the local stream of seasonal laborers on southern Coahuila's Hacienda de San Carlos in 1893, where he had harvested *ixtle* alongside José Silva. Soon, like the thousands of women and men who periodically crossed the border, Lira extended his journeys in 1903, when he traveled from Presa de Guadalupe to San Ygnacio, near Laredo, to clear land for onion fields. By 1906, he had extended his circuit to Del Rio, Texas, where he worked on the construction of a new onion-packing shed. Two years later, as the cotton frontier pushed onto the Texas coastal plain, he spent several seasons clearing mesquite and cactus from swathes of Nueces County in preparation for irrigated cultivation. And, beginning in 1910, he started to divide his search for work between Duval County, where he joined a cotton-chopping gang each year, and Nueces County, where he continued to clear land.[54] Lira's orbit demanded long journeys in ox carts and railroad cars to Laredo, early morning round-ups in gang labor for land clearing, week-long bouts of chopping, month-long stints of picking, and on and on, from one site to another across southwest Texas. In Lira's experience, the rapidly expanding frontier stretched his quest for work and provisions from deep in Mexico to the heart of Texas and beyond. Here grew an invisible but powerful dominion that enforced endless labor in order to acquire food and clothes at the company store.[55]

The company Vicente Lira kept on his journeys reveals still more about the new regime of consumption. In his annual round of work in Nueces County, for instance, he moved along knotted networks of kin and neighbors.[56] Among the newcomers who arrived between 1909 and 1919, about a third, like Vicente Lira, were agricultural laborers from southern Coahuila. This loose-knit com-

George Paul's first cotton field in Nueces County, Texas, 1908. Photograph, courtesy Robstown Collection, Harry Hunt Ransom Humanities Center, University of Texas, Austin.

munity of familiars was able to join together as they resisted pressures on the delicate balance they sought to maintain between work and consumption. Signal among these pressures were those of south Texas cotton farmers who sought to rationalize the work in their fields. They pressed the itinerant and tenant Mexican laborers to abandon their cultivation of corn and beans, to quit their customary garden plots, to drive their draft animals from common pasturage, and to contract with them or their associates for credit. A bare litany of a few cases highlights the landowners' tightening control: on J. B. Womack's farm, in 1911, five Mexican tenants found themselves forced to make credit arrangements with the owner's business partner. In 1912, on W. T. Moore's cotton operation, twelve Mexican tenants contracted to use their own draft animals for planting and cultivating, in exchange for favorable terms on their share of cotton production. Two years later, in 1914, Moore enforced contracts that made the tenants into laborers while still demanding the same contribution of draft power. By the 1920s, very few Mexican sharecroppers remained in Nueces County, for the terms of their contracts had erased their slim margins enabling survival.[57] Just as they seemed to forfeit all autonomy in terms of labor, so too did they in terms of consumption.

In the face of mounting pressure, women's maintenance of kinship and community relationships proved crucial, for these connections made possible

Mexican migrant workers in front of their home near Oso Bay, Nueces County, Texas, 1908. Photograph courtesy Robstown Collection, Harry Hunt Ransom Humanities Center, University of Texas, Austin.

male workers' itinerancy.[58] Especially among cotton choppers and pickers, the most seasonal and migratory of workforces, the work of women sustained community life. In one kin group of three families, for instance, all living in one compound in the south Texas town of Robstown, two sisters supported the family of a third, whose husband and father had fallen into peonage on a farm five hundred miles away in the Texas Panhandle. Such female networks enabled Mexican males to spread the extraordinary risks of their new lives among a number of allied households.[59] Like Vicente Lira's journeys, then, the collective enterprise that was migration depended on women's entrance into the spaces of provisioning, whether garden plot or market stall.

When Lira had begun his working life in the 1890s, he could find labor and provisions within a small compass. Over the decade between 1875 and 1885, for instance, Apolonio Mayorga, one of five hands on Rancho Calaveras, a grain and livestock ranch of 4,200 acres in Ben Bolt, Texas, worked the year round running cattle and sheep. Although his wages amounted to only seven cents a day, he also received monthly rations of corn, coffee, sugar, and tobacco. And with his miserably small earnings, he purchased clothes, shoes, bacon, and soap on credit from the ranch's tiny commissary, where he settled accounts at the end of each six months. Beginning in the late 1880s, signs of change were

D. W. Kinney General Store, Nueces County, Texas, ca. 1910. Photograph courtesy Robstown Collection, Harry Hunt Ransom Humanities Center, University of Texas, Austin.

already appearing, when the ranch hired several more men for two or three months of work, each of whom earned double Mayorga's wages but lacked his monthly rations. The new hands ran up more debt at the commissary than they could pay off at the end of their employment.[60] So onto the next job they traveled without a cent in their pockets, having earned nothing more than their keep for a few months. Here is evidence of one of the new kinds of provisioning, situated within the exploitive conditions facilitated by the borderlands' sparse settlement, the men's itinerancy, and the women's community-sustaining relationships.[61]

Over the next half century, the full immersion of Mexican laborers in a consumer economy resulted in their near complete exploitation.[62] In June 1927, for instance, on his five-thousand-acre cotton and livestock operation near Roma, Texas, Manuel Guerra hired three men recently arrived from Coahuila to chop cotton. As soon as they settled into the tiny shacks on the farm, Encarnación Escobar, Alonzo Ramírez, and Nicasio Benavides made credit purchases for lard, flour, knives, canned tongue and salmon, cumin, soap, meat, and thread. A week later, Escobar was back in Guerra's store to buy bacon, salt, canned tomatoes, sugar, coffee, chile con carne, gas, and lard, while Benavides bought a tablet, a razor, soap, and rope. Ramírez purchased very small amounts of canned corned beef, canned salmon, and gasoline on a continual basis. In the third week of their work, all three returned to buy more canned vegetables and staples.[63] As they walked the aisles of the store, they found an array of goods, ranging from foodstuffs (all of it canned or salted) to clothes (almost all work clothes, with few suits and dresses) to shoes (mostly work shoes), along with a small stock of tractor and truck parts. Variety there was, in the sense of a range of brands of necessities— P&G soap *and* Octagon laundry soap, Log Cabin syrup *and* Karo syrup—but no large selection of commodities. Most telling were the very close margins within which Guerra's laborers lived. In most weeks, migrant workers paid less than one dollar a week on their accounts. And in October 1930, when the Depression had already dogged rural Texas for four years, the thirteen cotton pickers who had just finished the season skirted a hazardous brink: five, among them Escobar, Ramírez, and Benavides, could pay nothing on their accounts.[64]

Not only did giant operations, like the Post operations in the Texas Panhandle, the Taft holdings in south Texas, and the De Bremond irrigated farms in southern New Mexico, succeed in tightly yoking work and consumption, but they also managed to harness state power for this purpose.[65] County courts did a brisk business enforcing the debts of laborers to company stores in Nueces and Cameron counties, as a bare recital of cases illustrates. Demetrio Casas and three fellow choppers, migrants from a hacienda near Bustamante, in Tamaulipas, in debt for shoes, socks, shirts, pants, and hats to a company store, were $17.50 short at the end of thinning cotton in 1908, and so were charged with theft. Melecio Pequeño and two other members of a picking gang from the hacienda of San Juan del Retiro, in Coahuila, were short $104 after sending remittances to their families, and so were sentenced to construct an all-weather road to their employers' cotton farm in 1910. Librado Flores and Lázaro Villanueva, crew leaders of migrant cotton choppers from Parras, in Coahuila, charged in 1914 with stealing four sacks of flour to feed a crew of forty-five who had been left without work and without food, found themselves digging irrigation ditches without pay. Lola Sánchez, a migrant cotton picker from the Hacienda de San Carlos, in Tamaulipas, in 1915 was sentenced to six months of labor on a cotton farm for the unauthorized use of six spoons, one towel, two sheets, one blanket, and six cups to feed and bed her family of four children.[66] In the worst case, helpless workers were forced into debt peonage, which became a standard form of coerced labor in the U.S. Southwest after 1915, much as it was across the U.S. South since the 1880s.[67]

In the face of mounting exclusion from the market for labor and for necessities, migrant workers sought new instrumentalities of collective response. One means at hand was class mobilization. On the giant Watts Farms in Cameron County, Texas, for instance, overseers enforced the monopoly of the company store. By 1910 surveillance of laborers' provisioning practices was so intense, that its foreman caught Ramón Rangel attempting to purchase a pound of macaroni from a store outside the operation. What is more, he had permission to beat Rangel and confiscate the pasta.[68] Watts Farms however missed something far more important than off-site shopping: its laborers had formed a defense organization, the Agrupación Protectora Mexicana. This informal union struck alliances with other groups of migrant agricultural laborers across south Texas: the groups exchanged information, distributed labor newspapers, raised funds for the support of local actions, and coordinated regional movements. Sustained by contributions from Mexican migrant workers throughout the Southwest, the Agrupación Protectora boycotted the Watts Farms' commissary during 1911 and 1912.[69] Even though their protest ultimately failed, the boycotters became part of the larger mobilization of an international agrarian working class, among whom were African American, Mexican, Mexican American, and European American field hands concentrated in Texas and the U.S. South; southeast Asian, Filipino, and Chinese sugar-cane workers in Hawai'i, Mexican, Japanese, Scandinavian, and Filipino farm workers in California and the U.S. Northwest; and Mexican pickers in the border states, as well as Colorado and points further north.[70] The boycott of the Watts Farms store was an effort of Mexican migrants to decouple consumption from work and to assert that the marketplace for goods should be free and fair, even when the one for labor was not.

Building on an earlier record of fitful success, these mobile communities took on a wider significance in the course of labor's vast uprising in the United States during the late 1930s.[71] In one town after another across Texas, migratory agricultural workers sought wider alliances. Beginning in 1936 with a series of conferences in Laredo, San Antonio, and Corpus Christi, local associations met with agents of the Southern Tenant Farmers Union and the CIO-aligned United Cannery, Agricultural, and Packing Workers, to organize the mobilization of field and packing-shed workers. By late 1938, the Cannery

Workers had succeeded in organizing fourteen locals across south Texas, from the pecan shellers of San Antonio to the cotton pickers of Palacios.[72] These organizing efforts sparked renewed efforts to break free of limits placed on consumption choices by both big packing operations and large farms. In one local after another, members sought not only to double wages—from a miserably low fifty cents to a dollar for picking one hundred pounds of cotton—and to break the power of big operations, but also to widen their access to stores and theaters and cafés and public services.[73] Over the next few years, across the entire southwest, migratory Mexican laborers galvanized an extraordinary movement that joined the demands of a mobilized class of workers *and* their consumption needs and desires *and* the drive of a new immigrant group for recognition *and* the claims of an aroused citizenry.[74]

Among the most remarkable of these locals was a spinach pickers' union that began in the south Texas town of Mathis in December of 1941. Urged on by Telésforo Oviedo, who, along with Emma Tenayuca, had led San Antonio's pecan shellers in 1937, this local grew from several informal revolving credit and mutual benefit associations that cotton and spinach workers had founded in Mathis and neighboring towns.[75] In a tent city of six hundred women, men, and children, almost all of whom picked and packed spinach every day, this remarkable movement fought to raise pay from seven cents to ten cents a bushel, to restrict children's working hours, and to improve water quality and sanitation in the tent village. Soon the members were mounting a broader drive, first to institute a night school, next to campaign against discrimination in local stores and theaters, and finally to desegregate public parks.[76] As the spinach season wound down in early March, Oviedo reported that organizers were already planning "to set up a good organization to demand a better price on the onions season that starts in May." As the migrant workers followed the season northward—to Robstown, Elsa, Falfurrias, Dallas, and Lamesa—they carried with them their capacity to organize collective defenses against exploitation and mobilize against exclusion from the marketplace for consumer goods.[77]

In a network of locals that now stretched from the border high into the Texas Panhandle, this company of six hundred migrant workers sustained a drive for rights—in fields and packinghouses, in schools, and in the marketplace. In Lamesa, a northern outpost of the expanding cotton kingdom of the Southwest, they challenged the town's segregation of stores and theaters. In a long letter to a Food, Tobacco, Agricultural, and Allied Workers Union organizer, Oviedo laid out both the promise and perils of this drive: "Where ever I have been I find a lot of places where the Mexican people is discriminated, but I have not do any thing due to the short period of time that remains on a certain place." And he continued: "Here is the latest example Roy's Cafe located at North First St. Lamesa Tex has a sign on the door that says *no Mexicans.*" A few days later, he wrote again to report that he had surveyed stores, cafés, and theaters in the town and discovered that most excluded Mexican workers. With support from Mexican American union locals, Texas and California civil rights organizations, and the Congress of Industrial Organizations, this movable community boycotted Shermer's Grocery Store and picketed Roy's Café and the Lamesa Theater during the month of October 1942. "You know," concluded Oviedo in his last letter from Lamesa, "this is dangerous at the present time, because there are a lot of Spanish speaking people that don't thinks it worth a while to fight for a country where they are not considered as civilized people."[78]

"A country where they are not considered as civilized people." Here we must understand that "civilized" stood for patterns of consumption rooted in provisioning that extended well beyond the bare necessities. In the face of such enormous condescension over the half century from the 1880s onward, Mexican migrants contended for decent work and steady provisions. By gaining a new repertory of collective action—the mobile working-class community, knit together from the myriad networks of migrating families; the labor local, built in the fires of class mobilization; the civil rights campaign, assembled in the course of political awakening—they played no small, no marginal part in the emergence of a new regime of consumption in the borderlands, despite their minimal purchasing power.[79] As it was elsewhere around the world where capitalism was in play, the market was the only place where work and the necessities of life could be secured. In each case, the exchange value placed upon each—wages and prices—would determine the contours of the never-ending regime of provisioning.

Abbreviations

AGN/CNA	Comisión Nacional Agraria, Archivo General de la Nación
AGN/DGG	Fondo Dirección General de Gobierno, Archivo General de la Nación
AGN/Gob	Fondo Gobernación, Archivo General de la Nación
AGN/GobPR	Fondo Gobernación Período Revolucionario, Archivo General de la Nación

AGN/Gonzalo Robles	Fondo Gonzalo Robles, Archivo General de la Nación
AGN/Obregón-Calles	Fondo Álvaro Obregón-Plutarco Elías Calles, Archivo General de la Nación
AGN/Trab	Fondo Trabajo, Archivo General de la Nación
AMS/P	Protocoloros Municipal, Archivo Municipal de Saltillo
AMS/Planos	Planos, Archivo Municipal de Saltillo
AMS/PM	Presidencia Municipal, Archivo Municipal de Saltillo
BCRO/45th DCR	Recorder's Office, 45th District Court Records, Bexar County, Texas
CCRO/CCR	Criminal Court Records, Cameron County, Texas, Recorder's Office
Condumex/Reyes	Fondo Bernardo Reyes, Centro de Estudios de la Historia Mexicana
DCC/A	Diocese of Corpus Christi (Texas), Archives
IEDC/AMG	Archivo Municipal de Guerrero, Instituto Estatal de Documentación Coahuila
IEDC/SigloXIX	Fondo Siglo XIX, Instituto Estatal de Documentación Coahuila
MRRG/OHC	Museum of the Republic of Rio Grande, Oral History Collection
NARA	National Archives Records Administration (United States)
NARA-SW/FHA	Farmers Home Administration, RG 96, Region 12, Rural Rehabilitation Case Files, Texas, National Archives Records Administration, Southwest Region
NCRO/NCCM	Chattel Mortgages, Nueces County Recorder's Office, Nueces County, Texas
NCRO/NCCR	Criminal Court Records, Nueces County Recorder's Office, Nueces County, Texas
NMSU/RGHC	Rio Grande Historical Collection, New Mexico State University, Las Cruces
OMA/SPA	Oblates of Mary Immaculate, Southern Provinces Archive
RAN/Saltillo	Registro Agrario Naciónal, Saltillo
SHSW/AFL	American Federation of Labor Papers, State Historical Society of Wisconsin
SHSW/Sapposs	David Sapposs Papers, State Historical Society of Wisconsin
TAMUK/STA/Allhands	James M. Allhands Collection, South Texas Archive, Texas A&M University, Kingsville
TAMUK/STA/Farias	Farias Family Collection, South Texas Archive, Texas A&M University, Kingsville
TTU/SC/Double U	Double U Company Records, Southwestern Collection, Texas Tech University

UCOL/WHC/Mine Mill	International Union of Mine, Mill, and Smelter Workers, Western Historical Collection, University of Colorado
UNC/SHC/STFU	Southern Tenant Farmers Union Papers (microfilm edition), Southern Historical Collections, University of North Carolina
UT/BLAC/Sáenz	José de la Luz Sáenz Papers, Benson Latin American Collection, University of Texas, Austin
UT/CAH/CF	Coleman-Fulton Pasture Company Collection, Center for American History, University of Texas, Austin
UT/CAH/Field	Henry M. Field Papers, Center for American History, University of Texas, Austin
UT/CAH/LMT	Labor Movement in Texas Collection, Center for American History, University of Texas, Austin
UT/CAH/Pierce	Jonathan E. Pierce Papers, Center for American History, University of Texas, Austin
UT/CAH/Sanders	Elias O. Sanders Papers, Center for American History, University of Texas, Austin
UT/CAH/TWR	Texas War Records, Center for American History, University of Texas, Austin
UTA/TLA/FTAAW	Food, Tobacco, Agricultural, and Allied Workers Papers, Texas Labor Archives, University of Texas, Arlington
UTA/TLA/Lambert	George Lambert Papers, Texas Labor Archives, University of Texas, Arlington
UTA/TLA/TexAFL-CIO	Texas AFL, CIO Council Papers, Texas Labor Archives, University of Texas, Arlington
UTPA/RGVHC/Guerra	Manuel Guerra Store Collection, Lower Rio Grande Valley Historical Collection, University of Texas, Pan American
UTPA/RGVHC/Shary	John H. Shary Collection, Lower Rio Grande Valley Historical Collection, University of Texas, Pan American
UTPA/TRHRD	Texas Regional Historical Resource Depository, University of Texas, Pan American
WSU/RALHUA/CIO	CIO Secretary-Treasurer Office Collection, Reuther Archives of Labor History and Urban Affairs, Wayne State University

Notes

Several readers have generously improved this paper, particularly Gergely Baics, Nicole Fabricant, Alexis McCrossen, Marc Rodriguez, Frank Safford, Steve Striffler, Mary Weismantel, and Patricia Zamudio. I owe a special debt to Jorge Coronado and Brodwyn Fischer, my collaborators in Northwestern University's Latin American and Caribbean Studies Program's Rockefeller Foundation project entitled "How the Poor Constitute Community." I especially acknowledge Alexis McCrossen's extensive editorial work on this essay.

Notes fully cite primary sources and specialized secondary sources. Full bibliographic details for all other citations are in the volume's selected bibliography.

1. On *enseres*, see José Silva, August 3, 1918, AMS/PM/161/1/14/49. For a description of tools and harvesting, see José C. Segura, *El maguey: memoria sobre el cultivo y beneficio de sus productos* (Mexico City, 1891), 187–92; Ramón González Rangel to Luis A. Aldaco, June 2, 1928, RAN/Saltillo/DT/I-II/Tanque de Emergencia, 110; Palma Barreta, undated memo, ca. 1944, AGN/Gonzalo Robles/3/51.

2. On old estates and new haciendas, see Poder, October 26, 1886, AMS/P/34/6/212–17; Venta, July 28, 1893, AMS/P/36/12/13/23–26; and Onésimo Gloria, March 22, 1924, RAN/Saltillo/DT/II-III/Gómez Farías, 32. On the Texas side of the story, see records of Caney Cattle & Pasture Company, J. B. Pierce Day Book, entries for May 30, 1907 and August 13, 1907; Matagorda County Drainage Commission Ledger, 1912–1914, entry for October 7, 1912; both in UT/CAH/Pierce.

3. Martín Domínguez to José Mijares, March 14, 1918, AMS/PM/161/1/14/51.

4. On the analysis of a world of radically delocalized places, see Sherry Ortner, "Field-work in the Postcommunity," *Anthropology and Humanism* 22 (1997): 61–80. Migration figures for 1911–1921 are derived from agrarian census schedules held in the archives of RAN/Saltillo and AMS/PM. See also Luis Aldaca, Informe, July 15, 1925, RAN/Saltillo/DT I/Presa de San Javier, 5.

5. On the 1917 evictions of recent migrants, see accounts in Informe, February 21, 1930; and Lázaro Calzada to CNA, May 12, 1933; both in RAN/Saltillo/DT/I-II-III/Aguanueva 145.

6. On provisioning and marketing, see Solicitud, January 11, 1921, AMS/PM/164/1/13; Juan R. Robles García de la Cadena, Memoria-técnica, February 23, 1923, RAN/Saltillo/DT II-III/32. On women's theft, see AMS/PM/146/6/17/43. On reciprocal relationships, compare the account of isolation of a young woman in 1901 (AMS/PM/144/2/5/2) with the petition of the women's Agrupación Agraria of San Miguel in 1925 (Pedro Cerda to Presidente Municipal [Saltillo], September 3, 1935, AMS/PM 178/9/33/85). On rotating credit and consumer cooperatives, see Acta, August 6, 1925, AMS/PM/168/3/ 40/94. On producers' cooperatives, see Cuestionario, March 2, 1919, AGN/Trab/171/25. For conceptual help, see Pamela Herd and Madonna Harrington Meyer, "Care Work: Invisible Civic Engagement," *Gender and Society* 16 (2002): 665–88, see esp. pp. 666–69, 674–76; Caroline Brettell, *Anthropology and Migration: Essays on Transnationalism, Ethnicity, and Identity* (Walnut Creek: Altamira Press, 2003), 43–44; Lynn Stephen, *Women and Social Movements in Latin America: Power from Below* (Austin: University of Texas Press, 1997), 191–93.

7. Demographers, anthropologists, sociologists, and historians have accumulated an impressive scholarly literature on the consequences of economic and political crises and a few have begun to draw connections between migrants' old homes and their new ones. For collections of recent historical and anthropological scholarship, see Friedrich Katz, ed., *Riot, Rebellion, and Revolution: Rural Social Conflict in Mexico* (Princeton: Princeton University Press, 1988); Joseph and Nugent, eds., *Everyday Forms of State Formation*;

Nugent, ed., *Rural Revolt in Mexico*; Roseberry, "Understanding Capitalism," 63–64; Berry, *No Condition Is Permanent*, 69–78, 159–80; Cohen, *Culture of Migration*, 30–48.

8. Bevir and Trentmann, "Markets in Historical Contexts"; Trentmann, "Beyond Consumerism"; Trentmann, "Knowing Consumers."

9. De Grazia, "Changing Consumption Regimes"; Appadurai, "Commodities and the Politics of Value," 6, 15, 29; Mankekar, " 'India Shopping,' " 82, 93.

10. Josiah McC.Heyman distinguishes between flow-conserving and flow-through strategies of consumption in "Organizational Logic of Capitalist Consumption," 179–83.

11. Appadurai, *Modernity at Large*, 67–68, 73–74, 83.

12. Klingle, "Spaces of Consumption," 95, 98–100, 107; Appadurai, "Grassroots Globalization," 6–7, 13, 17–18; Appadurai, "Deep Democracy," 34, 45–46; William Roseberry, "Beyond the Agrarian Question in Latin America," in Frederick Cooper, ed., *Confronting Historical Paradigms: Peasants, Labor, and the Capitalist World System in Africa and Latin America* (Madison: University of Wisconsin Press, 1993), 318–70, see esp. 342, 356–57; Ballantyne and Burton, "Bodies, Genders, Empires," 405–6.

13. Calhoun, "Is It Time to Be Postnational?," 240–43; Eric Wolf, *Pathways of Power: Building an Anthropology of the Modern World*, ed. Sydel Silverman (Berkeley: University of California Press, 2001), 166–83, 193–214, 247–50; William Roseberry, *Anthropologies and Histories: Essays in Culture, History, and Political Economy* (New Brunswick: Rutgers University Press, 1989), 188–96; James Ferguson, "Anthropology and Its Evil Twin: 'Development' in the Constitution of a Discipline," in Frederick Cooper and Randall M. Packard, eds., *International Development and the Social Sciences: Essays on the History and Politics of Knowledge* (Berkeley: University of California Press, 1997), 150–75, see esp. 168–69.

14. Eric Wolf, "Kinship, Friendship, and Patron-Client Relationships in Complex Societies," in Michael Banton, ed., *The Social Anthropology of Complex Societies*, Association of Social Anthropologists Monograph 4 (London: Routledge, 1966), 1–22. On local studies and structure and direction of globalization, see Benjamin Orlove, "Working in the Field: Perspectives on Globalization in Latin America," in William Loker, ed., *Globalization and the Rural Poor in Latin America* (Boulder: Lynne Rienner, 1999), 196–200; Sidney Mintz, "The Localization of Anthropological Practice: From Area Studies to Transnationalism," *Critique of Anthropology* 18 (1998): 117–33. On local and transnational networks of work and consumption, see Dohan, *Price of Poverty*, 11–13, 96–98.

15. François Chevalier, *La formación de los latifundios en México: Haciendas y sociedad en los siglos XVI, XVII y XVIII*, 3rd ed. (Mexico City: Fondo de Cultura Económica, 1999), 212–14, 224–25, 272–79, 338–41; Charles H. Harris, *A Mexican Family Empire: The Latifundio of the Sánchez Navarros, 1765–1867* (Austin: University of Texas Press, 1975), 246–54, 261–70; David Walker, *Kinship, Business, and Politics: The Martínez del Río Family in Mexico, 1824–1867* (Austin: University of Texas Press, 1986), 137–63, 226–27; Cosío, "Los empresarios y el crédito," 227–56.

16. Pérez Herrero, "El comportamiento," 194–95; Cerutti, "Empresariado y banca"; Cerutti, "Ferrocarriles"; Manuel Vargas, "La biología y la filosofía de La 'Raza' en México: Francisco

Bulnes y José Vasconcelos," in Aimer Granados García and Carlos Marichal, eds., *Construc-ción de las identidades latinoamericanas: Ensayos de historia intelectual (siglos XIX y XX)* (Mexico City: El Colegio de México, 2004), 159–78, see esp. 163–69.

17. My estimate of one store for every 500 people derives from a survey of the twenty-three surviving manuscript census schedules for the forty-two haciendas and seventy-nine ranchos in Saltillo in 1881 (AMS/PM/124/2/120). On density of stores in Macon County, Alabama, between 1910 and 1930, see evidence in Charles Spurgeon Johnson, *Shadow of the Plantation* (Chicago: University of Chicago Press, 1934), 15–16, 124.

18. On the timing of the growth of inequality in assets and income, see Coatsworth, "Economic and Institutional Trajectories," 41; Haber, Razo, and Maurer, *Politics of Property Rights*, 41–79. About the connections between railroad construction and new elites' domination of the countryside in the 1890s, see Ficker and Connolly, "Los ferrocarriles," 115–20; Ficker, *Empresa extranjera*, 276–79, 299–301. About the development of new towns, see François-Xavier Guerra, *Le Mexique de l'Ancien Régime a la Révolution* (Paris: Le Sorbonne, 1985), 487.

19. I have calculated the geographical distribution of public land transfers from data given in Holden, "Mexican State," 329–30. For the recomposition of northern elites, see especially Cerutti, *Burguesía, capitales e industria*, 141–63; Saragoza, *Monterrey Elite*, 31–71; Wasserman, *Capitalists, Caciques, and Revolution*, 48–53, 105, 110–12; Ruíz, *People of Sonora*, 38–40, 52–62.

20. Moreno, *Yankee Don't Go Home!* 17–23, 26, 38–39, 82–87. My characterization of a flexible adaptation of U.S. commercial ventures stems from reading twenty-five business organization handbooks and trade catalogs that circulated in New Mexico, Texas, Chihuahua, and Coahuila between 1880 and 1905, in the Amador Trade Catalogs Collection, NMSU/RGHC.

21. Charles Tilly, *Durable Inequality* (Berkeley: University of California Press, 1998), 21–22, 83–84, 91–96, pinpoints the structures of exploitation and exclusion within which rural peoples contended against inequality.

22. Almada, *La revolución*, 23–25; Kroeber, *Man, Land, and Water*, 164–181; Lloyd, "*Rancheros* and Rebellion"; Lloyd, *El proceso de modernización*, 97–108, 114–27; Alonso, *Thread of Blood*; Nugent, *Spent Cartridges*; Koreck, "Space and Revolution," 131–35.

23. On La Laguna, see Patricia Fernández de Castro, "Origen de las revueltas agrarias en La Laguna," in *Memoria del Congreso Internacional sobre la Revolución Mexicana* (San Luis Potosí: Instituto Nacional de Estudios Históricos de la Revolución Mexicana, 1991), 1:311–21; María Vargas-Lobsinger, *La hacienda de "La Concha": Una empresa algodonera de La Laguna, 1883–1917* (Mexico City: UNAM, 1984), 25–71. For the Compañía Agrícola de San Diego, see AGN/Trab/58/2/3, 8–10, 12–13.

24. The historian E. P. Thompson's work informs my argument here; see *Poverty of Theory and Other Essays* (New York: Monthly Review Press, 1978), 238–39, 289, 351–52 and *Customs in Common* (New York: New Press, 1991), 340–51.

25. Antonio Gramsci, *Quaderni del carcere*, ed. Gerratana, 3 vols. (Turin: G. Einaudi, 1975), 1:330; 2:868–69, 1058; 3:2283–84.

26. Adelman and Aron, "From Borderlands to Borders," 815–17, 837–40.

27. Aboites, *Norte precario*, 95–118; William Meyers, *Forge of Progress, Crucible of Revolt: Origins of the Mexican Revolution in La Comarca Lagunera, 1880–1911* (Albuquerque: University of New Mexico Press, 1994), 117–32; Juan Luis Sariego Rodríguez, *Enclaves y minerales en el norte de México: Historia social de los mineros de Cananea y Nueva Rosita, 1900–1970* (Mexico City: Centro de Investigaciones y Estudios Superiores en Antropología Social, 1988), 60–65, 100–107; Ngai, *Impossible Subjects*, 127–65; Aristide Zolberg, *A Nation by Design: Immigration Policy in the Fashioning of America* (New York and Cambridge: Russell Sage Foundation and Harvard University Press, 2006), 254–58.

28. García Martínez, "El espacio del (des)encuentro," 19–51; Valenzuela Arce, *Por las fronteras del norte*, 50–51; Michael Kearney, *Changing Fields of Anthropology: From Local to Global* (Lanham: Rowman and Littlefield, 2004), 252, 263.

29. For 1861 census of Hacienda de Guadalupe, see Padrón, 1861, IEDC/AMG/10/48. For the 1892 census of Hacienda de Guadalupe, see Padrón, 1892, IEDC/AMG/25/103.

30. On carts and oxen for transport, see Queja, January 24, 1885, IEDC/AMG/22/67. On timber cutting, see Ocurso, August 20, 1884, IEDC/AMG/22/53. On cotton cultivation, see Informe, August 26, 1895, IEDC/AMG/29/86. Concerning cotton cultivation in Texas and Mexico's northern borderlands, 1850–1965, see Foley, *White Scourge*; Walsh, *Building the Borderlands*.

31. On the collective defense of access to water, see Solicitud, July 30, 1884, IEDC/AMG/27/132.

32. On informal control of land, see Ocurso, March 5, 1894, IEDC/AMG/27/51; Ocurso, February 19, 1895, IEDC/AMG/27/22. On gardens and marketing, see Queja, October 19, 1895, IEDC/AMG/29/98; Enseres vendidos, March 24, 1898, IEDC/AMG/30/92. On resistance to male claimants, see F. Guardiola to Gobernador, October 20, 1924, IEDC/AMG/1924/3/2/4; Dotación de ejido, December 29, 1933, AGA/28/215. On links between consumption and household reproduction, see Carrier and Heyman, "Consumption and Political Economy," 362–64; Chamoux, "A propos du 'crédit invisible,' "; Benjamin Orlove and Shelly Diaz, "The Agrarian Household in Social and Cultural Context: An Examination of Andean Peasant Work Diaries," in David Small and Nicola Tannenbaum, eds., *At the Interface: The Household and Beyond* (Lanham: University Press of America, 1999), 55–72, see esp. 56–57.

33. On large agricultural operations, see Informe, 1913, AGN/Trab/58/2. On small plots, see Informe, August 26, 1895, IEDC/AMG/29/86. On local migration, see Ocurso, September 29, 1884, IEDC/AMG/22/56. On migration across the border, see telegram, L. Juárez to Gobernación, May 12, 1917, AGN/GOBPR, 215/56; Memorandum, March 10, 1921, AGN/Obregón-Calles/242-C7-S-7. On revolutionary bands, see issue of *Nueva Era* (Mexico City), August 9, 1911. On peasants' union and cooperative store, see F. Guardiola to Gobernación, February 15, 1925, AGN/DGG/F.2.82/9/12.

34. Eric Wolf, *Europe and the People without History* (Berkeley: University of California Press, 1982), 361–62, 379–80.

35. See the censuses of 1881, 1887, and 1896 in AMS/PM. See also Plano Aguanueva y Hedionda Grande (1893), AMS/Planos/1/4/120; Estadísticas (1891), AMS/PM/134/20; Diversas noticias and Dato (1898), AMS/PM/141/6/18/7, 10.

36. Compañía Mexicana de Máquinas, November 5, 1889, Protocolos (Ruperto González del Moral), 1888–91, AMS/P/46/2; Croquis, 1890, AMS/Planos/2/4/335; Minuta, April 8, 1898, Protocolos (Francisco Pérez), 1892–1910, no. 24, AMS/P/50/2.

37. Informe, June 8, 1887, AMS/PM/130/59; Ocurso, October 15, 1896, IEDC/SigloxIX/166/7572; Minuta, September 29, 1900, Minuta, November 17, 1909, both in Protocolos (Pedro C. Vega), Minutario 1907–15, AMS/P/64/18, 89/22.

38. Borrador de la noticia de los ranchos, 1887, AMS/PM/130/2/77; Cuenta del juez auxiliar, Gómez Farías, 1895, AMS/PM/138/1/6/8; Censo general, 1896, AMS/PM/139/7/4; Informe, September 9–10, 1900, AMS/PM/143/5/35.

39. Plano general, 1897, AMS/Planos/1/1/32; Queja, March 8, 1899, AMS/PM/142/3/5; Informe, March 31, 1901, AMS/PM/145/3/10; and Solicitud, March 14, 1901, AMS/PM/144/2/20/5; Protocolos (Pedro C. Vega), 1910, AMS/P/77/4; Solicitud, August 7, 1912, AGA/7/3251. About the 25 percent of the population with access to land, see Censo agropecuario (Saltillo, 1911), AMS/PM/154/3/11.

40. Oficio, April 25, 1908, AMS/PM/154/3/11/18; Oficio, May 5, 1911, AMS/PM/151/4/5/16; Oficio, May 16, 1911, AMS/PM/154/2/7/34; Solicitud, August 28, 1913, AMS/PM/156/1/9/32; Memorial, September 4, 1914, AGN/GobPR/154/45; Informe, September 4, 1917, AMS/PM/160/1/14/52.

41. Informe, February 23, 1923, AGA/7/325; Informe, August 7, 1924, AGN/CNA/XIX/142.

42. Censo agrário, 1911, AMS/PM/154/3/11/8, 18.

43. Oficio, May 5, 1911, AMS/PM/154/2/7/34; Informe, January 28, 1913, AMS/PM/156/1/9/8.

44. Informe, January 24, 1916, AMS/PM/159/1/12/11; Solicitud, March 6, 1917, AMS/PM/160/4/22.

45. Solicitud, January 24, 1919, AMS/PM/162/4/35; Francisco Acuña to Presidente Municipal, March 5, 1920, AMS/PM/163/5/19; Vicente Ortega to Secreteria de Trabajo, April 4, 1919; Memorandum, April 10, 1919, AGN/Trab/28/4, 7.

46. Oficio, May 5, 1911, AMS/PM/154/2/7/34; Informe, January 28, 1913, AMS/PM/156/1/9/8; Informe, January 24, 1916, AMS/PM/159/1/12/11; Solicitud, March 6, 1917, AMS/PM/160/4/22.

47. Informe, March 16, 1908, AMS/PM/151/4/5/9; Informe, March 23, 1908, AMS/PM/151/4/5/10; Orden 3a/252, January 8, 1910, AMS/PM/153/3/11/15; Memorandum, 1907, AGN/Gob/1a/907(13)/9; Bernardo Reyes to Ramón Corral, October 25, 1907, Condumex/Reyes/DLI/38/7379.

48. Memoria-técnica, February 23, 1923, RAN/Saltillo/DT II-III/Gómez Farías, 32.

49. On women's control of land, see Lista (Rancho de Vega, 1918), AMS/PM/159/2/31/20. On production and marketing, see Informe, July 15, 1925, RAN/Saltillo DT I/Presa de San Javier, 53; Planificación, August 1929, RAN/Saltillo/DT I-II-III/El Salitre, 49. On the

consolidation of marketing position, see Censo general agrario, Benito Juárez, September 1927, RAN/Saltillo/DT/I-II-III/Benito Juárez, 91; Maria del Bosque to Ciriaco Acosta, December 31, 1927, AMS/PM/171/3/36/2.

50. Sabas Sandoval to Presidente Municipal, November 13, 1925, AMS/PM/168/3/40/3. On the five unions near Presa de Guadalupe, see Ejido de Jagüey de Ferniza to Lázaro Cárdenas, June 5, 1934, AGN/DGG/2/382(3)38.

51. On the spread of cooperative stores in Coahuila, see Clemente García to Andrés Hernández, May 16, 1926, AMS/PM/169/2/41/42. For the statutes of the eleven rural unions, see AMS/PM/171/1/16; Norberto Alvarez to Presidente Municipal, June 24, 1926, AMS/PM/169/2/41/49; Domingo de la Rosa to Presidente Municipal, September 19, 1926, AMS/PM/169/2/41/107; Solicitud, June 23, 1931 and Solicitud, July 10, 1931, both in IEDC/1931/3/2/19; Memorial, May 12, 1931, IEDC/1931/3/2/19. For Tamaulipas, see *Segunda convención de la Liga de Comunidades Agrarias y Sindicatos Campesinos del Estado de Tamaulipas* (Mexico City, 1929), 106, 138, 163–64, 266. For Chihuahua, see "Constitución," August 26, 1928, AGN/DGG/2.382 (6) 5.

52. Concerning the most detailed of these censuses, see Memoria-técnica, February 23, 1923, RAN/Saltillo/DT II-III/Gómez Farías, 32.

53. Chamoux, *Indiens*, 155–56, 176–78, 196–97, 266–69; Gustavo Verduzco, *Campesinos itinerantes* (Zamora, Mich.: Colegio de Michoacán, 1982), 40–43, 58–59. On La Laguna, see Antonio Díaz and Félix Sandoval to Justino González, July 18, 1920, AGN/Trab/216/10/8; Jesús Hernández to Justino González, July 4, 1920, AGN/Trab/216/10/15; Juan Abásolo to Juan Torres, October 7, 1922, AGN/Trab/477/1/45. On Michoacán and Veracruz sugar plantations, see Dionisio Rodríguez to Adalberto Esteva, November 24, 1913; Esteva to Rodríguez, December 1, 1913, both in AGN/Trab/34/1/1–3. On the Tampico oil fields, see Andrés Araújo and Juan Saldaña to Secretaría de Trabajo, January 6, 1922; Araújo to Secretaría de Trabajo, March 17, 1922, both in AGN/Trab/322/1.

54. Depositions of J. H. Savage, July 11, 1916, and of W. D. King, July 11, 1916, *Texas v. José Antonio Arce et al.*, Webb County Criminal Court case no. 5209, June 23, 1916, UTPA/TRHRD/box TSL-5–21.

55. On journeys and provisions, see Denman Rumfield, oral testimony, March 10, 1876; Pedro Zepeda, oral testimony, March 16, 1876, both in MRRG/OHC/21, 22. On land-clearing gangs, see H. A. Shannon to John H. Shary, September 23, 1915, and John H. Shary to J. A. Miller, December 11, 1915, both in UTPA/RGVHC/Shary/box 15. On the migratory circuit, see Informe annuel (McAllen 1917), OMA/SPA/8H/85. Cindy Hahamovitch grasps the sharp break between older migratory labor systems and twentieth-century experiences in *Fruits of Their Labor*, 14–37, 116–32.

56. The following paragraphs are based on the reconstitution of 110 migrant families (811 persons) in Nueces County between 1909 and 1919, drawn from the marriage registers of five Mexican Catholic parishes (DCC/A), traced over two generations in the 1910 manuscript census schedules (NARA Microfilm Publication T624/1582), 1918 Selective Service records (UT/CAH/TWR), and Nueces County property tax, poll tax, mortgage, deeds, probate, and chattel mortgage registers (NCRO/NCCM). For fuller analysis, see Barton, "Land, Labor, and Community in Nueces," 194–96.

57. On the 102 Nueces County crop liens recorded for 1906–1926, see NCRO/NCCM. For the specific instances cited in the text, see H:111–12 (February 14, 1912), H:126–28 (March 1, 1912), L:74–75 (April 22, 1914), and 1:86–87 (April 27, 1923).

58. On networks of women, see *Texas v. Juan Zuñiga*, June 27, 1895, NCRO/NCCR/f.383. On the ways networks make it possible to find and take work in various places, see diary no. 15 (1908), 26, TAMUK/STA/Alhands; *Manuela B. Dávila v. T. J. Freeman*, November 2, 1912, BCRO/45th DCR/f.B-161.

59. In NCRO/NCCR, see the following cases: *Texas v. Rogerio Cavazos*, October 15, 1910, f. 3196; *Texas v. George Reyes*, April 2, 1920, September 13, 1921, f. 2299, 2393; *Texas v. Luis de León*, July 1, 1922, f. 2443; *Texas v. Jaime Gaitán*, July 31, 1922, f.2451; *Texas v. Juan Estrada*, May 17, 1927, f. 3120.

60. Caja . . . Daniel Valadez [1875–88], April 1, 1876, August 12, 1882, August 1, 1888, TAMUK/STA/Farias/box 691.

61. On migratory movement in the late 1880s and 1890s between Bustamante, Tamaulipas and Roma, Texas, see Claude Jaillet to Alexandre Certes, August 20, 1886, Archidiocèse de Lyon, Archives, Propagation de la Foi/F24/1377. On migratory movement in the late 1880s and 1890s between Sonora and the Pecos River Valley, see *El Valle del Bravo* [El Paso], October 26, 1889. Between Jiménez, Tamaulipas and Concepcion, Texas see *El Eco Liberal* [San Diego], January 25, 1891. Between Colombia, Nuevo Léon and Minera, Texas, see *El Defensor del Obrero* [Laredo]: 1 [1906–07], 317. By 1906–1907, such migration streams had spread from Matamoros to Ciudad Juárez (González Navarro, *La colonización en México*, 124, 127, 130, 132–33, 136–37). By 1920, they had become the mainstay of big-scale agriculture (Daniel, *Bitter Harvest*, 40–70; Guerin-Gonzales, *Mexican Workers*, 25–47).

62. Valdés, *Al Norte*, 8–29; Vargas, *Proletarians of the North*, 13–55.

63. Caja (November 1926–June 15, 1927), UTPA/RGVHC/Guerra/box 12; Libro auxiliar (June 7, 1927–June 28, 1927]), UTPA/RGVHC/Guerra/box 10.

64. Libro de Inventario, December 31, 1917; Saldo de Cuentas en Libro, December 10, 1930; both in UTPA/RGVHC/Guerra/box 13.

65. George Wilkes to C. W. Post, February 21, 1911, TTU/SC/Double U/box GC660; Stockholders Minutes, May 5, 1913, UT/CAH/CF/box 2E421; Diary, March 9, April 21, May 20, 1919, De Bremond Papers, in NMSU/RGHC. This is discussed at greater length in Barton, "Borderland Discontents."

66. *Texas v. Demetrio Casas et al.*, June 20, 1908, NCRO/NCCR/no. 1324; *Texas v. Melecio Pequeño et al.*, October 14, 1910, CCRO/CCR/no. 3185; *Texas v. Librado Flores*, October 15, 1914, *Texas v. Lázaro Villanueva*, October 15, 1914, and *Texas v. Lola Sánchez*, September 13, 1915, all in NCRO/NCCR, nos. 1746, 1747, and 1909. This paragraph analyzes all Nueces County criminal and civil cases involving goods purchased by Mexican laborers from company stores between 1890 and 1940 (N = 78) and all cases in Cameron County between 1900 and 1920 (N = 56).

67. *Texas v. Ylario Rodríguez*, May 11, 1915, *Texas v. Alberto García*, May 11, 1915, and *Texas v. S. Martínez*, November 27, 1915, all in NCRO/NCCR, nos. 1837, 1838, and 1957. See

articles in *La Prensa* (San Antonio), February 25, 1923, about the rapid expansion of peonage.

68. Watts Farms' orders in Order Book, March 8, June 8, August 16, August 22, 1906, UT/CAH/Field/2D141; and A. W. Mangum and Ora Lee, Jr., "Soil Survey of the Brownsville Area, Texas," in United States Department of Agriculture, Bureau of Soils, *Field Operations* (Washington, D.C.: Government Printing Office, 1907), 708, 710–12, 728. For success of both small and large operations to control purchases, see Elias O. Sanders diary, entry labeled "Cash out 1911," UT/CAH/Sanders; Double U Company payroll, August 1, 1911–July 30, 1912, TTU/SC/Double U.

69. *Regeneración* (Los Angeles), April 22, 1911, March 9, 1912. For the far reach of this network, see the account of Texas groups in *La Crónica* (Laredo), July 16 and September 28, 1911; David Sapposs's notes on a migratory Mexican crew in a timber camp in Hollowell, Louisiana, in "Louisiana Book II" [1913], SHSW/Saposs/ser. 4/box 28; and the account of a Mexican migrant workers' defense organization in Alexandria, Louisiana, in *Voice of the People* (New Orleans), December 4, 1913.

70. On the impact of radical farmworkers' movements, see Daniel, "In Defense of the Wheatland Wobblies," 485–509; Daniel, *Chicano Workers*, 1–27; Peck, *Reinventing Free Labor*, 158–90.

71. On the importance of these migrating communities, see Ernesto Galarza, Memorandum on Mexican Contract Workers in the United States, August 28, 1944, WSU/RALHUA/CIO/box 3. For the cohesion of such groups, see the testimony of the group that operated from Laredo to Michigan, another from Mercedes, Texas, to the Mississippi Delta, in U.S. Congress, House, *Hearings . . . Select Committee to Investigate the Interstate Migration of Destitute Citizens*, 76th Cong., 3rd sess., pt. 3 (1940) 1310–12, pt. 5 (1940) 1875–77, 1848–49, 1880. Stephen Pitti's *Devil in Silicon Valley* provides important context.

72. "Minutes, January 23, 1937, UT/CAH/LMT/box 2E310; Raymond Chavarría to John Brophy, September 31, 1937, WSU/RALHUA/CIO/box 51; George Lambert to H. L. Mitchell, November 11, 1937, UNC/SHC/STFU/reel 4; An Analysis, United Cannery, Agricultural Packing and Allied Workers of America, December 12 through 16, 1938, WSU/RALHUA/WDL/box 114.

73. *Official Proceedings of United Cannery, Agricultural, Packing, and Allied Workers of America, July 9th, 10th, 11th, and 12th, 1937* (Washington, D.C.: n.p., 1937), 4, 44–45, 65.

74. Tony Torres to Frank Morrison, May 13, 1938, SHSW/AFL/ser. 7/box 53/folder 21579; *UCAPAWA Yearbook: 2nd National Convention* (Washington, D.C.: n.p., 1939), 17; *El Progreso* (Corpus Christi), June 21, 1939; *Rocky Mountain News* (Denver), July 13, 1938; Facts and Figures on the Lettuce Workers' Strike, Salt River Valley, Arizona, UCOL/WHC/Mine Mill/box 131. On the blending of class, ethnic, and political mobilizations, see John Higham, *Hanging Together: Unity and Diversity in American Culture*, ed. Carl Guarneri (New Haven: Yale University Press, 2001), 210–12.

75. J. D. García to James Sager, July 11, 1938, UTA/TLA/Lambert/box 5; Telésforo Oviedo

to Donald Henderson, January 22, January 26, 1942, and Donald Kohler to Henderson, May 1942, all in UTA/TLA/FTAAW/box 1.

76. Oviedo to Henderson, February 21, February 26, 1942, UTA/TLA/TexAFL-CIO/ser. 16/box 5/folder 110–16–5–2. For working conditions, see Oviedo's letter in *La Prensa* (San Antonio), January 22, 1942.

77. Oviedo to Kohler, March 11, May 19, May 25, 1942, UTA/TLA/TexAFL-CIO/ser. 16/box 5/fol. 110–16–5–2. Farm Security Administration documentation informs my understanding of spinach workers' organization and strike, see Application for Rehabilitation, Enrique Garcia, July 29, 1938; Farm and Home Management Plan for Enrique Garcia, January 13, 1939; Farm Visit Report for Enrique Garcia, April 13, 1939; all in NARA-SW/FHA/box 233/fol. Garcia, Enrique 50–78–170492.

78. Oviedo to Kohler, October 12, October 20, and November 1, 1942, all in UTA/TLA/TexAFL-CIO/ser. 16/box 5/fol. 110–16–5–2. For Oviedo's list of stores, theaters, and public facilities, see Oviedo to J. Luz Sáenz, February 21, 1948, UT/BLAC/Sáenz/box 2/fol. 1.

79. For the intermingling of labor and civil rights, see especially García, *Mexican Americans*; Korstad, *Civil Rights Unionism*; Vargas, *Labor Rights Are Civil Rights;* Cohen, *Consumers' Republic.*

Robert Perez

Confined to the Margins
Smuggling among Native Peoples of the Borderlands

> The issue is, they set up a lifestyle they make attractive
> to those they've colonized psychologically. Historically,
> Indians here [Santa Barbara] are involved in the under-
> ground economy because they took all our resources
> and said "find a way to live." So we fell into the niches.
> I mean, you can't criminalize us for two hundred years
> and then say "go ahead and make your way." They
> make exclusionary laws, but we've always had these
> relationships across the border. . . . But they've criminal-
> ized our relationships. They've made it the king's forest,
> and how are we supposed to live now? We're not included
> in any of that. You know, most of our people are living
> in poverty here. We live in our cars while the *hueros*
> are in million-dollar houses. Do you know how much a
> house costs in Santa Barbara or Malibu? We can't afford
> a house in our land. So a lot of us grow and transport
> herb. It's like, whatever, we sell it to them anyway. It's
> simple, we have to survive.
>
> CHUMASH INDIAN, SANTA BARBARA, CALIFORNIA (2005)

Native peoples of the borderlands stand on the margins of consumer society, a position they were pushed into by Spanish, Mexican, Texan, and United States colonial regimes over the *longue durée*. Over the course of the past five centuries, they went from a position of relative abundance, and more importantly, self-sufficiency, to one of scarcity and dependency. Among the twenty-six Indian tribes who live in the United States and Mexico within 200 miles of the boundary line, the lands of the Kumeyaay, Cocopah, Tohono O'odham, and Texas Kicka-poo actually straddle the border. As many as 60 percent of borderlands native peoples live in poverty, while most of the rest hover just above the poverty line. In Mexico, tribes aboriginal to the borderlands face an even bleaker economic situation.[1] The imposition of the international boundary line through and adjacent to the lands of native peoples served to accelerate the course of the trajectory from abundance to scarcity, but not without opening up opportunities for resistance, including smuggling.

Native peoples responded to colonialism, nationalism, and consumer capitalism in a variety of ways: the Gilded Age *carte de visite* of a Chumash Indian posing with the febrile bow and arrow and the contemporary Chumash Indian's account of marijuana cultivation and trade are but two examples.[2] The essays in part II of this volume begin to account for the ways that native peoples rendered themselves, their lifestyles, and their crafts into commodities whose appeal in part derived from the exotic aura of the border. This essay examines another aspect of the Indians' role in the borderlands' economy—as participants in the underground economy. In doing so, it relies on evidence acquired from ethnographic interviews, historical sources ranging from missionary accounts to government reports, and contemporary journalistic reportage.

The genesis of European colonialism in the borderlands lies in Spain's conquest of the Aztec Empire and central Mexico in the 1520s. It did not take long before the conquistadors and missionaries turned their eyes northward in search of plunder and converts. In the 1560s, after large gold and silver deposits were discovered in Nueva Vizcaya (the present-day Mexican states of Chihuahua and Durango, and parts of Sinaloa, Sonora, and Chihuahua), Spanish mining, agriculture, and ranching operations began. By the early 1700s, Spanish colonialism had a foothold throughout what is known today as the U.S.-Mexico borderlands, with the exception of California, whose colonization began after 1769.

The first Europeans to enter what would become the borderlands observed the natural bounty celebrated in native people's oral traditions. Complex epistemologies and vast systems of historical and other knowledge are common to all the region's tribes. Native people who master these histories spend decades in training and are held accountable to a body of aboriginal scholars: they must learn song cycles numbering in the thousands and following a precise order. The Mohave people of the lower Colorado River today have a song cycle about their Creation that contains 525 songs and takes several nights

"Rafael Solares, a Santa Inez Chumash man," 1878. *Carte de visite* by Hayward & Muzzall, courtesy the Bancroft Library, University of California, Berkeley, ID BANC PIC 1989.061-PIC.

to sing sequentially. Each of these songs may serve as a reference point for a much longer story that provides an in-depth historical account of an event. According to one Mohave elder, the songs are a "map." He explains that "We have always lived along the river. This is our area. God put us here to protect our lands. We have been singing these songs since time immemorial."[3] The other native peoples of the region have similarly rich oral traditions and epistemologies based in songs, dance, and language. The oral traditions testify to a shared experience of abundance before European colonization.

Most native peoples' oral traditions cohere around the fact that their quality of life diminished greatly once Europeans arrived. An educator from the Chemehuevi tribe recounts a declension narrative that is similar to the stories of loss that inform most native peoples' contemporary understandings of their history:

> I can tell you one thing, as far as whether we had a better life before white people came. You know, one of the major aspects of our culture is traveling and visiting relatives and friends. A lot of our songs are maps, so you know that we traveled a lot. We lived in small family groups so we had to travel. If we can't visit people freely then we can't really live our lives in a traditional

manner and [our] quality of life is totally diminished. For us, the Spaniards and Mexicans never conquered our land. But ever since Americans got here life has been worse; it's not even debatable. First it was the army. And now we have the BLM [Bureau of Land Management], Forestry [Forestry Service], and sheriffs patrolling our lands, curtailing our activities. And of course the Border Patrol stop us when we go to visit relatives, and that's on this side of the border. It's worse when crossing the border. So yeah, life was better before. We were self-sufficient. I mean, we have a whole bunch of sheep songs, for example, that explain where people's hunting lands are. But where are the mountain sheep in our territory today? Or the deer even? They're rare because everything's been messed up and depleted. Anyone who thinks that we are living better now than before is totally ignorant of reality.[4]

In response to the suggestion that tales such as this are based on wishful thinking, an official of the Torres Martinez tribe of Desert Cahuilla Indians warns, "The idea that we are being nostalgic is based out of ignorance. People who say that, assume that this time, the present, is better, you know, because the idea of America is that it's a progressive country, so at this point we're supposed to be better off than we've ever been."[5] Native peoples' oral traditions, despite what might be characterized as a nostalgic tone, support the conclusion that the pre-contact borderlands was a region of abundance.

Corroborating the emphasis on abundance in native oral traditions are the accounts of early Spanish military officials and missionaries, who consistently remarked on the fertility and abundance of the land. The Jesuit missionary Luis Velarde noted in 1716 that the Pimería Alta, the land of the Pimas in northern Sonora, was more fertile than much of central Mexico, which was famed for its fecundity. Fellow Jesuits Daniel Januske and José Augustín de Campos noted much the same in 1723. A year later, no less a figure than the viceroy of New Spain wrote to the king of Spain that Nueva Vizcaya was "the most fertile and abundant province of New Spain." The Jesuit missionary Juan Nentvig was even more enthusiastic in 1764 when he reported that "though Sonora is the last in the order of conquest and farthest in location, it is definitely foremost, not only of the provinces named but possibly of all the others in this vast Mexican empire because of the fertility of the soil, the rich mines and placers, and the docility of the natives." He claimed that the unconquered tribes on the Gila River possessed a land that was "delightfully fruitful in wheat, corn, etc., and so much cotton that after harvest, because of

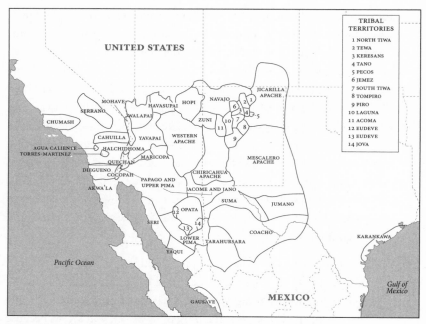

Lands of Native Peoples, Northern Mexico, ca. 1825.

the apathy of the natives, more remains in the field." Nentvig compared the Río Yaqui to the Nile in its capacity to irrigate extensive agricultural fields, noting that it flowed so mightily that dolphins were occasionally spotted swimming upriver from the Gulf of California.[6] Today the river's waters never reach the Yaqui pueblos from its headwaters in the Sierra Madre, because they have been diverted too extensively.[7]

Later missionary reports further testify to the pre-contact and early contact abundance of the other provinces of the contemporary borderlands. A Jesuit missionary wrote, "Sonora is altogether a blessed country. The fertility of the soil incites wonder. It produces incomparably all plants, trees, and growing things which require rich soil and warm air." To the east, a Franciscan missionary who spent several years in the late 1700s and early 1800s in the colony of Nuevo Santander, today's Texas-Tamaulipas borderlands, described "the fertility of its fields, the abundance and beauty of its waters, the mightiness of its river that flows into the Gulf of Mexico, the preciousness of its minerals, the lavishness with which in her nature is expressed and, in a word, the total sum of its bountiful proportions for human life."[8]

Observations about the health and vitality of the native people confirm the

Map detail, "La Californie ou Nouvelle Caroline: Teatro de los Trabajos, Apostolicos de la Compa. E Jesus en la America Septe," Paris: Nicholas de Fer, ca. 1720. Courtesy Library of Congress, Geography and Map Division.

picture of abundance given by oral traditions and early Spanish accounts of the region. For example, Andrés Pérez de Ribas, one of the first missionaries in Sonora, described the Seri Indians as "the tallest and most corpulent of all the nations of Nueva Vizcaya and even Europe, despite the fact that they have so little food." Pérez de Ribas, like most of the missionaries of the time, had a very narrow frame of reference as to what constituted "food." When Junipero Serra passed through northern Baja California on his way to San Diego in 1769, he found the health of the Indians near Ensenada inexplicable: "Food hardly appeals to them, as they are sturdy and robust." One missionary described the Pima's foodstuffs as being "in part bad, in part insipid and nauseating." He marveled that "these people live contentedly, reach a great age, and are much healthier on such fare than are others." The longevity and health of the native peoples astonished missionaries and travelers alike: one wrote that the Indians he encountered gave evidence "of the human body formed in all its perfection."[9]

Nevertheless, despite their own observations about the fecundity of the land and the health of the natives, Catholic missionaries believed that the native peoples of the region led woefully inadequate lives. Their lack of material possessions, ignorance of Christianity, disinterest in accumulation, and unwillingness to produce beyond their wants were all proof that a state of savagery prevailed in the midst of apparent abundance. One Jesuit, decrying the Indians' refusal to produce surplus goods, stated that "the Indians do not produce more than enough to satisfy their own needs and do not at all consider the advantages of producing more." He explained that "they do only such work as is unavoidable, and they are well satisfied with the fruit which nature herself plants." The native peoples' reluctance to "apply themselves to their cultivation with diligence and industry" was a common complaint. When among the Pimas in 1737, this same Jesuit observed, "that which they have they eat in a day, and they observe very exactly *nolite esse solliciti in crastinum* [not to be worried about tomorrow]."[10] Seen in this context, it is ironic but not surprising that in their attempt to appropriate the bounty of the region, the Spanish Empire and its agents created policies and institutions in the borderlands that served to create a genuine situation of scarcity for the previously well-supplied native people.

Spanish colonial policies effectively criminalized many aboriginal economic endeavors and trade relationships. Because concentrating the native population into a small number of towns facilitated policing and expropriating labor, the Spanish often relied on force to relocate Indians into missions and pueblos. Although the vast majority of Indians in the region had been village and town dwellers for centuries before the conquest, the Spanish often required heterogeneous groups to live together. What is more, relocated groups were forced to leave ancestral grounds. Native peoples were then required to labor in mining, construction, or agriculture; this history of forced labor is well-trodden ground, though its implications for Indian provisioning practices have not been closely studied. Although some Indians joined the missions of their own accord, in the end they were subject to the same coercive policies applied to their unwilling brethren. These policies and tactics continued for centuries; one of their many consequences was the willingness of some native peoples to enter into underground economic practices as a matter of cultural, social, and economic survival.

The immense growth of Spanish ranching and livestock operations in the borderlands during the seventeenth and eighteenth centuries further contributed to pushing native peoples to the economic margins. Spanish cattle ranching in New Spain resulted in such "cataclysmic landscape change," as one geographer has described it, that it could be considered "ecological colonialism." The ecological destruction of the borderlands multiplied the challenges Indians faced in terms of obtaining the necessities of life.[11] An Apache Indian interviewed at the turn of the nineteenth century recounted: "I could not remember having slept in a tepee covered with skins, though all our people had made them so before the *blue coats* [late-eighteenth-century Spanish soldiers and settlers sent to the frontier] came. Since then we had lacked enough hides even for clothing."[12] The presence of the Spanish disrupted aboriginal trade networks, intermarriage patterns, and ceremonial relationships among all Indians of the borderlands, whether conquered or not.

In the mid–eighteenth century, Spanish authorities attempted to eliminate threats unconquered Indians posed: thus began a period of all-out warfare against them. In 1750, the governor of Sonora called for the complete extermination of the Seris and appears to have favored the same plan for the Apaches.[13] Warfare against native peoples intensified in the ensuing decades, though it was largely ineffective in subjugating them. Under continual military attack and with their trade networks disrupted, the Apaches and Seris, among other tribes, became perpetual criminals—raiders and illegal traders— in the eyes of the Spaniards. In 1776, subjugation or extermination of "enemy Indians" became a central priority for the Spanish, though this goal was never fully realized.[14]

As the reduced and semi-conquered Indians of the borderlands sought to maintain their independence, at times they engaged in what today would be called "the underground economy," whether surreptitiously trading among themselves, raiding villages and ranches, or pursuing illicit trade with Spanish settlers.[15] Spanish accounts detailed extensive cattle raids during this period. For instance, the priest José Franco López claimed in 1785 that the Apaches alone were stealing at least seven thousand head of cattle a year in what would become present-day Texas.[16] Of particular importance are the activities that historian Pekka Hämäläinen has described among the Comanches, who were able to negotiate a position within the Spanish system that until the early 1800s allowed them to circumvent the trade prohibitions imposed on Apaches.[17] The constant conflict with some native peoples has been posited as one of the causes for the weakening of the Spanish Empire such that Mexico could achieve its independence. Only a quarter of a century later, independent Indians in Mexico's north had weakened the region such that it made the United States' land grab all the easier to accomplish shortly after the U.S.-Mexico War.[18]

Not only was warfare used in the attempt to quiet "enemy Indians," so too were gifts, especially in the form of rations. By way of demonstrating the extent of gifts as a mechanism Spanish officials employed to control native peoples, the historian F. Todd Smith estimates that in just two months of 1798, officials in San Antonio handed out gifts to 183 Lipan Apaches, 169 Comanches, 68 Tawakonis, 21 Hainais and Bidais, and 14 Tonkawas, despite treacherous overland trails, dried-up waterways, parsimonious treasury officials, and ever-increasing numbers of supplicants. Mexican officials faced similar constraints, finding that despite gifts, peace and stability on the northern frontier remained elusive. In the 1820s and 1830s, shortly after Mexican independence from Spain, "presents to Indians became fewer and shabbier, provoking 'humiliating' excuses from cash-poor northern Mexican officials and violent outbursts by Indian visitors."[19] In this context, where native peoples confronted hardship and hostility, they honed survival tactics that took into account the international boundary line.

By the mid-1850s, the cumulative effects of Spanish, Mexican, and Texan colonialism resulted in scarcity for nearly all the borderlands Indians. Mexican independence from Spain in 1821 does not appear to have substantially diminished participation in the underground economy, but in exacerbating conditions that imperiled the survival of native peoples, it pushed them further to the margins. Missionized Indians were confined to smaller geographic areas, as the number of *mestizo* settlers increased between 1800 and 1850. In the 1850s, European travelers through the western United States on their way to the gold fields of California encountered many tribes who were living in desperate conditions. Even tribes that had escaped the worst effects of Spanish and Mexican rule were caught up in the larger matrix of raiding, the Indian slave trade, and warfare.[20] As military effectiveness against the Apaches, Seris, and Comanches decreased, open raids became common. The tempo and intensity of Indian attacks on settler communities increased; that westward-moving Anglo-Americans traded weapons and were willing buyers of stolen goods only encouraged Indian raiding.[21]

The United States had assumed responsibility for the "Indian problem" in the borderlands under provisions of the Treaty of Guadalupe Hidalgo (1848), which ended the U.S.-Mexico War. The U.S. government hoped to end cross-border raids by signing treaties and isolating rebellious Indians on far-flung reservations. Tribes not conquered by Spain and Mexico found themselves confronted with the large and determined military of the United States.[22] When the boundary line was drawn up, Mexico and the United States perpetu-

"Mescalero Indians, into Las Cruces after supplies for their Agency, 112 miles distant," 1889. Photograph courtesy Archives and Special Collections, New Mexico State University Library, image ID 00010060.

In wagons and on foot, the Mescalero Apache traveled to Las Cruces, New Mexico to provision themselves; this seemingly orderly encounter stands in contrast to the cross-border raids that the Apache and other borderlands Indians had been known for prior to the 1880s.—A.M.

ated the Spanish regulation of Indians' physical mobility: Mexican presidios remained near the border, while the United States constructed its own line of forts north of the border. New laws in the United States further criminalized Indians, especially by limiting their ability to travel and move freely. Most Indians were confined to agencies, which would later become reservations, often far from centers of trade.[23] Participation in the underground economy became both necessary for survival and intertwined with native peoples' struggles to remain free of colonial domination.

These factors of marginalization, combined with a desire to maintain independence, figured in the formation of networks of dissent, a phenomenon that Josef Barton and Sarah Hill also explore in their essays in this part of the volume, and that Laura Serna touches on in her essay about Mexican cinema in part II of this volume. These networks united diverse Indian peoples: they planned rebellions, organized illegal religious gatherings, and coordinated raids on haciendas and non-Indian settlements. Actions such as these laid the foundations for smuggling and distribution networks among native people in the region that have been operational since the 1850s.

During the second half of the nineteenth century, the Indian underground economy consisted mostly of cross-border theft and livestock smuggling. Various Apache bands, the Kickapoos, and the Comanches utilized the border to what little advantage they could by stealing livestock in one country to sell in the other. Apaches living in Arizona raided Sonora and Chihuahua for horses and cattle.[24] Mexican and U.S. authorities reported Comanche livestock raids as far south as Zacatecas and Durango in the 1850s.[25] U.S. officials accused bands of Kickapoos, who had migrated to Coahuila from Texas during the 1860s, of stealing livestock in Texas to sell in Coahuila.[26] Some of the Lipan Apaches of the Big Bend region in south Texas—who also fled to Mexico during the 1860s—joined the underground economy of cross-border livestock rustling. Soon, U.S. and Mexican officials pursued them so relentlessly that the Lipan became "greatly incensed"—so much so that "according to reports received they have declared war against the world."[27]

Cross-border raiding was also a significant economic and political problem in the Alta/Baja California border region. The records of Abel Stearns, a ranch owner and prominent California citizen, depict a situation of frequent Indian rebellion and smuggling, primarily of livestock, on the California border during the 1850s and 1860s. One of his employees, José Arguello, reported that in the summer of 1854, Indians south of present-day Tijuana were stealing large numbers of horses. Stearns learned in late October 1860 that Indians from both Baja California and Alta California had killed many men and stolen their goods. The Indians were said to be "in rebellion," and it was warned that their cross-border alliance meant the "country was lost." A few months later, in January 1861, Stearns was told that three hundred Indians from San Diego and Baja, one hundred of them armed with rifles, were "in rebellion against the whites" and were "gathered in the area of Tecate" on the Mexican side of the border. During the next several years, the Indians of the California borderlands asserted their independence primarily through cross-border raiding and smuggling, rather than rebellion.[28]

By the end of the 1880s, Indians were no longer active in the cross-border livestock trade; more research is needed into Indian underground economic activities during the decades between 1890 and 1920. What might be called "technological colonialism"—barbed wire fences, railroads, heavy farm and mining machinery, and lightweight arms—joined with the violent policies of the Porfiriato in northern Mexico, the equally violent but also paternalistic policies of the U.S. government, and the organizational efforts of reformers seeking to solve what they saw as "the Indian problem" to hem in native peoples of the borderlands. As a result, native peoples were rendered unable to fully provision themselves, and thus entered into the matrix of the consumer

Ruidoso Store, near Fort Stanton, New Mexico, ca. 1880–1900. Photograph, Public Health Service Historical Photograph File, Record Group 90, National Archives Records Administration, ARC Identifier 596116.

This store and post office was near the Mescalero Apache reservation in southern New Mexico. The woven baskets and moccasins suggest an active trade of handicrafts for foodstuffs, such as the advertised sugar, molasses, and potatoes.—A.M.

economy, much as did the Mexican *ixtle* harvesters Joe Barton discusses in the previous essay.

U.S. policies toward Indians took a particularly paternalistic shape during the last decades of the nineteenth century, such that government policies, schools, and programs emanating from Indian agencies were all geared toward "civilizing the Indians." Just as "Americanization" of immigrants during this period focused in part on bringing them into line with market-oriented production and consumption, so did the proliferation of Indian schools, Indian agents teaching modern husbandry and home economics, and Protestant missionaries intent on conversion.[29] In seeking to "awaken wants," the civilizing mission—as other contributions to this volume also illustrate—was just as crucial to the arrival of consumer culture as railroads and department stores. Consider the oft-quoted 1896 speech of one prominent Indian reformer, Merrill Gates, who would a few years later serve as chairman of the U.S. Board of Indian Commissioners:

We have, to begin with, the absolute need of awakening in the savage Indian broader desires and ampler wants. To bring him out of savagery into citizenship we must make the Indian more intelligently selfish before we make him unselfishly intelligent. We need to awaken in him wants. In his dull savagery he must be touched by the wings of the divine angel of discontent. . . . Discontent with the teepee and the starving rations of the Indian camp in winter is needed to get the Indian out of the blanket and into trousers,—and trousers with a pocket in them, and with a pocket that aches to be filled with dollars![30]

The hope behind awakening wants was that Indians would enter into the modern labor market, that their desires would fuel greater work effort. Perhaps they did, but with opportunities to work hinged upon leaving behind inherited practices and beliefs, as well as familiar places, few native peoples were able to secure necessities, let alone satisfy "their wants."

Concomitant with the Spanish, Mexican, Texan, and American military campaigns and attempts to regulate Indian trade, mobility, and labor was the assault on aboriginal spirituality and ceremonial practice. Besides fermented alcoholic beverages made from corn, saguaro fruit, elderberry, and mescal, native people in the borderlands also used a variety of hallucinogenic plants, including datura (jimson weed), mushrooms, and peyote, in coming-of-age, initiation, and seasonal healing ceremonies.[31] One missionary's disparaging description of a Pima Indian ceremonial could be found in many similar iterations: "They drink as long as they can, and they are able to drink until they fall to earth just like blocks, completely devoid of reason and out of their heads. When the spirits heat their blood and have gone to their heads, there follow altercations, fights, blood-spilling, murder, and death, and even the most horrible revolts."[32] In contrast, the Tohono O'odham claimed that their physical survival depended on their consumption of *navait*, that they would literally starve without the saguaro cactus wine.[33] Consider a Tohono O'odham woman's 1846 elaboration on the drinking ceremony that followed a cactus harvest she attended with her father: "Then they began to drink. Making themselves beautifully drunk, for that is how our words have it. People must make themselves like plants in the rain and they must sing for happiness."[34] In some cases, native peoples' use of prohibited substances fomented political rebellion. For example, missionaries charged that prior to the Pima Rebellion of 1751, the leader had secretly organized drinking ceremonies in the mountains.[35] Spanish missionaries cast the use of these native sacraments as signs of rampant paganism, apostasy, and collusion with the devil, so along with civil authorities, they prohibited their trade and consumption. Indians

"Supai Charlie," 1908. Photograph by Henry G. Peabody, Library of Congress, Prints and Photographs Division, LC-USZ62-11267.

This Havasupai Indian man living in Arizona stands in front of a home built of local materials wearing clothing made of manufactured textiles and shoes likely made in a factory.—A.M.

defied the bans. And so *navait*, peyote, and other hallucinogens became the first "controlled substances" in the region: they were the original items of the aboriginal drug trade.[36]

While Anglo frontiersmen, merchants, and government officials introduced Indians to what in many cases became, and remains, a deadly trade in alcohol, the trade of aboriginal fermented beverages and hallucinogens among native peoples remained quiescent, though it was never absent, until the later years of the nineteenth century. In the 1880s and 1890s, native peoples' demand for ceremonial hallucinogens, especially peyote, increased. U.S. officials charged with overseeing Indians broke up peyote meetings, confiscating the hallucinogen and ceremonial items in the effort to halt its use. In frustration, the U.S. government banned peyote in 1899, which only transformed the substance into contraband. Because peyote only grows in south Texas and northern Mexico, many Indians relied on trade to obtain it. Thus as a result of the 1899 peyote laws, they found themselves involved in the first "drug smuggling" operations of the twentieth century. The transportation of peyote

**"The Saguaro Harvest—Pima,"
1907.** Photograph by Edward
Curtis, Library of Congress,
Prints and Photographs Division,
Edward S. Curtis Collection, LC-
USZ62–101252.

was a small-scale intra-Indian phenomenon that filled no one's pockets with dollars. It is very important to emphasize that Indian practitioners did not consider peyote a "drug," rather it was a necessary component of a developing pan-Indian religion. The divergent understandings between native peoples and colonizers about the natural world and its bounty were nothing new.[37]

The legacy of resistance to colonial domination and corresponding participation in the underground economy—whether smuggling livestock or peyote —meant that certain members of borderlands Indian tribes were well prepared to smuggle alcohol into the United States after the implementation of nationwide Prohibition in 1920. The congruity of some Indian lands with the borderline accounts, in part, for Indian participation in large-scale smuggling operations that usually included Mexican and U.S. nationals. For instance, in 1921 an official with the U.S. Immigration Service stationed on the Arizona border became convinced that Mexican nationals were smuggling whiskey into the United States with the help of what he called "a bad outfit" of Indians through the Cocopah reservation.[38] He enlisted a deputy sheriff to investigate. On the reservation, they found evidence that a wagon had met a boat that had crossed the river dividing the two nations; the wagon tracks led to a small house outside of which was parked an empty wagon and an automobile packed with boxes. Before the nosy immigration inspector and the sheriff could look into the boxes shots were fired. The federal official found himself surrounded by twenty-five or thirty armed Indians, whose leader backed his claim that he was a member of the Indian police force by showing a badge. The deputy sheriff, meanwhile, fled the scene. Back in Yuma, a posse of seven men, in addition to the deputy U.S. marshal and eight soldiers, was raised. When it got to the reservation, they found the inspector alive, but no sign of the smuggled contraband.[39] In the end, it appears that authorities found no evidence to implicate the "bad outfit" of Indians in smuggling.

To be sure, there are many similar such cases from the Prohibition era, but a few noteworthy things stand out in this particular case. First, the Mexicans smuggling whiskey into the reservation may well have been Cocopahs living on the south side of the border. Second, multiple organizations of armed agents found leave to patrol Indian lands on the grounds of enforcing Prohibition; this opening only widened over the course of the century, as laws multiplied in the effort to prevent the transit of contraband, whether banned substances or migrant laborers and their families. Finally, and more importantly, the Cocopah assumed to be smugglers demonstrated striking boldness in their show of strength in the face of aggressive tactics by federal agents, the sheriff's department, and the U.S. military.

With the repeal of Prohibition in 1933, large-scale smuggling of alcohol in the borderlands ended, but the militarization of the border hinted at in the 1921 Cocopah incident only accelerated. Over the next sixty years, the smuggling of people and contraband throughout the borderlands increased. The last two decades of the twentieth century and the first of the twenty-first saw an exponential growth in the militarization of the border; local, state, and federal agents from various branches of the U.S. government (Border Patrol, Customs, Drug Enforcement Administration, Department of Defense, Federal Bureau of Investigation, Department of the Interior, and Homeland Security, just to name a few) operate year-round along the border.[40] The increased surveillance of borderlands cities and ports of entry has pushed underground economic activity to less populated parts of the borderlands, which includes native peoples' lands. In response to the widening swathe of unofficial border crossings, the U.S. government has ramped up surveillance all along the border, which further detracts from native peoples' freedoms.

Unmanned Aerial Vehicle, U. S. Customs and Border Protection Agency, ca. 2004. Color photograph by Gerald Nino, CBP Photo Gallery, Website of U.S. Customs and Border Protection Agency, Department of Homeland Security.

Today Indian lands play a part in the transborder drug economy in two ways: they are one of many sites of drug cultivation and one of many pathways for smuggled drugs, which primarily include marijuana, cocaine, methamphetamines, and black-tar heroin. Many tribal peoples cannot escape the dual pressures exerted by drug runners and policing authorities. One leader of a tribe whose lands are adjacent to the border put it this way: "We have the undocumented and drug smugglers heading north and law enforcement heading south. We're smack in the middle."[41] Reports in 1994 indicated that the drug traffickers and the Mexican military were preying on the Tarahumara people in Chihuahua: the traffickers were clearing Tarahumara land, including ancient forests, to grow marijuana and opium poppies. With the land cleared, they forced the Tarahumaras and Pimas into the mountains to cultivate the crops. One man reported, "They say, we will kill your wife and rape your daughter and they often do."[42] Other Indians face the same problems as the Tarahumara. For example, drug traffickers began buying up the lands of the Pai Pai and Kiliwa Indians in Baja California in the 1980s; Indian leaders who protested were gunned down.[43] On the other hand, when gunmen executed two families of Pai Pais and their neighbors in the Baja California town of Ensenada in 1998, leaving a total of nineteen people dead, it was widely speculated that one of the Pai Pais, Fermín Castro, was himself the head of a small drug-smuggling operation of his own.[44]

As in previous generations, the economic incentive to participate in cross-border smuggling is tremendous. As early as 1916, Tohono O'odham leaders voiced their concerns about their tribe's inability to provision itself. One testified, "We are just as strong in our desire to hold this land as are the white people to get it from us." Another lamented, "What else do they want to do with us, have us live in the air like birds?" Joining this chorus of complaint about expropriation, another leader asked, "Why is it that after we have been pushed away from all of our rivers and mines and all valuable parts of our country, these few white men still insist on pushing us off this desert, our last foot-hold?"[45] Their concerns were prescient; in 2006, 40 percent of the families living on the reservation lived below the federal poverty line, while 42 percent of the adults were unemployed. The average per capita income was $8,000—$5,000 less than the average income of all Indians in the United States, and one-third the average income for all U.S. residents.[46]

The lands adjacent to the border provide certain smuggling opportunities. For instance, gates through which native peoples are allowed to pass to visit the other side are often unmanned. The San Miguel gate, for instance, which U.S. Tohono O'odhams pass through to visit relatives and tribal locales in Mexico, in the past decade has also served as an illegal port of entry for drugs.[47] Trafficking operations are said to pay thousands of dollars to tribal members with lands adjacent to the border, to store or transport contraband.[48] The Tohono O'odham reservation in southern Arizona, about three million acres of land that has a seventy-five-mile-long border with Mexico, illustrates the magnitude of drug smuggling's imprint on native peoples and their lands near the international boundary line. A fence does mark the border, but its barbed wire is easily cut. Furthermore, State Highway 86, which leads to Phoenix and California, runs through the reservation, making for an easy connection to two of the largest markets for illegal drugs and undocumented labor. In January 2003, when 6,081 pounds of marijuana, with an estimated street value near six million dollars, were seized on the reservation, Tohono O'odham tribal members were on both sides of the drug busts: Indian trackers in the Customs Service, known as "Shadow Wolves," found many of the bales of pot, while some of their fellow tribal members were arrested for smuggling.[49] Even prominent members of the tribe have been found guilty of participation in drug smuggling. For example, in 1999 Customs agents found 356 pounds of marijuana in the care of a Tohono O'odham tribal judge, the sister of the chairperson of the Tohono O'odham nation, whose brother was arrested six years later when police found 137 pounds of marijuana in his car.[50]

These drug busts are just a few of the many taking place across the extent of

"Shadow Wolves," ca. 2004. Color photograph by James R. Tourtellotte, CBP Photo Gallery, Website of U.S. Customs and Border Protection Agency, Department of Homeland Security.

The U.S. Customs and Border Protection Agency employs a group of Indians known as "shadow wolves" to help patrol for smuggling. These four men were at work on the Tohono O'odham reservation in southern Arizona, through which the international boundary line crosses.—A.M.

the international boundary, on nearby airstrips, and elsewhere in the United States, but it may be that the toll on native peoples of the region is greater than on others affected by the drug trade. One of many proposed solutions to the simmering conflict between drug smugglers and the authorities is to build a fence that would bar vehicles from crossing the border. For instance, the Tohono O'odham Tribal Council supports building a seventy-five-mile border fence, at more than a million dollars a mile, but other tribal members are against it.[51] One opponent explains, "That border continues to separate who we are."[52] If one considers the historical record, it is not unreasonable to conclude that the current militarization of the border, the havoc narcotics and human smuggling spread, and the proposed erection of a border fence are further manifestations of colonial power, only made worse by consumer capitalism.

The drug trade itself, illegal immigration, the consequent militarization of the border, and impoverishment have together exasperated many borderlands

Burlap backpacks with nearly a quarter of a ton of marijuana, Tohono O'odham reservation in southern Arizona, ca. 2004. Photograph by James R. Tourtellotte, CBP Photo Gallery, Website of U.S. Customs and Border Protection Agency, Department of Homeland Security.

Indians. Various accounts substantiate the fact that the crackdown on the border has intensified the restrictions on the mobility of the region's indigenous population. In 1996, Kumeyaay Indians, whose lands lie just south of the Baja border, expressed concern that increasingly restrictive policies were endangering transborder cultural and tribal relations. Oletha Lel, a Kumeyaay living on the U.S. side of the border, explains, "Up until the 1950s our people would commonly cross the border for community and cultural events without a problem. With the tightening of the border since then, we have begun to be divided. We didn't cross the border, the border crossed us."[53]

In response to the military buildup on the border, the Tohono O'odham Legislative Council passed a resolution in 2000 that decried "the arrest, deportation, seizure of vehicles and criminal prosecution" of many of its members.[54] An Apache informant from Texas adds his voice to the outcry:

> You can't travel anywhere near the border without getting harassed by the Border Patrol. If you have brown skin and especially if you got long hair, you're gonna get stopped and questioned. White people travel to Big Bend National Park and never have a problem. If we travel in the Big Bend, and remember that's our aboriginal territory, we have to run the gauntlet.

They just assume we're transporting drugs. It's like we fled the mission or went off the reservation every time we try to go somewhere. It's racial profiling, man. It's almost like, you might as well do it, you're gonna get blamed anyway.[55]

A Tohono O'odham corroborates, with his own account of out-of-control Border Patrol agents: "They're breaking into houses, doing random drug stops, cutting fences, and making their own roads. They chase people down."[56] Other tribal members are equally dismayed: "The O'odham are harassed and held at gunpoint during interrogations, as well as killed by the Border Patrol military."[57]

Even borderlands Indians whose lands are not adjacent to the borderline face increased restrictions on their mobility and actions. For example, the Cupeño and Luiseño Indians, who live on the Pala Reservation in northern San Diego County, constantly encounter the Border Patrol. One informant's story is revealing:

We were out there in Pala about a year ago and we had to gather some medicine for a friend of mine. There's this place out there near Gregory Canyon where we gather a lot of medicine. So we got the medicine and put it in little baggies and started going back and there was a Border Patrol right there just before Pala. And they stopped us and started asking us a lot of questions—where we were going, what we were doing—and he sees all these baggies with green plants. I told him we were going to Pala for a ceremony and eventually he let us go. But that was the second time that same day that we got stopped, 'cause earlier we were out there in Campo [a Kumeyaay reservation in eastern San Diego] to get something for this thing we had to do. There's a spring where we get this special water from, and we got stopped by the Border Patrol right there. Twice in one day, it sucked. It's crazy—how the car you drive, longhair, they just pinpoint you. People are always assuming things, like, Border Patrol is always assuming that you're Mexican, or whatever, illegal, or they assume you're smuggling drugs. They assume you're up to mischief.[58]

Another informant, a Cupeño resident of Pala, describes the effect of the Border Patrol on his life:

They set up their checkpoint on the road into Pala. Not even a mile away from home—they set up right on the outskirts of the reservation. And actually, that road is the main road to all the reservations. There's Pala, Pauma, Rincon, La Jolla, Santa Ysabel, Los Coyotes, Mesa Grande, all in consecutive order along that highway. So a lot of Indians drive that highway. The Border Patrol's a huge part of our life. . . . But if they were to pull us over and inspect our vehicles and we should have such medicines with us, the only thing that they could even think about is that it's got to be something illegal, or something in the wrong. No matter what it is, it's gotta be something. They have no idea what we're all about or what we use things for or anything. So they don't even have the right to look at the plants.[59]

The Border Patrol's lack of comprehension of some native peoples' practices and wholesale tendency to conflate brown skin and long hair with contraband reinforces distrust of the U.S. government. Combined with rampant poverty, suspicion fuels the willingness of borderlands Indians (and others) to enter into the underground economy.

Proximity to the border makes smuggling a viable economic strategy for some native peoples of the borderlands; poverty of resources and of opportunities in a consumer society makes it an appealing one. The colonization of native peoples, the criminalization of their sacraments, the drawing of a line— the border—through their territory, the expropriation of their lands, and the extensive effects of capitalist regimes of production and provisioning together account for the margins on which so many native peoples hover. Furthermore, the decisions some make to participate in drug cultivation and smuggling, are, ironically, only profitable and possible because of antidrug laws and efforts to seal borders. When poverty and marginalization are coupled with the palpable sense that the borderlands themselves provided better, more abundant lifestyles for their natives, before Europeans came, then sentiments such as the following will multiply: "Look, we had it good before white people took over. Maybe they thought we were ignorant savages, but by our own standards we were rich. We're just trying to get back to a point where we can at least live a decent life. For some of us, the drug trade is the only way to do it."[60]

Abbreviations

AB–HL	Abel Stearns Collection, Huntington Library
AGI–G	Archivo General de Indias, Guadalajara
AGN	Archivo General de la Nación
AMS	Archivo de la Mitra de Sonora, Hermosillo, University of Arizona Microfilm Collection 811

BIA-NARA-LN	United States Department of Labor, Immigration Service. Records of the Bureau of Indian Affairs, Yuma Agency, Record Group 75: National Archives and Records Administration–Pacific Region (Laguna Nigel)
HB	H. E. Bolton Papers, The Bancroft Library, University of California, Berkeley
ICT	*Indian Country Today* (Canastota, New York)
NAMP-DUSMM	National Archives Microfilm Publication 97, Dispatches from United States Ministers to Mexico, 1823–1906
NYT	*New York Times*

Notes

At early stages in the writing of this chapter, Alexis McCrossen made helpful suggestions about how to think about scarcity and abundance for native peoples in the precontact and colonial borderlands. In its later stages she added the illustrations and their captions, the map, some bibliographic references, as well as some material about gifting and raiding in the Spanish borderlands. The author has in his possessions transcripts, video recordings, or audio recordings of all the interviews cited in this chapter. The interviewees have all granted him permission to cite and quote their words. The Clements Department of History at Southern Methodist University paid the fees for reproduction and use of some of the essay's illustrations.

Notes fully cite primary sources and specialized secondary sources. Full bibliographic details for all other citations are in the volume's selected bibliography.

1. Arizona Commission of Indian Affairs, *2002–2003 Annual Report* (Phoenix, 2003); Center for California Native Nations, "An Impact Analysis of Tribal Government Gaming in California" (Riverside: University of California, 2006); Tina Faulkner, "Native Communities of the Borderlands," *Borderlines* 62 (1999), 2–3.

2. Interview with a Coastal Chumash tribal member, Ventura County, California, October 8, 2005.

3. The elder is quoted in Philip M. Klasky, "Song of the Land," *YES* (fall 2000).

4. Author's interview with John Smith, December 15, 2006, Redlands, California. See also author's interview with William Contreras, December 29, 2006, Palm Springs, California.

5. Author's interview with Contreras, *op. cit.*

6. El Marqués de Casafuerte, "Expediente sobre la conquista y reduccion de varias castas de Indios de la Provincia de Nueva Vizcaya, años de 1723 y 1724," AGI-G 171; Juan S. J. Nentvig, *Rudo Ensayo: A Description of Sonora and Arizona in 1764*, translated by Alberto Francisco Pradeau and Robert Ramussen (Tucson: University of Arizona Press, 1980), quotes pp. 4, 15, 9, and 19. See also Luis Velarde, "La Primera Relación de la Pimería Alta"; Daniel Januske, "Breve informe del estado presente en que se hallan los misiones de esta provincia de Sonora en 1723"; José Agustin de Campos, "Texto del

primer Documento de Campos, 1723"; all reprinted in Luis González, ed., *Etnologiá y misión en la Pimería Alta, 1715–1740* (Mexico City: Universidad Nacional Autónoma de México, 1977).

7. In August 2005 I visited the Yaqui pueblo of Raum, located on the banks of the Río Yaqui. Our host was an elderly Yaqui Pascola dancer. When I asked where the river was, he pointed to the dry sandy riverbed and said, "Ai mijo, eso es el río hoy (ay, my child, that is the river today)." I also observed the river farther north in the Sierra Madre where it still flows.

8. Ignaz Pfefferkorn, *Sonora: A Description of the Province*, translated by Theodore F. Treutlein (1756; Tucson: The University of Arizona Press, 1989), 42–43, 50, 74; Vincente de Santa María, *Relación Histórica de la Colonia del Nuevo Santander* (Mexico City: UNAM, 1973), 95.

9. "Father Andres Pérez de Ribas on the Seris, 1645," in Sheridan, ed., *Empire of Sand*, 21–26; Antonine Tibesar, ed., *Writings of Junípero Serra* (Washington, D.C.: Academy of American Franciscan History, 1955), 1:112; Pfefferkorn, *Sonora, op. cit.*, 200, 165; Nentvig, *Rudo ensayo, op. cit.*, 25; Santa María, *Relación histórica, op. cit.*, 95.

10. Pfefferkorn, *Sonora, op. cit.*, 42–43, 50, 74.

11. Sluyter, "Ecological Origins and Consequences of Cattle Ranching," 31.

12. Eve Ball and James Kaywaykla, *In the Days of Victorio: Recollections of a Warm Springs Apache* (Tucson: University of Arizona Press, 1970), 16.

13. Pfefferkorn, *Sonora, op. cit.*, 152,

14. It should be noted that mission Indians also suffered high mortality rates. See, for instance, Archibald, "Economy of the Alta California Mission."

15. Forbes, *Apache, Navaho, and Spaniard*, 158; Works, "Creating Trading Places."

16. Faulk, "Ranching in Spanish Texas." See also DeLay, *War of a Thousand Deserts*.

17. Hämäläinen, "Western Comanche Trade Center." See also Blackhawk, *Violence over the Land*, which addresses trade between empires in the early American West; Hämäläinen, *Comanche Empire*, 219–32; DeLay, *War of a Thousand Deserts*.

18. DeLay, "Independent Indians."

19. Smith, *From Dominance to Disappearance*, 34–53, quote p. 35.

20. Forbes, *Warriors of Colorado*.

21. Weber, *Mexican Frontier*, 95.

22. Bowen-Hatfield, *Chasing Shadows*, 2.

23. In California, for example, see the revisions to the law between 1855 and 1863 in *An Act for the Government and Protection of Indians* (1855 Cal. Statutes chap. 144; 1860 Cal Statutes chap. 231; 1863 Cal Statutes chap. 475; and 1863 Cal Statutes chap. 499). Similar laws were on the books of the New Mexico Territory.

24. "Depredations of Apache Indians from Arizona Territory into Mexico," April 24, 1874, no. 108 (NAMP-DUSMM, roll 48).

25. Inroads of Comanche Indians, Legation of the United States, Mexico, July 27, 1852, no. 18 (NAMP-DUSMM, roll 16).

26. Thomas Nelson to Department of State, April 22, 1872, no. 551 (NAMP-DUSMM, roll 46).

27. "Application of the Lipan and Comanche Indians to Cross into Mexico," March 20, 1875, no. 263 (NAMP-DUSMM, roll 51); "Depredations of American Indians into Mexico," March 15, 1879, no. 907 (NAMP-DUSMM, roll 51). Historian Brian DeLay shows that U.S. Army efforts to capture Indian raiders extended from the 1850s through the end of the 1870s. DeLay, "Independent Indians" and *War of a Thousand Deserts*.

28. Letters to Abel Stearns from José Arguello, June 21, 1854; from Guadalupe Estudillo de Arguello, October 28, 1860; from Juan Bandini, January 11, 1861; both in AB-HL. For a period account describing the U.S. cavalry unit's pursuit of Indian raiders across the border, see Schneider, "Border Incident of 1878."

29. About the connections between "Americanization" movements and the creation of modern consumers, see Heinze, *Adapting to Abundance*; Jacobson, *Barbarian Virtues*; Leach, *Land of Desire*.

30. Merrill Gates quoted in Berkhofer Jr., *White Man's Indian*, 173.

31. Russell, *Pima Indians*; Schaefer and Furst, eds., *People of the Peyote*.

32. Pfefferkorn, *Sonora, op. cit.*, 176–177.

33. Booth, " 'If We Gave Up.' "

34. Ruth Underhill and Maria Chona, *Autobiography of a Papago Woman* (Palo Alto: Stanford University Press, 1936), 11.

35. AGI-G, 419. In 1776, Mexican officials investigated the activities of a Pima Indian named Ambrosio from the village of Suaqui in Sonora. They accused him of teaching the "diabolical" peyote dance of the Indians of Tecoripa (Inquisiciones, vol. 1104, exp. 24, AGN).

36. Noemí Quezada, Martha Eugenia Rodríguez, and Marcela Suárez, eds., *Inquisición novohispana* (Mexico City: UNAM, 2000); Hernando Ruiz de Alarcón, *Treatise on the Heathen Superstitions that Today Live Among the Indians Native to this New Spain, 1629*, edited by J. Richard Andrews and Ross Hassig (Norman: University of Oklahoma Press, 1984). See also Mathewson, "Drugs, Moral Geographies, and Indigenous Peoples."

37. Stewart, *Peyote Religion*; Brandt, *Jim Whitewolf*, 129; Stewart, "History of Peyotism," 198–99; Kimber and McDonald, "Sacred and Profane Uses of the Cactus *Lophophora Williamsii*." See also Bonnie and Whitebread, *Marijuana Conviction*, 40–53.

38. Immigrant Inspector Alfred R. Dick to Immigration Service Inspector, January 18, 1921, file 6075, BIA-NARA-LN. See also Perramand, "Desert Traffic."

39. Ibid.; "Shooting Affray on Cocopah Indian Reservation," January 17, 1921, file 6075, BIA-NARA-LN.

40. Dunn, *Militarization of the U.S.-Mexico Border*.

41. John Pomfret, "As Border Crackdown Intensifies, A Tribe Is Caught in the Crossfire," *Washington Post*, September 15, 2006.

42. Brenda Norrell, "Tarahumaras Battle Logging, Drugs," ICT, January 12, 1994.

43. Sam Dillon, "Drug Gangs Devastate Indian Villages in Baja California," NYT, September 26, 1998.

44. Hilda Marella and Norman de la Vega, "Masacre en Ensenada," *La Opinión* (Los Angeles), September 18, 1998; Victor Clark, "Etnocido: Algunas communidades indigenas han sido infiltradas por los narcotraficantes," *La Opinión* (Los Angeles), December 4, 1998.

45. Minutes of Council with Papago Indians at Indian Oasis, September 21, 1916, BIA-NARA-LN.

46. Pomfret, "As Border Crackdown Intensifies," *op. cit.*

47. "CBP Border Patrol Seizes Cocaine Valued at Over $15 Million," press release dated February 17, 2005, Department of Homeland Security. The press release reports that Customs officers interdicted a 1979 brown Ford pickup when it crossed into Tohono O'odham lands in the U.S. carrying 472 pounds of cocaine hidden in the truck's false compartments.

48. "Drugs Invade via Indian Land," *USA Today*, August 6, 2003.

49. Department of Homeland Security press releases: "U.S. Customs Service Native American Trackers Seize 3,660 Pounds of Marijuana," January 14, 2003; "U.S. Customs Service Native American Trackers and Special Agents Seize 2,421 Pounds of Marijuana," January 29, 2003. See also Randal C. Archibold, "In Arizona Desert, Indian Trackers vs. Smugglers," NYT, March 7, 2007.

50. Michael Marizco, "O'odham Chairwoman's Brother Faces Drug-Smuggling Charges," *Arizona Daily Star*, September 27, 2005.

51. Pomfret, "As Border Crackdown Intensifies," *op. cit.* The Tohono O'odham Tribal Council allowed the Border Patrol to establish two permanent facilities on its land. The fence, a vehicle barrier, will cost more than $75 million.

52. Luke Turf, "New Push for Border Barrier Unfolds," *Tucson Citizen*, July 20, 2004.

53. "INS hassles Kumeyaay at US-Mexico border," *News from Indian Country*, November 30, 1996.

54. Brenda Norrell, "Border Racism Bars Indigenous Passage: Summit Unites Those Divided by Borders," ICT, December 20, 2000.

55. Author's interview with N. C., a Lipan Apache, Presidio, Texas, July 2005.

56. Brenda Norrell, "Tohono O'odham: Caretakers Protecting Sacred Mountain," ICT, March 24, 2004.

57. Brenda Norrell, "O'odham Meet with Tibetan Spiritual Leader," ICT, October 31, 2005.

58. Author's interview with G. C., a Desert Cahuilla Indian, Cabazon, California, September 21, 2005.

59. Author's interview with K. B., a Cupeño Indian, Cabazon, California, September 21, 2005.

60. Author's interview with John Smith, *op. cit.*

Peter S. Cahn

Using and Sharing
Direct Selling in the Borderlands

When Georgina came to Texas from Guerrero, Mexico, in 1987, she followed the path of many undocumented workers. She quickly immersed herself in a wearying routine of work. From nine in the morning until six at night, she performed clerical duties at an insurance claims company. After sleeping for a few hours, she then went to work for a cleaning service, starting her six-hour shift at two in the morning. As her English improved, she replaced the insurance job with a position at McDonald's. Eventually she rose to the rank of manager at the restaurant, but by then she had married a fellow migrant and had had five children. Even with her husband working two jobs, they never had sufficient money to cover all their expenses.

For extra income, Georgina enrolled as a Mary Kay distributor, offering skin care products and cosmetics to her co-workers and neighbors while earning a commission. In this she also followed an established path. Female residents of the proletarian neighborhoods in Ciudad Juárez, many of them migrants from Mexico's interior, have long supplemented their income with direct selling. When sociologist María Patricia Fernández-Kelly conducted fieldwork there in the 1980s, she found that although their supervisors frowned on it, many women sold cosmetics in the *maquila* factories, where customers appreciated the chance to purchase beauty products on credit. The *maquila* workers also reported that they enjoyed the social contact of home parties.[1]

Like women in Ciudad Juárez, Georgina never achieved significant earnings with direct selling, but she appreciated the economic cushion it gave her. So, in 2000, when one of her fellow Mary Kay beauty consultants told her about a new direct-selling company that focused on nutritional supplements, Georgina warned her that she had no interest in joining another company. Her friend persisted, so Georgina agreed to try one of the company's products, a coffee designed to promote weight loss. One taste of Omnilife's Cafetino won her over. Reflecting on her decision to become an Omnilife distributor, Georgina jokes that her children say she is "99 percent coffee." More than just liking coffee, she has always been attracted to "natural" products and tries to avoid doctors and allopathic medicine. In her view, working at McDonald's had left her overweight; the vitamin powders pitched by the new company promised a wholesome alternative to risky diets. Thus convinced, Georgina left Mary Kay to enroll in Omnilife.

Though the desire to generate commission checks motivates Georgina, what she and other direct sellers spend on products for their own use often exceeds what they earn from sales. Well-known firms such as Avon, Tupperware, and Amway, as well as newer companies like Omnilife, base their business on a model known as *direct selling*, which an industry trade group explains "is the sale of a consumer product or service, person-to-person, away from a fixed retail location."[2] Though the companies don't acknowledge it in publicity, direct sellers like Georgina devote more energy to consuming products than they do to selling them. Direct-selling companies downplay the labor of selling to highlight the contrast between the leisurely work of distributors and the arduous work typical of low-wage workers, especially migrants like Georgina who cobble together several physically taxing jobs.

As the companies frequently remind distributors, you cannot recommend a product that you have not tried. Through consumption, successful direct sellers necessarily undergo a transformation, manifest in improved health, appearance, or relationships. But what is more, their consumption forms the basis for persuading others to sample the company's products. Distributors must first use cosmetics or vitamin powders before their efforts to peddle them to others will succeed. Health and nutrition products, in particular, lend themselves to inspiring stories of the miraculous. By using the products, direct sellers come to embody the claims of the company to potential clients. The transformed body serves as the most effective advertising, and therefore obtaining it is the first work-related task of the aspiring direct salesperson.

Direct-selling companies ban the word "selling" in their training sessions and literature, and replace it with the language of "sharing" and "inviting." The bulk of direct-sales' corporate rhetoric—as evidenced in mass rallies and orientation sessions—encourages representatives to use products consistently and copiously. This logic inverts the traditional economic calculation in which productive activity leads to consumptive power; in the direct-selling industry, consumption precedes financial gain. The ready reception of this message illustrates how certain economic actors invest consumption with productive powers. As direct-selling companies multiply throughout the United States and Mexico, they disseminate their message about the primacy of consumption to an ever-wider audience.

In this essay I document how participation in direct selling by Mexican migrants like Georgina signals their desire for respite from the poorly paid, grueling labor that typifies production. I conducted fieldwork in August 2004 with Omnilife distributors in the Dallas–Fort Worth area and attended a weekend training session with Omnilife's founder, Jorge Vergara, in San Antonio. My findings show that in the face of scarce resources and limited access to vital services like health care, participants in direct-selling schemes assent to the elevation of consumption as a path to material success and physical well-being. Considering the genesis of one direct-sales company in the borderlands together with the drives of its participants reveals a pattern characteristic of a late-capitalist, transnational economy: orientation toward consumption over one toward production.

Selling in the Borderlands

Direct selling has long been a mainstay for the distribution of consumer goods in the borderlands. In the early 1900s, for instance, Yankee peddlers sold their eclectic array of goods on credit throughout the predominantly rural United States.[3] For decades, men dominated the ranks of door-to-door sellers, but in the 1880s, the company now called Avon began to recruit women in rural areas across the United States to sell perfume. Avon's founder envisioned his saleswomen not merely as the foot soldiers of product distribution, but as "directors of consumption." By 1930, the company counted twenty-five thousand distributors nationwide, over 80 percent of whom lived in towns of fewer than 2,500 people, mostly west of the Mississippi. Not only did rural women like these women lack access to department stores, they relied on their social networks for information about products. After the Second World War, suburban housewives living in the U.S. West were recruited to the ranks of "Avon ladies" on the assumption that they would be willing to work to purchase non-necessary consumer goods, like cosmetics, but not to pay household bills.[4]

Among many women who defied these expectations were Mary Kay Rogers

"Sea of Cadillacs," Dallas, Texas, Photograph, ca. 2005. Courtesy Mary Kay Inc.

and Mary Crowley, who, as single mothers living in Houston and Dallas respectively, became distributors for Stanley Home Products, a company that innovated the "party plan" in which distributors led in-home demonstrations of its household cleansers. By her account, near the end of the Second World War, Mary Kay held three in-home demonstrations a day, eventually becoming one of the company's highest earners. A few years later Crowley attended one of the parties, where she found affinity with Mary Kay's belief "about God's being a God of abundance who wanted us to have lots of good things, both material and spiritual." After a stint with the Dallas-based direct-sales firm World Gift, each woman established her own direct-sales company: Mary Kay sold cosmetics and Mary Crowley sold home decorations and gifts. Both women parlayed small initial investments into multimillion-dollar companies that helped make Texas synonymous with direct selling. Along the way they innovated signature rewards for their distributors: the Mary Kay Cadillac, now known as a "career car," is an iconic symbol of late-twentieth-century consumer culture in the United States.[5]

Texas's reputation for nurturing direct selling—which stems from a combination of a spirit of entrepreneurship, an uncomplicated acceptance of consumption for consumption's sake, and a steady flow of migrants seeking work, income, and opportunity—has attracted many other firms to the region. In 1989, a trio of entrepreneurs with experience in the direct-selling sector chose Carrollton, Texas, near Dallas, for the headquarters of their new nutritional supplement firm, named Omnitrition. Unlike cosmetics and decorations, Omnitrition's energy drinks and weight-loss powders appealed to men as well as women. Initially, the company's most profitable and visible distributor was Jerry Rubin, the former anticapitalist activist. Journalists dubbed his transformation "yippie turned yuppie," but he defended his decision to champion direct selling by explaining that it was a solution to rampant under- and unemployment.[6]

Rubin persuaded independent scientists Durk Pearson and Sandy Shaw to market their "designer foods" through Omnitrition's network of distributors. Pearson and Shaw, based in Los Angeles, had achieved national prominence as proponents of taking megadoses of vitamins to slow aging. They experimented on themselves and then published their findings as *Life Extension: A Practical Scientific Approach*, which included photographs of the authors in skimpy bathing suits making bodybuilding poses. The book and its sequels sold nearly two million copies while helping to promote the "free radical" theory of aging. This idea proposes that antioxidants found in vitamins can counteract the environmental and nutritional pollutants that cause cell damage and disease. With these sorts of promises and its wide array of drinkable antioxidants, Omnitrition reached sales of thirty-eight million dollars in its second year.[7]

The company soon expanded internationally. Mexico, due to its proximity, ample pool of unemployed, and tradition of herbal medicine, made a logical first choice. In addition, Mexicans were familiar with direct selling, especially due to the presence of Avon. Since 1957, Mexico has been the company's third-largest market. Mexican receptivity to direct selling is clear: for example, the direct-sales firm Herbalife achieved astounding sales of two million dollars worth of vitamin supplements during its first six weeks of operations in Mexico, and Amway recruited some 170,000 Mexican distributors in its first years of operations in the country. When Omnitrition set up its Mexican headquarters in Mexico City in 1991, Jorge Vergara, a former Mexican Herbalife distributor, agreed to run the division.[8]

As Vergara established Omnitrition as a viable competitor to Herbalife and Amway in Mexico, the company's Texas-based founders faced legal troubles. Disillusioned former Omnitrition distributors brought a class-action suit against the company, claiming that its marketing plan constituted an illegal

Onmilife storefront, Mockingbird Lane, Dallas, Texas, February 2008. Photograph by Adam Herring, courtesy of photographer.

Omnilife operates five wholesale stores for distributors in Texas, including this one in Dallas.

pyramid scheme. Such accusations have dogged multilevel marketers, those direct sellers who compensate distributors based on a percentage of the sales of their recruits, since a Federal Trade Commission investigation of Amway in 1979. Because Amway required that its distributors sell some product to customers each month, the FTC ruled that it was not a pyramid scheme, though the company paid a fine for misrepresenting potential earnings to new recruits. When the case against Omnitrition reached the Ninth Circuit Court of Appeals in 1996, the company relied on the "Amway defense," asserting that its compensation plan required distributors to resell product, not merely to hoard inventory to qualify for bonuses. The court rejected this argument, stating that no evidence existed that Omnitrition enforced its bonus requirements. The Supreme Court let stand the ruling that Omnitrition was an illegal pyramid scheme.[9] In the aftermath, the company scrambled to revise its compensation plan such that retail sales were emphasized. Although the lawyers prevailed in court, one of the founding partners kept the rights to the company's name.[10]

As scandal enveloped Omnitrition in the United States, Vergara established his independence from the U.S. company, changed his company's name to Omnilife, and relocated its headquarters to his hometown, Guadalajara, one of Mexico's largest industrial centers. Vergara quickly opened distribution centers across Mexico while pursuing ambitious plans for international expansion. Mexicans in the United States, many of whom were familiar with the products due to time spent in Mexico, represented a logical target for expansion. For Omnilife's corporate headquarters in the United States, Vergara chose Austin, Texas, partially due to the sizable population of peoples of Mexican descent in the region, but also in hopes of capitalizing on the state's demonstrated enthusiasm for direct selling.[11]

Becoming a Distributor

Omnilife has expanded its catalog of products beyond Pearson's and Shaw's original line of designer foods, though all the products still aim to supply large quantities of vitamins. Distributors choose from over eighty vitamin powders, which they dissolve in bottles of company-produced water and drink between meals. The sweet, citrus-flavored powders turn the water yellowish-orange in color. Although in recent years the company has introduced carbonated beverages in aluminum cans and 200 ml bottles, the fluorescent-hued water bottle remains Omnilife's trademark. Jorge Vergara, never media-shy, ensures that every photograph of him includes his bottle of product close at hand.

Following the free-radical theory of aging, Omnilife contends that most humans do not attain optimal nutrition through their diets, and those who manage to eat balanced meals still expose themselves to harmful pesticides and chemicals that the modern food industry increasingly employs. In company literature and training sessions, Omnilife presents its products as equivalent to food, though with concentrated nutrients and without harmful substances. Since the powders contain nothing more than what healthy people should be eating, consumers need no prescription to take them and can drink as many bottles as they feel necessary. As vitamin supplements, the products avoid U.S. government regulation, due to a 1999 federal case where Pearson and Shaw successfully challenged the Food and Drug Administration's right to verify the health claims made on labels of nutritional supplements.[12]

Since her first taste of Omnilife's coffee, Georgina's enthusiasm for the products has not diminished. She begins every day with a hot cup of Cafetino. Then, during the day, she drinks a bottle mixed with Omnilife supplements Kenyan and Magnus, which give her mental and physical energy. In the Texas heat, she drinks a vitamin called EgoLife, which rehydrates the body. She takes chewable pills designed to prevent diabetes and puts a calcium supplement in her children's breakfast cereal. Like Pearson and Shaw, Georgina maintains that most contemporary diets pollute the body with contaminants. She has witnessed how the powders can cleanse the body of toxins, including kidney stones or other noxious substances that Omnilife users have expelled. Pointing to a display of Omnilife bottles on the wall of her office, she calls the product line her "medicine cabinet."

No clinical evidence supports the theory that megadoses of antioxidants prevent the formation of free radicals in the human body. In one study, participants who received beta carotene supplements, a popular antioxidant, showed higher rates of lung cancer than the control group. When a *Newsweek* reporter asked Jorge Vergara for proof that his product works, he replied simply, "I take it every day. We have over a million distributors and five million customers."[13] For the mostly working-class consumers of Omnilife's supplements, the experiences of their family and friends hold more weight than studies published in medical journals. They require no chemical analysis of the product content to believe in its transformative properties. As Vergara reminds his distributors, their task is not to convince, but to take the powders, feel the results, and share their stories. This alone will be enough to win over a client.

Distributors invest so much confidence in the products that they commonly put them to uses not suggested by the company. In his public appearances, Vergara comments favorably about the novel uses for the products that he learns about from his distributors. A man in Argentina told him about using the company's anticellulite gel as a topical Viagra. A woman explained that she mixes several powders into a liquid, which she then administers as eye drops. In my fieldwork, I met Omnilife customers who fashion facial masks by mixing several powders into a paste, feed the vitamins to their pet birds, or inject the products into their veins. Despite these creative applications, Omnilife distributors do not avoid sickness altogether. Yet when they fall ill, they assert that the sickness would have been much more severe had they not been diligently taking the products.

Committing to taking multiple products daily, as the company urges, requires a significant financial outlay. On average, a box of thirty packets of vitamin powder retails for nearly thirty dollars. Georgina offers her clients individual packets of the vitamin powders, making the cost less burdensome. Many clients, like Georgina, lack health insurance, so a medical emergency can devastate them economically. Vitamin supplements can prevent future illness or alleviate existing symptoms, she believes. If a customer wants to buy an entire box, she advises that it makes more sense to enroll in the company, which entitles the distributor to purchase products at a wholesaler's discount. Becoming a distributor costs about twenty dollars. In exchange, the company provides a kit that includes a sample product, a promotional video and magazine, a manual of regulations, and a distributor number, which can be used to make purchases at distribution centers.

When distributors first enroll, they qualify to purchase the product at a 20 percent discount. Each product also carries a point value that correlates to its cost. As distributors increase their point totals through subsequent purchases, their discount increases to a maximum of 40 percent. At that level, called bronze distributor, they can recruit other distributors into their organizations to ascend in rank to silver, then gold, and finally diamond distributor. Georgina decided to make bronze as quickly as she could after enrolling. This required her to purchase about four hundred dollars of product every two weeks for two consecutive months. Despite the large initial outlay, she felt it was worthwhile because she could sample a range of the products en route to reaching the maximum discount level.

After four years as an Omnilife bronze distributor, Georgina has not risen further in the company hierarchy. Advancing to the next level, silver, requires that a distributor enroll three recruits, each of whom must earn one hundred dollars every two weeks in commission checks. Georgina counts three distributors below her, but none of them generates a commission check. Mostly, her recruits purchase Omnilife products for their own consumption, not for selling to others. If she reached silver status, Georgina could claim a larger portion of her network's sales volume in commissions. She doesn't divulge how much money she earns from her full-time commitment to Omnilife, but she mentions that her husband still works two jobs.

Still, she remains optimistic about her potential for growth in Omnilife. Georgina explains, "As Jorge [Vergara] says, we're people who take care of people. We don't look for money." By framing her direct-selling work as a service profession, Georgina measures success in terms of people helped, not money earned. Taking the weight-loss products helped her husband drop several waist sizes on his pants. More dramatically, she recommended Omnilife products to a woman with uterine cancer. The vitamins seemed to work so thoroughly that the woman's doctor expressed amazement that the cancer had disappeared. Georgina keeps a binder in her office with such powerful testimonies illustrated by before and after photographs. This focus on health outcomes enables her to stay motivated in Omnilife even without the tangible financial rewards that some of the superstar distributors featured in the company magazine have experienced. Georgina concerns herself with the proper consumption of the products, not with strategies for expanding her business.

Omnilife's most richly compensated distributor, who happens to be Jorge Vergara's first cousin, claims a monthly gross income of two hundred thousand dollars. Of course, such outsized earnings are the exception. For the distributors I talked to, participation in Omnilife either supplements income from more traditional employment or provides no earnings at all. The lack of consistent profit does not deter distributors from enthusiastically consuming the products. To the contrary, many enroll merely to purchase the company's products at a discount. Despite the company's efforts to discourage treating the products as prescription medicine, most distributors first learn about Omnilife while searching for relief from a physical or mental illness. Like Georgina, they approach direct selling primarily as a natural remedy for a condition that medical professionals fail to treat. Unlike Georgina, who dedicates herself to Omnilife as a career, most distributors remain ignorant of the byzantine rules of the compensation system. Their immediate priority is to improve their health by drinking bottles of product.

Motivating Consumers

Jorge Vergara understands that only a tiny percentage of distributors treat Omnilife as a business. He is also aware that a multilevel compensation scheme requires massive numbers of base-level distributors to generate revenue for those above them in the pyramid. Omnilife wages a constant communications campaign to recruit new distributors and to encourage them to consume once they enroll. The loudest voice in this effort is Jorge Vergara's. From his growing commercial empire in Guadalajara, Vergara commands multiple media for disseminating his message to the three million Omnilife distributors spread across eighteen countries. He is the sole owner of a company that produces quarterly magazines, biweekly newsletters, annual videos, Internet radio shows, biannual mass rallies, motion pictures, and music discs. Most visibly, Vergara owns the Chivas, a professional soccer team in Guadalajara and one of Mexico's most storied sports franchises. He capitalized on the popularity of the Chivas name among Mexican Americans by fielding an expansion team in Los Angeles as part of Major League Soccer.[14]

Vergara maintains a frenzied travel schedule, repeating his message to Spanish-speaking groups in Latin America and the United States. He offers his own story as proof that before an entrepreneur can achieve wealth, she or he must become a diligent consumer. When he publicly recounts his rise to riches, Vergara emphasizes his inauspicious start to minimize the distance between him and his working-class audience. As he tells it, he dropped out of high school to work selling Volkswagens. He switched to selling real estate for a major industrial conglomerate but fell victim to downsizing in the 1980s. Upon returning to his hometown of Guadalajara, Vergara invested in ventures ranging from pork wholesaling to an Italian restaurant, but ended up eating more food than he sold. In a few years, he was "fat, sick, and broke." A friend invited him to try Herbalife's weight loss products. When he took the pills conscientiously, he felt and looked better, so he began to recommend them to others.

At an August 2004 rally in San Antonio, Texas, Vergara tailors his speech for residents of the borderlands. Georgina drives from Dallas with her family to make a vacation out of the event before her children's school year starts. Downtown San Antonio's ornate Majestic Theater hosts the event, part of Vergara's weeklong sweep through the United States called the Gira del Sí (the Yes Tour). I purchase a ticket for ten dollars in the lobby of the theater, then walk into an antechamber at the back of the orchestra section. There, company employees staff two tables selling nutritional products along with memorabilia. While we wait for the 10 a.m. start, distributors dance in the aisles to driving dance music pumped from giant speakers flanking the stage. One group, wearing Chivas uniforms, unfurls a banner that announces "Dallas–Ft. Worth." A busload of distributors from Houston sports matching T-shirts they have designed for the occasion. The minimalist metallic set and single table and stool on the stage contrast with the fanciful castle turrets that frame the proscenium. About five hundred people partially fill the ground floor seats when the event begins.

Two giant screens on either side of the stage amplify Jorge Vergara's image as he strides to the table with a bottle of orangish drink in one hand and a cordless microphone in the other. He looks stylish, with his hair slicked back and dressed in a black suit with a white shirt open at the collar. Resting his bottle on the table, he asks the crowd, "Are you all Tejanos?" This prompts a raucous shouting of hometowns: Ciudad Juárez, Tampico, Chihuahua, Austin, Dallas. The cheering fades as Vergara sits on the stool and addresses his remarks to the mostly migrant audience. He acknowledges the undocumented status of some migrants in the audience but assures them that they need no papers to achieve their dreams. What they will have to do is break with the usual routine of backbreaking labor. "I knew a 'permanent tourist' who earned one thousand dollars a month working in a McDonald's and had to live with ten other people. I tried to motivate him to earn more, but that's all he wanted because it was more than he made in Mexico. You can't convince anyone who doesn't have the desire to change."

Majestic Theater marquee, San Antonio, Texas, August 2004. Photograph by Peter S. Cahn. The theater hosted an Omnilife rally where Jorge Vergara was the host.

Strenuous work not only compensates migrants poorly, he claims, but also it leaves them susceptible to illness. Vergara's message resonates with Georgina, who experienced both meager wages and unwanted weight gain when she worked at McDonald's. Vergara asserts that all migrants to the United States compromise their health:

> You can count the years you've been in the United States like rings on a tree with all the fat you've accumulated. If you order salmon from Alaska, how long does it take to get to San Antonio? Two weeks. It takes six months to bring Washington apples to San Antonio. Imagine what happens when you eat it. Our food starts with insecticides and pesticides. Chickens are the most contaminated animals in the world. They give them growth hormones so they grow to maturity in five weeks. I know you're saying, "I came to learn how to make money, and you're scaring me. What *can* I eat?"

When migrants in Texas opt for fast food or nonorganic produce to save time and money, says Vergara, they really damage themselves further. Even if migrants enjoyed the time and resources to choose healthy foods, they would still lack sufficient nutrition for optimum health. Improvement starts not with intensifying their work rhythm, he continues, but with supplementing

Jorge Vergara addresses the crowd at the Omnilife rally in San Antonio, August 2004. Photograph by Peter S. Cahn.

their diet. Vergara suggests that they take the OmniPlus supplement five times a day.

Vergara solicits testimonials from audience members who have experienced positive results with Omnilife's products. A woman volunteers that she applied OmniPlus topically to her swollen toes. Shortly after, the swelling subsided. "I've been using the products for a year and a half, and they've changed my life. I give thanks to you." A man describes a baby whose mother took OmniPlus daily when pregnant and gave it to the child daily from birth. The child learned quickly to turn over by himself and never got colicky.

Vergara asks who has lost weight with the Omnilife products. He steps down from the stage and winds through the aisles, repeating the number of kilograms dropped that audience members call out to him. Then he turns the microphone over to the director of Omnilife's line of cosmetics. Her claims for the beauty products echo Vergara's comments about the supplements: they are 100 percent natural, with no chemicals. She also solicits testimonials from the audience about how the shampoos and cosmetics have helped them correct health problems.

Around 2 p.m., she hands the microphone back to Jorge Vergara for a final explanation of how consumption of the products can lead to financial gain. Vergara reduces the formula for success to the pithy phrase, "Use and share." He elaborates, "Don't chase money. That's why you came to the United States, and you didn't find it. Don't chase money; chase results to help people. It depends on you—no one else—how much you earn." Earning money in Omnilife does not result from the physically demanding labor that most migrants encounter in the United States. Vergara reverses this formula. Rather than sacrificing their health for money, migrants can generate income by taking care of their health.

In Omnilife, improving health requires the consistent and copious consumption of vitamin powders. As friends and neighbors notice the salubrious effects, they will ask how they too can achieve the same benefits. The more a distributor drinks, the more conspicuous her physical improvement will be. Vergara encourages his audience to "imagine yourself in a village in Mexico scratching your belly while earning five thousand dollars a month." Far from the arduous work they find in the borderlands, migrants hear in Omnilife the promise of earning more money while enjoying a relaxing lifestyle in their home country.

Life for most Mexican migrants in the borderlands involves more than just ceaseless work; it also subjects them to ongoing vulnerability. "Permanent tourists," those who have overstayed their visas, must navigate work and leisure without alerting authorities to their undocumented status.[15] In Omnilife, Mexican migrants have the opportunity for public recognition without fear of reprisals. At the end of the San Antonio rally, Vergara calls to the stage several distributors to award them cash bonuses for high sales volume. He also presents keys to new cars to three couples for maintaining consistently high purchase volumes. In their acceptance speeches, the winners demonstrate how thoroughly they have assimilated the importance of consumption. A man who won a Toyota pickup assures the audience, "Anyone can win a truck; just take the product."

A Dallas couple originally from Chihuahua shares how their success in Omnilife translates to respect in their community. Olivia worked ironing shirts in a laundry for 250 dollars a week. Her husband worked two jobs that left him only four hours for sleep. Even so, they could afford only a tiny apartment, which was so small that they took turns with their daughter sleeping in the one bedroom. When Olivia began to take the product, she found that her migraine headaches disappeared. She followed Vergara's advice to "use and share," soon building an organization and collecting a monthly commission of six thousand dollars.

Although she and her husband had become U.S. citizens after ten years in the country, they still faced discrimination. Olivia decided to build a home with multiple bedrooms in an exclusive Dallas neighborhood. When the contractor told her that only Anglos could live in that subdivision, she showed him her paycheck; he built the house, making them the first Mexican-Americans in the neighborhood. As her husband exclaims from the San Antonio stage: "This man [Vergara] released me from slavery. Today I'm living the American dream, but with a Mexican company." Demonstrating Vergara's point about the futility of wage labor, they have both quit their grueling jobs to devote themselves full time to Omnilife.

Training Consumers

No matter how much Vergara travels throughout the United States and Latin America giving motivational rallies, not every distributor can dedicate an entire Sunday to hearing him speak. Once the collective effervescence of the San Antonio event wears off, Georgina and her network of distributors must keep their enthusiasm for the products without the guarantee of a paycheck, let alone a sizeable one. High turnover constantly bedevils all direct-selling firms.[16] Low barriers to entry and minimal requirements for active membership make it relatively easy to abandon the company. Those who do stay as independent resellers may set their own prices for the products or even offer competing brands alongside Omnilife's powders. Ensuring conformity to corporate philosophy and policies poses a constant challenge for Omnilife. Vergara's investments in media help disseminate his message to as many distributors as possible. The most effective way to impart Vergara's lessons about consumption, however, is in the thrice-weekly training sessions held in support centers.

Any enrolled distributor may open a support center to provide counsel for her organization and to attract new recruits. Georgina opened hers after three years in the company. Omnilife allows her to use the corporate logo in her advertising as long as she identifies herself as an "independent distributor." The company provides no other material resources for establishing support centers, aside from general advice. Omnilife suggests that centers hold orientation meetings about proper product consumption on Tuesdays and Saturdays. Training in the business plan for enrolled distributors takes place on Thursdays. In practice, many centers deviate from this schedule, but they do hold both product and business meetings each week. Although the company does not specify a script for session leaders to follow, the trainings are highly standardized in recommending the plan to "use and share."

Georgina's support center occupies a rectangular room in the interior of a single-story office building near the Texas Rangers stadium in Arlington. I pass a tax preparer, a travel agency, and a print shop before reaching the door that reads "Omnilife U.S.A. Centro De Apoyo Oficial. Distribuidores Independientes" (Official Support Center. Independent Distributors). Below the stenciled writing, Georgina has posted a handwritten sign advertising free English classes. Inside, she sits behind a desk with a computer, phone, fax, and printer. On the far end of the room, I see two tables with white plastic chairs next to a whiteboard, which serve as the classroom. Shelves on the wall closest to the desk hold a display of the products. Next to them, open boxes of Kenyan (for mental function) and Magnus (for energy) vitamin powders advertise packets for one dollar each. In the opposite corner, a television and VCR share a table with a stack of Omnilife promotional videos. Among the decorations behind the desk, I notice a photograph of Georgina posing with Jorge Vergara.

The idea to offer English classes is Georgina's innovation. She explains that it helps increase the traffic at the support center. Although she does not force anyone to try the Omnilife products, the students almost always notice the display and ask about the powders. If students want more information about Omnilife, she directs them to attend one of the three training sessions she holds each week. Ostensibly, the meetings alternate between orientations to the product line and tips for business success. In practice, little differentiates the two types of meetings, both of which encourage greater vitamin consumption as the solution to either physical or financial problems.

On a Thursday evening in July 2004, I attend a business meeting for already enrolled distributors. Shortly after 7 p.m., I join seven women and four men watching an Omnilife-produced video in Spanish, with English subtitles. I notice that most of the guests carry a bottle of Omnilife product with them. When the video ends, Georgina turns on the lights and asks who is here for the first time. She welcomes me as the only newcomer, then turns the meeting over to Jesús, a distributor visiting from Mérida, Yucatán. Since Jesús comes from Mexico, the birthplace of Omnilife, Georgina suggests that we "soak ourselves" in his knowledge.

Jesús asks us to arrange our chairs in a circle. His relaxed speaking style and small stature give him an avuncular air. He begins by saying that when we invite a guest to an Omnilife meeting, we have to give her a sample of the product. "It's 2 percent chatting and 98 percent product," he quips. The products' advanced formulation ensures that their nutrients enter the bloodstream immediately, causing a warm feeling within fifteen minutes, signaling that it works. Hearing this advice and realizing that I arrived without a bottle of product, Georgina bustles to bring me a bottle of company water and two packets of Magnus energy powder. (When the meeting ends, she charges me three dollars.) Jesús recounts his own introduction to Omnilife, which also serves as an example for how consuming the product precedes recruitment. One of his coworkers left the company where Jesús worked in Mexico. When they saw each other again by chance six months later, the once-obese man looked thin. Jesús asked him how he had lost so much weight and heard the name Omnilife for the first time. That same day Jesús registered as a distributor, in order to have access to the products.

Taken properly, he remarks, the products sell themselves. His sponsor did not have to convince Jesús to join Omnilife; he did not even have to broach the topic. So visible was his weight loss that Jesús asked him about the products. From this anecdote, Jesús extrapolates that all the work in Omnilife is about consuming products, not peddling them. "The company doesn't need or look for sellers. It looks for consumers," he states. The prospect of selling door-to-door may deter many potential distributors, but consuming health drinks does not seem so daunting. "99.9 percent of the people in this country who work suffer stress," Jesús claims. He encourages his audience not to limit their business just to friends and relatives. Still, he admits that many people distributors approach will reject their offers to try the supplements.

Successful distributors talk to everyone about the products. While this may sound burdensome or in violation of social norms, Jesús reminds us that we should not consider these conversations work. He describes a recent encounter he had with a woman in Dallas who brushed him off, saying she sold Herbalife. He greeted her as a colleague, told her she had "divine eyes," and left his contact information. A few days later the woman called him, identifying herself as the one with the "divine eyes." She confided that few clients liked Herbalife's products and asked Jesús to enroll her in Omnilife.

His anecdotes sought to emphasize how Omnilife's business plan could work for anyone. In contrast with the stress-filled work migrants usually perform, success in Omnilife requires only that the distributors "use and share." Dallas and Fort Worth, he emphasizes, hold special promise. "The best multilevel companies have been born in Dallas." His hometown in Mexico, which is much smaller than Dallas, supports some seven hundred Omnilife distributors who receive monthly commission checks from the company. He estimates that the comparable number in Dallas is only sixty, leaving ample room for growth. Since multilevel companies tend to gain members during times of economic downturn, he advises his audience to "take advantage of the crisis. The path has been cleared. Just follow it. We're capable. It's not important if you've been to university or if you're illiterate." Omnilife provides all the resources its distributors need to reap the rewards of the multilevel system. The only obstacle to achieving success is a distributor's own self-imposed limitations. It is as simple as beginning to drink the product.

Jesús ends his comments at 9 p.m, but the audience keeps him another half hour to ask questions. They do not ask for clarification about Omnilife's complex compensation plan. Nor do they share examples of their own successful recruiting practices. All they want to know is which product to take for their specific ailments. In keeping with Vergara's distinction, Jesús emphasizes that the products function as food, not as medicine. Even so, the women and men in Georgina's support center treat Jesús like a doctor dispensing prescriptions. Many write down his recommendations on a notepad. One woman wants to know what to give her cousin's husband, who suffers from back problems. A man complains of tingling in his leg. A woman with migraines and a man with knee pain also ask Jesús for advice. In each case, he recommends taking Omnilife products multiple times a day over several weeks.

Toward the end of the meeting, a man—a client of one of the women present—enters the room. I see a pus-filled wound on his shin. A workplace accident mangled one of his legs, he explains. He has been through a skin graft and medical care, but still lacks feeling in his foot. Without asking further questions, Jesús prescribes Power Maker. When the man says that he already consumes Power Maker, Jesús names three other products to take in conjunction. He encourages the despondent man: "First have faith in the Lord. He left you with your leg. Prayer and the product practically work miracles." Georgina, who is listening to the man, offers her own testimonial of using Power Maker to treat an ulcer. As nutritional supplements, Omnilife's powders do not treat diseases or heal injuries in a targeted way as medicines do. Jesús clarifies, "The products don't cure. They regenerate the damaged part of your body." He leaves vague the mechanics of this process, though he assures the man that the larger the quantity of product taken, the faster the recovery.

Miracles, like the ones Jesús promises and Georgina collects in her binder, motivate distributors to consume Omnilife's products conscientiously. While expensive medicines and specialized medical care may be out of reach for many borderlands residents, obtaining the benefits of Omnilife products requires only a trip to the distribution center. In relative terms, the high prices of the vitamin powders do not seem so unreasonable. Georgina acknowledges that the products are expensive, but adds, "They're worthwhile. It's more expensive to go to the hospital." Many distributors also equate consuming the products with taking medicine, developing a testimonial of recovery that bypasses medical professionals. They share their stories of self-healing with as many people as possible. Personal anecdotes of miraculous results outweigh scientific evidence in proving the efficacy of vitamin supplements and present routes to health easily available to undocumented migrants. Just as work in Omnilife offers an alternative to the burdens of the formal economy, so do its products offer an alternative to the uncertainties of allopathic medicine.

Conclusion

Direct sellers have long found the U.S.-Mexico borderlands fertile ground. During the period when few retail outlets reached residents of the U.S. West, door-to-door Avon representatives brought the glamour of cosmetics to rural areas. Companies like Mary Kay, Home Interiors & Gifts, and Omnitrition made Texas their headquarters. With their growth, direct-sales companies turned to neighboring Mexico as a recruiting ground for additional distributors and consumers. By the 1990s, the proliferation of Tupperware parties and catalogs of cosmetics familiarized most Mexicans with direct selling.[17] After learning multilevel marketing from a U.S.-based company, Jorge Vergara tailored its system to his native Mexico. He determined that the Mexican palate favors sweet powders over Herbalife's tasteless pills. He also decided to issue paychecks twice a month, as is the Mexican custom. As his company began to grow beyond central Mexico, he looked to the borderlands for expansion. From its base in Austin, Texas, Omnilife returned direct selling to its country of origin.

In many ways, the burgeoning population of undocumented Mexican migrants makes the borderlands well suited for direct selling. Shoppers across the country may have increased access to retail options, but the appeal of direct selling still holds for "permanent tourists." All the Omnilife publications come in Spanish, and all the employees at the wholesale centers speak Spanish, which prevents communication problems. Moreover, most independent distributors allow customers to pay for their orders in installments, without charging interest. Most importantly, companies do not require that representatives demonstrate legal status, higher education, or willingness to work a set schedule. With this flexibility comes the possibility of earning additional income. Few distributors reach the level of Olivia and her husband, who built their own house from their Omnilife profits. Still, for Georgina, working in

Omnilife offers an "emotional" paycheck. She improves her own health and gains satisfaction from helping others to feel better.

In her previous jobs, Georgina never felt the same sense of purpose. She performed unskilled labor, often in isolation: filing, cleaning, and cooking. She endured the numbing work because the pay enabled her to meet her family's consumption needs. Traditionally, migrant workers have followed the same pattern, accepting physically demanding jobs as a way to save money for durable goods or to support relatives in their sending community. Georgina's job as an Omnilife distributor demands work, too: attending motivational meetings, reading company literature, leading training sessions, and recruiting interested clients. But in multilevel marketing, consumption precedes any productive labor. Before she could invest the energy in building her network of recruits to ascend the ranks of prosperity, she first had to take the products.

At the San Antonio rally, Vergara disparaged Mexicans toiling at McDonald's for minimum wage. No matter how diligently they work, their employer would reward them with little possibility for advancement and increased risk of obesity. This perspective contrasts with the rhetoric in Mexico, where the work ethic of migrants to the United States merits praise. As president, Vicente Fox defended the contributions Mexicans make to the U.S. economy by claiming that migrants fill jobs that no U.S. citizen wants. Vergara, on the other hand, frames low-wage toiling not as noble sacrifice but as misdirected energy. He faults fast-food workers like Georgina for lack of vision. Perhaps they eke out a living, but at the same time they damage their health and fail to realize their potential. Instead of glorifying productive labor, Vergara celebrates consumption as the path to material rewards and physical healing.

Downplaying production has the effect of also devaluing steady income. Omnilife's motto, "people taking care of people," reminds distributors not to pursue clients purely for monetary gain, but to recast selling as helping people in need. In the early days of door-to-door sales, companies treated peddling as a trade, complete with scripts and quotas for giving product demonstrations. Georgina and other Omnilife distributors devote almost no time to rehearsing the dynamics of client interactions. Their goal is to provide a service, not sell a product. Other direct-sales professionals and aspirants along the borderlands interpret their work in the same way. They measure success in the number of people benefited, not in the amount of money earned. Helping, in these cases, always implies introducing clients to life-altering products and instructing them in their uses. The products best suited to direct selling are those that appeal to a wide range of consumers and require frequent replenishment.[18]

That the products offered do not have an obvious competitor in the retail market works to prevent price comparisons. Nutritional supplements fit the profile; so do sex toys.

Passion Parties, a direct-sales company based in California that offers lotions, clothes, and vibrators to women through home parties, reports that the southern United States dominates its market. One Dallas-area distributor made national headlines when local police arrested her for violating a Texas statute that outlaws the sale of any device for stimulating the genitals. In her defense, the distributor cast her work as educational and therapeutic: "Most of what I teach I learned after I was forty. . . . One woman had been married five years and had never had an orgasm."[19] The city later dropped the charges against her, but she continued her educational campaign by mounting a legal challenge to the state's legislation.

Sex-toy parties give a modern twist to the traditional gender roles associated with many direct sellers like Mary Kay and Avon. They overturn the stereotype of the sexually passive woman who sacrifices her own pleasure for her family's benefit. But the empowerment possible at an all-female sex-toy party does not offer women true power.[20] Direct sellers still suffer from vulnerabilities inherent to the industry: no health care, no guaranteed salary, no employer benefits. In the same way that the notion of providing help substitutes for earning an income, the rhetoric of entrepreneurship in direct selling substitutes for job stability. Yet, in male-dominated societies like Mexico's, women whose work closely resembles their domestic duties receive more approval than those women who enter the corporate world. Seen as a service profession, direct selling does not threaten stereotypical gender norms and keeps women grounded in the realm of consumption.

To maximize Omnilife's reach in the borderlands, Jorge Vergara gently challenges the customary correlation between women and consumption. Starting from his own example, he stresses that both men and women must take responsibility for proper consumption. Although women dominate the lower ranks of Omnilife distributors, as they ascend the hierarchy, their husbands tend to join the business, so that nearly all top-level leaders are married couples. Men confide in their testimonials at meetings how they feel embarrassed at first to be taking and recommending brightly colored vitamin powders. Once they begin to experience health benefits, however, their shame disappears. Omnilife's catalog of products includes a supplement specifically for regulating men's hormones. The prominent exposure Vergara gives to his soccer teams and images of players taking the products further reassure men that participating in the company does not compromise their masculinity. Omnilife's rhetoric also neutralizes the common assumption that only women concern themselves with consuming. Men, too, must purchase and take the products so that they may function more effectively as men.

Bringing men into direct selling validates the claim that Omnilife's products benefit everyone who takes them. In the borderlands, environmental pollution, chemical additives, and the popularity of fast food conspire to make most people susceptible to disease. Since we can no longer depend on our diets to provide the necessary nutrients, urges Vergara, we must nourish our cells through supplementation. The company's supplements "go to where your body needs them most," Georgina explains to me. Omnilife's competitors market their vitamins with the imprimatur of a scientific advisory board and lectures by biologists accompanied by PowerPoint slides. Omnilife, by contrast, no longer mentions scientists Durk Pearson and Sandy Shaw in its promotional material, nor does it reveal who formulates its more recent products. Vergara merely asserts that scientific testing has confirmed the products' worth, then invites satisfied customers to give their testimonials.

Without laboratory evidence to bolster the health claims of its products, Omnilife endows consumption itself with redemptive powers. Every meeting, publication, and rally features inspiring testimonials like Olivia's that begin with taking the product and end with realizing a dream. Olivia does not deny the work she devotes to reaching her goal, but the work she undertakes centers on drinking the vitamin powders. Consumption alone unlocks the potential to improve physical health while increasing financial wealth. To avoid an illegal pyramid structure that prioritizes the business opportunity over retail sales, Omnilife and other direct sellers require that their distributors meet minimum purchase requirements. Yet, little selling takes place in direct selling. Rather, distributors consume the products themselves, tell friends and family about them, and enroll other distributors who will consume the vitamins and recommend them to more people.

For Mexican migrants in the United States, the promise of Omnilife turns the liabilities of the formal economy into advantages in the informal one. Direct selling does not privilege legal status, education, or language skills. It fosters community instead of atomizing an already fragmented population. It purports to relieve wage laborers from physically demanding work and offers them a chance to use their efforts to help others. Through direct selling, migrants come to value consumption as a primary activity, not the potential reward for productive behavior. Few sustain the vision put forward in Omnilife's testimonials—experienced distributors estimate that 90 percent of potential recruits they approach will reject their advances, and Georgina commonly sees defection among her roster of already-enlisted distributors. These facts point to the tenuousness of an economic strategy that glorifies consumption in a climate of scarcity. That Omnilife continues to find willing distributors throughout the U.S.-Mexico borderlands, however, illustrates the appeal of a message that ascribes transformative powers to consumption.

Notes

I'd like to thank the University of Oklahoma's College of Arts and Sciences for supporting my fieldwork in Texas.

Notes fully cite primary sources and specialized secondary sources. Full bibliographic details for all other citations are in the volume's selected bibliography.

1. Fernández-Kelly, *For We Are Sold*, 162.

2. Direct Selling Association, "About Direct Selling," http://www.dsa.org, accessed September 19, 2002.

3. Biggart, *Charismatic Capitalism*, 20.

4. Manko, " 'Ding Dong! Avon Calling!' " 5; Manko, "Depression-Proof Business Strategy," 142, 147; Cohen, *A Consumers' Republic*, 287.

5. Paul Rosenfield, "Beautiful Make-up of Mary Kay," *Saturday Evening Post*, October 1981, 61; Mary Kay Ash, *Mary Kay* (New York: Harper and Row, 1981), 16; Jim Underwood, *More Than a Pink Cadillac: Mary Kay Inc.'s Nine Leadership Keys to Success* (New York: McGraw-Hill, 2003), 12; Enid Nemy, "Mary Kay Ash, Builder of Beauty Empire, Dies at 83," *New York Times*, November 24, 2001; Mary C. Crowley, *Think Mink!* (Old Tappan, NJ: Fleming H. Revell Company, 1976), 48; Anne Bagamery, "Please Make Me Feel Special," *Forbes*, March 28, 1983, 89.

6. Jennifer Files, "Baby Boomers Are Prime Market for Company's Food Supplements," *Dallas Morning News*, July 19, 1992; Daniel Akst, "Freedom Is Still Rubin's Motto," *Los Angeles Times*, January 21, 1992; James Kim, "Rubin's New Angle: 'Nutrition for Masses': From Yippie to Yuppie," *USA Today*, March 8, 1990; Jerry Rubin, "The Flee Generation," *Success*, March 1992, 32.

7. Durk Pearson and Sandy Shaw, *Life Extension: A Practical Scientific Approach* (New York: Warner Books, 1982); "Can You Live Longer? What Works and What Doesn't," *Consumer Reports* 57 (1992): 7; Files, "Baby Boomers," *op. cit.*

8. Hayden, *When Nature Goes Public*; Zacarías Ramírez Tamayo, "Avon sigue tocando puertas: En medio de una feroz competencia, la empresa de ventas directas sigue abriendo las puertas del consumidor nacional," *Expansión*, February 1, 1995; Patricia Hinsberg, "Herbalife, Mexican Officials Feuding," *Daily News of Los Angeles*, May 20, 1988; Xardel, *Direct Selling Revolution*, 107; Daniel J. McCosh, "Omnilife for the Masses: Somewhere between Evangelist and Pitchman," *Latin CEO: Executive Strategies for the Americas* 2 (2001): 43–48.

9. Yumiko Ono, "On a Mission: Amway Grows Abroad, Sending 'Ambassadors' to Spread the Word," *Wall Street Journal*, May 14, 1997; Craig Barkacs, "Multilevel Marketing and Antifraud Statutes: Legal Enterprises or Pyramid Schemes?" *Academy of Marketing Science Journal* 25 (1997): 176–78.

10. Omnitrition, "History," http://www.omnitrition.com, accessed July 26, 2004.

11. Jonathan Friedland, "Mexican Health Mogul Says Omnilife May Be the Answer," *Wall Street Journal*, March 2, 1999.

12. Nestle, *Food Politics*, 266.

13. Ruth Kava, *Vitamins and Minerals: Does the Evidence Justify the Supplements?* (New York: American Council on Science and Health, 1995), 11; Alan Zarembo, "The Art of Sockless Marketing," *Newsweek*, June 25, 2001, 66.

14. Marina Delaunay, "El Planeta de Jorge Vergara," *Expansión*, November 13, 2002: 55–68; David Davis, "Conquistador in Cleats," *Los Angeles Times Magazine*, March 13, 2005.

15. Chavez, *Shadowed Lives*.

16. Thomas Wotruba and Pradeep Tyagi, "Met Expectations and Turnover in Direct Selling," *Journal of Marketing* 55 (1991): 24–35.

17. Ariel de Vidas Anath, "Tupperware en el rancho: Las Interconexiones globales en un pueblo Nahua de la Huasteca Veracruzana." Paper presented at the meeting Comercio y Movilidades Urbanas en Tiempos de Metropolización, Mexico City, June 2005; Gutiérrez Zúñiga, "Estrategias de motivación en redes de mercadeo en Guadalajara," 47–63.

18. Friedman, *Birth of a Salesman*, 203–5; Everett R. Smith, "Economic Future," *Harvard Business Review* 4 (1926): 326–32.

19. Jennifer Senior, "Everything a Happily Married Bible Belt Woman Always Wanted to Know About Sex but Was Afraid to Ask," *New York Times Magazine*, July 4, 2004; Glenna Whitley, "Sex Toy Story: You Can't Buy a Vibrator in Burleson, but There Are Plenty of Dildos," *Dallas Observer*, April 8, 2004.

20. Merl Storr, *Latex and Lingerie: Shopping for Pleasure at Ann Summers* (Oxford, UK: Berg, 2003).

Sarah Hill

El Dompe, *Los Yonkes*, and *Las Segundas*
Consumption's Other Side
in El Paso–Ciudad Juárez

Three decades before the 1994 North American Free Trade Agreement (NAFTA), Mexico carved out a thirty-kilometer territory along its northern border for a "free trade zone." There, factories that produced goods for export to the United States lured Mexicans to work, while stores selling duty-free American merchandise soaked up their factory paychecks. The resulting uptick in American consumption, particularly of the most American of commodities—the automobile—prompted a new slang term that Mexican American youth in El Paso invented to poke fun at the cautious driving habits of Ciudad Juárez residents who ventured into El Paso to shop and visit. They called the wheezing Chevys, Fords, and Chryslers that crept around El Paso's poorer neighborhoods "*fronchis.*" A contraction of "Frontera Chihuahua," *fronchi* is an abbreviation stamped plainly in dark green on the amber-colored license plates of all vehicles that had been *fronterizado* (borderized): legally imported to border cities like Ciudad Juárez, but whose use in Mexico was restricted to the thirty-kilometer northern border free trade zone.

These cars stood out in color-coded hues from the newish Mexican-manufactured Nissans and Volkswagens (and some Fords, it must be said) that bore regular Chihuahua license plates, whose coloring varied from year to year but which notably lacked the moniker "Frontera." Unlike *fronchis*, vehicles with "CHIH MEX" plates could travel throughout Mexico, where they could be repeatedly sold in regional used-car markets. *Fronchis*, by contrast, were limited to the free trade zone, so as not to depress prices for Mexican-manufactured vehicles, either new or resale. So, while the term *fronchi* in El Paso enabled Mexican American youth to signal their own distinction from Mexican nationals (with whom they were sometimes confused), in Juárez, *fronchi* license plates marked their drivers as not entirely Mexican, but rather Mexicans tied by secondhand imports to American culture. *Fronchis* piloted their relics of American manufacturing might more or less freely back and forth across the international boundary, but only within clearly delimited internal borders that established *fronchi* cars and their drivers as hybrid subjects, neither fully Mexican, nor unequivocally American.

If *fronchis* compromised the authentic Mexicanness of their *fronchi* drivers, so did much of the rest of *juarense* consumer culture. For most of the twentieth century, El Paso stores offered better prices and a richer array of goods than their *juarense* counterparts.[1] Ciudad Juárez had always been a remote outpost of the Mexican nation; thousands of miles from the central valley of Mexico, Juárez shoppers had, since the city's inception (as the Paso del Norte), obtained from the United States everything residents required but could not provision locally. By the mid–twentieth century, the high cost of freighting Mexican-made goods to Ciudad Juárez yielded an anemic retail market there, while lower American freight costs enhanced El Paso's dynamic retail sector. Soon, Mexicans who could cross the border to shop came to prefer American brands.[2] Those who could not cross the border either paid dearly in Juárez for Mexican-made merchandise, or they turned to the lively trade in secondhand American goods that emerged alongside the flow of new goods across the border. Consumer culture along Mexico's northern border was thus inextricably bound up in American consumer culture on the other side of the border. And as *fronchis* demonstrate, Mexican *fronterizo* consumer culture often absorbed things gotten rid of in the United States. In this way, both Americans and Mexicans along the border came to rely on the vibrant economy of discards, secondhand merchandise, and in some cases, the quintessential unwanted, used-up good: trash itself.

Beginning in the late nineteenth century, mass consumption in the United States grew in tandem with services for convenient and sanitary disposal of unwanted and used-up goods. What might be termed "mass disposal" thus is fundamental to mass consumption in the United States, despite its invisibility: as long as consumers can quickly, easily, and painlessly discard virtually anything, disposal in the United States poses no impediment to further purchasing.[3] To understand how this is so takes only imagining the alternative:

Undated Frontera Chihuahua license plate, "Fronchi," on 1960s Ford Futura, central Juárez, June 2006.
Photograph by Sarah Hill.

what would consumer behavior in the United States look like if prospective shoppers could not rid themselves of broken dishes, old television sets, out-dated clothes, or inoperative automobiles? Consumption in the contemporary United States virtually requires cheap and easy disposal of previously purchased items.

In contrast to the norms of disposal throughout the United States, disposal in the El Paso–Juárez metroplex for the last 120 years has been somewhat more visible—and more complicated. Here, as in other twin cities along the border, discarded goods do not simply disappear into undifferentiated, buried mounds of trash. Instead, they get siphoned off into streams feeding active, vibrant salvaged-goods markets. Many materials and goods that simply end their short lives in landfills throughout most of the United States endure in reincarnated form as recovered, repaired, and renewed merchandise in Ciudad Juárez, a foreign city that profits handsomely from Americans' abandonment of their earlier historical practice of what Strasser called "object stewardship"—the careful preservation of materials to ensure their continued utility.[4] Juárez is not unique in this respect (used European clothing, for example, journeys across Africa nowadays in a burgeoning secondhand trade that mimics the global production system), but full understanding of consumer culture in the borderlands requires some attention to its corollary: disposal culture.[5] In the El Paso–Juárez metroplex, consumption and disposal form two elements of a multi-stranded, unitary process, one that has given rise to a local idiom of disposal/recovery that makes visible what otherwise tends toward invisibility in the rest of the United States: the relation between consumption and disposal.

This essay explores some folk naming practices like *fronchi* that have sprung up in the fertile soil of rejected-goods traffic across the border. I discuss the naming of three sites of consumption/disposal in the pages that follow—*el dompe* (the dump), *los yonkes* (junkyards), and *las segundas* (secondhand markets)—to show that the border itself makes disposal different than anywhere else in either Mexico or the United States. Taken together, these sites shed light on the collision of two features of the U.S.-Mexico borderlands that shape their consumer culture: on the one hand, the border's role in fueling the Mexican federal government's historic ambivalence about provisioning Mexican citizens living near the U.S. border, and on the other, U.S. residents' exploitation of the border itself in their need to get rid of unwanted objects. Entwined in this political economy of acquisition/disposal run threads of race, class, gender, and national identity, weaving together a thick cloak of waste and recovery. Naming practices in the market of secondhand and discarded goods reveal a distinct local cultural formation, subject to conditions over which borderland consumers and disposers have little control but which they nonetheless creatively mark through an inventive borderlands idiom.

Some of the terms described here resonate throughout the borderlands and are common features of border Spanglish. Like any slang, this argot binds its users together in a shared community of purposeful distinction from other communities, contributing in important ways to a common border experience from Tijuana to Brownsville.[6] However, in this essay I look at what makes these terms distinct and unique in Juárez–El Paso. To most border residents, as well as observers, such terms as *dompe* and *yonke* form part of the taken-for-granted lexicon that defines the borderlands' inherent hybridity. Nonetheless, such a view overlooks how these terms differ in historic and particularly local tensions of trade and identity. The stories that I relate are purposefully local accounts that unveil rich, complicated histories of stasis and change in patterns of consumption and disposal between El Paso and Juárez.[7] Other border communities might possess their own etymological histories rather than share a generic linguistic history marked by common borderisms.

One of the characteristic elements of borderline inventions in El Paso—

Juárez is that they do not uniformly encompass the variegated social strata of the vast two cities. In other words, not only do the twin cities' linguistic idiosyncrasies make little sense anywhere else in either Mexico or the United States (though some of the terms may trade in the currency of other border cities); they also make little sense across the entirety of Juárez–El Paso. They do show how the two cities and their waste recovery/consumer disposal practices are tangled in a Gordian knot of mobile goods and transported meanings. "*Fronchi*" is here a case in point: it worked as a joke only on the U.S. side of the Chihuahua-Texas border. And like any cultural formation, *fronchi* is not static. Because of border languages' contingent character in a changing global marketplace in which both sides are only tenuously situated, idiomatic expressions appear, flourish, mutate, and disappear over time. *Fronchi*, a comical term that needed little elaboration from the 1970s to 1990s, is now a sign lacking a signifier and with nothing to signify because the Mexican federal government has dispensed with plain alphanumeric license plates in favor of airbrushed decorative ones. These new license plates still distinguish between *fronterizado* vehicles and national ones, but more subtly, and they have not (yet) given rise to a new playful moniker for the cars' owners.

Of Dumps and *El Dompe*: The Mexican Nature of Garbage

In 1995, I asked Guadalupe, a homesteader on Ciudad Juárez's then-active landfill, how she wound up living there.[8] She answered without hesitation, "We had just arrived [to Juárez] to look for *maquila* [factory] jobs. We were told we could find work at '*el dompe*,' which we thought was a *maquila*. So we took the bus here"—she paused, giving me a wry smile before continuing—"and of course saw that this is not a *maquila*." Desperately poor, and with no money for the return bus fare back to her rented lodging, Guadalupe spent the rest of the day gleaning cans, bottles, and other discarded scrap. Seasoned scavengers suggested that she camp out, because some land at *el dompe* would soon be for sale. Within weeks she and her husband built a shanty, and they eventually began formal land payments. By the time I met Guadalupe, two years after she had arrived at *el dompe*, several dozen other immigrant families from elsewhere in Mexico had stumbled onto the real estate available there for similar reasons: they had not known what "*el dompe*" meant.[9]

To English-language speakers familiar with Spanish, "*dompe*" might not seem an opaque term: it sounds like "dump" with an added accent (dump-A), suggesting that it means—as Guadalupe and her future neighbors quickly discovered—the place for garbage. But to Mexicans living anywhere in Mexico but the border, Guadalupe's confusion would be very understandable: in Mexican Spanish, *basurero* describes the place where *basura* (garbage or trash) goes, and *tiradero* describes the place where thrown-away things (*tirados*) wind up. So why in Juárez did the *basurero* (or *tiradero*) get called "*el dompe*"? The short answer most readily offered whenever I have asked is that *dompe* is slang; people tell me: "*Dompe* comes from 'dumping,'" (or *dompear*).[10] But this response just begs other questions: why use the English language to describe an activity engaged in by Mexicans, in Mexico? And how did English-language terminology migrate across the border, given that Mexicans already have a Spanish term for the activity (waste disposal), which is as elemental to life in Mexico as it is in the United States? Considering some characteristics of early cross-border garbage disposal between Ciudad Juárez and El Paso will help sort out how consumption, garbage disposal, and materials reclamation became an entangled set of activities across the international boundary, such that Juárez's *basurero* became *el dompe*.

To date, no one I have spoken with can recall a time when the term *dompe* was a neologism in Juárez. Retired city engineers and others knowledgeable about public works history insist that the slang term has circulated in common currency since their childhoods, and perhaps since the border existed. One elderly city engineer, eighty-six-year-old Francisco Ochoa, thoughtfully suggested to me in June 2006 that *dompe* became a common term in Juárez because so much of the city fled to El Paso as refugees in 1914, when Pancho Villa's occupying army drove them across the border: "The rich [Mexicans] settled in Sunset Heights, and the poor settled in Chihuahuita [El Paso's "Mexican" neighborhood"], and they took on American customs that became part of Juárez later as they came and went back and forth across the border." Ochoa's reasoning may indeed have some basis in historical fact.

Before 1880, both El Paso and Juárez were small, dusty adobe villages, according to travelers' accounts, which Amy Greenberg's essay in this volume details. The 1880 census counted merely 736 residents in the village of Franklin (as it was then called), Texas; but when, in 1881 and 1882, three railroads arrived to link El Paso to the rest of the continental United States, the town's population grew nearly tenfold, to roughly 5,000.[11] In the summer of 1882, an El Paso municipal ordinance declared that the Rio Grande would be the only site for the disposal of a long list of discarded materials, including rubbish and garbage. The code mandated that "no person in the City of El Paso shall throw into or deposit upon any public street highway or grounds, or upon any private premises or anywhere, except in such places as may be designated for that purpose, any glass, broken ware, dirt, rubbish, old clothes, garbage, or filth and any person so offending shall be fined in any sum not exceeding ten dollars for each offense." It then designated the Rio Grande River "as the place of deposit for all such material."[12]

Municipal records from Juárez, by contrast, do not include codes governing trash hauling or garbage burial until well into the twentieth century.[13] This is perhaps not surprising, because typically disposal becomes a public concern only when population pressures and the amount of material stuff consumed—and discarded—by urban residents reach a certain critical mass.[14] Through the 1880s, Juárez remained relatively unchanged. Low-lying adobe structures added to its "quaint" "Old World" character, according to visitors from El Paso, despite the fact that in 1882 and 1883 two Mexican national rail lines finally brought the town into a transportation network with the rest of Mexico. In fact, the only structure not built of adobe, in 1883, was a railway office.[15] And though Juárez's population grew—doubling in two years—its pace of development remained much slower than its northern neighbor. Despite a few years when Juárez merchants prospered due to the *zona libre*, El Paso assumed a lead in commercial and industrial development.[16] The confluence of five rail lines at the border provided the opportunity for El Paso merchants to launch business interests in the interior of Mexico, bypassing entirely Mexico's remote little outpost—Juárez—across the river, which seemed ever more locked in the past as El Paso surged toward modernity.[17] In 1896, El Paso's *City Directory* boasted of El Paso's continentwide supremacy in ore refining and in other heavy industries, while "an easy walk or drive takes the visitor or sojourner into that quaint adobe town [Juárez], with its seventeenth century method of living and work. A trip to the Holy Land would not more completely put him in a 'foreign country.'"[18]

The well-grounded fears of Juárez's eclipse by its upstart northern neighbor prompted a group of *juarense* businessmen in 1881 to appeal to the central Mexican government for relief from import duties on basic goods. They lamented, "Jealousy comes from contemplating those situated on the other side of the river, given their preponderance of commercial and industrial developments. And while they become grander at our expense, we find no object, no matter how cheap or expensive, that their warehouses do not stock, yielding our sad situation that we must demand the most vital articles as flour, corn, wheat and beef, as we see ourselves ruined and impoverished watching the disappearance of our residents and capital and with them our last hope for improvement."[19] This complaint would become a staple feature of the struggle of *juarense* merchants, who to this day contend with the decided preference of *juarense* shoppers for stores on the other side of the border.[20] Moreover, the grounds of the complaint, "El Paso's preponderance of commercial and industrial developments," points to the likelihood that residents of El Paso were acquiring more goods than their neighbors in Juárez. No doubt a greater volume of waste and discards originated in El Paso than Juárez. So, at the outset of El Paso's modern history, it possessed both a population density and access to goods that made trash disposal a more urgent problem than it was for neighboring Juárez.[21]

While it seems that Juárez had no municipally designated area for dumping, this does not mean that no disposal site existed. Felipe Talavera, director of the Juárez Municipal Archives, told me that before Juárez had an actual *basurero*, everyone used the river (primarily employing *carretas*, the services of mule-driven carters).[22] But the fact that the town lacked municipal garbage codes, while its neighbor to the north possessed a designated dump (albeit also in the river), suggests that the idea of an official municipal dumping ground first appeared—as retired engineer Francisco Ochoa speculated—as an American custom. The customs that became associated with "dumping" in 1880s and 1890s El Paso might have provided a template for how to handle discarded materials in Juárez when its population density and participation in the consumer market were large enough to necessitate a common, publicly managed site.

El Paso codified still more practices associated with dumping, while Juárez left the activity unregulated. In April 1886, the city established a patronage monopoly for waste carting: the city scavenger. Appointed by the City Council for a two-year term, the scavenger paid a bond for the right to charge residents a fee to collect all refuse in the city—including streets and alleyways—and haul it to the city dumping grounds. The ordinance effectively outlawed private householder dumping, as well as what may have been a number of other carting operations. In order to protect residents against the monopolistic abuse of the scavenger, the ordinance set the carting rates. During the first year of the scavenger's contract, residents paid twenty-five cents a week for three pickups, which was the equivalent of about a quarter of a day's work for most, who earned about $1.00 a day.[23] From the 1880s onward, city ledgers in El Paso indicate both income and expenses from the city scavenger. Here again, the contrast with Juárez is notable; no corresponding office existed, and the city recorded no accounts associated with waste hauling.

The custom of the scavenger office in El Paso indicates further distinctions

"Leather Goods Made Repaired and Exchanged," El Paso Trunk Factory, 1910s. Photograph by Otis Aultman, courtesy Aultman Collection, A5344, El Paso Public Library.

between disposal practices in the two communities. As the name suggests, the city scavenger engaged not simply in the business of cleaning city streets and carting off wastes. The scavenger also received exclusive rights to mine the city's waste stream for recoverable materials (another ordinance in 1886 declared that only the scavenger had access to the city dumping grounds). If evidence from the waste trades elsewhere in the United States serves as any guide, city scavengers in El Paso probably profited not from the collected household fees, but in the market for recovered materials. Beginning in 1896, El Paso city directories show a number of junk dealers and materials processors trading in all manner of detritus and refuse, amassing, sorting, refining and selling their materials to various industries.[24] It is unclear from the records whether the scavenger sold to or competed with El Paso's existing waste traders, whose large numbers suggest a lively market for scrap materials. In contrast to El Paso, Juárez directories (such as exist) indicate no businesses dedicated to materials recovery, perhaps reflective of the fact that practically no industries in the city (other than cottage) could have made use of recovered materials.

Just as it was elsewhere in the United States, waste disposal at El Paso's dump was secondary to materials recovery. At the turn of the twentieth century, dumps served primarily as centralized recovery repositories where armies of scavengers worked—in the most appalling conditions—feeding the supply chain of small-scale industrial buyers of waste materials.[25] But materials recovery is only a viable business—small-scale or otherwise—in the context of production needs. If no manufacturers require a supply of materials recovered from the waste stream, there exists no market demand to recover such materials. Since Juárez had little local industry, there was no market for scavenged materials in Juárez; that market lay on the north side of the border, in El Paso. Thus, any scavenging that took place along Juárez's banks of the Rio Grande—and surely there was scavenging there—probably fed the much more robust scrap market on the other bank.

The name *dompe* for dump might have come into common usage in the 1890s because, as newspapers and city records show, "Mexicans" made up the scavenging labor force under non-Mexican bosses.[26] Few of El Paso's junk dealers between 1896 and 1917 appear to have been Mexican; their Ashkenazi surnames—Blott, Bloch, Rosenberg, and Trachtenberg—are consistent with those of waste traders elsewhere in the United States.[27] And until 1908, when El Paso's Democratic "Ring" first rewarded a "Mexican," Frank Alderete, with the scavenger concession, none of the city scavengers possessed Hispanic surnames or given names.[28] Nonetheless, it appears that, regardless of who was awarded the scavenger office or ran junk businesses, those who carted, sorted, and managed materials for Jewish, Anglo, and other ethnic bosses were Mexican, and that Mexicans were intimately associated with waste hauling. For example, from the 1880s, the city dumping grounds were located along the river (by ordinance), not far from the "Mexican" neighborhood of Chihuahuita. In 1911, a newspaper reporter ventured there to observe "a little band of Mexicans who eke out a living delving into the trash and garbage of the city." Informal haulers—Mexicans living on the city's south side and particularly young boys—posed a persistent problem for the scavenger's monopoly: they used their own carts to intercept trash in "American" neighborhoods or charged rates that undercut the scavenger's fees for carting.[29] A garbage haulers' strike identified the aggrieved workers as Mexican, listing only Hispanic surnames on a petition for higher wages.[30] Thus, in the "American" city of El Paso (as promotional literature from the city emphasized), dumping possessed a distinctly Mexican character.

If dumping in the city had meant, at the turn of the twentieth century, something akin to "recovering materials for industry," then it is unsurprising that the concept of dumping should become Hispanicized for the Mexican workers primarily engaged in recovery. Eventually, of course, Juárez grew in size and required its own dumping grounds. But the bulk of manufacturing remained, until the late 1960s, on the U.S. side of the border. Thus, dumping/recovering—regardless of the side of the border—supplied a U.S. market. Perhaps this is why Juárez's eventual *basurero* became known locally as *el dompe*.

In the early 1970s, long after El Paso had closed its dump and turned to the modern, industrial technology of landfilling, a scrappy band of scavengers on Juarez's city dump had cornered the regional market for recovered materials. By then, resource recovery had squarely repositioned itself on the Mexican side of the border. In 1972, a curious fight erupted between the scavenging cooperative and the local office of the Mexican Treasury (Secretaria de Hacienda): because much of the packaging recovered by the scavengers came from dry and canned goods bought in El Paso but consumed in Juárez, the Treasury wanted to charge import duties. The scavengers' cooperative protested loudly and publicly, taking out newspaper ads that asked, rhetorically, "What nationality is garbage?" The cooperative prevailed, but even as it did, the economic basis of the city was undergoing a dramatic change, with heavy industry moving far from the border, and light, export-oriented manufacturing on the verge of an unprecedented explosion in the region due to the arrival of *maquiladoras*. But certain "customs" of waste handling, as former city engineer Francisco Ochoa musingly called them, remained vibrant, thanks to cheap labor and robust networks of materials traders that kept consumer recovery vital.

Yonkes: The Linguistic Politics of Car Parts

In the summer of 2006, while driving Juárez's main north-south artery, a Mexican academic friend of mine wondered out loud why the businesses amassed along this highway called their wares "*autopartes usadas.*" Native to a ranching hamlet on the far eastern end of the U.S.-Mexico border, my friend grew up in the hybrid idioms of border Spanish and English. Nonetheless, this particular phrasing struck him as curious. The conventional names of the businesses we sped past—*yonkes*—seemed self-explanatory to him. He recognized *yonke* as an Hispanicization of a common American term, the *junkyard*; like *dompe*, *yonke* sounds like *junk* with an accented "A" on the end. Indeed, *yonkes*' self-conscious business presentation makes them seem like junkyards, with vast fenced areas of desert containing acres of automotive cadavers, their hoods and doors yawning to show their vital components. Although my friend's hometown possessed no *yonkes*, the etymology of *yonke* seemed obvious. *Autopartes usadas*, on the other hand, did not make sense;

Yonke El Pitufo, **south central Juárez, June 2006.** Photograph by Sarah Hill.

why "explain" *yonke* with *autopartes usadas* (a direct appropriation of "used auto parts), he mused, when *refacciones* (repair parts) would serve suitably? Why explain one imported concept (*yonke*) with yet another (*autopartes usadas*) that was not nearly as legible as *yonke*?

I found myself again struck by the way that certain American terms seem to have simply migrated across the border, weaving themselves into *juarense* everyday speech. *Juarenses*, and many others, I found, take this for granted. For example, in his closely observed essay on scavengers in Tijuana, author Luis Alberto Urrea blandly notes that on the border, junkyards become *yonkes* and dumps become *dompes*, tautologically reinforcing a commonsense notion that lexical migrations simply happen, yielding—to paraphrase Eric Wolf— words without history.[31] Nonetheless, in the case of *yonke*, we can trace at least part of a history leading to an explanation of why *yonkes* in Juárez call themselves vendors of *autopartes usadas*.

Recall that *fronchis* are worn-out American cars; they hunger constantly for spare parts. Thus, with the mass migration of used American cars across the border, a market system for feeding them replacement parts—also used— migrated with them. As Juárez's population grew along with the *maquila-doras* in the 1970s and 1980s, so too grew the market for *fronchis*, which provided both status and affordable transportation for working-class families living in the sprawling settlements that fanned out over nearly sixty-five square miles. These vehicles ferried around the very workers who toiled in automotive plants making components for new GMs, Dodges, and Fords exported to U.S. dealerships. To procure parts to keep an aged but ever-expanding fleet of cheap cast-off vehicles viable, *juarenses* turned to *los yonkes*, where they could find acres and acres of used vehicles ready to be cannibalized for components.

Like *el dompe*, it is not immediately clear why businesses that have counterparts throughout Mexico—used auto parts vendors—would bear an English language–origin name on the border. Colloquially, in central Mexico, people call these businesses *deshuesaderos* or "de-boners," a term which seems to be regarded as slang, since it often appears captured by quotation marks in newspaper stories and official documents, and followed with "*tianguis de autos*" (automobile marketplaces).[32] Mexico also has a name for secondhand car parts: *chatarra*. Ironically, *chatarra* translates into *junk*.[33] These terms likely lack *yonke*'s currency on the border, because historically no Mexican equivalents existed in the interior of the country: *yonkes* specialize in imported used automobile parts to serve in the repair of used *imported* automobiles. When junkyards began opening up in Juárez, chock-full of American junkers, they might have purposefully mimicked American junkyards and hence imported their very name: *yonke*. As in my queries about *el dompe*, thus far I have not found anyone in Juárez who knows how long Juárez has had *yonkes*, nor who thinks that the question merits inquiry. Similar to explanations I was given about *el dompe*, the president of the Juárez Association of Yonkeros, Héctor Lozoya, told me in August 2005 that some years earlier, his organization found that *yonkes* had been in Juárez as long as "there was a border."[34]

This history is not without controversy: both the material and symbolic matters of *yonkes* have been a thorn in the side of government officials who seek to regulate the flow of American goods—used and otherwise—into border cities. As businessmen or capitalist boosters, these government officials were also eager to exploit the economic opportunities the border made available. However, throughout the twentieth century, they have, as Mexican nationalists who perceived the border as both a "threat and an opportunity," danced carefully around the issue of *ayanquando* ("yankifying"), notes Antonio Bermúdez, not only a mid-century Juárez mayor, but also the first director of PRONAF (discussed at length in Evan Ward's essay in this volume).[35] Such claims of concern for Mexican nationality only thinly veil the class bias at the heart of such worries. Mid-twentieth-century elites often complained about American dilution of *juarense* consumer culture, though they themselves trafficked freely back and forth across the boundary line. They feared, nonetheless, that the "weakly" cultured working class could not withstand

Auto Partes Usadas (Yonke) Japon, **south central Juárez, June 2006.** Photograph by Sarah Hill.

the forces of apparent "yankification" inherent in the consumption of American goods.[36]

Another mayor, Jaime Bermúdez (nephew of Antonio Bermúdez), shared this ambivalence about American goods, at least in his dealings with the yonkeros. During his term in office (1983–86) he imposed a new restriction on the *yonkes*: the businesses could no longer call themselves *yonkes*. According to Yonkeros Association President Lozoya, Bermúdez said to him: "I'm not going to give you even a single new permit for another *yonke*." Bermúdez, who reportedly thought the American name carried negative associations, did not try to shut down *yonkes* (likely difficult, since *yonkes* had federal permission to import used, inoperative vehicles), but he did want them to dignify the American discards they imported with something other than imported slang. Bermúdez required that such businesses call themselves "*autopartes usadas.*"

The yonkeros dutifully complied with the new requirements. Lozoya's business, for example, changed its name from Yonke Japón (he specializes in parts for Japanese imports, a further layer of irony) to Autopartes Usadas Japón. Curiously, however, Lozoya claimed that his business promptly dropped off, as did that of the other formerly denominated *yonkes*, because his primary customers "didn't know what *autopartes* meant." Lozoya soon had the white walls surrounding his junkyard repainted, again, so that while he stuck to the letter of the law, he made a concession to the idiom of his customers. The revised signage read: "Autopartes Usadas (Yonke) Japón."

When I asked Lozoya why he thought his clientele could not make sense of *autopartes usadas*, he explained that most of his customers come from El Paso. So Bermúdez's objection to the nationality of the slang, but not the merchandise, begins to make some sense. By the time Bermúdez came to office, Juárez had dwarfed its northern neighbor, thanks in no small measure to the *maquila* program of which he was one of the founders and chief beneficiaries. (Through the ownership and management of real estate leased to American factories Bermúdez reaped millions of dollars.) And yet, as was consistent with the half century of mayors who preceded him, Bermúdez wanted to profit personally from the prospects the border offered while restricting its impact on consumer habits that he saw as unacceptably threatening to Mexican nationality.

As Juárez began to dominate the regional market for used auto parts in the 1970s (effectively putting El Paso's automobile junkyards out of business by the end of the decade), the *yonkes* no doubt supplied an important source of foreign revenue for the city. In contrast to the customary northward flow of revenues out of the city (both shopping in El Paso and *maquila* development do little for the city coffers), *yonkes* generated business taxes, property taxes, and so forth, inverting the usual order of things in Juárez. With *yonkes*, U.S. residents (mostly Mexican in nationality or ethnicity) travel to Juárez specifically to acquire used goods that have been imported to Mexico. Yet, no matter how important these businesses were to the city during Bermúdez's administration, he apparently could not stomach the name *yonke*. Bermúdez's fears of what his uncle called "*yankifying*" did not extend to the Americanization of Mexican industry in the *maquila* sector. But his concerns did arise when *juarenses* adopted what he seemed to consider degenerate American customs—the term *junk/yonke* instead of the more respectable English-language origin "used auto parts." Whatever the case may be, it reveals *juarense* elites' discomfort with their city's integration into the American consumer market, for new, used, and junked stuff.

I suspect that Bermúdez's selection of an American-origin neologism (*autopartes*) shows both a veneration of things American and a desire to dress up used versions a bit. Bermúdez could have opted for genuinely Mexican nomenclature, such as *refacciones usados* (used spare parts) or *negocios de chatarra* (*chatarra* shops). Instead, he seems to have wanted the fact of their foreign origins to remain clear, albeit in a sanitized fashion. Curiously, the somewhat comical redundancy of the *yonkes'* signage has more recently become an unexpectedly useful symbolic tool in the Yonkeros Association's struggles for

Totem constructed by Yonkeros Association, made of crushed automobile cubes (a form of signage no longer in common usage for *yonkes*), south central Juárez, June 2006. Photograph by Sarah Hill.

legitimacy. While Bermúdez might have fretted over the denigrated second-hand form of "*yankification*" represented in the name *yonkes*, the yonkeros' concerns subsequently came to center on the difference between themselves as registered, duty-paying, law-abiding businesses and the unregistered, "illegal" *yonkes* whose numbers have exploded in recent years. Such businesses, according to Lozoya, deal in *chuecos*—"crooked" merchandise sold without license or proper taxes. In 2005, 450 registered members of the Yonkeros Association competed for customers among themselves and with an estimated 225 illegal *yonkes* around the city, whose exterior walls and signage reference their illegality. Since the illegal *yonkes* are not registered, they do not bother with cumbersome mandated nomenclature. They call themselves, simply, *yonkes* (when they have painted signs), or in lieu of verbal signage, they indicate their wares with fences made of crushed, cubed automobiles, a formerly universal symbol in Juárez for yonkeros.

In 2006, *yonkes* lined both sides of Juárez's north-south arteries. With the city spreading southward, they had gradually moved southward too, wherever land was abundant and cheap enough to warehouse vast fleets of cars. For many in El Paso (Mexican, American, and otherwise), the *yonkes* are not only the main source of used auto parts on the border; they are also the most visible reminder of a thriving underworld of car thievery, chop shops, and reselling that explains the persistently high auto insurance rates in El Paso. For Lozoya and his fellow legitimate yonkeros, and for Americans who know the term, *yonkes* are tangled up with anxieties about the border region's crooked practices (business and cultural) that often seem to bear down upon the efforts of legitimate businesses.

But in the evolving marketplace for auto components along a dissolving trade boundary, *yonkes* face an emerging threat: that they are not American enough. The Yonkeros Association more recently has sought to help its members not only to establish their legitimacy but also to compete on price, quality, and service in a marketplace that has seen the arrival of a new kind of American import: franchises offering discount spare parts and discount auto repairs. In 2005 the Yonkeros (unsuccessfully) petitioned for city land to build an installation where all 450 members could relocate. Their plan accommodated air-conditioned areas where customers could relax while awaiting repairs. They wanted to develop the *yonkes'* business image such that they could sever the association between criminality and used auto parts. The failed plan would have given them a fighting chance against, on the one hand, the AutoZones, Pep Boys, and the like that skim their most prosperous customers, and on the other, illegal *yonkes* that continue to poach on the lower end of the market.

Meanwhile, the language on the border for conveying the expanding penetration of American automobiles and parts into the Mexican economy of used merchandise itself keeps expanding. In August 2005, Mexican president Vicente Fox removed the prohibitions against individuals importing cars from the United States. The national coverage of the policy change introduced slang terms from Mexico's interior used to describe vehicles that entered the country across the northern border. In Mexico City, such vehicles, called "chocolate," are said to be illegally left behind by "migrants": that is, Mexicans who live and work for long periods in the United States. In Juárez, "chocolate" soon appeared in the war of words to distinguish among imported vehicles. At my request, Eduardo Barrera asked his graduate class in epistemology at the Autonomous University of Ciudad Juárez in 2005 to explain the difference between *chocolate* and "*chueco.*" No clear consensus emerged: some students said that *juarenses* do not use the term *chocolate*, others reported that *chueco* means a vehicle that lacks a title and plates (indeed, *chocolate* does not appear in the university's extensive slang glossary, first compiled in 1985, while *chueco* does). But one student explained that *chocolate* refers to vehicles that are "tolerated," despite being illegal.[37]

Importers in Mexico City strenuously decried Fox's executive order. Guillermo Rosales Zarate, government relations director of the Mexican Association of Automobile Distributors, declared that the policy legalized contraband. (The analogy of opposition to legalizing "illegal" immigrants in the United States comes readily to mind.) With little else effective at hand (the executive order is, after all, a done deal), Rosales resorted to an old trick: the attempt to reclassify a transient object with unambiguously negative value. He suggested that the soon-to-be-legal *chocolate* was, in effect, "garbage": "We want to be business partners with the U.S. and Canada, not their largest *basurero de chatarra automovile.*"[38] In this he upped the ante—by turning *chatarra* into *basura*, or junk into trash.

Las Segundas: From Secondhand to Global Market Subordination

When I first began research at *el dompe* (October 1994), I met a former RCA factory supervisor who was at that time struggling to set herself up in business as a neighborhood seamstress. Socorro was talented, but she disliked the penurious self-exploitation that selling homemade special-occasion dresses required. She constantly found herself torn between wanting to earn a reasonable income for herself (which she sorely needed) and the pain of telling young girls that they could not afford all the extra frills they desired on their first-communion or *quinceañera* dresses. One place that Socorro found she could achieve a slight advantage was in her choice of fabric stores. If she traveled by bus to *el centro*, bypassed the Mexican fabric stores in and around Avenida Lerdo, and walked across the bridge to El Paso, she could procure her materials at a favorable price. However, Socorro chastised herself every time she did so, calling this shopping "*malinchando,*" a term that comes from the name of Malinche, the Indian princess who was Cortéz's consort and who served as his translator during the conquest of Mexico. To *malinchear* is to act as a traitor (and, it almost goes without saying, to act as a female traitor). So in crossing the river to purchase fabric, Socorro avoided the (slightly) more pricey Mexican vendors, and in so doing, sold them out.

Several years later, when her seamstress prospects foundered, Socorro briefly set up a small stand in an ersatz market that had gradually become a permanent fixture down the mountain from the Juárez dump, on the paved grounds of a giant parish church. I once went to visit her with my research

assistant, who told me that Socorro was working in "*las segundas*"—the secondhand market. To my surprise, Socorro was not selling anything used,
however, nor were most of the other vendors. Under a loosely tied plastic tarp
that shielded her from the sun but also captured its heat like a convection
oven, she sat limply behind a table filled with dusty plastic hair accessories:
the classic *fayuca* (contraband) of the city's growing underground import
econnomy. That the market called *las segundas* offered little that was secondhand posed no paradox for *juarenses*.[39] The fact of the merchandise's new
or secondhand status was not as relevant a distinction as it once was, nor was
the nationalist distinction that had once made Socorro compare herself with
Malinche.

The sheer volume of stuff available to purchase in Juárez—new, secondhand, or even thirdhand—has grown in tandem with the global volume of
consumer goods. Ironically Juárez's reinvention as a major industrial city
engaged in export-oriented commodity production exemplifies the conditions under which the global trade in finished consumer goods has surged. In
this sense, the Mexican predilection for creative reuse—"Mexican" recycling,
as Claudio Lomnitz calls it—is coming under the same influences that fostered
the American tendency to simply throw something away once it is out of
fashion, modestly marred, or reveals a tiny defect.[40] Furthermore, the nature
of consumption in *las segundas* is more important than the status of the goods
as new or secondhand, or as Chinese or American. Like *yonkes*—which no
longer strictly refer to junkyards but now to businesses that both sell *and*
install used automobile parts—*las segundas* now refers to markets that might
sell used goods, or might sell cheap Asian *fayuca*, or both. To *juarenses*, it does
not really matter, because *las segundas* has always clearly indicated that what
these markets provide is access to goods from elsewhere. Whether used or new,
the market sells imports and a shopping experience of a particular kind:
bargaining and haggling based on the purported second-class or secondhand
quality of the merchandise under consideration.

At the same time, however, there remain some clear and well-known distinctions that *juarenses* recognize in the array of *segundas* around the city. For
example, the market known as "*los cerrajeros*," where hundreds of stalls are set
up and torn down every day in one of Juárez's oldest working-class neighborhoods, La Chaveña, is still largely dedicated to used merchandise. Vendors
ferry most of it in small lots from across the border. Initially, the market
specialized in locks—*cerrajero* means locksmith—that the vendors likely collected in exchange for the locks that they repaired. Over time, the market

Household appliances for sale in *Los Cerrajeros*, north central Juárez, June 2003. Photograph by Sarah Hill.

incorporated tools, appliances, and kitchenwares, many acquired from flea markets, garage sales, pawn shops, and Goodwill shops throughout the U.S. Southwest. Thus, no one expects to find locksmiths in the *cerrajeros* market anymore, although everyone expects to find vendors who continue to tinker. Now, however, they tinker with used imported and domestic merchandise, repairing fans, air conditioners, power tools, TVs, phones, and so forth, in order to resell them to cash-poor *juarenses* who scrupulously inspect and test the wares.

One curious feature of Socorro's two efforts to establish a business (first as a seamstress and second as a market vendor) is that her guilt of *malinchando* was slightly misplaced. Socorro's conflict over patronizing vendors in El Paso suggests that historically, *malinchando* in Juárez speaks specifically to the competition between American and Mexican retailers, but what is more, to the disparity between the two sides of the border that they represent. What made her shopping trips a form of *malinchando* was that when she crossed the border to the United States, she betrayed her side. The El Paso stores she went to were not exactly American: Socorro, as do most other Mexicans, called these shops "*los chinos.*" The stores on El Paso Street, mostly owned by Koreans and Chinese, have come to rely almost exclusively on a Mexican working-class clientele who cannot drive to El Paso's distant malls and big-box discount stores. They stock not goods made in the U.S., but imports. The only thing that is "American" about the stores is the sales tax of 8.25 percent they collect for the state of Texas and the county of El Paso.

Socorró did not express any guilt of *malinchando* when she purchased her Asian-import hair ornaments to sell in her stall in the *segunda*. And why should she? She had not crossed the border. Nevertheless, her simple act of buying Asian imported goods did contribute to the steady shift rocketing through the foundation of both Juárez's and Mexico's economy. Her simple, guilt-free act of wholesale consumption was one of millions of prosaic, quotidian acts that illuminate the changes in the very nature of the borderlands and of consumer culture. When I first met Socorro, Juárez's export industry was booming, but by 2004, many industrial parks were virtual ghost towns, eerily quiet and still, with hardly a worker in sight, and their once carefully landscaped grounds turned into fields of billowing tumbleweeds and droning locusts. The number of factories had declined by a third, and the number of workers employed in them had dropped off nearly as much. Television production, which Juárez used to dominate for the North American market, is now practically nonexistent, even though overall factory employment had recovered somewhat in 2005 and 2006.[41] The reason? China's cheaper labor— nearly a quarter of the cost of Juárez labor—had struck a body blow to the Mexican *maquiladora* industry.

Perhaps the fabric that Socorro purchased in 1994–95 in *los chinos* did not come from China, but within little more than a decade it would have, thanks to the end of the thirty-one-year-old international Multi-Fiber Agreement, which has been widely predicted to eliminate all obstacles to China's global dominance in textile production. In the latest ironic twist to the historical complications between nationalism, secondary goods, and cross-border consumption, El Paso stores now sell venerable Mexican branded items—and iconic Mexican imagery—that is manufactured in neither the United States nor Mexico, but in China.[42]

How the Border Crossed Goods, Bads, and Traffic in Trash

During the run-up to the 1994 North American Free Trade Agreement (NAFTA), some Mexican border scholars observed that the once denigrated northern border had recently achieved a historically unprecedented cultural valuation among Mexican intellectuals and policymakers: it would become the laboratory of Mexico's future.[43] Indeed, as NAFTA has unfolded, the internal borders within Mexico that kept export-oriented production and foreign-goods importation isolated to the region adjacent to the border with the United States have disappeared. Now Blockbuster, Wal-Mart, and Kentucky Fried Chicken are as likely to operate in Ciudad Juárez as they are in Oaxaca, Cuernavaca, or Dallas. Venues such as a bar in Guadalajara, calling itself Bar Yonke Recycle, suggest that the border's once-unique slang has left footprints on cultural formations across Mexico. In a few hours of travel around Mexico, via World Wide Web, I discovered in early 2007 that the cultural formation that used to be distinct to the border—the peculiar American English–inflected language of discard and recovery—has migrated southward, settling not just in every border city and township but even deep in the interior of the country. Businesses calling themselves *yonkes* now range across the states of Sonora, Baja California (del Norte), and Tamaulipas. Some describe themselves as selling *autopartes*— one in Quereterro even calls itself Autopartes Yonke Outlet.[44]

But in the meantime, the threads of Mexican trade that once got knotted with American import slang might now be unraveling in the face of a dramatically transformed global economy. Throughout Juárez's markets, the impact of China is everywhere. China is now the world's leading purchaser of recovered materials. The cooperative that won the right to declare Juárez's garbage "Mexican" is practically out of business, having been seriously hampered by the city's closure of *el dompe* following the establishment of a sanitary landfill in October 1994. Brokers from Mexico's Pacific coast and southern California have contacts with buyers in China—foundries, paper plants, and so forth, so Juárez materials buyers contend with them, instead of locals. Perhaps, in the not-too-distant future, a new language will emerge to mark this extraordinary turn of fortune.

Abbreviations

EPT	*El Paso Times*
DJ	*Diario de Juárez*
IOH	Institute of Oral History, University of Texas, El Paso Library, Special Collections

Notes

I thank a Richard Carly Hunt Fellowship from the Wenner Gren Foundation for Anthropological Research and the College of Arts and Sciences at Western Michigan University for support in writing here. I am indebted to Eduardo Barrera for his willingness to test some of the ideas explored in this essay. I thank my colleague Kristina Wirtz and the participants in the Ethnohistory Seminar at the University of Pennsylvania for a lively discussion about goods, bads, and brands, and also David Grazian, who provided insightful commentary. And finally, my appreciation goes to Alexis McCrossen, Mauricio Tenorio, and two anonymous reviewers for their close reading of the essay and very helpful corrections and suggestions for revision.

Notes fully cite primary sources and specialized secondary sources. Full bibliographic details for all other citations are in the volume's selected bibliography.

1. This has been the long-term character of the border, though in particular moments the "free zone" on the Mexican side has given advantage to *juarense* merchants over their El Paso counterparts. Martinez, *Border Boom Town*, 7, 113–25; Hill, "Wasted Resources"; García, *Desert Immigrants*, 9–32; González de la Vara, *Breve historia de Ciudad Juárez*, 112–16.

2. Martínez, *Border Boom Town*, 129–31; Hill, "Wasted Resources." See also Antonio J. Bermúdez, *Recovering Our Market Future: A Task in the Service of Mexico* (Mexico City: n.p., 1968), 109–21, 133; Miranda René Mascareñas, Oral History Interview Transcript, 1976, IOH, 91–97.

3. Strasser, *Waste and Want*, 161–201. See also Heather Rogers, *Gone Tomorrow: The Hidden Life of Garbage* (New York: New Press, 2005), 77, 79–101; Jeff Ferrell, *Empire of Scrounge: Inside the Urban Underground of Dumpster Diving, Trash Picking, and Street Scavenging* (New York: New York University Press, 2005).

4. Strasser, *Waste and Want*, 21–68.

5. Hansen, *Salaula*.

6. On slang, see Connie Eble, *Slang and Sociability* (Chapel Hill: University of North Carolina Press, 1996), esp. pp. 11–24.

7. Scholars of the El Paso–Juárez metroplex have written against the tendency to homogenize the borderlands by analyzing the cities' complex systems of internal borders of race, class, nationality, and gender. See especially Vila, *Crossing Borders*; Wright, *Disposable Women*.

8. Some of the material in this section appears in longer form in Hill, "Wasted Resources."

9. I discuss this real estate development at length in Hill, "Domesticated Responsibility"; Sarah Hill, "The Environmental Divide: Neoliberal Incommensurability at the U.S.-Mexico Border," *Urban Anthropology* 30, nos. 2–3 (2001): 157–87.

10. A glossary of Juárez slang provides little guidance here. It defines *dompe* as *basurero*, notes its origin as "English": "*que significa basurero*" (which means dump), and then points to four lexicons of Mexican-American slang as references for the term (i.e., indicating that it is widely used by Mexican Americans). Ricardo Aguilar Melantzón, *Glosario del calo de Ciudad Juárez*, translated by Federico Ferro Gay, 2nd ed. (Las Cruces, N.M.: Joint Border Institute, New Mexico State University, 1989), 57.

11. León, *Mariano Sanmiego*, 5.

12. El Paso City Council, *Minutes*, July 10, 1882, Southwest Collection, El Paso Public Library, El Paso, Texas.

13. City records and council minutes held in the Municipal Archives of Ciudad Juárez show no evidence that comparable codes for waste disposal existed in Juárez before the 1920s. The city sanitation department existed by the mid–twentieth century.

14. See especially Martin Melosi, *Garbage in the Cities: Refuse, Reform and The Environ-*

ment, 1880–1980 (Chicago: Dorsey Press, 1981). Ritual pollution is, of course, another matter. See Mary Douglas, *Purity and Danger: An Analysis of the Concepts of Pollution and Taboo* (London: Routledge, 1966); Michael Thompson, *Rubbish Theory: The Creation and Destruction of Value* (Oxford: Oxford University Press, 1979).

15. Frederick Albion Ober, *Travels in Mexico and Life Among the Mexicans* (Boston: Estes & Lauriat, 1887), 598–99.

16. González de la Vara, *Breve historia de Ciudad Juárez*, 119–24; García, *Desert Immigrants*, 15–28.

17. Martinez, *Border Boom Town*, 31–34.

18. *1896–97 Evans & Worley's Directory of the City of El Paso* (Dallas, 1896), 3.

19. Petition to the state government, published in *Periodico Oficial del Estado de Chihuahua*, September 3, 1881. Cited in Chávez, *Historia de Ciudad Juárez*, 293, author's translation.

20. Future iterations of these complaints are discussed in Martinez, *Border Boom Town*, 129–31; González de la Vara, *Breve historia*, 156–59; Hill, "Wasted Resources."

21. Even during Juárez's brief commercial heyday of 1885–1890, most of what was purchased in Juárez was *used* in El Paso, and thus, in turn, disposed of there, too.

22. Author interview, June 2006.

23. The account in this paragraph is drawn from historian Mario T. García's *Desert Immigrants*. In his account of the Democratic "Ring" and a reformist political movement of the 1910s, he refers to the city scavenger as a client of the "Ring" (p. 32). It is unclear whether all El Paso residences paid scavengers' fees. García reports that in 1900, common laborers earned eighty-eight cents a day in Juárez, while their counterparts earned a dollar across the river (p. 35). In 1909 the Dillingham Commission reported that the railroads paid their "Mexican" laborers a dollar a day (p. 39). The smelter that would become ASARCO's massive refinery in 1901 was charged in 1887 with underpaying forty Mexican contract workers at a rate of fifty cents a day (p. 52).

24. Carl Zimring, *Cash for Your Trash: Scrap Recycling in America* (New Brunswick: Rutgers University Press, 2006).

25. Martin Melosi, *The Sanitary City: Urban Infrastructure in America from Colonial Times to the Present* (Baltimore: Johns Hopkins University Press, 2000); Martin Melosi, "The Fresno Sanitary Landfill in American Cultural Context," *The Public Historian* 24 (2002): 17–35. For other accounts of scavenging, see Benjamin Miller, *Fat of the Land: Garbage in New York—The Last Two Hundred Years* (New York: Four Walls Eight Windows, 2000); Melosi, *Garbage in the Cities*, op. cit.

26. *EPT*, May 21, 1913; *EPT*, January 28, 1911, 11. In common parlance there was no distinction at the turn of the century, in El Paso, between Mexican nationals and U.S. citizens of Mexican descent. Both were called—and called themselves—"Mexican."

27. Zimring, *Cash for Your Trash*, op. cit. Zimring contends that immigrant Jews almost exclusively dominated the waste trades. Nonetheless, in some cities other immigrant groups—Italians in San Francisco and Dutch in Chicago—established enclaves in waste carting and scrap businesses. See also Stewart Perry, *San Francisco Scavengers: Dirty*

Work and the Pride of Ownership (Berkeley: University of California Press, 1978); David Pellow, *Garbage Wars: The Struggle for Environmental Justice in Chicago* (Cambridge: MIT Press, 2002).

28. García, *Desert Immigrants*, 72.

29. EPT, May 21, 1913, 12.

30. EPT, January 28, 1911, 11; EPT, February 7, 1914, 6.

31. Urrea, *Across the Wire*, 4; Eric Wolf, *Europe and the People without History* (Berkeley: University of California Press, 1982).

32. My thanks to Mauricio Tenorio for alerting me to *deshuesaderos*. E-mail communication, May 2006. "Tianguis" is the Nahautl word for "market."

33. A May 2006 nutritional campaign to ban packaged, high-fat, high-carbohydrate foods in Mexican schools was dubbed an effort to outlaw "*comida chatarra.*" "Prohibe Cámara comida chatarra en esculeas," DJ, December 9, 2005.

34. In my August 8, 2005, conversation he said first that *yonkes* had been around since there was a border, and then later said they had been around since the 1920s–1930s. So he might have meant two different things: that *yonkes*—dealers in cross-border junk (i.e., scrap)—have been around since there was a border, and that *yonkes* specializing in car parts have been around since there were cars on the border.

35. Cited in Barrera, "The U.S.-Mexican Border," 188–90; Antonio J. Bermúdez, *Gaceta Municipal: Informe que Rinde El Ayuntamiento Constitucional* (Ciudad Juárez: Ayuntamiento de Ciudad Juárez, 1943), 11.

36. I discuss this issue at greater length in Hill, "Wasted Resources."

37. Melantzón, *Glosario del calo*, op. cit., 50. "Something illegally obtained; cripple" (translation in the original).

38. "Mexico autoriza importar vehículos de EU y Canadá," *La Opinion* (Los Angeles), August 23, 2005.

39. While the term "seconds" might mean factory seconds to U.S. consumers, historically in Juárez "segundas" refers to secondhand markets. Of course "segundas" could come to mean "factory seconds and overstocks" in Juárez, given the nature of the merchandise now sold in *segundas*.

40. Lomnitz, *Deep Mexico*, 118.

41. Melissa Wright, personal communication, May 2005.

42. DJ, August 6, 2005.

43. Barrera, "U.S.-Mexican Border," 188.

44. From a series of postings about the Spanish equivalent for the word "landfill," December 1, 2004, on the wordreference.com language forum, http://forum.wordrefer ence.com/showthread.php?t=6964, accessed January 22, 2006.

REFLECTIONS

South El Paso St., 216–222, El Paso, Texas, 1980. Photograph by David Kaminsky, Library of Congress, Prints and Photographs Division, HABS TEX, 71-ELPA, 4–14.

Howard Campbell and Josiah McC. Heyman

The Study of Borderlands Consumption
Potentials and Precautions

The juxtaposition of concentrated wealth and extreme poverty forms the contours of everyday life and consumer culture in the borderlands. The 2,000-mile boundary between the United States and Mexico is the only place in the world where a developed country shares a border with a developing country. This is not by chance, as American prosperity is contingent upon the exploitation of cheap Mexican labor and abundant natural resources. Yet, although the United States is the wealthiest nation in the world, Mexico, despite the poverty of over half its people, possesses the twelfth-largest world economy. Indeed, Mexican telecom entrepreneur Carlos Slim Helú now outranks Microsoft's founder Bill Gates as the richest person on the planet. Despite Mexico's relative poverty, extraordinary pockets of prosperity and lavish consumer lifestyles exist in Mexico, its northern states, and its border cities, including Monterrey, Tijuana, and Ciudad Juárez. The close proximity of the two distinct national cultures and their complex intertwining of scarcity and abundance, along with government and private attempts to wall off and militarize the border, shape the consumer society of the borderlands. Despite these factors, border peoples have long histories of zigzagging, slantwise movements in which they transgress or avoid international barriers and create individual and collective strategies of survival, subsistence, and meaning.[1]

It is thus too simple to study border consumption as if Mexico and the United States are two monolithic societies: capitalist and traditionalist, rich and poor. Rather, we must envision a region in which two immensely varied and interpenetrating

Lowriders at the University of Texas at El Paso, October 1998. Photograph by Laura Trejo, courtesy of photographer.

The lowrider parade here pictured in a university stadium underscores the complexity of identity politics in the border region.—A.M.

societies mutually constitute each other. The enormous "monumentalism"of the two national cultural identities and the breadth and depth of distinct cultural practices on each side of the boundary allow us to speak broadly of Mexican and U.S. people engaging in a series of cultural encounters in the region.[2] Many residents, it must be remembered, never cross the border; much of their practical and meaningful experience is thoroughly oriented toward the interiors of their own nations.[3] Within the space of the borderlands, we should be open to both national frames and cross-border frames for the study of consumer culture. Beyond the immediate border region, a geographically wide range of interactions take place between the two nations, such as the consumption of Mexican news and entertainment programming in Spanish-language media throughout each nation, or the vast and dense web of telephone conversations using inexpensive phone cards sold throughout both countries, complete with insignias of popular Mexican soccer teams, or the ubiquity of Coca-Cola and Hollywood movies. It is thus clear that practices and mandates associated with a consumer economy bind the two nations together, and not just along the border, as Evan Ward's essay about the emergence of a "new" borderlands along Mexico's Pacific and Gulf coasts amply illustrates.

The study of consumerism in the border region demands a broad perspective on the provisioning and production of daily life that ought to inform and enrich the scholarly tendency toward focusing on possession and display in the fashioning of identity. Understanding consumption-provisioning systems is as important as inquiry into the making of habits, tastes, and wants over time. As anthropologists, we view consumption as the use of materials and energy in the production of daily life—food, shelter, clothing, and so forth. The material making and renewal of existence, furthermore, occurs through the complex interplay between the agency of consumers and the structures regulating prices, credit, and markets.[4] The specific phenomenon of consumerism emerges when people purchase, rather than make, a large portion of the items used for their material and symbolic life.[5] Each item and activity of consumption is simultaneously loaded with symbolic meanings and a material process of daily existence. Some, but only some, consumption involves identity construction. In terms of the border region, this means carefully unpacking that which does speak to the two national cultural "monuments" and their relations to each other, and that which has primarily practical and personal meanings.

Upon arrival in the region, various European groups and their descendents, motivated at first by imperialism and then later by nationalism, erected and dismantled barriers to trade and consumption. As Robert Perez's essay about native peoples in the borderlands in this volume shows, New Spain's corporatist colonial regulations involved widespread (if highly incomplete) restrictions on local production and importation from non-Spanish sources. Further, the regulations sought to differentiate communities in terms of sanctioned consumer goods and practices. In the late colonial period, these barriers gradually weakened, a trend that continued after Mexico became independent, despite challenging economic conditions throughout the nation. The process of drawing the contemporary U.S.-Mexico boundary between 1848 and 1853 put into play issues relating to consumption—saliently gender and domesticity—as Amy Greenberg deftly brings out in her essay in this volume. Despite the examples Perez and Greenberg line up, in our view, the border as a functioning region of interchange only emerged in the late nineteenth and early twentieth centuries.[6] It was then, for the first time, that capital, resources, labor, and consumer goods flowed across what was a wide-open border.

At no point since the 1880s has the sort of flux that Josef Barton and Rachel St. John describe completely stopped, but the postrevolutionary (post–1920) Mexican nationalist project did reimpose a degree of corporatism in shaping

Twenty-First Century Housing in the Mexican Borderlands, Anapra, Mexico, June 2001. Photograph by Laura Trejo, courtesy of photographer.

Evident here in the Juárez environs are several consumption-provisioning systems characteristic of the border region: one of the several protruding wires likely connects the house to the electric grid; salvaged tires and pallets set the yard's boundaries; boxes, rebar, and tar paper constitute the walls of the house. The streetlights, telephone wires, and billboard promising *"energia a domicilio"* further highlight the dependency on utilities, one of the most important features of consumption-provisioning systems. There is no sign in the photograph of the source of water, the necessity whose supply is least dependable in the border region.—A.M.

Mexican consumer structures. National regulations protected domestic industries and gave Mexican commercial houses privileged access to Mexican and foreign consumer goods. This era created a rather marked "Mexicanness" both in the practice and meaning of consumption, but again, it was incomplete. The border was precisely its place of leakage and eventual breakdown, with the rampant growth of vice tourism in border cities such as St. John details for Tijuana, with the extensive smuggling of consumer goods from the United States (termed *fayuca*), with the back-and-forth migration of people, and, after 1965, with a new system of export-oriented manufacturing resulting in the construction of what would become thousands of *maquiladoras*. Mexico's foreign debt, and behind it the ugly marriage of a greedy national elite with a brutal international banking regime, tore down the foundations of the inward-developing system. By the 1980s, amid the ruins of the national project, a new consumer structure grew: its central features include a high volume of imported goods (Asian as well as North American), advanced capitalist consumer firms, notably U.S. or U.S.-style chain and big-box retailers, and Mexican mass media conglomerates whose reach extends through Latin America and the United States.

Living on the border provides income-generating opportunities (legal and illegal work and commerce) for many Mexicans that translate into greater consumer options than would be available to them in the national economy. U.S. border towns cater to these consumers such that today, poorer Mexicans walk across the border to shop in downtown El Paso's dollar stores, while shoppers from throughout the state of Chihuahua cram shopping malls, Wal-Marts, and other big-box retail centers. The billion-dollar contraband drug economy pumps up consumer spending (on staple items as well as luxury goods such as suvs, or the garish narco-mansions of East Juárez and West El Paso, occupied by wealthy Americans and Mexicans). This illicit economy also fuels the growth of money-exchange houses, expensive restaurants, bars, hotels, and high-end retail stores, but rampant drug violence disrupts everyday consumer activity and scares off investors and tourists. Mysteriously large deposits of cash bolster the border banking and finance sectors; the border region has more banks per capita than any other region in the United States or Mexico. These structural facts, along with the complex social identities border residents fashion for themselves, give the border's consumer culture a unique texture and style.

Yet, despite stylish scholarly research and artistic representations, border consumption habits are not strictly or even primarily a matter of overt identity choices. It is important to draw a distinction between the "normal" practices of consumption (such as Mexican *fronterizos* buying U.S. milk in local supermarkets) and explicitly identity-oriented consumption (such as purchasing compact discs of the *narcocorrido* musical genre). Our point is not to devalue poor people's deployment of ethnic or national taste when making buying decisions—in fact, this volume amply demonstrates the contrary—but to point out that everyday consumption also involves other types of discretion, particularly because limited access and purchasing power so severely curtails choice. Understanding how border residents negotiate consumption-provisioning systems—that is, taking class into consideration—is as important as inquiry into habits, tastes, and wants that together shape identity.

The essays by Barton and Peter Cahn together make the point that border consumer patterns in the aggregate are the result of broad movements of working people creatively adapting to changes in the regional economy and society. Barton shows how the new consumer practices of Mexican migrants during the first third of the twentieth century were collective responses to

Mrs. Estella Cortez, Corpus Christi, Texas, 1949. Photograph by Russell Lee, courtesy Russell Lee Photograph Collection, Box 3y183, negative no. e_r1_13918af_0004, Center for American History, University of Texas, Austin.

Signs of Mrs. Cortez's engagement with various consumption-provisioning systems are evident in the interior of this home in the border region at mid-century. Mrs. Cortez, who is washing her hands before giving her brother-in-law a hypodermic to treat tuberculosis, does not have running water or electricity. She does have access to foodstuffs, health care, and medicine, all necessities whose transformation into commodities has created considerable hardship and opportunity. Consider the branded canned, bottled, and sacked goods, which include insignia of an Indian (Calumet baking power) and of an African American (Aunt Jemima), perhaps from a chain grocery like Piggly Wiggly or the A&P.—A.M.

political and economic processes rather than individual choices in a free marketplace for goods and labor. Cahn's fieldwork on the appeal to border people of direct selling for companies like Amway, Mary Kay, and Omnilife shows the transformative power of consumption activity for poor migrants surviving on the edges of the mainstream economy. Akin to drug trafficking, direct selling often entails constant consumption of the product one sells—reversing the production-consumption cycle. It, too, promises economic independence and self-realization through informal means that bypass mainstream economic institutions and procedures.

Adaptation, as should be clear, should be a signpost in all studies of consumption: Sarah Hill's, Laura Isabel Serna's, and Lawrence Culver's essays serve as a corrective to the tendency of many border scholars to distill this complex process to "hybridization." Hill's ethnographic study illustrates the fluidity of pragmatic border consumers amidst inequality; in renaming secondhand U.S. goods in Ciudad Juárez street markets and *yonkes*, they make them Mexican. Here we see the limitations of hybridity as a framework, for as Hill demonstrates, nationalist meanings assert themselves in the Mexican marketplace, even when the goods being traded are used imports. Serna's historical study shows that border crossing resulted not in simplistic bricolage of two national cultures but rather in an endogenous U.S.-side Spanish-language film industry with overt Mexican themes, imagery, and heroes. Lawrence Culver unearths another fine example of the troubled course of hybridization: initially Anglos sought the exotic leisure of Southwestern homes precisely because they were emblematic of "the Other," but by the 1950s all that remained of hybridity in their progeny, the ranch house, was the demand for cheap Mexican labor to build it, maintain it, and clean it.

Celebrating border hybridity could prevent one from recognizing that it is frequently lived and viewed quite differently in Mexico than in the United States. Whereas many U.S. academics are quite charmed by the postmodern play of border hybrid cultures, Mexican intellectuals may view them with a great deal of apprehension, especially as a sign of American imperialism and portent of cultural contamination. Additionally, class and symbolic capital differences cross-cut national differences in hybridity, which also means there are "hybridities and hybridities." Upper-class Mexicans, "Hispanic yuppies," or "Anglo yuppies" have greater freedom than do working-class Mexicanos on either side of the border. It is vital to examine how power shapes consumer practices on the border and elsewhere. The various groups of consumers are, of course, linked through processes as diverse as labor migration and trans-national big-box retailers, but the lack of direct access to the other nation and explicit nationalistic and racist (in some cases) rejections of the identity of the "other side" shape divergent consumer practices and styles. Many border residents resist hybridity more fervently than do their compatriots living in the interior: they espouse nationalist, ethnic, or racist reasons for wishing to "buy American" or to maintain their *mexicanidad*.

Global neoliberal economic flows, unreliable practices of governance, and a virulent "drug war" are restructuring relations between states, corporations, and civil society, despite the increasingly high pitch of nationalism. The essays in this volume clearly establish and exemplify the rewards of a view from the border: they bring us in touch with concrete social settings and diverse local practices in a manner that highlights the structures of power that overlay and overdetermine individual action. Additionally, they bring to light border consumers' complex maneuvers to achieve economic survival and meaning.

Editor's Note

I want to thank Professors Heyman and Campbell for bringing their formidable scholarly and experiential knowledge of the border, its people, and its cities to bear on the essays in this volume. I illustrated and wrote the captions for their essay; the Clements Department of History at Southern Methodist University partially funded the illustrations' permission and use fees.

Notes

Full bibliographic details are in the volume's selected bibliography.

1. Campbell and Heyman, "Slantwise."
2. On monumentality, see Renato Rosaldo, *Culture and Truth* (Boston: Beacon Press, 1989), especially chap. 9.
3. Martinez, *Border People*, 52–53, 61, 77–78.
4. Carrier and Heyman, "Consumption and Political Economy."
5. Heyman, "Organizational Logic of Capitalist Consumption."
6. Lorey, *U.S.-Mexican Border*, 35ff.; Campbell and Heyman, "Slantwise."

Mauricio Tenorio-Trillo

On *La Frontera* and Cultures of Consumption
An Essay of Images

I

On the morning of October 16, 1909, in an elaborate carriage drawn by black horses, leaving his military escort behind, so as not to infringe the sovereignty of the neighboring nation, president Porfirio Díaz—former *caudillo* of sundry revolutions and anti-interventionist wars—crossed the bridge over the Rio Grande between Ciudad Juárez and El Paso. El Chamizal, a then-disputed territory, was declared neutral, but once in official U.S. territory, an aged president Díaz descended from his carriage, dressed in full military uniform and carrying all the insignias as chief of government, as symbol of the state, and as commander-in-chief of all the Mexican armies. U.S. War Secretary Jacob M. Dickinson—a former Confederate soldier—saluted him. "You are the first Chief of Executive of a nation to cross our border," he claimed, marking the event as historic. William H. Taft, it was reported, then became the first U.S. president to venture into foreign territory while heading to an elegant banquet in Ciudad Juárez, organized in honor of the lawyer, former governor general of the Philippines, and commander-in-chief of the United States.[1] The two presidents had a private meeting at the Chamber of Commerce in El Paso, only attended by Chihuahua's governor Enrique Creel, who served as interpreter. No one knows what really was discussed, especially since less than a year later the Pact of Ciudad Juárez—signed between high Porfirian authorities and revolutionary factions, with the unofficial approval of U.S. authorities and financiers—established a peaceful transition to what was a dangerous terra incognita for both nations: a Mexico with no Díaz.

Taft-Diaz Meeting, El Paso, October 16, 1909. Photograph by Otis Aultman, courtesy Aultman Collection, A5989, El Paso Public Library.

The pact seemed to work until the election of Francisco I. Madero as president. The rest is history.

What was discussed at the meeting between Taft and Díaz is less important than what was indeed performed by both presidents: namely, the border. The meeting constituted the true inauguration, the final mark of existence, of a hitherto illusory boundary between two modern nation-states that by then had existed for nearly a century. It does not really matter whether Díaz was the first Mexican president to cross the border, or whether Taft was the first U.S. president to visit a foreign nation (Theodore Roosevelt had been in Panama before).[2] The border was a lax line that was in constant dispute from its very inception, as Amy S. Greenberg's contribution to this collection makes clear.[3] What is important is that the entire paraphernalia of the Taft-Díaz meeting made visible to the world that the border existed, though even then it was hard to clearly map it cartographically, economically, and, above all, humanly.

The border had been a legal aspiration but not a physical entity: depending on the moment and circumstances, it did and did not exist. The conception of the U.S.-Mexican border was a long and complex process beyond the mere local mapping disputes. What Díaz crossed was indeed a triumph in itself—

Dinner Party, El Paso, May 1911. Photograph by Otis Aultman, courtesy Aultman Collection, A5146, El Paso Public Library.

This photograph of a dinner party at El Paso home of newspaperman Frank Wells Brown, honoring Francisco Madero Jr., (seated male furthest to the left), and his family, as well as his revolutionary companions Giuseppe Garibaldi, well-known arms dealer Lazaro de la Garza, and the German double agent Felix Sommerfeld (seated at the head of the table), renders the border differently than as a line dividing two nations. It is likely that this dinner was held just days after the Battle of Juarez, in which various revolutionary factions together triumphed, securing Madero's claim to the presidency. The wallpaper, chandeliers, lace curtains, decorative vases, not to mention full settings of silver cutlery and fine china, all suggest that the line that distinguishes abundance from scarcity should not be drawn between Americans and Mexicans. Instead, this line cuts through the two nations and the borderlands in far more complex patterns than the distinguishing marks of "nationality" could possibly encompass.—A.M.

finally Mexico was a state and a nation so clearly defined and recognized as to have a physical border that could be imagined and reproduced as definitive in all sorts of ways. Teddy Roosevelt's reform and expansion of the U.S. state, including the economic, cultural, and political integration of the Southwest into the nation, paralleled Díaz's consolidation of the Mexican state, which included connecting the outlying territory to central Mexico through large railroad networks and industrial development. The border became real, because it meant what it was supposed to mean to begin with—that the mythical nations on either side were now consolidated, separate states.

And thus the line divided more than two jurisdictions and sovereignties—for this was long imagined as a line that would divide two worlds, two civilizations, two races, two religions, two languages. Or rather, this was always meant to be the division between the West and the "non-West," the modern and the backward. As such, the border worked when it did not really exist, as in 1848, or in the 1920s, or in the 1950s, or today. The two American boundary commissioners, John Russell Bartlett and William Emory, subscribed to this vision, as Amy S. Greenberg lucidly discusses in one of this volume's essays. This civilizational barrier is what one character in Lawrence Culver's essay, Charles Fletcher Lummis, promoted in order to attract investment and colonization in the Alta and Baja Californias. And such ontological difference, as Rachel St. John's contribution shows, was what was reenacted in Tijuana for U.S. audiences to enjoy. Indeed, the civilizational barrier seems so matter-of-fact and important that the contributions to this volume attest to how difficult it is to question the past, present, and future existence of what was performed in 1909 for the first time by two presidents. Most of this volume's contributions seek to expose the random and unstoppable historical construction of a border region, but the border has become such a mighty political, economic, and cultural category that at times, alas, in dismantling it, we ourselves create but another episode in its intellectual construction.[4]

Of course, the borderlands were not then, and are not now, such a barrier to civilization, nor are they a dividing line between one place with it and another without. The border had to be painfully constructed as a civilizational barrier, as much as it had to be maintained as such—unlike, for instance, the Canadian border with the U.S. or the Guatemalan border with Mexico. For Díaz, the Guatemalan border was a constant source of political and military, but not "ontological" problems (to be or not to be Mexico). A border line, a border zone, borderlands, real, visible, clearly demarcated . . . those were the final marks of larger historical processes—the formation of nations and states in the context of the conquest of native peoples and the collapse of competing European empires. Ever since, we, scholars, have imagined the in and outs thanks to the possibility of such a border and also have projected the line back and forth in time, seeking the border in the eighteenth or nineteenth centuries, and in space, finding it in segregated Chicago or Los Angeles, or in *agringado* San Miguel Allende or Baja California, or in the realization of a globalized versus an unglobalized world.[5]

However, as this volume shows, the meaning of the border is constantly shifting. *Frontera, línea, escape, paso, garita, zona libre, zona de tolerancia*, or frontier, borderlands, border, limit, sin, free zone, duty free: somehow all terms involve patterns of consumption and circulation of merchandise. Consumption, therefore, is a singular tool with which to study the changing—in

Medallion marking spot where U.S. and Mexican nations meet, ca. 2003–2005. Photograph by James R. Tourtellotte, Customs and Border Patrol Photo Gallery, Website of U.S. Customs and Border Protection Agency, Department of Homeland Security.

Neither this medallion, nor the sarsaparilla bottle first marking the border in the 1850s, nor the various concrete and wooden markers, nor the walls and fences so in vogue today, can fully transform the border from abstract ideal to visible reality.—A.M.

time, space, and morals—meanings of the borderlands. Once both nation-states incorporated their respective territories and connected them through railroad lines, fiscal agencies, and educational and judiciary institutions, then the bordering situation acquired names of very different connotations both in English and Spanish. *Frontera* and *línea* seemed clear demarcations of two sovereignties: the end of one nation, the beginning of another. But until very recently in Spanish, *frontera* and *línea* were intrinsically connected to *paso*, *garita*, or *aduana*, very important for the fiscal existence of both states and for the consumption patterns in Mexico—*fayuca* (contraband) was, until NAFTA, synonymous with *frontera*.

The most important merchandise in the borderlands, however, has been always human labor. Mexicans were never included in the accumulating immigration restrictions the United States erected between the Chinese Exclusion Act (1882) and the First Quota Act (1920). Merchandise and people legally and illegally passed over and back again. Even during the Mexican Revolution, when hundreds of thousands of Mexicans crossed the border, the border was not seen as a site in which there was a serious migration problem. *La línea* as synonym for migration policy is a late development. Not until the 1920s was the U.S. Border Patrol established.[6] Even with its militarizing presence, as Robert Perez characterizes it, *la frontera* as a migratory *rite de passage* and as a national security threat is a very recent phenomenon.

In Spanish, *la línea* never took the mythical connotation of the English word *frontier*, except when talking about Native Americans, whom both nation-states—Mexico and the United States—were willing and in agreement about controlling and hopefully exterminating, as Perez's essay delineates. *La frontera* became a frontier, with all its cultural connotations in English, in the twentieth century, but in a less bucolic and romantic way than we might imagine. In Mexico, it became *el Norte*: the adventure, hope, and opportunity of an economic escape. Hence, contemporary Mexico's mythic "West" is the North, and its allure is shown by *remesas* (remittances), the narrative themes of popular Mexican and Central American cultures, and in the local popular heroes in the interior, say, Michoacán or Zacatecas.

What ought to be understood is that the border came to represent the possibility of escape through consumption for both sides. For Americans it meant sexual adventure, alcohol, and drugs, or else Mexican arts and crafts and images of a pristine lost world, of solidarity and community, with which many U.S. travelers and intellectuals sought to remedy their dismay with U.S. urban growth and industrialism. For Mexicans, the border also offered an escape, from violence during the revolution, from poverty at all times, but also from a rigid class structure that possession of commodities could, and still can, subvert. The border thus provides Mexicans and U.S. nationals an opportunity to escape, by making consumption, of whatever is desired, possible.[7]

As the contributions by Lawrence Culver and Rachel St. John show, the border region also became a *zona de tolerancia*, offering affordable sex and sin for nationals of both sides. In the zone, the jurisdictions of both nations seemed far away, though they were, in fact, present. The border was there because there was a borderless situation. Where the rule of law existed, national "morals" and nationalist values bumped up against each other. In fact, the Porfirian state created the border in the 1880s and 1890s with railroad routes and fiscal tariffs, each of which made the borderline's presence all too conspicuous.[8] But somehow, since the end of the nineteenth century, the region that was "*de paso*" (a temporary way station en route to somewhere) gained fame as a site of moral and legal flexibility. U.S. consumers soon appropriated the *zona de tolerancia* and *zona libre* on the way to temporary bliss of a bargain found, a rush acquired.

When leftist president Lázaro Cárdenas decided to ban prostitution and gambling throughout Mexico, he was not thinking exclusively about the border. Except for some forms of anarchism, in the 1920s and 1930s the Left often, in Mexico or Moscow, blended with a sort of Victorian belief in the value of the family, women's role as mothers, homophobia, and stringent notions of hygiene and sanitation that extended to sexual practices. Salvador Novo, a Mexico City dandy (often mocked by 1920s and 1930s revolutionary intellectuals), believed that Cárdenas's measures would not work, as "no one can ban hunger by decree." Prostitution and gambling moved not only to Las Vegas, Nevada but also illegally to Chicago and to Mexico City, where the 1930s and 1940s were epic decades recounted in all sorts of sinful anecdotes. The border had moved, literally, to major urban centers in each nation.

But in terms of consumption, the conviction that the border symbolized ontological differences of lasting dichotomies demands criticism and research. Let me mention but one dichotomy that is present in some of this volume's contributions—that between the Mexican elite and poor. In terms of consumption, Mexican elites are axiomatically cast as Europeanized, Americanized, modernized, racist, individualistic, consumerist, and globalized, in contrast with the Mexican poor, who are aprioristically considered traditional, rural, and anti-urban, somehow really Mexican, not consumerist, not racist, not individualistic, and not yet globalized. Although Josef Barton's essay for this collection shows that elites and poor contributed to the emergence of global economies, there seems to be a consensus about the real existence of this division, even in Barton's lucid account, through which he wishes to show that there is "globalization from below." It assumes an original pristine state of the Mexican poor, as if until the late nineteenth century they had remained community-based, rural, traditional. Very likely, northern Mexican peoples were Catholics and consumers who had a long history of migration and adaptation, starting especially in the late eighteenth century. But somehow we tend to see them as the carriers of historical fixedness and non-Westernness.

In the study of consumption in the borderlands, to maintain this sharp cultural distinction between rich and poor reinforces Mexico's ontological distinction vis-à-vis the United States. For if Mexico's poor were considered consumerist and westernized as its elites, then radical cultural differences between U.S. and Mexican cultures would be very difficult to maintain. Different they would be, but not in the sense of two opposed civilizations. The borderlands, as a source of legal and illegal opportunities, would cease to represent the land of clashes of civilizations, and instead the laxity of rules and regulations, of new riches, legal or illegal, and also of old and new forms of misery, whether in the railroad construction of the past or the *maquiladoras* of the present, would dominate our vision. The borderlands is, above all, a testing zone of different cultural patterns of consumption that do not adhere to notions of consumers as traditional and poor *or* modern and elite. *Narco nouvelles riches* consume what would be seen by old Monterrey, Saltillo, or Mexico City elites as gaudy, but they are vast consumers of Mexican, U.S, Asian, and European products.

I grew up witnessing in La Piedad, Michoacán the trendy nature of electronic and automotive fashions every December, when migrants would come back with all sorts of new products that we, the "Europeanized" middle classes, had never seen: the first wireless remote control Sony Trinitron television I saw in my life, the first lowrider car, the first electronic watch. And this was not because I was backward, but because Mexico existed under a sort of protective Franquism in which we were forced to consume Mexican products. While the higher classes and migrant workers had forged pathways that allowed them to consume foreign-made goods, Mexican nationalism, in the form of prohibitive tariffs, restricted the consumption of the middle classes. Often the migrants would run out of money and would sell the products before returning to the States. My grandfather bought a Sony Trinitron, but I was condemned to watch old Mexican Tin Tan and Dolores del Río (each frontier products) movies through the uncanny-looking bobbleish sticker that read SONY affixed to the screen, as my elitist provincial lawyer grandfather asked us never to remove the sticker. Commodity *fetischismus* was as strong for him as for the migrant worker who sold him the TV—it was *fayuca*, but in the form of the waste left by migrant workers in La Piedad. Stories such as this one could join Sarah Hill's intriguing ethnography of waste between opulence and poverty.[9]

II

In 1889, the Sociedad Mexicana de Consumo attempted to organize a great commercial exhibition in Mexico City in order to teach Mexicans how to consume. Mexicans were, according to the president of the society, Antonio Medina y Ormaechea, happy with *pulque*, a pair of sandals, and cheap cotton trousers. In fact, in late-nineteenth-century economic thought, the absence of consumption habits was considered an obstacle to economic growth, and it was a dogma that low-class Mexicans, regardless of their income, had very primitive consumption habits.[10] Such dogma rose out of deeply seated historical biases about the character of Mexicans and Americans. That is, it was believed on the one hand that Mexicans naturally engaged in primitive forms of consumption that gave the collective unit (family, community) primacy over the individual, while Americans, on the other hand, naturally followed individualistic consumption habits, which were cast as modern. Thus the U.S.-Mexican border came to be the natural ground to look at the encounter of tradition and modernity, a perspective that this volume, in part, perpetuates.

The conceptual consensus, in part rising out of a reflexive sense that primitive and civilized, or traditional and modern, meet and clash at the border, unites the volume's different chapters. The authors show us how certain patterns of consumption defined the border: how, for instance, romantic dreams of an "old Mexico" led to real estate speculation and a tourist industry peddling at first the "authentic," and then the forbidden. They also admirably move beyond historiographies centered on the nation-state, but in so doing they at times perpetuate an unquestioned assumption: the existence of two clearly demarcated and opposed U.S. and Mexican cultures, defined historically, culturally, or racially. The belief that U.S. and Mexican cultures are separate entities is linked, in turn, to ideas about Americanization, Mexicanization, hybridization, and nationalization that also course through the volume.

The conviction that the two nations are different in essential ways needs some revision. First, Mexicans and Americans have long been consumers, according to their means, to the social definitions of their needs, and to the merchandise available to them. Nineteenth-century economists tended to consider "native" clothing, sombreros, or *pulque* as outside the realm of consumption. In fact, most of what we call "traditional" clothing symbolized patterns of consumption established, transformed, and demanded by Spanish and Indian authorities in different cities and towns. In the 1880s, Mexican authorities were surprised by how much of the collective income of towns was used to organize the yearly celebration of the *santo patrón del pueblo*. Flowers, special clothing, food, different decorations, parties, beverages, books, papers, wood, fireworks . . . all demanded lots of consumption that extended beyond local commerce. In early-twentieth-century Mexico City, the massive consumption of *pulque* astounded sanitary, fiscal, and religious authorities. In the 1930s, a drink produced in northern Mexico—beer—surpassed it. A blend of Mexican and foreign propaganda techniques sold beer throughout the country. Perhaps the state, with its connections to northern breweries and concerns for social hygiene, promoted the shift in tastes and habits away from home-brewed *pulque*. National and foreign hygienists believed that rather than experimenting with useless U.S.-style prohibition or continuing with the dan-

"The Queens of Tijuana," ca. 1925. Photographic postcard, courtesy DeGoyler Archives, Southern Methodist University, Dallas, Texas. Thanks to Andrea Boardman for identifying and locating this image.

Mexicali Pilsner and other beers brewed and bottled in Northern Mexico sated the thirst of U.S. nationals during the twenties, and extended their appeal throughout Mexico during the 1930s.—A.M.

gerous *pulque*, whose sanitary conditions were hard to control, beer had to triumph as soon as possible.[11] Beer, a border product, won the contest.

On the other hand, historians are only beginning to understand the consumption habits of peasants and the urban poor. In Mexico City, in the 1920s, Jewish and Lebanese immigrants demonstrated, long before Avon or Omnlife —the interesting recent cases studied by Peter S. Cahn in this volume—that with innovative forms of credit, Mexico City's poor could become active consumers.[12] Some Jews and Lebanese established themselves as small ambulant retailers in northern Mexico and the southwestern U.S. In the city, these vendors went door to door selling religious images, fabrics, socks, cloth, and basic hardware on installment payments. And the vendors and clients kept trying new products, some of them made in the United States: medicines, knitting supplies, and eventually movies. According to various recollections from these vendors, collected in the 1980s through oral histories, very rarely did they encounter problems. Mexicans, they said, were great consumers and good clients.[13] Often Polish or Aleppo Jews, the peddlers sold *santitos*; whether this is a sin is for the Pope to say. But the lesson is interesting for the analysis of patterns of consumption at the border. No one in Mexico City, of course, thought that to buy a *santito* from "*el alemán*"—as the peddlers were often called, and wanted to be called rather than being identified as Jews—was a threat to either their religiosity or their Mexicanness. The form of credit was also an innovation that was quite acceptable for consumers and profitable for the peddlers, many of whom eventually became successful *Mexican empresarios*.

Though scarcity marked what we know as the border region, whatever consumption took place there before the real conception of the border cannot easily be related to national identities. Mexican gold and silver coins circulated throughout the region and the world, and no American thought that to have them or exchange them was an un-American thing to do. Mexican food is a world commodity, as is Frida Kahlo, but they are also, and perhaps more importantly, U.S. commodities. Industrialized products started to reach the U.S. Southwest and northern Mexico in the late nineteenth century; to consume tinned food became standard even in these far reaches before the turn of the century, as Barton's inventory of one of the grocery stores in south Texas suggests. In fact, once the border was truly real, it became not a zone where national identities faced off, but a place where collective dreams of all sorts and styles of consumptions proliferated: the utopia of gold, of the television, of the stereo, of the *Troca*, of sex (for Mexicans), and the allure of exotic adventures, alcohol, cheap labor, nannies, and sex (for U.S. citizens).

Indeed, the prism of consumption raised concerns about the national. But I have the impression that these were a more metropolitan, interior preoccupation, rather than a thing of the borderlands. Even at the turn of the twentieth century, Mexican intellectuals were alarmed about the insertion of U.S. English into Mexico City's Spanish, or about the overwhelming presence of U.S. products in their capital city. These concerns were not as strong in the borderlands. But U.S. travelers and Mexican intellectuals in the capital were complaining, because they wanted their pristine Mexico. In 1890s Mexico City, Henry Adams felt betrayed by the lack of Mexican exoticism—Mexico was too American—and in 1919 a U.S. radical, Charles Phillips, saw in the omnipresence in Mexico City of the Singer sewing machine, the Oliver typewriter, and Libby's potted beef, "the modern age of Mexico":

> Mexican cities mean nothing without
> Oliver, Singer, and Libby
> Lift up your voices, O Comrades and shout
> Oliver, Singer, and Libby![14]

He, like many U.S. travelers, commentators, and intellectuals, wanted Mexico to conform to the image of a rural and communitarian place, a utopia just south of the border.

El Grullense #1, Redwood City, California, June 2007. Photograph by Adam Herring, courtesy of photographer.

Three of the well-known El Grullense taco stands occupy vacated fast-food chain buildings—A&W Root Beer—in the Silicon Valley town known as "little Jalisco." As often as Mexican food start-ups move into run-down sites abandoned by national chains, these same national chains are moving into territories previously dominated by the mom-and-pop store and taco stand: borderland cities now host numerous McDonald's and Sonics, while the cities in Mexico's interior are home not only to American fast-food chains but also to local ones, including the Guatemalan *Pollo Campanero* found as far north as Dallas, Texas. These restaurants tend to offer foods high in caloric content and low in price.—A.M.

Curiously, though this volume's contributions do not deal with it, food can be seen as an extremely revealing historical phenomenon, especially on the U.S.-Mexican border. Moving from central Mexico to the border, or from New England to the deserted Southwest, the path went from relative caloric abundance to profound scarcity. But for Mexico at some point in the twentieth century this path changed, and the closer to the border one got, the cheaper the calories became, in a way that Mexico had not known: after all, until the 1920s Mexico's great problem was very low demographic growth, largely due to the scarcity of foodstuffs. Today, more and more cheap calories are accessible everywhere, not only in the borderlands; their consumption is a mark of racial and class standing in the United States, and more and more a common phenomenon in low-income families throughout Mexico. This is an unprecedented fact in the history of humankind. For centuries, poverty resulted in low caloric consumption; now we have extremely high caloric consumption in the midst of misery.[15] The consequent poor health, particularly obesity, renders the contrast between opulence and poverty (within Mexico and within the United States, as well as between the two countries) all the more compelling.

Along these lines, the importance of tourist consumption along the border comes into focus; as Lawrence Culver shows, "important landmarks of twentieth-century consumer culture" came from but also went beyond the U.S.-Mexico border.[16] In contrast, Rachel St. John argues that the political and cultural allure of a tourist border was that it "created a commodified Mexican culture that was simply meant to amuse and entertain." This same version of Mexican culture, Evan Ward argues, is what Cancún offers up at a much better advantage than border cities could—its Mayan-themed architecture, ubiquitous air conditioning, and sandy beaches combine to draw hundreds of thousands of tourists. In each place—Lummis's "Great Southwest" of the turn of the twentieth century, the Tijuana of the twenties, and the Cancún of the nineties—promoters drawing distinctions between the United States and Mexico called upon "theming," a practice that had its origins in 1880s international exhibitions, with their prominent "Streets of Cairo" or "Mexican Town" or "History of Habitation" exhibits, where Mexico was often somehow included. 1950s Disneyland, just on the southern edge of Los Angeles, was but a continuation of this trend.

In sum, consumption patterns are indispensable for understanding the borderlands and the two nations as well. We know that since the eighteenth century, European, Mexican, and U.S. settlers and travelers considered these territories as tough and dangerous places, constantly subjected to the cruelty of nature and attacks by "*indios bárbaros*." Scarcity, as Alexis McCrossen remarks, defined the region, although the patterns of consumption, commerce, and exchange prior to the mid–nineteenth century are only marginally understood, despite the efforts of Robert Perez in the first part of his essay in this volume. Population was scarce, and life was difficult. How the region went from scarcity to various forms of abundance lending themselves to consumption and interactions that could be labeled "Mexican," "American," "national," "transnational," "Mexicanizing," "Americanizing," "modern," "global," "uprooting," "communitarian," or "hybrid" is the story the contributions to this volume tell in variegated ways.

It is a story that says as much about the social transformation of the border as it does about the intellectual struggle to overcome the category *border* as an unquestioned barrier between civilizations. For if the story of consumption in the border is that of gradual globalization but with strong "bordering" marks—racial, cultural, national, ethnic, and economic distinctions—then the story of the border as a concept has moved from the invisible line between radically opposed imagined ontologies to the massive ecological, social, political, and economic presence of borderlands between two "worlds" which are conceived of as more than two nations. Mexico and the United States constitute two assumed civilizations that were, and are, nevertheless totally, in human and economic terms, integrated. Hence, though the United States and Mexico have long shared a common history and destiny, the border has become a power zone that attracts and repels multinational economic interests and common people seeking daily subsistence.

Legally, the border went from a loose line to fixed boundary, while in the *imaginaires* of both nations it went from a fixed boundary to a loose social and cultural line that, notwithstanding, is still assumed to be an unchanging boundary. It is precisely the consumption of products, of ideas, of human labor that has blended Mexico and the United States into *one* human unit that makes obsolete our fixed distinction of the United States and of Mexico as ontological antinomies.

III

In 1861, the influential Swiss American scientist, Louis Agassiz, upon learning of the Confederate bombing of Fort Sumter (1861), said, "They will Mexicanize the country." Mexicanizing meant political instability and violence, to be sure—the Civil War made the United States one with the Americas, where modern violent struggle to create unified nation-states was the norm. But it would also mean, for Agassiz, a Mexico-like racial chaos and promiscuity, which was supposed to emerge from the end of slavery, emancipation, and the massive migration of free blacks to the North.[17] Agassiz's theories never defeated those of his great enemy, Charles Darwin. But his racial views of what could happen to the United States in light of Mexico's racial promiscuity were then, and are still now, a common fear. A recent iteration of this fear came from Samuel Huntington's formulation of "The Hispanic Challenge."[18] Paradoxically, the idea of the borderlands might help to conquer this racist prediction, but to a great extent race has been what underpins the category of borderlands in anthropological, ethnographic, political, and historical scholarship. I share my doubts about this racialization, but alas, I do not have a solution. In historicizing and critiquing race there is no need to indulge in the current academic obsession with race. Racializing from the point of view of the present—though with commendable progressive political goals—an already racialized past only reinforces the centrality of race in real life, in our

"A Storefront, San Antonio, Texas," 1949. Photograph by Russell Lee, courtesy Russell Lee Photograph Collection, Center for American History, University of Texas at Austin.

The San Antonio store selling "the finest Latin American records" speaks to transnational patterns of cultural consumption. In the 1920s, U.S. recording companies set up temporary studios in the hotels of San Antonio and other Texas cities, where they paid Mexican musicians for nothing more than the sessions. Similar efforts in Texas and elsewhere resulted in "race records" recorded by and meant for African Americans. But, by the 1940s, U.S. record companies no longer sought out Mexican musicians; until the 1970s, small independent labels produced a handful of American-born performers of Mexican and Tejano music, and record stores like this one imported records from Mexico and the rest of Latin America.—A.M.

narratives, and into the present. What is there to do? In general, thanks to their transnationalism, these volume's contributions show the importance of race without necessarily reproducing racial marking as a necessary intellectual or political argument.

Race, however, is a tricky category of historical analysis. Ethnic markers, for instance, can be said to be important in past and present commercial markets, but do these markers grant more identity to their consumers than the very fact of consuming? Is the fact that Mexicans in the 1940s bought more Agustín Lara records than, say, Frank Sinatra albums, more important than the fact that for the first time in Mexico's history Mexicans of all classes and throughout the nation consumed the same cultural product through RCA records and the prominent radio station XEW—*la voz de la América Latina desde México*"?

Laura Serna's insightful analysis of movies and theaters in the border high-

Poster for "Nigga, the romantic style" posted in Tlalpan, Mexico City, June 4, 2007. Digital photograph by Thomas Aleto, courtesy photographer.

This poster pasted on a wall in Mexico City reveals the complexity and depth of the contemporary trade in racialized popular culture, rather than the extent of Mexico's "Americanization."—A.M.

lights many aspects of the complexity that arise when race is considered. Were theater entrepreneurs *ethnic* because they were Mexicans who offered conditions for Mexican consumers that racialized U.S. commercial spaces denied them, or were they *ethnic* because they were selling something radically different than what U.S. film entrepreneurs were producing? Why "*ethnic*"? Could a successful Jewish Mexican entrepreneur, Jacobo Granat, who in the 1930s became an owner of various theaters in the north of Mexico and in the capital, be considered equally ethnic?[19] Were Mexicans in Serna's account Americanized because of their attitudes toward blacks, expressed when they resisted being seated with African Americans in Texas's segregated theaters, or were they simply racist, as were the poor and small merchants in Durango, Torreón, or Mexico City, especially against the Chinese?

Race, we know today, is a dubious biological fact, to say the least. But race in the border, to be sure, was and is an overwhelming reality. In the second half of the nineteenth century, the border became a scenario for the worst expressions of racial prejudice. Lynching people of Mexican descent gave voice to what historian Richard Hofstadter called in the 1950s "ethnic nationalism," an expression of anguish about lost status and extinction of privilege.[20] But Mexicans, of all classes also had their racial prejudices. Except for some well-known cases, Mexico's history has no record of massive lynching or slaughter of U.S. citizens, but it does offer ample evidence of the murder and harassment of Spaniards and Chinese. Racisms have chaotically blended along the border, with various outcomes. U.S. immigration quotas produced a Mexican Jewish community in Mexico City. Institutionalized racism in Mexico enlarged California's Chinese communities. Overwhelming class distinctions added to U.S. racism against Mexicans. And the color line as deeply divides Mexican migrants in the border region and throughout the United States as it does white Americans.

IV

"*Cerré con fuerza [los ojos] y vi cuánto silencio arrastra el río*" (I closed my eyes and I saw how much silence the river swept along)—thus ends one of the short stories by *fronteriza* writer Rosario Sanmiguel.[21] The dividing river is of silence, because it is a pause, a hide, a circumspection, an escape, but also because it is an intriguing cultural product, despite or because of violence and misery. It is a cultural product that has become popular merchandise lately. Borderlands as a cultural "*denominación de origen*" is in. The border has attracted high and low cultural efforts, in English and Spanish: novels by Gabriel Trujillo Muñoz, Daniel Sada, Carlos Fuentes, Arturo Pérez-Reverte, or the late Roberto Bolaños, art exhibits in Tijuana and San Diego, *grupero* music, and Hollywood thrillers with *fronterizo* topics. The 2005 film *Brokeback Mountain* incorporated into the vanguard rendition of gay cowboy erotica one protagonist's trip to the border in search, of course, of escape, of cheap sex, and of alcohol. He could have said, too, with his gay escape to the border: "*cuánto silencio arrastra el río.*"

Patterns of consumption in the borderlands ought to include the consideration of borderlands as recent cultural product in itself. New York or Mexico City seem to some passé, simply old cultural canons, surpassed by *la frontera*. It seems that we went from the Mexico of *Under the Volcano* or of *Los de abajo* (another *fronterizo* product, first published in San Antonio, Texas) to (as a critic put it commenting on the literature of the border), "*el anuncio de que todo es posible aunque nada sea auténtico*" (the statement that everything is possible though none of it is authentic).[22] The new authenticity is *la frontera*, the kingdom of the ephemeral, the post-, the fragmentary, the hybrid.

As a historian, of course, I do not doubt the cultural richness of the border-

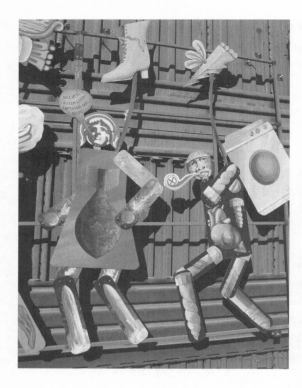

Detail of Nogales Border Wall Mural, Nogales, Mexico, by Alberto Morackis and Guadalupe Serrano. Photograph by Steev Hise, November 29, 2005, courtesy of photographer.

The depiction here of three interrelated forms of consumption—that of cheap labor (as represented by the migrant bodies made of screws), that of necessities and decencies (the shoes and washing machine), and that of borderlands culture (the mural itself)—serves to critique the commodification of humans, the stuff of life, and art.—A.M.

lands, though I would hesitate to call them an unprecedented or a unique phenomenon. But then again, I am for *vicio* (vice) and *oficio* (craft), a *chilango* (city slicker), and also—worse—a scholar working in U.S. universities. Moreover, I have spent fifteen years in and out of Barcelona, being a minor observer of the European project in contrast with the identity struggles of post-Franco Spain. That is, I am particularly ill equipped to understand how the U.S.-Mexico border is, to quote a classic (Anzaldúa), "*una herida supurante*" (a weeping wound).

In Mexico or the United States or elsewhere, in terms of culture and consumption, is not *fronterizo* the indispensable state of things? The border is geography, a line, but it is something else. It is transnationalism, experimentation, the boom of the *lumpen*, clashes, drugs, and irreverence—cultural encounters of all kinds. But to the historian's ears this sounds like business as usual. In literature, for instance, to inhabit frontiers has been, for American English, the name of the game. What is literature in American English without the input of people who are Jewish, Chinese, Puerto Rican, Irish, Mexican, African, Hindus, or *mojados*? Literature changes in borders, but in frontiers it lives. It is the same in Spanish, nor is this a new development. Rubén Darío, Alfonso Reyes, José Vasconcelos, Paul Groussac, or Jorge Luis Borges wrote the until-then unsayable in Spanish because they lived in between cultural borders (the Americas, Europe, Japan, India, the United States). The odd thing was not the cultural frontiers, but the blind faith in the existence of clearly defined and fixed national cultures.

Indeed, the U.S.-Mexico border, as this volume's contributions dealing with contemporary topics show, is home to a new phenomenon. *Maquilas* and the new role of Mexican women are a true novelty in Mexico and on the border. But the border has been at the center of twentieth-century political and cultural life in both the United States and Mexico. For Mexican analysts it is rather simple to see and accept the importance of the North in the examination of anything Mexican. For analysts of the United States, however, it seems that it would be a sort of historical degradation to see and admit that since that great first nation-alistic *rite de passage*–the U.S.-Mexico War—Mexico has been essential in the definition of what Huntington would call the "Anglo-Saxon creed."

We can read great icons of Mexico's twentieth-century culture in *fronterizo* key. José Vasconcelos, Mexico's most prominent thinker of the first half of the twentieth century, was not only the *chilango* ideologue of the "cosmic race," but the man who grew up in the borderlands, who, as he recalled, almost became a Texano George de Santayana—but he declined the offer of his U.S. high school teacher to take a scholarship at the University of Texas, and instead moved to Mexico City. His love for the classics came from late-nineteenth-century U.S. public libraries, and his hatred of gringos and Protestants came from the border. Also, Octavio Paz's *Laberinto de la soledad* is but a collection of essays written by a young Mexican diplomat witnessing, in the 1940s, Mex-ico in and from Los Angeles. What we are seeing in the current literary consumption of *fronterizo* is more of the same. The new literature from the border, I have the impression, could be seen as a return to the same old water spring in view of the cultural aridness of the Anáhuac Valley. And the spring always provides something, but not what first-generation U.S. populists found in their imagined Mexico—utopias of communal life and bucolic origins—but in a *maudit*, disconcerting fashion, as someone who digs in what is always true: misery, vice, vileness, violence, but also plentiful cultural creativity.

Editor's Note

An expression of thanks to Professor Tenorio-Trillo is hardly sufficient as acknowledg-ment for the passion and knowledge he brought to reading and thinking about the essays in this volume. What is more, reading an early draft of his reflection on the volume inspired me as I worked to frame the volume's chapters in my introductory essay and to illustrate the entire volume with worthy images. It was a special pleasure to illustrate and write the captions for Professor Tenorio's essay; the Clements Department of History at Southern Methodist University partially funded the illustrations' permission and use fees.

Notes

Notes fully cite primary sources and specialized secondary sources. Full bibliographic details for all other citations are in the volume's selected bibliography.

1. As reported by the *New York Times*, October 17, 1909.

2. Santa Ana had crossed the border before but he was either not a president, or he had not reached the border with the United States, but rather with the Republic of Texas. The Brazilian Emperor Pedro II visited the 1876 Philadelphia Centennial Exhibition.

3. Recent contributions have advanced the examination of this cartographic moment in the history of both nations, see especially Rebert, *Gran Línea*; Craib, *Cartographic Mexico*; and Amy S. Greenberg's bibliographical references in her essay in this volume. There remains much to do in examining the mutual spatial formation between Mexico and the United States, which very likely parallels the mythical mutual construction of each nation's nationalism, one as the antinomy of the other.

4. Some recent studies have sought to historicize the construction of this ontological division: Reséndez, *Changing National Identities*; Truett and Young, eds., *Continental Crossroads*; Truett, *Fugitive Landscapes*; Young, *Catarino Garza's Revolution*.

5. Evan Ward's analysis of PRONAF (1961–65) in his essay in this volume covers a poorly known period of Mexican history and Antonio Bermúdez, an important personality who deserves analysis. Though Ward examines Mexican policies without referring to the "civilizational gap" I here discuss, he does argue that the program adopted and adapted American promotional and industrial techniques. And indeed it did. The problem is, why are these techniques considered "American"? We need to start challenging the notion that everything capitalist or modern is "American." When various U.S. artists went to Mexico to learn mural painting with Diego Rivera, they were not purely adapting and adopting a Mexican art; they were involved in a global trend that included Italian, French, Spanish, German, and Mexican art. The historian Daniel Rodgers has shown how difficult it is to consider purely American the many policies and ideas of the U.S. Progressive Era, and the same should be done for the arts and culture. Daniel Rodgers, *Atlantic Crossings: Social Politics in a Progressive Age* (Cambridge: Harvard University Press, 1999).

6. Dirk Raat, "The Diplomacy of Suppression: *Los Revoltosos*, Mexico and the United States, 1906–1911," *Hispanic American Historical Review* 56 (1976): 529–50; Dirk Raat, "U.S. Intelligence Operations and Covert Actions in Mexico 1900–1947," *Journal of Contemporary History* 22 (1987): 615–38.

7. Bunker, " 'Consumers of Good Taste.' " See also Casasola, ed., *México, ¿quieres tomarte una foto conmigo?*; Moreno, *Yankee, Don't Go Home!*

8. See Jáuregui, "Vino viejo y odres nuevos"; Riguzzi, *¿La reciprocidad imposible?*

9. Sarah Hill points out an interesting avenue for further historical research. Already Alma Guillermoprieto's amazing essay about *pepenadores* in 1980s Mexico City, published in *The Heart That Bleeds* (New York: Vintage Books, 1994), has inspired some graduate students to pursue the history of garbage, but there remains a lot to be done, especially between Mexico and the United States. The first thing that a Mexican learns in the United States is that nothing is repaired, everything is replaced by new parts, new models, new things.

10. Antonio de Medina y Ormaechea, *Iniciativa para celebrar el Primer Centenario de la Independencia de México con una Exposición Universal* (Mexico City: n.p., 1893); *La Exposición Universal del Primer Centenario Mexicano* (Mexico City: n.p., 1894).

11. See the memoirs of the great physician Hans Zinsser who in the early 1930s visited Mexico: Hans Zinsser, *As I Remember Him. The Biography of R.S.* (Boston: Little, Brown, and Company, 1940). About the beer industry and its expansion in Monterrey, see Haber, *Industry and Underdevelopment*; Saragoza, *Monterrey Elite*.

12. Omnilife is similar to an earlier border health consumption pattern. As Alexis McCrossen briefly mentions in one of her essays in this volume, "Disrupting Boundaries," U.S. pseudo-doctor John R. Brinkley established the most powerful radio station in northern Mexico in the 1920s and 1930s, XER, broadcasting his "cures" to the U.S. Southwest and northern Mexico. See Ortiz Garza, *Una radio entre dos reinos*.

13. This assertion is based on my examination of memoirs and oral history interviews with various immigrants to Mexico City. See especially the translation from the Yiddish of David Zabludowsky, *Años pasados*. I have also looked into 154 interviews of Jews in Mexico (done mostly in the 1980s), a project of the Institute of Contemporary Jewry, The Hebrew University of Jerusalem.

14. I deal with this material in "The Brown Atlantis," in *City upon a Lake*, forthcoming.

15. See Cullather, "Foreign Policy of the Calorie."

16. See LeFalle-Collins and Goldman, *Spirit of Resistance*; Oles, *South of the Border*; Boardman, *Destination México*.

17. Anecdote told in Nathaniel S. Shaler, *The Autobiography of Nathaniel Southgate Shaler* (Boston: Houghton Mifflin, 1909), as quoted in Louis Menand, *The Metaphysical Club* (New York: Farrar, Straus and Giroux, 2001), 102.

18. Samuel Huntington, *Who Are We?: The Challenges to America's National Identity* (New York: Simon and Schuster, 2004); Fernando Escalante, ed., *Otro sueño americano: En torno a quiénes somos de Samuel P. Huntington* (Mexico City: Paidós, 2004). For similar arguments but from the other side of the identity debate, see González, *Culture of Empire*. See also David Hollinger, *Postethnic America* (New York: Pantheon Books, 1995); José Antonio Águilar Rivera, *El sonido y la furia: La persuasión multicultural en México y Estados Unidos* (Mexico City: Santillana Ediciones Generales, 2004).

19. He then sold his theaters to the most successful theater owner from the 1930s to the

1950s, a U.S. entrepreneur who lived in Mexico, William Jenkins. Institute of Contemporary Jewry, oral history interview. See also Andrew Paxsman, "Golden Age Monopoly: How William Jenkins Came to Control the Mexican Film Industry," unpublished paper in author's possession. Seth Fein's dissertation, "Hollywood and United States–Mexico Relations," is indispensable to understanding the cultural exchange in the Mexican movie industry.

20. According to William D. Carrigan and Clive Webb, there were more than 500 men of Mexican origins lynched in the United States from the 1870s to 1930s. More research needs to be done on the subject. Carrigan and Webb, "The Lynching of Persons of Mexican Origin or Descent in the United States, 1848 to 1928," *Journal of Social History* 37 (2003): 411–38; Coerver and Hall, *Texas and the Mexican Revolution*; de León, *They Called Them Greasers*; Limón, "El Primer Congreso Mexicanista de 1911."

21. Rosario Sanmiguel, "Bajo el puente," *Quimera* 258 (June 2005): n.p.

22. Nuria Vilanova, "Literatura y frontera: De México a Estados Unidos," *Quimera* no. 258 (2005): n.p. See also María Socorro Tabuenca Córdoba, "Outlining U.S.-Mexico's Border Identities, and the Ciudad Juárez Cultural Movement", delivered at the colloquium *México y Estados Unidos: Nuevas posiciones y contraposiciones*, Rice University, April 1, 2006.

Selected Bibliography

EDITOR'S NOTE: Full citations for primary sources and specialized secondary sources are in the essays' endnotes.

Aboites Aguilar, Luis. *Norte precario: Poblamiento y colonizacion en México, 1760–1940.* Mexico City: El Colegio de México, 1995.

Adams, John. *Bordering the Future: The Impact of Mexico on the United States.* Westport: Greenwood Press, 2006.

Adams, Thomas Jessen. "Making the New Shop Floor: Wal-Mart, Labor Control, and the History of the Postwar Discount Retail Industry in America." In Lichtenstein, ed., *Wal-Mart,* 213–29.

Adelman, Jeremy, and Stephen Aron. "From Borderlands to Borders: Empires, Nation-States, and the Peoples In Between in North American History." *American Historical Review* 104 (1999): 814–41.

Adkisson, Richard, and Linda Zimmerman. "Retail Trade on the U.S.-Mexico Border during the NAFTA Implementation Era." *Growth and Change* 35 (2004): 77–89.

Adshead, Samuel. *Material Culture in Europe and China, 1400–1800.* London: Palgrave, 1997.

Agnew, Jean-Christophe. "Coming Up for Air: Consumer Culture in Historical Perspective." In Brewer and Porter, eds., *Consumption and the World of Goods,* 19–39.

Alisky, Marvin. "Early Mexican Broadcasting." *Hispanic American Historical Review* 34 (1954): 513–52.

Almada, Francisco. *La revolución en el estado de Chihuahua,* 2 vols. Mexico City: Biblioteca del Instituto Nacional de Estudios Historicos de la Revolución Méxicana, 1964–65.

Alonso, Ana María. *Thread of Blood: Colonialism, Revolution, and Gender on Mexico's Northern Frontier.* Tucson: University of Arizona Press, 1995.

Alvarez, Robert, Jr. *Familia: Migration and Adaptation in Baja and Alta California, 1880–1975.* Berkeley: University of California Press, 1991.

——. *Mangos, Chiles, and Truckers: The Business of Transnationalism.* Minneapolis: University of Minnesota Press, 2005.

Anderson, Benedict. *Imagined Communities: Reflections on the Origin and Spread of Nationalism.* 1983. 2nd. ed. London: Verso, 1991.

Anderson, Joan, and James Gerber. *Fifty Years of Change on the U.S.-Mexico Border: Growth, Development, and Quality of Life*. Austin: University of Texas Press, 2008.

Anderson, Joan, and Egbert Wever. "Borders, Border Regions and Economic Integration: One World, Ready or Not." *Journal of Borderlands Studies* 18 (2003): 27–38.

Andreas, Peter. *Border Games: Policing the U.S.-Mexico Divide*. Ithaca: Cornell University Press, 2000.

——. "The Escalation of U.S. Immigration Control in the Post-NAFTA Era." *Political Science Quarterly* 113 (1998–99): 591–615.

Appadurai, Arjun. "Commodities and the Politics of Value." In Appadurai, ed., *The Social Life of Things*, 3–63.

——. "Deep Democracy: Urban Governmentality and the Horizon of Politics." *Public Culture* 14 (2002): 21–48.

——. "Grassroots Globalization and the Research Imagination." *Public Culture* 12 (2000): 1–20.

——. *Modernity at Large: Cultural Dimensions of Globalization*. Minneapolis: University of Minnesota Press, 1996.

——, ed. *The Social Life of Things: Commodities in Cultural Perspective*. New York: Cambridge University Press, 1986.

Archibald, Robert. "The Economy of the Alta California Mission, 1803–1821." *Southern California Quarterly* 58 (1976): 227–40.

Aron, Cindy. *Working at Play: A History of Vacations in the United States*. New York: Oxford University Press, 1999.

Arreola, Daniel. *Tejano South Texas: A Mexican American Cultural Province*. Austin: University of Texas Press, 2002.

——, ed. *Hispanic Spaces, Latino Places: Community and Cultural Diversity in Contemporary America*. Austin: University of Texas Press, 2004.

Arreola, Daniel, and James Curtis. *The Mexican Border Cities: Landscape Anatomy and Place Personality*. Tucson: University of Arizona Press, 1993.

Astorga, Luis. "Drug Trafficking in Mexico: A First General Assessment." Discussion Paper No. 36, Management of Social Transformation, UNESCO, 1999. http://www.unesco.org/most/astorga.htm, accessed June 2008.

——. *El siglo de las drogas*. Mexico City: Espasa-Calpe Mexicana, 1996.

Astorga, Pablo, Ame Berges, and Valpy Fitzgerald. "The Standard of Living in Latin America during the Twentieth Century." *Economic History Review* 58 (2005): 765–96.

Avila, Eric. *Popular Culture in the Age of White Flight: Fear and Fantasy in Suburban Los Angeles*. Berkeley: University of California Press, 2004.

Babb, Sarah. *Managing Mexico: Economists from Nationalism to Neo-liberalism*. Princeton: Princeton University Press, 2004.

Bacon, David. *The Children of NAFTA: Labor Wars on the U.S./Mexico Border*. Berkeley: University of California Press, 2004.

Bakewell, Peter. *History of Latin America: 1450 to the Present*. Malden: Blackwell Publishing, 2004.

Balderrama, Francisco, and Raymond Rodríguez. *Decade of Betrayal: Mexican Repatriation in the 1930s*. 1995. Albuquerque: University of New Mexico Press, 2006.

Bales, Kevin. *Disposable People: New Slavery in the Global Economy*. 1999. Berkeley: University of California Press, 2004.

Ballantyne, Tony, and Antoinette M. Burton. "Bodies, Genders, Empires: World History in Perspective." In Ballantyne and Burton, eds., *Bodies in Contact*, 1–15.

——, eds. *Bodies in Contact: Rethinking Colonial Encounters in World History*. Durham: Duke University Press, 2005.

Bane, Mary Jo, and Rene Zenteno. "Poverty and Place in North America." Harvard University, John F. Kennedy School of Government, Faculty Research Working Papers Series. RWP05–035. April 2005. http://ksgnotes1.harvard.edu/research/wpaper .NSF/rwp/RWP05–035, accessed February 2006.

Barger, William. "Furs, Hides, and a Little Larceny: Smuggling and Its Role in Early California's Economy." *Southern California Quarterly* 85 (2003): 381–412.

Barrera, Eduardo. "The U.S.-Mexican Border as Post-NAFTA Mexico." In McAnany and Wilkinson, eds., *Mass Media and Free Trade: NAFTA and the Cultural Industries*, 3–29.

Barton, Josef. "Borderland Discontents: Mexican Migration in Regional Contexts, 1880–1930." In Marc S. Rodriguez, ed., *Repositioning North American Migration History: New Directions in Modern Continental Migration, Citizenship, and Community*, 157–74. Rochester: University of Rochester Press, 2005.

——. "Land, Labor, and Community in Nueces: Czech Farmers and Mexican Laborers in South Texas, 1880–1930." In Frederick C. Luebke, ed., *Ethnicity on the Great Plains*, 190–209. Lincoln: University of Nebraska Press, 1980.

Bartra, Armando. The Seduction of Innocents: The First Tumultuous Moments of Mass Literacy in Postrevolutionary Mexico." In Gilbert Joseph and Daniel Nugent, eds., *Everyday Forms of State Formation: Revolution and the Negotiation of Rule in Modern Mexico*. 2nd ed., 301–25. Durham: Duke University Press, 1994.

Basante, Marcela Terrazas. "Los especuladores y el debate parlamentario norteamericano en torno al Tratado de la Mesilla." In Ana Rosa Suárez Arguello and Marcela Terrazas Basante, eds., *Política y negocios: Ensayos sobre la relación entre México y los Estados Unidos en el siglo XIX*, 293–378. Mexico City: UNAM, 1997.

Bauer, Alfred. *Goods, Power, History: Latin America's Material Culture*. New York: Cambridge University Press, 2001.

Baughman, James. *The Republic of Mass Culture: Journalism, Filmmaking, and Broadcasting in America since 1941*. Baltimore: Johns Hopkins University Press, 2006.

Beatty, Edward. "Approaches to Technology Transfer in History and the Case of Nineteenth-Century Mexico." *Comparative Technology Transfer and Society* 1 (2003): 167–97.

——. "Commercial Policy in Porfirian Mexico: The Structure of Protection." In Bortz and Haber, eds., *The Mexican Economy, 1870–1930*, 205–52.

——. *Institutions and Investment: The Political Basis of Industrialization in Mexico before 1911*. Palo Alto: Stanford University Press, 2001.

Beck, Ulrich. *What Is Globalization?* Translated by Patrick Camiller. Cambridge: Polity Press, 2000.

Bederman, Gail. *Manliness and Civilization: A Cultural History of Gender and Race in the United States, 1880–1917.* Chicago: University of Chicago Press, 1995.

Beezley, William. *Judas at the Jockey Club and Other Episodes of Porfirian Mexico.* 1987. Rev. ed., Lincoln: University of Nebraska Press, 2004.

Bell, Samuel, and James Smallwood. "*Zona Libre*: Trade and Diplomacy on the Mexican Border, 1858–1905." *Arizona and the West* 24 (1982): 119–52.

Benson, Susan Porter. "Gender, Generation, and Consumption in the United States: Working-Class Families in the Interwar Period." In Strasser, McGovern, and Judt, eds., *Getting and Spending*, 223–40.

——. *Household Accounts: Working-Class Family Economies in the Interwar United States.* Ithaca: Cornell University Press, 2007.

——. "Living on the Margin: Working-Class Marriages and Family Survival Strategies in the United States, 1919–1941." In de Grazia, ed., *The Sex of Things*, 212–43.

Berger, Dina. *The Development of Mexico's Tourism Industry: Pyramids by Day, Martinis by Night.* New York: Palgrave Macmillan, 2006.

Berglund, Barbara. "Western Living *Sunset* Style in the 1920s and 1930s: The Middlebrow, the Civilized, and the Modern." *Western Historical Quarterly* 37 (2006): 133–57.

Berkhofer, Robert, Jr. *The White Man's Indian: Images of the American Indian from Columbus to the Present.* New York: Vintage Books, 1979.

Berry, Sara. *No Condition Is Permanent: The Social Dynamics of Agrarian Change in Sub-Saharan Africa.* Madison: University of Wisconsin Press, 1993.

Bértola, Luis, and Jeffrey Williamson. "Globalization in Latin America before 1940." In Bulmer-Thomas, Coatsworth, and Cortes-Conde, eds., *The Cambridge Economic History of Latin America, Volume 2: The Long Twentieth Century*, 11–56.

Best, Amy. *Fast Cars, Cool Rides: The Accelerating World of Youth and Their Cars.* New York: New York University Press, 2006.

Betts, Dianne, and Daniel Slottje. *Crisis on the Rio Grande: Poverty, Unemployment, and Economic Development on the Texas-Mexico Border.* Boulder: Westview Press, 1994.

Bevans, Charles, ed. *Treaties and Other International Agreements of the United States of America, 1776–1949.* Washington, D.C.: Government Printing Office, 1968–1976.

Bevir, Mark, and Frank Trentmann. "Markets in Historical Contexts: Ideas, Practices and Governance." In Mark Bevir and Frank Trentmann, eds., *Markets in Historical Contexts: Ideas and Politics in the Modern World*, 1–24. New York: Cambridge University Press, 2004.

Bhabha, Homi. *The Location of Culture.* New York: Routledge, 1994.

Biggart, Nicole Woolsey. *Charismatic Capitalism: Direct Selling Organizations in America.* Chicago: University of Chicago Press, 1989.

Blackhawk, Ned. *Violence over the Land: Indians and Empires in the Early American West.* Cambridge: Harvard University Press, 2006.

Blaisdell, Lowell. *The Desert Revolution: Baja California, 1911*. Madison: University of Wisconsin Press, 1962.

Blanke, David. "Consumer Choice, Consumer Agency, and New Directions in Rural Consumer History." *Agricultural History* 81 (2007): 182–204.

———. "Consumer Culture during the Gilded Age and Progressive Era." H-SHGAPE, November 1996, http://www.h-net.org/~shgape/bibessays/consumer.html, accessed November 7, 2007.

———. *Sowing the American Dream: How Consumer Culture Took Root in the Rural Midwest*. Athens: Ohio University Press, 2000.

Blaszczyk, Regina Lee. *Imagining Consumers: Design and Innovation from Wedgwood to Corning*. Baltimore: Johns Hopkins University Press, 2000.

Bliss, Katharine. "The Science of Redemption: Syphilis, Sexual Promiscuity, and Reformism in Revolutionary Mexico City." *Hispanic American Historical Review* 79 (1999): 1–40.

Block, Alan A. "European Drug Traffic and Traffickers Between the Wars: The Policy of Suppression and its Consequences." *Journal of Social History* 23 (1989): 315–37.

Blumin, Stuart. *The Emergence of the Middle Class: Social Experience in the American City, 1760–1900*. New York: Cambridge University Press, 1989.

Boardman, Andrea. *Destination México, A Foreign Land a Step Away: U.S. Tourism to Mexico, 1880s–1950s*. Dallas: DeGolyer Library, Southern Methodist University, 2001.

Bonacich, Edna, and Khaleelah Hardie. "Wal-Mart and the Logistics Revolution." In Lichtenstein, ed., *Wal-Mart*, 163–87.

Bonifaz de Novelo, Maria Eugenia. "The Hotel Riviera del Pacífico: Social, Civic, and Cultural Center of Ensenada." *Journal of San Diego History* 29 (1983): 77–85.

Bonnie, Richard, and Charles Whitebread. *The Marijuana Conviction: A History of Marijuana Prohibition in the United States*. New York: Lindesmith Center, 1999.

Boorstin, Daniel J. *The Image: A Guide to Pseudo-Events in America*. 1961. New York: Macmillan Publishing, 1987.

Booth, Peter. "'If We Gave Up the Making of Nawait, It Would Mean Starvation': Saguaro Wine Defenders of Tohono O'Odham Land and Way of Life." *Journal of Arizona History* 46 (2005): 375–96.

Bordo, Michael, and Marc Flandreau. "Core, Periphery, Exchange Rate Regimes, and Globalization." In Bordo, Taylor, and Williamson, eds., *Globalization in Historical Perspective*, 417–72.

Bordo, Michael, Alan Taylor, and Jeffrey Williamson, eds. *Globalization in Historical Perspective*. Chicago: University of Chicago Press, 2003.

Bortz, Jeffrey. "Prices and Wages in Tijuana and San Diego: A Binational Comparative Overview." In David Lorey, ed., *The United States–Mexico Border Statistics since 1900*, 445–55. Los Angeles: University of California, Los Angeles, Latin American Center Publications, 1990.

Bortz, Jeffrey, and Stephen Haber, eds. *The Mexican Economy, 1870–1930: Essays on the*

Economic History of Institutions, Revolution, and Growth. Palo Alto: Stanford University Press, 2002.

Bowe, John. *Nobodies: Modern American Slave Labor and the Dark Side of the New Global Economy*. New York: Random House, 2007.

Bowen-Hatfield, Shelley. *Chasing Shadows: Apaches and Yaquis along the United States–Mexico Border, 1876–1911*. Albuquerque: University of New Mexico Press, 1998.

Bowman, Kirk. "The U.S.-Mexico Border as Locator of Innovation and Vice." *Journal of Borderlands Studies* 9 (1994): 51–67.

Brandt, Allan. *The Cigarette Century: The Rise, Fall, and Deadly Persistence of the Product that Defined America*. New York: Basic Books, 2007.

Brandt, Charles, ed. *Jim Whitewolf: The Life of a Kiowa Apache Indian*. Ann Arbor: University of Michigan Press, 1969.

Breen, T. H. " 'Baubles of Britain': The Consumer Culture of Eighteenth-Century America and the Coming Revolution." *Past and Present* 119 (1988): 73–104.

——. *The Marketplace of Revolution: How Consumer Politics Shaped American Independence*. New York: Oxford University Press, 2004.

Brewer, John, and Roy Porter, eds. *Consumption and the World of Goods*. London: Routledge, 1993.

Brewer, John, and Frank Trentmann, eds. *Consuming Cultures, Global Perspectives: Historical Trajectories, Transnational Exchanges*. New York: Berg, 2006.

Bright, Brenda Jo. " 'Heart Like a Car' ": Hispano/Chicano Culture in Northern New Mexico." *American Ethnologist* 25 (1998): 583–609.

——. "Nightmares in the New Metropolis: The Cinematic Poetics of Low Riders." In Joe Austin and Michael Willard, eds., *Generations of Youth: Youth Cultures and History in Twentieth-Century America*, 412–26. New York: New York University Press, 1998.

Britton, John. *Revolution and Ideology: Images of the Mexican Revolution in the United States*. Lexington: University Press of Kentucky, 1995.

Brooks, James. *Captives and Cousins: Slavery, Kinship, and Community in the Southwest Borderlands*. Chapel Hill: University of North Carolina Press, 2001.

Brouwer, Kimberly, et al. "Trends in Production, Trafficking, and Consumption of Methamphetamine and Cocaine in Mexico." *Substance Use and Misuse* 41 (2006): 707–27.

Brown, Jonathan. "The Structure of the Foreign-Owned Petroleum Industry in Mexico, 1880–1938." In Brown and Knight, eds., *The Mexican Petroleum Industry*, 1–35.

Brown, Jonathan, and Alan Knight, eds. *The Mexican Petroleum Industry in the Twentieth Century*. Austin: University of Texas Press, 1992.

Brown, Stephen. *Revolution at the Checkout Counter: The Explosion of the Bar Code*. Cambridge: Harvard University Press, 1997.

Bruegel, Martin. *Farm, Shop, Landing: The Rise of Market Society in the Hudson Valley, 1780–1860*. Durham: Duke University Press, 2002.

Buenger, Victoria, and Walter Buenger. *Texas Merchant: Marvin Leonard and Ft. Worth*. College Station: Texas A&M University Press, 2008.

Bulmer-Thomas, Victor, John Coatsworth, and Roberto Cortes-Conde, eds. *The Cambridge Economic History of Latin America: Volume 1: The Colonial Era and the Short Nineteenth Century*. New York: Cambridge University Press, 2006.

——, eds. *The Cambridge Economic History of Latin America, Volume 2: The Long Twentieth Century*. New York: Cambridge University Press, 2006.

Bunker, Steven. " 'Consumers of Good Taste': Marketing Modernity in Northern Mexico, 1890–1910." *Mexican Studies/Estudios Mexicanos* 13 (1997): 227–69.

Burke, Timothy. *Lifebuoy Men, Lux Women: Commodification, Consumption, and Cleanliness in Modern Zimbabwe*. Durham: Duke University Press, 1996.

Bushman, Richard. *The Refinement of America: Persons, Houses, Cities*. New York: Vintage Books, 1992.

Cabeza de Baca, Vincent. "Moral Renovation of the Californias: Tijuana's Political and Economic Role in American-Mexican Relations, 1920–1935." Ph.D. diss., University of California, San Diego, 1991.

Cabeza de Baca, Vincent, and Juan Cabeza de Baca. "The 'Shame Suicides' and Tijuana." In Wood, ed., *On the Border*, 145–76.

Cadava, Geraldo. "Ethnic Histories of Tucson and the Arizona-Sonora Borderlands, 1940–1990." Ph.D. diss., Yale University, 2008.

Cahill, Rick. *Border Towns of the Southwest: Shopping, Dining, Fun and Adventure from Tijuana to Juárez*. Boulder: Pruett Publishing Company, 1987.

Calavita, Kitty. *Inside the State: The Bracero Program, Immigration, and the INS*. New York: Routledge, 1992.

Calder, Lendol. *Financing the American Dream: A Cultural History of Consumer Credit*. Princeton: Princeton University Press, 1999.

Calderón, Roberto R. *Mexican Coal Mining Labor in Texas and Coahuila, 1880–1930*. College Station: Texas A&M University Press, 2000.

Calhoun, Craig. "Is It Time to Be Postnational?" In Stephen May, Tariq Modood, and Judith Squires, eds., *Ethnicity, Nationalism, and Minority Rights*, 231–56. New York: Cambridge University Press, 2004.

Camarillo, Albert. *Chicanos in a Changing Society: From Mexican Pueblos to American Barrios in Santa Barbara and Southern California, 1848–1930*. Cambridge: Harvard University Press, 1979.

Campbell, Colin. *The Romantic Ethic and the Spirit of Modern Consumerism*. New York: Blackwell, 1987.

Campbell, Howard. "Chicano Lite: Mexican-American Consumer Culture on the Border." *Journal of Consumer Culture* 5 (2005): 207–33.

——. "Drug Trafficking Stories: Everyday Forms of Narco-Folklore on the U.S.-Mexico Border." *International Journal of Drug Policy* 16 (2005): 326–33.

——. "A Tale of Two Families: The Mutual Construction of 'Anglo' and Mexican Ethnicities along the US-Mexico Border." *Bulletin of Latin American Research* 24 (2005): 23–43.

Campbell, Howard, and Josiah McC. Heyman. "Slantwise: Beyond Domination and Resistance on the Border." *Journal of Contemporary Ethnography* 36 (2007): 3–30.

Canclini, Néstor García. *Consumers and Citizens: Globalization and Multicultural Conflicts*. Translated by George Yúdice. Minneapolis: University of Minnesota Press, 2001.

——. *Hybrid Cultures: Strategies for Entering and Leaving Modernity*. Translated by Christopher L. Chiappari and Silvia L. López. Minneapolis: University of Minnesota Press, 1995.

Carr, Lois, and Lorena Walsh. "Changing Lifestyles and Consumer Behavior in the Colonial Chesapeake." In Carson, Hoffman, and Albert, eds., *Of Consuming Interests: The Style of Life in the Eighteenth Century*, 59–166.

Carreras de Velasco, Mercedes. *Los mexicanos que devolvió la crisis*. Mexico City: Secretaría de Relaciones Exteriores, 1973.

Carrier, James, and Josiah Heyman. "Consumption and Political Economy." *Journal of the Royal Anthropological Institute*, new series 3 (1997): 355–73.

Carson, Cary, Ronald Hoffman, and Peter Albert, eds. *Of Consuming Interests: The Style of Life in the Eighteenth Century*. Charlottesville: University of Virginia Press, 1994.

Casasola, Gustavo, ed. *México, ¿quieres tomarte una foto conmigo?: Cien anos de consumo*. Mexico City: Procuraduría Federal del Consumidor, 1996.

Casey, Emma, and Lydia Martens, eds. *Gender and Consumption: Domestic Cultures and the Commercialisation of Everyday Life*. Aldershot, UK: Ashgate, 2007.

Castells, Manuel, and Alejandro Portes. "World Underneath: The Origins, Dynamics, and Effects of the Informal Economy." In Alejandro Portes, Manuel Castells, and Lauren A. Benton, eds., *The Informal Economy: Studies in Advanced and Less Developed Countries*, 11–40. Baltimore: Johns Hopkins University Press, 1989.

Castillo, Debra, Maria Gudelia Rangel Gomez, and Bonnie Delgado. "Border Lives: Prostitute Women in Tijuana." *Signs* 24 (1999): 387–422.

Castillo Berthier, Héctor. *La sociedad de la basura: Caciquismo en la Ciudad de México*. Mexico City: UNAM, 1990.

Ceballos Ramírez, Manuel, ed. *Encuentro en la frontera: Mexicanos y norteamericanos en un espacio común*. Mexico City: El Colegio de México, 2001.

Cerutti, Mario. *Burguesía, capitales e industria en el norte de México: Monterrey y su ámbito regional (1850–1910)*. Mexico City: Alianza Editorial, 1992.

——. "Empresariado y banca en el norte de México (1870–1930)." In Mario Cerutti and Carlos Marichal, eds., *La banca regional en México, 1870–1930*, 174–96. Mexico City: Fondo de Cultura Económica, 2003.

——. "Ferrocarriles y actividad productiva en el norte de México, 1880–1910." In Carlos Marichal, ed., *Historia de las grande empresas en México, 1850–1930*, 176–204. Mexico City: Fondo de Cultura Económica, 1997.

Chacón, Justin, and Mike Davis. *No One Is Illegal: Fighting Violence and State Repression on the U.S.-Mexico Border*. Chicago: Haymarket Books, 2006.

Chamoux, Marie-Noëlle. *Indiens de la Sierra: La communauté paysanne au Mexique*. Paris: L'Harmattan, 1981.

——. *Prêter et emprunter: Pratiques de crédit au Mexique (XVIe–XXe siècle)*. Paris: Maison des Sciences de l'Homme, 1993.

———. "A propos du 'crédit invisible.'" In Chamoux, ed., *Prêter et emprunter*, 213–220.

Chandler, Alfred. *The Visible Hand: The Managerial Revolution in American Business.* Cambridge: Harvard University Press, 1977.

Chappell, Ben. "Lowrider Cruising Spaces." In Anja Bandau and Marc Priewe, eds., *Mobile Crossings: Representations of Chicana/o Cultures*, 51–62. Trier, Germany: WVT, 2006.

———. "Lowrider Space: A Critical Encounter of Knowledge." Ph.D. diss., University of Texas at Austin, 2003.

Chatriot, Alain, Marie-Emmanuelle Chessel, and Matthew Hilton, eds. *The Expert Consumer: Associations and Professionals in Consumer Society.* Aldershot, UK: Ashgate, 2006.

Chávez, Armando. *Historia de Ciudad Juárez.* Mexico City: PAX, 1991.

Chavez, John. *The Lost Land: The Chicano Image of the Southwest.* Albuquerque: University of New Mexico Press, 1984.

Chavez, Leo. *Shadowed Lives: Undocumented Immigrants in American Society.* Fort Worth: Harcourt Brace Jovanovich, 1992.

Chen, Xiangming. *As Borders Bend: Transnational Spaces on the Pacific Rim.* Lanham: Rowman and Littlefield, 2005.

Chin, Elizabeth. *Purchasing Power: Black Kids and American Consumer Culture.* Minneapolis: University of Minnesota Press, 2001.

Clark, Christopher. *The Roots of Rural Capitalism: Western Massachusetts, 1780–1860.* Ithaca: Cornell University Press, 1990.

Clark, Clifford, Jr. *The American Family Home, 1800–1960.* Chapel Hill: University of North Carolina Press, 1986.

Clarke, Sally. *Trust and Power: Consumers, the Modern Corporation, and the Making of the United States Automobile Market.* New York: Cambridge University Press, 2007.

Clunas, Craig. "Modernity, Global and Local: Consumption and the Rise of the West." *American Historical Review* 104 (1999): 1497–511.

Coatsworth, John. "Economic and Institutional Trajectories in Nineteenth-Century Latin America." In Coatsworth and Taylor, eds., *Latin America and the World Economy since 1800*, 23–54.

———. *Growth against Development: The Economic Impact of Railroads in Porfirian Mexico.* DeKalb: Northern Illinois University Press, 1981.

———. "Obstacles to Economic Growth in Nineteenth-Century Mexico." *American Historical Review* 83 (1978): 80–100.

Coatsworth, John, and Alan Taylor, eds. *Latin America and the World Economy since 1800.* Cambridge: Harvard University/David Rockefeller Center for Latin American Studies, 1998.

Coerver, Don, and Linda Hall. *Texas and the Mexican Revolution: A Study in State and National Border Policy, 1910–1920.* San Antonio: Trinity University Press, 1984.

Cohen, Deborah. "Masculine Sweat, Stoop-Labor Modernity: Gender, Race and Nation in Mid–Twentieth Century Mexico and the U.S." Ph.D. diss., University of Chicago, 2001.

Cohen, Jeffrey. *The Culture of Migration in Southern Mexico*. Austin: University of Texas Press, 2004.

Cohen, Lizabeth. *A Consumers' Republic: The Politics of Mass Consumption*. New York: Vintage, 2003.

——. "From Town Center to Shopping Center: The Reconfiguration of Community Marketplaces in Postwar America." *American Historical Review* 101 (1996): 1050–81.

Collins, Jane Lou. *Threads: Gender, Labor, and Power in the Global Apparel Industry*. Chicago: University of Chicago Press, 2003.

Comaroff, Jean, and John Comaroff. "Millennial Capitalism: First Thoughts on a Second Coming." In Jean Comaroff and John Comaroff, eds., *Millennial Capitalism and the Culture of Neoliberalism*, 1–56. Durham: Duke University Press, 2001.

Conn, Steven. *Museums and American Intellectual Life, 1876–1926*. Chicago: University of Chicago Press, 1998.

Cook, Scott. *Understanding Commodity Cultures: Explorations in Economic Anthropology with Case Studies from Mexico*. Lanham: Rowman and Littlefield, 2004.

Cooper, Frederick, ed. *Confronting Historical Paradigms: Peasants, Labor, and the Capitalist World System in Africa and Latin America*. Madison: University of Wisconsin Press, 1993.

Cooper, Frederick, and Randall Packard, eds. *International Development and the Social Sciences: Essays on the History and Politics of Knowledge*. Berkeley: University of California Press, 1997.

Corona, Ignacio, and Alejandro Madrid. "Ideology, Flux, and Identity in Tijuana's Nortec Music." In Corona and Madrid, eds., *Postnational Musical Identities*, 99–117.

——, eds. *Postnational Musical Identities: Cultural Production, Distribution, and Consumption in a Globalized Scenario*. Lanham: Rowman and Littlefield, 2007.

Coronado, Raúl Jr. "Selena's Good Buy: Texas Mexicans, History, and Selena Meet Transnational Capitalism." *Aztlán: A Journal of Chicano Studies* 26 (2001): 59–100.

Cowie, Jefferson. *Capital Moves: RCA's 70-Year Quest for Cheap Labor*. Ithaca: Cornell University Press, 1999.

——. "Century of Sweat: Subcontracting, Flexibility, and Consumption." *International Labor and Working-Class History* 61 (2002): 128–40.

Craib, Raymond. *Cartographic Mexico: A History of State Fixations and Fugitive Landscapes*. Durham: Duke University Press, 2004.

Crawford, Margaret. "The World in a Shopping Mall." In Michael Sorkin, ed., *Variations on a Theme Park: Scenes from the New American City*, 3–30. New York: Hill and Wang, 1992.

Cross, Gary. *An All-Consuming Century: Why Commercialism Won in Modern America*. New York: Columbia University Press, 2000.

——. "Corralling Consumer Culture: Shifting Rationales for American State Intervention in Free Markets." In Daunton and Hilton, eds., *The Politics of Consumption*, 283–300.

Cullather, Nick. "The Foreign Policy of the Calorie." *American Historical Review* 112 (2007): 337–64.

Culver, Lawrence. "The Island, the Oasis, and the City: Santa Catalina, Palm Springs, Los Angeles, and Southern California's Shaping of American Life and Leisure." Ph.D. diss., University of California, Los Angeles, 2004.

Curtis, James. "Mexicali's Chinatown." *Geographical Review* 85 (1995): 335–48.

Curtis, James, and Daniel Arreola. "*Zonas de Tolerencia* on the Northern Mexico Border." *Geographical Review* 81 (1991): 333–46.

Daniel, Cletus. *Bitter Harvest: a History of California Farmworkers, 1870–1941*. Ithaca: Cornell University Press, 1981.

——. *Chicano Workers and the Politics of Fairness: The FEPC in the Southwest, 1941–1945*. Austin: University of Texas Press, 1991.

——. "In Defense of the Wheatland Wobblies: A Critical Analysis of the IWW in California." *Labor History* 19 (1978): 485–509.

Daunton, James, and Matthew Hilton, eds. *The Politics of Consumption: Material Culture and Citizenship in Europe and America*. Oxford: Berg, 2001.

Dávila, Arlene. *Latinos, Inc.: The Marketing and Making of a People*. Berkeley: University of California Press, 2001.

Davis, Mike. *Magical Urbanism: Latinos Reinvent the U.S. City*. London: Verso, 2000.

de Grazia, Victoria. "Changing Consumption Regimes in Europe, 1930–1970: Comparative Perspectives on the Distribution Problem." In Strasser, McGovern, and Judt, eds., *Getting and Spending*, 59–84.

——. "Empowering Women as Citizen-Consumers." In de Grazia, ed., *The Sex of Things*, 275–86.

——. *Irresistible Empire: America's Advance through 20th-Century Europe*. Cambridge: The Belknap Press of Harvard University Press, 2005.

——, ed. *The Sex of Things: Gender and Consumption in Historical Perspective*. Berkeley: University of California Press, 1996.

de León, Arnoldo. *They Called Them Greasers: Anglo Attitudes toward Mexicans in Texas, 1821–1900*. Austin: University of Texas Press, 1983.

de Vries, Jan. "Between Purchasing Power and the World of Goods: Understanding the Household Economy in Early Modern Europe." In Brewer and Porter, eds., *Consumption and the World of Goods*, 85–132.

——. "The Industrial Revolution and the Industrious Revolution." *Journal of Economic History* 54 (1994): 249–70.

——. *The Industrious Revolution: Consumer Behavior and the Household Economy, 1650 to the Present*. New York: Cambridge University Press, 2008.

Dear, Michael, and Gustavo Leclerc, eds. *Postborder City: Cultural Spaces of Bajalta California*. New York: Routledge, 2003.

DeLay, Brian. "Independent Indians and the U.S.-Mexican War." *American Historical Review* 112 (2007): 35–69.

——. *The War of a Thousand Deserts: Indian Raids and the U.S.-Mexican War*. New Haven: Yale University Press, 2008.

——. "The Wider World of the Handsome Man: Southern Plains Indians Invade Mexico, 1830–1846." *Journal of the Early Republic* 27 (2007): 83–113.

Delgadillo, Willivaldo, and Maribel Limongi. *La mirada desenterrada: Juárez y El Paso vistos por el cine (1896–1916)*. Ciudad Juárez: Cuadro x Cuadro, 2000.

Delgado, Grace. "At Exclusion's Southern Gate: Changing Categories of Race and Class among Chinese *Fronterizos*, 1882–1904." In Truett and Young, eds., *Continental Crossroads*, 183–208.

Deloria, Philip. *Playing Indian*. New Haven: Yale University Press, 1998.

Delpar, Helen. *The Enormous Vogue of Things Mexican: Cultural Relations between the United States and Mexico, 1920–1935*. Tuscaloosa: University of Alabama Press, 1992.

DeLyser, Didia. *Ramona Memories: Tourism and the Shaping of Southern California*. Minneapolis: University of Minnesota Press, 2005.

Dermota, Ken. "Snow Business: Drugs and the Spirit of Capitalism." *World Policy Journal* 16 (1999–2000): 15–24.

Desmond, Jane. *Staging Tourism: Bodies on Display from Waikiki to Sea World*. Chicago: University of Chicago Press, 1999.

Deverell, William. *Whitewashed Adobe: The Rise of Los Angeles and the Remaking of Its Mexican Past*. Berkeley: University of California Press, 2005.

Diehl, Philip. "The Effects of Peso Devaluation on Texas Border Cities." *Texas Business Review* 57 (1983): 120–25.

Dohan, Daniel. *The Price of Poverty: Money, Work, and Culture in the Mexican-American Barrio*. Berkeley: University of California Press, 2003.

Donohue, Kathleen. *Freedom from Want: American Liberalism and the Idea of the Consumer*. Baltimore: Johns Hopkins University Press, 2003.

Dorman, Peter. "Globalization, the Transformation of Capital, and the Erosion of Black and Latino Living Standards." In Cecilia Conrad, ed., *African Americans in the U.S. Economy*, 185–92. Lanham: Rowman and Littlefield, 2005.

Dorsey, Margaret. *Pachangas: Borderlands Music, U.S. Politics, and Transnational Marketing*. Austin: University of Texas Press, 2006.

Driscoll, Barbara. *Tracks North: The Railroad Bracero Program of World War II*. Austin: Center for Mexican-American Studies, University of Texas, 1999.

Dunn, Timothy. *The Militarization of the U.S.-Mexico Border, 1978–1992: Low-Intensity Conflict Doctrine Comes Home*. Austin: Center for Mexican-American Studies, University of Texas, 1996.

Durand, Jorge, Douglas Massey, and Emilio Parrado. "The New Era of Mexican Migration to the United States." *Journal of American History* 86 (1999): 518–36.

Dye, Victoria. *All Aboard for Santa Fe: Railway Promotion of the Southwest, 1890s to 1930s*. Albuquerque: University of New Mexico Press, 2005.

Easterlin, Richard. "The Worldwide Standard of Living since 1800." *Journal of Economic Perspectives* 14 (2000): 7–26.

Edberg, Mark. *El Narcotraficante: Narcocorridos and the Construction of a Cultural Persona on the U.S.-Mexico Border*. Austin: University of Texas Press, 2004.

Elias, Judith. *Los Angeles: Dream to Reality, 1885–1915*. Los Angeles: Santa Susana Press, 1983.

Elvins, Sarah. "Shopping for Recovery: Local Spending Initiatives and the Great Depression in Buffalo and Rochester, New York." *Journal of Urban History* 29 (2003): 670–93.

Emory, Deborah. "Running the Line: Men, Maps, Science, and the Art of the United States and Mexico Boundary Survey, 1849–1856." *New Mexico Historical Review* 75 (2000): 221–65.

Escoto Ochoa, Humberto. *Integración y desintegración de nuestra frontera norte*. Mexico City: Editorial Stylo, 1949.

Faulk, Odie B. "Ranching in Spanish Texas." *Hispanic American Historical Review* 44 (May 1965): 257–66.

——. *Too Far North . . . Too Far South*. Los Angeles: Westernlore Press, 1967.

Fein, Seth. "Hollywood and United States–Mexico Relations in the Golden Age of Mexican Cinema." Ph.D. diss., University of Texas, 1996.

Fejes, Fred. "The Growth of Multinational Advertising Agencies in Latin America." *Journal of Communication* 30 (1980): 36–49.

Felsenstein, Daniel, and Daniel Freeman, "Gambling on the Border: Casinos, Tourism Development, and the Prisoner's Dilemma." In Krakover and Gradus, eds., *Tourism in Frontier Areas*, 95–114.

Fernández, Linda, and Richard Carson, eds. *Both Sides of the Border: Transboundary Environmental Management Issues Facing Mexico and the United States*. Boston: Kluwer Academic Publishers, 2002.

Fernández, Raul. *The United States–Mexico Border: A Politico Economic Profile*. Notre Dame: University of Notre Dame Press, 1977.

Fernández-Kelly, María Patricia. *For We Are Sold, I and My People: Women and Industry in Mexico's Frontier*. Albany: State University of New York Press, 1983.

Fernández-Kelly, María Patricia, and Jon Shefner, eds. *Out of the Shadows: Political Action and the Informal Economy in Latin America*. University Park: Pennsylvania State University Press, 2006.

Ferrat, Carlos. "Mexico, the Latin American Nation: A Conversation with Carlos Rico Ferrat." Interview by David Thelen. *Journal of American History* 86 (1999): 467–80.

Ficker, Sandra Kuntz. *Empresa extranjera y Mercado interno: el Ferrocarril Central Mexicano, 1880–1907*. Mexico City: Colegio de México, 1995.

——. "The Import Trade Policy of the Liberal Regime in Mexico, 1870–1900." In Rodríguez, ed., *The Divine Charter*, 305–38.

——. "Institutional Change and Foreign Trade in Mexico, 1870–1911." In Bortz and Haber, eds., *The Mexican Economy*, 161–204.

Ficker, Sandra, and Priscilla Connolly. "Los ferrocarriles y la formación del espacio económico en México, 1880–1910." In Sandra Ficker and Priscilla Connolly, eds., *Ferrocarriles y obras públicas*, 105–37. Mexico City: Instituto Mora, 1999.

Fifer, J. Valerie. *American Progress: The Growth of the Transport, Tourist, and Information Industries in the Nineteenth-Century West*. Chester: Globe Pequot Press, 1988.

Findlay, Ronald, and Kevin O'Rourke. "Commodity Market Integration, 1500–2000." In Bordo, Taylor, and Williamson, eds., *Globalization in Historical Perspective*, 13–64.

Foley, Neil. *The White Scourge: Mexicans, Blacks, and Poor Whites in Texas Cotton Culture*. Berkeley: University of California Press, 1997.

Forbes, Jack D. *Apache, Navaho, and Spaniard*. Norman: University of Oklahoma Press, 1960.

——. *Warriors of the Colorado: The Yumas of the Quechan Nation and Their Neighbors*. Norman: University of Oklahoma Press, 1965.

Fowler, Gene, and Bill Crawford. *Border Radio: Quacks, Yodelers, Pitchmen, Psychics, and Other Amazing Broadcasters of the American Airwaves*. Austin: University of Texas Press, 2002.

Fox, Claire. "Fan Letters to Cultural Industries: Border Literature about Mass Media." In Sadowski-Smith, ed., *Globalization on the Line*, 121–46.

——. *The Fence and the River: Culture and Politics at the U.S.-Mexico Border*. Minneapolis: University of Minnesota Press, 1999.

Fox, Richard, and T. J. Jackson Lears, eds. *The Culture of Consumption: Critical Essays in American History, 1880–1980*. New York: Pantheon Books, 1983.

Fox, Stephen. *The Mirror Makers: A History of American Advertising*. 1984. London: Heineman, 1990.

Francaviglia, Richard. "The Geographic and Cartographic Legacy of the U.S.-Mexican War." In Richard Francaviglia and Douglas Richmond, eds., *Dueling Eagles: Reinterpreting the U.S.-Mexican War, 1846–1848*, 1–18. Arlington: University of Texas at Arlington, 2000.

Francois, Marie Eileen. *A Culture of Everyday Credit: Housekeeping, Pawnbroking, and Governance in Mexico City, 1750–1920*. Lincoln: University of Nebraska Press, 2006.

Frank, Dana. *Buy American: The Untold Story of Economic Nationalism*. Boston: Beacon Press, 1999.

——. *Purchasing Power: Consumer Organizing, Gender, and the Seattle Labor Movement, 1919–1929*. New York: Cambridge University Press, 1994.

Franko, Patrice. *The Puzzle of Latin American Economic Development*. 2003. Lanham: Rowman & Littlefield, 2007.

Franz, Kathleen. *Tinkering: Consumers Reinvent the Early Automobile*. Philadelphia: University of Pennsylvania Press, 2005.

French, William E. *A Peaceful and Working People: Manners, Morals, and Class Formation in Northern Mexico*. Albuquerque: University of New Mexico Press, 1996.

Friedman, Walter. *Birth of a Salesman: The Transformation of Selling in America*. Cambridge: Harvard University Press, 2004.

Furlough, Ellen, and Carl Strikwerda, eds. *Consumers against Capitalism? Consumer Cooperation in Europe, North America, and Japan, 1840–1990*. Lanham: Rowman & Littlefield, 1999.

Gabbert, Ann. "Prostitution and Moral Reform in the Borderlands: El Paso, 1890–1920." *Journal of the History of Sexuality* 12 (2003): 575–604.

Gamio, Manuel. *Mexican Immigration to the United States: A Study of Human Migration and Adjustment*. Chicago: University of Chicago Press, 1930.

——. *Número, procedencia y distribución geográfica de los immigrantes mexicanos en los Estados Unidos*. Mexico City: Talleres Gráficos de la Nación, 1930.

Ganster, Paul, and David Lorey. *Borders and Border Politics in a Globalizing World*. Lanham: Rowman & Littlefield, 2004.

——, eds. *The U.S.-Mexican Border Into the Twenty-first Century*. Lanham: Rowman & Littlefield, 2008.

Garcia, Juan Ramon. *Operation Wetback: The Mass Deportation of Mexican Undocumented Workers in 1954*. Westport: Greenwood, 1980.

García, Mario. *Desert Immigrants: The Mexicans of El Paso, 1880–1920*. New Haven: Yale University Press, 1981.

——. *Mexican Americans: Leadership, Ideology, and Identity, 1930–1960*. New Haven: Yale University Press, 1989.

Garcia, Matt. *A World of Its Own: Race, Labor, and Citrus in the Making of Greater Los Angeles, 1900–1970*. Chapel Hill: University of North Carolina Press, 2001.

García Martínez, Bernardo. "El espacio del (des)encuentro." In Manuel Ceballos Ramírez, ed., *Encuentro en la frontera: Mexicanos y norteamericanos en un espacio común*, 19–51. Mexico City: Colegio de México, 2001.

Garon, Sheldon, and Patricia Maclachlan, eds. *The Ambivalent Consumer: Questioning Consumption in East Asia and the West*. Ithaca: Cornell University Press, 2006.

Garvey, Ellen. *The Adman in the Parlor: Magazines and the Gendering of Consumer Culture, 1880s to 1910s*. New York: Oxford University Press, 1996.

de la Garza, Rodolfo, and Briant Lowell, eds. *Sending Money Home: Hispanic Remittances and Community Development*. Lanham: Rowman and Littlefield, 2002.

George, Rosemary. "Homes in the Empire, Empires in the Home." *Cultural Critique* 26 (1993–94): 95–127.

Gereffi, Gary, and Miguel Korzeniewicz, eds. *Commodity Chains and Global Capitalism*. Westport: Greenwood Press, 1994.

Gereffi, Gary, and Donald Wyman. *Manufacturing Miracles*. Princeton: Princeton University Press, 1990.

Gerth, Karl. *China Made: Consumer Culture and the Creation of the Nation*. Cambridge: Asia Center, Harvard University, 2003.

Glickman, Lawrence. *Buying Power: Consumer Activism in America from the Boston Tea Party to the Twenty-First Century*. Chicago: University of Chicago Press, 2009.

——. *A Living Wage: American Workers and the Making of Consumer Society*. Ithaca: Cornell University Press, 1997.

Goetzmann, William. *Army Exploration in the American West, 1803–1863*. New Haven: Yale University Press, 1959.

——. "The United States–Mexican Boundary Survey, 1848–53." *Southwestern Historical Quarterly* 62 (1958): 164–90.

Gómez-Galvarriato, Aurora. *The Evolution of Prices and Real Wages in Mexico from the Porfiriato to the Revolution*. Mexico City: Centro de Investigación y Docencia Económicas, 1997.

——. *Foreign and Mexican Companies In Mexico's First Age of Globalization, 1885-1910*. Mexico City: Centro de Investigación y Docencia Económicas, 2004.

——. "The Impact of Revolution: Business and Labor in the Mexican Textile Industry, Orizaba, Veracruz, 1900–1930." Ph.D. diss., Harvard University, 1999.

——. *The Political Economy of Protectionism: The Evolution of Labor Productivity, International Competitiveness, and Tariffs in the Mexican Textile Industry, 1900–1950*. Mexico City: Centro de Investigación y Docencia Económicas, 2001.

——. "Premodern Manufacturing." In Bulmer-Thomas, Coatsworth, and Cortes-Conde, eds., *The Cambridge Economic History of Latin America: Volume 1*, 357–94.

Gómez-Galvarriato, Aurora, and Gabriela Recio. "The Indispensable Service of Banks: Commercial Transactions, Industry, and Banking in Revolutionary Mexico." *Enterprise and Society* 8 (2007): 68–105.

González, Gilbert. *Culture of Empire: American Writers, Mexico, and Mexican Immigrants, 1880–1930*. Austin: University of Texas Press, 2004.

González, Guadalupe, and Maria Tienda, eds. *The Drug Connection in U.S.-Mexican Relations*. San Diego: Center for U.S.-Mexican Studies, University of California, San Diego, 1989.

González de la Vara, Martín. *Breve historia de Ciudad Juárez y su región*. Las Cruces: New Mexico State University, 2002.

González Navarro, Moisés. *La colonización en México, 1877–1910*. Mexico City: n.p., 1960.

Goodovitch, Tomer. "Legalization of Casino Gambling in a Frontier Region: The Israeli Experience." In Krakover and Gradus, eds., *Tourism in Frontier Areas*, 83–94.

Graebner, Norman. *Empire on the Pacific: A Study in American Continental Expansion*. New York: Ronald Press, 1955.

Greenberg, Amy. *Manifest Manhood and the Antebellum American Empire*. New York: Cambridge University Press, 2005.

Greenberg, Emily. *Financial Missionaries to the World: The Politics and Culture of Dollar Diplomacy, 1900–1930*. Durham: Duke University Press, 2003.

Greenberg, James. "The Tragedy of Commoditization: The Political Ecology of the Colorado River Delta's Destruction." *Research in Economic Anthropology* 19 (1998): 133–49.

Gruesz, Kirsten. *Ambassadors of Culture: The Transamerican Origins of Latino Writing*. Princeton: Princeton University Press, 2002.

Guerin-Gonzales, Camille. *Mexican Workers and American Dreams: Immigration, Repatriation, and California Farm Labor, 1900–1939*. New Brunswick: Rutgers University Press, 1994.

Guo, Chiquan, Arturo Vasquez-Parraga, and Yongjian Wang. "An Exploration Study of Motives for Mexican Nationals to Shop in the U.S.: More Than Meets the Eye." *Journal of Retailing and Consumer Services* 13 (2006): 351–62.

Gutiérrez, David. *Walls and Mirrors: Mexican Americans, Mexican Immigrants and the Politics of Ethnicity*. Berkeley: University of California Press, 1995.

Gutiérrez Zúñiga, Cristina. "Estrategias de motivación en redes de mercadeo en Guadalajara." In Miguel Hernández Madrid and Elizabeth Juárez Cerdi, eds., *Religión y cultura: Crisol de transformaciones*, 47–63. Zamora: El Colegio de Michoacán, 2003.

Gutmann, Matthew. "For Whom the Taco Bells Toll: Popular Responses to NAFTA South of the Border." *Critique of Anthropology* 18 (1998): 297–315.

Habell-Pallán, Michelle. *Loca Motion: The Travels of Chicana and Latina Popular Culture*. New York: New York University Press, 2005.

Haber, Stephen. *Industry and Underdevelopment: The Industrialization of Mexico, 1890–1940*. Stanford: Stanford University Press, 1989.

——. "The Political Economy of Industrialization." In Bulmer-Thomas, Coatsworth, and Cortes-Conde, eds., *The Cambridge Economic History of Latin America, Volume 2*, 537–84.

Haber, Stephen, Armando Razo, and Noel Maurer. *The Politics of Property Rights: Political Instability, Credible Commitments, and Economic Growth in Mexico, 1876–1929*. New York: Cambridge University Press, 2003.

Hahamovitch, Cindy. *The Fruits of Their Labor: Atlantic Coast Farmworkers and the Making of Migrant Poverty, 1870–1945*. Chapel Hill: University of North Carolina Press, 1997.

Hale, Grace. *Making Whiteness: The Culture of Segregation in the South, 1890–1940*. New York: Vintage, 1999.

Hall, Dawn, ed. *Drawing the Borderline: Artists-Explorers of the U.S.-Mexico Boundary Survey*. Albuquerque: The Albuquerque Museum, 1996.

Hämäläinen, Pekka. *The Comanche Empire*. New Haven: Yale University Press, 2008.

——. "The Western Comanche Trade Center: Rethinking the Plains Indian Trade System." *Western Historical Quarterly* 29 (1998): 833–62.

Hanchett, Thomas. "U.S. Tax Policy and the Shopping-Center Boom of the 1950s and 1960s." *American Historical Review* 101 (1996): 1082–1110.

Hansen, Ellen. "The Difference a Line Makes: Women's Lives in Douglas, Arizona, and Agua Prieta, Sonora." In Martha Loustaunau and Mary Jo Bane, eds., *Life, Death, and In-Between on the U.S.-Mexico Border: Así Es la Vida*, 77–94. Westport: Praeger/Greenwood, 1999.

Hansen, Karen. *African Encounters with Domesticity*. New Brunswick: Rutgers University Press, 1992.

——, ed. *Salaula: The World of Second Hand Clothing and Zambia*. Chicago: University of Chicago Press, 2000.

Hansen, Lawrence. "The Origins of the *Maquila* Industry in Mexico." *Comercio Exterior* 53 (2003): 1–16.

Hardwick, Jeffrey. *Mall Maker: Victor Gruen, Architect of an American Dream*. Philadelphia: University of Pennsylvania Press, 2004.

Harner, John. "*Muebles Rústicos* in Mexico and the United States." *Geographical Review* 92 (2002): 354–71.

Hart, John. *Empire and Revolution: The Americans in Mexico since the Civil War*. Berkeley: University of California Press, 2002.

Hart, Keith. "Commoditisation and the Standard of Living." In Sen and Hawthorn, eds., *The Standard of Living*, 70–93.

Haskell, John. "John Russell Bartlett (1805–1886): Bookman." Ph.D. diss., George Washington University, 1977.

Hayden, Cori. *When Nature Goes Public: The Making and Unmaking of Bioprospecting in Mexico*. Princeton: Princeton University Press, 2003.

Heinze, Andrew. *Adapting to Abundance: Jewish Immigrants, Mass Consumption, and the Search for American Identity*. New York: Columbia University Press, 1990.

Heldmann, Philipp. "Negotiating Consumption in a Dictatorship: Consumer Politics in the GDR in the 1950s and 1960s." In Daunton and Hilton, eds., *The Politics of Consumption*, 185–202.

Hernandez, Maria, and Melissa Marquez. "White House Department Store Offered Elegance and Service." *Borderlands* 24 (spring 2006). http://epcc.edu/nwlibrary/borderlands/24/whitehouse.htm, accessed April 22, 2007.

Hernández, Omar, and Emile McAnany. "Cultural Industries in the Free Trade Age: A Look at Mexican Television." In Joseph, Rubenstein, and Zolov, eds., *Fragments of a Golden Age*, 389–414.

Hernández Sáenz, Luz María. "Smuggling for the Revolution: Illegal Traffic of Arms on the Arizona-Sonora Border, 1912–1914." *Arizona and the West: A Quarterly Journal of History* 28 (1986): 357–77.

Herzog, Lawrence. *From Aztec to High Tech: Architecture and Landscape across the Mexico–United States Border*. Baltimore: Johns Hopkins University Press, 1999.

——. "Globalization of the Barrio: Transformation of the Latino Cultural Landscapes of San Diego, California." In Arreola, ed., *Hispanic Spaces, Latino Places*, 103–24.

——. "The Political Economy of Tourism Development in the San Diego–Tijuana Trans-Frontier Metropolis." In Dennis Judd, ed., *The Infrastructure of Play: Building a Tourist City*, 215–45. Armonk: M. E. Sharpe, 2002.

——. *Where North Meets South: Cities, Space, and Politics on the US-Mexico Border*. Austin: Center for Mexican American Studies, University of Texas, 1990.

——, ed. *Shared Space: Rethinking the U.S.-Mexico Border Environment*. San Diego: Center for U.S.-Mexican Studies, University of California, 1999.

Heyman, Josiah. "The Emergence of the Waged Life Course on the United States–Mexico Border." *American Ethnologist* 17 (1990): 348–59.

——. *Finding a Moral Heart for U.S. Immigration Policy: An Anthropological Perspective*. Washington, D.C.: American Anthropological Association, 1998.

——. "Imports and Standards of Justice on the Mexico–United States Border." In Orlove, ed., *The Allure of the Foreign*, 151–84.

——. *Life and Labor on the Border: Working People of Northeastern Sonora, Mexico, 1886–1986*. Tucson: University of Arizona Press, 1991.

——. "The Organizational Logic of Capitalist Consumption on the Mexico–United States Border." *Research in Economic Anthropology* 15 (1994): 175–238.

——. "The Political Ecology of Consumption: Beyond Greed and Guilt." In Susan Paulson and Lisa Gezon, eds., *Political Ecology across Spaces, Scales and Social Groups*, 113–32. New Brunswick: Rutgers University Press, 2005.

——. "Working for Beans and Refrigerators: Learning about Environmental Policy from Mexican Northern-Border Consumers." In Maurice J. Cohen and Joseph Murphy, eds., *Exploring Sustainable Consumption: Environmental Policy and the Social Sciences*, 137–55. Amsterdam: Pergamon, 2001.

Hibino, Barbara. "Cervecería Cuauhtemoc: A Case Study of Technological and Industrial Development in Mexico." *Mexican Studies/Estudios Mexicanos* 8 (1992): 23–43.

Hickerson, Nancy. *The Jumanos: Hunters and Traders of the South Plains*. Austin: University of Texas Press, 1994.

Hietala, Thomas. *Manifest Design: American Exceptionalism and Empire*. 1985. Rev. ed., Ithaca: Cornell University Press, 2003.

Hill, Jane. "*Hasta La Vista*, Baby: Anglo Spanish in the American Southwest." *Critique of Anthropology* 13 (1993): 145–76.

Hill, Ronald, and Jeannie Gaines. "The Consumer Culture of Poverty: Behavioral Research Findings and Their Implications in an Ethnographic Context." *Journal of American Culture* 30 (2007): 81–95.

Hill, Ronald, Elizabeth Hirschman, and John Bauman. "Consumer Survival during the Great Depression: Reports from the Field." *Journal of Macromarketing* 17 (1997): 107–27.

Hill, Sarah. "Domesticated Responsibility: The Making of the U.S.-Mexico Border Environment." Ph.D. diss., Johns Hopkins University, 2000.

——. "Wasted Resources of *Mexicanidad*: Consumption and Disposal on Mexico's Northern Frontier." In Walsh, ed., *The Social Relations of Mexican Commodities*, 157–85.

Hilmes, Michele. *Only Connect: A Cultural History of Broadcasting in the United States*. 2002. 2nd ed., Belmont: Thomson Wadsworth, 2007.

Hilton, Matthew. *Consumerism in Twentieth-Century Britain: The Search for a Historical Movement*. Cambridge: Cambridge University Press, 2003.

——. "Consumers and the State since the Second World War." *Annals of the American Academy of Political and Social Science* 611 (2007): 66–81.

Hoffman, Abraham. *Unwanted Mexican Americans in the Great Depression: Repatriation Pressures, 1929–1939*. Tucson: University of Arizona Press, 1974.

Hoganson, Kristin. *Consumers' Imperium: The Global Production of American Domesticity, 1865–1920*. Chapel Hill: University of North Carolina Press, 2007.

——. "Stuff It: Domestic Consumption and the Americanization of the World Paradigm." *Diplomatic History* 30 (2006): 571–94.

Holden, Robert. "The Mexican State Manages Modernization: The Survey of the Public Lands in Six States, 1876–1911." Ph.D. diss., University of Chicago, 1986.

Hoopes, James. "Growth through Knowledge: Wal-Mart, High Technology, and the Ever Less Visible Hand of the Manager." In Lichtenstein, ed., *Wal-Mart*, 83–104.

Hopkins, Terence, and Immanuel Wallerstein. "Commodity Chains in the World Economy Prior to 1800." *Review of the Fernand Braudel Center* 10 (1986): 157–70.

Horowitz, Daniel. *The Anxieties of Affluence: Critiques of American Consumer Culture, 1939–1979*. Amherst: University of Massachusetts Press, 2004.

——. *The Morality of Spending: Attitudes toward the Consumer Society in America, 1875–1940*. Baltimore: Johns Hopkins University Press, 1985.

Horowitz, Roger, Jeffrey Pilcher, and Sydney Watts. "Meat for the Multitudes: Market Culture in Paris, New York City, and Mexico City over the Long Nineteenth Century." *American Historical Review* 109 (2004): 1055–83.

Hu-Dehart, Evelyn. "The Chinese in Baja California Norte, 1910–1934." *Proceedings of the Pacific Coast Council on Latin American Studies*. San Diego: San Diego State University Press, 1985–1986.

——. "Coolies, Shopkeepers, Pioneers: The Chinese of Mexico and Peru, 1849–1930." *Amerasia* 15 (1989): 91–116.

——. "Globalization and Its Discontents: Exposing the Underside." *Frontiers: A Journal of Women Studies* 24 (2003): 244–60.

——. "Immigrants to a Developing Society: The Chinese in Northern Mexico, 1875–1932." *Journal of Arizona History* 21 (1980): 275–312.

——. "Racism and Anti-Chinese Persecution in Sonora, Mexico, 1876–1932." *Amerasia* 9 (1982): 1–27.

Hufbauer, Gary Clyde, and Jeffrey Schott. NAFTA *Revisited: Achievements and Challenges*. Washington, D.C.: Institute for International Economics, 2005.

Hurley, Andrew. *Diners, Bowling Alleys, and Trailer Parks: Chasing the American Dream in Postwar Consumer Culture*. New York: Basic Books, 2002.

Hyde, Anne Farrar. *An American Vision: Far Western Landscape and American Culture, 1820–1920*. New York: New York University Press, 1990.

Iglesias Prieto, Norma. *Beautiful Flowers of the Maquiladora: Life Histories of Women Workers in Tijuana*. Translated by Michael Stone and Gabrielle Winkler. Austin: University of Texas Press, 1997.

Jacobs, Meg. "'How About Some Meat?': The Office of Price Administration, Consumption Politics, and State Building from the Bottom Up, 1941–1946." *Journal of American History* 84 (1997): 910–41.

——. "Inflation: The Permanent Dilemma of the American Middle Classes." In Olivier Zunz, Leonard Schoppa, and Nobuhiro Hiwatari, eds., *Postwar Social Contracts under Stress*, 130–53. New York: Russell Sage, 2002.

——. *Pocketbook Politics: Economic Citizenship in Twentieth-Century America*. Princeton: Princeton University Press, 2005.

——. "The Politics of Plenty: Consumerism in the Twentieth-Century United States." In Daunton and Hilton, eds., *The Politics of Consumption*, 223–40.

Jacobson, Matthew Frye. *Barbarian Virtues: The United States Encounters Foreign Peoples at Home and Abroad, 1876–1917*. New York: Hill and Wang, 2000.

Jakle, John, and Keith Sculle. *The Gas Station in America*. Baltimore: Johns Hopkins University Press, 2002.

Jameson, Fredric, and Masao Miyoshi, eds. *The Cultures of Globalization*. Durham: Duke University Press, 1998.

Jáuregui, Luis. "Vino viejo y odres nuevos: La historia fiscal en México." *Historia Mexicana* 52 (2003): 725–71.

Johnson, Benjamin. *Revolution in Texas: How a Forgotten Rebellion and Its Bloody Suppression Turned Mexicans into Americans*. New Haven: Yale University Press, 2005.

Joseph, Gilbert, Anne Rubenstein, and Eric Zolov, eds. *Fragments of a Golden Age: The Politics of Culture in Mexico since 1940*. Durham: Duke University Press, 2001.

Joseph, Gilbert, and Daniel Nugents, eds. *Everyday Forms of State Formation: Revolution and the Negotiation of Rule in Modern Mexico*. Durham: Duke University Press, 1994.

Kamikihara, Shizue, and Jim Simmons. "Toward a Corporate Geography for Mexico." Eaton Chair in Retailing, Ryerson University, 1998, http://www.ecr.ryerson.ca/Jim/JimNote7.html, accessed September 5, 2008.

Kanbur, Ravi. "The Standard of Living: Uncertainty, Inequality and Opportunity." In Sen and Hawthorn, eds., *The Standard of Living*, 59–69.

Kannelos, Nicolas. *A History of Hispanic Theatre in the United States: Origins to 1940*. Austin: University of Texas Press, 1990.

Kaplan, Amy. *The Anarchy of Empire in the Making of U.S. Culture*. Cambridge: Harvard University Press, 2002.

Kasson, John. *Amusing the Million: Coney Island at the Turn of the Century*. New York: Hill and Wang, 1978.

Katz, Friedrich. *The Secret War in Mexico: Europe, the United States and the Mexican Revolution*. Chicago: University of Chicago Press, 1981.

Kazimi, Camilla, Felipe Cuamea, Juan Alvarez, Alan Sweedler, and Matt Fertig. "Emissions from Heavy-Duty Trucks at the San Diego–Tijuana Border Crossing." *Journal of Borderlands Studies* 14 (1999): 1–15.

Kerig, Dorothy. "Yankee Enclave: The Colorado River Land Company and Mexican Agrarian Reform in Baja California, 1902–1944." Ph.D. diss., University of California, Irvine, 1988.

Kimber, Clarissa T., and Darrel McDonald. "Sacred and Profane Uses of the Cactus *Lophophora Williamsii* from the South Texas Peyote Gardens." In Steinberg, Hobbs, and Mathewson, eds., *Dangerous Harvest*, 182–208.

Klasson, Henry. "T. C. Power & Bro.: The Rise of a Small Western Department Store." *Business History Review* 66 (1992): 671–772.

Klein, Alan. *Baseball on the Border: A Tale of Two Laredos*. Princeton: Princeton University Press, 1999.

Klingle, Matthew. "Spaces of Consumption in Environmental History." *History and Theory* 42 (2003): 94–110.

Knight, Alan. "The Politics of the Expropriation." In Brown and Knight, eds., *Mexican Petroleum Industry*, 90–128.

Koehn, Nancy. *Brand New: How Entrepreneurs Earned Consumers' Trust from Wedgewood to Dell*. Boston: Harvard Business School Press, 2001.

Komlos, John. *The Biological Standard of Living in Europe and America, 1700–1900.* Studies in Anthropometric History. Aldershot, UK: Variorum Press, 1995.

Kopinak, Kathryn. *Desert Capitalism: Maquiladoras in North America's Western Industrial Corridor.* Tucson: University of Arizona Press, 1996.

Koreck, María Teresa. "Space and Revolution in Northeastern Chihuahua." In Nugent, ed., *Rural Revolt in Mexico*, 147–170.

Korstad, Robert. *Civil Rights Unionism, Tobacco Workers and the Struggle for Democracy in the Mid-Twentieth-Century South.* Chapel Hill: University of North Carolina Press, 2003.

Kortheuer, Dennis. "The Compagnie du Boléo: The Making of a Town and Company in the Porfirian Frontier, 1885–1900." Ph.D. diss., University of California, Irvine, 2001.

Koszarski, Richard. *An Evening's Entertainment: The Age of the Silent Feature Picture, 1915–1928.* Berkeley: University of California Press, 1994.

Kraidy, Marwan. *Hybridity, or the Cultural Logic of Globalization.* Philadelphia: Temple University Press, 2005.

Krakover, Shaul, and Yehuda Gradus, eds. *Tourism in Frontier Areas.* New York: Lexington Books, 2002.

Kroeber, Clifton. *Man, Land, and Water: Mexico's Farmlands Irrigation Policies, 1885–1911.* Berkeley: University of California Press, 1984.

Kroen, Sheryl. "Renegotiating the Social Contract in Post-War Europe: The American Marshall Plan and Consumer Democracy." In Brewer and Trentmann, eds., *Consuming Cultures, Global Perspectives*, 251–78.

Kun, Josh. *Audiotopia: Music, Race, and America.* Berkeley: University of California Press, 2005.

——. "The Aural Border." *Theatre Journal* 52 (2000): 1–21.

Laird, Pamela. *Advertising Progress: American Business and the Rise of Consumer Marketing.* Baltimore: Johns Hopkins University Press, 1998.

Lamar, Howard. *The Far Southwest, 1846–1912: A Territorial History.* New Haven: Yale University Press, 1966.

Langley, Lester. *MexAmerica: Two Countries, One Future.* New York: Crown Publishers, 1988.

Leach, William. *Land of Desire: Merchants, Power, and the Rise of a New American Culture.* New York: Pantheon Books, 1993.

Lears, Jackson. *Fables of Abundance: A Cultural History of Advertising in America.* New York: Basic Books, 1994.

——. "From Salvation to Self-Realization: Advertising and the Therapeutic Roots of the Consumer Culture, 1880–1930." In Fox and Lears, eds., *The Culture of Consumption*, 1–38.

——. *No Place of Grace: Antimodernism and the Transformation of American Culture, 1880–1920.* 1983. Chicago: University of Chicago Press, 1994.

——. "Reconsidering Abundance: A Plea for Ambiguity." In Strasser, McGovern, and Judt, eds., *Getting and Spending*, 449–66.

Lebergott, Stanley. "Through the Blockade: The Profitability and Extent of Cotton Smuggling, 1861–1865." *Journal of Economic History* 41 (1981): 867–88.

Lebhar, Godfrey. *Chain Stores in America, 1859–1959.* New York: Chain Store Publishing, 1959.

Lee, Erika. "Enforcing the Borders: Chinese Exclusion along the U.S. Borders with Canada and Mexico, 1882–1924." *Journal of American History* 89 (2002): 54–86.

———. "Orientalisms in the Americas: A Hemispheric Approach to Asian American History." *Journal of Asian American Studies* 8 (2005): 235–56.

LeFalle-Collins, Lizzetta, and Shifra Goldman. *In the Spirit of Resistance: African-American Modernists and the Mexican Muralist School.* New York: American Federation of Arts, 1996.

León, Ricardo. *Mariano Sanmiego: Medio siglo de la vida fronteriza.* Ciudad Juárez: Universidad Autónoma de Ciudad Juárez, 2006.

Levinson, Marc. *The Box: How the Shipping Container Made the World Smaller and the World Economy Bigger.* Princeton: Princeton University Press, 2006.

Lichtenstein, Nelson. "Wal-Mart: A Template for Twenty-First-Century Capitalism." In Lichtenstein, ed., *Wal-Mart,* 3–30.

———, ed. *Wal-Mart: The Face of Twenty-First-Century Capitalism.* New York: The New Press, 2006.

Liebs, Chester. *Main Street to Miracle Mile: American Roadside Architecture.* Baltimore: Johns Hopkins University Press, 1995.

Limón, José. "El Primer Congreso Mexicanista de 1911." *Aztlán* 5 (1974): 85–117.

Lindert, Peter, and Jeffrey Williamson. "Does Globalization Make the World More Unequal?" In Bordo, Taylor, and Williamson, eds., *Globalization in Historical Perspective,* 227–76.

Lloyd, Jane-Dale. *El proceso de modernización capitalista en el noroeste de Chihuahua, 1880–1910.* Mexico City: Universidad Iberoamericana, Departamento de Historia, 1987.

———. "*Rancheros* and Rebellion: The Case of Northwestern Chihuahua, 1905–1909. In Nugent, eds., *Rural Revolt in Mexico,* 107–33.

Lomnitz, Claudio. *Deep Mexico, Silent Mexico: An Anthropology of Nationalism.* Minneapolis: University of Minnesota Press, 2001.

———. "Times of Crisis: Historicity, Sacrifice, and the Spectacle of Debacle in Mexico City." *Public Culture* 15 (2003): 127–47.

Longstreth, Richard. *City Center to Regional Mall: Architecture, the Automobile and Retailing in Los Angeles, 1920–1950.* Cambridge: MIT Press, 1997.

———. "The Diffusion of the Community Shopping Center Concept during the Interwar Decades." *The Journal of the Society of Architectural Historians* 56 (1997): 268–93.

———. *The Drive-In, the Supermarket, and the Transformation of Commercial Space in Los Angeles, 1914–1941.* Cambridge: MIT Press, 1999.

López-Alonso, Moramay. "Growth and Inequality: Living Standards in Mexico, 1850-1950." *Journal of Latin American Studies* 39 (2007): 81–106.

López-Córdova, Ernesto. "Globalization, Migration, and Development: The Role of Mexican Migrant Remittances." *Economia: The Journal of Latin American and Caribbean Economic Association* 6 (2005): 217–47.

Lord, Kenneth, Sanjay Putrevu, and H. G. Parsa. "The Cross-Border Consumer: Investigation of Motivators and Inhibitors in Dining Experiences." *Journal of Hospitality & Tourism Research* 28 (2004): 209–29.

Lorey, David. *United States–Mexico Border Statistics since 1900*. Los Angeles: University of California, Los Angeles, Latin American Center Publications, 1990.

——. *The U.S.-Mexican Border in the Twentieth Century: A History of Economic and Social Transformation*. Wilmington: Scholarly Resources, 1999.

Loza, Steven. "Assimilation, Reclamation, and Rejection of the Nation-State by Chicano Musicians." In Corona and Madrid, ed., *Postnational Musical Identities*, 137–50.

Lustig, Nora. *Mexico: The Remaking of an Economy*. 1992. 2nd ed., Washington, D.C.: Brookings Institution Press, 1998.

MacCannell, Dean. *The Tourist: A New Theory of the Leisure Class*. 1976. 2nd ed., Berkeley: University of California Press, 1999.

Macias-González, Victor. "The *Lagartijo* at *The High Life*: Masculine Consumption, Race, Nation, and Homosexuality in Porfirian Mexico." In Robert McKee Irwin, Edward McCaughan, and Michelle Rocio Nasser, eds., *The Famous 41: Sexuality and Social Control in Mexico, 1901*, 227–49. New York: Palgrave, 2003.

——. "Mexicans 'of the Better Class': The Elite Culture and Ideology of Porfirian Chihuahua and Its Influence on the Mexican American Generation, 1876–1926." M.A. thesis, University of Texas, El Paso, 1995.

Maclachlan, Patricia. *Consumer Politics in Postwar Japan: The Institutional Boundaries of Citizen Activism*. New York: Columbia University Press, 2002.

Mankekar, Purnima. " 'India Shopping': Indian Grocery Stores and Transnational Configuration of Belonging." *Ethnos* 67 (2002): 75–98.

Manko, Katina Lee. "A Depression-Proof Business Strategy: The California Perfume Company's Motivational Literature." In Philip Scranton, ed., *Beauty and Business: Commerce, Gender, and Culture in Modern America*, 142–68. New York: Routledge, 2001.

——. " 'Ding Dong! Avon Calling!' Gender, Business, and Door-to-Door Selling, 1890–1955." Ph.D. diss., University of Delaware, 2001.

Marchand, Roland. *Advertising the American Dream: Making Way for Modernity, 1920–1940*. Berkeley: University of California Press, 1985.

Maril, Robert Lee. *Patrolling Chaos: The U.S. Border Patrol in Deep South Texas*. Lubbock: Texas Tech University Press, 2004.

Márquez, Graciela. "Commercial Monopolies and External Trade." In Bulmer-Thomas, Coatsworth, and Cortes-Conde, eds., *The Cambridge Economic History of Latin America: Volume 1*, 395–422.

——. "Tariff Protection in Mexico, 1892–1909: *Ad Valorem* Tariff Rates and Sources of Variation." In Coatsworth and Taylor, eds., *Latin America and the World Economy since 1800*, 402–44.

Marti, Judith. "Nineteenth-Century Views of Women's Participation in Mexico's Markets." In Linda J. Seligman, ed., *Women Traders in Cross-Cultural Perspective: Mediating Identities, Marketing Wares*, 27–44. Stanford: Stanford University Press, 2001.

Martinez, Oscar. *Border Boom Town: Ciudad Juárez since 1848*. Austin: University of Texas Press, 1978.

——. *Fragments of the Mexican Revolution: Personal Accounts from the Border*. Albuquerque: University of New Mexico Press, 1983.

——. "Surveying and Marking the U.S.-Mexico Boundary: The Mexican Perspective." In Hall, ed., *Drawing the Borderline*, 13–22.

——, ed. *Border People: Life and Society in the U.S.-Mexico Borderlands*. Tucson: University of Arizona Press, 1994.

——, ed. *U.S.-Mexico Borderlands: Historical and Contemporary Perspectives*. Wilmington: Scholarly Resources, 1996.

Marx, Thomas. "The Development of the Franchise Distribution System in the U.S. Automobile Industry." *Business History Review* 59 (1985): 465–74.

Mason, William. "Adobe Interiors in Spanish California." *Southern California Quarterly* 70 (1988): 253–63.

Massey, Douglas, Jorge Durand, and Nolan J. Malone. *Beyond Smoke and Mirrors: Mexican Immigration in an Era of Economic Integration*. New York: Russell Sage Foundation, 2002.

Massey, Douglas, and Zai Liang. "The Long-Term Consequences of a Temporary Worker Program: The U.S. Bracero Experience." *Population Research and Policy Review* 8 (1989): 199–226.

Massey, Douglas, and Emilio Parrado. "Migradollars: The Remittances and Savings of Mexican Migrants to the USA." *Population Research and Review* 13 (1994): 3–30.

Mathewson, Kent. "Drugs, Moral Geographies, and Indigenous Peoples: Some Initial Mappings and Central Issues." In Steinberg, Hobbs, and Mathewson, eds., *Dangerous Harvest*, 11–23.

Matt, Susan. *Keeping Up with the Joneses: Envy in American Consumer Society, 1890–1930*. Philadelphia: University of Pennsylvania Press, 2002.

May, Lary. *Screening Out the Past: The Birth of Mass Culture and the Motion Picture Industry*. New York: Oxford University Press, 1980.

Maynes, Mary Jo. "Gender, Labor, and Globalization in Historical Perspective: European Spinsters in the International Textile Industry, 1750–1900." *Journal of Women's History* 15 (2004): 47–66.

Mayo, John. "Consuls and Silver Contraband on Mexico's West Coast in the Era of Santa Ana." *Journal of Latin American Studies* 19 (1987): 389–411.

McAnany, Emile, and Kenton Wilkinson, eds. *Mass Media and Free Trade: NAFTA and the Cultural Industries*. Austin: University of Texas, Austin, 1996.

McCants, Anne. "Goods at Pawn: The Overlapping Worlds of Material Possessions and Family Finance in Early Modern Amsterdam." *Social Science History* 31 (2007): 213–38.

McCrossen, Alexis. *Holy Day, Holiday: The American Sunday*. Ithaca: Cornell University Press, 2000.

McCusker, John, and Russell Menard, eds. *The Economy of British America, 1607–1789.* Chapel Hill: University of North Carolina Press, 1991.

McDonald, James. "NAFTA and Basic Food Production: Dependency and Marginalization on Both Sides of the US/Mexico Border." *Research in Economic Anthropology* 15 (1994): 129–43.

——. "The Narcoeconomy and Small-town, Rural Mexico." *Human Organization* 64 (2005): 115–25.

McElvaine, Robert. *The Great Depression: America, 1929–1941.* 1984. 2nd ed. New York: Time Books, 1993.

McGovern, Charles. *Sold American: Consumption and Citizenship, 1890–1945.* Chapel Hill: University of North Carolina Press, 2006.

McKanna, Clare, Jr. "Prostitutes, Progressives, and Police: The Viability of Vice in San Diego, 1900–1930." *Journal of San Diego History* 35 (1989): 44–65.

McKenzie, David. "Beyond Remittances: The Effects of Migration on Mexican Households." In Maurice Schiff and Caglar Ozden, eds., *International Migration, Remittances and the Brain Drain,* 123–47. New York: Palgrave McMillan, 2005.

Medina, Martin. "Informal Transborder Recycling on the U.S.-Mexico Border: The *Cartoneros* of Nuevo Laredo." *Journal of Borderlands Studies* 16 (2001): 19–40.

——. "Scavenging on the Border: A Study of the Informal Recycling Sector in Laredo, Texas and Nuevo Laredo, Mexico." Ph.D. diss., Yale University, 1997.

Merish, Lori. *Sentimental Materialism: Gender, Commodity Culture, and Nineteenth-Century American Literature.* Durham: Duke University Press, 2000.

Metz, Leon. *Border: The U.S.-Mexico Line.* El Paso: Mangan Books, 1990.

——. *Desert Army: Fort Bliss on the Texas Border.* El Paso: Mangan Books, 1988.

Mexicali: Una historia. Vol. 1. Mexicali: Universidad Autónoma de Baja California, Instituto de Investigaciones Históricas, 1991.

Meyer Cosío, Rosa María. "Los empresarios y el crédito en el México independiente." In Rosa María Meyer Cosío, ed., *Identidad y prácticas de los grupos de poder en México, siglos XVII–XIX: Seminario de formación de grupos y clases sociales,* 227–56. Mexico City: Instituto Nacional de Antropología e Historia, 1999.

Micheletti, Michele, Andreas Follesdal, and Dietlind Stolle, eds. *Politics, Products, and Markets: Exploring Political Consumerism Past and Present.* Edison: Transaction Press, 2003.

Miller, Michael Nelson. *Red, White, and Green: The Maturing of Mexicanidad, 1940–1946.* El Paso: Texas Western Press, 1998.

Miquel, Angel. *Por las pantallas de la Ciudad de México: Periodistas del cine mudo.* Guadalajara: Universidad de Guadalajara, 1995.

Mishra, Prachi. "Emigration and Wages in Source Countries: Evidence from Mexico." *Journal of Development Economics* 82 (2007): 180–99.

Mitchell, Pablo. *Coyote Nation: Sexuality, Race, and Conquest in Modernizing New Mexico, 1880–1920.* Chicago: University of Chicago Press, 2005.

Mitchell, Stacy. *Big-Box Swindle: The True Cost of Mega-Retailers and the Fight for America's Independent Businesses.* Boston: Beacon Press, 2006.

Montemayor, Alma. *Cien años de cine en Chihuahua*. Chihuahua: Instituto Chihua-huense de las Culturas, 1998.

——. "El cine silente en la Ciudad de Chihuahua." In Eduardo de la Vega Alfaro, ed., *Microhistorias del cine en México*, 79–95. Mexico: Universidad de Guadalajara, 2001.

Mora, Carl. *Mexican Cinema: Reflections of a Society, 1896–1980*. Berkeley: University of California Press, 1982.

Mora-Torres, Juan. *The Making of the Mexican Border: The State, Capitalism, and Society in Nuevo León, 1848–1910*. Austin: University of Texas Press, 2001.

Morales, Ed. *Living in Spanglish: The Search for Latino Identity in America*. New York: St. Martin's Press, 2003.

Moran, Kristin. "The Development of Spanish-Language Television in San Diego: A Contemporary History." *Journal of San Diego History* 50 (2004): 42–54.

Moreno, Julio. "J. Walter Thompson, the Good Neighbor Policy, and Lessons in Mexican Business Culture, 1920–1950." *Enterprise & Society* 5 (2004): 254–80.

——. *Yankee Don't Go Home! Mexican Nationalism, American Business Culture, and the Shaping of Modern Mexico, 1920–1950*. Chapel Hill: University of North Carolina Press, 2003.

Morris, Stephen. *Gringolandia: Mexican Identity and Perceptions of the United States*. Lanham: Rowman and Littlefield, 2005.

Mosco, Vincent, and Dan Schiller. "Integrating a Continent for a Transnational World." In Mosco and Schiller, eds., *Continental Order?*, 1–34.

——, eds. *Continental Order? Integrating North America for Cybercapitalism*. Lanham: Rowman & Littlefield. 2001.

Mraz, John. "Today, Tomorrow, and Always: The Golden Age of Illustrated Magazines in Mexico, 1937–1960." In Joseph, Rubenstein, and Zolov, eds., *Fragments of a Golden Age*, 116–58.

Nader, Ralph. *Unsafe at Any Speed: The Designed-In Dangers of the American Automobile*. New York: Grossman Publishers, 1965.

Naím, Moisés. *Illicit: How Smugglers, Traffickers and Copycats are Hijacking the Global Economy*. New York: Doubleday, 2005.

Nater, Laura. "Colonial Tobacco: Key Commodity of the Spanish Empire, 1500–1800." In Topik, Marichal, and Frank, eds., *From Silver to Cocaine*, 93–117.

Nestle, Marion. *Food Politics: How the Food Industry Influences Nutrition and Health*. Berkeley: University of California Press, 2002.

Nevins, Joseph. *Operation Gatekeeper: The Rise of the 'Illegal Alien' and the Making of the U.S.-Mexican Boundary*. New York: Routledge, 2002.

Newman, Kathy. *Radio Active: Advertising and Consumer Activism, 1935–1947*. Berkeley: University of California Press, 2004.

Ngai, Mae. *Impossible Subjects: Illegal Aliens and the Making of Modern America*. Princeton: Princeton University Press, 2004.

Niblo, Stephen. *Mexico in the 1940s: Modernity, Politics, and Corruption*. Wilmington: Scholarly Resources, 1999.

Nickles, Shelley. " 'More Is Better': Mass Consumption, Gender, and Class Identity in Postwar America." *American Quarterly* 54 (2002): 581–622.

Nugent, Daniel. *Spent Cartridges of Revolution: An Anthropological History of Namiquipa, Chihuahua*. Chicago: University of Chicago Press, 1993.

——, ed. *Rural Revolt in Mexico: U.S. Intervention and the Domain of Subaltern Politics*. Durham: Duke University Press, 1998.

Oberle, Alex. "*Se Venden Aquí*: Latino Commercial Landscapes in Phoenix, Arizona." In Arreola, ed., *Hispanic Spaces, Latino Places*, 240–51.

Oberle, Alex, and Daniel Arreola. "Mexican Medical Border Towns: A Case Study of Algodones, Baja California." *Journal of Borderland Studies* 19 (2004): 1–18.

Ochoa, Enrique C. *Feeding Mexico: The Political Uses of Food since 1910*. Wilmington: Scholarly Resources, 2000.

O'Day, Patrick, and Angelina López. "Organizing the Underground NAFTA." *Journal of Contemporary Criminal Justice* 17 (2001): 232–42.

Ohmann, Richard. *Selling Culture: Magazines, Markets, and Class at the Turn of the Century*. New York: Verso, 1998.

Ojeda de la Peña, Norma. "Transborder Families and Gendered Trajectories of Migration and Work." In Denise Segura and Patricia Zavella, eds., *Women and Migration in the U.S.-Mexico Borderlands*, 327–40. Durham: Duke University Press, 2007.

Ojeda-Benitez, Sara, Carolina Armijo de Vega, and Elizabeth Ramírez-Barreto. "The Potential for Recycling Household Waste: A Case Study from Mexicali, Mexico." *Environment and Urbanization* 12 (2000): 163–73.

Olegario, Rowena. *A Culture of Credit: Embedding Trust and Transparency in American Business*. Cambridge: Harvard University Press, 2006.

Oles, James. *South of the Border: Mexico in the American Imagination, 1914–1947*. Washington, D.C.: Smithsonian Institution Press, 1993.

Olney, Martha. "Avoiding Default: The Role of Credit in the Consumption Collapse of 1930." *Quarterly Journal of Economics* 114 (1999): 319–35.

——. *Buy Now, Pay Later: Advertising, Credit, and Consumer Durables in the 1920s*. Chapel Hill: University of North Carolina Press, 1991.

Orlove, Benjamin, ed. *The Allure of the Foreign: Imported Goods in Postcolonial Latin America*. Ann Arbor: University of Michigan Press, 1997.

Ortiz Garza, José Luis. *Una radio entre dos reinos: La increíble historia de la radiodifusora mexicana más potente del mundo en los años 30*. Buenos Aires: J. Vergara, 1997.

Ortiz-Gonzales, Victor. *El Paso: Local Frontiers at a Global Crossroads*. Minneapolis: University of Minnesota Press, 2004.

Ownby, Ted. *American Dreams in Mississippi: Consumers, Poverty, and Culture, 1830–1998*. Chapel Hill: University of North Carolina Press, 1999.

Papademetriou, Demetrios, and Deborah Meyers, eds. *Caught in the Middle: Border Communities in an Era of Globalization*. Washington, D.C.: Carnegie Endowment for International Peace, 2001.

Pardinas, Juan. "Fighting Poverty in Mexico: Policy Challenges." In Susan Kaufman

Purcell and Luis Rubio-Friedberg, eds., *Mexico under Fox*, 65–86. Boulder: Lynne Rienner, 2004.

Paredes, Américo. *A Texas-Mexican Cancionero: Folksongs of the Lower Border*. Urbana: University of Illinois Press, 1976.

Paredes, Mari Castañeda. "The Reorganization of Spanish-Language Media Marketing in the United States." In Mosco and Schiller, eds., *Continental Order?* 120–35.

Patrick, Michael. "A Preliminary Assessment of NAFTA's Impact on the Texas Border Economy." *Journal of Borderlands Studies* 11 (1996): 23–50.

Patrick, Michael, and William Renforth. "The Effects of the Peso Devaluation on Cross Border Retailing." *Journal of Borderlands Studies* 11 (1996): 25–41.

Paxman, Andrew, and Alex Saragoza. "Globalization and Latin Media Powers: The Case of Mexico's Televisa." In Mosco and Schiller, eds., *Continental Order?*, 64–85.

Payan, Tony. *The Three U.S.-Mexico Border Wars: Drugs, Immigration, and Homeland Security*. Westport: Praeger Security, 2006.

Peck, Gunther. *Reinventing Free Labor: Padrones and Immigrant Workers in the North American West, 1880–1930*. New York: Cambridge University Press, 2000.

Pells, Richard. *Not Like Us: How Europeans Have Loved, Hated, and Transformed American Culture since World War II*. New York: Basic Books, 1997.

Peña, Devon. *The Terror of the Machine: Technology, Work, Gender, and Ecology on the U.S.-Mexico Border*. Austin: The Center for Mexican-American Studies, University of Texas, 1997.

Peñaloza, Lisa. "*Atravesando Fronteras*/Border Crossings: A Critical Ethnographic Exploration of the Consumer Acculturation of Mexican Immigrants." *Journal of Consumer Research* 21 (1994): 32–54.

——. "Multiculturalism in the New World Order: Implications for the Study of Consumer Behavior." In Karin Ekström and Helene Brembeck, eds., *Elusive Consumption*, 87–109. Oxford: Berg, 2004.

Pence, Katherine. "Shopping for an 'Economic Miracle': Gendered Politics of Consumer Citizenship in Divided Germany." In Chatriot, Chessel, and Hilton, eds., *The Expert Consumer*, 105–20.

Perales, Monica. "Smeltertown: A Biography of a Mexican American Community, 1880–1973." Ph.D. diss., Stanford University, 2003.

Pérez Herrera, Octavio. *La zona libre: Excepción fiscal y conformación histórica de la frontera norte de México*. Mexico City: Dirección General del Acervo Histórico Diplomático de la Secretaría de Relaciones Exteriores, 2004.

Pérez Herrero, Pedro. "El comportamiento de las élites económicas en México en tres momentos de apertura comercial." In Agueda Jiménez Pelayo, ed., *Élites y poder: México y España, siglos XVI al XX*, 184–205. Guadalajara: Universidad de Guadalajara, 2003.

Perkmann, Markus, and Ngai-Ling Sum, eds. *Globalization, Regionalization and Cross-Border Regions*. London: Palgrave, 2002.

Perramond, Eric. "Desert Traffic: The Dynamics of the Drug Trade in Northwestern Mexico." In Steinberg, Hobbs, and Mathewson, eds., *Dangerous Harvest*, 209–20.

Phillips, Keith, and Roberto Coronado. "Texas Border Benefits from Retail Sales to Mexican Nationals." Working Paper, Federal Reserve Bank of Dallas. October 2005. http://www.dallasfed.org/research/pubs/fotexas/fotexas_phillips.html, accessed November 14, 2007.

Piketty, Thomas, and Emmanuel Saez. "Income Inequality in the United States, 1913–1998." *Quarterly Journal of Economics* 118 (2003): 1–39.

Pilcher, Jeffrey. "Fajitas and the Failure of Refrigerated Meatpacking in Mexico: Consumer Culture and Porfirian Capitalism." *The Americas* 60 (2004): 411–29.

——. "From 'Montezuma's Revenge' to 'Mexican Truffles': Culinary Tourism across the Rio Grande." In Lucy M. Long, ed., *Culinary Tourism*, 76–96. Lexington: University Press of Kentucky, 2003.

——. "Industrial Tortillas and Folkloric Pepsi: The Nutritional Consequences of Hybrid Cuisines in Mexico." In James L. Watson and Melissa Caldwell, eds., *The Cultural Politics of Food and Eating: A Reader*, 235–50. Malden: Blackwell, 2005.

——. *Que Vivan Los Tamales! Food and the Making of Mexican Identity*. Albuquerque: University of New Mexico Press, 1998.

——. *The Sausage Rebellion: Public Health, Private Enterprise, and Meat in Mexico City, 1890–1917*. Albuquerque: University of New Mexico Press, 2006.

——. "Taco Bell, *Maseca*, and Slow Food: A Postmodern Apocalypse for Mexico's Peasant Cuisine?" In Richard Wilk, ed., *Fast Food/Slow Food*, 69–82. Lanham: Rowman Altamira, 2006.

——. "Tex-Mex, Cal-Mex, New Mex, or Whose Mex?: Notes on the Historical Geography of Southwestern Cuisine." *Journal of the Southwest* 43 (2001): 659–79.

Piñera Ramírez, David, and Jesús Ortiz Figueroa, eds. *Historia de Tijuana: Edición conmemorativa del centenario de su fundación, 1889–1989*, vol. 1. Tijuana: Universidad Autónoma de Baja California, Centro de Investigaciones Históricas, 1989.

Pitrone, Jean Maddern. *F. W. Woolworth and the American Five and Dime: A Social History*. Jefferson: McFarland and Company, 2003.

Pitti, Stephen. *The Devil in Silicon Valley: Northern California, Race, and Mexican Americans*. Princeton: Princeton University Press, 2003.

Plascencia, Luis F. B. "Low Riding in the Southwest: Cultural Symbols in the Mexican Community." In Mario T. García et al., eds., *History, Culture and Society: Chicano Studies in the 1980s*, 141–75. Ypsilanti: Bilingual Press/National Association for Chicano Studies, 1983.

Pletcher, David. *The Diplomacy of Trade and Investment: American Economic Expansion in the Hemisphere, 1865–1900*. Columbia: University of Missouri Press, 1998.

Pollan, Michael. *The Omnivore's Dilemma: A Natural History of Four Meals*. New York: Penguin Press, 2006.

Pomeroy, Earl. *In Search of the Golden West: The Tourist in Western America*. New York: Knopf, 1957.

Portes, Alejandro, Manuel Castells, and Lauren Benton, eds. *The Informal Economy: Studies in Advanced and Less Developed Countries*. Baltimore: Johns Hopkins University Press, 1989.

Potter, David. *People of Plenty: Economic Abundance and the American Character*. Chicago: University of Chicago Press, 1954.

Presthold, Jeremy. *Domesticating the World: African Consumerism and the Genealogies of Globalization*. Berkeley: University of California Press, 2008.

———. "On the Global Repercussions of East African Consumerism." *American Historical Review* 109 (2004): 755–82.

Price, John. *Tijuana: Urbanization in a Border Culture*. Notre Dame: University of Notre Dame Press, 1973.

Princen, Thomas, Michael Maniates, and Ken Conca, eds. *Confronting Consumption*. Cambridge: MIT Press, 2002.

Prock, Jerry. "The Peso Devaluations and Their Effect on Texas Border Economies." *Inter-American Economic Affairs* 37 (1984): 83–92.

Proffitt, T. D., III. *Tijuana: The History of a Mexican Metropolis*. San Diego: San Diego State University Press, 1994.

Raikes, Philip, Michael Jensen, and Stefano Ponte. "Global Commodity Chain Analysis and the French *filière* Approach: Comparison and Critique." *Economy and Society* 29 (2000): 390–417.

Rajagopal, Arvind. "The Violence of Commodity Aesthetics: Hawkers, Demolition Raids, and a New Regime of Consumption." *Social Text* 19 (2001): 91–113.

Ramírez, Elizabeth. *Footlights across the Border: A History of the Spanish-Language Professional Theatre on the Texas Stage*. New York: Peter Lang, 1990.

Ramos, Raúl. *Beyond the Alamo: Forging Mexican Ethnicity in San Antonio, 1821–1861*. Chapel Hill: University of North Carolina Press, 2008.

Raucher, Alan R. "Dime Store Chains: The Making of Organization Men, 1880–1940." *Business History Review* 65 (spring 1991): 130–63.

Ravallion, Martin. "The Debate on Globalization, Poverty and Inequality: Why Measurement Matters." *International Affairs* 79 (2003): 739–53.

Rebert, Paula. *La Gran Línea: Mapping the United States–Mexico Boundary, 1849–1857*. Austin: University of Texas Press, 2001.

Recio, Gabriela. "Drugs and Alcohol: U.S. Prohibition and the Origins of the Drug Trade in Mexico, 1910–1930." *Journal of Latin American Studies* 34 (2002): 21–43.

Reeve, Agnesa Lufkin. *From Hacienda to Bungalow: Northern New Mexico Houses*. Albuquerque: University of New Mexico Press, 1988.

Renouard, Joe. "The Predicaments of Plenty: Interwar Intellectuals and American Consumerism." *Journal of American & Comparative Cultures* 30 (2007): 54–67.

Reséndez, Andrés. *Changing National Identities at the Frontier: Texas and New Mexico, 1800–1850*. New York: Cambridge University Press, 2005.

———. "Getting Cured and Getting Drunk: State versus Market in Texas and New Mexico, 1800–1850." *Journal of the Early Republic* 22 (2002): 77–103.

———. "Masonic Connections, Pecuniary Interests, and Institutional Development Along Mexico's Far North." In Rodríguez, ed. *The Divine Charter*, 109–32.

Richards, Thomas. *The Commodity Culture of Victorian England: Advertising and Spectacle, 1851–1914*. Stanford: Stanford University Press, 1990.

Richardson, Chad. *Batos, Bolillos, Pochos, & Pelados: Class and Culture on the South Texas Border*. Austin: University of Texas Press, 1999.

Richardson, Chad, and Rosalva Resendiz. *On the Edge of the Law: Culture, Labor, and Deviance on the South Texas Border*. Austin: University of Texas Press, 2006.

Riguzzi, Paolo. *¿La reciprocidad imposible?: La política del comercio entre México y Estados Unidos, 1877–1938*. Mexico City: El Colegio de México, 2003.

Roche, Daniel. *A History of Everyday Things: The Birth of Consumption in France, 1600– 1800*. 1997. Translated by Brian Pearce. Cambridge: Cambridge University Press, 2000.

Rockman, Seth. *Scraping By: Wage Labor, Slavery, and Survival in Early Baltimore*. Baltimore: Johns Hopkins University Press, 2008.

Rodgers, Daniel. *The Work Ethic in Industrial America, 1850–1920*. Chicago: University of Chicago Press, 1978.

Rodríguez, Jamie E., ed. *The Divine Charter: Constitutionalism and Liberalism in Nineteenth-Century Mexico*. Lanham: Rowman and Littlefield, 2005.

Rodríguez, Néstor, and Jacqueline Hagan. "Transborder Community Relations at the U.S.-Mexico Border: Laredo/Nuevo Laredo and El Paso/Ciudad Juárez." In Papademetriou and Meyers, eds., *Caught in the Middle*, 88–116.

Romero, Matías. *Mexico and the United States: A Study of Subjects Affecting Their Political, Commercial, and Social Relations, Made with a View to Their Promotion*. New York: G. P. Putnam, 1898.

Romero, Robert Chao. "Transnational Commercial Orbits." In William Deverell and David Igler, eds., *A Companion to California History*, chap. 13. Hoboken: Wiley-Blackwell, 2008.

Romo, David Dorado. *Ringside Seat to a Revolution: An Underground Cultural History of El Paso and Juárez: 1893–1923*. El Paso: Cinco Puntos Press, 2005.

Roseberry, William. "Understanding Capitalism—Historically, Structurally, Spatially." In David Nugent, ed., *Locating Capitalism in Time and Space: Global Restructurings, Politics, and Identity*, 61–79. Stanford: Stanford University Press, 2002.

Rosenberg, Emily S. "Ordering Others: U.S. Financial Advisers in the Early Twentieth Century." In Laura Ann Stoler, ed., *Haunted by Empire: Geographies of Intimacy in North American History*, 405–24. Durham: Duke University Press, 2006.

Rothman, Hal. *Devil's Bargains: Tourism in the Twentieth-Century American West*. Lawrence: University Press of Kansas, 1998.

——, ed. *The Culture of Tourism, the Tourism of Culture: Selling the Past to the Present in the American Southwest*. Albuquerque: University of New Mexico Press, 2003.

Ruíz, Ramón Eduardo. *On the Rim of Mexico: Encounters of the Rich and Poor*, 1998. Boulder: Westview Press, 2000.

——. *The People of Sonora and Yankee Capitalists*. Tucson: University of Arizona Press, 1988.

Ruíz, Vicki L. "The Flapper and the Chaperone." In *Out of the Shadows: Mexican Women in Twentieth-Century America*. New York: Oxford University Press, 1998.

Russell, Frank. *The Pima Indians*. Washington, D.C.: GPO, 1908.

Rydell, Robert. *All the World's a Fair: Visions of Empire at American International Expositions, 1876–1916*. Chicago: University of Chicago Press, 1984.

Ryscavage, Paul. *Income Inequality in America: An Analysis of Trends*. Armonk: M. E. Sharpe, 1999.

Sadowski-Smith, Claudia, ed. *Globalization on the Line: Culture, Capital, and Citizenship at U.S. Borders*. New York: Palgrave, 2002.

Salas, Miguel. *In the Shadow of the Eagles: Sonora and the Transformation of the Border during the Porfiriato*. Berkeley: University of California Press, 1997.

Saldaña-Portillo, María Josefina. "In the Shadow of NAFTA: *Y Tu Mama También* Revisits the National Allegory of Mexican Sovereignty." *American Quarterly*, special issue edited by Mary Dudziak and Leti Volpp, "Legal Borderlands: Law and the Construction of American Borders," 57 (2005): 751–77.

Saldívar, José David. *Border Matters: Remapping American Cultural Studies*. Berkeley: University of California Press, 1997.

Salvucci, Richard. "Export-Led Industrialization." In Bulmer-Thomas, Coatsworth, and Cortes-Conde, eds., *The Cambridge Economic History of Latin America, Volume 2*, 249–92.

——. "The Origins and Progress of U.S.-Mexican Trade, 1825–1884: 'Hoc opus, hic labor est.'" *Hispanic American Historical Review* 71 (1991): 697–735.

Salzinger, Leslie. *Genders in Production: Making Workers in Mexico's Global Factories*. Berkeley: University of California Press, 2003.

——. "Manufacturing Sexual Subjects: 'Harassment,' Desire, and Discipline on a Maquiladora Shopfloor." In Segura and Zavella, eds., *Women and Migration in the U.S.-Mexico Borderlands*, 161–83.

Samponaro, Frank, and Paul Vanderwood. *Border Fury: A Picture Postcard Record of Mexico's Revolution and U.S. War Preparedness, 1910–1917*. Albuquerque: University of New Mexico Press, 1988.

Sánchez, George. *Becoming Mexican American: Ethnicity, Culture, and Identity in Chicano Los Angeles, 1900–1945*. New York: Oxford University Press, 1993.

Sánchez, Roberto. "Binational Cooperation and the Environment at the U.S.-Mexico Border: A Mexican Perspective." In Herzog, ed., *Shared Space*, 53–71.

Sánchez-Ruiz, Enrique. "Globalization, Cultural Industries, and Free Trade: The Mexican Audiovisual Sector in the NAFTA Age." In Mosco and Schiller, eds., *Continental Order?*, 86–119.

Sandos, James. "Northern Separatism during the Mexican Revolution: An Inquiry into the Role of Drug Trafficking, 1910–1920." *The Americas* 41 (1984): 191–214.

Sandoval, David. "The American Invasion of New Mexico and Mexican Merchants." *Journal of Popular Culture* 35 (2001): 61–73.

Santiago, Myrna. *The Ecology of Oil: Environment, Labor, and the Mexican Revolution, 1900–1938*. New York: Cambridge University Press, 2006.

Saragoza, Alex. *The Monterrey Elite and the Mexican State, 1880–1940*. Austin: University of Texas Press, 1988.

———. "The Selling of Mexico: Tourism and the State, 1929–1952." In Joseph, Rubenstein, and Zolov, eds., *Fragments of a Golden Age*, 91–115.

Scanlon, Jennifer. *Inarticulate Longings: The Ladies' Home Journal, Gender, and the Promises of Consumer Culture*. New York: Routledge, 1995.

Schaefer, Stacy, and Peter Furst, eds. *People of the Peyote: Huichol Indian History, Religion, and Survival*. Albuquerque: University of New Mexico Press, 1996.

Schantz, Eric. "All Night at the Owl: The Social and Political Relations of Mexicali's Red-Light District, 1909–1925." In Wood, ed., *On the Border*, 91–144.

———. "The Mexicali Rose and Tijuana Brass: Vice Tours of the U.S.-Mexico Border, 1910–1965." Ph.D. diss., University of California, Los Angeles, 2001.

Schelonka, Greg. "RockIn' La Frontera: Mexican Rock, Globalization, and National Identity." In Corona and Madrid, ed., *Postnational Musical Identities*, 151–70.

Schivelbusch, Wolfgang. *Disenchanted Night: The Industrialization of Light*. 1983. Translated by Angela Davies. Berkeley: University of California Press, 1988.

Schlosser, Eric. *Reefer Madness: Sex, Drugs, and Cheap Labor in the American Black Market*. New York: Houghton Mifflin, 2003.

Schmidt, Leigh Eric. *Consumer Rites: The Buying and Selling of American Holidays*. Princeton: Princeton University Press, 1995.

Schneider, Friedrich, and Dominik Enste. "Shadow Economies around the World: Size, Cause and Consequences." *Journal of Economic Literature* 38 (2000): 77–114.

———. *The Shadow Economy: An International Survey*, 2002. New York: Cambridge University Press, 2007.

Schneider, George, ed. "A Border Incident of 1878 from the Journal of Captain John S. McNaught." *Southwestern Historical Quarterly* 70 (October 1966): 314–20.

Schreiber, Rebecca. "The Cold War Culture of Political Exile: U.S. Artists and Writers in Mexico, 1940–1965." Ph.D. diss., Yale University, 2000.

Schroeder, Richard. *Lone Star Picture Show: Nickelodeons to Deluxe Theaters, 1908–1921*. College Station: Texas A&M Press, 2001.

Scranton, Philip. *Endless Novelty: Specialty Production and American Industrialization, 1865–1925*. Princeton: Princeton University Press, 1997.

Scrivano, Paolo. "Signs of Americanization in Italian Domestic Life: Italy's Postwar Conversion to Consumerism." *Journal of Contemporary History* 40 (2005): 317–40.

Segura, Denise, and Patricia Zavella, eds. *Women and Migration in the U.S.-Mexico Borderlands*. Durham: Duke University Press, 2007.

Seligman, Brad. "Patriarchy at the Checkout Counter: The *Dukes v. Wal-Mart Stores, Inc.*, Class Action Suit." In Lichtenstein, ed., *Wal-Mart*, 231–42.

Sellers, Charles. *The Market Revolution: Jacksonian America, 1815–1846*. New York: Oxford University Press, 1991.

Sen, Amartya. "Globalization, Inequality and Global Protest." *Development* 45 (2002): 11–16.

———. *Inequality Re-examined*. 1992. Cambridge: Harvard University Press, 2007.

———. "The Standard of Living: Lecture I, Concepts and Critiques." In Sen, *The Standard of Living*, 1–19.

——. *The Standard of Living*, edited by Geoffrey Hawthorn. Cambridge: Cambridge University Press, 1988.

Sepúlveda, César. *La frontera norte de México: Historia, conflictos, 1762–1975*. Mexico City: Editorial Porrúa, 1976.

Serna, Laura Isabel. "'As a Mexican I Feel It's My Duty': Citizenship, Censorship, and the Campaign Against Derogatory Films in Mexico, 1922–1930." *The Americas* 63 (2006): 225–44.

——. "'We're Going Yankee': American Movies, Mexican Nationalism, Transnational Cinema, 1917–1935." Ph.D. diss., Harvard University, 2006.

Shammas, Carole. "Changes in English and Anglo-American Consumption from 1550 to 1800." In Brewer and Porter, eds., *Consumption and the World of Goods*, 177–205.

——. "How Self-Sufficient Was Early America?" *Journal of Interdisciplinary History* 13 (1982): 247–72.

Sheridan, Thomas, ed. *Empire of Sand: The Seri Indians and the Struggle for Spanish Sonora, 1645–1803*. Tucson: University of Arizona Press, 1999.

Shi, David. *The Simple Life: Plain Living and High Thinking in American Culture*. New York: Oxford University Press, 1985.

Simmons, Jim, and Shizue Kamikihara. "Field Observations from the U.S.-Mexico Border." Eaton Chair in Retailing, Ryerson University, March 2000, http://www.ecr.ryerson.ca/Jim/JimNote8.html, accessed September 5, 2008.

Simonett, Helena. *Banda: Mexican Musical Life across Borders*. Middletown: Wesleyan University Press, 2001.

——. "Quest for the Local: Building Musical Ties between Mexico and the United States." In Corona and Madrid, ed., *Postnational Musical Identities*, 119–36.

Sklair, Leslie. *Assembling for Development: The Maquila Industry in Mexico and the United States*. 1989. 2nd ed., San Diego: Center for U.S.-Mexican Studies, University of California, 1993.

Slesnick, Daniel. *Consumption and Social Welfare: Living Standards and Their Distribution in the United States*. New York: Cambridge University Press, 2001.

——. *Living Standards in the United States: A Consumption Based Approach*. Washington, D.C.: AEI Press, 2000.

Sluyter, Andrew. "The Ecological Origins and Consequences of Cattle Ranching in Sixteenth-Century New Spain." *Geographical Review* 86 (1996): 161–77.

Smith, F. Todd. *From Dominance to Disappearance: The Indians of Texas and the Near Southwest, 1786–1859*. Lincoln: University of Nebraska Press, 2005.

Smulyan, Susan. *Selling Radio: The Commercialization of American Broadcasting, 1920–1934*. Washington, D.C.: Smithsonian Institution Press, 1994.

Spector, Robert. *Category Killers: The Retail Revolution and Its Impact on Consumer Culture*. Boston: Harvard Business School Press, 2005.

Spener, David. "The Logic and Contradictions of Intensified Border Enforcement in Texas." In Peter Andreas and Timothy Snyder, eds., *The Wall around the West: State Borders and Immigration Controls in North America and Europe*, 115–37. Lanham: Rowman and Littlefield, 2000.

St. John, Rachel. "Line in the Sand: The Desert Border between the United States and Mexico, 1848–1934." Ph.D. dissertation, Stanford University, 2005.

Staples, Anne. "*Policía y Buen Gobierno*: Municipal Efforts to Regulate Public Behavior, 1821–1857." In William Beezley, Cheryl English Martin, and William E. French, eds., *Rituals of Rule, Rituals of Resistance: Public Celebrations and Popular Culture in Mexico*, 115–26. Lanham: Rowman and Littlefield, 1994.

Staudt, Kathleen. *Free Trade?: Informal Economies at the U.S-Mexico Border*. Philadelphia: Temple University Press, 1988.

——. "Informality Knows No Borders? Perspectives from El Paso–Juárez." *SAIS Review* 21 (2001): 123–30.

Staudt, Kathleen, and Irasema Coronado. *Fronteras No Mas: Toward Social Justice at the U.S.-Mexico Border*. New York: Palgrave Macmillan, 2002.

Stavans, Ilan. *Spanglish: The Making of a New American Language*. New York: Harper-Collins, 2003.

Stearns, Peter. *Consumerism in World History: The Global Transformation of Desire*. New York: Routledge, 2001.

——. "Stages of Consumerism: Recent Work on the Issues of Periodization." *Journal of Modern History* 69 (1997): 102–17.

Steigerwald, David. "All Hail the Republic of Choice: Consumer History as Contemporary Thought." *Journal of American History* 93 (2006): 385–403.

Steinberg, Michael K., Joseph J. Hobbs, and Kent Mathewson, eds. *Dangerous Harvest: Drug Plants and the Transformation of Indigenous Landscapes*. New York: Oxford University Press, 2004.

Steiner, André. "Dissolution of the 'Dictatorship over Needs'? Consumer Behavior and Economic Reform in East Germany in the 1960s." In Strasser, McGovern, and Judt, eds., *Getting and Spending*, 167–86.

Stern, Alexandra. "Buildings, Boundaries, and Blood: Medicalization and Nation-Building on the U.S.-Mexico Border, 1910–1930." *Hispanic American Historical Review* 79 (1999): 41–81.

——. *Eugenic Nation: Faults and Frontiers of Better Breeding in Modern America*. Berkeley: University of California Press, 2005.

Steward, Omer Call. "The History of Peyotism in Nevada." *Nevada Historical Society Quarterly* 25 (1982): 197–209.

——. *Peyote Religion: A History*. Norman: University of Oklahoma Press, 1987.

Stoddard, Ellwyn, and John Hedderson. *Trends and Patterns of Poverty on the United States–Mexico Border*. Borderlands Research Monograph Series no. 3. El Paso: University of Texas, El Paso, 1987.

Stole, Inger. *Advertising on Trial: Consumer Activism and Corporate Public Relations in the 1930s*. Urbana: University of Illinois Press, 2006.

Stone, Michael C. "*Bajito y Suavecito*: Lowriding and the 'Class' of Class." *Studies in Latin American Popular Culture* 9 (1990): 85–126.

Storper, Michael. "Lived Effects of the Contemporary Economy: Globalization, Inequality, and Consumer Society." *Public Culture* 12 (2000): 375–409.

Storrs, Landon R. Y. *Civilizing Capitalism: The National Consumers' League, Women's Activism, and Labor Standards in the New Deal Era*. Chapel Hill: University of North Carolina Press, 2000.

Strasser, Susan. "Making Consumption Conspicuous: Transgressive Topics Go Mainstream." *Technology and Culture* 43 (2002): 761–62.

——. *Satisfaction Guaranteed: The Making of the American Mass Market*. Washington, D.C.: Smithsonian Institution Press, 1989.

——. *Waste and Want: A Social History of Trash*. New York: Metropolitan Books, 1999.

——. "Woolworth to Wal-Mart: Mass Merchandising and the Changing Culture of Consumption." In Lichtenstein, ed., *Wal-Mart*, 31–56.

Strasser, Susan, Charles McGovern, and Matthias Judt, eds. *Getting and Spending: European and American Consumer Societies in the Twentieth Century*. New York: Cambridge University Press, 1998.

Sturman, Janet. *Zarzuela: Spanish Operetta, American Stage*. Urbana: University of Illinois Press, 2000.

Sunstein, Carl. *The Second Bill of Rights: FDR's Unfinished Revolution and Why We Need It More Than Ever*. New York: Basic Books, 2004.

Sweeny, Gary. "Drawing Borders: Art and the Cultural Politics of the U.S.-Mexico Boundary Survey, 1850–1853." In Hall, ed., *Drawing the Borderline*, 23–77.

Tarrow, Sidney. *The New Transnational Activism*. New York: Cambridge University Press, 2005.

Taylor, Arnold. *American Diplomacy and the Narcotics Traffic, 1900–1939: A Study in International Humanitarian Reform*. Durham: Duke University Press, 1969.

Taylor, Lawrence. "The Wild Frontier Moves South: U.S. Entrepreneurs and the Growth of Tijuana's Vice Industry, 1908–1935." *Journal of San Diego History* 48 (2002): 204–29.

Taylor, Paul. *An American-Mexican Frontier: Nueces County, Texas*. Chapel Hill: University of North Carolina Press, 1934.

Tebbutt, Melanie. *Making Ends Meet: Pawnbroking and Working-Class Credit*. New York: St. Martin's Press, 1983.

Tedlow, Richard. *New and Improved: The Story of Mass Marketing in America*. Boston: Harvard Business School, 1996.

Tenorio-Trillo, Mauricio. *Artilugio de la nación moderna*. Mexico City: Fondo de Cultura Económica, 1998.

——. "The Cosmopolitan Mexican Summer, 1920–1949." *Latin American Research Review* 32 (1997): 224–42.

——. *Mexico at the World's Fairs: Crafting a Modern Nation*. Berkeley: University of California Press, 1996.

Thompson, Kristin. *Exporting Entertainment: America in the World Film Market, 1907–1934*. London: British Film Institute, 1985.

Thompson, Mark. *American Character: The Curious Life of Charles Fletcher Lummis and the Rediscovery of the Southwest*. New York: Arcade Publishing, 2001.

Thompson, Noel. "Social Opulence, Private Asceticism: Ideas of Consumption in Early Socialist Thought." In Daunton and Hilton, eds., *The Politics of Consumption*, 51–68.

Tiefenbacher, John. "*La Frontera Química*: Toxic Emissions and Spills along the U.S.-Mexican Border." *Journal of Borderlands Studies* 13 (1998): 57–77.

Tiersten, Lisa. *Marianne in the Market: Envisioning Consumer Society in Fin-de-Siècle France*. Berkeley: University of California Press, 2001.

Tilly, Chris. "Wal-Mart in Mexico: The Limits of Growth." In Lichtenstein, ed., *Wal-Mart*, 189–259.

Timmons, Wilbert H. *El Paso: A Borderlands History*. El Paso: Texas Western Press, 1990.

Timothy, Dallen, ed. *Tourism and Political Boundaries*. London: Routledge, 2001.

Timothy, Dallen, and Richard W. Butler. "Cross-Border Shopping: Canada and the United States." *Annals of Tourism Research* 22 (1995): 16–34.

Tomes, Nancy. "Merchants of Health: Medicine and Consumer Culture in the United States, 1900–1940." *Journal of American History* 88 (2001): 519–47.

Topik, Steven, Carlos Marichal, and Zephyr Frank, eds. *From Silver to Cocaine: Latin American Commodity Chains and the Building of the World Economy, 1500–2000*. Durham: Duke University Press, 2006.

Toro, María Celia. "The Internationalization of Police: The DEA in Mexico." *Journal of American History* 86 (1999): 623–40.

——. *Mexico's "War" on Drugs: Causes and Consequences*. Boulder: Lynne Rienner, 1995.

Trentmann, Frank. "Beyond Consumerism: New Historical Perspectives on Consumption." *Journal of Contemporary History* 39 (2004): 373–401.

——. "Bread, Milk and Democracy: Consumption and Citizenship in Twentieth-Century Britain." In Daunton and Hilton, eds., *The Politics of Consumption*, 129–64.

——. *Free Trade Nation*. London: Oxford University Press, 2008.

——. "Knowing Consumers: Histories, Identities, Practices. An Introduction." In Frank Trentmann, ed., *The Making of the Consumer: Knowledge, Power and Identity in the Modern World*, 7–32. New York: Berg, 2006.

——. "The Modern Evolution of the Consumer: Meanings, Knowledge, and Identities Before the Age of Affluence." In Brewer and Trentmann, eds., *Consuming Cultures, Global Perspectives*, 19–70.

Truett, Samuel. *Fugitive Landscapes: The Forgotten History of the U.S.-Mexico Borderlands*. New Haven: Yale University Press, 2006.

Truett, Samuel, and Elliott Young. "Making Transnational History: Nation, Regions, and Borderlands." In Truett and Young, eds., *Continental Crossroads*, 2–32.

——, eds. *Continental Crossroads: Remapping U.S.-Mexico Borderlands History*. Durham: Duke University Press, 2004.

Urrea, Luis Alberto. *Across the Wire: Life and Hard Times on the Mexican Border*. New York: Anchor Doubleday, 1993.

Valdés, Dennis Nodín. *Al Norte: Agricultural Workers in the Great Lakes Region, 1917–1970*. Austin: University of Texas Press, 1991.

Valenzuela Arce, José Manuel, ed. *Por las fronteras del norte: Una aproximación cultural a la frontera México–Estados Unidos*. Mexico City: Fondo de Cultura Económica, 2003.

Van Binsbergen, Wim, and Peter Geschiere, eds. *Commodification: Things, Agency and Identities*. Berlin: LIT, 2005.

Van Schendel, Willem, and Itty Abraham, eds. *Illicit Flows and Criminal Things: States, Borders and the Other Side of Globalization*. Bloomington: Indiana University Press, 2005.

Van Young, Eric. *Hacienda to Market in Eighteenth-Century Mexico: The Rural Economy of the Guadalajara Region, 1675–1820*. Berkeley: University of California Press, 1981.

Vanderwood, Paul. *Juan Soldado: Rapist, Murderer, Martyr, Saint*. Durham: Duke University Press, 2004.

Vargas, Zaragosa. *Labor Rights Are Civil Rights: Mexican American Workers in Twentieth-Century America*. Princeton: Princeton University Press, 2005.

———. *Proletarians of the North: A History of Mexican Industrial Workers in Detroit and the Midwest, 1917–1933*. Berkeley: University of California Press, 1993.

Vaughan, Mary Kay. "Transnational Processes and the Rise and Fall of the Mexican Cultural State: Notes from the Past." In Joseph, Rubenstein, and Zolov, eds., *Fragments of a Golden Age*, 471–87.

Vaughan, Mary Kay, and Stephen Lewis, eds. *The Eagle and the Virgin: Nation and Cultural Revolution in Mexico, 1920–1940*. Durham: Duke University Press, 2006.

Vázquez, Josefina Zoraida, and Lorenzo Meyer. *The United States and Mexico*. Chicago: University of Chicago Press, 1985.

Velasco Ortiz, Laura. "Women, Migration, and Household Survival Strategies: Mixtec Women in Tijuana." In Segura and Zavella, eds., *Women and Migration*, 341–59.

Venkatesh, Alladi. "Ethnoconsumerism: A New Paradigm to Study Cultural and Cross-Cultural Consumer Behavior." In Janeen Arnold Costa and Gary Bamossy, eds., *Marketing in a Multicultural World: Ethnicity, Nationalism, and Cultural Identity*, 26–67. Thousand Oaks: Sage, 1995.

Venkatesh, Sudhir Alladi. *Off the Books: The Underground Economy of the Urban Poor*. Cambridge: Harvard University Press, 2006.

Vernon, Raymond. *Storm over the Multinationals*. Cambridge: Harvard University Press, 1977.

Vila, Pablo. *Border Identifications: Narratives of Religion, Gender, and Class on the U.S.-Mexico Border*. Austin: University of Texas Press, 2005.

———. *Crossing Borders, Reinforcing Borders: Social Categories, Metaphors and Narrative Identities on the U.S.-Mexico Border*. Austin: University of Texas Press, 2000.

———, ed. *Ethnography at the Border*. Minneapolis: University of Minnesota Press, 2003.

Vogel, Ronald. "Crossing the Border for Health Care: An Exploratory Analysis of Consumer Choice." *Journal of Borderlands Studies* 10 (1995): 19–44.

Voss, Stuart. *On the Periphery of Nineteenth-Century Mexico*. Tucson: University of Arizona Press, 1982.

Voth, Hans-Joachim. "Living Standards during the Industrial Revolution: An Economist's Guide." *American Economic Review* 93 (2003): 221–26.

——. *Time and Work in England, 1750–1830*. Oxford: Oxford University Press, 2000.

Wald, Elijah. *Narcocorrido: A Journey into the Music of Drugs, Guns, and Guerrillas*. New York: HarperCollins, 2002.

——. "Polka *Contrabandista*: Mexican Ballads in the Modern Age." In Rachel Rubin and Jeffrey Melnick, eds., *American Popular Music: New Approaches to the Twentieth Century*, 211–30. Amherst: University of Massachusetts Press, 2001.

Wallerstein, Immanuel. *The Modern World System: Capitalist Agriculture and the Origins of the European World-Economy in the Sixteenth Century*. New York: Academic Press, 1974.

Walsh, Casey. *Building the Borderlands: A Transnational History of Irrigated Cotton Along the Mexico-Texas Border*. College Station: Texas A&M University Press, 2008.

——. " 'A Rosy Future': Cotton and Regional Development in Mexico's Northern Borderlands, 1920–1965." In Walsh, ed., *The Social Relations of Mexican Commodities*, 19–54.

——, ed. *The Social Relations of Mexican Commodities: Power, Production, and Place*. La Jolla: Center for U.S.-Mexican Studies, University of California, San Diego, 2003.

Walsh, Lorena. "Peopling, Producing, and Consuming in Early British America." In Cathy Matson, ed., *The Economy of Early America: Historical Perspectives and New Directions*, 124–45. University Park: Pennsylvania State University Press, 2006.

Ward, Evan. *Packaged Vacations: Tourism Development in the Spanish Caribbean*. Gainesville: University Press of Florida, 2008.

Ward, Peter. *Colonias and Public Policy in Texas and Mexico: Urbanization by Stealth*. Austin: University of Texas Press, 1999.

Warman, Arturo. *El campo mexicano en el siglo xx*. Mexico City: Fondo de Cultura Económica, 2001.

——. *La historia de un bastardo: Maíz y capitalismo*. Mexico City: UNAM, 1988.

Wasserman, David. "The Borderlands Mall: Form and Function of an Imported Landscape." *Journal of Borderlands Studies* 11 (1996): 69–88.

——. *Capitalists, Caciques, and Revolution: The Native Elite and Foreign Enterprise in Chihuahua, Mexico, 1854–1911*. Chapel Hill: University of North Carolina Press, 1984.

——. *Persistent Oligarchs: Elites and Politics in Chihuahua, Mexico, 1910–1940*. Durham: Duke University Press, 1993.

Webb-Vignery, June. *Jacome's Department Store: Business and Culture in Tucson, Arizona, 1896–1980*. New York: Garland, 1989.

Weber, David. *The Mexican Frontier, 1821–1846: The American Southwest under Mexico*. Albuquerque: University of New Mexico Press, 1982.

——. "Turner, the Boltonians, and the Borderlands." *American Historical Review* 91 (1986): 66–81.

Webster, Grady, and Conrad Bahre, eds. *Changing Plant Life on La Frontera: Observations on Vegetation in the United States/Mexico Borderlands*. Albuquerque: University of New Mexico Press, 2001.

Weeks, William. *Building the Continental Empire: American Expansion from the Revolution to the Civil War*. Chicago: Ivan R. Dee, 1996.

Weems, Robert, Jr. " 'Bling-Bling' and Other Recent Trends in African-American Consumerism." In Cecilia Conrad, ed., *African Americans in the U.S. Economy*, 252–57. Lanham: Rowman & Littlefield, 2005.

——. *Desegregating the Dollar: African American Consumerism in the Twentieth Century*. New York: New York University Press, 1998.

Weigle, Marta, and Barbara Babcock, eds. *The Great Southwest of the Fred Harvey Company and the Santa Fe Railway*. Phoenix: The Heard Museum, 1996.

Weiner, Richard. *Race, Nation and Markets: Economic Culture in Porfirian Mexico*. Tucson: University of Arizona Press, 2004.

Werne, Joseph Richard. "Partisan Politics and the Mexican Boundary Survey, 1848–1853." *Southwestern Historical Quarterly* 90 (1987): 329–46.

——. "Pedro García Conde: El trazado de límites con Estados Unidos desde el punto de vista mexicano (1848–1853)." *Historia Mexicana* 36 (1986): 113–29.

Wildt, Michael. "Changes in Consumption as Social Practice in West Germany during the 1950s." In Strasser, McGovern, and Judt, eds., *Getting and Spending*, 301–16.

Williams, Allan, and Gareth Shaw, eds. *Tourism and Economic Development: European Experience*. 1988. 3rd ed., West Sussex: John Wiley & Sons, 1998.

Williams, Rosalind. *Dream Worlds: Mass Consumption in Late Nineteenth Century France*. Berkeley: University of California Press, 1982.

Willoughby, Randy. "Crouching Fox, Hidden Eagle: Drug Trafficking and Transnational Security—A Perspective from the Tijuana-San Diego Border." *Crime, Law and Social Change* 40 (2003): 113–142.

Wilson, Chris. *The Myth of Santa Fe: Creating a Modern Regional Tradition*. Albuquerque: University of New Mexico Press, 1997.

Wilson, Ron, and Wimai Dissanayake, eds. *Global/Local: Cultural Production and the Transnational Imaginary*. Durham: Duke University Press, 1996.

Wilson, Tamar. *Subsidizing Capitalism: Brickmakers on the U.S.-Mexican Border*. Albany: State University of New York Press, 2005.

Winseck, Dwayne, and Robert Pike. *Communications and Empire: Media, Markets, and Globalization, 1860–1930*. Durham: Duke University Press, 2007.

Woloson, Wendy. "In Hock: Pawning in Early America." *Journal of the Early Republic* 27 (2007): 35–81.

Wood, Andrew Grant. "Anticipating the Colonias: Popular Housing in El Paso and Ciudad Juárez, 1890–1923." *Journal of the Southwest* 43 (2001): 493–504.

——, ed. *On the Border: Society and Culture between the United States and Mexico*. Lanham: SR Books, 2004.

Woods, Gerald. "A Penchant for Probity: California Progressives and Disreputable Pleasures." In William Deverell and Tom Sitton, eds., *California Progressivism Revisited*, 99–114. Berkeley: University of California Press, 1994.

Wocks, Martha. "Creating Trading Places on the New Mexican Frontier." *Geographical Review* 82 (1992): 268–81.

Wright, Melissa. "Crossing the Factory Frontier: Gender, Place and Power in a Mexican Maquiladora." *Antipode: A Journal of Radical Geography* 29 (1997): 278–302.

——. "The Dialectics of Still Life: Murder, Women and Maquiladoras." *Public Culture* 11 (1999): 453–74.

——. *Disposable Women and Other Myths of Global Capitalism*. New York: Routledge, 2006.

——. "Maquiladora Mestizas and a Feminist Border Politics: Revisiting Anzaldúa." *Hypatia: A Journal of Feminist Philosophy* 13 (1998): 114–31.

Wrobel, David, and Patrick Long, eds. *Seeing and Being Seen: Tourism in the American West*. Lawrence: University Press of Kansas, 2001.

Xardel, Dominique. *The Direct Selling Revolution*. Cambridge: Blackwell Business, 1994.

Yoskowitz, David, and Michael Pisani. "Penetration of the Mexican Peso into U.S. Retail Operations: An Examination of Texas Firms along the Mexican Border." *Journal of Borderlands Studies* 17 (2002): 53–62.

Young, Elliott. *Catarino Garza's Revolution on the Texas-Mexico Border*. Durham: Duke University Press, 2004.

Young, Gay, ed. *The Social Ecology and Economic Development of Ciudad Juárez*. Boulder: Westview Press, 1986.

Yúdice, George. *The Expediency of Culture: Uses of Culture in the Global Era*. Durham: Duke University Press, 2003.

Zakim, Michael. *Ready-Made Democracy: A History of Men's Dress in the American Republic, 1760–1860*. Chicago: University of Chicago Press, 2003.

Zhang, Sheldon. *Smuggling and Trafficking in Human Beings: All Roads Lead to America*. New York: Praeger, 2007.

Zolov, Eric. *Refried Elvis: The Rise of the Mexican Counterculture*. Berkeley: University of California Press, 1999.

Zorrilla, Luis. *Historia de las relaciones entre México y los Estados Unidos de América, 1800–1958*. 2 vols. Mexico City: Editorial Porrúa, 1965–66.

Zukin, Sharon. *Point of Purchase: How Shopping Changed American Culture*. New York: Routledge, 2005.

Contributors

Josef Barton is an associate professor of history at Northwestern University, where he has been on the faculty since receiving his Ph.D. from the University of Michigan (1971). He first published an account of peasants encountering modernity in 1975, titled *Peasants and Strangers: Italians, Rumanians, and Slovaks in an American City, 1890–1950* (Harvard University Press). Professor Barton takes up a similar theme in a book titled *The Edge of Endurance: Mexican Peasants in Migration*, forthcoming from Cornell University Press. He co-directs a Rockefeller Foundation project, "How Do the Poor Constitute Community?"

Peter S. Cahn is an associate professor of anthropology at the University of Oklahoma, where he has been on the faculty since receiving his Ph.D. in sociocultural anthropology from the University of California, Berkeley (2001). After completing his first book, *All Religions Are Good in Tzintzuntzan: Evangelicals in Catholic Mexico* (University of Texas Press, 2003), he began researching the religious elements of direct selling in Mexico. Professor Cahn's book-length ethnographic account titled *The Great Commission: Direct Sales and Direct Faith in Mexico*, is forthcoming from Duke University Press.

Howard Campbell is a professor of cultural anthropology at the University of Texas, El Paso. He received a Ph.D. in anthropology from the University of Wisconsin, Madison (1990). Among his publications is an account of indigenous activism in Oaxaca, Mexico, titled *Mexican Memoir: A Personal Account of Anthropology and Radical Politics in Oaxaca* (Greenwood, 2001). Professor Campbell's recent publications include ethnographic accounts of female drug smugglers, corruption, narco-folklore, and Mexican American consumer culture in the borderlands.

Lawrence Culver is an assistant professor in the Department of History at Utah State University, where he has been on the faculty since receiving his Ph.D. in history from the University of California, Los Angeles, in 2004. His book-length study of Santa Catalina, Palm Springs, Los Angeles, and Southern California, titled *The Frontier of Leisure: Southern California and the Shaping of Modern America*, is forthcoming from Oxford University Press.

Amy Greenberg is a professor of history and women's studies at Pennsylvania State University, where she has been on the faculty since receiving a Ph.D. in history from

Harvard University (1995). She is the author of *Manifest Manhood and the Antebellum American Empire* (Cambridge University Press, 2005) and *Cause for Alarm: The Volunteer Fire Department in the Nineteenth Century City* (Princeton University Press, 1998). Professor Greenberg is currently at work on a history of the U.S.-Mexico War, titled *War for Empire: The 1846 U.S.-Mexico War and the Transformation of America*.

Josiah McC. Heyman is a professor of anthropology at the University of Texas, El Paso, where he also serves as chair of his department. He received a Ph.D. in anthropology from the City University of New York (1988). His book *Life and Labor on the Border: Working People of Northeastern Sonora, Mexico, 1886–1986* (University of Arizona Press, 1991) is a landmark account of the impact of consumer capitalism on the people of Sonora, Mexico.

Sarah Hill is an assistant professor of anthropology and environmental studies at Western Michigan University. Since receiving a Ph.D. in cultural anthropology from Johns Hopkins University (2001), she has been writing about the culture of waste along the U.S.-Mexico border during the past one hundred years. In March of 2006, Professor Hill cofounded a university–community partnership, Bronco Biodiesel, to power public fleets with diesel fuel made from used cooking oil. Among Professor Hill's publications is an essay titled "Metaphoric Enrichment and Material Poverty: The Making of Colonias," in a volume edited by Pablo Vila, *Ethnography at the Border* (University of Minnesota Press, 2003).

Alexis McCrossen is an associate professor of history at Southern Methodist University, where she has been on the faculty since receiving a Ph.D. in the history of American civilization at Harvard University (1995). The recipient of several awards, including a National Endowment for the Humanities Fellowship supporting her work on the material culture and political economy of timekeeping in the United States, she has published on the history of Sunday in the United States, timekeeping in U.S. cities, and other aspects of U.S. culture and society.

Robert Perez is an assistant professor of ethnic studies at the University of California, Riverside, where he also received a Ph.D. in history (2003). He has held a number of prestigious fellowships supporting his study of the historical experiences of the aboriginal peoples of the vast region comprised of California, Arizona, New Mexico, Texas, Sonora, and Chihuahua. Professor Perez seeks in his publications to draw historical connections between precolonial aboriginal societies, colonialism, and the modern situation.

Laura Isabel Serna is an assistant professor of history at Florida State University. After receiving a Ph.D. in the history of American civilization from Harvard University (2006), she held a two-year postdoctoral fellowship at Rice University's Humanities Research Center, where she revised her dissertation (winner of the American Studies Association's Ralph Henry Gabriel Prize in 2006 and the Society for Cinema and Media

Studies' Best Dissertation Prize in 2007) into a book about the reception of American silent film in Mexico during the 1920s. The book, titled *Making Cinelandia: American Films and Mexican Film Culture before the Golden Age, 1916–1936*, is forthcoming from Duke University Press.

Rachel St. John is an assistant professor of history at Harvard University, where she has been teaching since receiving her Ph.D. from Stanford University in 2005. Professor St. John is currently revising her dissertation titled *Line in the Sand: The Desert Border between the United States and Mexico, 1848–1934*. The book, which focuses on the spatial transformation of the western U.S.-Mexico boundary line, is forthcoming from Princeton University Press.

Mauricio Tenorio-Trillo is a professor of history at the University of Chicago and research professor in the History Division of the Centro de Investigación y Docencia Económicas, Mexico City. After receiving a Ph.D. in history from Stanford University in 1993, he joined the History Department at the University of Texas, Austin. Professor Tenorio-Trillo has published extensively in both English and Spanish, including *Mexico at the World's Fairs: Crafting a Modern Nation* (University of California Press, 1996); *El urbanista* (*The Urban Planner*) (Fondo de Cultura Económica, 2004); and with Aurora Gómez-Galvarriato, *El Porfiriato* (Fondo de Cultura Económica USA, 2006).

Evan R. Ward is an associate professor of history at Brigham Young University. After he received a Ph.D. in history from the University of Georgia (2000), he taught at the University of North Alabama. After publishing on U.S.-Mexican environmental relations, including the book *Border Oasis: Water and the Political Ecology of the Colorado River* (University of Arizona Press, 2003), Professor Ward turned his attention to post–Second World War tourism in Florida, the Caribbean, and Mexico in a book titled *Packaged Vacations: Tourism Development in the Spanish Caribbean* (University Press of Florida, 2008).

Index

A&P, 21

Abundance: institutions of, 11–13; native peoples and, 249–53, 269; paradigm of, xvii, 12; religion and, 277; scarcity and, 27, 345; senses of deprivation and, 63; surplus as, 11, 26, 254; U.S. national identity and, 35–36, 53

Acapulco, 7, 206

Adobe. *See* Houses

Advertising: as institution of abundance, 11–13, 17, 23, 25; Mexican stereotypes in, 120–21; for Southern California real estate, 187–88; for Tijuana, 114, 122–23, 129; for tourist attractions, 113, 119; during U.S.-Mexico War, 95–96; vice tourism and, 128–29. *See also* Branding; Marketing

African Americans, 22, 126, 150, 346–49

Agriculture: 28–29; in northern Mexico, 28–29, 217–18, 223–25; in Texas, 229–30; in the United States, 17; in U.S. Southwest, 28–29, 95, 171, 183

Agrupación Protectora Mexicana, 234

Agua Caliente Indians, 182–83

Agua Caliente Resort, Tijuana, 128–29

Albuquerque, New Mexico, 14, 173

Alcabala, 95

Air transportation, xviii, 197, 203, 207–8, 211; airports, 128, 205

Alarcón, Juan de la Cruz, 151, 154, 162

Alcázar Theater, El Paso, 151, 158, 162

Americanization: of border cities, 15, 41 n. 30, 130–31; commercial, 97; Porfirio Díaz's effort to counteract, 15–16; of *fronterizos*, 106, 310–11; globalization and, 79 n. 75; through Hollywood movies, 144, 151, 155–56; of immigrants to United States, 272 n. 29; of Mexico, 341, 343; as modernization, 162; racism and, 348; of North American native peoples, 106, 259–60; of U.S. Southwest, 15, 102–3

Amway, 275, 278–79

Anglo-Americans, 15, 90, 98–99, 119–22, 144, 168–92, 331, 340–43

Antimodernism. *See* Modernity

Apache, 161, 257–58; Mescalero, 257–59

Architecture, xix, 22, 185–87, 189–90, 200, 208–9

Arizona, 4, 19–20, 36, 260, 265–68

Article 27 of Mexican Constitution (1917), 31

Artículos ganchos program, 55

Arts and Crafts movement, 185, 187–88

Austin, Texas, 150, 280, 292

Automobiles, 21, 32–33, 115, 188, 203, 277, 287, 298–300, 322 n. 34; *fronchis*, 298–99; junkyards and, 308–15. *See also* Low riders

Avon Company, 275–76, 278, 292

Baja California, Mexico, 36, 113–18, 127, 132–33, 135, 197, 204–5, 253, 258, 264

Banks: Banco de México, 197, 204–6; in

Horse racing, 126–28
Hotels: Agua Caliente (Tijuana), 128, 130; in Cancún, 209–10; Desert Inn (Palm Springs), 182; Fred Harvey (railroad), 173–74; Metropole (Catalina Island), 178; in Mexico since 1960s, 54–55, 200
Houses: adobe, 14–15, 103, 110 n. 36, 185–86, 215; Anglo-American, 15, 90, 98–100; California bungalow, 187–88; as civilizing institution, 91, 98–101; consumer culture and, 35, 169, 184, 191; floors of, 91, 99–100; *jacal* [hut], 217; in Los Angeles, 176; magazines devoted to, 185; of Mexican migrants, 231, 287–88; narco-mansions, 329; of native American, 94, 104, 255, 261; ranch-style, 189–92; Southwest-style, 185–87; of squatters, 62, 302, 328; U.S. opinions of Mexican, 84, 99; vacation, 188–89; windows for, 99–100. *See also* Charles Fletcher Lummis
Houston, Texas, 277
Hunting clubs, 118
Hybrid cultures, 49, 62, 70 n. 2, 330–31, 341

"Illegal alien": as site and symbol of economic anxiety, 65–66
Image, 25–26, 48
Imagined community, 8
Immigration: through illegal networks, 64, 67; of refugees during Mexican revolution, 27, 149; to United States, 11–12, 100–1, 178; U.S. attitudes toward, 5, 31, 68; from United States during 1930s, 26–27. *See also* Migration
Imperial Valley, California, 29, 117, 128
Imports, 6–9; duties on, 11; Mexican, 15, 26, 54–55, 202, 308, 310, 315–18, 328–29, 340; into northern Mexico, 15–16, 19, 26, 42 n. 32, 36, 55–57, 95–96, 105, 298. *See also* Tariffs

Import substitution policies: in Latin America, 196–97; in Mexico, 54, 202, 340; proponents of, 198
Indians. *See* Native peoples; Indigenous peoples
Indigenismo, 53, 153–54, 208–9
Industrialization. *See* Manufacturing; Border Industrialization Program
Industrious revolution, 6, 9; North American native peoples and, 254; productivity and, 11–12, 17
Inequality: global, 49, 69; income in the United States, 27, 56; in U.S.-Mexico borderlands, 59, 70 n. 2
Inflation, since 1970s, 56–57
Informal economy, 61–66, 68, 330. *See also* Direct selling
Information age, 25
INFRATUR. *See* FONATUR
International Amusement Company, 151, 154, 162
International Pictures Company, 151, 154, 162
Investment in Mexico, 13, 15, 51, 174, 197, 206–10
Isleta Pueblo, New Mexico, 185
Itinerant movie exhibitors, 146–47, 159–60

Jácome Department Store, Tucson, 19–20
Jews, as entrepreneurs, 348; as peddlers, 342–43
Johnson, Jack, 126
Juárez. *See* "Ciudad Juárez"
Juárez Association of Yonkeros, 310–15
Junk, 306, 308, 310

Kitchen Debates (1959), 52–53
Kitchens, 330
Kleptomaniac, 65

Laborers: African American, 178, 183; agricultural, 183, 217–18, 229–32; child,

Narcotics. *See* Controlled substances

National identity: advertising and, 18; consumption and, 342–43; ethnicity and, 180; perceptions of, xix, 25–26, 341; Mexican, 143–44, 155, 161–62, 208–9; social hierarchies based upon, 149; Spanish, 8; U.S., 7, 15

Nationalism: American, 6–7, 26; consumer goods and, 41 n. 30, 69, 330; Mexican, 8, 143–44, 153–55, 201, 318, 327–28; movies and, 157, 160–61; scholarship and, 49, 70 n. 3. *See also* Americanization; *Mexicanidad*

Nationalization, Mexican, 5, 29, 31, 53, 55, 198–99, 328

Nation building, x, xvi, 3–5, 36–38, 143–44, 154–55; role of border and borderlands in, 49, 53, 66, 161, 333–37

Native Americans. *See* Native peoples

Native peoples (North American), 8, ceremonial practices of, 260–61; as consumers, 259–60; "drug wars" and, 264–69; health of, 252–53; homes of, 184; images of, 37, 101, 161, 250; as laborers, 171; labor of, 169, 182–83, 254; lands of, 248–53, 262, 264–265; oral traditions of, 249–51; rebellion of, 260–61; raiding by, 10, 92, 255–58; on Santa Fe Trail, 9; Spanish colonialism and, 249, 253–56; standard of living before 1500s, 249–53, 269; subjugated, 104, 255–56; U.S. Boundary Commission and, 87, 93, 101–2, 104, 106

Nativism, 5, 31, 65–68

Necessities, 34, 48, 174, 222–23, 236, 255

Necessity, xv–xvii, 26, 63, 228

Neoliberalism, 51, 62–69, 331. *See also* North American Free Trade Agreement; *Zona libre*

New Deal, 36

New Mexico, 7–9, 51, 60, 110 n. 36

New Spain. *See* Mexico

Newspapers, 25, 85, 158

Nieman Marcus Department Store, Dallas, 20

Nogales, Sonora and Arizona, 4, 18, 33

Nordhoff, Charles, 170–72

North American Free Trade Agreement (NAFTA) (1994), 50–51, 62–69, 318–19. *See also* Trade regulation

Northern Mexicans: attitude toward central Mexico, 92–93, 97; lawlessness of, 97. *See also* Mexican North; U.S.-Mexico borderlands

Northern Mexico. *See* Mexican North

El Nuevo Mundo, Ciudad Chihuahua, 152

Nuevo Laredo, Tamaulipas, 48

Nutritional supplements. *See* Herbalife; Omnilife; Omnitrition

Oaxaca, 7

Obraje. See Manufacturing

Omnilife, 275

Omnitrition, 278–80

Operation Intercept (U.S.) (1969), 32

Operation Wetback (U.S.) (1954), 67

Oviedo, Telésforo, 236–37

Packaging of consumer goods, 23, 220

Padilla, Félix, 159

Pala Indian Reservation, California, 268–69

Palm Springs, California, 177–78, 182–84, 187–89

Pani, Mario, 200

Passion Parties, 294

Patman, Wright, 21

Patriotism. *See Mexicanidad*; Nationalism

Peasants, 220

Peddlers, 65–68, 276, 342–43

Pesciado, Joe, 180–81

Peso devaluations, 56–57, 59, 207, 210

Peyote, 261–62

Photographs: of the borderlands, xix, 48;

Alexis McCrossen is an associate professor of history at Southern Methodist University. She is the author of *Holy Day Holiday: The American Sunday* (2000).

Library of Congress Cataloging-in-Publication Data
Land of necessity : consumer culture in the United States–Mexico borderlands / edited by Alexis McCrossen.
p. cm.
Includes bibliographical references and index.
ISBN 978-0-8223-4460-5 (cloth : alk. paper)
ISBN 978-0-8223-4475-9 (pbk. : alk. paper)
1. Consumption (Economics)—Mexican-American Border Region. 2. Consumption (Economics)—Social aspects—Mexican-American Border Region. 3. Mexican-American Border Region—Economic conditions. 4. Mexican-American Border Region—Social conditions. I. McCrossen, Alexis.
HC137.M46L36 2009
306.30972′1—dc22   2008055241